Tolley's Taxwise II
2008/09

Inheritance Tax
Taxation of Trusts and Estates

Authors:
Sue Jones CTA TEP ATT BSc (Hons) (Oxon)
Michael Waterworth MA (Cantab) of Lincoln's Inn, Barrister

Members of the LexisNexis Group worldwide

United Kingdom	LexisNexis, a Division of Reed Elsevier (UK) Ltd, Halsbury House, 35 Chancery Lane, London, WC2A 1EL, and London House, 20–22 East London Street, Edinburgh EH7 4BQ
Argentina	LexisNexis Argentina, Buenos Aires
Australia	LexisNexis Butterworths, Chatswood, New South Wales
Austria	LexisNexis Verlag ARD Orac GmbH & Co KG, Vienna
Benelux	LexisNexis Benelux, Amsterdam
Canada	LexisNexis Canada, Markham, Ontario
China	LexisNexis China, Beijing and Shanghai
France	LexisNexis SA, Paris
Germany	LexisNexis Deutschland GmbH, Munster
Hong Kong	LexisNexis Hong Kong, Hong Kong
India	LexisNexis India, New Delhi
Italy	Giuffrè Editore, Milan
Japan	LexisNexis Japan, Tokyo
Malaysia	Malayan Law Journal Sdn Bhd, Kuala Lumpur
New Zealand	LexisNexis NZ Ltd, Wellington
Poland	Wydawnictwo Prawnicze LexisNexis Sp, Warsaw
Singapore	LexisNexis Singapore, Singapore
South Africa	LexisNexis Butterworths, Durban
USA	LexisNexis, Dayton, Ohio

© Reed Elsevier (UK) Ltd 2008

Published by LexisNexis

A CIP Catalogue record for this book is available from the British Library.

ISBN: 9 780754 534785

Typeset by Letterpart Ltd, Reigate, Surrey

Printed in the UK by CPI William Clowes Beccles NR34 7TL

Visit LexisNexis at www.lexisnexis.co.uk

ABOUT THIS BOOK

For over 25 years Tolley's Taxwise II has provided practitioners with a practical means of keeping up to date with changing legislation relating to inheritance tax and trusts. This is achieved by way of worked examples, which have been updated annually to illustrate the major changes introduced by the Finance Act.

The publication is useful as a manual for staff, also acting as a training aid, as well as giving guidance as to the layout of computations. The examples are supplemented with explanatory notes explaining the law and practice relating to the issue illustrated.

The Taxwise publications are invaluable for students enabling them to apply their theoretical knowledge to practical examples of the types used by examiners in professional examinations.

Coverage

A selection of examples on inheritance tax, taxation of trusts and taxation of estates, based on the legislation current for 2008–09, complete with annotated solutions.

The examples are preceded by a summary on page (xi) of the relevant provisions of Finance Act 2008, which received Royal Assent on 21 July 2008.

The book is not an exhaustive work of reference but it shows the treatment of the points that are most likely to be encountered.

The contents list starting on page (v) shows the broad coverage of each example. In addition, there is a general index at the back of the book to assist in the location of specific points.

All statutory references in the inheritance tax sections of the book are to the Inheritance Tax Act 1984 unless otherwise stated.

References to ITTOIA 2005 are to the Income Tax (Trading and Other Income) Act 2005.

The authors

Sue Jones, CTA, TEP, ATT, BSc (Hons), Technical Officer for the Low Incomes Tax Reform Group (LITRG); Michael Waterworth, MA (Cantab) of Lincoln's Inn, Barrister, continuing the original work of Arnold Homer, FCA, CTA, TEP, and Rita Burrows, MBA, ACIS, CTA.

Companion publications

Tolley's Taxwise I 2008–09 (covering Income Tax and National Insurance, Corporation Tax, Capital Gains Tax and Stamp Duty).

Contents

Contents

CAPITAL TRANSFER TAX – RATES FROM 13 MARCH 1975 TO 14 MARCH 1988

Nil-rate threshold	From	To
£15,000	13.03.1975	26.10.1977
£25,000	27.10.1977	25.03.1980
£50,000	26.03.1980	08.03.1982
£55,000	09.03.1982	14.03.1983
£60,000	15.03.1983	12.03.1984
£64,000	13.03.1984	05.04.1985
£67,000	06.04.1985	17.03.1986
£71,000	18.03.1986	16.03.1987
£90,000	17.03.1987	14.03.1988

INHERITANCE TAX – RATES FROM 15 MARCH 1988

Since 15 March 1988 there has been a single rate of inheritance tax of 40% (halved for some lifetime transfers), applicable where the gross cumulative chargeable transfers exceed a stipulated threshold:

Threshold	Fixed by	Applicable to following transfers
110,000	FA 1988	Between 15 March 1988 and 5 April 1989
118,000	Statutory Instrument	Between 6 April 1989 and 5 April 1990
128,000	Statutory Instrument	Between 6 April 1990 and 5 April 1991
140,000	Statutory Instrument	Between 6 April 1991 and 9 March 1992
150,000	F(No 2)A 1992, FA 1993 and FA 1994	Between 10 March 1992 and 5 April 1995
154,000	Statutory Instrument	Between 6 April 1995 and 5 April 1996
200,000	FA 1996	Between 6 April 1996 and 5 April 1997
215,000	FA 1997	Between 6 April 1997 and 5 April 1998
223,000	Statutory Instrument	Between 6 April 1998 and 5 April 1999
231,000	Statutory Instrument	Between 6 April 1999 and 5 April 2000
234,000	Statutory Instrument	Between 6 April 2000 and 5 April 2001
242,000	Statutory Instrument	Between 6 April 2001 and 5 April 2002
250,000	FA 2002	Between 6 April 2002 and 5 April 2003
255,000	Statutory Instrument	Between 6 April 2003 and 5 April 2004
263,000	Statutory Instrument	Between 6 April 2004 and 5 April 2005
275,000	Finance Act 2005 s 98	Between 6 April 2005 and 5 April 2006
285,000	Finance Act 2005 s 98	Between 6 April 2006 and 5 April 2007
300,000	Finance Act 2005 s 98	Between 6 April 2007 and 5 April 2008
312,000	Finance Act 2006 s 155	Between 6 April 2008 and 5 April 2009
325,000	Finance Act 2006 s 155	Between 6 April 2009 and 5 April 2010
350,000	Finance Act 2007 s 4	Between 6 April 2010 and 5 April 2011

INCOME TAX RATES

Income tax rate bands have altered dramatically from 2007/08 to 2008/09.

Earnings, pensions, taxable state benefits, self-employed profits up to £34,800 are taxed at the rate of 20% (now basic rate) except income from savings.

Savings income (broadly, bank and building society interest) is regarded as the part of taxable income which is taxed next. The definition of income to be treated as savings income is contained in ITA 2007 s 18. FA 2008 s 3 introduces a new 10% starting rate for savings income only, with a limit of £2,320. If taxable non-savings income (ie earnings and pensions etc as mentioned above) is more than this limit, then the 10% savings rate will not be applicable and savings income will be taxed in full at 20%.

What this means is that if an individual has total income including savings of between £6,035 and £8,355 – the 10% rate will apply to at least part of their savings income. For people over 65 who are receiving the higher personal allowance these limits will be increased.

However, if the personal allowance has been utilised against non-savings income (as explained above) but the remaining non-savings income is less than £2,320 – the balance of the £2,320 against can be used to tax savings income at the 10% rate. Only the balance of savings income remaining is then chargeable at 20%.

There are no changes to the taxation of dividends or distributions from unit trusts (but not interest) – they are taxable at the 10% rate and form the last tranche of income and so are taxed at the highest appropriate rate of tax. For an individual paying tax at 40% on their other taxable income they will pay tax at 32.50% on their dividends.

Taxable income over £34,800 will be taxed at the 40% higher rate (apart from dividends) whether or not it is savings income.

RATES FOR TRUSTS AND ESTATES

Special trust rates

The 'trust rate' (ITA 2007 s 9) applies to income of discretionary and accumulation and maintenance trusts.

The 2008/09 rate is 40%.

The 'dividend trust rate' (ITA 2007 s 9) applies to company dividends and other distributions (including share buy-backs) of discretionary and accumulation and maintenance trusts. In addition it applies to some dividend income received by all trusts.

The 2008/09 rate is 32.5%.

The special trust rates do not apply to the first £1,000 of relevant income, instead that will be charged at the standard rate, ie the income tax rate applicable to that type of income.

Trust income not liable at special rates

Trustees of other trusts and personal representatives of deceased's estates are charged at the dividend rate of 10% on dividend income, and the basic rate of 20% on savings income and non-savings income.

Trusts with vulnerable beneficiaries

Trusts with vulnerable beneficiaries are able to elect irrevocably for the income and gains of the trust to be taxed as if the income belonged to the vulnerable beneficiary. See question 45.

CAPITAL GAINS TAX

Total net gains of individuals for 2008/09 not exceeding £9,600 (2007/08 £9,200) are exempt. Gains in excess of the annual exemption are taxed at a flat rate of 18%.

Personal representatives are entitled to the annual exemption, currently £9,600 for the tax year of death and the next two tax years. Gains not covered by the exemption are taxed at 18%.

Gains of trusts in which the settlor retains an interest are taxed as the settlor's gains. For other trusts, the trustees are entitled to an annual exemption (AE) of £4,800 (2007/08 £4,600), divided equally between trusts created by the same settlor after 6 June 1978, subject to a minimum exemption of £960 for each trust (2007/08 £920). From 2008/09 gains in excess of the exemption are charged at 18% for all types of trust (previously 40%).

Taper relief has been abolished with effect from 6 April 2008 and replaced by a more limited entrepreneurs' relief (discussed below in Examples 36 and 40).

SUMMARY OF PROVISIONS OF FINANCE ACT 2008 RELATING TO INHERITANCE TAX, INCOME TAX, CAPITAL GAINS TAX AND TAXATION OF TRUSTS AND ESTATES

Finance Act 2008 reference		*Example*
ss 1–5 and Sch 1	*Income tax rates*	*44 and 39*

FA 2008 ss 1–5 together with Sch 1 abolish the 10% starting rate for individuals and reduce the basic rate from 22% to 20%. The higher rate remains at 40%.

Tax on taxable income such as earnings, pensions, taxable state benefits, self-employed profits up to £34,800 is levied at the basic rate of 20% but there is an exception for income from savings.

Savings income is treated separately. FA 2008 s 3 introduces a new 10% starting rate for savings income only, with a limit of £2,320. If taxable non-savings income (i.e. earnings and pensions etc. as mentioned above) is more than this limit, then the 10% savings rate will not be applicable and savings income will be taxed in full at the rate of 20%.

The result is that if an individual has total income including savings of between £6,035 and £8,355 – the 10% rate will apply to at least part of their savings income. The limits of £6,035 and £8,355 apply only to someone getting the basic personal allowance. For people over 65 who are receiving the higher personal allowance these limits will be increased.

However, if the personal allowance has been utilised against non-savings income but the remaining non-savings income is less than £2,320 – the balance of the £2,320 against can be used to tax savings income at the 10% rate. Only the balance of savings income remaining is then chargeable at 20%.

Taxable income over £34,800 will be taxed at the 40% higher rate (apart from dividends) whether or not it is savings income.

s 8 and Sch 2	*Capital gains tax*	*36, 40 and 47*

FA 2008 s 8 and Sch 2 set out a radical reform of capital gains tax from 2008/09 and later years.

The annual exemption and the rules for losses remain. The annual exemption for 2008/09 is set at £9,600 for individuals and £4,800 for trustees.

FA 2008 s 8 sets the rate of capital gains tax at 18% for individuals, personal representatives and trustees. Sch 2 provides that in respect of some disposals entrepreneurs' relief will be available and a lower effective rate of 10% will be applicable.

FA 2008 s 8 and Sch 2 para 5 repeals some of the special rules for UK resident 'settlor-interested' settlements (including TCGA 1992 ss 77 to 79) because the single rate of CGT means that those rules are no longer required.

FA 2008 s 8 and Sch. 2 paras 11 to 20 amend the rules in Chapter 4 of Part 2 of the Finance Act (FA) 2005 for the taxation of the income and gains of settlements for vulnerable persons. The broad effect of these rules is that the tax paid in respect of such income and gains should be no higher than would be the case if the income and gains arose directly to the vulnerable person.

FA 2008 s 8 and Sch 2 paras 23 to 56 abolish taper relief and make a variety of consequential amendments. Para 25 of the Schedule repeals TCGA 1992 s 2A and thus abolishes taper relief.

FA 2008 s 8 and Sch 2 paras 57 to 71 abolish the kink test relating to the disposal of assets held at 31 March 1982. Assets held at 31 March 1982 are treated as though they had been acquired at their market value on that date, so that gains or losses relating to changes in value prior to that date are not taken into account for CGT purposes. The abolition of the kink test for CGT purposes means that in future the gains accruing on all disposals of assets owned at 31 March 1982 will be based on their market value at that date, so effectively 'rebasing' all allowable expenditure to 31 March 1982.

FA 2008 s 8 and Sch 2 paras 72 to 76 provide for the abolition of halving relief for capital gains tax purposes.

FA 2008 s 8 and Sch 2 paras 77 to 83 abolish indexation allowance. Indexation allowance was frozen as at April 1998, so that it was only available in relation to increases in the RPI between the date of acquisition of the asset in question (or, if later, 31 March 1982) and April 1998. For disposals on or after 6 April 2008 it is no longer available.

FA 2008 s 8 and Sch 2 paras 84 to 100 contain rules relating to the identification of assets disposed of with a view to simplifying pooling of fungible assets.

s 9 and Sch 3   *Entrepreneurs' relief*   *36 and 40*

FA 2008 s 9 and Sch 3 introduce entrepreneurs' relief, a form of substitute for taper relief. The effect is that the first £1 million of gains arising on or in connection with disposals of the whole or part of a business (including, in certain circumstances, disposals of shares or securities) are charged to capital gains tax at 4/9ths of the main capital gains tax rate (which, so long as the main rate is 18%, amounts to an effective rate of 10%). The relief has effect for disposals on or after 6 April 2008.

FA 2008 Sch 3 inserts new ss 169H to 169S into TCGA 1992 which allow for entrepreneurs' relief to apply to individuals and trustees who dispose of the whole or part of a trading business, or of shares in a trading company in which they have a qualifying interest.

Entrepreneurs' relief may be available in respect of gains made by individuals on the disposal of:

–   all or part of a trading business the individual carries on alone or in partnership;

–   assets of the individual's or partnership's trading business following the cessation of the business;

–   shares in (and securities of) the individual's 'personal' trading company (or holding company of a trading group);

–   assets owned by the individual and used by his / her 'personal' trading company (or group) or trading partnership.

The first £1 million of gains will qualify for the relief which effectively taxes qualifying gains at 10%. Gains in excess of £1 million will be charged to CGT at the rate of 18%.

Where a claim is made in respect of a qualifying business disposal the relevant gains are to be aggregated, with any relevant losses being deducted. The resulting amount is to be reduced by 4/9ths but if the total of current gains less losses and the amounts resulting in relation to earlier relevant qualifying business disposals (if any), exceeds £1 million, the reduction is to be made in respect of only so much (if any) of the amount resulting as (when added to that total) does not exceed £1 million.

The amount arrived at is to be treated as a chargeable gain accruing at the time of the disposal to the individual or trustees by whom the claim is made. An individual will be able to make claims for relief on qualifying disposals made on or after 6 April 2008. Claims may be made on more than one occasion up to a 'lifetime' limit of £1 million. Disposals on or before 5 April 2008 do not affect the lifetime limit. The £1 million limit will only begin to diminish when the relief is claimed.

Trustees will be able to claim relief on certain disposals of business assets and company shares and securities where a 'qualifying beneficiary' has a qualifying interest in the business in question.

For the disposal to qualify for entrepreneurs' relief to a qualifying beneficiary must have been an officer or employee of the company throughout a period of one year ending not more than three years before the disposal or a qualifying beneficiary must have carried on the business throughout a period of one year ending not more than three years before the disposal and ceases to do so on the date of the disposal or within three years before then. Some relief will be available in respect of any life interest beneficiaries who work for the company if the disposal is of shares or securities or an interest in shares or securities in the company.

There is a disposal of trust business assets when:

(a)   there is a disposal by trustees of assets which are part of the settled property of the settlement and are shares in or securities of a company, or interests in such shares or securities; or assets that have been used for the purposes of a business, or interests in such assets ('settlement business assets');

(b)   there is an individual in relation to a the settlement who has have an interest in possession (other than an interest in possession which has a fixed term) in the whole of the settled property of the settlement or in a part of the settled property that contains the settlement business assets (a 'qualifying beneficiary').

In relation to the disposal of settlement business assets a 'relevant condition' is been satisfied. The nature of the relevant condition depends upon whether the settlement business assets are shares in or securities of a company (or interests in such shares or securities), in which case the company should have been the qualifying beneficiary's personal company and the qualifying beneficiary must have been an officer or employee of the company throughout a period of one year ending not more than three years before the disposal. If the settlement business assets are assets (or interests in assets) that have been used for the purposes of a business the relevant condition is that the qualifying beneficiary has carried on the business throughout a period of one year ending not more than three years before the disposal and ceases to do so on the date of the disposal or within three years before then.

s 10 and Sch 4   *Inheritance tax: transfer of unused nil-rate band*   *1 and 34*

FA 2008 s 10 and Sch 4 allow a claim to be made for the part of the nil-rate band unused on the death of a spouse or civil partner to be added to the surviving spouse or civil partner's own nil-rate band when they die, to give a larger IHT nil-rate band to be applied against the survivor's estate.

*FA 2008 s 10
and Sch 4
para 2 inserts a
new s 8A into
IHTA 1984*

The new section 8A applies where (a) immediately before the death of a person (a 'deceased person'), the deceased person had a spouse or civil partner ('the survivor'), and (b) the deceased person had unused nil-rate band on death.

This new provision is to take effect in relation to cases where the survivor's death occurs on or after 9 October 2007 FA 2008 Sch 4 para 9(1).

This will apply where the IHT nil-rate band of the first deceased spouse or civil partner was not fully used in calculating the IHT liability of their estate. When the surviving spouse or civil partner dies, the unused amount may be added to their own nil-rate band. The claim must be made within 24 months from the end of the month in which the surviving spouse or civil partner dies.

The key provisions are to be found at s 8A(2) to (4). They are in the following terms:

(2)   For the purposes of this section a person has unused nil-rate band on death if—

$M > VT$

where—

M is the maximum that could be transferred by the chargeable transfer made (under section 4 above) on the person's death if it were to be wholly chargeable to tax at the rate of nil per cent.; and

VT is the value actually transferred by that chargeable transfer (or nil if there is no such chargeable transfer).

(3) Where a claim is made under this section, the nil-rate band maximum at the time of the survivor's death is to be treated for the purposes of the charge to tax on the death of the survivor as increased by the percentage specified in subsection (4) below (but subject to subsection (5) and section 8C below).

(4) That percentage is—

$(E \div NRBMD) \times 100$

where—

E is the amount by which M is greater than VT in the case of the deceased person; and

NRBMD is the nil-rate band maximum at the time of the deceased person's death.

The term 'nil-rate band maximum' is defined by s 8A(7) to mean 'the amount shown in the second column in the first row of the Table in Schedule 1 to [IHTA 1984] (upper limit of portion of value charged at rate of nil per cent.) and in the first column in the second row of that Table (lower limit of portion charged at next rate).'

A claim may be made by the personal representatives of the survivor within the permitted period, or (if no claim is so made) by any other person liable to the tax chargeable on the survivor's death within such later period as HM Revenue & Customs (HMRC) may specify. The 'permitted period' referred is:

(a) the period of two years from the end of the month in which the survivor dies or (if it ends later) the period of three months beginning with the date on which the personal representatives first act as such, or

(b) such longer period as HMRC may specify.

A claim made within either of the periods mentioned above may be withdrawn no later than one month after the end of the period concerned.

The new provisions make provision for re-marriage by the survivor (or the formation of a new civil partnership) but IHTA 1984 ss 8A(5) and 8C (which deals with deferred charges) limit the uplift in the nil-rate band to 100%. If the amount of the increase in the nil-rate band maximum at the time of the survivor's death effected by the provisions would exceed the amount of that nil-rate band maximum, the amount of the increase is limited to the amount of that nil-rate band maximum. The effect is that an unused nil-rate band can be carried forward from one marriage or civil partnership to the next where, for example, the survivor has survived more than one person who had unused nil-rate band on death but that there is an overall cap on the uplift available.

s 24

Residence and domicile: periods of residence

FA 2008 s 24 introduces changes to the way in which the UK treats days of arrival and departure when day-counting tests are relevant to determining residence status for tax purposes. Previous practice was to ignore both days of arrival and departure.

With effect from 6 April 2008, days where an individual is present in the UK at the end of the day will now be counted, unless the individual is in the UK as a passenger in transit.

s 67   *Income of beneficiaries under settlor-interested settlements*   46

FA 2008 s 67 amends ITTOIA 2005 s 685A and rectifies an anomaly of the trusts modernisation legislation. It affects individuals who receive discretionary income payments from a settlor-interested trust and who also receive savings or dividend income. The new provision provides that such income from a settlor-interested trust is treated as one of the highest slices of income.

s 118 Sch 39   *General: time limits for assessments, claims etc*

This provides for the alignment of time limits for HMRC to make an assessment to correct the income tax and capital gains tax due from a taxpayer. It also aligns the descriptions of taxpayer behaviours used in setting time limits, using the terms at Schedule 24 to Finance Act 2007. The Schedule further provides for the alignment of time limits for taxpayers to make claims.

s 119   *Correction and amendment of tax returns*

Section 119 allows an HMRC officer to make a correction to a tax return where he has reason to believe it is incorrect as a result of other information available. As now, the taxpayer will be able to reject the correction if he or she does not agree.

s 122 Sch 40   *Penalties for failure to notify etc*   5

FA 2008 s 122 and Sch 40 amend Schedule 24 to the FA 2007 (penalties for errors) to extend its application to further taxes, levies and duties. This provides for a single legal framework for penalties to be imposed on taxpayers who make errors in documents that they send to HMRC. The further taxes are environmental taxes (aggregates levy, climate change levy, landfill tax); excise duties (alcohols, tobacco, oils, gambling and air passenger duty); stamp duties (stamp duty land tax, stamp duty reserve tax); inheritance tax, insurance premium tax, pension schemes and petroleum revenue tax. The penalty would be related to the amount of tax understated, the underlying behaviour giving rise to the understatement and the extent of disclosure by the taxpayer.

The new provisions for incorrect returns will provide for penalties in line with FA 2007 Sch 24, which are based on the amount of tax understated, the nature of the behaviour and the extent of disclosure by the taxpayer. There will be no penalty where a taxpayer makes a mistake but there will be a penalty of up to:

–   30% for failure to take reasonable care;

–   70% for a deliberate understatement; and

–   100% for a deliberate understatement with concealment.

Each penalty is substantially reduced where the taxpayer makes a disclosure (takes active steps to put right the problem), more so if this is unprompted.

For an unprompted disclosure of a failure to take reasonable care the penalty could be reduced to nil.

Where a taxpayer discloses fully when prompted by a challenge from HMRC each penalty could be reduced by up to a half.

The other significant change is to introduce a penalty on a third party who deliberately supplies false information to, or withholds information from a person intending to cause that person to give HMRC an inaccurate document.

Where a return is incorrect because a third party has deliberately provided false information or deliberately withheld information from the taxpayer, with the intention of causing an understatement of tax due, it will be possible to allow a penalty to be charged on the third party.

For failure to notify a taxable activity there will be no penalty unless there is tax due but unpaid as a result, nor where the taxpayer has a reasonable excuse for the failure. Otherwise there will be a penalty of:

– 30% of tax unpaid for non-deliberate failure to notify;

– 70% of tax unpaid for a deliberate failure to notify; and

– 100% of tax unpaid for a deliberate failure with concealment.

Each penalty will be substantially reduced where the taxpayer makes a disclosure (takes active steps to put right the problem), more so if this is unprompted.

s 123 Sch 41   *Penalties for failure to notify etc*

FA 2008 s 123 Sch 41 provide for penalties to be imposed on persons who have an obligation to notify HMRC that they are chargeable to tax, liable to register for tax etc., and fail to do so. This would create a single legal framework for penalising failure to comply with a notification obligation across all relevant taxes and duties, based on the same principles used for penalising incorrect returns contained in Schedule 24 to FA 2007.

s 140   *Charge on termination of interest in possession where new*
interest acquired

FA 2008 s 140 amends s 53(2A) of IHTA 1984 (exceptions from charge on termination of interest in possession) with effect from 22 March 2006 to give effect to the true intention of FA 2006.

s 141   *Interest in possession settlements: extension of transitional period*

FA 2008 s 141 substitutes 'October' for 'April' in ss 49C, 49D and 49E of IHTA 1984 in order to extend the duration of transitional serial interests by six months.

Question

(i)   Outline the basic principles of inheritance tax.

(ii)   'Disposition', 'transfer of value', 'chargeable transfer', 'potentially exempt transfer' and 'relevant property' are primary terms which need to be considered when determining whether an inheritance tax liability arises on a transaction. Explain the meaning of each term, demonstrating how the terms are linked together.

(iii)   Explain the term 'nil-rate band' and how the transfer of the nil-rate band works in practice.

(iv)   Explain how inheritance tax can become payable at death in respect of transfers of value already made in lifetime.

(v)   Outline the exemptions from inheritance tax.

(vi)   Explain the 'grossing up' of a lifetime transfer.

Answer

(i) **Basic principles of inheritance tax**

Introduction of inheritance tax

Inheritance tax applies from 18 March 1986 having replaced capital transfer tax. As most of the capital transfer tax legislation was retained, the Capital Transfer Tax Act 1984 was renamed the Inheritance Tax Act (IHTA) 1984.

Transfers between spouses and civil partners

A husband and wife or civil partners are separate chargeable persons for inheritance tax, each being able to take advantage of any available reliefs and exemptions.

Chargeable transfers and potentially exempt transfers

Lifetime transfers of value may be completely exempt from inheritance tax (see part (iv)). If they are not exempt, they are divided between *chargeable transfers* and *potentially exempt transfers* (see part (ii)), the essence of inheritance tax being that chargeable gifts are accumulated for seven years. The tax cost of gifts depends upon whether or not the sum of the accumulated gifts plus the present chargeable transfer exceeds the threshold at which tax becomes payable on the scale applicable at the time of the chargeable transfer. The present nil-rate threshold is £312,000 (applicable to transfers on and after 6 April 2008) and this will increase to £325,000 for 2009/10 and £350,000 for 2010/11, with tax being charged at 40% on the excess over that amount, or 20% for certain lifetime transfers (see below).

Position on death

On death, the chargeable estate is added to the chargeable transfers made in the previous seven years to determine the tax liability. In addition, transfers made in that seven year period that were potentially exempt now become chargeable because of the death. In charging those potentially exempt transfers, chargeable transfers made within seven years before each particular gift are taken into account even though the scale of tax used is that applicable at the date of *death*. Tax will only be payable to the extent that the total transfers less any unused annual exemption at the time of the gift (see note 6) exceed the nil threshold in force at the date of death and a tapering relief is available as indicated in (iii) below.

If a donor survives a *potentially exempt transfer* by seven years, it will not attract inheritance tax unless the donor retains an interest in or benefits from the gifted property, in which case the seven year survivorship period only starts to run from the time the interest or benefit ceases.

Where the donor has avoided a pre-owned asset income tax charge by making an election under FA 2004 Sch 15.21 or 15.22 then the asset is treated for inheritance tax as a gift with reservation and the seven year survivorship period starts from the time that the donor ceases to have any benefit or enjoyment from the property (see Example 23).

Chargeable lifetime transfers

Where a lifetime transfer (or deemed transfer) is *chargeable to inheritance tax when made*, the tax is calculated at one half of the then scale rates (see above), the rate applicable to each transfer being arrived at by aggregating it with accumulated chargeable transfers in the previous seven years. If the donor should die within seven years after the chargeable transfer, tax is recalculated at the full rate, but using the scale of rates in force at the date of death, and a tapering relief is available as indicated in (iii) below.

Calculation of tax

Because the inheritance tax threshold is increased annually (unless Parliament decides otherwise) and because tax rates may also change, it should be borne in mind that the correct starting point for calculating tax on a chargeable transfer is the cumulative chargeable transfers within the previous seven years. The tax on the transfer should then be calculated using a cumulative tax figure for the earlier transfers based on the *current* scale of rates (or the scale of rates at death, where tax or additional tax arises as a result of the donor's death within seven years). That cumulative tax figure will often not represent the tax that has actually been paid, but it is the simplest way to make the tax calculation (see the example in part (iii)).

Trusts

Where property is held in trust, the inheritance tax treatment depends on the type of trust. The detailed provisions relating to trusts are dealt with in Examples 42 to 65.

From 22 March 2006 there are special rules for trusts that are created:

1.   on death by a parent for a minor child who will be fully entitled to the assets in the trust at age 18, or

2.   on death for the benefit of one life tenant in order of time only (more than one such interest may be created on death as long as the trust capital vests absolutely when the life interest comes to an end), or

3.   either in the settlor's lifetime or on death for a disabled person.

The IHT treatment for trusts which do not satisfy these rules follows the mainstream IHT rules for 'relevant property' trusts. Relevant property is settled property in which there is no interest in possession (see Example 52).

A relevant property trust is any trust in which the beneficiary's interest is not one of the following (the list is not exhaustive):

(a)   an interest in excluded property, (see Example 3);

(b)   an interest in property held for charitable purposes only, whether for a limited time or otherwise, property held in accumulation and maintenance settlements including from 22 March 2006;

(c)   an interest in a trust for bereaved minors (s 71A) or an Age18–25 trusts (s 71D);

(d)   an interest in property held on trusts for disabled people settled before 10 March 1981;

(e)   an interest in property held in approved maintenance funds for historic buildings;

(f)   an interest in property held in pensions schemes (but not benefits which, having become payable under a fund or scheme, become comprised in a settlement);

(g)   an interest in property held on a settlement with an interest in possession settled on or after 22 March 2006 which is an immediate post death interest (IPDI) (s 49A) or a transitional serial interest (TSI) (s 49B);

(h)   an interest in property applied to pay a lump sum death benefit within FA 2004, s 168(1) (registered pension scheme lump sum death benefits) from the date of death of the scheme member to the date when the payment is made by the pension scheme;

(i)   an interest in possession existing before 22 March 2006 and still continuing.

A limited exception is given to Accumulation & Maintenance (A & M) trusts which allow the advance of capital to be delayed until the beneficiary is 25. It permits the relevant property rules to apply only when the beneficiary reaches the age of 18, so that the theoretical maximum exit charge will be 4.2% when the beneficiary turns 25. However, for trust property settled after 21 March 2006, this exception applies *only* where one of the beneficiary's parents has died and the funds come from the will of that parent or through a trust established under the Criminal Injuries Compensation Scheme.

For interest in possession (IIP) trusts which commenced before 22 March 2006 (see (i) above) the capital is to be treated as part of the life tenant's taxable estate. Interests in possession which commenced after 21 March 2006 will be subject to these rules only if they relate to either:

(a)   a bare trust; or

(b)   an immediate post-death interest; or

(c)   a disabled person's interest.

Otherwise, IIP trusts are subject to the 'relevant property' rules.

(ii)   **Dispositions, transfers of value, potentially exempt transfers and chargeable transfers**

Chargeable transfers and transfers of value

IHTA 1984 Part I incorporates a number of sections in arriving at the definition of a *chargeable transfer of value*:

s 1 Inheritance tax shall be charged on the value transferred by a *chargeable transfer*.

s 2(1) A *chargeable transfer* is any transfer of value made by an individual other than an exempt transfer. (It is provided in s 2(3), however, that references to chargeable transfers include references to occasions on which tax is payable by discretionary trusts.)

s 3(1) A *transfer of value* is any disposition made by a person (the transferor) as a result of which the value of his estate immediately after the disposition is less than it would be but for the disposition and the amount by which it is less is the value transferred by the transfer. Unless otherwise provided, 'transfers of value' include events on which tax is chargeable (such as deemed transfers when someone with an interest in possession dies, or chargeable occasions in relation to discretionary trusts) (s 3(4)).

s 3(2) Any diminution in the value of the estate brought about by the disposal of 'excluded property' is ignored.

s 10 Furthermore any disposition which is not intended to confer any gratuitous benefit on any person and *either* was made at arm's length between unconnected persons *or* was such as might have been expected to be made in a transaction at arm's length between unconnected persons is *not* a transfer of value.

A *chargeable transfer of value* is therefore the difference between the value of the transferor's estate before and after the transfer less any exemptions and ignoring disposals of excluded property (as to which see Example 3).

A person's estate is defined by s 5(1) as the aggregate of all the property to which he is beneficially entitled, except that the estate of a person immediately before his death does not include excluded property. 'Property' includes rights or interests of any description, but does not include 'settlement powers', ie powers over, or exercisable directly or indirectly in relation to, settled property or a settlement (s 272).

Dispositions

The term *disposition* is not defined but case law has determined that the word has no special or technical meaning (*Ward v CIR* (1956)). It therefore covers any act by which a person deliberately divests himself of the beneficial ownership of his property. The legislation extends its meaning where there are associated operations (ss 268 and 272), deliberate failure to exercise a right (s 3), and alterations of rights attaching to shares in a close company (s 98) (see Example 22). Certain dispositions are not transfers of value (see s 10 above and Example 2).

Potentially exempt transfers

The concept of a *'potentially exempt transfer'* is contained in s 3A, which was introduced by FA 1986 and extended by F(No 2)A 1987. Any lifetime transfer of value which:

1.   is made by an individual on or after 18 March 1986, and

2.   would but for this provision be a chargeable transfer, and

3.   is an absolute gift to another individual, or

4.   arises because a life tenant with an interest in possession uses his own assets to buy a reversionary interest in the trust property,

is 'potentially exempt' from inheritance tax. It will therefore initially be treated as an *exempt transfer*. However if the transferor's death then occurs during the next *seven* years the transfer becomes a *chargeable transfer*. Any tax on the gift is paid by the transferee.

To come within the definition of a gift to an individual, the value transferred must be attributable to property that becomes part of the individual's estate, or as a result of which the individual's estate is increased.

Potentially exempt transfers which become chargeable transfers are charged to inheritance tax at their value at the time of the transfer, but using the rates applicable at the time of death. Where such transfers have occurred more than *three* years before death any tax due on that particular transfer is reduced by tapering relief, as in (iii) below. Even though the potentially exempt transfers have become chargeable transfers, no tax is payable (and tapering relief is not therefore relevant) if when added to the chargeable transfers in the previous seven years they do not exceed the nil threshold in force at the date of death. The nil-rate band available in respect of the death estate is, however, correspondingly reduced.

The definition of potentially exempt transfer covers virtually all lifetime transfers except those into and out of mainstream trusts.

(iii)   **Transfer of the nil-rate band and nil-rate band archive**

Nil-rate band archive since March 1975

For inheritance tax purposes the nil-rate band is the amount of the estate or lifetime gift on which there is no inheritance tax to pay. If the estate, including any assets held in trust and transfers of value made within seven years of death, is less than the nil-rate band, no inheritance tax will be due on it.

The limit for determining whether an estate can qualify as an excepted estate remains at £300,000 until 6 August 2008.

The table below shows the different nil-rate bands in use for deaths up to 2010/11:

From	To	Nil-rate band
13.03.1975	26.10.1977	£15,000
27.10.1977	25.03.1980	£25,000
26.03.1980	08.03.1982	£50,000
09.03.1982	14.03.1983	£55,000
15.03.1983	12.03.1984	£60,000
13.03.1984	05.04.1985	£64,000
06.04.1985	17.03.1986	£67,000
18.03.1986	16.03.1987	£71,000
17.03.1987	14.03.1988	£90,000
15.03.1988	05.04.1989	£110,000
06.04.1989	05.04.1990	£118,000
06.04.1990	05.04.1991	£128,000
06.04.1991	09.03.1992	£140,000
10.03.1992	05.04.1995	£150,000

06.04.1995	05.04.1996	£154,000
06.04.1996	05.04.1997	£200,000
06.04.1997	05.04.1998	£215,000
06.04.1998	05.04.1999	£223,000
06.04.1999	05.04.2000	£231,000
06.04.2000	05.04.2001	£234,000
06.04.2001	05.04.2002	£242,000
06.04.2002	05.04.2003	£250,000
06.04.2003	05.04.2004	£255,000
06.04.2004	05.04.2005	£263,000
06.04.2005	05.04.2006	£275,000
06.04.2006	05.04.2007	£285,000
06.04.2007	05.04.2008	£300,000
06.04.2008	05.04.2009	£312,000
06.04.2009	05.04.2010	£325,000
06.04.2010	05.04.2011	£350,000

Transfer of the nil-rate band between spouses and civil partners

FA 2008 s 10 and Sch 4 (para 2 inserts a new section 8A into IHTA) introduces legislation to allow a claim to be made to transfer any unused IHT nil-rate band on a person's death to the estate of their surviving spouse or civil partner who dies on or after 9 October 2007. This will apply where the IHT nil-rate band of the first deceased spouse or civil partner was not fully used in calculating the IHT liability of their estate. When the surviving spouse or civil partner dies, the unused amount may be added to their own nil-rate band. The claim must be made within 24 months from the end of the month in which the surviving spouse or civil partner dies.

Death of first spouse or civil partners – records

The transferable allowance will be available to all survivors of a marriage or civil partnership who die on or after 9 October 2007, no matter when the first partner died or dies subsequently.

The claim to transfer unused nil-rate band must be made by the personal representatives when the surviving spouse or civil partner dies and not when the first spouse or civil partner dies.

No action need be taken on the first death. The transfer of unused nil-rate band applies only on the death of the second spouse or civil partner, so there is no need to agree the amount that is transferable on the first death but it is necessary to keep certain records that will be needed on the death of the second spouse or civil partner.

The information and documents to be kept comprise:

(i)   a copy of the HMRC return (form IHT205 or IHT200; in Scotland, forms C1 and C5);

(ii)   a copy of the deceased's will (if any);

(iii)   a copy of any documents, such as a Deed of Variation, executed after the death of the first spouse or civil partner, that change who benefits from their estate;

(iv)   any valuation(s) of assets that pass under will or intestacy other than to the surviving spouse or civil partner;

(v)   any evidence to support the availability of relief (such as agricultural or business relief) where the relievable assets pass to someone other than to the surviving spouse or civil partner.

But there can be other assets that are chargeable when someone dies such as:

(i)   assets owned jointly with another person;

(ii)   assets held in trust from which the first to die was entitled to benefit and which are treated as forming part of their estate on death;

(iii)   any lifetime gifts made by the first to die in the seven years before their death;

(iv)   any gifts made by the first to die where they did not give up possession and use of the assets, or where they retained a right to use the asset through an arrangement (a gift with reservation of benefit); and

(v)   where the first to die was over 75, any alternatively secured pension fund from which they received a pension.

If any of these apply to the estate of the first person to die, the personal representatives will need to pass on information about these assets as well, for example:

- details of the assets concerned and evidence of their values;

- details about any exemptions and/or relief taken into account in arriving at the chargeable values.

The personal representatives will be able to obtain copies of some of the documents required from public records bodies:

- copies of grants of representation or confirmation and copies of wills are available from the Court Service (for England & Wales, www.hmcourts-service.gov.uk, for Scotland www.scot-courts.gov.uk, and for Northern Ireland www.courtsni.gov.uk); and

- copies of death certificates and marriage certificates are available from the General Register Office (for England & Wales www.gro.gov.uk, for Scotland www.gro-scotland.gov.uk, and for Northern Ireland www.groni.gov.uk).

These will give the value of the first estate that was declared for probate/confirmation and will also provide information about who inherited the assets that passed under the deceased's will or intestacy.

However, it will not provide any information about other assets that are chargeable when someone dies (list above).

The personal representatives will need to make enquiries of those who inherited the first estate to see if they can recall whether or not there may have been other assets that were chargeable on the first death. If values are known, they should be included on the claim form; if values are not known, the personal representatives should complete the claim form to the best of their ability and explain the position to HMRC when they make their claim. If there is no evidence that any other assets were chargeable, the personal representatives can make their claim based on the information they have from the documents already mentioned.

With regard to agreeing values of assets such as houses or household goods and whether a relief such as agricultural or business relief applies, it will only be necessary to agree values where such assets pass to chargeable beneficiaries on the first death (ie someone other than the surviving spouse or civil partner). This will be done when the surviving spouse or civil partner dies, but only where it is necessary to do so because the amount of the unused nil-rate band may affect the amount of IHT to pay on the second death. Similarly, if a farm is left to, say, a son and the personal representatives of the first death consider that agricultural relief is due against the whole property, the extent to which the relief is due will be established, if it is necessary, on the second death.

Form IHT216

If the gross value of the estate of the second spouse or civil partner to die is below the IHT nil-rate band that applies when they die, no claim need be made for transfer of the unused nil-rate band.

If a claim is necessary to transfer the unused part of the nil-rate band of the first spouse or civil partner to die, because the gross value of the second estate is above the nil-rate band that applies on their death, the personal representatives will need to fill in form IHT200.

Under s 8B personal representatives dealing with the estate of the surviving spouse or civil partner can make a claim to transfer the unused nil-rate band from the estate of the first spouse or civil partner to die. They will need to fill in a claim form IHT216 available online, or from the helpline on 0845 30 20 900, and send it to HMRC together with the copy documents requested.

The form IHT216 is a request for information about the estate of the first spouse or civil partner to die and is necessary to calculate the amount of the nil-rate band that was unused. A calculation can then be made to determine the extent to which the nil-rate band available to the survivor may be increased and use that revised nil-rate band to calculate the inheritance tax payable on the survivor's estate.

The form should be sent to HMRC at the same time as form IHT200 for the estate of the survivor together with the documents requested (for example, the death certificate of the first spouse or civil partner to die, a copy of their will and the marriage certificate).

Mechanics of the transfer (IHTA s 8 as amended by s 8A)

The increased nil-rate band does not replace the single nil-rate band available to the survivor that determines whether or not their estate is an excepted estate.

Where a valid claim to transfer unused nil-rate band is made, the nil-rate band that is available when the surviving spouse or civil partner dies will be increased by the proportion of the nil-rate band unused on the first death. For example, if on the first death the chargeable estate is £162,500 and the nil-rate band is £325,000, 50% of the nil-rate band would be unused. If the nil-rate band when the survivor dies is £350,000, then that would be increased by 50% to £525,000.

The amount of the nil-rate band that can be transferred does not depend on the value of the first spouse or civil partner's estate. Whatever proportion of the nil-rate band is unused on the first death is available for transfer to the survivor.

Even if all the assets passing under the will are left to the surviving spouse or civil partner, there may be other components of the aggregate chargeable 'estate' on death for IHT purposes (such as assets in trust, or gifts to other people made within seven years of death). If present, these may use up some or all of the nil-rate band in the normal way, and so reduce the amount of unused nil-rate band that may be available for transfer.

The rules apply in the same way whether the first spouse or civil partner to die leaves a will or dies intestate.

The rules allow unused nil-rate band to be transferred from more than one deceased spouse or civil partner, up to a limit of one additional nil-rate band. Therefore, if someone has survived more than one spouse or civil partner, then on their death the personal representatives may be able to claim additional nil-rate band from more than one of the relevant estates. A separate claim form should be completed for each spouse or civil partner who died before the deceased.

However, the total additional nil-rate band accumulated for this purpose is limited to a maximum of the amount of the nil-rate band in force at the relevant time. This is set out in the example of Martin below.

Existing wills

The new rules will not change the effect of existing wills. So people who have, for example, a nil-rate band trust written into their will do not have to take any action as a result of this measure. But if someone wants to change their will to take account of the new rules, that change can usually be made by a codicil, rather than having to rewrite the will.

If the nil-rate band was fully used when the spouse or civil partner died and a nil-rate band discretionary trust was set up under their will and the remaining spouse or civil partner's estate exceeds the nil-rate band on death, they will have made full use of the two nil-rate bands that are available and no transfer will be possible.

If the spouse or civil partner died more than two years previously, there is nothing that can be done to terminate the trust. Any changes to the trust may give rise to a separate charge to inheritance tax on the trust itself.

If the spouse or civil partner died less than two years previously, an appointment of the trust assets in the remaining spouse or civil partner's favour (before the second anniversary of their death, but not within the three months immediately following the death) would normally be treated for IHT purposes as if the assets had simply been left to them outright. Ending the trust in this way would mean that the nil-rate band was not used on the first death, and so the amount available for eventual transfer to the remaining spouse or civil partner's estate would be increased appropriately.

If a person executed an Instrument of Variation to create a nil-rate band discretionary trust and use up the nil-rate band on their death – the position is the same as above – if their spouse or civil partner died less than two years previously, an appointment of the trust assets in a remaining spouse or civil partner's favour (before the second anniversary of their death, but not within the three months immediately following the death) would normally be treated for IHT purposes as if the assets had simply been left to them outright. Ending the trust in this way would mean that the nil-rate band was not used on the first death. An appointment made in this way after the Instrument of Variation which created the trust is valid and will not be barred as a subsequent variation.

Where individuals leave assets on trust with a life interest for their surviving spouse or civil partner, with the remainder passing on their spouse or civil partner's death to someone else (for example their children), there is no IHT to pay on the first death because spouse or civil partner exemption applies. So if the entire estate is left in trust to the surviving spouse or civil partner, the nil-rate band would be available for transfer to the estate of the survivor on their eventual death in the same way as if the estate had been left to them absolutely.

Any additional nil-rate band is only relevant in establishing whether or not any tax is payable on the estate of the survivor – it does not replace the individual nil-rate band amount that determines the excepted estate limit for reporting purposes. If when the survivor dies, their gross estate exceeds the individual nil-rate band amount applicable at the time of their death, the estate cannot qualify as an excepted estate. The personal representatives will still need to deliver form IHT200 and make their claim for the transferable nil-rate band on the death of the survivor.

First death before 18 March 1986 (FA 2008 Sch 4 paras 10 and 11)

Inheritance tax was introduced with effect from 18 March 1986, but before this date other estate taxes (capital transfer tax (CTT) and estate duty) applied. Where a surviving spouse dies on or after 9 October 2007 and their spouse died before the introduction of the current inheritance tax provisions, a claim may still be made for the nil-rate band of the surviving spouse to be increased by reference to unused allowances of their spouse.

Where the first spouse died between 13 March 1975 and 18 March 1986 then the estate would have been subject to CTT. Any transfers to the spouse would have been exempt from tax in the same way as under the current rules. The transfer of nil-rate band provisions will operate in these cases in the same way as it works for inheritance tax. So that if on the death of the first spouse all their estate was transferred to their surviving spouse, then a claim may be made on the death of the surviving spouse to increase the nil-rate band by 100%.

For CTT, initially, all the gifts made during an individual's lifetime were to be taken into account when they died, although this was limited to gifts within seven years of the death during the first seven years of CTT and this was subsequently cut from an unlimited cumulation to a period of ten years in 1981.

Before 13 March 1975 estate duty applied. Under estate duty there was no tax-free transfer permitted between spouses until 21 March 1972, when a tax-free transfer between spouses of up to £15,000 was introduced. For estate duty, settled property in which the deceased had a life interest was not always aggregable with the estate on death.

Where the first spouse died between 21 March 1972 and 13 March 1975 a claim to transfer the nil-rate band to the surviving spouse will be based on the amount of the tax-free band that was unused on the death of the first spouse. For example, a husband died in 1973 and left an estate valued at £10,000, which was all transferred to his wife. As this was all within the spouse's exemption, the individual tax-free band was unused. In this case the full amount of that allowance may be transferred, and a claim may be made on the death of the surviving spouse to increase the nil-rate band by 100%.

Where any part of the first spouse's individual tax-free band was used then there will be a proportionate reduction in the amount by which the nil-rate band of the surviving spouse may be increased.

Similarly, where the first spouse died before 21 March 1972 the transfer of nil-rate band will be based on the proportion of the individual tax-free band that was unused on the death of the first spouse. However, as there was no relief from estate duty for transfers to spouses, any transfer made on the death of the first spouse will use up part of the tax-free band and so reduce the amount by which the nil-rate band of the surviving spouse may be increased.

Other issues

Lifetime gifts

Gifts and any other assets that are chargeable on the first death (eg assets in trust or assets owned jointly with a son or daughter) all utilise the nil-rate band in the normal way and reduce the amount that may be available for transfer.

The unused nil-rate band can only be transferred to be used against an estate when a person dies. If they were to die within seven years of making an immediately chargeable lifetime transfer, so that additional tax is payable on the gift as a result of their death, the transferred nil-rate band will be used in the normal way and may reduce any additional tax due as a result of the death – but the unused nil-rate band cannot be transferred against the tax due on a lifetime transfer at the time the transfer is made.

Low value estates

At present, the excepted estate rules remain as they are; so if the surviving spouse or civil partner's estate exceeds the single nil-rate band at their death (and assuming surviving spouse or civil partner exemption and charity exemption is not available), the estate cannot qualify as an excepted estate even though there may be no tax to pay because of transferred nil-rate band. So for the time being at least the surviving spouse or civil partner's personal representatives must deliver form IHT200 and make a claim to transfer the unused nil-rate band.

If the estates of both spouses or civil partners do not exceed one nil-rate band – the executors should still work out how much of the nil-rate band is available for transfer as the circumstances of the individual's spouse or civil partner may change before they die. But if, when they die, their estate remains below a single nil-rate band and provided they have not remarried or entered into a new civil partnership, there is no need for their personal representatives to make a claim to transfer unused nil-rate band.

Jointly owned assets

If all of the deceased's assets were jointly owned and so pass automatically to the surviving spouse or civil partner without the need to take out a grant of representation or confirmation (in Scotland) on the first death then provided there were no other assets chargeable to IHT on the deceased's death, the whole of the nil-rate band is unused and can be transferred to the surviving spouse or civil partner's estate. The personal representatives can make a claim to transfer the unused nil-rate band. Any other assets chargeable on death, such as gifts made within seven years of the death, will start to use up the nil-rate band.

It will be very important for the surviving spouse or civil partner to keep information about any assets (that they know about) that pass to others by survivorship, because the value of those assets will affect the proportion of nil-rate band that their personal representatives will be able to claim. The same applies to any other assets that are chargeable to IHT on the deceased's death such as gifts made within seven years that are not covered by one or other of the exemptions.

Consecutive deaths within a short period

If both parties to a marriage or civil partnership have died, one shortly after the other, the appropriate forms to apply for a grant in the estate of the first person to die should be completed in the normal way. This will establish how much of the nil-rate band is unused on the first death. The extent of the second estate should then be computed by adding together the value of that person's own assets and any assets they inherited from the estate of the first spouse to die.

If this does not exceed the single nil-rate band available to the estate of the second spouse or civil partner to die, there is no need to transfer the unused nil-rate band from the first death. Provided the other conditions are satisfied, a grant as an excepted estate can be applied for.

If this does exceed the single nil-rate band, form IHT200 will need to be completed for the estate of the second spouse or civil partner to die. A provisional claim should also be made to transfer the unused nil-rate band which should be based on the information available at the time of the claim. The claim form should indicate that the value is an estimate and the personal representative should provide the final figure once it is known. The estimated amount of the nil-rate band that can be transferred can be used to work out the tax payable on the second death.

If husband and wife or civil partners die at the same time, the same basic principle applies – if there is any nil-rate band unused on death of one spouse or civil partner, it can be transferred to the estate of the other, if required.

Marital changes

If the first spouse or civil partner died during the marriage or civil partnership and:

- the surviving spouse or civil partner subsequently remarried/formed a new partnership but is now divorced – the personal representatives can make a claim to transfer any unused nil-rate band from the first husband/civil partner's estate to the remaining spouse or civil partner's estate as a result of a claim made by the personal representatives.

- the surviving spouse or civil partner remarries or enters into another civil partnership and they die before their new spouse or civil partner – the nil-rate band available to the surviving spouse or civil partner will be increased by any unused amount of the deceased spouse or civil partner's nil-rate band and this is claimable by the personal representatives.

- the surviving spouse or civil partner dies leaving all their assets to their new spouse or civil partner, then again, the full amount of the nil-rate band on their death is available for transfer to their new spouse or civil partner. But the maximum that can be added to anyone's own nil-rate band is 100% of the nil-rate band applicable to their death.

If an ex-spouse or civil partner has died without remarrying, the personal representatives cannot claim to transfer the unused nil-rate band to ex-spouse or civil partner's estate as the marriage must still be in force at the date of death (see Example 4 – Martin below).

Conditionally exempt property

This will depend on whether the surviving spouse or civil partner dies before the conditional exemption ceases. Where the conditional exemption ceases before the surviving spouse or civil partner dies, the charge on cessation of the exemption will apply in the usual way – and if this exhausts the nil-rate band, there will then be nothing left to transfer to the surviving spouse or civil partner.

If, however, the surviving spouse or civil partner dies first and their personal representatives transfer the unused nil-rate band, the amount transferred will not be available for use when the conditional exemption ceases. Nevertheless, if this is some considerable time after the surviving spouse or civil partner dies, the charge on cessation of the exemption will still reflect any increase in the nil-rate band that has occurred between death and cessation.

Examples of how the new rules will work

Example 1

Ben dies on 14 April 2008 with an estate of £400,000, which he leaves entirely to his spouse, Amanda.

Amanda dies on 17 June 2009 leaving an estate of £600,000 equally between her two children. When Amanda dies the nil-rate band is £325,000. As 100% of Ben's nil-rate band was unused, the nil-rate band on Amanda's death is doubled to £650,000. As her estate is £600,000 there is no IHT to pay on Amanda's death.

Example 2

Jane dies on 27 May 2008, with an estate of £312,000. She leaves legacies of £41,600 to each of her three children with the remainder to her spouse Keith. The nil-rate band when Jane dies is £312,000.

Keith dies on 15 September 2009 leaving his estate of £500,000 equally to his three children; the nil-rate band when Keith dies is £325,000.

Jane used up 40% ((41,600 x 3)/312,000 = 40%) of her nil-rate band when she died, which means 60% is available to transfer to Keith on his death. So Keith's nil-rate band of £325,000 is increased by 60% to £520,000. As Keith's estate is only £500,000 there is no IHT to pay on his death.

Example 3

Cassie dies on 14 April 2009 with an estate of £450,000, which she leaves entirely to her civil partner, Sally.

Sally dies on 17 June 2009 leaving an estate of £675,000 which she leaves equally between her two nieces. When Sally dies the nil-rate band is £325,000. As 100% of Cassie's nil-rate band was unused, the nil-rate band on Sally's death is doubled to £650,000. This leaves £25,000 chargeable to IHT on her death.

Example 4

Martin dies on 14 April 2008 with an estate of £250,000, leaving £124,800 to his son Thomas and the remainder to his spouse Pamela.

The nil-rate band when Martin dies is £312,000 so 60% of his nil-rate band is unused. Pamela later marries Will who dies on 14 May 2010 and also leaves 60% of his nil-rate band unused. Pamela dies on 14 June 2010 with an estate of £750,000 when the individual nil-rate band is £350,000.

Pamela's nil-rate band is increased to reflect the transfer from Martin and Will, but the amount of increase is limited to 100% of the nil-rate band in force at the time. So Pamela's nil-rate band is £700,000, leaving £50,000 chargeable to IHT on her death.

Nil-rate band transfer and Capital Gains Tax (FA 2008 Sch 4 para 8)

TCGA 1992 s 274 provides that where the value of an asset in a deceased person's estate has been ascertained for IHT purposes, that value also has effect for CGT purposes. The value of an asset transferred from a deceased's estate will not be determined for CGT purposes until a subsequent disposal of that asset. So generally, where the value of an asset needs to be ascertained for IHT purposes, this will occur on the death of the individual and so before the value of that asset is ascertained for CGT purposes.

In some cases the transfer of the nil-rate band will mean that, to calculate how much nil-rate band can be transferred from the first deceased spouse's estate, the value of assets in that estate will need to be determined when the second spouse dies.

In these circumstances, if the value of the asset differs from any already agreed for CGT purposes, TCGA 1992 s 274 would require CGT to be recalculated on the basis of the value agreed for IHT purposes.

Consequently, the requirement under TCGA 1992 s 274 to use the IHT valuation for CGT purposes will not have effect where the valuation of an asset does not have to be ascertained for IHT purposes on the death of an individual.

So, for example, if the IHT valuation of an asset does not have to be ascertained until the death of the surviving spouse in order to establish the nil-rate band that may be transferred, then TCGA 1992 s 274 will not require that value to be used for any CGT calculation.

(iv)   **Tax chargeable on lifetime transfers following transferor's death**

Apart from tax becoming payable because a transfer which was potentially exempt becomes chargeable, additional tax may be due on chargeable lifetime transfers made within seven years before death, on which tax is recalculated by reference to the full rate at death.

Three points have to be taken into account in calculating such tax:

1.   If, because of a change in rate or for any other reason, the tax calculated at death is less than that calculated at the time of the gift, no repayment of tax is due.

2.   Lifetime gifts which are reckoned at death are brought in at their value at the time of the gift, but using the later rates applicable at the time of death (although if the value of the gift has fallen before death, the death value may sometimes be substituted).

3.   The tapering relief reduces the tax, not the value of the gift, for the purpose of calculating the tax payable by the following percentages:

Years between gift and death	% reduction in tax payable
0 to 3	0
3+ to 4	20
4+ to 5	40
5+ to 6	60
6+ to 7	80

(IHTA 1984 s 7).

Even though tax is only payable on most lifetime gifts if the donor does not survive them by *seven years*, it will still be necessary to keep records for inheritance tax purposes of lifetime transfers for up to 14 years.

Illustration

Edward, having used his available exemptions, makes a lifetime gift of £145,000 cash to a discretionary settlement on 31 May 1995. Although this is a chargeable transfer, no tax is payable since it is below the chargeable limit.

Edward makes a lifetime gift of £183,000 cash to Christopher on 30 April 2002. No tax is payable at that time since the first £6,000 of the gift is covered by two years' annual exemptions of £3,000 each, and the balance of £177,000 is a potentially exempt transfer.

Edward dies on 31 March 2009, leaving an estate at death of £235,000.

The tax arising at death is calculated as follows:

On £177,000 of the gift on 30.4.2002, which was within seven years before death

Having been a potentially exempt transfer, the gift of £177,000 is now chargeable by reference to the scale in force at 31.3.09:

	£	Tax on scale at time of death £
Gift within previous seven years (31.May 1995)	145,000	–
Gift on 30 April 2002 (183,000 – 6,000 exempt, see part (iv))	177,000	4,000*
	322,000	4,000*

(* 322,000 – 312,000 = 10,000 @ 40%)

Tax on £177,000 potentially exempt transfer now chargeable	4,000
Less: tapering relief (80% for surviving 6 years but not 7)	3,200
Tax payable by donee, Christopher	800

On estate at death 31 March 2009

	£	£
Gift within previous seven years (30 April 2002)	177,000	–
Estate at death	235,000	40,000*
	412,000	40,000*

(* 412,000 – 312,000 = 100,000 @ 40%)

Tax payable on estate at death	£40,000*

The gift of £145,000 to the discretionary settlement was made more than seven years before death (almost 14 years in fact), but because of the seven year accumulation period it has to be taken into account in calculating the tax on the gift to Christopher on 30 April 2002, since that gift was made within seven years after the gift to the trust and within seven years before Edward's death. The tax chargeable on the gift to Christopher is therefore calculated at the rates applicable to transfers between £145,000 and £322,000. (Had the gift of £145,000 been *potentially exempt*, it would have become totally exempt on 31 May 2002, and would not have been taken into account in calculating the tax on the potentially exempt transfer of £177,000 that became chargeable because of Edward's death.)

The gift to the discretionary settlement is excluded from the accumulation seven years after it was made, that is at 31 May 2002, so that it does not enter into the cumulative total at death on 31 March 2009. The tax on the death estate is calculated at the rates applicable to transfers between £177,000 and £412,000. Note that in the death estate calculation, the tax on the gift of £177,000 is shown as nil, whereas the tax actually chargeable, before tapering relief, was £4,000. This is because the tax on the earlier cumulative transfers is a notional figure, based on the scale at death, in order to give the correct starting point for the calculation of tax on the death estate (see part (i)).

(v) **Inheritance tax exempt transfers**

Most transfers of value made by an individual are *potentially exempt*, only becoming chargeable if the donor dies within seven years after the gift (s 3A).

There are however some transfers which are *completely exempt*:

(a) *Transfers between spouses and civil partners* (s 18).

This applies to all lifetime and death transfers between spouses including property to be held on trust for the transferee spouse except where the transferee spouse is foreign domiciled and the transferor spouse is UK domiciled, when transfers are only exempt to a cumulative total of £55,000. See Example 3(d) for more detailed information on this point.

The definition of spouse includes civil partners. This enables same sex couples who have performed a civil ceremony to have the same tax position as a married couple (FA 2005 s 103). In the case of *Burden v UK* (Application no. 13378/05) it was decided that sisters in their eighties who had lived together all their lives did not qualify for the exemption.

(b)   *Small gifts to same person* (s 20).

Any outright lifetime gifts to any one person in any one tax year are exempt up to the value of £250.

(c)   *Normal expenditure out of income* (s 21).

To obtain exemption the gift must be:

1.   Part of the donor's normal expenditure.

2.   Made out of income (taking one year with another).

3.   Such as will not reduce the donor's available net income (after all other similar transfers) below that required to maintain his usual standard of living.

An example would be payment of a life insurance or stakeholder pension premium for the benefit of another. HMRC will normally look for a pattern of giving in relation to this exemption.

(d)   *Gifts in consideration of marriage* (ss 22 and 57).

A gift of up to £5,000 by a parent of a party to a marriage; of £2,500 by a lineal ancestor; of £2,500 by one party to the marriage to the other; or of £1,000 by any other person is exempt providing it is a lifetime gift made in consideration of the marriage. If it is a marriage settlement it must be primarily for the benefit of the parties to the marriage, their issue or the spouses of such issue. The limit applies to gifts by any one donor for any one marriage. For this exemption 'children' include step-children, adopted and illegitimate children.

A civil partnership ceremony is deemed, for taxation, to be the equivalent of a marriage and therefore gifts in consideration of a civil ceremony, to the limits set out above, will be exempt transfers.

(e)   *All gifts to charities or registered community amateur sports clubs, either outright or held on trust for charitable purposes only or, in the case of a sports club, held for the purposes of the club or another registered club or an eligible sports governing body or a charity* (s 23 and FA 2002 Sch 18.9).

All such gifts are exempt whether in lifetime or on death.

(f)   *Gifts to political parties* (s 24).

Gifts to a qualifying political party, whether in lifetime or on death, are wholly exempt.

(g)   *Gifts for national purposes* (s 25 and Sch 3).

All such qualifying gifts are exempt whether in lifetime or on death.

(h)   *Maintenance funds for heritage property* (s 27 and Sch 4).

On a claim being made, transfers into a settlement established for the maintenance, repair or preservation of heritage property are exempt providing a Treasury direction is made in respect of the property under Sch 4. The exemption applies in lifetime or on death. A claim must be made within two years of the date of transfer or such longer period as HMRC may allow.

(i)   *Gifts to housing associations* (s 24A).

Gifts of land to a registered housing association are exempt whether in lifetime or on death.

(j)   *Employee trusts* (s 28).

Transfers by individuals of shares or securities in a company to a trust for the benefit of employees of the company are exempt, providing detailed conditions are satisfied.

HMRC concession F20 exempts certain compensation payments made to World War 2 survivors or their estates — see Example 3 part (a). As indicated in (ii) above, certain property that is not exempt is nonetheless left out of account because it is 'excluded property'. Details of excluded property are also in Example 3 part (a).

Where an exempt beneficiary settles a claim against a deceased's estate out of his own resources the exemption is abated. This could occur, for example, where a claim is made for financial provision against an estate by a non-exempt beneficiary (eg a child or mistress of the deceased). If, instead of the estate meeting the claim, an exempt beneficiary met the liability (eg spouse, charity etc) then tax would be avoided, since that part of the estate passing to the exempt beneficiary rather than to the non-exempt beneficiary would not have attracted tax. Section 29A provides that any such value transferred by the exempt beneficiary is treated as a chargeable part of the deceased's estate.

Annual exemption (s 19).

For those *lifetime transfers* which are not completely exempt there is an annual exemption.

The first £3,000 of transfers in any tax year are exempt provided they are completed in the lifetime of the individual. Any unused portion of the exemption may be carried forward for one year only for use in the following tax year after the exemption for that following year has been completely used.

The annual exemption is applied to lifetime transfers that are not completely exempt in strict chronological order. In the case of a lifetime transfer which does not give rise to an immediate charge, it is only the balance over and above any available exemptions, including any annual exemptions, which is a potentially exempt transfer, as illustrated in part (iii) above in relation to the gift by Edward.

Availability of exemptions to trusts

With the exception of (b), (c) and (j), the above exemptions are available to interest in possession trusts, subject in the case of the annual and marriage exemptions to certain conditions (s 57 — see Example 55 explanatory note 4).

The exemptions are not available on transfers out of discretionary trusts (except for certain transfers to employee trusts or charitable trusts — see Example 59 explanatory note 10).

Conditional exemption for heritage property (s 30).

On a claim being made within two years of the event, exemption is granted, subject to conditions, for the transfer of property that is designated by the Treasury as of pre-eminent national, scientific, historic, artistic or scenic interest (eg works of art and historic buildings). This applies to transfers on death and to lifetime transfers where the property has been owned for six years or more by the transferor and/or his spouse, or where it passed to the transferor on the death of another. Tax may be chargeable if the conditions are no longer satisfied — see explanatory note 4.

(vi)   **'Grossing up' of a lifetime transfer**

'Grossing up' is a term that applies where the donor pays the inheritance tax arising on the making of a chargeable transfer. The donor is therefore effectively making two dispositions, one directly to the transferee and the second to HMRC in respect of a liability arising on the first disposition. The value of the donor's estate is reduced on each occasion and the inheritance tax is calculated by reference to the reduction in the value of the donor's estate.

Illustration

Mr Smith has already made chargeable transfers of £312,000 and has used up all his available exemptions. He makes a chargeable transfer of £8,000 to a discretionary settlement on 1 May 2008 and agrees to pay the inheritance tax. The rate of tax on lifetime gifts over £312,000 is one half of 40%, ie 20% so that the £8,000 received into the settlement must represent 80% of the gross gift, so the gross gift is 100/80ths of the net gift = £10,000.

The calculation is as follows:

	Gross £	Tax £	Net £
Cumulative chargeable transfers to date	312,000	–	312,000
1 May 2008 Gift to discretionary settlement			
Net			8,000
Grossed up			
$\dfrac{100}{80} \times 8,000$	10,000	2,000	
Cumulative chargeable transfers carried forward	322,000	2,000*	320,000

(*322,000 – 312,000 = 10,000 @ 20%)

If Mr Smith's previous transfers had been £306,000 instead of £312,000, the position would have been:

	Gross £	Tax £	Net £
Cumulative chargeable transfers to date	306,000	–	306,000
1 May 2008 Gift to settlement within nil band	6,000	–	6,000
Remaining net gift			2,000
Grossed up			
$\dfrac{100}{80} \times 2,000$	2,500	500	
Cumulative chargeable transfers carried forward	314,500	500*	314,000

(*314,500 – 312,000 = 2,500 @ 20%)

A potentially exempt transfer never has to be grossed up. This is because the transferor is never personally liable for the tax. If tax is payable it is because of the death of the transferor within the next seven years. In that event the donee is primarily responsible for the tax.

Explanatory Notes

Normal expenditure out of income

1. 'Normal expenditure out of income' was considered in the case of *Bennett and Others v CIR* (1994), where it was held that there was no fixed minimum period during which the expenditure must be incurred. All that was required was for the pattern of actual or intended payments to have been

established, and for the pattern of payments to be intended to remain in place for a sufficient period to be regarded as a regular feature of the transferor's annual expenditure, and that the item in question conformed with that pattern.

Gifts in consideration of marriage or civil ceremony

2.   Whether a gift is in consideration of a marriage or civil ceremony is a question of fact. A gift made on the occasion of a marriage or civil ceremony or one made conditionally upon the marriage/civil ceremony taking place, whilst usually qualifying, is not automatically in consideration of marriage/civil ceremony. This is an involved legal point and reference to appropriate judicial decisions should be made if the point requires consideration in greater depth.

Gifts to political parties

3.   Exemption is not given for gifts to all political parties, but only to those where, at the last general election preceding the transfer:

(a)   Two members of that party were elected to the House of Commons, or

(b)   One member of that party was elected to the House of Commons and no fewer than 150,000 votes were given to candidates of that party (s 24(2)).

Heritage property

4.   The conditions under which exemption is available for heritage property and the circumstances in which inheritance tax becomes payable are dealt with in Example 29.

Gifts to housing associations

5.   Land is not defined for the purpose of the s 24A exemption on gifts to housing associations. It would appear therefore that buildings are included, since they are within the definition of land in the Interpretation Act 1978 Sch 1.

Annual exemption

6.   The treatment of the annual exemption outlined in part (v) of the example appears to conflict with s 19(3A), which provides that if a potentially exempt transfer becomes a chargeable transfer because of the donor's death within seven years, any annual exemption which has not been used then becomes available, and is given against the earliest transfer if there is more than one. An annual exemption which has already been given on chargeable transfers in the same year is not to be disturbed, even if some or all of the potentially exempt transfers that have become chargeable were made before the transfers against which the annual exemption had been utilised. But potentially exempt transfers that become chargeable take priority over chargeable transfers in a *later* tax year, so that where an unused annual exemption had been carried forward and used in the following tax year, the exemption is to be given instead against the potentially exempt transfers, and the tax on the transfers which originally used it has to be recomputed.

The provisions of s 19(3A) are, however, redundant when considered in the light of the definition of 'potentially exempt transfer' in s 3A, namely that a potentially exempt transfer is a transfer that would be a chargeable transfer but for s 3A. Any part of a transfer covered by the annual exemption is an exempt transfer, and therefore would not be a chargeable transfer apart from s 3A. It follows that if a potentially exempt transfer becomes chargeable there cannot possibly be any available annual exemption to use against it. Despite the fact that a drafting error makes s 19(3A) meaningless, no action has been taken to correct it.

The capital gains tax gifts holdover relief provisions of TCGA 1992 s 260 are available against a slice of any lifetime gift, to the extent that it is covered by the inheritance tax annual exemption. Capital gains tax gifts relief is dealt with in the companion to this book, Tolley's Taxwise I 2008/09. See Example 25 part A (c) for the interaction between the annual exemption and business and agricultural property relief.

Voidable transfers

7.   A transfer which is set aside by enactment or rule of law (eg bankruptcy) is not counted as a transfer for inheritance tax purposes, and neither is the transfer back (s 150 — voidable transfers).

Dispositions that are not transfers of value

8.   This example deals with transfers of value that are wholly or partly exempt. Example 2 at part (a) illustrates that there are certain dispositions which are not treated as transfers of value at all.

Tapering relief

9.   It should be noted that even though transfers may immediately or subsequently be chargeable transfers, no tax is payable until the cumulative total exceeds the nil threshold. Any transfers within that nil rate slice do not attract any tax, later transfers above the threshold bearing the whole of the tax payable (subject to tapering relief if available). Since the transfers within the nil rate slice never attract any tax, the tapering relief that applies when a donor survives a gift by more than three years but less than seven is irrelevant on those transfers.

Illustration

A wealthy married couple who have made no previous gifts want to know how much cash they could give away on 4 April 2009 without any possibility of inheritance tax ever being payable on the gifts. (No specific exemptions are available.)

Each spouse could give £318,000, making a total of £636,000. £6,000 each would be covered by the current and previous years' annual exemptions, leaving potentially exempt transfers of £312,000 each. If they both then died the next day, the potentially exempt gifts would become chargeable, but they would be covered by the nil threshold. Tax at 40% would be payable on each of their chargeable estates at death, since the nil threshold would have been used up by the lifetime gifts.

If they survived for seven years, they could in the meantime each make annual gifts amounting to the £3,000 annual exemption plus any annual increase in the nil threshold and after the seven years they could then make further gifts equal to the then nil threshold each, because their initial potentially exempt gifts would become completely exempt at that point. Tapering relief would not be relevant no matter how long they survived, since all gifts would be either exempt or covered by the nil threshold. Again tax at the full rate would be paid on the whole of their chargeable death estates, since the nil threshold would have been fully used against lifetime gifts.

Failure to exercise a right

10.   As indicated in part (ii) of the example, the failure to exercise a right is a disposition for inheritance tax under s 3. Such a disposition is treated as made at the latest time that the right could have been exercised. On the other hand, s 10 provides that any disposition that is not intended to confer a gratuitous benefit is not a transfer of value.

Where an employee dies in service after the earliest age at which he could have retired, and a lump sum death benefit is held in trust for his dependants, the employee could be regarded as having failed to exercise his right to take the pension. HMRC have, however, stated that they will not take this point in genuine cases of deferred retirement, and will only do so where there is evidence that the intention of deferring benefits was to increase the estate of someone else.

Similar provisions apply in respect of Registered Pension Schemes from 6 April 2006. The legislation is to be found in FA 2006, Sch 22.

An IHT charge can arise in a scheme member's lifetime under IHTA 1984 s 3(3), if they do not exercise their right to take pension benefits. The charge applies at the latest time when the right could be exercised i.e. immediately before death. For example, if a scheme member did not take their pension when their life expectancy was seriously impaired, and this resulted in an enhanced death benefit being paid to their beneficiaries, then IHT could apply.

Currently, by concession, IHT is not charged in respect of these enhanced death benefits where the beneficiary is a spouse, civil partner or person who is financially dependant on the scheme member. Nor is IHT applied where a scheme member chooses not to exercise a right at a time when this choice does not trigger a charge (for example, choosing not to take a pension when they are in good health) and does not subsequently vary that choice, even when a reduction in their life expectancy would in strictness trigger an IHT charge.

In addition, payments arising in these circumstances which are made to charity will also be exempted from IHT.

Fall in value of gift before donor's death

11.   For detailed notes on the relief where the value of a gift has fallen before the donor's death see Example 12.

Question

(a) Consider whether the following are 'transfers of value':

  (i)   School fees paid for the education of the transferor's son.

  (ii) School fees paid for the education of the transferor's grandson.

  (iii) Sums paid to a sister of the transferor for her maintenance.

  (iv) An entitlement to a bonus as sales director of a family company, and to a dividend on a holding of shares therein, both of which have been waived.

  (v)   Payment by a sole trader of £30,000 compensation for loss of office to a former employee.

  (vi) A loan of £50,000 to a friend.

(b) Charles, a widower, made the following gifts (after all exemptions other than the annual exemption):

(i)	10 July 1995	£66,000 to grandson
(ii)	20 May 1999	£239,000 to a discretionary settlement — on condition that the trustees paid the inheritance tax due
(iii)	12 June 2000	£37,000 to nephew
(iv)	20 October 2001	£185,000 to a discretionary settlement — on condition that the trustees paid the inheritance tax due
(v)	1 January 2005	£250,000 to an accumulation and maintenance settlement for his grandchildren

On 8 August 2008 Charles died leaving an estate of £400,000. By his will he left £200,000 to the Save the Children Fund and the balance to his daughter absolutely.

Calculate the inheritance tax payable on each of the gifts in lifetime and on death, and on the death estate.

Answer

(a)   **Dispositions that are not transfers of value**

Certain dispositions are not transfers of value:

1.   Dispositions which are not intended to confer any gratuitous benefit and made on arm's length terms (s 10).

2.   Expenditure on family maintenance (s 11). This covers dispositions:

    (a)   For the maintenance of the transferor's spouse, or former spouse if made on dissolution or annulment of the marriage (s 11(1) and (6)) (the same rules now apply to civil partnerships), or

    (b)   For the maintenance, education or training of a child for a period ending not later than the tax year in which the child becomes eighteen years of age or, after attaining that age, ceases to undergo full-time education or training.

    For this purpose 'child' includes:

      (i)   A child of the transferor by marriage or previous marriage (s 11(1) (6)).

      (ii)   An illegitimate child of the transferor (s 11(4)).

      (iii)   A child who is not in the care of a parent (but dispositions to such a child for a period ending after the year in which he reaches age eighteen will not be exempt unless the child was in the care of the transferor for substantial periods before he became eighteen) (s 11(2)).

    or

    (c)   Made for the reasonable care and maintenance of a dependent relative (s 11(3)). The term 'dependent relative' is defined in s 11(6).

3.   A waiver or repayment of remuneration (s 14), and a waiver of dividends made within twelve months before any right to the dividend has accrued (s 15).

4.   Expenditure which is allowable as a deduction in computing a person's profits or gains for income or corporation tax (s 12).

5.   Transfers to employee trusts by close companies (s 13).

6.   A grant of an agricultural tenancy for full consideration (s 16).

7.   Deeds of variation within s 142.

The position in the six situations given is therefore:

  (i)   *School fees for education of transferor's son*

    Leaving aside the possibility that the school fees were paid out of income and therefore may be exempt as annual expenditure out of income, school fees paid for the education of the transferor's son will not be a transfer of value providing the son is under eighteen or in full-time education or training.

  (ii)   *School fees for education of transferor's grandson*

    If the school fees for the grandson were not paid out of income then they will be a transfer of value unless the grandson is under eighteen and is not in the care of one of his parents; or the grandson is over eighteen and is not in the care of one of his parents *and* was in the care of his grandparent for substantial periods before reaching the age of eighteen.

(iii)   *Gifts for maintenance of sister*

Again leaving aside the question of non-chargeable payments out of income, gifts to the transferor's sister for her maintenance would be a transfer of value unless the sister was a dependent relative by reason of old age or infirmity *and* the amounts were reasonable for her care and maintenance, or unless she was not in the care of a parent and was either under eighteen years of age or if over eighteen, had been in the care of the transferor for substantial periods before reaching age eighteen and in that event was still in full time education or training.

(iv)   *Waiver of remuneration and dividends*

The waiver of remuneration is not a transfer of value, nor is the dividend waiver if waived within twelve months before any right to it has accrued.

(v)   *Compensation for loss of office*

So long as the compensation payment is allowed in computing profits, it will not be a transfer of value.

(vi)   *Loan to a friend*

If someone lends money or property for a prolonged period, or denies himself the opportunity to recall the money or property, the property is then worth less in the owner's hands than it was before. Thus if the £50,000 is lent free of interest for a fixed term of ten years and after making the loan the lender requires the cash, the only way to obtain it is to assign the debt to someone else. But for how much? Not £50,000, because the assignee will want a commercial return, which he will obtain by paying sufficiently below £50,000 to compensate for having to wait for the remainder of the ten years before the capital sum becomes repayable. A transfer of value will thus arise on the difference between the amount lent and the discounted present value of the future right to repayment.

If however the loan is at commercial rates of interest and repayable on demand or on reasonable notice, then there will be no diminution in its value, and a transfer of value will not arise.

If the various conditions stated above were not satisfied, the payments would be transfers of value, against which the current and previous years' annual exemptions could be used if available.

To the extent that the amounts in (iii) and (v) were not covered by the annual exemption, they would be potentially exempt transfers and therefore only brought into account if the donor died within the next seven years.

If the school fees under (i) and (ii) are not within the 'family maintenance' exemption and are not by way of settlement, it is possible that the transfers could be regarded as chargeable transfers of value (subject to any other available exemptions) rather than potentially exempt transfers because for a transfer to an individual to be potentially exempt, the transferee's estate must be increased by the transfer, which would not directly apply in these two instances. Similarly, any transfer of value arising out of the loan at (vi) would be a chargeable transfer rather than a potentially exempt transfer unless the estate of the borrower could be regarded as increased by the value of the right to have the loan on favourable terms.

(b)   **Charles — inheritance tax position on lifetime gifts and on estate at death**

Tax payable in lifetime

				Gross £	Tax £
10 July 1995 —	gift to grandson			66,000	
	Less: Annual exemptions	1995/96	3,000		
		1994/95	3,000	6,000	
Potentially exempt transfer				60,000	
20 May 1999 —	gift to discretionary settlement			239,000	
	Less: Annual exemptions	1999/00	3,000		
		1998/99	3,000	6,000	
Lifetime chargeable transfer (one half rates)				233,000	400*

(* 233,000 – 1999/00 threshold 231,000 = 2,000 @ 20%)
Inheritance tax payable by trustees £400.

				Gross £	Tax £
12 June 2000 —	gift to nephew			37,000	
	Less: Annual exemption	2000/01		3,000	
Potentially exempt transfer				34,000	

			Gross £	Tax on 2001/02 scale
			233,000	–
20 Oct 2001 —	gift to discretionary settlement	185,000		
	Less: Annual exemption 2001/02	3,000		
Lifetime chargeable transfer (one half rates)			182,000	34,600*
			415,000	34,600*

(* 415,000 – 2001/02 threshold 242,000 = 173,000 @ 20%)
Inheritance tax payable by trustees £34,600.

				Gross £	
1 Jan 2005 —	gift to accumulation and maintenance settlement			250,000	
	Less: Annual exemptions	2004/05	3,000		
		2003/04	3,000	6,000	
Potentially exempt transfer				244,000	
20 May 2006 —	exclude transfer seven years earlier			(233,000)	
				182,000	

On death of Charles — 8 August 2008

	Gross £	Tax (using 2008/09 rates) £

Transfers within seven years before death i.e.
    9 August 2001 to 8 August 2008:
    20 October 2001 — gift to discretionary settlement
        Cumulative *chargeable* transfers within previous seven
        years

	Gross £	Tax (using 2008/09 rates) £
(ie 21 October 1994 – 20 October 2001 — see explanatory note 3)	233,000	
Chargeable transfer (full rates)	182,000	41,200*
	415,000	41,200*

(* 415,000 – 312,000 = 103,000 @ 40%)
1 January 2005 — gift to accumulation and maintenance settlement
Cumulative *chargeable* transfers within previous seven years

(ie 2 January 1998 – 1 January 2005)	415,000	41,200
Chargeable transfer	244,000	97,600
	659,000	138,800*

(* 659,000 – 312,000 = 347,000 @ 40%)
8 August 2008 – date of death
Cumulative chargeable transfers within previous seven years

		Gross £	Tax £
(182,000 + 244,000) (ie 9 August 2001 – 8 August 2008)		426,000	45,600*
Estate on death	400,000		
Less: Exempt – Legacy to charity	200,000	200,000	80,000
		626,000	125,600**

(* 426,000 – 312,000 = 114,000 @ 40%)
(** 626,000 – 312,000 = 314,000 @ 40%)

Inheritance tax payable — lifetime

		£
(i)	Grandson	nil
(ii)	trustees of 1999 discretionary settlement	400
(iii)	nephew	nil
(iv)	trustees of 2001 discretionary settlement	34,600
(v)	trustees of accumulation and maintenance settlement	nil

Inheritance tax payable — death

	£	£
By grandson, trustees of 1999 discretionary settlement and nephew (excluded as gifts were made more than seven years before death)		nil
By trustees of 2001 discretionary settlement		
Tax due on death scale	41,200	
Less: Tapering relief 80% (6–7 years)	32,960	
	8,240	
Less: Paid on lifetime transfer	34,600	nil
(No repayment will be made to the trustees)		
By trustees of accumulation and maintenance settlement		
Tax due on death	97,600	
Less: Tapering relief 20% (3–4 years)	19,520	78,080

	£	£
By personal representatives		80,000
		158,080

Explanatory Notes

Dispositions for family maintenance

1. The distinction between school fees paid for the education of the transferor's son and his grandson illustrates how carefully the wording of a section has to be considered, particularly since the heading of a section is often widely descriptive, in this case being 'disposition for maintenance of family' (s 11). Broadly speaking, transfers for the maintenance of one's own children are not chargeable if the child is either under eighteen or in full time education. Transfers for the maintenance of other persons are chargeable (in the absence of other exemptions) unless the child is *not* in the care of a parent and if over eighteen, was in the care of the transferor for substantial periods before reaching age eighteen and is still in full time education or training.

Potentially exempt transfers to grandson and nephew

2. The gifts to grandson and nephew in part (b) are made after 17 March 1986 and are outright gifts by an individual to another individual, and are therefore potentially exempt transfers in so far as they exceed the available annual exemptions.

    Since the transferor did not die within seven years after the gifts, the potentially exempt transfers become exempt transfers, so there is no inheritance tax liability on them and they are not taken into account in the figure of cumulative chargeable transfers. For more detailed notes see Example 4 explanatory note 6.

Cumulation of transfers

3. When calculating the tax on a transfer, the tax on the brought forward figure is always recalculated on the current scale, and it may, or may not, represent the tax that was actually paid on the earlier transfers. This gives the correct starting point to calculate the tax on the current transfer. Now that there is only one rate of tax, this will only be relevant where the cumulative transfers are below the nil threshold applicable at the date of the current transfer, because later lifetime transfers will be at 20% and death transfers at 40%.

4. In the example the cumulative chargeable transfers within seven years before 20 October 2001 exclude the 10 July 1995 and 12 June 2000 transfers (as potentially exempt transfers that became exempt transfers after seven years), but include the 20 May 1999 transfer, whereas the total as at 1 January 2005 includes both the 20 May 1999 and 20 October 2001 transfers. On death the 20 October 2001 chargeable transfer and the 1 January 2005 potentially exempt, now chargeable, transfer are included.

Question

In connection with inheritance tax:

(a) Explain the meaning and inheritance tax treatment of excluded property for both domiciled and non-domiciled individuals.

(b) Briefly describe the circumstances in which a charge to tax may arise on property comprised in a settlement.

(c) Discuss the basic overseas aspects of IHT and explain the non-domiciled spouse exemption.

Answer

(a)   **Excluded property**

'Excluded property' is defined in IHTA 1984 ss 6 and 48.

If a person is not domiciled in the UK, the following types of asset may be treated as excluded property and no inheritance tax is chargeable:

●   Foreign property owned by individuals domiciled outside the UK (s 6(1)).

●   Settled property – settled property situated outside the UK is excluded property if the settlor was domiciled outside the UK at the time the property was settled. Reversionary interests are also generally excluded property (s 48(3)).

●   Visiting armed forces – emoluments and tangible movable property of members of visiting forces (other than British citizens, British Dependent Territories citizens or British Overseas citizens) and certain staff of allied headquarters are excluded property. For inheritance tax purposes, HMRC will not take periods spent on duty in the UK into account in deciding whether a transferor is resident, domiciled or deemed to be domiciled here (ss 6(4) and 155(1)).

●   Former employees of ex-colonial governments – there are special rules about pensions paid to former employees of former colonial governments. On the death of a former employee any pension payable under the Government of India Act 1935 s 273, or an equivalent scheme under the Overseas Pensions Act 1973 s 2, is exempt.

●   Pension payments and gratuities – certain other pension payments and gratuities are treated as being paid abroad and there is no inheritance tax due on such pensions on the estate of a deceased pensioner who dies whilst domiciled abroad.

●   National Savings Certificates and small savings – if an individual is domiciled in the Channel Islands or the Isle of Man and holds National Savings Certificates and certain other forms of small savings, they are excluded property. The deemed domicile provisions do not apply (s 6(3)).

●   Non-sterling accounts with a bank or the Post Office – balances on non-sterling accounts with a bank or the Post Office are excluded from inheritance tax on death if they are held by:

    –   an individual not domiciled, resident or ordinarily resident in the UK, or

    –   trustees not domiciled, resident or ordinarily resident in the UK on behalf of an individual with an interest in possession in the account, if the settlor was not domiciled in the UK when the settlement was made.

●   Holdings in Authorised unit trusts (AUTs) and Open-ended investment companies (OEICs) are excluded property if held by an individual not domiciled in the UK or if held in a trust made by a settlor not domiciled or not deemed domiciled in the UK when making the trust (s 6(1A) and s 48(3A)).

●   FOTRA securities first issued before 30 April 1996 are exempt from tax if a person is neither domiciled nor ordinarily resident in the UK (s 6(2)).

●   For FOTRA securities first issued after 29 April 1996 new conditions apply which mean that domicile is not relevant. An individual needs to be not ordinarily resident in the UK to benefit from the exemption. From 6 April 1998 the new conditions apply to all British Government Securities, except 3½% War Loan 1952 or later.

By HMRC concession F19, a decoration awarded for valour or gallant conduct is to be treated for inheritance tax as excluded property if it is shown never to have been transferred for consideration in money or money's worth.

By HMRC concession F20, ex gratia compensation payments of £10,000 made by the Government to British survivors of Japanese imprisonment or their spouses, and various other modest amounts paid by European bodies to slave labourers and other World War 2 victims or their spouses, or payments of such compensation made to the person's personal representatives, are left out of account in calculating the value of the person's estate for inheritance tax.

Excluded property is generally outside the scope of inheritance tax, because inheritance tax is not charged on the lifetime disposal of such property nor on such property passing at death (ss 3(2) and 5(1)). A charge to tax in respect of a lifetime transfer of non-excluded property can, however, be affected by excluded property, because excluded property is taken into account when measuring the value of the estate before and after the transfer of non-excluded property. If, for example, someone owned shares in a company in their own right, and had an interest in possession in shares in the company under a settlement made by a non-UK domiciled settlor, the two holdings together constituting a controlling interest, and a transfer was made of the shares held directly which reduced the combined holding to a minority holding, the loss to the donor's estate would reflect the fall in value of the combined holding.

Apart from the point made in the above paragraph, excluded property is treated in the same way as property that is exempt.

Certain other property, although not within the definition of 'excluded property', is also outside the scope of inheritance tax as follows:

Cash options under approved annuity schemes (s 152);

Overseas pensions, in valuing an estate at death (s 153);

Property passing as a result of death on active military service (s 154).

Foreign currency bank accounts, on the death of an individual not domiciled, resident or ordinarily resident in the UK (s 157).

Works of art, normally kept overseas, physically present in the UK on the death of a foreign owner are excluded if brought into the UK solely for public exhibition, cleaning or restoration (HMRC concession F7).

(b) **Charge to tax on property comprised in a settlement**

The charge to tax on property comprised in a settlement depends upon the type of settlement.

(i) If the settlement has a beneficiary taxed *interest in possession* (see Chapter 52), broadly where one or more persons are entitled to the income, the property in the settlement is deemed to belong to the person who is entitled to that interest and any liability will arise when that person's interest in the property comes to an end, for example, if he makes a sale or gift of his interest, or his interest ceases by reason of a death or marriage or other reason. Like any other transfer in lifetime, however, the cessation of the life interest may be potentially exempt. This will apply where the trust property is transferred to an individual, or to another interest in possession settlement or to an accumulation and maintenance trust or a disabled trust. The transfer will only become a chargeable transfer if the life tenant who has given up his interest dies within the next seven years, the tax being computed by taking into account transfers within the seven years before the now chargeable transfer and calculating tax on the death scale.

(ii) If there is *no interest in possession* (eg the settlement is a discretionary settlement — broadly where the beneficiaries only have a hope as distinct from a right to receive the income arising) then a charge to tax will occur on the tenth anniversary of the creation of the trust and at ten yearly intervals thereafter. The tax is charged on the value of the 'relevant property' in the trust at 30% of the effective rate (called the 'principal charge').

The lifetime rate of tax is used to calculate the effective rate, and the maximum possible charge is 30% of 20%, ie 6%.

As it would be possible to avoid the forthcoming principal charge to tax on a discretionary settlement by distributing assets between ten-year anniversaries, an 'exit charge' arises when property ceases to be relevant property. The tax on the amount leaving the settlement is charged at the appropriate fraction of 30% of the effective rate, the appropriate fraction depending on the number of complete quarters that have elapsed since the creation of the trust or the last ten year anniversary as the case may be.

(c) **Transfers between spouses when wife not domiciled in the UK**

Since 1 January 1974, a wife's domicile is not necessarily the same as the domicile of her spouse or civil partner. It is based on similar criteria as those for individuals who are able to have an independent domicile. But, if a woman married before 1974 and had acquired her husband's domicile, she will retain this until she legally acquires a new domicile.

Non-domiciled spouse or civil partner exemption on transfers on death and life are restricted to a total of £55,000:

- where the deceased/donor is domiciled in the UK, and

- the transferee spouse or civil partner is not domiciled in the UK,

and, for the purpose of the exemption, domicile includes deemed domicile. See Example 15 for more information on the effects of domicile for IHT purposes (s 18(2)).

As regards the transfer of the nil-rate band – this restriction may mean that bequests to the surviving spouse or civil partner will use up some of the nil-rate band available on the non-domiciled individual's death; but anything unused remains available for transfer and can be claimed by the personal representatives of the surviving spouse or civil partner when they die.

For example, Mr and Mrs Hill live in the UK. Mr Hill is UK domiciled but his wife is domiciled in Fiji. Mr Hill owns a house in Cornwall – an area his wife likes particularly so he decides to gift the house to her as a birthday present. The property is worth £355,000 at the time of the gift. Had Mrs Hill been UK domiciled the whole gift would have been an exempt transfer, but under s 18(2) only £55,000 of the gift remains exempt and the remaining £300,000 becomes a potentially exempt transfer. Mr Hill will need to live for a further seven years if the gift is to become exempt from IHT.

In 2001, Mr Cliff, who was domiciled in the UK, transferred £200,000 to Mrs Cliff, who was not domiciled in the UK. Of this transfer, £55,000 is exempt under s 18(2), and £145,000 is a potentially exempt transfer and assumed to be exempt. Mr Cliff dies in 2009 and leaves all his property to Mrs Cliff, who remains domiciled outside the UK. Even though Mr Cliff has survived for seven years after making the transfer, the limited exemption under s 18(2) has all been used and is not available on Mr Cliff's death.

In 2000 Mr Brink transfers a UK property worth £500,000 to Mrs Brink. Both are domiciled outside the UK. Exemption under s 18(1) is available in full. In 2008 Mr Brink is deemed to be domiciled in the UK and a year later gives £100,000 to Mrs Brink who remains domiciled outside the UK. The limited exemption under s 18(2) is not then available because the amount of exemption already conferred under s 18 as a whole exceeds £55,000.

Effects of domicile on inheritance tax

Domicile means the legal system with which a person is most closely connected. This will normally be a country, but it may be a State within a country if it has its own legal system.

HMRC explains domicile as follows:

'Domicile is not the same as nationality or residence. Broadly speaking, you have your domicile in the country that is your "real" or permanent home. Everyone acquires a domicile of origin at birth. This is generally the country that your father considered to be his 'home country' at the date of your birth. If you have a domicile of origin outside the UK, then this is likely still to apply unless you have chosen to remain in the UK permanently or indefinitely. In most cases an individual's domicile is obvious.'

So domicile can be loosely thought of as the place to which someone will ultimately return even though they may be absent from it from time to time, or even for a very long time.

Any liability to UK inheritance tax depends on a person's domicile at the time they make a transfer of value.

Domicile of origin

A 'domicile of origin' is normally taken as the father's domicile at the time when the child is born but may in fact not be the country of birth. For example, if Jack is born in Germany while his father is working there, but the father's permanent home is in the UK, Jack's domicile of origin is the UK.

Domicile of dependency

Until a person can legally change it by acquiring a domicile of choice, their domicile will be the same as that of the person on whom they are legally dependent. If that person's domicile changes, the dependant automatically acquire the same domicile in place of their domicile of origin. This is known as a domicile of dependency.

Deemed domicile

There is a concept of 'deemed domicile' for inheritance tax. Even if a person is not domiciled in the UK under general law they will be treated as if they are domiciled in the UK at the time of a transfer if:

- they were domiciled in the UK within the three years immediately before the transfer, or

- they were resident in the UK in at least 17 of the 20 tax years ending with the year in which they make a transfer.

Generally, if an individual is domiciled, or deemed to be domiciled, in the UK, inheritance tax applies to their assets wherever they are situated. Similarly, inheritance tax applies to settled property in the UK. It does not apply to settled property outside the UK, unless the settlor was domiciled, or deemed to be domiciled, in the UK when the property was settled.

The location of assets is subject to general law as amended by any special provisions in a double taxation agreement. The normal rules for the more common types of asset are that:

- rights or interests in or over immovable property and chattels are situated where the property is located;

- registered shares or securities are situated where they are registered;

- coins and bank notes are situated wherever they happen to be at the time of the transfer;

- bearer securities are situated where the certificate of title is located at the time of the transfer;

- goodwill is situated where the business, to which it is attached, is carried on;

- an interest in a partnership is situated in the country whose law governs the partnership agreement;

- debts are situated where the debtor resides;

- bank accounts are situated at the branch where the account is kept.

If a person is domiciled abroad, inheritance tax applies only to their UK assets. However, if an individual is domiciled abroad there is no charge on excluded assets. See Example 3(a) for a list of excluded assets for non-domiciled individuals.

The deemed domicile rules do not apply to a taxable reversionary interest in settled property. Inheritance tax is not due if the reversionary interest is situated outside the UK, and the person beneficially entitled to it is domiciled outside the UK.

Domicile of choice

A person can legally acquire a new domicile, a domicile of choice, from the age of 16. To do so, they must leave the country in which they are now domiciled and settle in another country, and in addition provide irrefutable evidence that they intend to live there permanently or indefinitely.

The fact of living in another country for a long time, although an important factor, does not prove an individual has acquired a new domicile and as might be expected, there is a substantial body of case law on this topic.

Double taxation treaties and IHT

The UK has a number of bilateral treaties for taxes on estates, gifts and inheritances.

For the purpose of the agreement, the treaties permit:

- The country in which the transferor is (or in the case of a death, was) domiciled to tax all property wherever it is, and the other country to tax only specified types of property, such as immovable property, in its territory.

- Where the person is doubly taxed there are rules for deciding which country gives credit for the other's tax. Where, exceptionally, the relief given by a treaty would be less than that given by unilateral relief the person receives the benefit of unilateral relief.

If there is no treaty and the transfer is liable to inheritance tax and also to a similar tax imposed by another country with which the UK does not have an agreement, an individual may be able to get relief under unilateral relief provisions.

Credit is given against inheritance tax for the tax charged by another country on assets situated in that country. For this purpose, UK law determines the location of the asset. If the tax that is charged on the asset by the other country exceeds inheritance tax on that asset, the credit is limited to the amount of inheritance tax.

Credit is also given where both the UK and another country impose tax on assets that are situated:

- in a third country, or

- both in the UK under UK law and in the other country under that country's law.

In these cases the credit is a proportion of the tax. The proportionate credit is computed by the formula:

$$\frac{A}{(A + B)} \times C$$

A is the inheritance tax, B is the overseas tax and C is whichever of A or B is the lesser.

If the UK and two or more other countries charge the same asset to tax – the above applies but with modifications.

Example 1

Kirsty is domiciled in Xanadu, but is also treated as domiciled in the UK. She makes a gift of property situated in Shangrila.

UK inheritance tax (A) £1,500,

Xanadu inheritance tax (B) £500,

C is the smaller of A and B £500,

The amount to be set against UK inheritance tax is:

$$\frac{£1,500}{(£1,500 + £500)} \times £500 = £375$$

Balance of UK tax due is £1,125.

Example 2

Jamie is domiciled in Shangrila but holds shares in a Xanadu company, which maintains a duplicate share register in the UK. Under UK law the shares are regarded as situated in the UK, but Xanadu law regards them as situated in Xanadu. Jamie dies (but his estate is not liable to Shangrilan tax).

UK inheritance tax (A) £500,

Xanadu inheritance tax (B) £2,000,

C is the smaller of A and B £500,

The amount to be set against UK inheritance tax is:

$$\frac{£500}{(£500 + £2,000)} \times £1,000 = £200$$

Balance of UK tax due is £300.

Explanatory Notes

Reversionary interest

1.   'Reversionary interest' is defined in s 47 as a future interest under a settlement, whether vested or contingent. Where, for example, property is settled on A for life, then to B absolutely, B (sometimes called the remainderman) has a reversionary interest in the settled property.

Deemed UK domicile

2.   See 3(c) for a detailed explanation of deemed domicile.

For related points and the treatment of foreign currency bank accounts see Example 27. Example 27 also illustrates excluded property held by a non-UK domiciled person. For the treatment of reversionary interests see Example 58.

Meaning of 'settlement'

3.   For inheritance tax purposes a settlement is defined as any disposition or dispositions of property whereby the property is for the time being:

(a)   held in trust for persons in succession, or for any person subject to a contingency (s 43(2)(a))

(b)   held by trustees on trust to accumulate the whole or any part of any income of the property, or with power to make payments out of that income at the discretion of the trustees or some other person, with or without the power to accumulate surplus income (s 43(2)(b))

(c)   charged or burdened (otherwise than for full consideration in money or money's worth) with the payment of any annuity or other periodical payment for a life or any other limited or terminable period (s 43(2)(c)).

Also treated as a settlement is a lease of property for the duration of a person's life or persons' lives, unless the lease was granted for full consideration in money or money's worth.

The words 'settlement' and 'trust' are usually regarded as being interchangeable, although as can be seen from the definition, 'settlement' has a wider coverage. Any reference in IHTA 1984 to a trustee, in relation to a settlement where there would otherwise be no trustees, is to any person in whom the settled property or its management is vested (s 45).

Classes of settlement

4.   For inheritance tax purposes settlements may be considered to fall into four main classes:

(a)   Interest in possession settlements.

(b)   Settlements in which there is no interest in possession (usually but not exclusively discretionary trusts).

(c)   Accumulation and maintenance trusts.

(d)   Certain other special types of settlement, eg trusts for the benefit of employees, protective trusts and charitable trusts.

The distinction between settlements in which there is an interest in possession and settlements where there is no such interest is fundamental to an understanding of the inheritance tax legislation. The position is dealt with in detail in the section of this book dealing with settlements and trusts.

The inheritance tax settlement provisions do not apply to registered pension schemes.

Adding property to a settlement

5.   With regard to heading (v) in part (a) of the example, HMRC take the view that a separate settlement is made when property is put into an existing settlement, so that even if a settlement of foreign property was made when the settlor was not UK domiciled, any further foreign property added to the settlement at a time when the settlor was UK domiciled would not be excluded property (Tax Bulletin February 1997).

Question

Mr C T Tax made the following lifetime gifts:

20 November 2001   £254,000 to a discretionary trust
11 January 2003   £60,000 to his sister, Ann
3 May 2005   £86,000 to his daughter, Joan
4 April 2006   £90,000 to his son, Ben.

Mr C T Tax died on 2 April 2009 leaving an estate of £620,000 equally to Ben and Joan.

(i)   Compute the tax payable by reason of the death of Mr C T Tax.

(ii)   Would the tax payable be different if Mr C T Tax had not made gifts to his children in 2005 and 2006 totalling £176,000 but had left an estate of £796,000 instead of £620,000?

(iii) Show the tax payable in lifetime and on death if the circumstances were as in (i) except that instead of giving £90,000 to Ben on 4 April 2006, Mr C T Tax transferred £90,000 to a discretionary trust (the trustees paying the tax) on:

(a)   4 March 2006

(b)   6 April 2007.

Answer

(i)   **Inheritance tax position of Mr C T Tax**

Tax payable in lifetime

			£	£
20 Nov 2001	gift to discretionary trust			254,000
	Less: Annual exemptions	2001/02	3,000	
		2000/01	3,000	6,000
	Chargeable transfer			248,000
	Tax payable by trustees (on 2001/02 scale) 248,000 − 242,000 = 6,000 @ 20%		£1,200	
11 Jan 2003	gift to Ann			60,000
	Less: Annual exemption	2002/03		3,000
	Potentially exempt transfer			57,000
3 May 2005	gift to Joan			86,000
	Less: Annual exemptions	2005/06	3,000	
		2004/05	3,000	6,000
	Potentially exempt transfer			80,000
4 April 2006	gift to Ben – potentially exempt transfer			90,000

On death of Mr C T Tax 2 April 2009

Potentially exempt transfers since 3 April 2002 now become chargeable transfers:

	Gross £	Tax (using rates at 2 April 2009) £
Cumulative transfers in seven years before gift to Ann		
20 November 2001 — discretionary trust	248,000	–
11 January 2003 — gift to Ann	57,000	–
	305,000	–
3 May 2005 — gift to Joan	80,000	29,200*
	385,000	29,200*
(*385,000 − 312,000 =73,000 @ 40%)		
4 April 2006 — gift to Ben	90,000	36,000
	475,000	65,200
20 November 2008		
Deduct transfer made more than seven years previously (ie prior to 21 November 2001)	248,000	
Cumulative transfers in seven years before death	227,000	–
Estate chargeable on death	620,000	214,000*
	847,000	214,000*

(* 847,000 − 312,000 = 535,000 @ 40%)

	£
Inheritance tax payable:	
By Ann on gift made 11 January 2003:	nil
By Joan on gift made 3 May 2005:	
As gift is made more than 3 but not more than 4 years	
before death tax payable is 80% × £29,200 =	23,360
By Ben on gift made 4 April 2006:	
As gift is within 3 years of death there is no reduction	
in the tax payable	36,000
By Estate	214,000
Tax payable by reason of death of Mr C T Tax	273,360

(ii)   **If no lifetime gifts made to children — position on death of Mr C T Tax 2 April 2009**

	Gross £	Tax £
Cumulative transfers in seven years before death		
(ie 3 April 2002 – 2 April 2009)		
11 January 2003	57,000	–
Estate chargeable on death	796,000	216,400*
	853,000	216,400*
(* 853,000 – 312,000 = 541,000 @ 40%)		
Tax with gifts to children (part (i))		273,360
Tax without gifts to children — estate	216,400	
Tax on gift to Ann — as above	nil	216,400
Additional tax because of chargeable transfers made within		
seven years before lifetime gifts to children		£56,960

(iii)   **Inheritance tax position of Mr C T Tax with gift to discretionary trust instead of to Ben**

(a)   **Gift to discretionary trust on 4 March 2006**

Tax payable in lifetime

		Gross £	Tax on 2001/02 scale £
20 November 2001 —	chargeable transfer	248,000	1,200
11 January 2003 and 3 May 2005 —	potentially exempt transfers £57,000 and £80,000 as before		

		Gross £	Tax on 2005/06 scale £
Cumulative transfers before gift to discretionary trust on 4 March 2006		248,000	–
4 March 2006 —	gift to discretionary trust	90,000	12,600*
		338,000	12,600*

(* 338,000 – 275,000 (using 2005/06 scale) = 63,000 @ 20%)

			Tax on 2005/06 scale £

Tax payable by trustees   £12,600

On death of Mr C T Tax 2 April 2009

		Gross £	*Tax (using rates at 2 April 2009)* £
Cumulative transfers in seven years prior to gift to Ann		248,000	–
11 January 2003 —	gift to Ann	57,000	–
		305,000	–
3 May 2005 —	gift to Joan	80,000	29,200*
		385,000	29,200*
(* 385,000 – 312,000 = 73,000 @ 40%)			
4 March 2006 —	gift to discretionary trust	90,000	36,000
		475,000	65,200

Inheritance tax payable by Ann on gift made 11 January 2003		nil
Inheritance tax payable by Joan on gift made 3 May 2005 80% × £29,200 (tapering relief as before)		23,360
Additional inheritance tax payable by trustees — as gift is made more than 3 but not more than 4 years before death tax payable is:		

	£	£
Tax on death scale	36,000	
Less 20% tapering relief	7,200	
	28,800	
Less paid in lifetime	12,600	16,200

Tax on estate:

	£
Cumulative transfers as above	475,000
Deduct transfer made more than seven years previously	248,000
	227,000
Estate chargeable on death	620,000
	847,000

Tax payable (847,000 – 312,000 = 535,000 @ 40%)	214,000
	£253,560

(b)   **Gift to discretionary trust on 6 April 2007**

Tax payable in lifetime

		Gross £	*Tax on 2001/02 scale* £
20 November 2001 —	chargeable transfer	248,000	1,200

		Gross £	Tax on 2001/02 scale £
11 January 2003 and 3 May 2005 —	potentially exempt transfers £57,000 and £80,000 as before		
Cumulative transfers before gift to discretionary trust on 6 April 2007 (c/f)		240,000	

		Gross £	Tax on 2007/08 scale £
Cumulative transfers before gift to discretionary trust on 6 April 2007 (b/f)		248,000	–
6 April 2007 — gift to discretionary trust	90,000		
Less: Annual exemptions 2007/08	(3,000)		
2006/07	(3,000)	84,000	6,400*
		332,000	6,400*

(* 332,000 – 300,000 (using 2007/08 scale) = 32,000 @ 20%)
Tax payable by trustees   £6,400

On death of Mr C T Tax 2 April 2009

	Gross £	Tax (using rates at 2 April 2009) £
Cumulative transfers in seven years prior to gift to Ann (as above)	248,000	–
11 January 2003 — gift to Ann	57,000	–
	305,000	–
3 May 2005 — gift to Joan	80,000	29,200*
	385,000	29,200*
(* 385,000 – 312,000 = 73,000 @ 40%)		
6 April 2007 — gift to discretionary settlement	84,000	33,600
	469,000	62,800
20 November 2008 Deduct transfer more than seven years previously (ie prior to 21 November 2001)	248,000	
Cumulative transfers in seven years before death	221,000	–
Estate chargeable on death	620,000	211,600*
	841,000	211,600*

(* 841,000 – 312,000 = 529,000 @ 40%)

Inheritance tax payable by Ann on gift made 11 January 2003	nil
Inheritance tax payable by Joan on gift made 3 May 2005 80% × £29,200 (tapering relief as before)	23,360

Additional inheritance tax payable by trustees on gift made 6 April 2007 (no tapering relief because within 3 years before death):

	Gross £	Tax (using rates at 2 April 2009) £
Tax on death scale	33,600	
Less paid in lifetime	6,400	27,200
Tax payable by estate		211,600
		£262,160

The total tax payable is £2,400 more than in iii(a):

	(a) £	(b) £
Ann	–	–
Joan	23,360	23,360
Trustees	28,800	33,600
Estate	214,000	211,600
Total tax payable	266,160	268,560
Paid in lifetime by trustees	12,600	6,400
Due on death	260,700	262,160

The increase in the tax payable arises as follows:

Loss of tapering relief on transfer to trust, since gift now less than three years before death (36,000 @ 20%)	7,200
Less: Reduction of trust transfer by 2007/08 and 2006/07 exemptions, saving 6,000 @ 40%	(2,400)
Consequential reduction in cumulative transfers at death, saving a further 6,000 @ 40%	(2,400)
	£2,400

The inheritance tax liability can therefore vary depending on the timing and amounts of lifetime gifts. C T Tax had the same value of assets in each of the above examples. The total tax payable by the first discretionary trust remains constant at £1,200, being a lifetime gift made more than seven years before death. The tax payable on death plus gifts made within seven years before death is:

(i)	(ii)	(iii)(a)	(iii)(b)
£273,360	£216,400	£266,160	£268,560

The reduction of £56,960 in (ii) is due to non-aggregation of the gift to the first discretionary trust with other lifetime gifts (see explanatory note 6). The reduction of £7,200 in (iii)(a) compared with (i) is because the chargeable gift to the trust of £90,000 on 4 March 2006 was more than three years before death, thus giving rise to taper relief of £7,200. The difference in tax payable in (iii)(a) and (iii)(b) is explained above.

Explanatory Notes

Potentially exempt transfers to sister and children

1.   As the transfers to the sister and to the children are gifts by one individual to another they are potentially exempt, after deducting available annual exemptions from the earliest gift in any tax year. Accordingly no tax is payable at the time.

Inheritance tax liability arising on death

2.   On the death of Mr C T Tax a liability arises both on his estate at death and also on transfers made within seven years before death.

The additional charge on death is the tax due using the scale in force on the date of death less any tax paid on that gift during lifetime. If the tax already paid exceeds that now due no refund will arise. Any tax due is payable primarily by the donee (see Example 5).

Tapering relief on lifetime transfers

3.   Transfers which were potentially exempt in lifetime become chargeable if the donor dies within seven years after the lifetime transfer. They are chargeable on their value when made, but at the full scale rate at the time of death. Where the period between the gift and death exceeds three years then the tax calculated on the full scale rate is reduced as follows:

Years between transfer and death	*Percentage reduction*	*Percentage of full rate tax due*
3 to 4	20	80
4+ to 5	40	60
5+ to 6	60	40
6+ to 7	80	20

Thus, in part (i) of the example Ann's gift would attract an 80% reduction as the gift is made more than six but less than seven years before death. In fact no tax is payable on the gift and therefore the taper relief is lost. Joan can claim a 20% reduction as her gift was more than three but less than four years before death, but Ben cannot claim any reduction as his gift was within three years of death.

Calculating tax on potentially exempt transfers that become chargeable

4.   When computing the tax on potentially exempt transfers which have become chargeable it is necessary to take into account other *chargeable* transfers made within *seven years before those transfers* even though those transfers themselves may not be subject to any uplift on death because they were made more than seven years before the date of death. Thus when computing any tax on the gifts in January 2003, May 2005 and April 2006 the cumulative chargeable transfers include the gift into settlement in November 2001. However when computing the tax due on the estate at death, the November 2001 chargeable transfer is excluded since it was made more than seven years prior to death. Even if it had exceeded the nil threshold at death, the November 2001 transfer could not have attracted additional tax, since Mr C T Tax survived it by seven years.

Interaction of annual exemption with chargeable/potentially exempt transfers

5.   Part (iii) of the example illustrates the provisions relating to the annual exemption where there are both chargeable lifetime transfers and potentially exempt transfers within the same year. The detailed notes are in Example 1. The annual exemption is given against transfers in strict chronological order, thus the gift to Joan on 3 May 2005 (which is otherwise potentially exempt) receives the benefit of the annual exemptions, even though no tax would be payable if C T Tax survived for more than seven years. No exemptions are accordingly available to reduce the chargeable lifetime transfer on 4 March 2006 in part (iii) (a) and tax of £12,600 is immediately payable by the trustees. Note that if the gifts in (iii) (a) to Joan on 3 May 2005 and to the discretionary trust on 4 March 2006 had occurred in reverse order then the annual exemptions of £6,000 would reduce the chargeable transfer to the trust to £84,000 and the tax immediately payable to £11,400. This benefit would have been retained if C T Tax had lived for more than seven years. In fact death occurs within that period, so that the annual exemptions reduce the transfer on which Joan is chargeable and have not been wasted by being used against a potentially exempt transfer that never became chargeable.

Cumulation with earlier chargeable transfers

6.   It is not always appreciated that making gifts within seven years before death rather than leaving a correspondingly greater amount at death can increase the overall tax liability. This occurs because of the need, in calculating the tax payable on a potentially exempt transfer which becomes chargeable, to include *chargeable* transfers made within the seven years before the gift. (Potentially exempt transfers are never taken into account unless the donor dies within seven years after making them, in which case they become chargeable transfers.) Thus a period of up to fourteen years might need to be taken into account to calculate the inheritance tax liability arising on a death. The earlier transfers (ie years 8–14 before death) are eliminated after seven years and are therefore not included in calculating the liability on the estate at the date of death. The additional charge is often mitigated by the tapering provisions set out at note 3 above and the amount chargeable is reduced by use of lifetime exemptions. However, as shown in parts (i) and (ii) of this example those provisions are insufficient to cover the additional charge arising through having to include the earlier gifts in calculating the tax payable on the potentially exempt transfers, the additional tax payable by reason of the lifetime transfers to the children being as follows:

	£
Savings:	
Reduction in chargeable estate because of lifetime gift to Joan	
Annual exemptions 2005/06 and 2004/05 (6,000 @ 40%)	2,400
Tapering relief on Joan's gift (29,200 – 23,360)	5,840
	8,240
Additional liability:	
Gift of £248,000 20 November 2001 accumulated with gifts made 11 January 2003, 3 May 2005 and 4 April 2006 but not with estate, Causing lifetime gifts to Joan and Ben to exceed nil threshold (73,000 + 90,000) = £163,000 @ 40%	65,200
Net additional liability as in part (ii) of the example	£56,960

This problem only arises when transfers that were immediately chargeable in lifetime are taken into account in calculating the tax on potentially exempt transfers that become chargeable. If, for example, C T Tax's transfer on 20 November 2001 had been a potentially exempt transfer, the transfers to Ann, Joan and Ben would still have become chargeable transfers, but the potentially exempt transfer on 20 November 2001, more than seven years before C T Tax's death, would then be totally exempt and would not enter into the cumulative total.

Interaction with capital gains tax

7.   Where a gifted asset is a chargeable asset for capital gains tax, that tax needs to be considered in addition to inheritance tax. Capital gains tax is not payable on death, and there is normally an automatic uplift of base values to the probate value, unless the probate value of the asset has not been *ascertained* for inheritance tax (which would be the case, for example, if no inheritance tax was payable on the estate) (TCGA 1992 s 274). In that event the acquisition value for capital gains tax is the open market value at the date of death (TCGA 1992 s 272 — see Example 38 explanatory note 1). If an election has been made to avoid a pre-owned asset income tax charge then the asset is included within the estate at death for inheritance tax. However that election does not apply for capital gains tax and the value will remain at the capital gains tax value at the time of transfer (normally open market value at date of original gift) (TCGA 1992 s 18 see Example 23 explanatory note 13).

On gifts made in lifetime, capital gains tax may be payable unless the gain is deferred under the gifts holdover relief provisions — either the business gifts relief of TCGA 1992 s 165 or the relief under TCGA 1992 s 260 for gifts that are *immediately* liable to inheritance tax (such as gifts to discretionary trusts). Consequently, capital gains tax may be paid on a potentially exempt transfer, and if the donor dies within seven years the gift will also be liable to inheritance tax (unless covered by reliefs or exemptions). There is no direct relief against inheritance tax for the capital gains tax paid, although the chargeable estate at death will have been reduced by the capital gains tax paid or owing.

If the capital gains tax gifts holdover relief *is* available, and the potentially exempt transfer becomes liable to inheritance tax, any inheritance tax payable is deducted in computing the donee's gain when he eventually disposes of the asset (TCGA 1992 s 165(10)). The same applies in relation to the inheritance tax on a gift to which capital gains holdover relief under TCGA 1992 s 260 applied because the gift was immediately chargeable to inheritance tax (s 260(7)). The inheritance tax taken into account in each case to reduce the capital gain is the amount finally payable, after any adjustments following death.

For detailed coverage on capital gains tax see the companion to this book, Tolley's Taxwise I 2008/09.

Question

(a)   When is inheritance tax due to be paid:

    (i)   on chargeable lifetime transfers?

    (ii)   when it arises because of death?

(b)   Who is accountable for the inheritance tax arising on:

    (i)   chargeable lifetime transfers?

    (ii)   potentially exempt transfers which become chargeable at death?

    (iii)   the estate at death?

    (iv)   settled property in which the deceased enjoyed a life interest?

(c)   What penalties can be charged for incorrect returns or understatement of IHT due?

Answer

(a)   Due date of payment of inheritance tax

Payment of inheritance tax may sometimes be made by instalments, but otherwise the due date is as follows (s 226):

(i)	Lifetime chargeable transfers between 6 April and 30 September	30 April in following year
	Lifetime chargeable transfers between 1 October and 5 April	6 months after end of month in which transfer was made
(ii)	Death, including tax on what were previously potentially exempt transfers and additional tax on chargeable lifetime transfers	6 months after end of month in which death occurred

The personal representatives must, however, pay any tax for which they are liable when they deliver their account in connection with their application for a grant of probate or administration, even if this is earlier than the due date shown above. This will be before they have access to the funds. However certain financial institutions may be prepared to release the funds of the deceased before probate is granted by way of an electronic transfer to HMRC against an inheritance tax reference (see explanatory note 11).

Interest on unpaid inheritance tax is charged at the rate of 4% from 6 January 2008 (see also explanatory note 1).

(b)   Liability for payment of inheritance tax

(i)   Chargeable lifetime transfers

On chargeable lifetime transfers of property not already comprised in a settlement, primary liability for payment of tax rests with the *donor* except in the case of any extra tax payable on death which is primarily the responsibility of the *donee*. The personal representatives are only liable if the additional tax exceeds the value of the asset in the hands of the recipient, or if the tax is not paid by the recipient (s 204).

The donor and donee may, however, agree between them who is to pay the tax, and if the donor is to pay the tax the transfer has to be grossed up, because the extent to which the donor's estate is depleted is the transfer to the donee plus the tax paid. If the donee pays the tax grossing up is not necessary.

Grossing up does not apply on a potentially exempt transfer since tax is not payable in the donor's lifetime.

A return for inheritance tax because of a chargeable transfer in lifetime has to indicate who is to pay the tax.

In the case of lifetime transfers of property comprised in a settlement, the primary liability is that of the trustees.

(ii)   Potentially exempt transfers which become chargeable

The liability on potentially exempt transfers which become chargeable at death is primarily that of the donees. The donee is also primarily responsible where property subject to reservation of an interest by the deceased becomes liable to tax on death.

(iii)   **Estate at death**

The personal representatives are liable to pay the tax on property which is not immediately before death included in a settlement, or owned jointly by the deceased and others as joint tenants (usually called the 'free estate').

They are also liable to pay the tax on UK land which is included in a settlement but which devolves on them in their capacity as personal representatives.

Property owned by the deceased and others as joint tenants is not dealt with by the personal representatives because it becomes the property of the other owner(s) and any tax attributable to the value of that property is payable by the person(s) in whom it is vested (s 200(1)(c)).

See explanatory note 8 as to who bears the tax.

(iv)   **Settled property in which deceased had life interest**

For settled property other than that in (iii) above, the liability rests with the trustees of the settlement.

(v)   **Discretionary trusts – ten-year anniversary**

A form IHT100d will be due for completion in respect of each ten-year event (in conjunction with form IHT100). The submission deadline is one year after the end of the month in which the event took place. Penalties for late delivery will be charged under IHTA 1984 s 245.

The due dates for payment of any tax due are:

Event	Tax due date
6 Apr – 30 Sep	30 Apr next year
1 Oct – 31Oct	30 Apr
1 Nov – 30 Nov	31 May
1 Dec – 31 Dec	30 Jun
1 Jan – 31 Jan	31 Jul
1 Feb – 28/9 Feb	31 Aug
1 Mar – 31 Mar	30 Sep
1 Apr – 5 Apr	31 Oct

Other persons liable for payment

In addition to the persons mentioned above, certain other people may be liable to pay inheritance tax, but usually only where tax remains unpaid after the due date.

This is because of s 199, which is headed 'Dispositions by transferor' and imposes a liability on:

1.   The transferor

2.   Any person whose estate is increased by the transfer

3.   In respect of tax attributable to the value of any property, any person in whom the property is vested, whether beneficially or otherwise, at any time after the transfer or who is beneficially entitled to an interest in possession in the property

4.   Where property has become settled property, any person for whose benefit any of the property or income from it is applied.

Where more than one person is liable for the same tax then each of them may be called upon for the whole amount (s 205).

Section 199 poses a problem for personal representatives, because the deceased's estate is liable for tax on potentially exempt transfers in the seven years before death (even though the liability would not arise if the tax was paid, as it ought to be, by the donee), and the personal representatives may not be able to trace all such transfers. HMRC have, however, stated that they would not usually pursue the personal representatives for any such unpaid tax if, after making full enquiries and doing all in their power to disclose all lifetime transfers to HMRC, the personal representatives had obtained a certificate of discharge and distributed the estate before a chargeable lifetime transfer came to light (Law Society's Gazette 13 March 1991).

(c)   **Penalties (Finance Act 2008 amendments)**

Any person for inheritance tax purposes who understates their tax liability, whether deliberately or by failing to take reasonable care in completing returns, will be subject to a revised penalty regime introduced in FA 2008 s 122, s 123 and Sch 40. This legislation is intended to extend the provisions enacted in FA 2007 Sch 24. The penalty will be determined by the amount of tax understated, the nature of the behaviour giving rise to the understatement and the extent of disclosure by the taxpayer.

New penalties for failure to notify are expected to have effect for failure to meet notification obligations that arise on or after 1 April 2009.

It is expected that for incorrect returns, the new rules will be effected by Treasury Order for return periods commencing on or after 1 April 2009 where the return is due to be filed on or after 1 April 2010.

Incorrect returns

The new provisions for incorrect returns will provide for penalties in line with FA 2007 Sch 24, which are based on the amount of tax understated, the nature of the behaviour and the extent of disclosure by the taxpayer. There will be no penalty where a taxpayer makes a mistake but there will be a penalty of up to:

- 30% for failure to take reasonable care;
- 70% for a deliberate understatement; and
- 100% for a deliberate understatement with concealment.

Each penalty is substantially reduced where the taxpayer makes a disclosure (takes active steps to put right the problem), more so if this is unprompted.

For an unprompted disclosure of a failure to take reasonable care the penalty could be reduced to nil.

Where a taxpayer discloses fully when prompted by a challenge from HMRC each penalty could be reduced by up to a half.

Third party providing false information or withholding information

Where a return is incorrect because a third party has deliberately provided false information or deliberately withheld information from the taxpayer, with the intention of causing an understatement of tax due, it will be possible to allow a penalty to be charged on the third party.

For failure to notify a taxable activity there will be no penalty unless there is tax due but unpaid as a result, nor where the taxpayer has a reasonable excuse for the failure. Otherwise there will be a penalty of:

- 30% of tax unpaid for non-deliberate failure to notify;
- 70% of tax unpaid for a deliberate failure to notify; and
- 100% of tax unpaid for a deliberate failure with concealment.

Each penalty will be substantially reduced where the taxpayer makes a disclosure (takes active steps to put right the problem), more so if this is unprompted.

The Act also includes provision for appeals against penalty notices.

In addition FA 2008 Sch 36 para 39 applies to a person who fails to comply with an information notice or deliberately obstructs an officer during an inspection authorised by a first tier tribunal – the penalty is £300 and continues at £60 per day (para 40) for each day on which the failure or obstruction continues.

Explanatory Notes

Rates of interest on unpaid and overpaid inheritance tax

1. As stated in part (a) of the example, the current rate of interest on unpaid inheritance tax is 4%.

    Previous interest rates from 6 December 2003 were:

6.12.03 to 5.9.04	6.9.04 to 5.9.05	6.9.05 to 5.9.06	6.9.06 to 5.8.07	6.8.07 to 5.1.08	From 6.1.08
3%	4%	3%	4%	5%	4%

    Where tax is overpaid, the overpayment carries interest in favour of the taxpayer from the date on which the payment was made at the same rate as overdue tax carries interest (s 235). In making interest calculations, IR Capital Taxes use a denominator of 366 for interest on overdue tax and 365 for interest on overpaid tax, whether or not a leap year is involved (March 1997 CTO Newsletter). In both cases this gives a slight advantage to the taxpayer.

Treatment of interest on overdue and overpaid tax

2. Interest charged on overdue tax does not qualify for tax relief, nor is interest received on an overpayment taxable (ss 233(3) and 235). HMRC have issued a statement of practice (SP 6/95) indicating that they do not automatically initiate an assessment that would lead to a repayment of tax if the amount involved is £25 or less, although the repayment will be made if claimed.

    Where payments are made before IR Capital Taxes notify the amount due, if their calculation shows a balance of tax due of less than £20 it will not be collected and if less than £10 is overpaid it will not be repaid unless claimed by the taxpayer (HMRC Inheritance Tax: Customer Guide (online version only)). Payments in advance do not attract interest, which only runs from the date that tax is due for payment (see Example 28 for an illustration).

Conditionally exempt transfers

3. Where tax has not been paid because a transfer was conditionally exempt (works of art and historic buildings etc), or because of the relief for woodlands, and it later becomes payable on those objects, buildings or woodlands, the due date is six months after the end of the month in which the event by reason of which it is chargeable occurs (s 226(4)), following which interest then runs (s 233).

Different payment dates re one transaction

4. It should be noted that tax can be due at different times in respect of one transaction. If, for example, a chargeable transfer was made to a discretionary trust on 1 May 2008, the tax would be payable on the lifetime transfer on 30 April 2009. Any additional tax payable as a result of the subsequent death of the donor would be due six months after the end of the month in which the donor died. Therefore if the donor died on 21 May 2008 the additional tax would be payable on 30 November 2008, some five months before the date for payment of the original liability.

Payment by instalments

5. Tax may be paid by equal yearly instalments over ten years on qualifying assets in respect of transfers on death; chargeable lifetime transfers if the donee pays the tax; and transfers of settled property

where the property concerned continues to be comprised in the settlement (eg termination of an interest in possession without the property leaving the settlement; or ten yearly charges on trusts without an interest in possession) (s 227). The first instalment is due for payment on death transfers and on additional liabilities arising because of the death of the donor six months after the end of the month in which the death occurred. The first instalment on lifetime chargeable transfers is due on the normal due date as indicated in part (a)(i) of the example.

The instalment option applies to the following assets:

(a) Land of any description, wherever situated.

(b) Shares which gave the transferor control immediately prior to the transfer.

(c) Unquoted shares and securities (unquoted being defined as not listed on a recognised stock exchange (ss 227(1AA) and 228(5)):

   (i)   where tax cannot be paid without undue hardship (s 228(1)(c)); or

   (ii) for shares only, where they are valued in excess of £20,000 and either the nominal value of the shares is not less than 10% of the nominal value of all the shares of the company at that time or, if the shares are ordinary shares, their nominal value is not less than 10% of the nominal value of all ordinary shares in the company at that time (s 228(3)); or

   (iii) where the tax payable on the shares or securities, together with the tax on the other instalment assets, amounts to 20% or more of the tax payable by the same person on the same transfer (s 228(2)). This applies only to transfers on death.

(d) A business or an interest in a business.

(e) Timber, when a chargeable transfer is made following its being left out of account on a previous death (s 229).

The facility to pay by instalments is only available on potentially exempt transfers which become chargeable transfers if the transferee still owns the qualifying property at the time of the transferor's death, (or, for transfers of property qualifying for business or agricultural relief, replacement property).

The instalment option on unquoted shares is not available for tax payable in consequence of the donor's death, unless the shares are still unquoted when the donor dies (or if earlier, when the donee dies) (s 228(3A)). This applies to both controlling and non-controlling holdings.

Unquoted shares include those dealt in on the Alternative Investment Market.

See Example 59 explanatory note 11, in relation to the instalment option and the ten yearly charge on a discretionary settlement.

6. In the case of land, except land that forms part of a business (as distinct from land owned by partners or directors and occupied by their business) or land that qualifies for agricultural property relief, interest is charged on the *total* amount of tax for the time being remaining unpaid, the interest being added to each instalment as it falls due. Interest is also charged on any instalment that is paid late.

   In the case of land that forms part of a business, land qualifying for agricultural property relief and all other assets in (b) to (e) of note 5 above (excluding shares in an investment company) interest is not charged unless an instalment is paid late, in which case the interest is charged only on the late instalment and not on the full amount of the deferred tax (s 234).

Sale of instalment property

7. If instalment property is sold, the outstanding tax becomes payable immediately (s 227(4)). This explains why a lifetime transferor cannot pay tax on his chargeable transfer by instalments, because he cannot direct the actions of the transferee. If instalment property was comprised in a potentially

exempt transfer and then disposed of by the donee, the instalment option would not be available to the donee if a charge to inheritance tax subsequently arose because of the donor's death within seven years.

Incidence of tax

8.   The question of who is liable to pay inheritance tax is complex and is dealt with in IHTA 1984 ss 199 to 214. HMRC have powers to collect tax from a wide range of persons, but in most cases tax would be paid by the persons indicated in part (b) of the example.

Where tax is unpaid there is normally a HMRC charge on the property concerned, however, this cannot take priority over an existing valid charge (s 237). No HMRC charge may be imposed on personal or movable property vested in personal representatives (other than settled property in which the deceased had a life interest). The HMRC charge can also apply in relation to outstanding tax and interest on assets from which heritage reliefs have been withdrawn.

The person who is liable to pay inheritance tax because of death is not necessarily the person who ultimately bears the tax. Tax on death is borne as follows:

Tax relating to a life interest of the deceased in settled property is borne by the trust funds and thus reduces the value of the funds for the person who becomes entitled to them, or to an interest in them.

Tax relating to property nominated to others during the lifetime of the deceased or held jointly by the deceased and others as joint tenants is payable out of that property, and hence borne by the nominees or joint tenants.

In the absence of specific provisions in the will, tax on all other property, both real and personal, wherever situated in the UK, is a testamentary expense payable out of the residue of the estate and thus borne by the residuary legatees (s 211). This is most important in relation to the drafting of wills and if it is intended that any particular asset should bear its own tax, this should be expressly provided in the terms of the will.

The tax on property situated abroad is a charge on that property.

Income tax relief re loan to pay inheritance tax

9.   Income tax relief is available in respect of interest paid for a period of up to one year on a loan raised by personal representatives to pay inheritance tax on personalty (ie all property other than freehold land and buildings) in order to obtain probate. Any excess interest over income of the estate in the tax year of payment may be carried back against the income of the estate in the preceding tax year(s) and any remaining excess is carried forward against future income of the estate (ITA 2007 s 405).

Obtaining an IHT reference number

10.   Before a personal representative can make the first payment of inheritance tax they must obtain an inheritance tax reference number and payslip. They can do this by applying for an IHT reference online or by using the Form D21 application for an inheritance tax reference. The application for a reference should be made at least three weeks before the expected date of any payment.

HMRC will send a note of the reference number and a pre-referenced payslip by post which should be used to pay the tax. The payslip can be used only for payments regarding a particular estate.

Electronic transfer of inheritance tax from participating financial institutions

11.   Most banks and building societies are able to accept instructions from personal representatives to make a payment of inheritance tax, by electronic transfer, before probate is obtained. They will need to complete Form D20 for each bank or building society making the transfer of funds.

If a personal representative wishes to use this facility they must contact HMRC at IR Capital Taxes, Ferrers House, PO Box 38, Castle Meadow Road, Nottingham NG2 1BB or telephone 0845 30 20 900 or fax 0115 974 2526.

HMRC will then allocate an IHT reference number to the estate. When the personal representative is ready to apply for probate (or letters of administration) they will send the form of authority (included with the probate pack) to the bank/building society. They in turn will transfer funds to HMRC electronically. HMRC will provide the personal representative with a receipt which must be presented to the Court Service to obtain the grant.

Question

You have been asked by the chairman of your company for advice on the inheritance tax position on the death of his father.

The following information is available:

1.   The chairman's father died on 1 March 2009.

2.   His estate comprised:

   (a)   Freehold house and land valued for probate at £500,000. This property was owned jointly by the deceased and his wife (who survived him) as joint tenants.

   (b)   Stocks and shares:

      (i)   £100,000 6% bonds valued @ 92–96.

             Interest is payable half-yearly on 30 June and 31 December.

      (ii)   £20,000 5% stock valued @ 86–88 ex dividend.

             Interest is payable half-yearly on 31 March and 30 September.

(c)	Bank deposit account	£24,305
	Accrued interest (net of 20% tax)	£1,000
(d)	Proceeds of an insurance policy	£27,990
(e)	Personal chattels	£20,000

3.   He was life tenant of a trust fund, the assets of which amounted to £216,000, including gross accrued non-savings income to 1 March 2009 of £1,000 (taxable at 22%). The trust funds are payable to the chairman on the death of his father.

4.   Debts and funeral expenses amounted to £2,675.

5.   By his will the deceased bequeathed legacies of £5,000 to each of two grandchildren, a legacy of £5,000 and the personal chattels to his widow and the residue to your chairman.

6.   There had been no lifetime transfers.

Prepare a statement showing the amount of inheritance tax payable, who is accountable for the payment, and upon whom the burden falls.

Answer

Estate of Chairman's Father

Date of death 1 March 2009

	£	£	£
Property jointly owned with spouse			
Freehold house – half share		250,000	
Less: devolving on widow by survivorship		250,000	–
Free estate			
£100,000 6% bonds @ 93		93,000	
£20,000 5% stock @ 86½% ex dividend	17,300		
Add: net interest 31 March 2009 (£1,000 less 20%)	800	18,100	
Bank deposit account, including accrued interest (net of income tax)		24,305	
Proceeds of insurance policy		27,990	
Personal chattels		20,000	
Accrued income from trust fund to 1 March 2009 (£1,000 less 20%)		800	
		184,195	
Less: debts and funeral expenses		2,675	
		181,520	
Less: spouse exemption			
Legacy	5,000		
personal chattels	20,000	25,000	156,520
Settled property			
Trust fund		216,000	
Less: gross accrued income		1,000	215,000
			371,520
Inheritance tax due on death (2008/09 scale)			
Inheritance tax payable on (371,520 – 312,000) = 59,520 @ 40%			£23,808

$$\text{Estate rate} = \frac{23,808}{371,520} \times 100 \qquad = \qquad 6.4083\%$$

Payable by executors	156,520 @	6.4083%	10,030
Payable by trustees of trust fund	215,000 @	6.4083%	13,778
	£371,520		£23,808

The tax payable by the executors will fall on the residue of the estate, so that the two grandchildren will receive their £5,000 legacies in full, with the chairman receiving the balance of residue after legacies and inheritance tax.

The tax payable by the trustees will reduce the trust fund remaining for the chairman.

Explanatory Notes

Quoted securities — valuation, sale within twelve months of death

1.   Quoted securities are valued cum div at a price one-quarter up on the buying and selling quoted market prices. Thus the 6% bonds at 92–96 are valued at 92 + (¼ × (96 – 92)) = 93. If the midpoint between the highest and lowest recorded bargains gives a lower figure, then this is used instead (TCGA 1992 s 272(3)).

Where securities are quoted ex div then it is necessary to add the full amount of impending dividend or interest less lower rate tax to the above valuation.

Relief may be claimed if quoted securities are sold for less than the death valuation within twelve months after death. All securities sold have to be aggregated to determine whether there is any relief. In arriving at the aggregate sale proceeds the sale values are taken *before* deducting any expenses of sale. The relief is restricted if any purchase of quoted securities takes place in the period beginning at the date of death and ending two months after the date of the last sale within the twelve months period after death (ss 178–189). See Example 11 for a detailed illustration.

Life interest in settlement — accrued income

2.   Accrued income of a life interest in a trust fund forms part of the free estate of the deceased life tenant and not part of the settled property, the trustees having a liability to pay the accrued income less the appropriate rate of tax to the estate of the deceased life tenant (the appropriate rate being the rate of 10% on dividend income (covered by the tax credits), the lower rate on other savings income and the basic rate on non-savings income).

Joint tenancy and tenancy in common

3.   Assets held jointly by husband and wife (or civil partners) are deemed to be held on a joint tenancy unless this has been specifically rebutted.

The characteristic of a joint tenancy is that there are no separate shares which can be disposed of, so that on the death of a joint tenant his share automatically merges with that of the survivor. It therefore follows that the intestacy rules do not apply to the distribution of such assets.

There can be a joint tenancy between persons who are not husband and wife or civil partners, but this has to be specifically created (whereas with husband and wife and civil partners it is implied).

If husband and wife (or civil partners) have specifically rebutted the joint tenancy and in other cases of joint ownership where a joint tenancy has not been specifically created, the ownership is on the basis of a tenancy in common. This means that there are separate shares which do not merge on death and which can therefore be independently dealt with by will or under an intestacy.

Had the chairman's father and mother owned the house in this example as tenants in common, his will would have covered the disposition of his share, and for it to have been exempt it would have had to be devised to his widow as distinct from accruing to her by survivorship in the circumstances of the joint tenancy indicated in the example.

4.   Had the house been owned by say the chairman's father and his uncle, the position would have been:

(a)   If held as tenants in common (which is presumed unless specifically rebutted) the will would cover the disposition of the share and it does not automatically go to the survivor.

The share would be exempt if devised/bequeathed to a spouse or a charity but otherwise would be chargeable.

(b)   If held under a specifically created joint tenancy the share of the deceased would automatically merge with the survivor's share. The share would accordingly be chargeable on the death of the chairman's father since clearly its devolution to the uncle would not be exempt.

In both cases, however, the value of the share in the property would be affected by the joint ownership in that the difficulty of dealing with the share would be taken into account in making the valuation.

5.   Where the property is held jointly by husband and wife or civil partners, whether as joint tenants or tenants in common, the related property provisions do not permit any such reduction in value, because the legislation provides that the whole is first valued and then divided pro rata between the part owners. For the detailed provisions see Example 10.

6.   As indicated in note 4 property held jointly may or may not be liable to inheritance tax.

Further, it may or may not form part of the estate for the purposes of applying for a grant of probate or administration and in administering the estate.

If it is held under joint tenancy with accrual to the survivor it does not technically form part of the estate (although it may be liable to tax, depending on who the other joint tenant is) and is not therefore comprised in the probate summary in the HMRC account.

This is one reason why the value of published estates often does not accord with what the public expects to see in that the value of assets held as a joint tenant will not be included in the total.

7.   In the administration of the estate all that is required in relation to assets held on a joint tenancy is the registration of the death, for example by a building society or bank in the case of joint accounts, or the placing of a death certificate with the title deeds in the case of properties, the share in the asset itself having accrued by survivorship.

A share of an asset held as a tenant in common does form part of the estate, will appear in the probate summary in the HMRC account and will require dealing with by the personal representative as distinct from accruing by survivorship.

Position of surviving spouse where private residence owned as tenants in common

8.   As indicated in note 3, where the home is held by husband and wife or civil partners as tenants in common, the will of the deceased will deal with that person's share, and in order to avoid wasting the inheritance tax nil-rate band of the first to die, the share may be left other than to the survivor. In order to protect the survivor's right to remain in the home, however, it has been common for wills to provide for the surviving partner to be allowed to remain in the property free of charge, the share then passing, say, to the children. Such a provision has been held in *CIR v Lloyd's Private Banking Ltd* to create an interest in possession in favour of the survivor, so that the whole property is chargeable on the second death. Any such arrangement would need to be on the basis of an understanding between the parties, rather than by stipulation in the will. This could, of course, lead to other problems, for example if family relationships do not remain harmonious.

Position of co-habitees

9.   Care needs to be taken where unmarried couples share a house that was purchased in the name of only one of them. If it is intended that the ownership of the property is to be regarded as shared, the purchaser could make a written declaration that the property was held on trust for himself and the co-habitee as joint tenants in equal beneficial shares, and the treatment would then be as indicated in note 4 above, so that on the first death the survivor would acquire the deceased's share. Such a declaration would not represent a transfer of value by the purchaser to the extent that the other had contributed to the cost. Any amount not so covered would be a potentially exempt transfer.

In the absence of such a declaration the legal position is complex and HMRC may argue that, even if the co-habitee has made substantial direct or indirect contributions to the cost of the property (for example by sharing mortgage payments, cost of alterations and household bills generally), the whole property is chargeable on the death of the legal owner (see also Example 10 part A re valuing the share of a co-habitee).

Calculation of inheritance tax

10.   In the example, the legacy to the widow (cash and chattels) is exempt under s 18 and is therefore deducted from the free estate before the inheritance tax calculation is made.

11.   As no lifetime transfers had been made the scale rates apply to the taxable value of the estate without aggregation with any earlier transfers, giving an estate rate of 6.4083%. The tax is then payable by the executors and by the trustees of the settled property on presentation of the probate papers. Interest is payable from 30 September 2008, being six months after the end of the month in which the death occurred (s 226(2) and s 233(1)).

12.   Had the trust funds in which the chairman's father had a life interest devolved on his death to his widow, either for her lifetime or absolutely, they would have been left out of the inheritance tax calculation because of the surviving spouse exemption. There would then have been no tax payable on the death, since the £156,520 free estate would have been below the £312,000 threshold.

Question

Christopher died on 20 March 2009 at which date his assets were valued at:

Quoted investments	£156,000
Cash at bank	£5,312
Life policies on his own life, producing	£47,500

Outstanding liabilities at 20 March 2009 were £5,714 and the funeral expenses amounted to £1,748. The quoted investments were sold by the executors on 28 September 2009 for £150,000, less expenses of sale of £2,500 giving net proceeds of £147,500.

By his will Christopher gave the residue of his estate to his daughter absolutely.

Christopher had not made any chargeable transfers before 5 April 2003 but since then he had made the following cash gifts:

2003	26	April	Recognised charity	£110,000
2005	2	June	Discretionary trust	£293,000
	24	December	Daughter	£60,000
2006	20	February	Godson (on the occasion of his marriage)	£1,600
2007	24	December	Daughter	£90,000
2008	2	June	Discretionary trust	£62,000

Christopher had agreed to pay any tax due on the lifetime gifts.

Compute:

(a)   The original amounts of tax payable on the lifetime gifts, stating the due dates for payment.

(b)   The additional amount of tax payable on the gifts following Christopher's death, showing who is liable for the tax, and stating the due date for payment.

(c)   The amount of inheritance tax payable by the executors, stating the due date for payment.

Answer

Inheritance tax payable in Christopher's lifetime

	£	Gross £	Tax on 2005/06 scale £	Net £
26 April 2003				
Gift to charity	110,000			
Less: Exempt transfer (s 23)	110,000	–	–	–
2 June 2005 (explanatory note 1)				
Settlement on discretionary trust	293,000			
Less: Annual exemptions				
2005/06	3,000			
2004/05	3,000	6,000		
Net transfer, grossed up	287,000	290,000	3,000	287,000
24 December 2005				
Gift to daughter —				
Potentially exempt transfer	60,000			
20 February 2006				
Gift to godson	1,600			
Less: Marriage exemption (s 22)	1,000			
Potentially exempt transfer	600			
24 December 2007				
Gift to daughter	90,000			
Less: Annual exemptions				
2007/08	3,000			
2006/07	3,000	6,000		
Potentially exempt transfer	84,000			

	£	Gross £	Tax on 2008/09 scale £	Net £
2 June 2008 (explanatory note 1)				
Chargeable transfers within previous seven years		290,000	–	290,000
Settlement on discretionary trust	62,000			
Less: Annual exemption 2008/09	3,000			
	59,000			
Net transfer, grossed up (*358,250 – 312,000 = 46,250 @ 20%)		68,250	9,250	59,000
		358,250	9,250	349,000

On Christopher's death – 20 March 2009

	Gross	Tax on 2008/09 scale
	£	£
Gifts within seven years before death:		
Accumulation before first such gift	–	–
2 June 2005		
Settlement on discretionary trust	290,000	–
24 December 2005		
Gift to daughter	68,250	18,500*
(*358,250 – 312,000 = 46,250 @ 40%)		
	358,250	18,500
20 February 2006		
Gift to godson	600	240
24 December 2007	358,850	18,740
Gift to daughter	84,000	33,600
2 June 2008	442,850	52,340
Settlement on discretionary trust	68,250	27,300
Cumulative transfers in seven years prior to death	511,100	79,640

Estate of Christopher deceased

	Date of death 20 March 2009	
	£	£
Quoted investments		156,000
Cash at bank		5,312
Life policies		47,500
		208,812
Less: Liabilities	5,714	
Funeral expenses	1,748	
Inheritance tax re settlement 2 June 2008	8,000	15,462
Value on death		193,350
Less: Loss on sale of quoted securities		
Probate value	156,000	
Proceeds (before expenses)	150,000	6,000
Chargeable to inheritance tax on death		187,350
	£	£
Cumulative transfers in seven years before death	511,100	79,640
Chargeable estate and tax thereon	187,350	74,940
	698,450	154,580

Summary

(a)   The original amounts of inheritance tax payable on chargeable lifetime gifts were as follows:

Gift	Tax payable	Due date
2 June 2005	£3,000	30 April 2006
2 June 2008	£8,000	30 April 2009

(b)   The additional amounts of inheritance tax payable by reason of the death of Christopher are:

By discretionary trust

Amounts payable by trustees re transfers to discretionary trust made on:

2 June 2005 —	On death	–		
	Paid on original transfer	3,000		–
(No amount repayable)				–
				–
2 June 2008 —	On death	24,500		
	Payable on original transfer	9,250		15,250
By daughter			£	15,250

24 December 2005 Gift		18,500		
Less: tapering relief as gift is made more than 3 but not more than 4 years before death – 20%		3,700		14,800
24 December 2007 Gift				33,600
			£	48,400

By godson				
20 February 2006 Gift		240		
Less: tapering relief as above — 20%		48	£	192

The tax is payable in each case on 30 September 2009.

(c)   The amount of inheritance tax payable by the executors is £74,940. It is payable on 30 September 2009 (ie six months after the end of the month in which the death occurred), or if earlier, upon the application for a grant of probate.

Interest runs from 30 September 2009 (ie six months after the end of the month in which the death occurred).

If tax had been paid on the estate before relief was claimed for the shares sold at a loss (amounting to £6,000 @ 40% = £2,400), the amount paid would have been £77,340 and the £2,400 reduction due to the fall in value of the shares would be repaid with interest from 30 September 2009 (or the date of payment if later) once the claim for fall in value was made.

Explanatory Notes

Grossing up lifetime gifts to discretionary trust

1.   The gift to the discretionary trust on 2 June 2005 is a chargeable lifetime transfer liable to inheritance tax at one half of the full rate. As Christopher has agreed to pay the tax on the transfer the net chargeable gift must be grossed up using the 2005/06 lifetime table. The net transfer of £287,000 exceeds the nil band of £275,000 by £12,000, which is grossed up using the 20% lifetime rate. The calculation is therefore:

	Net £	Gross £
Nil band	275,000	275,000
Net amount within 20% rate band is	12,000	
Grossed up		

	Net £	Gross £
$12,000 \times \dfrac{100}{80}$		15,000
	287,000	290,000

The second transfer to the discretionary trust on 2 June 2008 must also be grossed up. Tax on the cumulative transfers brought forward is recomputed on the 2008/09 scale to give the starting point for later transfers. As the cumulative total of £290,000 does not exceed the 2008/09 nil threshold of £312,000, the second transfer to the discretionary trust of £59,000 falls within the 20% band to the extent of £37,000, the gross equivalent of which is:

	Net £	Gross £
Nil band	312,000	312,000
Net amount within 20% rate band	37,000	
Grossed up		
$37,000 \times \dfrac{100}{80}$		46,250
	349,000	358,250

The gross chargeable transfer is therefore (15,000 + 46,250 =) £61,250.

Potentially exempt transfers

2.   The other gifts are all potentially exempt transfers. They are reduced by the marriage exemption on the gift to the godson and the annual exemptions on the gift to the daughter on 24 December 2006 for the purposes of any future charge to inheritance tax.

Recomputation of tax following Christopher's death

3.   On the taxpayer's death, gifts within seven years before death must be reconsidered and the tax recomputed using the scale applicable at the date of death (s 7). If the original gift required grossing up, the originally calculated grossed up gift is used in the second calculation. The tax payable is the difference between that now calculated and the amount previously paid (Sch 2.2). If the amount paid exceeds the revised amount due on the new scale no refund of tax is made.

Quoted securities

4.   Quoted securities sold within the twelve months following death by the person liable to account for the inheritance tax thereon must be aggregated and if the resulting sale proceeds are lower than the probate value of those securities a claim may be made for the loss to be deducted from the probate value (ss 178–189). For this purpose proceeds means sale value *before* deducting any expenses of sale. For detailed notes see Example 8.

Due date of payment of tax

5.   Inheritance tax is payable on lifetime transfers six months after the end of the month in which the transfer was made, or at the end of April in the following tax year if this is later (s 226).

Inheritance tax on the estate at death (other than tax payable by instalments, as to which see Example 9) is payable on the delivery of the HMRC account. The account is submitted in conjunction with the application for a grant of probate or administration, which is usually made within twelve months after death. Interest runs from six months after the end of the month in which death occurred (s 226(2)(3)).

Inheritance tax on potentially exempt transfers that become chargeable and the additional inheritance tax on chargeable lifetime transfers made within seven years before death is payable by the transferee six months after the end of the month in which the death occurred (s 226).

Question

(a)   On 31 May 2007 X died leaving a net estate included in the application for probate at £351,250. Application for probate was made on 2 March 2009 and inheritance tax of £15,700 was paid on that date. Interest of £117 was also paid.

(b)   The executors subsequently became aware that certain assets valued at £12,500 had been omitted from the Inland Revenue Account.

(c)   Before his death the deceased had contracted for certain alterations to be made to the house in which he resided. The work was completed on 10 June 2008 and the valuation for probate which was subsequently made had taken the improved condition of the house into account. The contractors were now requesting payment of their final account amounting to £9,500, which had not been deducted from the value of the estate for probate purposes, since it was not clear at that time whether all alterations had been paid for by progress payments.

(d)   Prior to his death the deceased had made an unsecured loan of £8,000 to the company XZ Ltd, which loan had been included in the value of the estate for probate at its face value. On 1 May 2008 the company had gone into liquidation and it was now clear that nothing would be available for the unsecured creditors.

(e)   In order to pay the cash legacies the executors had to sell all the deceased's quoted securities. They did this on 1 April 2009 as follows:

   (i)   2,000 £1 shares in CD plc, quoted at death at 219p–223p with recorded bargains of 219p, 220p and 222p, were sold at 190p.

   (ii)   4,000 £1 shares in DE plc, quoted at death at 109p–116p with recorded bargains of 109p, 109½p and 111p, were sold at 87½p.

   (iii) 12,000 6% preference shares in DE plc, quoted at death at 53p–61p with no recorded bargains, were sold at 60p.

Advise the executors how they should proceed, and calculate the inheritance tax and interest payable or repayable if the position were finalised on 2 September 2009, assuming the rate of interest on unpaid and overpaid inheritance tax in force since 6 January 2008 (4%) remains unchanged.

Answer

The executors should submit a corrective account which should include the omitted assets and other amendments (s 217).

Quoted securities (see explanatory note 1)

Where quoted securities are sold by the persons liable to account for the inheritance tax thereon within twelve months after death at an aggregate value that is lower than probate value, relief may be claimed for the loss. In arriving at the aggregate value the sale values taken into account are the gross proceeds *before* deducting selling expenses. In this case the position is:

	Death Value		Realised Value	
2,000 shares in CD plc	@ 220p	4,400	@ 190p	3,800
4,000 shares in DE plc	@ 110p	4,400	@ 87½p	3,500
12,000 6% preference shares in DE plc	@ 55p	6,600	@ 60p	7,200
		£15,400		£14,500

A reduction of £900 (£15,400 – £14,500) is available on a claim being made (ss 178–189).

Alterations to the house

The deceased had placed the contract for the work to be done and therefore he or his estate is liable for the cost, the value of his house having reflected the work done and that increased value being included in the net estate.

Unsecured loan to XZ Ltd

The loan must be valued at the price it would have realised on a sale on the open market at the time of death (s 160). The market value at the date of death in the circumstances outlined would be nil. Since the value included in the net estate was £8,000, a reduction of £8,000 will be made. The valuation is not affected by an event *after* death. Here the liquidation had commenced *before* death but the proper value *as at death* has been ascertained later.

After making the appropriate adjustments the revised inheritance tax will be:

Value per account submitted at the time of the application for probate		351,250
Omitted assets		12,500
		363,750
Less: Loss on quoted securities	900	
Additional debt	9,500	
Reduction in value of loan to XZ Ltd	8,000	18,400
Adjusted estate		£345,350
Inheritance tax on 2008/09 death scale		
(345,350 – 312,000 = 33,350 @ 40%)		13,340
Amount paid		15,700
Repayment due		£2,360
Interest overpaid 1 December 2008 to 1 March 2009		
90 days @ 4% × £2,360		£23
Inheritance tax overpaid		2,360
Interest overpaid		23
		2,383
Interest thereon (185 days @ 4% 2 March 2009 to 2 September 2009)		48
Total repayable		£2,431

Explanatory Notes

Valuation of quoted securities

1.   Quoted securities are valued at cum div prices at the lower of:

(a)   ¼ up from the lower of the closing prices

(b)   The midpoint of recorded bargains.

X's estate therefore included the following values:

						Lower
Value of CD plc shares						
(a) ¼ (223 – 219) = 1	+ 219	=	220	)		220p
(b) ½ (219 + 222)		=	220.5	)		
Value of DE plc shares						
(a) ¼ (116 – 109) = 1.75	+ 109	=	110.75	)		110p
(b) ½ (109 + 111)		=	110	)		
Value of DE plc preference shares						
(a) ¼ (61 – 53) = 2	+ 53	=				55p
(b) N/A						

Relief for a fall in value of quoted securities

2.   The relief for a fall in value of quoted securities sold in the twelve months following death is not available if the person who claimed the relief purchases further quoted securities of a value equal to or greater than the proceeds of sale within the period beginning with the date of death and ending two months after the date of the last sale in that twelve months. If the reinvestment does not amount to the whole of the sale sproceeds the relief is withdrawn proportionately (s 180). For an illustration see Example 11.

3.   *All* sales of quoted securities, whether at a loss or at a profit, which take place in the period of twelve months following the death must be included in the computation for relief (s 179).

4.   The provisions giving relief where securities are sold at a loss within twelve months after death also apply to securities for which the quotation is suspended, or which are cancelled, within that period. For details see Example 11.

Interest on overpaid tax

5.   The repayment of inheritance tax, including the interest overpaid, carries interest against the Revenue from the due date (or the date of payment if later) to that of repayment, at the same rates at which tax (if outstanding) would have carried interest against the taxpayer (s 235) (see Example 5 explanatory note 1).

6.   The original tax and interest will have been calculated as follows:

Net estate per original grant application	£351,250
Tax on (351,250 − 312,000) = £39,250 @ 40%	£15,700
Interest at 4% pa from 1 December 2008 to 1 March 2009 (91 days)	£157

Provisional figures in HMRC Account

7.   Personal representatives need to take care when including provisional figures in the HMRC Account, because HMRC are taking a harsher attitude to penalties where asset values are understated — see Example 33 explanatory note 10.

Question

Smith, who had been in partnership with his son for many years, died on 5 April 2009. He had made a lifetime gift on 12 November 2003 of £182,000. He had subsequently made gifts to use his annual exemptions but had made no other transfers of value.

The value of his estate at the date of his death was agreed as follows:

	£
Stocks and shares	10,000
Cash at bank	2,000
Furniture and effects	4,000
Interest as a partner in partnership of Smith & Son	200,000
His house, 5 Side Street	350,000
Let agricultural land (owned and let on same lease for 20 years)	173,000
His outstanding debts were:	
General household bills	7,250
Income tax and capital gains tax	11,000

His funeral expenses amounted to £2,750.

Under his will his whole estate passed to his son absolutely.

Where possible the inheritance tax in connection with his death is being paid by instalments. The first instalment and the inheritance tax not payable by instalments was paid on 1 January 2010. The second instalment was paid on 1 January 2011.

Calculate the inheritance tax and interest payable on those two dates, assuming the rate of interest on unpaid inheritance tax in force since 6 January 2008 (4%) remains unchanged.

Answer

Estate of Smith deceased

Date of death 5 April 2009

£

Non-instalment option property

Stocks and shares		10,000
Cash at bank		2,000
Furniture and effects		4,000
		16,000

Less: Funeral expenses	2,750	
General household bills	7,250	
Income tax and capital gains tax	11,000	21,000
Amount to be deducted from instalment option personalty		(5,000)

Instalment option property

Freehold house		350,000
Let agricultural land	173,000	
Less: agricultural property relief 50%	86,500	86,500
Personalty – Interest as a partner in partnership of Smith & Son	200,000	
Less: balance of debts as above		
(see explanatory notes 3 and 4)	(5,000)	
	195,000	
Less: business property relief 100%	195,000	–
Chargeable to inheritance tax at death		436,500

				£	Tax on 2008/09 scale £
November 2003 — Gift			182,000		
Less: Annual exemptions	2003/04	3,000			
	2002/03	3,000	6,000	176,000	
Chargeable estate				436,500	120,200*
				612,500	120,200*

(* 612,500 – 312,000 = 300,500 @ 40%)
Tax on estate at death is therefore: £120,200

Part attributable to house

$$\frac{350,000}{436,500} \times 120,200 \qquad\qquad 96,380$$

Part attributable to agricultural land

$$\frac{86,500}{436,500} \times 120,200 \qquad\qquad 23,820$$

£120,200

The tax may be paid by ten equal annual instalments in each case. Interest on the tax relating to the house is charged on the *total* amount for the time being remaining unpaid, the interest being added to each instalment as it falls due, and interest is also charged on the instalment if it is paid late. In respect of land qualifying for agricultural relief, interest is payable only on the amount of the instalment if it is paid late.

The amounts of tax and interest payable are therefore:

	£	£
On 1 January 2010		
Re agricultural land:		
Instalment due 31 October 2009	2,382	
Interest thereon from 31 October 2009 to 31 December 2008		
£2,382 × 4% × 62/365	16	2,398
Re house:		
Instalment due 31 October 2009	9,638	
Interest thereon from 31 October 2009 to 31 December 2009		
£9,638 × 4% × 62/365	65	9,703
Total tax and interest due		12,101
On 1 January 2011		
Re agricultural land:		
Instalment due 31 October 2010	2,382	
Interest thereon from 31 October 2010 to 31 December 2010		
£2,382 × 4% × 62/365	16	2,398
Re house:		
Instalment due 31 October 2009 (10,119 + 68)	9,638	

	£	£
Interest thereon from 31 October 2009 to 31 December 2009		
£9,638 × 4% × 62/365	65	
Interest on unpaid tax of (£96,380 less 1st instalment of £9,638)		
£86,742 × 4% × 1 year	3,470	13,173
Total tax and interest due		15,571

Explanatory Notes

Recomputation of tax following donor's death

1. Where gifts are made within seven years before the donor's death, tax has to be recomputed on the death scale in force at the date of death and any additional tax arising is payable by the donee (but no tax is repayable should the tax on the current scale be less than the lifetime tax originally paid).

Payment by instalments

2. Tax may be paid by equal yearly instalments over ten years on certain assets where they are transferred on death. The instalment facility is also available for chargeable lifetime transfers where the donee pays the tax, and, so long as the assets are still owned by the donee, in respect of additional tax or tax on potentially exempt transfers that becomes payable on death. The detailed notes on the assets qualifying for this treatment are in Example 5. Smith's instalment assets are his freehold house and agricultural land. His partnership interest would also have qualified but as it attracts 100% business property relief no tax is payable in respect of that asset.

Debts payable out of estate

3. Debts payable out of a deceased's estate are payable primarily from personalty (ie property other than freehold land and buildings) unless charged against specific property, in which case the deduction is against that property (s 162(4)). It could be argued that the liabilities are to be deducted pro-rata against the non-instalment personalty (£16,000 in this example) and the instalment personalty (£200,000 in this example). Since the instalment personalty in the example qualifies for 100% business property relief, the effect would be to increase the chargeable estate by the proportion of the debts set against that property. It is understood that in practice it is accepted that the debts reduce non-instalment option personalty before instalment option personalty.

Business property relief

4. Business property relief is given at the rate of 100% or 50% on relevant business property (for detailed notes see Example 25). In the case of a business or an interest in a business the value is defined as the value of the assets used in the business (including goodwill) reduced by the liabilities incurred for the purpose of the business (s 110). Even if any of the taxation liabilities in this example relate to the business they were not incurred for the purpose of the business and do not affect the business property relief. Section 104 provides, however, that business property relief is given on such part of the value transferred as is attributable to relevant business property. In this example the excess of liabilities over non-instalment option personalty reduces the value transferred in respect of the partnership interest. The excess of £5,000 therefore reduces the amount on which 100% business property relief is given.

Agricultural property relief

5. Agricultural property relief on agricultural property let before 1 September 1995 is at the rate of 50% (subject to special transitional provisions for certain property owned since before 10 March 1981 and let within a farming family). See Example 25 for details.

Interest on overdue tax

6.   Where tax is not paid on the due date, interest is payable thereon, currently at 4% (from 6 January 2008), in respect of transfers made on death and on the tax or additional tax payable on gifts within the seven previous years. The detailed provisions and the rates of interest prior to 6 January 2008 are in Example 5. HMRC use a denominator of 366 when calculating interest on overdue tax, as shown in the example (and a denominator of 365 when calculating interest on overpaid tax) — see Example 5 explanatory note 1.

7.   Although land is one of the assets qualifying for the instalment treatment as indicated in note 2 above, interest is charged not only on the amount of any instalment paid late but also on the *total* amount of tax remaining unpaid, the interest being added to each instalment as it falls due (s 227(3)). (This does not apply to land that forms part of a business or qualifies for agricultural property relief.) Thus in the example, interest arises re the freehold house on the balance of tax outstanding after deducting the first instalment, in addition to the interest that is due on the overdue instalment. The amount on which interest will be calculated at 31 October 2011 is £77,104, being the previous balance of £86,742 less the second instalment of £9,638. Further interest will arise if the third instalment is paid late, and so on.

Question

A.

Inheritance tax is charged on the value transferred by a chargeable transfer.

How is property valued for this purpose, and how is the value affected if the property is 'related property'?

Comment upon the basis applicable to the following property:

(a)   Unquoted securities

(b)   Farm cottages and farmhouses

and the effect on that valuation of

(i)   A special purchaser

(ii)   Capital gains tax.

B.

A testator who was a widower died in November 2008 leaving a freehold property, Blackacre. The value as at the date of his death is agreed by the executors with HMRC as being £400,000 and inheritance tax is paid on that basis.

What effect will there be, if any, on the inheritance tax payable in respect of Blackacre if eighteen months after his death the executors sell Blackacre for (i) £350,000 or (ii) £450,000?

Answer

A. Valuation of property

The amount on which inheritance tax is charged on a chargeable transfer of value is the difference between the value of the transferor's estate before and after the transfer less any exemptions and ignoring disposals of excluded property (s 3).

The value of property is the price which it ought reasonably to be expected to fetch if sold on the open market at the time. The value is not, however, to be reduced on the ground that the whole property is to be placed on the market at one time (s 160).

With regard to open market value, it has been held by the Land Tribunal in the case of *Walton (exor of Walton decd) v CIR* (1994), that the interest of a partner in a non-assignable agricultural tenancy should be valued according to the extent to which the partnership profits were enhanced as a result of not paying a full market rent, rather than by reference to the vacant possession value compared with the tenanted value.

Valuation on death

The valuation of property on death is dealt with in ss 171–177. These sections provide that the value shall be that immediately prior to death, but taking into account changes in the value of the estate resulting from the death (other than changes relating to life interests or property passing by survivorship). However, allowances are to be made for reasonable funeral expenses (s 172) and for expenses incurred in administering or realising property situated outside the United Kingdom not exceeding five per cent of the value of that property, where the expense is incurred because of the situation of the property (s 173). Thus the deduction is limited to the additional cost of administering the property because it is situated outside the United Kingdom.

In some circumstances where the value of property has fallen between the date of a gift and the donor's death, the lower value may be taken into account to compute the tax or additional tax payable by the donee. The value in the accumulation for later transfers, including that on death, is not, however, altered.

Where a death estate includes quoted securities and they are sold, cancelled or the quotation is suspended within twelve months after the date of death, then a claim may be made for relief for the fall in value under ss 178–189. Similarly if the estate includes land which is sold within four years after death, ss 190–198 apply as detailed in part B below.

When valuing assets in a deceased's estate, care must be taken to ensure that all parts of an asset included in the estate are aggregated when considering its value, eg if the deceased owned a half share of a house personally and had a life interest in the other half then the value to be used will be that of the whole, allocated equally between the free estate and the settled property.

By comparison, if the deceased owned a half share of a house personally and the other half is owned by a co-habitee then the value of the deceased's share should be reduced by a discount, typically 15%, to reflect the fact that any purchaser would have to share the house with the co-habitee (*Wright & Another v CIR* (1982)). See Example 6 explanatory note 9 re establishing that co-habitees do actually share the ownership of the property.

Valuation of lifetime transfers

Similar valuation rules apply in relation to lifetime transfers, except where the property transferred is a life interest in a settlement. In that event s 52(1) provides that the value transferred is treated as being equal to the value of the property in which the life interest subsisted. Where a life tenant also owns property of a similar kind (eg shares in the same company) in his own right, the value of the life interest is valued independently. If therefore someone owned shares both directly and as a life tenant, and the combined holding gave a controlling interest, a gift of the shares owned directly that reduced the combined holding to a minority holding would be valued so as to reflect the loss of control, whereas a transfer of the life interest would be valued only in terms of the life interest shares, even though the life tenant's estate had fallen in value by a greater amount.

Related property

Special rules apply to calculate the value of an asset to which the related property rules apply (s 161). These rules do not apply if the asset is sold within three years after death and relief is claimed under s 176 (see explanatory note 4).

The related property rules provide that property is related to the property in a person's estate if it is:

(a)   Property belonging to his spouse.

(b)   Property which was the subject of an exempt transfer by the taxpayer or his spouse to a charity, political party, national heritage body or housing association after 15 April 1976 and which is owned by that body or has been owned by that body at any time in the previous five years.

If it produces a higher value than its unrelated value, the value of the property in the transferor's estate will be:

$$\frac{\text{Value of that property at unrelated value}}{\text{Value of that property and the related property at unrelated value}} \times \text{Related value of total}$$

In arriving at this proportion for shares or debentures etc of the same class, the respective unrelated values are deemed to be equivalent to the number of shares held (s 161).

For example, the shareholders of Related Ltd are Mr R 40%, Mrs R 25%, Discretionary trust created by Mr R in 1970 15%, Others 20%.

An 80% shareholding is valued at £80,000

A 65% shareholding is valued at £58,500

A 40% shareholding is valued at £24,000

A 25% shareholding is valued at £15,000

A 15% shareholding is valued at £ 4,500

The inheritance tax values of the shares held by Mr & Mrs R would be:

$$\text{Mr R } \frac{40}{65} \times \text{£58,500 for a 65\% holding } = \text{£36,000}$$

$$\text{Mrs R } \frac{25}{65} \times \text{£58,500 for a 65\% holding } = \text{£22,500}$$

since these are higher than £24,000 (for a 40% holding) and £15,000 (for a 25% holding) respectively.

Unquoted securities

Section 168 refers to *unquoted shares and securities* and states that the valuation is to be made on the basis that the prospective purchaser has available all the information which a prudent purchaser might reasonably require in an arm's length transaction.

Farm cottages and farmhouses

Section 169 deals with *farm cottages* occupied by agricultural employees. In valuing such agricultural property no account is to be taken of any value attributable to the fact that the cottages are suitable for residential purposes of any other persons. If the cottage is occupied by a retired employee or the retired employee's widow(er) it is deemed to be occupied by an employee provided it is occupied under a statutorily protected tenancy or under a lease granted to the employee (and surviving spouse) for life as part of his contract of employment.

In a Lands Tribunal decision in the Antrobus case it has been decided that only the agricultural value of a farmhouse qualifies for agricultural buildings allowance, not its full market value, which will often be much higher.

A special purchaser

A problem arises when the property to be valued could be the subject of a bid by a *special purchaser*. For example, a piece of land with a normal value of £100,000 might be worth more to an adjoining landowner for the value that it would add to his own holding. Although he might be prepared to bid up to, say £170,000, he would, in fact, only usually make the bid necessary to obtain the land. That might well be very little more than its normal market value. The value of such property will therefore be between its normal value and the highest price that a special purchaser would pay.

Capital gains tax

If the asset to be transferred will give rise to a liability to *capital gains tax* and the *donee* bears that tax, then the value transferred is reduced by the tax paid (s 165). Capital gains tax may be held over on the disposal of certain property otherwise than under a bargain at arm's length if a claim is made under the provisions of TCGA 1992 s 165 or s 260. In this event the inheritance tax value is not altered, and any inheritance tax payable, either immediately or as a result of the donor's death within seven years, is deducted in computing the chargeable gain arising when the donee eventually disposes of the asset (but not so as to create or increase a loss).

B. Blackacre — sale after death above or below probate value of £400,000

Sale below probate value

If Blackacre is the only sale of land involved, then relief is available under s 191 for the reduction in value. This is given by comparing the value at death with the gross sale value of all land sold within three years after death, and with land sold at a loss within the fourth year after death.

If the result of a disposal is a net adjustment which is less than £1,000 (or 5% of the value at death if lower) then no adjustment will be made for that disposal (s 191(2)).

The relief can only be claimed if the land was sold to an unconnected person by the 'appropriate person', ie the person liable to pay the inheritance tax on the land at death (eg personal representative or trustee of settlement).

In arriving at the *sale value* there are provisions to substitute for the *sale price*, the best consideration which could reasonably have been obtained at the time of sale.

If a claim for relief is made, all sales within the *three* year period (except those covered by the de minimis rule above) must be taken into account, ie including sales at a profit. Sales at a profit in the *fourth* year are not taken into account.

Sale above probate value

If the property increases in value no additional inheritance tax is payable on the increase providing no claim for a reduction in value of other properties has been made (but capital gains tax at 18% *is* payable subject to any exemptions and reliefs available to the executors). Such a sale may, however, influence the agreement of a value on death. (See also explanatory note 7.)

Therefore if the executors sell Blackacre for £350,000 on the open market eighteen months after the date of death, and the estate does not sell any other land, a claim under s 191 should be made, reducing the value of the estate by £50,000. If the property were sold in similar circumstances for £450,000 the executors would be liable for capital gains tax on a gross gain of £50,000, reduced by the capital gains tax annual exemption.

Explanatory Notes

Open market value

1. The 'open market value' rule is the general valuation rule applicable to both lifetime and death transfers. There are, however, a number of special rules relating to particular assets, some of which are dealt with in the example.

   The special rules relating to valuation of quoted securities on death are dealt with in Examples 6, 8 and 11. The provisions for claiming relief for a fall in value of a gift before the donor's death are dealt with in Example 12. See also Example 38 explanatory note 1 for differences in valuation for capital gains tax and inheritance tax purposes.

Valuation of life policies

2. The valuation of life insurance policies on the life of the transferor depends on whether it is a lifetime or death transfer. Market value applies to a lifetime transfer but the policy cannot normally be valued at less than the premiums paid (s 167). For death transfers the policy is valued as having matured.

Associated operations

3. The valuation to be placed on a particular asset will be affected if it is disposed of as part of a series of associated transactions (see Example 22).

Related property

4. Where property in a death estate has been valued under the related property rules, and the property is sold within three years after the death, a claim may be made under s 176 for the value of the property immediately before the death to be redetermined as if the related property rules did not apply. This does *not* mean substituting the *sale proceeds* for the probate value.

   A claim may only be made if:

   (a) The property is sold either by the personal representatives or the person in whom the property is vested.

   (b) The sale is at arm's length for a freely negotiated price and not made in conjunction with a sale of any of the related property.

   (c) The vendor and purchaser are totally unconnected.

   (d) The vendor does not have a right to reacquire the property.

Valuation at death

5. Although the value of property at death is deemed to be its value immediately prior to death, the valuation may anticipate the effect of the death, but not the effect of the sale of the assets. For example, the value of unquoted shares in a company would be affected by the death of the sole director who ran the business and this could be taken into account. But if someone had a large

holding of shares, the availability of which affected the market and caused the price to drop, the drop in price could not be taken into account in arriving at the death valuation, since the drop would be attributable to the *sale* not to the *death*.

6.   Where an estate at death includes a building society account on which demutualisation profits in the form of a cash bonus and/or shares will arise, but the date when the benefits will be received is not determined at the date of death, the value of the rights in the demutualisation will be taken into account in the death valuation, but it will be discounted to reflect the degree of uncertainty or delay at the time of death.

Sale of land after death

7.   Valuation adjustments have to be made where the legal interest in land sold within four years after death is not the same as that held at death, and in connection with leases, exchanges and compulsory purchase (ss 192–198).

In order to qualify for relief under s 191, the sale of the land must actually take place. In the case of *Jones v CIR* (1997), contracts had been exchanged within the (then) three year period, but the sale did not take place and the intended purchaser forfeited his deposit. It was held that s 191 relief was not available.

HMRC Capital Taxes will not consider a claim under s 191 when there is not a chargeable transfer and as a consequence there is no appropriate person. This would arise where, for instance, 100% agricultural property relief would be due. This was confirmed in the case of *Stonor & Mills (Dickinson's Executors) v CIR* (SpC 288, 2001), where the executors sold land within three years of death at figures considerably in excess of the probate values. This did not increase the inheritance tax, because the value of the estate was covered by exemptions and the nil band, so no tax was payable. The executors' attempt to have the values revised under s 191 failed because the Special Commissioners upheld the Revenue's view that there was no 'appropriate person' who could make a claim.

Interaction of inheritance tax and capital gains tax gifts holdover relief

8.   If an asset is transferred in lifetime and a holdover election for capital gains tax is made under TCGA 1992 s 165 or s 260, any inheritance tax paid is allowed as a deduction in computing the chargeable gain when the donee disposes of the asset. This will also apply if the transfer is a potentially exempt transfer for inheritance tax purposes and a death occurs within seven years, causing inheritance tax then to be payable. But the inclusion of inheritance tax as an allowable cost cannot have the effect of creating an allowable loss. Where a potentially exempt transfer is made on which capital gains holdover relief is not available so that capital gains tax is payable, there is no set-off against inheritance tax should the potentially exempt transfer become chargeable on the donor's death. See Example 4 explanatory note 7 for further details (full details of when a chargeable capital gain may be held over under TCGA 1992 s 165 or s 260 are in companion book Tolley's Taxwise I 2008/09).

Question

When X, a widower, died on 7 April 2008 his own assets included a policy on his own life which produced £21,600. As soon as the proceeds of the policy were available his executors invested the whole sum in a new issue of 28,000 shares in AB plc, doing so in July 2008.

He owned at death:

5,000	50p	ords in AB plc quoted at 75–79 with bargains done at 75, 75½ and 78
5,000	£1	ords in CD plc quoted at 121–129 with bargains done at 121 and 123
20,000	£1	ords in EF plc quoted at 240–242 but with no recorded bargains
15,000	£1	ords in GH plc quoted at 252–256 with a single bargain at 252
10,000	£1	ords in IJ plc quoted at 4–6 with no recorded bargains
1,000	50p	ords in KL plc quoted at 92–96 with bargains at 93 and 95

His executors made the following sales:

1 February 2009:	5,000	shares in CD plc sold for £7,500 gross
3 March 2009:	20,000	shares in EF plc sold for £40,550 gross
23 March 2009:	15,000	shares in GH plc sold to the residuary beneficiary Y for £37,000 gross
12 April 2009:	33,000	shares in AB plc sold for £26,400 gross

X had also received equally with his brother the income from a settled fund set up under the will of his father. The trust assets at the date of X's death were:

8,000	50p	ords in AB plc
12,000	£1	ords in EF plc
20,000	£1	ords in MN plc quoted at 251–256 with bargains done at 251, 251½ and 253

On 5 May 2008 the trustees sold half the shares in EF plc (6,000 shares) for £13,800 gross which they used to pay the inheritance tax in respect of half the trust fund in connection with X's death. They then retired and appointed new trustees. There was a dispute about the devolution of X's half share of the trust fund and the new trustees sold half the shares in AB plc on 24 February 2009 (4,000 shares) for £3,120 gross which they used to pay the cost of Counsel's Opinions etc. It is agreed that X's son S is entitled to X's half share of the trust fund absolutely and the new trustees accordingly transferred to him half of the shares in MN plc plus the remaining cash capital in hand. On 15 March 2009 S sold for £27,000 gross, the 10,000 shares in MN plc which were transferred to him.

In each sale or purchase, the expenses incidental to that sale or purchase may be taken to be equal to 1% of the gross sale or purchase price.

On 23 November 2008 IJ plc went into liquidation and the shares were subsequently cancelled without payment of dividend.

The Stock Exchange suspended the shares in KL plc on 5 March 2009, the market value of the 1,000 shares on 7 April 2009 being £400.

Appropriate claims for relief are made.

HMRC point out that at the time of the sale by the executors of the 15,000 shares in GH plc to the residuary beneficiary, such shares were quoted at 253–256, with a single recorded bargain at 253.

Calculate the original and revised values for taxation purposes placed on each holding of shares as at the date of death of X.

Answer

(1)   **Valuation of X's own shares**

				£	£
Date of death 7 April 2008					
5,000	50p	ord in AB plc	@ 76	3,800	
5,000	£1	ord in CD plc	@ 122	6,100	
20,000	£1	ord in EF plc	@ 240½	48,100	
15,000	£1	ord in GH plc	@ 252	37,800	
10,000	£1	ord in IJ plc	@ 4½	450	
1,000	50p	ord in KL plc	@ 93	930	97,180

Less relief for loss on shares sold, cancelled or suspended within one year after death:

		£	£
AB plc —	Sold more than one year after death (12 April 2009)		–
CD plc —	Sale price (1 February 2009)	7,500	
	Probate value	6,100	1,400
EF plc —	Sale price (3 March 2009)	40,550	
	Probate value	48,100	(7,550)
GH plc —	'Best price' (23 March 2009)	37,950	
	Probate value	37,800	150
KL plc —	Suspended security — market value	400	
	Probate value	930	(530)
Reduction in value			£(6,530)

	£
Acquisition of 'qualifying investments' —	
Shares in AB plc purchased by executors	21,600
Total value of disposals within year —	
(£7,500 + £40,550 + £37,950 + £400)	86,400

Reduction in value on death is therefore restricted by

$$\frac{21,600}{86,400} \qquad \text{ie } ¼$$

	£
Claim for reduction in probate value ¾ × 6,530	4,898
	92,282

The value of each holding on death then becomes:

		£
Shares in	AB plc	3,800
	CD plc (£ 6,100 + ¾ of £1,400)	7,150
	EF plc (£48,100 – ¾ of £7,550)	42,438
	GH plc (£37,800 + ¾ of £150)	37,912
	IJ plc	450
	KL plc (£930 – ¾ of £530)	532
		£92,282

(2)   **Valuation of Trust Fund (in which X has a one half interest)**

Date of death 7 April 2008   £   £

8,000	50p	ord in AB plc	@ 76	6,080	
12,000	£1	ord in EF plc	@ 240½	28,860	
20,000	£1	ord in MN plc	@ 252	50,400	£85,340

Relief for loss on shares sold within one year after death:

				£	£
EF plc	Sale price (5 May 2008)			13,800	
	Probate value				
	6,000	@ 240½		14,430	(630)
AB plc	Sale price (24 February 2009)			3,120	
	Probate value				
	4,000	@ 76		3,040	80
MN plc	Sale by beneficiary cannot affect position				–
Reduction in value					(550)

Value of shares taxable on death of X		
	½ of £85,340	42,670
Less:	Reduction in value	
	½ of £550	275
		£42,395

The value of each holding on death then becomes:			
Shares in	AB plc	½ of (£6,080 + £80)	3,080
	EF plc	½ of (£28,860 – £630)	14,115
	MN plc	½ of £50,400	25,200
			£42,395

Explanatory Notes

Quoted securities

1.   The notes to Examples 6 and 8 relating to shares sold within twelve months after death apply also to this example, but the problems of partial reinvestment and a partial interest in trust property are also considered here.

2.   Listed shares and securities are valued at the lower of:

(a)   The lower closing price plus one-quarter of the difference between the lower and higher closing prices; or

(b)   Half way between the highest and lowest recorded bargains for the day of valuation.

The respective valuations are therefore:

Own Shares	Closing Prices	Bargains	Lower
AB plc	75 + 1/4 (79 − 75) = 76		
	$\dfrac{75 + 78}{2}$	= 76½	76
CD plc	121 + 1/4 (129 − 121) = 123		
	$\dfrac{121 + 123}{2}$	= 122	122
EF plc	240 + 1/4 (242 − 240) = 240½	None	240½
GH plc	252 + 1/4 (256 − 252) = 253	252	252
IJ plc	4 + 1/4 (6 − 4) = 4½	None	4½
KL plc	92 + 1/4 (96 − 92) = 93		
	$\dfrac{93 + 95}{2}$	= 94	93
Trust Shares			
MN plc	251 + 1/4 (256 − 251) = 252¼		
$\dfrac{251 + 253}{2}$		= 252	252

Where a death occurs on a Sunday or other day for which no prices are available, the price of each individual item may be taken for either the first day before or after the death for which prices are available. Units in an approved unit trust are valued at the manager's buying price (ie the lower of the two prices quoted). If no price was published on the date of death the last published price before death should be used.

Sales within twelve months after death

3.   When qualifying securities are sold at an overall loss within twelve months after death, s 179 enables the 'appropriate person', ie the personal representatives or trustees accounting for the tax, to claim a reduction in the value of those securities at the time of death. 'Qualifying securities' means quoted securities or holdings in authorised unit trusts. 'Quoted securities' means securities listed on a recognised stock exchange (ss 178(1) & 272). Securities on the Alternative Investment Market (AIM) are unquoted.

To compute the reduction, if any, *all* qualifying securities sold within one year after death by the appropriate person are taken into account (s 179(1)(a)). The total sale proceeds, or if higher, the best consideration which could reasonably have been obtained for them at the time of sale, are substituted for probate value at death (s 179(1)(b)). No allowance is made for expenses (s 178(5)).

Thus the sale of shares in AB plc by the executors is ignored as it occurred more than twelve months after death.

Actual selling prices before expenses are substituted for probate value for the holdings by the deceased in CD plc and EF plc (subject to explanatory notes 5 and 6).

The shares in GH plc were sold to the residuary beneficiary for £37,000 but if they had been sold on the Stock Exchange they would probably have made 15,000 × 253 = £37,950.

HMRC would normally use the same valuation rules as for date of death ie the lower of

Closing Prices	*Bargains*	*Lower*
$253 + \frac{1}{4}(256 - 253) = 253\frac{3}{4}$	253	253

A claim cannot be restricted to disposals with losses; all disposals must be included in the computation.

Shares cancelled or in which dealings suspended

4.   If dealings in quoted shares are suspended as at the first anniversary of death, and the then market value is lower than the value at death, the security may be deemed to have been sold at its market value twelve months after death (s 186B). The shares in KL plc are therefore deemed to have given rise to a notional loss of £530. In practice it will be difficult to arrive at a market value of shares in which dealings are suspended. No guidance has been given as to how such a market value is to be arrived at.

Under s 186A, if a qualifying security is cancelled within twelve months after death, it may be treated as sold twelve months after death for £1. Shares are sometimes cancelled in company reorganisations, but the apparent intention of s 186A is to deal with company liquidations. Cancellation does not, however, take place when liquidation commences, but at the time the liquidation is completed. It would be rare for a company whose shares had a significant value on death to go into liquidation and for the liquidation to be completed within the required twelve month period. It appears, therefore, that s 186A does not meet its objective. One possible solution where shares have a significant value at death but then become worthless is to undertake a deed of variation to direct the shares to an exempt beneficiary, such as a charity. The value would not then be included in the chargeable estate.

It has been assumed that the liquidation of IJ plc in the example was not completed before 7 April 2009.

Sales followed by reinvestment

5.   To prevent the appropriate person selling investments and reacquiring them shortly afterwards s 180 provides that, if any qualifying investments are acquired in the same capacity within a period beginning on the date of death and ending two months after the date of the last sale (or deemed sale), then the claim shall be reduced by the proportion which the purchase prices of all such qualifying purchases bears to the aggregate sale prices used in the claim.

In this example the executors had invested £21,600 in quoted securities during the relevant period. The total relief is therefore reduced by the proportion which that investment bears to the sale values of securities disposed of or deemed to be disposed of within twelve months after death (ie CD plc + EF plc + GH plc + KL plc = £86,400) giving actual relief of

$$£6,530 - \left(\frac{21,600}{86,400} \times 6,350\right) = £4,898$$

The purchase does not have to be made out of the proceeds of sale of the securities sold. Any purchase of qualifying shares made during the period commencing with the date of death and ending two months after the date of the last sale, whether before or after the sale, and irrespective of the source of the purchase money, reduces the amount of relief available.

6.   The relevant proportion of gain or loss is then added to or subtracted from probate value at death of each security included in the claim for reduction in value to give the revised value for inheritance tax. That revised value is also deemed to be market value at date of death for capital gains tax (s 187).

Thus the value of the shares in AB plc is unaltered because they are not sold within twelve months after death and therefore not included in the s 179 claim;

The value of the shares in CD plc is increased by ¾ of the gain on sale, £1,400;

The value of the shares in EF plc is reduced by ¾ of the loss on sale, £7,550;

The value of the shares in GH plc is increased by ¾ of the notional gain of £150 on disposal, notwithstanding the fact that the actual proceeds showed a loss;

The value of the shares in IJ plc remains unaltered because they were not cancelled within twelve months after death;

The value of the shares in KL plc is reduced by ¾ of the notional loss on suspension, £530.

Shares forming trust property in which deceased had a part interest

7.   As the trust assets have not been appropriated into separate funds for X and his brother, the entirety of the trust fund has to be calculated at the death of X (s 186) but only the one half proportion representing his life interest is included in the computation of tax due. This has the effect of treating a part of the securities disposed of as belonging to the non taxable part of the trust and therefore restricts the relief claimable. In this example one half of the trust fund is taxable and therefore only one half of the computed reduction in value is claimable.

8.   The trustees of a settled fund are treated as a single and continuing body (s 178(4)) and therefore the computation includes the sales of shares by the old and new trustees.

   However the beneficiary is not the same person as the trustees and was not himself accountable for the tax on the death even though he ultimately bore the burden of its payment by receiving less funds from the trust and therefore the disposal by S as beneficiary of shares in MN plc transferred to him by the trustees is not included in the calculation of relief.

Investments not found until more than twelve months after death

9.   The relevant sale must take place within twelve months of the date of death for relief for loss to be available. In the case of *Exors of CE Lee v IRC* (SpC 349 2002) the documents relating to the investment were not found until more than twelve months after death. The shares had lost value. The value for inheritance tax was market value at date of death. Relief for loss in value was not available.

Question

Pilling, who had been a widower since 1990, died on 3 May 2008. He was survived by a son and daughter – twins born in 1953. Mrs Pilling had an estate of £175,000 and there is no available nil-rate band to carry forward to be utilised on Pilling's death.

For many years up to 5 April 2001, Pilling had made regular gifts, fully using the annual exemption for inheritance tax, but he had not made any chargeable transfers.

Pilling had made the following gifts after 5 April 2001:

15 June 2002	To nephew £203,400 in securities.
15 April 2003	10,000 £1 shares in Black plc, a listed company, to his niece. The shares were worth £13.00 each at the date of the gift. On 3 December 2002 Black plc was taken over by White plc and in exchange for her Black plc shares, Pilling's niece was given 15,000 White plc shares of 25p each, those shares being worth £7.00. At Pilling's death they were worth £2.80 each.
25 December 2003	Motor car worth £12,600 to his nephew. Two days before Pilling's death the car was totally destroyed by fire. The insurance compensation was £5,000.
4 July 2005	Cash gift of £63,000 to his grandson in consideration of his marriage, which took place on that date.

At the time of his death Pilling owned 3,200 ordinary shares in Briggs and Pilling Ltd; he had subscribed for these shares when the company was formed in 1957 and they were valued at £55 per share on his death. The company has an issued capital of 5,000 ordinary shares and is engaged in demolition contracting.

His other assets comprised quoted investments and personal chattels with a total value of £240,700. He had a bank overdraft of £33,100 and his funeral expenses were £1,100.

By his will, which was made immediately after the death of his wife in 1990, Pilling left his shares in Briggs and Pilling Ltd to his son, with the residue of his estate divided equally between his son and his daughter.

Pilling's son accepts that because he will receive the legacy of the shares in Briggs and Pilling Ltd, his sister or her family should have a larger share in the residue of the estate. In September 2008 they ask you for advice on dealing with their father's estate in the most efficient way in relation to inheritance tax. The son is married with two children whose ages are 13 and 10; the daughter is a widow whose only child is Pilling's grandson who was married in July 2005.

(a)   Calculate the inheritance tax payable as a result of Pilling's death, stating the due date of payment.

(b)   List the points that you would bring to the attention of Pilling's son and daughter in connection with altering the terms of Pilling's will.

Answer

(a) **Inheritance tax payable as a result of Pilling's death on 3 May 2008 Lifetime transfers**

Lifetime transfers

				Gross	Tax on 2008/09 scale
	Potentially exempt transfers now chargeable:		£	£	£
June 2002	Nephew — securities		203,400		
	Less: Annual exemptions 2002/03	(3,000)			
	2001/02	(3,000)	197,400		–
April 2003	Niece — shares		130,000		
	Less: Annual exemption 2003/04	(3,000)	127,000	4,960*	
	(324,400 – 312,000 = 12,400 @ 40% = £4,960)			324,400	4,960
December 2003	Nephew — car			12,600	5,040**
July 2005	Grandson		63,000		
	Less: Marriage exemption	(2,500)			
	Annual exemptions 2005/06	(3,000)			
	2004/05	(3,000)	54,500	21,800	
				391,500	

*   On a claim by the niece, tax on her gift may be recomputed as follows:

Value of gift	130,000
Value on death (15,000 @ £2.80)	42,000
Reduce transfer by	£88,000
Giving chargeable transfer of (117,000 – 88,000) = £29,000	

When this is added to the chargeable transfers brought forward of £197,400, the total is £226,400, which is below the nil threshold, so that the inheritance tax payable by the niece is reduced to nil.

**   Tapering relief of 40% will be available to the nephew on the gift on 25 December 2003, because it was made between 4 and 5 years before death. Inheritance tax payable will be 60% × £5,040 = £3,024.

		£	Due date
Tax payable on PETs which became chargeable because of Pilling's death within 7 years:			
15 June 2002	By nephew	nil	
15 April 2003	By niece (after claim re fall in value)	nil	
25 December 2004	By nephew (after tapering relief)	3,024	30 November 2008
4 July 2005	By grandson	21,800	

Pilling's estate at death

		Date of death 3 May 2008	
		£	£
Shares in Briggs and Pilling Ltd 3,200 @ £55		176,000	
Less: 100% business property relief		176,000	–
Quoted investments and personal chattels			240,700
			240,700
Less: Debts and funeral expenses (33,100 + 1,100)			34,200
Chargeable estate at death			206,500

Since the lifetime transfers exceed the nil threshold, the tax payable by the personal representatives is £206,500 @ 40%, ie £82,600. The due date of payment is 30 November 2008, or when they deliver their account with their application for probate if earlier.

(b)   **Points to be brought to attention of Pilling's son and daughter in connection with altering the terms of Pilling's will**

1.   Pilling's son and daughter may vary the way in which the estate is distributed, providing they do so within two years after the date of his death. Both the son and daughter must sign the instrument of variation. The personal representatives will not be required to sign, since the variation will not result in any additional tax being payable by them. The variation will be treated for inheritance tax as if it had applied at the date of death (see explanatory note 7).

2.   The variation is also effective for capital gains tax purposes (providing a statement to that effect is included within the deed – TCGA 1992 s 62(6) and (7)), so that the ultimate beneficiaries who receive any chargeable assets directly will be treated as having acquired them at market value at the date of Pilling's death.

3.   For income tax purposes, any income arising on the assets before the variation is still treated as belonging to the original beneficiary and taxed at his/her tax rates. If that person is assessed to higher rate tax on the income, it may be thought appropriate for the tax to be paid by whoever receives the income.

4.   If Pilling's son and daughter already have adequate income, they may wish to provide in the instrument of variation that some or all of Pilling's estate is transferred direct to their children. In the case of Pilling's son's infant children the funds would be held in trust until they reached age 18 or married before that time. If, however, Pilling's son gives up some or all of his entitlement in favour of his own infant children this would be treated as a parental settlement and the income arising from the assets would be treated as Pilling's son's income so long as his children were infant and unmarried, unless the funds were transferred by way of accumulation and maintenance settlement and the income was accumulated. There would be no problem in relation to Pilling's daughter, since her son is married, nor in relation to any transfer by Pilling's son to his nephew.

Explanatory Notes

Fall in value of gift before death

1.   If the value of a gift has fallen between the date of gift and the date of death, a claim may be made for the tax to be computed as if the value transferred were reduced by the reduction in value of the asset. The recomputation does not affect the amount of the chargeable transfer taken into account in the figure of cumulative transfers for the purpose of computing the tax on any later chargeable transfers

or on death. The relief does not apply to wasting chattels and hence the car value is not reduced in this example (s 131). If the asset is shares and there is a reorganisation or takeover prior to death, the original shares and the new holding are treated as the same property (s 135).

2. A claim for the relief must be made by the person liable to pay the tax. So, following a claim by Pilling's niece, the value of the shares given to her is reduced by £88,000 in computing the tax payable.

3. These provisions also apply where the asset has been sold prior to death by the transferee or his spouse, providing it was a bona fide sale at arm's length to an unconnected person (s 131(3)). In this case the relief applies to the difference between the value transferred and the sale proceeds.

4. If the property to which the claim for reduction of value relates qualified for business property relief (or agricultural property relief) then that relief is also reduced proportionately. This will only be relevant where the relief is less than 100%.

5. If the original gift was a chargeable lifetime transfer on which the donor paid the tax, the *original* amount of tax would be added to the recomputed transfer.

Cumulative transfers exceed nil threshold

	Gross £	Tax £	Net £
Net gift of 10,000 shares worth £4 each to discretionary trust			40,000
Grossed up $\left(\times \dfrac{100}{80}\right)$	50,000	10,000	
		(½ rate)	
Shares worth £3 each on death within seven years			
Recomputed gift 10,000 @ £3	30,000		
Add tax on original gift	10,000	40,000	16,000
		(full rate)	

Additional tax payable because of death within seven years after the gift is £6,000 (£16,000 – £10,000), subject to any available taper relief.

Increase in value of gift before death

6. If the value of a gift has *increased* between the date of gift and the date of death, the death scale is nonetheless only applied to the original chargeable transfer.

Deeds of variation

7. Deeds of variation do not have to be sent to HMRC Capital Taxes unless the variation results in additional tax becoming payable then the beneficiaries and personal representatives must send a copy of the variation to HMRC Capital Taxes within six months and notify them of the amount of additional tax payable (IHTA 1984 s 218A). See Example 34 for further details, in particular explanatory note 5.

Cross references

8. For further notes on exemptions, see Example 1; business property relief, see Example 25; dates of payment, see Example 5 and the treatment of liabilities in relation to the instalment option and business property relief, see Example 9.

Question

Hartford, who had never married, owned and operated a farm in Cheshire until his death on 31 May 2008

Hartford had made two lifetime gifts as follows. On 14 October 1993 he gave £112,700 to his sister Providence. On 25 September 2000 he gave £148,500 to his cousin Lansing in consideration of Lansing's marriage, which took place on that date.

The assets owned by Hartford at the time of his death were valued for probate as follows:

	£
Freehold farm in Cheshire (agricultural value £640,000)	780,000
Quoted investments, personal possessions and bank balances	335,500

Debts due at death and funeral expenses (all allowable in calculating inheritance tax) totalled £7,280.

Hartford was also life tenant of a family trust in which his interest had commenced on the death of a brother on 25 November 2002, when the value of the trust fund was £83,800, out of which inheritance tax of £18,500 was paid as a result of the brother's death. On 31 May 2008 the trust fund consisted of quoted investments valued at £153,850 (including accrued income £2,410) and there was also undistributed income due to Hartford amounting to £3,730.

By his will, which was made in February 1999, Hartford made charitable bequests totalling £100,000 and also left £30,000 to a qualifying political party. The farm was left absolutely to his cousin Lansing and the residue was to be held in trust for Sally (born 1998) the infant child of his deceased sister Augusta. Hartford was Sally's legal guardian at the time of his death.

(a) State the points relating to taxation that should have been taken into consideration when drafting the terms of the trust created by Hartford's will for his sister's infant child.

(b) Calculate the inheritance tax payable as a result of Hartford's death, stating the persons responsible for payment of the tax and the amount payable by each.

(c) State what difference, if any, it would have made to the calculations in (b) if the gifts to Providence and Lansing had been made one year later, ie 14 October 1994 and 25 September 2001 respectively.

Answer

(a)   **Hartford — Tax points in relation to drafting trust for sister's children**

A trust for a bereaved minor is a trust for the benefit of a person:

- under the age of 18; and

- at least one of whose parents, or as the case may be step-parent or person having parental responsibility eg legal guardian, has died.

A bereaved minor's trust created under the terms of a will or intestacy is not a relevant property settlement. Unlike accumulation and maintenance settlements where no interest in possession subsists in the settled property and the income from that settled property is to be accumulated so far as not applied for the maintenance, education or benefit of a beneficiary – the 'bereaved minor' can be given an interest in possession immediately.

In this case settled property is held on a bereaved minors trust for the benefit of Augusta's minor child – Sally, where the trust is established under the will of Hartford as the legal guardian with parental responsibility for her.

Whilst Sally is under the age of 18 – if any of the capital of the settled property is applied it must be applied for her benefit only. She must, prior to or upon the attainment of the age of 18 years, be absolutely entitled to the settled property and also absolutely entitled to any income arising there from and any income that has been accumulated.

If the trust property is not so applied then whilst Sally is under the age of 18 years the income arising there from, if any, must be a full entitlement or the income must not be applied for the benefit of any other person.

A charge to tax arises:

(i)   under s 70/71 – if the trustees make a 'disposition' which reduces the value of the settled property. 'Disposition' includes an omission to exercise a right, unless not deliberate, which is treated as made at the latest time the right could have been exercised;

(ii)   where settled property on bereaved minor's trusts ceases to be property which satisfies the necessary conditions of s 71A

The rate of the tax charge is determined by reference to the Hartford's cumulative transfers in the seven years preceding the date on which the settlement commenced, as well as the settlement's cumulative transfers in the ten years preceding the anniversary.

Tax is calculated using the following rates:

(i)   where the whole of the relevant property has been comprised in the settlement throughout the ten-year period ending immediately before the ten-year anniversary, at 30% of the effective rate;

(ii)   and where the whole or part of the relevant property was not relevant property or was not comprised in the settlement throughout the ten years ending immediately before the ten-year anniversary, at 30% of the effective rate reduced by one-fortieth for each successive 'quarter' in the ten-year period which expired before the property became, or last became, relevant property.

The 'effective rate' is the rate found by expressing the tax chargeable as a percentage of the amount on which tax is charged on an assumed chargeable transfer by an assumed transferor.

The rates used are as follows:

		Cumulative total
0.25% for each of the first 40 quarters	10%	10%
0.20% for each of the next 40 quarters	8%	18%
0.15% for each of the next 40 quarters	6%	24%
0.10% for each of the next 40 quarters	4%	28%
0.05% for each of the next 40 quarters	2%	30%
Maximum rate chargeable after 50 years		30%

To look at an example of how this works:

Say that on 31 May 2019, Hartford's will settlement fails to qualify as a bereaved minors trust and the claw back provisions apply. The settlement was valued at £1,250,000 on 31 May 2008 and at £2,500,000 on 31 May 2019. There will be a charge to IHT on the whole of the value of the settlement on 31 May 2019. The period from 31 May 2008 to 31 May 2019 is 44 complete quarters charged at the s 70(6) rate:

				Cumulative total
0.25% for each of the first	40	quarters	10%	10%
0.20% for each of the next	4	quarters	0.8%	10.8%
	44			10.8%

The IHT charge is 10.8% × £2,500,000 = £270,000

No charge arises:

(i)   on Sally becoming absolutely entitled to the settled property (not necessarily in fixed shares) on or before attaining the specified age of 18 years; or

(ii) on Sally's death before her attaining the specified age of 18 years;

(iii) on funds being paid or applied for Sally's advancement or benefit; or

(iv) on the payment of costs or expenses attributable to the trust property.

The rate charged may be reduced if any of the property is, or was excluded property.

(b)   **Inheritance tax payable as a result of Hartford's death on 31 May 2008**

				£
Estate at death was as follows:				
Freehold farm in Cheshire			780,000	
Less: agricultural property relief 100% × 640,000	640,000			
business property relief 100% × 140,000	140,000		780,000	–
Quoted investments, personal possessions and bank balances				335,500
Accrued income from trust fund*				2,410
Undistributed income due from trust fund*				3,730
(* Assumed to be net of income tax)				
				341,640
Less: debts and funeral expenses				7,280
				334,360
Less: charitable bequests			100,000	
qualifying political party bequest			30,000	130,000
				204,360
Settled property (153,850 – 2,410)				151,440
				355,800

The only lifetime transfers made by Hartford were the potentially exempt transfer to Providence on 14 October 1993, which became completely exempt on 14 October 2000, and the potentially exempt transfer to Lansing on 25 September 2000, which became completely exempt on 25 September 2007.

The tax payable on the death estate is therefore:

$355,800 - 312,000 = 43,800$ @ 40%   17,520

Less: quick
succession relief $20\% \times 18,500 \times \dfrac{65,300}{83,800}$ 2,883   £14,637

Payable as to $\dfrac{204,360}{355,800} \times 14,637 = £8,407$ by Hartford's personal
representatives

and as to $\dfrac{151,440}{355,800} \times 14,637 = £6,230$ by trustess of settled property

(c)

If the transfers to Providence and Lansing had been made a year later, the transfer to Providence would have been a potentially exempt transfer that became completely exempt on 14 October 2001. The transfer to Lansing would have been within seven years before Hartford's death and would thus become a chargeable transfer. The position would therefore be:

Cumulative transfers at Hartford's death:			*Gross* £	*Tax* £
25 September 2001	Gift to Lansing	148,500		
	Less: Marriage exemption	(1,000)		
	Annual exemptions			
	2001/02	(3,000)		
	2000/01	(3,000)		
	PET now chargeable		141,500	–
Estate at death			355,800	74,120
			497,300	74,120**

(** $497,300 - 312,000 = 185,300$ @ 40%)
Tax on estate at death   74,120

Less: quick succession relief $20\% \times 18,500 \times \dfrac{65,300}{83,800}$

                                                                2,883   £71,237

Payable as to $\dfrac{204,360}{355,800} \times 71,237 = £40,916$ by Hartford's personal representatives

		Gross £	Tax £
Cumulative transfers at Hartford's death:			

and as to $\dfrac{151,440}{355,800} \times 71,237 = £30,321$ by trustees of settled property

Thus the transfer to Lansing would not itself attract tax, since it was below the nil threshold, and the tapering relief of 80% for transfers within six and seven years before death would not therefore be relevant, but the transfer would take up £141,500 of the nil band otherwise available to the death estate. The tax on the death estate would accordingly increase by £141,500 @ 40% = £56,600 (ie 71,237 – 14,637).

Explanatory Notes

Will trusts

1.   When property is left by a will into a trust the normal rules for settlements apply (see Examples 52 to 63). Accordingly if the settlement had an interest in possession then the settlement would be deemed to be part of the estate of the person with that interest, as in the case of Hartford in this example. However, when the beneficiaries are minors it is usual to retain a degree of discretion over the income of the settlement and where that is done the rules relating to discretionary settlements apply (see Example 60).

Transfer to Providence

2.   Providence would have no liability as a result of Hartford's death whether her gift had been made on 14 October 1993 or 14 October 1994. As a potentially exempt transfer the gift becomes completely exempt after seven years. In computing the liability on the gift to Lansing if it had been made on 25 September 2001, only chargeable transfers in the previous seven years are taken to form the opening figures. The gift to Providence, being potentially exempt, and subsequently completely exempt, is not taken into account.

Cross references

3.   For notes on agricultural property relief and business property relief, see Example 25; for notes on exemptions, see Example 1; and quick succession relief, see Example 21.

Question

Thomas died on 20 December 2008.

He left an estate valued at £400,000 after payment of all debts and funeral expenses.

By his will he gave a pecuniary legacy of £206,000 to his son Dick, with the residue of his estate to his wife.

He had on 31 December 2005 made a gift of £217,000 to Dick. This was the only gift made by Thomas since 2000.

Calculate the inheritance tax payable in consequence of Thomas's death.

Answer

Lifetime transfer

			£
31 December 2005			
Gift to Dick			217,000
Less: Annual exemptions	2005/06	3,000	
	2004/05	3,000	6,000
Potentially exempt transfer			211,000

Inheritance tax payable on death of Thomas 20 December 2008

	Gross £	Tax on 2008/09 scale £
By Dick		
31 December 2005		
Gift — potentially exempt transfer now chargeable	211,000	–

By Estate
Tax is payable on the grossed up equivalent of the £206,000 legacy to Dick when added to an inheritance tax accumulation of £211,000 using the 2008/09 scale:

	Gross £	Tax £	Net £
Before death	211,000	–	211,000
Pecuniary legacy (see working note)	276,000	70,000	206,000
	487,000	70,000	417,000
Tax payable by estate			
(£487,000 – 312,000 @ 40%) = £175,000 @ 40%		£70,000	

The estate will accordingly be divided as follows:

	£	£
Gross estate		400,000
To HMRC — payment of inheritance tax		70,000
To Dick		206,000
To Wife (exempt transfer)		
(ie) £400,000 estate – £206,000 to Dick	194,000	
Less: Tax on Dick's legacy	70,000	124,000
		400,000

Working Note

As cumulative net transfers of £417,000 exceed £312,000 the 40% rate of tax applies to the excess of £105,000, giving a gross equivalent for that part of the legacy of:

$$\frac{100}{60} \times £105,000 = £175,000$$

with tax payable of £70,000.

Explanatory Notes

Potentially exempt transfer on 31 December 2005

1.   The gift made on 31 December 2005, in so far as it exceeded the available annual exemptions, was a potentially exempt transfer that became a chargeable transfer on the death of Thomas (s 19). It is then chargeable using the rates applicable at death. The lifetime gift attracts the nil rate band before the estate at death and accordingly no tax is due on that gift. If a liability had arisen it would be payable by the transferee.

Pecuniary legacies

2.   On death, the residue left to the wife is exempt (s 18) but it cannot be ascertained until the tax payable by the estate has been calculated. Tax is payable on the pecuniary legacy and since the legatee receives the actual amount of the legacy, the tax payable is found by grossing it up (ss 36–42).

3.   The amount received by the widow is much less than she at first sight appears entitled to:

Estate		400,000
Dick's legacy		206,000
Apparent entitlement		£194,000

but in fact she gets:

Estate		400,000
Dick's legacy	206,000	
after tax of	70,000	276,000
		£124,000

4.   Contrast the above with the position if the will had left a legacy of £206,000 to the widow and the residue (£194,000) to Dick. Then the taxable estate would be:

Value on death at 20 December 2008		400,000
Less: Exempt legacy – wife		206,000
Chargeable to inheritance tax on death		£194,000

Inheritance tax due on death		2008/09 scale
	£	£
Chargeable transfers accumulation at death	211,000	–
Chargeable estate	194,000	37,200*
	405,000	37,200*

(* 405,000 – 312,000 = 93,000 @ 40%)

The estate would then be divided:

	£	£
Gross estate		400,000

	£	£
To HMRC – payment of inheritance tax		37,200
To Wife		206,000
To Dick	194,000	
Less: Tax on residue	37,200	156,800
		400,000

The widow is better off by more than Dick is worse off, HMRC being the loser:

	Legacy to Dick *Residue to widow*	*Legacy to widow* *Residue to Dick*	*Difference* *£*
Dick	206,000	156,800	(49,200)
Widow	124,000	206,000	82,000
HMRC	70,000	37,200	(32,800)
	£400,000	£400,000	

There is nothing to prevent the widow making a personal gift to Dick from her own resources, covered in part by available exemptions and the amount reckonable being a potentially exempt transfer. If, however, a claim was made by Dick against the estate for an increased share of the estate and that claim was settled by Thomas's widow out of her own assets rather than out of assets from the estate, then s 29A would operate to treat that amount as being a payment out of the estate, reducing accordingly the exempt amount to the widow (claims under the Inheritance (Provision for Family and Dependants) Act 1975 that are settled out of the estate are already treated as if they were effected by the will (s 146)).

Question

Samuel Smith died on 31 March 2009 leaving net estate valued as follows:

	£
His half share in the business of S and D Smith carried on in partnership for many years (his brother, David Smith, owning the other half share)	400,000
An office building occupied by S and D Smith	430,000
Bank and building society accounts	34,600
Quoted securities	82,300
Half share in the matrimonial home and contents, valued at £545,000, being held by himself and Mrs Smith (who survived him) as joint tenants	272,500
Life assurance policies on his own life — amount receivable	132,400
A house in France (there are no additional costs of administration because of the situation overseas)	140,800

He made bequests of £100 to each of three grandchildren and £5,000 to his daughter on her reaching the age of twenty-five or her earlier marriage.

He left £18,000 to charities and £100 to a political party.

He left his widow a legacy of £150,000.

The house in France was left to his daughter with the stipulation that she bore any inheritance tax applicable to it.

His share in the partnership business together with the office building occupied by the partnership was left to his son with the stipulation that he bore any tax thereon.

The residue of the estate was left equally to his son and daughter. He had made no lifetime transfers.

(a) Calculate the inheritance tax payable and show by whom it would be borne.

(b) Explain the position regarding capital gains tax on the assets comprised in the estate.

Answer

(a)   **S Smith deceased**

	Date of death 31 March 2009		
	£	£	£
Share in matrimonial home and contents		272,500	
Less: Exempt because of devolution on widow		272,500	–
House in France (see explanatory notes 4 and 5)			140,800
Half share in S and D Smith		400,000	
Less: 100% business property relief		400,000	–
Office building occupied by S and D Smith		430,000	
Less: 50% business property relief		215,000	215,000
Residuary estate			
Bank and building society accounts		34,600	
Quoted securities		82,300	
Life assurance policy proceeds		132,400	
		249,300	
Less: Exempt legacies			
Gifts to charities	18,000		
Gift to political party	100		
Legacy to widow	150,000	168,100	81,200
Total estate on which inheritance tax is payable			437,000

Comprising:

Estate before reliefs and exemptions (*after* jointly owned assets which pass directly to widow)	1,220,100
Less: Business property relief	615,000
	605,100
Less: Exempt legacies	168,100
	£437,000
Tax payable on estate (437,000 – 312,000) = £125,000 @ 40%	£50,000

Which would be borne as follows:		*Tax*	*Borne by*
Matrimonial home		–	
House in France	$\dfrac{140,800}{437,000} \times 50,000 = 16,110$	16,110	Daughter
Office Building	$\dfrac{215,000}{437,000} \times 50,000 = 24,600$	24,600	Son

Which would be borne as follows:		Tax	Borne by
Residue	$\dfrac{81,200}{437,000} \times 50,000 = 9,290$	9,290	Son and daughter out of residue
		$\underline{\hphantom{00}}$	
		£50,000	

The tax on the house in France and on the office building could be paid by instalments over ten years so long as the daughter and son retained the assets.

(b)   Capital gains tax position on death

There is no capital gains tax charge on death. The legatees or devisees who receive chargeable assets acquire them for capital gains tax purposes at the probate value, so that the increase in value during the ownership of the deceased escapes capital gains tax.

Explanatory Notes

Joint tenancies and tenancies in common

1.   For details of joint tenancies (and tenancies in common), see the explanatory notes to Example 6. Since Smith's matrimonial residence and contents are jointly owned with his wife as joint tenants, they automatically accrue to his widow who survived him, and are thus left out of the calculation of the estate for inheritance tax because of the spouse exemption.

Had the house been held under a tenancy in common, then husband and wife would each be entitled to a separate share, which would have formed part of the residue of the estate which devolved on the son and daughter, Smith's one half share of the value then being included in the calculation of the chargeable estate.

Life insurance

2.   The example illustrates that life insurance on one's own life swells the chargeable estate where the proceeds are payable to the estate. A preferable alternative is where the policy is taken out by the taxpayer on his own life but a trust is created in favour of his children, so that the proceeds of the policy eventually fall into the trust fund as distinct from the estate.

Any gifts will have occurred yearly as the taxpayer has maintained the policy by paying the premiums. They will usually be exempt as payments out of the donor's income. The proceeds in the form of the trust fund are received by the beneficiaries without any inheritance tax liability, since the beneficiaries have always had a right to the capital of the trust fund (which has now become cash instead of a life policy).

Alternatively the children of a taxpayer could themselves take out and maintain a policy on the life of their parent on a 'life of another' basis with the same inheritance tax advantages.

3.   Another advantage of life policies not belonging to the estate is that the beneficiaries have cash without waiting for the grant of probate. The policy monies do not belong to the deceased and their receipt does not depend upon the grant of probate. They are paid upon proof of death — the death certificate. This is often a useful way of putting the dependants in funds for family necessities, or to pay inheritance tax, as well as mitigating the inheritance tax charge.

Foreign property and domicile

4.   Property situated abroad does not escape inheritance tax unless the taxpayer is also domiciled abroad. Domicile has a specially extended meaning for inheritance tax.

Effects of domicile on inheritance tax

Domicile is a legal concept and so differs from nationality or residence. An individual is domiciled in the country where they have their permanent home and they can only have one domicile at any given time. Any liability to UK inheritance tax depends on a person's domicile at the time they make a transfer of value.

Domicile of origin

A 'domicile of origin' is normally taken as the father's domicile at the time when the child is born but may in fact not be the country of birth. For example, if Jack is born in Germany while his father is working there, but the father's permanent home is in the UK, Jack's domicile of origin is the UK.

Domicile of dependency

Until a person can legally change it by acquiring a domicile of choice, their domicile will be the same as that of the person on whom they are legally dependent. If that person's domicile changes, the dependant automatically acquire the same domicile in place of their domicile of origin. This is known as a domicile of dependency.

Deemed domicile

For inheritance tax purposes, there is a concept of 'deemed domicile'. Even if a person is not domiciled in the UK under general law they will be treated as if they are domiciled in the UK at the time of a transfer if:

● 	they were domiciled in the UK within the three years immediately before the transfer; or

● 	they were resident in the UK in at least 17 of the 20 tax years ending with the year in which they make a transfer.

As a general rule – if an individual is domiciled, or deemed to be domiciled, in the UK, inheritance tax applies to their assets wherever they are situated. Similarly, inheritance tax applies to settled property in the UK. It does not apply to settled property outside the UK, unless the settlor was domiciled, or deemed to be domiciled, in the UK when the property was settled.

The location of assets is subject to general law as amended by any special provisions in a double taxation agreement. The normal rules for the more common types of asset are that:

● 	rights or interests in or over immovable property and chattels are situated where the property is located;

● 	registered shares or securities are situated where they are registered;

● 	coins and bank notes are situated wherever they happen to be at the time of the transfer;

● 	bearer securities are situated where the certificate of title is located at the time of the transfer;

● 	goodwill is situated where the business, to which it is attached, is carried on;

● 	an interest in a partnership is situated in the country whose law governs the partnership agreement;

● 	debts are situated where the debtor resides;

● 	bank accounts are situated at the branch where the account is kept.

If a person is domiciled abroad, inheritance tax applies only to their UK assets. However, if an individual is domiciled abroad there is no charge on excluded assets. See Example 3 (a) for a list of excluded assets for non-domiciled individuals.

The deemed domicile rules do not apply to a taxable reversionary interest in settled property. Inheritance tax is not due if the reversionary interest is situated outside the UK, and the person beneficially entitled to it is domiciled outside the UK.

Domicile of choice

A person can legally acquire a new domicile, a domicile of choice, from the age of 16. To do so, they must leave the country in which they are now domiciled and settle in another country, and in addition provide irrefutable evidence that they intend to live there permanently or indefinitely.

The fact of living in another country for a long time, although an important factor, does not prove an individual has acquired a new domicile and there is a substantial body of case law on this topic.

Double taxation treaties and IHT

The UK has a number of bilateral treaties for taxes on estates, gifts and inheritances.

For the purpose of the agreement, the treaties allow:

- the country in which the transferor is (or in the case of a death, was) domiciled to tax all property wherever it is, and the other country to tax only specified types of property, such as immovable property, in its territory.

- where the person is doubly taxed there are rules for deciding which country gives credit for the other's tax. Where, exceptionally, the relief given by a treaty would be less than that given by unilateral relief the person receives the benefit of unilateral relief.

If there is no treaty and the transfer is liable to inheritance tax and also to a similar tax imposed by another country with which the UK does not have an agreement, an individual may be able to get relief under unilateral relief provisions.

Credit is given against inheritance tax for the tax charged by another country on assets situated in that country. For this purpose, UK law determines the location of the asset. If the tax that is charged on the asset by the other country exceeds inheritance tax on that asset, credit is limited to the amount of inheritance tax.

Credit is also given where both the UK and another country impose tax on assets that are situated:

- in a third country; or

- both in the UK under UK law and in the other country under that country's law.

In these cases the credit is a proportion of the tax. The proportionate credit is computed by the formula:

$$\frac{A}{(A + B)} \times C$$

A is the inheritance tax, B is the overseas tax and C is whichever of A or B is the lesser.

If the UK and two or more other countries charge the same asset to tax – the above applies but with modifications.

Example 1

Kirsty is domiciled in Xanadu, but is also treated as domiciled in the UK. She makes a gift of property situated in Shangrila.

UK inheritance tax (A) £1,500,

Xanadu inheritance tax (B) £500,

C is the smaller of A and B £500,

The amount to be set against UK inheritance tax is

$$\frac{£1,500}{(£1,500 + £500)} \times £500 = £375$$

Balance of UK tax due is £1,125.

Example 2

Jamie is domiciled in Shangrila but holds shares in a Xanadu company, which maintains a duplicate share register in the UK. Under UK law the shares are regarded as situated in the UK, but Xanadu law regards them as situated in Xanadu. Jamie dies (but his estate is not liable to Shangrilan tax).

UK inheritance tax (A) £500,

Xanadu inheritance tax (B) £2,000,

C is the smaller of A and B £500,

The amount to be set against UK inheritance tax is

$$\frac{£500}{(£500 + £2,000)} \times £1,000 = £200$$

Balance of UK tax due is £300.

5. Where property is situated abroad, an allowance of up to a maximum of 5% of the value of the property may be claimed in respect of the additional expenses incurred in administering or realising that property because it is situated overseas (s 173).

Treatment of specific gifts and gifts of residue where there are exempt beneficiaries

6. Detailed notes on business and agricultural property relief are in Example 25.

In this example the interests in the partnership business and related office building were left specifically to the son and thus did not attract any exemption from inheritance tax, as they would have done if left to a surviving spouse or to a charity. There are various ways in which a deceased may have dealt with business or agricultural property in his will, and the effect is as follows (s 39A):

(a) Business or agricultural property left specifically to a non-exempt beneficiary (as it was to the son in this example) — BPR/APR reduces the value of the business/agricultural property, reducing the tax accordingly, and it is not affected by any exempt legacies.

(b) Business or agricultural property left specifically to an exempt beneficiary, such as to a spouse (or as part of residue to an exempt beneficiary) — BPR/APR wasted, since no tax payable on the property in any event.

(c) Business or agricultural property left as part of residue that goes wholly to a non-exempt beneficiary, where there are no pecuniary or other specific gifts to exempt beneficiaries — BPR/APR reduces the value of the residue, reducing the tax accordingly.

(d) Business or agricultural property left as part of residue to a non-exempt beneficiary where there are pecuniary or other specific gifts to exempt beneficiaries, or where the residue is left partly to an exempt beneficiary (eg half to son, half to spouse) — BPR/APR is applied rateably to the exempt and non-exempt parts of the estate, and is thus wasted to the extent that it is attributed to exempt legacies or exempt residue.

For the technical way in which this is expressed in the legislation and the complications where part of the residue is exempt from tax and part is chargeable, see Example 17.

7.   The exempt legacies in this example, which are pecuniary legacies rather than legacies of specific property, are paid out of assets not subject to business property relief and the business property relief is therefore fully available.

If the will had merely left the legacies as stated with the residue to the son and daughter, without specifically leaving the partnership share and office building to the son, then the relief for business property would be spread rateably between the exempt and non-exempt parts of the estate, that relating to the exempt part then being wasted as follows:

$$\text{Maximum business property relief } 615,000 \times \frac{\text{Exempt estate} 168,100}{\text{Total estate} 1,220,100} = £84,732$$

The full business property relief would still be deducted from the business property in ascertaining what tax relates to that property from an instalment option point of view (see note 10), the reduction in relief being regarded as reducing the exempt legacies. The estate liable to inheritance tax would become:

Estate before reliefs and exemptions as before			1,220,100
Less:	Business property relief		615,000
			605,100
Less:	Exempt legacies	168,100	
	Restricted by reference to business property relief	84,732	83,368
			£521,732
Comprising:			
	House in France		140,800
	Residue as before	249,300	
	Business property	830,000	
Less:	100%/50% business property relief	615,000	215,000
			464,300
Less:	Exempt legacies	83,368	380,932
			£521,732

Tax payable would be (521,732 − 312,000) = £209,732 @ 40% £83,893

Which would be borne as follows:

Daughter	$\dfrac{140,800}{521,732} \times 83,893$	22,640
Residuary legatees	$\dfrac{381,070}{521,732} \times 83,893$	61,253
		£83,893

8.   Similarly if the partnership share and office building formed part of the residue and the matrimonial home had not been held under a joint tenancy (and thus formed part of the estate), but £272,500 in respect thereof had been left as a specific gift to the widow, the position would be:

Estate before exemptions and reliefs as before			1,220,100
Add matrimonial home			272,500
			£1,492,600

Maximum business property relief is restricted by

$$615,000 \times \frac{\text{Exempt estate} \left(168,100 \ + \ 272,500\right)}{\text{Total estate}} = \frac{440,600}{1,492,600} = £181,541$$

The estate liable to inheritance tax becomes:

Estate			1,492,600
Less: Business property relief			615,000
			877,600
Less: Exempt legacies		440,600	
Restricted by reference to business property relief		181,541	259,059
			£618,541

Comprising:

House in France				140,800
Matrimonial home			272,500	
Residue as before		249,300		
Business property	830,000			
Less: 100%/50% business property relief	615,000	215,000		
		464,300		
Less: Exempt legacies		259,059	205,241	477,741
				£618,541

Tax payable would be (618,541 − 312,000) = £306,541 @ 40%   £122,616

Which would be borne as follows:

Daughter

$$\frac{140,800}{618,541} \times 122,616 \qquad\qquad\qquad 27,911$$

Residuary legatees

$$\frac{477,741}{618,541} \times 122,616 \qquad\qquad\qquad 94,705$$

£122,616

9.   The above shows that on S Smith's estate the increase in the inheritance tax payable if the business property is part of the residue is as follows:

	If exempt legacies were £168,100	*If exempt legacies were £440,600*
Tax payable	83,893	122,616
Compared with tax payable as per part (a) of example	50,000	50,000
	£33,893	£72,616

Although the exempt legacies are the *cause* of the higher tax, they do not themselves *bear* any of it. It is borne rateably by the residuary estate and by the specific legacies that bear their own tax under the terms of the will, as shown in notes 7 and 8.

10.   In note 7, the tax of £61,253 borne by the residuary legatees would relate to the respective parts of residue as follows:

Business property

$$\frac{215,000}{464,300} \times 61,253 \qquad\qquad 28,364$$

Remainder of residue

$$\frac{249,300}{464,300} \times 61,253 \qquad\qquad 32,889$$

$$£61,253$$

In note 8, the tax of £94,624 borne by the residuary legatees would relate to the respective parts of residue as follows:

Business property

$$\frac{215,000}{464,300} \times 94,705 \qquad\qquad 43,854$$

Remainder of residue

$$\frac{249,300}{464,300} \times 94,705 \qquad\qquad 50,851$$

$$£94,705$$

The tax relating to the business property could be paid by instalments if the conditions were satisfied (see Example 5 explanatory note 5).

Question

Mr Algernon died on 3 September 2008. His estate contained the following:

	Value at date of death £
Main residence	725,000
Proceeds from insurance policy	300,000
Quoted shares	775,000
Bank account	185,000
Other possessions	40,000
Mortgage on main residence	(25,000)

Mr Algernon's will which was executed in 2006 required that:

1.   his daughter receive £324,000 free of all taxes;

2.   his son John receive £400,000 bearing its own taxes;

3.   his wife receive one-half of the residue, the other half to pass into a trust for his grandchildren, and the division into equal shares to be made before deduction of inheritance tax thereon.

Mr Algernon had made no lifetime transfers.

Advise the trustees as to the amount of funds they can expect from Mr Algernon's estate.

Answer

Death of Mr Algernon 3 September 2008 — calculation of inheritance tax

His estate on death amounted to:	£	£
Main residence	725,000	
Less: Mortgage thereon	25,000	700,000
Insurance policy		300,000
Quoted shares		775,000
Bank account		185,000
Other possessions		40,000
Gross estate		2,000,000

Stage 1

Gross up specific gifts which do not bear their own tax as though they alone were chargeable to inheritance tax on death:

	£
Legacy to daughter (see explanatory note 5)	324,000
Tax thereon	8,000
Gross gift	332,000

Stage 2

Using gross gift as calculated in Stage 1, divide the estate between exempt and non-exempt parts:

	Exempt £	Non-Exempt £	£
Gross estate			2,000,000
Gross legacy to daughter		332,000	
Legacy to John bearing its own tax		400,000	
Residue (£1,268,000)			
Wife	634,000		
Trust		634,000	
	634,000	1,366,000	2,000,000

Stage 3

Calculate the inheritance tax on the non-exempt estate at Stage 2:

1,366,000 – 312,000 = £1,054,000 @ 40% = £421,600

Stage 4

Using the tax computed at Stage 3, recompute the grossing up of specific gifts not bearing their own tax:

$$\text{Legacy to daughter } 324,000 \times \frac{1,366,000}{1,366,000 - 421,600} = £468,640$$

Stage 5

Using the revised gross gifts re-divide the estate between exempt and non-exempt parts:

	Exempt £	Non-Exempt £	£
Gross estate			2,000,000
Legacy to daughter as in Stage 4		468,640	
Legacy to John		400,000	
Residue (£1,131,360)			
Wife	565,680		
Trust		565,680	
	565,680	1,434,320	2,000,000

Stage 6

Calculate the inheritance tax on the revised non-exempt part of the estate and calculate the effective rate of tax:

1,434,320 – 312,000 = £1,122,320 @ 40% = £448,928

$$\frac{448,928}{1,434,320} \times 100 = 31.2990\% \text{ effective rate}$$

Stage 7

The residue of the estate is therefore as follows:	£	£	£
Gross estate			2,000,000
Less: Inheritance tax payable			448,928
			1,551,072
Less: Legacy to daughter		324,000	
Legacy to John	400,000		
Less IHT thereon at 31.2990%	125,196	274,804	598,804
Residue			952,268

However none of the charge to inheritance tax is to fall on the exempt part due to the spouse.

The estate is therefore distributed as follows:	£	£	£
Daughter			324,000
John			274,804
			598,804
Tax on legacies at 31.2990% (per Stage 6) at grossed up value (per Stage 4) 468,640+ 400,000 = £868,640 × 31.2990%		271,875	
Residue before tax (2,000,000 – (598,804 + 271,875))	1,129,321		
Half to widow			564,660
Half to A & M Trust	564,661		
Less: Tax @ 31.2990% on £565,680 (per Stage 5)	177,052	177,052	
	387,609		387,609
Inheritance tax		448,927	448,927
Gross estate			2,000,000

The trustees may therefore expect to receive £387,609.

Explanatory Notes

Incidence of tax on deceased's estate

1.   The calculation of the inheritance tax and the distribution of the estate is not straightforward where on a person's death part of the estate is the subject of an exempt transfer (for example, to the surviving spouse) and part is chargeable.

2.   The incidence of tax on a deceased's estate is as follows:

Tax relating to a life interest of the deceased in settled property is payable out of the trust funds.

Tax relating to nominated and jointly held property of the deceased is payable out of that property.

The tax on property situated abroad is a charge on that property.

In the absence of specific provisions in the will, tax on all other property, both real and personal, wherever situated in the UK, is a testamentary expense payable out of the residue of the estate.

Partially exempt legacies

3.   Thus, although the widow's share of the estate is exempt, the tax on specific legacies must come out of the residue (unless the will specifically provides that the legacy is to bear its own tax).

If the residue then remaining is left partly to the widow and partly by way of chargeable transfer, the tax on the residue must be borne in accordance with the will. This is subject to s 41, which provides that notwithstanding the terms of the will, none of the tax on either a specific gift or a gift of residue is to fall on the gift if the gift is exempt.

Re Benham

In the case of *Re Benham's Will Trusts* (1995) it was held that the plain intention of the deceased's will was that each beneficiary should *receive* the *same amount* and that this was not inconsistent with s 41. Consequently the non-exempt shares of residue had to be grossed up so that the after tax amounts were equal. This had the effect of increasing both the tax charged on the estate and the shares of non-exempt residuary beneficiaries at the expense of exempt beneficiaries, which was contrary to the accepted practice and was not the view taken by the Capital Taxes Office. In 1999 a different High Court judge came to the opposite conclusion in the case of *Re Ratcliffe (deceased)*. He referred to the *Benham* approach as the 'net division' approach and the previously accepted approach as the 'gross division' approach, and held that the 'gross division' approach was correct on the facts of the case. The case has not been taken to appeal, but is generally regarded as overriding the *Benham* decision except on facts very close to those arising in *Benham*. Even so, it would be sensible to review the wording of wills where there is partly exempt residue, to ensure that it is clear whether the division of residue is to take place before or after deducting the tax on the residue.

Stages in tax calculation

4.   Unless the cumulative lifetime transfers exceed the nil threshold the method of calculation is complex (ss 36 to 42). The procedure is straightforward where lifetime transfers exceed the nil threshold, because all grossing calculations are at the same rate, ie 100/60 (see note 7).

Where, as in this example, the lifetime transfers are less than the nil threshold, there are seven stages in the calculation, the first six of which are notional calculations used in order to ascertain the effective rate of inheritance tax on the estate.

The stages are as follows:

(1)   Gross up specific gifts which do not bear their own tax as though they were the only chargeable transfers made at death (s 38(1) and (3)).

(2)   Using the grossed up gifts arrived at in (1) divide the estate between exempt and non-exempt parts.

(3)   Compute tax on the *notional* non-exempt part of the estate.

(4)   Once again gross up specific gifts which do not bear their own tax but using the tax arrived at in (3) (s 38(4) and (5)). This replaces Stage 1.

(5)   Using the revised gross gifts in (4) re-divide the estate between exempt and non-exempt parts.

(6)   Compute tax on the non-exempt part and calculate the effective rate of tax (s 38(1)).

(7)   Distribute the estate in such a way that the tax, if any, on the gifts in the will not bearing their own tax comes out of the whole of the residue, and the tax on the residue falls on the part of the residue that is not exempt (s 41).

5.   The grossing up calculation in Stage 1 of the example on the legacy to the daughter is as follows:

Cumulative net transfers of £324,000 exceed £312,000 by £12,000. This is grossed up using the 40% tax rate.

	Gross £	Tax £	Net £
	312,000	–	312,000
Gross equivalent $\dfrac{100}{60} \times 12,000$	20,000		12,000
and tax thereon		8,000	
	332,000	8,000	324,000

6.   The calculation of tax on the trustees' share of the residue is based upon their notional share of residue ie £565,680 per Stage 5 not their actual share of £564,661 at Stage 7. This method is used by HMRC Capital Taxes. Views have been expressed that the tax should be based upon the actual share of residue (ie £564,661 @ 31.2990% = £176,733 compared with £177,052 as computed). This does not appear to follow the requirement that none of the tax as computed is to fall on the spouse or other exempt transfers. Instead it recomputes the tax yet again.

Calculation if lifetime transfers exceed nil band

7.   If Mr Algernon had made cumulative lifetime transfers of £312,000, the seven stage calculation would not be necessary and the position would be as follows:

	Gross £	Tax £	Net £
Inheritance tax accumulation at death on 2008/09 scale	312,000	–	312,000
Legacy to daughter grossed up 324,000 × 100/60	540,000	216,000	324,000
Legacy to John	400,000	160,000	240,000
Leaving residue of 2,000,000 – (540,000 + 400,000) = £1,060,000, of which half, ie £530,000, is exempt, so that non-exempt residue is	530,000	212,000	318,000
	1,782,000	588,000	1,194,000

The estate would therefore be distributed as follows:

Daughter — legacy	324,000
John — legacy	240,000

Widow's share of residue		530,000
Trust's share of residue	530,000	
Less tax @ 40%	212,000	318,000
Inheritance tax:		
On legacies — daughter	216,000	
John	160,000	
On Trust's share of residue	212,000	588,000
		£2,000,000

The same procedure would apply if the lifetime transfers had been any amount in excess of £312,000.

Further examples

8. For further illustrations of the treatment of partially exempt legacies, including the provisions in relation to settled property, business and agricultural relief and intestacy, see Examples 17 and 18.

Grandchildren's trust

9. If the will was executed in 2005, it is likely that the grandchildren's trust would have been an accumulation and maintenance settlement in accordance with IHTA 1984 s 71. Had Mr Algernon died before 22 March 2006, this would have allowed the funds to have been accumulated without the trust fund becoming relevant property (and subject to the ten-yearly and exit charges regime).

However, since Mr Algernon died after 21 March 2006, any trust for his grandchildren would constitute relevant property unless it was an immediate post-death interest in possession under section 49A. That would require the grandchildren to have an interest in possession in the fund from the date of their grandfather's death and for this to arise under either the will or the law of intestacy. Consequently, it would not be possible for a post-death deed of variation to be entered into to allow the trust terms to be varied to allow it to qualify. (Such a variation would, in any event, require more than merely a change in the administrative powers to qualify for IHT purposes (s 142)).

Question

On 1 January 2005 X, who had made no previous lifetime transfers, gave £123,000 to his daughter D and on 1 November 2005, £81,500 each to his daughter E and his son S.

On 1 June 2008 X died leaving an estate which, after payment of all debts and funeral expenses, was valued at £250,000, after deduction of business property relief of £150,000.

By his will he left business property valued at £120,000 (before business property relief of £60,000) equally to his daughter E and his wife W free of tax, £25,000 to a charity, a pecuniary legacy of £20,000 to his son S and the residue of his estate equally (before inheritance tax thereon) to W and three children D, S and E.

X was entitled for life to income of the residuary estate of his father (who died in 1973) with remainder to his son S. The assets of that settlement were valued at £100,000 on 1 June 2007.

Calculate the inheritance tax payable on X's death.

Answer

X — inheritance tax accumulation

			£
1 January 2005			
Gift to D			123,000
Less: Annual exemptions 2004/05		3,000	
2003/04		3,000	6,000
Potentially exempt transfer			117,000
1 November 2005			
Gift to E			81,500
Gift to S			81,500
			163,000
Less: Annual exemption 2005/06 (split equally)			3,000
Potentially exempt transfers			160,000

On death of X — 1 June 2008

	Gross £	Tax on 2008/09 scale £
PET to D — 1 January 2005	117,000	–
PETs to E and S — 1 November 2005	160,000	–
Inheritance tax accumulation at death	277,000	–

No tax payable on lifetime transfers since below nil threshold.

Estate on Death

Free estate	400,000	
Less: Business property relief	150,000	250,000
Settled property		100,000
		£350,000

Summary of specific gifts with business property relief

		£	£
To wife — W	½ of business property	60,000	
	Less: BPR of 50%	30,000	30,000
To daughter — E	½ of business property	60,000	
	Less: BPR of 50%	30,000	30,000
			60,000

17.3 PARTIALLY EXEMPT LEGACIES (AFFECTED BY TRUST FUNDS, BUSINESS AND AGRICULTURAL PROPERTY RELIEF)

Summary of specific gifts without business property relief

To charity — exempt	25,000
To son — S	20,000
	45,000

Division of estate to compute exempt transfers

(1) Allocate balance of business property relief pro-rata to specific and non-specific gifts after excluding specific gifts with such relief:

			Before BPR	*After BPR*
Estate			400,000	250,000
Less: Specific gifts of business property			120,000	60,000
			£280,000	£190,000
Specific gift to charity	25,000	$\times\dfrac{190,000}{280,000}=$		16,964
to son — S	20,000	$\times\dfrac{190,000}{280,000}=$		13,572
Residue	235,000	$\times\dfrac{190,000}{280,000}$		159,464
	£280,000			£190,000

Gross up specific gifts that do not bear their own tax (as distinct from being exempt):

Half of business property (after BPR) to E	30,000
Legacy to S (after BPR)	13,572
	£43,572

	Gross £	Tax £	Net £
Inheritance tax accumulation at death	277,000	–	277,000
Specific gifts	49,287	5,715	43,572
	326,287	5,715	320,572(*)

* *Grossed up*

Net		Gross
312,000		312,000
8,572	× 100/60	14,287
£320,572		£326,287

(2) Divide estate after business property relief between exempt and non-exempt parts, using notional gross gifts per (1):

		Exempt	Non-exempt	Total
		£	£	£
Business property to wife		30,000		30,000
To E	$\dfrac{30,000}{43,572} \times 49{,}287$		33,935	33,935
Legacy to S	$\dfrac{13,572}{43,572} \times 49{,}287$		15,352	15,352
Charity	$\dfrac{190,000}{280,000} \times 25{,}000$	16,964		16,964
Residue — balance				153,749
Wife (¼)		38,437		
Children (¾)			115,312	
		85,401	164,599	250,000

(3)   Inheritance tax payable on non-exempt estate:

	Gross	Tax
	£	£
Accumulation at death	277,000	–
Non-exempt estate	164,599	51,840*
	441,599	51,840*

(* 441,599 – 312,000 = 129,599 @ 40%)

(4)   Re-gross specific gifts:

$$£43{,}572 \times \frac{164{,}599}{(164{,}599 - 51{,}840)} = £63{,}604$$

(5)   Re-divide estate

		Exempt £	Non-exempt £	Total £
Business property to wife		30,000		30,000
to E	$\dfrac{30,000}{43,572} \times 63,604$			
			43,792	43,792
Legacy to S	$\dfrac{13,572}{43,572} \times 63,604$		19,812	19,812
Charity — specific gift after BPR		16,964		16,964
Residue				110,568
				139,432
Wife (¼)		34,858		
Children (¾)			104,574	
		81,822	168,178	250,000

(6) Inheritance tax payable on non-exempt estate:

		Gross £	Tax £
Accumulation at death		277,000	–
Non-exempt estate	168,178		
Settled property	100,000	268,178	93,271*
		545,178	93,271*

(* 545,178 – 312,000 = 233,178 @ 40%)

Effective rate $\dfrac{93,271}{268,178} \times 100 = 34.78\%$

Inheritance tax payable by

Personal representatives	168,178	× 34.78% =	58,492
Trustees of settled property	100,000	× 34.78% =	34,779
	£268,178		£93,271

(7) Distribution of free estate:

Estate at death			400,000
Less: Inheritance tax			58,492
			341,508
Less: Exempt legacies			
To wife		60,000	
charity		25,000	85,000
			256,508
Legacies not bearing their own tax			
To E		60,000	
S		20,000	80,000

Net residue		£176,508

Distribution of net residue so that no inheritance tax relates to widow

Legacies to E and S (at grossed up value stages (4) and (5)) at final effective rate of 34.78%

Tax thereon = £63,604 × 34.78% = £22,121

Estate on death			400,000
Exempt legacies	— wife	60,000	
	— charity	25,000	
Legacies not bearing own tax			
	— E	60,000	
	— S	20,000	
	— tax thereon	22,121	187,121
Residue before tax			£212,879
Net residue as at stage (7) above			176,508
One quarter of residue before tax to widow ¼ × 212,879			53,220
Balance equally to children:			£123,288
D			£41,096
S			£41,096
E			£41,096

Summary of division of estate and trust funds

		£	£
To Son S from trustees of settled property		100,000	
Less:	Inheritance tax thereon	34,779	65,221
To charity			25,000
To E	legacy	60,000	
	share of residue	41,096	101,096
To S	legacy	20,000	
	share of residue	41,096	61,096
To D	share of residue		41,096
To wife	legacy	60,000	
	share of residue	53,220	113,220
Inheritance tax (including that on settled property)			93,271
			£500,000

Explanatory Notes

Same-day transfers

1. The first step is to compute the inheritance tax accumulation at death.

2. Where two or more transfers are made on the same day they are treated except in certain special circumstances as one transfer and the effective rate of tax on the total transfer is applied to the individual transfers (s 266(2)).

Interest in possession in settled property

3.   Settled property in which the donor had an interest in possession is treated as belonging to the donor absolutely for inheritance tax purposes, although the tax relating to the settlement is payable by the trustees of the settlement (ss 49 and 200(1)(b)). An interest in possession which existed prior to 22 March 2006 continues to be treated in this way despite the changes wrought by FA 2006.

Partially exempt legacies and business and agricultural property relief

4.   In order to compute the tax payable on death the rules for partially exempt transfers must be applied (ss 36–42). These are detailed in Example 16.

      Where an estate is entitled to business property or agricultural property relief and there are specific gifts then special rules apply in computing the inheritance tax payable, as follows:

      (a)   Specific gifts of relevant business or agricultural property are taken at their value reduced by BPR or APR.

      (b)   Specific gifts other than in (a) above are taken at the appropriate fraction of their value (s 39A), that is:

$$\text{Specific gift} \times \frac{\text{Assets transferred (net of BPR/APR) less specific gifts of business/agricultural property (net of BPR/APR)}}{\text{Assets transferred (before BPR/APR) less specific gifts of business/agricultural property (before BPR/APR)}}$$

      A specific gift is any gift other than a gift of residue or of a share in residue (s 42). It therefore covers both specific legacies of particular property and general (ie pecuniary) legacies.

      Where specific gifts are tax-free then the grossing up rules are applied to the value so reduced, as shown on page 17.3.

Gifts out of different funds

5.   Section 40 provides that where gifts take effect separately out of different funds (for example where a deceased has a free estate and a life interest in a settlement, and gifts are made out of the free estate), the partial exemption rules in ss 36–39A are to be applied separately to the gifts taking effect out of each of those funds. The rate of tax used to gross up the gifts is arrived at by looking at each fund separately and in isolation. In the example, therefore, the tax on the non-exempt estate at stage (3) that is used to re-gross the specific gifts is arrived at by taking into account only the free estate and not the settled property.

Pecuniary legacies

6.   Where a will provides a pecuniary legacy (a gift of cash like the legacy of £20,000 to S), then the legatee receives the amount stated and any inheritance tax relating to that legacy is borne by the residue of the estate unless the will provides that the legatee is to bear the tax (s 211). For further notes on this point see Example 5 explanatory note 8.

Re Benham and Re Ratcliffe

7.   Where a will provides that the residuary shares are computed on the residue after deduction of inheritance tax, there were conflicting views in *Re Benham* and *Re Ratcliffe* on how the shares of residue should be calculated. It is now generally regarded as settled that the established approach in dealing with partly exempt estates is correct — see Example 16 explanatory note 3.

Question

Jones died intestate on 10 June 2008 survived by his wife and two children.

He had made no chargeable lifetime transfers.

His estate according to the account accompanying the application for a grant of administration consisted of:

  5,000   £1 shares in A plc quoted at 1088–1092 with recorded bargains at 1088, 1089, 1090 and 1091

10,000   £1 shares in B plc quoted at 295–297 with a sole recorded bargain at 295

  8,000   50p shares in C plc quoted at 60–69 with bargains at 61, 61½, 62 and 63

10,000   shares in the Hong Kong Bank valued at £70,000

	£
Cash at bank	87,569
Policy on his life, insuring	150,000
Salary accrued due to date of death (net)	1,625
Rents from his father's will trust (net of basic rate income tax)	
accrued due	645
apportionment to date of death	621
Furniture and effects	10,500

His debts were shown as:

Funeral expenses	1,650
General household bills (electricity, gas, etc)	220
Daughter, under a deed of covenant dated 1 January 1992	
binding his legal personal representatives to pay her on his death	5,000

Under the will of his father who had died in 1985 he also had a life interest in a house, No 12 High Street, valued at £170,000, which passed on his death to his children equally. The rent due to Jones at death is indicated above.

A grant of administration was obtained on 14 February 2009 when inheritance tax amounting to £2,630 and £16 interest was paid by the intended administrators on the basis of the above information.

The administrators subsequently discover:

(1)   Jones is entitled to a pecuniary legacy of £10,000 free of tax under the will of his brother who died on 4 August 2007. Inheritance tax amounting to £13,000 had been paid on the brother's estate valued at £100,000.

(2)   There was an outstanding income tax liability of £750.

(3)   There were bonuses totalling £47,250 attaching to the life policy.

(4)   The value of the shares in the Hong Kong Bank is agreed at £70,000, but death duties amounting to the sterling equivalent of £7,000 and £420 interest had to be paid locally because the shares were registered there. The additional cost of employing a local agent to make title to the shares, including agreeing the value with the local fiscal authorities, amounted to a sterling equivalent of £4,150.

(5)   The remaining values were agreed with HMRC.

A corrective account is lodged and the final adjustment to the inheritance tax payable is made on 5 November 2009, the trustees also paying any tax and interest attributable to the trust funds on that day.

Given that the 'statutory legacy' payable to the spouse on an intestacy when the intestate leaves issue is £125,000 with the spouse also taking the personal chattels and a life interest in one half of the residue, whilst the other half of the residue devolves on the issue:

(a)   Calculate the inheritance tax and interest paid by or repaid to the administrators on 5 November 2009.

(b)   Show the distribution of the free estate and trust funds upon Jones's death and the allocation of the tax payable.

Assume that the rate of interest on tax overpaid or repaid is 3% pa throughout.

Answer

(a)   **Estate of Jones (after submission of corrective account)**

Free estate			Date of Death 10 June 2008 £	£
Quoted shares:				
5,000 £1 shares in A plc	@ 1089		54,450	
10,000 £1 shares in B plc	@ 295		29,500	
8,000 50p shares in C plc	@ 62		4,960	88,910
Cash at bank				87,569
Policy on life			150,000	
Bonuses thereon			47,250	197,250
Salary due				1,625
Rents accrued due to date of death				
(after basic rate income tax) (645 + 621)				1,266
Furniture and effects				10,500
Legacy due from unadministered estate of brother				10,000
Chattels abroad				
10,000 shares in the Hong Kong Bank			70,000	
Less: Costs of administration (maximum 5%)			3,500	66,500
				463,620
Less:	Funeral expenses		1,650	
	General household debts		220	
	Income tax		750	
	Covenanted debt — no deduction possible since			
	no consideration was given		–	2,620
				461,000
Settled property				
Father's will trust				170,000
Inheritance tax payable on				631,000

The statutory legacy of £125,000 plus furniture and effects £10,500 and one half of the residue in trust for the widow are exempt transfers. To determine the amount deemed to be transferred to the trust for the widow it is necessary to apply the 'double grossing up' rules that apply to partially exempt residues.

Division of estate to compute exempt transfer

(1)   Gross up specific gifts not bearing own tax:

Covenanted gift to daughter D	£5,000
As there were no lifetime transfers and value is below £312,000, its grossed up value is	£5,000

(2)   Divide estate between exempt and non-exempt parts, using notional gross gifts:

		Exempt	Non-exempt	Total
Specific gift			5,000	5,000
To Wife	Statutory legacy	125,000		125,000
	Furniture etc	10,500		10,500

		Exempt	Non-exempt	Total
	½ of residue (life interest)	160,250		
To Children	½ of residue		160,250	320,500
		£295,750	£165,250	£461,000

(3)   Inheritance tax payable on non-exempt estate:

	Gross	Tax
Inheritance tax accumulation at death	–	–
Non-exempt estate	£165,250	£–

As the value of the non-exempt estate is less than £312,000 (excluding settled property), it is not necessary to re-gross up the specific gift, or to re-divide the estate. The inheritance tax payable is therefore:

		Gross	Tax
Non-exempt estate	165,250		
Settled property	170,000	£335,250	£9,300*

(* 335,250 – 312,000 = 23,250 @ 40%)

	£
Inheritance tax on chargeable estate	9,300
Less: Quick succession relief	
$100\% \text{ of } \dfrac{10,000}{100,000} \times £13,000$	1,300
	8,000

Less: Relief for overseas tax — re Hong Kong   )
          Bank shares. Amount paid £7,000 but   )
          restricted to inheritance tax attributable to   )
          that property   )

$\dfrac{66,500}{631,000}$	$\times 8,000 =$	843
		7,157

Tax payable by administrators $\dfrac{165,250}{335,250} \times £8,000 = 3,943 - 843$	3,100
Less: already paid	2,630
Additional tax payable	470
Interest on £470 at 3% from 1.1.09 to 5.11.09 = 309 days	12
Total payable by the administrators 5.11.09	482

Tax payable by the trustees of father's will trust

	Gross	Tax
$\dfrac{170,000}{335,250} \times £8,000 =$		4,057
Interest at 3% from 1.1.09 to 5.11.09 = 309 days		103
Total payable by the trustees 5.11.09		£4,160

(b)   Distribution of funds and allocation of tax payable

		£	£
Daughter	— specific gift		5,000
Widow	— Cash	125,000	
	Chattels	10,500	
	½ of residue as at (a) (2)	160,250	295,750
Children —	½ of residue as at (a) (2)	160,250	
	Less: inheritance tax payable	3,100	157,150
Inheritance tax payable by administrators			3,100
			461,000
Inheritance tax payable by trustees of father's will trust			4,160

The interest payable on overdue tax will be dealt with through the income accounts of the estate and the trust.

Explanatory Notes

Partially exempt legacies — intestacy

1.   The notes to Examples 16 and 17 also apply to this example. The example highlights the fact that an intestacy will often create partially exempt residue. See in particular Example 17 note 5 regarding the treatment to be adopted where a partly exempt estate consists of free estate and an interest in settled property. The rules relating to distribution on intestacy are set out at explanatory note 6 below.

For further details on:

Corrective and supplementary accounts	see Example 8
Administration of foreign assets	see Example 15
Quick succession relief	see Example 21
Double taxation relief	see Example 28 and Example 3(c)

Valuation of quoted shares

2.   Quoted shares are valued at the lower of

(a)   One quarter up on lower quoted closing price

(b)   Midpoint of bargain prices, thus:

Closing Price		*Bargains*	*Lower*
Shares in A plc	1088 + ¼ (1092 − 1088) = 1089		

$$\frac{1088 + 1091}{2} = 1089\frac{1}{2} \qquad\qquad 1089$$

B plc	295 + ¼ (297 − 295) = 295½	295	295
C plc	60 + ¼ (69 − 60) = 62¼		

$$\frac{61 + 63}{2} = 62 \qquad\qquad 62$$

Covenanted gift

3.   The non-deductible covenanted sum is treated as a specific gift and thus does not bear its own tax (s 38(6)).

Double tax relief

4.   Double tax relief is available where tax is charged both abroad and in the UK. For detailed notes see Example 28 explanatory note 6. The relief is given as a reduction of the tax on the relevant property (s 159). In this example therefore the relief reduces the tax on the non-settled part of the estate.

The additional costs of administering or realising assets abroad may be deducted if shown to be attributable to the situation of the property, up to a maximum of 5% of the value of the property (s 173).

Intestacy rules for dividing estates

5.   When a person dies without leaving a will, or leaves a will that does not fully dispose of his estate, then the rules of intestacy apply to the estate not disposed of by will. These rules determine to whom the estate is to be distributed. The inheritance tax rules then determine the amount of tax to be paid, with the amounts allocated to the spouse being exempt transfers. Section 211 provides that the tax payable is to be borne by the residue of the estate as a general testamentary expense. This is subject to s 41, which provides that none of the tax on residue is to fall on any part of the residue that is exempt. Thus, in this example, although the widow's share of the estate is exempt, the tax, if any, on specific legacies must come out of residue and the tax on the residue must be borne wholly by the chargeable part of the estate. The rules for calculating the tax are set out in ss 38 to 42.

6.   The rules of intestacy for England and Wales provide that the estate is to be distributed as set out below.

Those surviving	*Those entitled to the estate*
Spouse/civil partner — no issue, parent, brother, sister or issue thereof	Spouse/civil partner absolutely
Spouse/civil partner and issue	Spouse/civil partner takes: (i) Personal chattels (ii) £125,000 (iii) Life interest in ½ of residue Issue share other ½ of residue (on statutory trust to 18) and take spouse's/civil partner's share on his (her) death.
Spouse/civil partner, no issue but parent(s)	Spouse/civil partner takes: (i) Personal chattels (ii) £200,000

Those surviving	*Those entitled to the estate*
	(iii) ½ of residue absolutely
	Parent(s) share ½ of residue absolutely.
Spouse/civil partner, no issue or parents but brothers or sisters of the whole blood (or issue thereof)	Spouse/civil partner takes:
	(i) Personal chattels
	(ii) £200,000
	(iii) ½ of residue absolutely
	Brothers and sisters (or their issue) share ½ of residue absolutely
No spouse/civil partner but issue	Issue take all absolutely
	(held on statutory trust if under 18)
No spouse/civil partner or issue but	
Parent(s)	Take absolutely
Brothers and sisters of the whole blood	Take absolutely
Brothers and sisters of the half blood	Take absolutely
Grandparents	Take absolutely
Uncles and aunts (whole blood)	Take absolutely
Uncles and aunts (half blood)	Take absolutely
(Each category takes the whole estate to the exclusion of any later category.)	
No relatives mentioned above	The Crown

'Issue' means children, grandchildren, great grandchildren etc. Where someone entitled to a share is deceased but has surviving children, the children will take the deceased's parent's share (and so on for grandchildren etc).

From 1 January 1996 a spouse (and since 5 December 2005, a civil partner) does not inherit under the intestacy rules unless he/she survives the deceased by at least 28 days.

7.   The rules of intestacy applying to the distribution of an estate in Scotland are as follows:

1. Prior rights

After debts and other liabilities have been met, a widow, widower or a surviving civil partner has a certain *'prior rights of a surviving spouse or civil partner'* in the deceased person's estate, where no will has been left.

He or she is entitled to the dwelling house of the deceased in which the surviving spouse or civil partner was resident at the time of the deceased's death, plus up to the value of £24,000 any furnishings and furniture of that house. (In certain cases, eg where the house is a farmhouse or part of a shop, or where the house is worth more than £300,000 the entitlement is not to the house itself, but to its value up to £300,000).

The surviving spouse or civil partner is also entitled to the first £42,000 out of the estate if the deceased left children or descendants of children or to the first £75,000 if the deceased left no children or descendants.

Prior rights are a first claim on the estate, before legal rights (see below).

2. Legal rights

A surviving spouse or civil partner and children are entitled to certain 'legal right' out of the deceased person's moveable estate. In Scots law, heritable property means land and buildings, while moveable property includes such things as money, shares, cars, furniture and jewellery.

The surviving spouse or civil partner is entitled to one-third of the deceased's moveable estate if the deceased left children or descendants of children, or to one-half of it if the deceased left no such children or descendants.

The children are collectively entitled to one-third of the deceased's moveable estate if the deceased left a spouse or civil partner, or to one-half of it if the deceased left no spouse or civil partner. Each child has an equal claim. Where a child would have had a claim had he (she) not died before his (her) parent, his (her) descendants may claim his (her) share by the principle known as representation.

3. *Other rights on intestacy*

After any prior rights and legal rights have been satisfied, the remainder of the intestate estate, both heritable and moveable, devolves (without distinction between heritable and moveable estate) in the following order, any surviving relative in an earlier group taking precedence, thereby precluding any surviving relatives in a later group from succeeding to any part of the estate, *viz:*

(a)   Children take the whole.

(b)   Either or both parents and brothers and sisters – half to parent or parents and half to brothers and sisters.

(c)   Brothers and sisters take the whole.

(d)   Either or both parents take the whole.

(e)   Husband or wife or civil partner – surviving spouse or civil partner takes the whole.

(f)   Uncles or aunts (on either parent's side) take the whole.

(g)   Grandparent or grandparents (on either side) take the whole.

(h)   Brothers and sisters of any grandparents (on either side) take the whole.

(i)   Ancestors of intestate remoter than grandparents, on both paternal and maternal sides generation by generation successively take the whole, but if no ancestors survive in any generation their brothers and sisters come before ancestors of the next more remote generation.

(j)   Finally, the Crown, failing any relatives in the foregoing categories, takes the whole.

The application of the foregoing order of succession is subject to three general principles:

(i)   There is no preference for male persons, or in regard to age. For instance, brothers do not rank before sisters, or elder brothers before younger (except in relation to succession to such things as titles and coats of arms).

(ii)   There is representation in all branches of succession, ie where any relative who would, if alive, have been entitled to succeed to the whole or any part of the intestate estate has predeceased leaving children, such children take equally among them the share which their deceased parent would have received if in life. If, however, the persons taking by representation are all in the same degree of relationship to the deceased, each individual takes an equal share.

(iii)   In the case of collaterals, ie brothers and sisters of the deceased or of an ancestor of the deceased, both those of the full blood and those of the half blood are entitled to succeed, but collaterals of the full blood have preference: if there are no collaterals of the full blood, the collaterals of the half blood rank without distinction as between those related through the father or mother.

4. Adopted children

The position of adopted children is the same as that of natural children for the purposes of succession. Thus an adopted child has the same rights of succession in relation to its adoptive parent's estate as a natural child, and adoptive parents have the same rights of succession that they would have, had they been natural parents of the child.

Question

I B Smart, aged 62 and in poor health, and his wife aged 55 and in excellent health, were worried about their potential inheritance tax liability on death. They had not made any chargeable transfers. They had two children, John aged 22 who is a director of the family trading company, Smart & Co Ltd, and Jill aged 24, who are married with one child aged 6 months.

Their estates consisted of:

	I B Smart	Mrs Smart
Shares in Smart & Co Ltd	49 shares	49 shares
Freehold offices rented at £10,600 pa to Smart & Co Ltd	£130,000	–
Villa in Spain valued at	£176,000	–

They also owned as joint tenants their private residence, valued at £304,000, and had joint accounts at building societies totalling £196,000.

Mr Smart had recently retired from the family company and was drawing a pension of £40,000 pa. This pension would increase by 3% pa and on his death a 2/3rds pension would be payable to Mrs Smart.

The estimated value of the shares in Smart & Co Ltd is:

100% holding	£1,230 per share
98% holding	£1,224 per share
51% holding	£1,200 per share
49% holding	£1,000 per share
2% holding	£100 per share

There are 100 shares in issue.

No dividends have been declared.

Mr and Mrs Smart wished to continue to live in their main residence but to spend four weeks per year in Spain. They believed that their personal expenditure would require the whole of the rent on the offices as well as the pension but were prepared to forgo the rent on the overseas property of £5,000 pa (rent £500 per week in season). They did not wish to give away any cash.

The wills of Mr and Mrs Smart each provide for the whole of their estates to be left to the surviving spouse for life and on the death of the survivor to be divided equally between the children.

After talking informally to an acquaintance who is a personal finance consultant they attempted to mitigate their liability by Mr Smart giving all of his shares in Smart & Co Ltd to John and the holiday home to Jill, reserving the right to use it rent free when they wished. Both gifts were made on the same day. They did not alter their wills.

Nine months after effecting the above Mr and Mrs Smart were involved in a boating accident in Spain. Mrs Smart died immediately and Mr Smart six weeks later.

Assuming that:

(1)   all values are unaltered;

(2)   the current legislation remains throughout;

(3)   2008/09 rates apply throughout; and

(4)   the personal representatives of Mr and Mrs Smart neglect to elect to take advantage of the provisions under IHTA 1984 s 8A (transfer of nil-rate band between spouses):

(a)   Set out the inheritance tax liabilities on the assumption that Mr Smart had not undertaken the above proposals.

(b)   Set out the inheritance tax liabilities which do arise following his actually having effected the proposals in May 2008.

(c)   Compute the tax liabilities on the assumptions that the following proposals had instead been adopted:

    (i)   Mr Smart to give the Spanish property to Jill.

    (ii)   Mrs Smart to give a 47% interest in Smart & Co Ltd to John.

    (iii)   The freehold office premises to be transferred to Mrs Smart.

    (iv)   The building society accounts to be transferred into Mrs Smart's sole ownership.

    (v)   Mr and Mrs Smart to pay open market rent of £500 per week when they visit the Spanish property.

    (vi)   Each of their wills to provide that on death a discretionary trust should be created for the benefit of the surviving spouse, children and grandchildren, with specific bequests to the trustees of the business property, shares and residue of the estate (the house passing to the spouse by survivorship).

(d)   Compare the tax liabilities in the three situations had the deaths occurred nine years later rather than nine months, all values and tax rates remaining the same.

Answer

I B Smart — gifts with reservation

    (a)   If proposals had not been implemented

    Death of Mrs Smart

	£	£
Estate:		
Shares in Smart & Co Ltd (explanatory note 3)		
49 × £1,224	59,976	
Less: 100% business property relief	59,976	–
½ share of jointly owned assets:		
Freehold house	152,000	
Building society accounts	98,000	250,000
Not chargeable because of spouse/civil partner exemption – no inheritance tax payable		250,000

    Death of Mr Smart

	£	£	£
Estate:			
Freehold house		304,000	
Property in Spain		176,000	
Freehold offices	130,000		
Less: 50% business property relief	65,000	65,000	545,000
Shares in Smart & Co Ltd			
98 × £1,224 (one half owned by Mr Smart and one half life interest from Mrs Smart)		119,952	
Less: 100% business property relief		119,952	–
Building society accounts			196,000
Estate chargeable to inheritance tax			741,000
Tax payable (at 2008/09 rates) (741,000 – 312,000 = 429,000 @ 40%)			171,600

    (b)   If proposals were implemented in May 2008

    Death of Mrs Smart

Exempt as before — all to Mr Smart for life or absolutely as the surviving joint tenant.

    Death of Mr Smart

    (1)   *Charging gift with reservation in death estate and ignoring the gift to Jill*

	£	£
Freehold house	304,000	
Property in Spain (gift with reservation)	176,000	
Freehold offices (no BPR as no control)	130,000	610,000
Shares in Smart & Co Ltd		
49 × £1,000 (life interest from Mrs Smart)	49,000	
Less: 100% business property relief	49,000	–

	£	£
Building society accounts		196,000
		806,000

Tax on gifts made within seven years before death

Shares to John

before transfer	$\frac{49}{98} \times (98 \times £1,224) =$	59,976
after transfer — no shares held		nil
		59,976
Less: 100% business property relief		59,976
		nil

As the shares still qualify for business property relief at 100% no amount is chargeable on death.

Inheritance tax payable on death

	Gross £	Tax £
Cumulative transfers within seven years before death	–	–
Estate on death	806,000	197,600*
	806,000	197,600*

(* 806,000 – 312,000 = 494,000 @ 40%)
Tax payable on estate at death (which is the total tax payable
as a result of Mr Smart's death, since no tax was payable on
gifts within previous seven years)   £197,600

(2) *Charging gift to Jill and ignoring the value of the gift in the death estate*

Death estate as above		806,000
Less: property in Spain		176,000
		£630,000

Tax on gifts made within seven years before death

Shares to John as above			–
Property in Spain to Jill			176,000
			176,000
Less: Annual exemptions	2008/09	3,000	
	2007/08	3,000	6,000
PETs now chargeable			£170,000

No tax payable since 2007/08 threshold is not exceeded.

Inheritance tax payable on death

	Gross £	Tax £
Cumulative transfers within seven years before death	170,000	–
Estate on death	630,000	195,200*
	800,000	195,200*

(* 800,000 – 312,000 = 488,000 @ 40%)

Tax payable on estate at death	195,200
Add tax on gifts within previous seven years	–
Total tax payable as a result of Mr Smart's death	£195,200

As the first calculation is greater than the second, that is deemed to be the one that determines the tax liabilities. The effect is that the whole of the tax will be payable out of Mr Smart's estate, and borne equally between John and Jill.

(c)   If alternative proposals had been adopted

Death of Mrs Smart

	£	£
Estate:		
Business property	130,000	
Less: 50% business property relief	65,000	65,000
Freehold house – ½	152,000	
Less: Exempt on devolution to spouse	152,000	–
Shares in Smart & Co Ltd		
2 × £1,200 (related property = 51%)	2,400	
Less: 100% business property relief	2,400	–
Building society accounts		196,000
Chargeable to inheritance tax		261,000

Gifts within seven years before death

			Gross £	Tax £
Shares to John				
before transfer	$\dfrac{49}{98} \times (98 \times £1,224) =$		59,976	
after transfer	$\dfrac{2}{51} \times (51 \times £1,200) =$		2,400	
			57,576	
Less: 100% business property relief			57,576	
			nil	
Cumulative transfers within seven years before death			–	
Estate on death			261,000	–

				Gross £	Tax £
No tax payable since threshold is not exceeded				261,000	–

Death of Mr Smart

Estate:

				Gross £	Tax £
Freehold house					304,000
Shares in Smart & Co Ltd					
49 shares @ £1,000			49,000		
Less: 100% business property relief			49,000		–
					304,000

Gifts within seven years before death

				Gross £	Tax £
To Jill					
Spanish property			176,000		
Less: Annual exemptions	2008/09	3,000			
	2007/08	3,000	6,000	170,000	–
Cumulative transfers within seven years before death				170,000	–
Estate on death				304,000	64,800*
				474,000	64,800*

(* 474,000 – 312,000 = 162,000 @ 40%)

Tax payable on estate at death   £64,800

(d)   Comparative tax liabilities if deaths had occurred nine years later

(a)   *No change — as above*

£171,600

(b)   *Original proposals*

If the donor survived the gifts (including the gift with reservation) by more than seven years, there would be no charge to tax on the gifts and therefore the double charges regulations would not apply. The Spanish property would, however, still be included in Mr Smart's estate, so the position would be:

	Gross £	Tax £
Cumulative transfers within previous seven years	–	–
Estate on death (including Spanish property)	806,000	197,600*

* (806,000 – 312,000 = 494,000 @ 40%)

(c)   *Revised proposals*

Mrs Smart

	Gross £	Tax £
Cumulative transfers within previous seven years	–	–
Estate on death	261,000	–

Mr Smart

Cumulative transfers within previous seven years	–	–
Estate on death (within nil rate)	304,000	–

Explanatory Notes

Effect of different scenarios on tax liabilities

1.   This example illustrates that it is possible to increase the liability to inheritance tax by making gifts without considering their tax implications.

The tax liability on the second death if none of the proposals were adopted would amount to £171,600 (nil liability on first death).

If the first proposals were adopted then following the earlier death of Mrs Smart the tax liability on the death of Mr Smart would be increased by £26,000 to £197,600.

Whereas if the second proposals had been adopted then on the first death (Mrs Smart) no tax would be payable and on the second death (Mr Smart) £64,800 would be payable. An overall reduction of £106,800 would arise.

If Mr Smart had predeceased his wife then the tax liabilities under the proposals at (c) would have become:

Mr Smart

	£	£
Gifts within seven years before death		
— property to Jill (176,000 – 6,000 annual exemptions)		170,000
Estate on death:		
Shares in Smart & Co Ltd		
49 shares @ £1,200 (related property 51%)	58,800	
Less: 100% business property relief	58,800	–
Freehold house —	152,000	
Exempt since devolving on Mrs Smart	152,000	–
		170,000

No tax is payable since threshold is not exceeded.

		£	£
Mrs Smart			
Gifts within seven years before death (as before)			–
Estate on death:			
Freehold house		304,000	
Office premises		130,000	
Shares in Smart & Co Ltd			
2 × £100	200		
Less: 50% business property relief	100	100	
Building society accounts		196,000	630,100
			630,100
Tax payable (630,100 – 312,000 = 318,100 @ 40%)			£127,240

Taking both deaths together the tax is £127,240.

Thus the reduction from £171,600 would be £44,360.

In considering how best to mitigate inheritance tax liabilities, one has to remember the continuing need for the income from the business property, and that the personal residence cannot be transferred (except to each other) whilst the Smarts remain in residence (such a transfer would be a gift with reservation and therefore ineffective). However the second proposals would mitigate the potential liabilities regardless of who died first. Furthermore after the earlier death of Mr Smart, Mrs Smart could possibly start to make use of the annual exemption by making gifts to her children or grandchildren if her capital was likely to increase by unspent income.

Transfers to discretionary trust

2.   The amounts transferred to the discretionary trust on the death of Mrs Smart would be potentially liable to further inheritance tax charges, as although she had made no transfers in the seven years before her death, the initial value of the property comprised in the settlement (being the values *before* business property relief) is above the inheritance tax threshold of £300,000, ie:

Business property	130,000
Shares in Smart & Co Ltd	2,400
Building society accounts	196,000
	£328,400

A liability will arise if there are any exits from the settlement within ten years. The initial rate applicable to such exits would be +arrived at as follows:

(328,400 – 312,000) @ 20% = £3,280, which is an effective rate on £328,400 of 0.999%. The actual rate is 30% of the effective rate, ie 30% of 0.999% = 0.3000%.

$$\text{The initial rate would be } 0.3\% \times \frac{x}{40}$$

where x is the number of complete quarters since the creation of the settlement.

A liability at or after ten years would only occur if the assets increased in value to the extent that after business property relief their value exceeded the then threshold (which is usually increased annually by at least the rate of inflation). For detailed notes on discretionary trusts see Examples 59 to 63, particularly Example 62 explanatory note 5.

In the event that the property was appointed absolutely to the beneficiaries within two years after death (following the later death of Mr Smart) it will be deemed to have been transferred by Mrs Smart under her will (s 144) and no further tax would be payable. See Example 63 explanatory note 5.

Related property; valuations for capital gains tax

3.   The related property rules apply to the shares in Smart & Co Ltd and accordingly it is necessary to look at the appropriate proportion of the value of the combined holdings of Mr and Mrs Smart before and after the transfer. Furthermore the entitlement to business property relief depends on the total related shares held by Mr and Mrs Smart (but not the discretionary settlement). Business property relief is not available on the office premises if the combined holding drops below 51%. See Examples 10, 22 and 26 for the related property rules and Example 25 for the rules relating to business property relief.

The related property provisions are not relevant for capital gains tax. For capital gains tax purposes, the value of an asset in the hands of a beneficiary is its open market value at the date of death (TCGA 1992 s 62). It is, however, provided by TCGA 1992 s 274 that if the value of an asset has been *ascertained* for inheritance tax, the same value applies for capital gains tax. But if shares qualify for

100% business property relief, their value will not require to be ascertained for inheritance tax, so that the normal open market value rule will apply for capital gains tax. The beneficiary's acquisition value may thus be lower than the inheritance tax value, since it will be based on the number of shares held by the beneficiary in isolation. See Example 38 explanatory note 1 for further comments on this point.

Gifts with reservation

4.   FA 1986 s 102 and Sch 20 provide in respect of gifts on or after 18 March 1986 that if an asset is transferred and

(a)   possession and enjoyment of the property is not bona fide assumed by the donee at or before the beginning of the relevant period, (ie the period beginning seven years before the donor's death or on the date of the gift if later) or

(b)   at any time in the relevant period the property is not enjoyed to the entire exclusion, or virtually to the entire exclusion, of the donor and of any benefit to him by contract or otherwise,

then the gift is treated as property within the donor's estate as at the date of death.

The gifts with reservation provisions do not apply if or to the extent that the transfer is covered by one of the following inheritance tax exemptions (as to which see Example 1):

—   transfers between spouses/civil partners (s 18)

—   small gifts (s 20)

—   gifts in consideration of marriage or registration of a civil partnership (s 22)

—   gifts to charities (s 23)

—   gifts to political parties (s 24)

—   gifts to housing associations (s 24A)

—   gifts for national purposes etc (s 25)

—   maintenance funds for historic buildings (s 17)

—   employee trusts (s 28).

If it can be shown that the property ceased to be subject to a reservation prior to death then the donor is treated as making a potentially exempt transfer of the property at the time that the reservation ceased (FA 1986 s 102(4)). Such a transfer could not be reduced by annual exemptions.

The initial gift is still a transfer of value, although it may be potentially exempt (after deducting available annual exemptions). If it is potentially exempt then it will not be charged to tax if the donor survives seven years.

These provisions are illustrated in the example. The proposed gift of the Spanish property to Jill will not remove the property from Mr Smart's chargeable estate if Mr and Mrs Smart continue to use the property rent free. If, however, the gift was made nine years before Mr Smart's death as in part (d) of the example, the gift would escape tax, but the value of the property would be brought into his estate if the reservation was not released. If say he had released the reservation between three and four years before his death he would be treated as making a further potentially exempt transfer to Jill equal to the value of the property at that time (not reduced by any annual exemptions) and following his death tax would be charged, subject to tapering relief of 20%, but the value of the property would be excluded from his estate.

An exception to the gifts with reservation rules is made when either

(i)   full consideration is given for any right of occupation or enjoyment retained or assumed by the donor and the property is land or chattels, or

(ii)   in the case of land, the donor later occupies the property as a result of a change of circumstances that was unforeseen at the time of the original gift and the benefit provided by the donee to the donor only represents reasonable provision for the care and maintenance of an elderly or infirm relative.

Thus the occupation by Mr and Mrs Smart of the Spanish property at full rent would be sufficient to nullify the reservation of benefit, as would any occupation rent free by Mr Smart after the boating accident.

Continuing gifts made under the terms of a regular premium insurance policy effected before 18 March 1986 are not caught by the gifts with reservation rules, unless the policy is altered after that date.

There are special rules to provide for the benefits reserved to be followed through when the original property is substituted by replacement property, with appropriate adjustments if the donee provides consideration.

5.   The gifts with reservation legislation was strengthened following the decision in *Ingram v CIR* (1999). The House of Lords held that the rules did not apply to Lady Ingram, who created a rent-free lease for herself of her freehold property and then gave away the freehold.

Under FA 1986 ss 102A, 102B and 102C, gifts of interests in land or shares of interests in land made on or after 9 March 1999 will be treated as gifts with reservation if there is some significant interest, right or arrangement which enables or entitles the donor to occupy the land to a material degree without paying full consideration.

6.   The provisions do not apply where the gift is covered by one of the inheritance tax exemptions listed in note 4, nor where exception (i) or (ii) in note 4 applies. Nor do they apply where, despite some negligible benefit retained, the donor is virtually excluded from any enjoyment of the land, or to gifts made more than seven years after the interest etc was created, or where the donor cannot occupy or enjoy the land until the interest given away expires (for example when a lease terminates).

7.   Where there is a gift of an undivided share of an interest in land, the donor and donee may both occupy the land providing the donor receives no other benefit at the donee's expense in connection with the gift (ie the donee pays no more than his fair share of the outgoings) (s 102B(4), giving effect to existing Revenue practice as stated in their letter of 18 May 1987 to the Law Society Gazette following a ministerial statement in Standing Committee G on 10 June 1986).

8.   For further comments on gifts with reservation relating to land see Example 23. For the interaction of the gifts with reservation provisions and business and agricultural property relief, see Example 25 explanatory note 9.

9.   Under FA 1986 s 102ZA the termination of a pre-22 March 2006 interest in possession or of an IPDI, a disabled person's interest or a transitional serial interest during the lifetime of the beneficiary is treated as a gift of the property in which the interest subsists. If the beneficiary continues to benefit the property will now be subject to the gifts with reservation rules.

Pre-owned assets

10.   Since 6 April 2005 where a potential inheritance tax liability does not arise under the gifts with reservation provisions a free-standing income tax charge will apply to the benefit of using an asset that was formerly owned by the taxpayer. A similar charge will apply to the use of assets at low cost or to the use of assets purchased with funds provided by the taxpayer. The charge applies to tangible and intangible assets. For details see Example 23.

Relief for double charges

11.   Making a gift with reservation as outlined in notes 4 and 5 is one of the occasions within the inheritance tax legislation where it is possible to get a double charge to tax. There are regulations to eliminate such double charges (SI 1987/1130). The operation of the regulations for gifts with

reservation where the original gift was potentially exempt is illustrated in the example. See Example 20 for the other occasions when double charges arise and the detailed provisions of the regulations and Example 23 for interaction with the pre-owned assets provisions.

More than one double charge

12. When most lifetime transfers were potentially exempt, there were few occasions in practice where the double charges regulations could come into effect. Following FA 2006, many more gifts are not potentially exempt and the occasions on which the double charges regulations will apply are increased. The regulations are very complex, and even so they do not cover the possibility of a single donor being affected by more than one occasion of double charge, such as for example if Mr Smart had made a cash gift to his daughter, in addition to the gift with reservation, and the daughter had then made a loan back to Mr Smart. No guidance has been given on the procedure to be followed in such a case.

Same day transfers

13. Where transfers that are or become chargeable transfers are made on the same day, the annual exemption is apportioned between them (s 19(3)(b)) even if one of the transfers was chargeable immediately and the other was potentially exempt. For detailed notes on this point, see Example 24 explanatory note 1.

Capital gains implication of gifts with reservation

14. Where there are gifts with reservation, not only is the inheritance tax chargeable on the higher of the two bases as indicated in the example, but for capital gains tax the tax-free uplift to market value on death does not apply. Instead the donee's capital gains tax cost will be the market value at the date of the gift plus taper relief from that date (subject to any available holdover relief claims).

Question

(a)   Albert, a bachelor aged 70, sold his business for cash in the 1990s and subsequently carried out the following:

   May 2002   Gave his younger sister Beryl cash of £142,000 (no previous gifts having been made)

   June 2002   Created a discretionary trust with cash of £254,500, the trustees paying any tax due. The potential beneficiaries of the trust were his brothers and sisters and their children.

   In June 2003 Beryl died. During her lifetime she had made an unsecured interest-free loan of £136,000 to her son's business. On her death she left to Albert the debt due from her son.

   In July 2008 Albert died, leaving an estate of £321,000, including the £136,000 debt due from his nephew's business.

   Calculate the tax payable as a result of Albert's death.

(b)   In July 2008 Andrew died, aged 87. He had been a widower for many years and had supported his only grandson Barry in his business ventures. In May 2004 Andrew had made a gift of £166,000 to Barry to help launch a new product in his business.

   In June 2004 Andrew had created a discretionary trust with cash of £294,000, including as beneficiaries his only daughter Clarice, her children and Barry's children. The trustees paid any tax due.

   In June 2005 Andrew was taken ill and had to move into a nursing home. He sold his house and received a loan from Barry of £100,000 to help fund the fees.

   In July 2008 the value of Andrew's estate was £50,000, excluding the debt of £100,000 to Barry.

   Calculate the tax payable as a result of Andrew's death.

Answer

Double charges regulations

    (a)   **Tax payable as a result of Albert's death**

    Lifetime gifts

			£	£
May 2002	Gift to Beryl			142,000
Less: Annual exemptions	2002/03	3,000		
	2001/02	3,000		6,000
Potentially exempt transfer				136,000

		Gross £	Tax on 2002/03 scale £
June 2002	Gift to discretionary trust	254,500	900*

(* 254,500 – 250,000 = 4,500 @ 20%)
Tax payable by trustees   £900

On death of Albert — July 2008

    (1)   *Including loan inherited from Beryl in Albert's estate and ignoring gift to Beryl in May 2002*

		Gross £	Tax on 2008/09 scale £
June 2002	Gift to trust	254,500	–
July 2008	Estate on death	321,000	105,400*
		575,500	105,400*

(* 575,500 – 312,000 = 263,500 @ 40%)

Tax payable by trust	–
(No repayment of tax of £900 paid at time of gift)	
Tax payable by estate	105,400
Total tax payable	£105,400

(Note that if Albert had died earlier than June 2008, i e less than five years after Beryl's death, quick succession relief would have been available by reference to the tax paid in Beryl's estate on the £136,000 left to him by Beryl — see Example 21.)

(2)   *Including gift to Beryl in May 2002 and ignoring value of gift back in Albert's estate*

			Gross £	Tax on 2008/09 scale £
May 2002	Gift to Beryl		136,000	–
June 2002	Gift to trust		254,500	31,400*
			390,500	
July 2008	Estate at death (excluding £136,000 loan)		185,000	74,000
			575,500	105,400

(* 390,500 – 312,000 = 78,500 @ 40%)

	Gross £	Tax on 2008/09 scale £
Tax payable by Beryl's estate on gift from Albert		–
Tax payable by trust	31,400	
Less: tapering relief 80% (6 to 7 yrs)	25,120	
	6,280	
Less: tax already paid at time of gift	900	5,380
Tax payable by Albert's estate		74,000
Total tax payable as a result of Albert's death		£79,380

As (1) shows the higher amount of tax payable, that calculation is used to calculate the tax liabilities (see explanatory note 4).

(b)   Tax payable as a result of Andrew's death

Lifetime gifts

		£	£
May 2004 — Gift to Barry			166,000
Less: Annual exemptions	2004/05	3,000	
	2003/04	3,000	6,000
Potentially exempt transfer			160,000

		Gross £	Tax on 2004/05 scale £
June 2004	Gift to discretionary trust	294,000	6,200*

(* 294,000 – 263,000 = 31,000 @ 20%)

Tax payable by trustees			£6,200

On death of Andrew — July 2008

(1)   *Excluding £100,000 of May 2004 gift and not deducting debt in Andrew's death estate*

		Gross £	Tax on 2008/09 scale £
May 2004	Gift to Barry	160,000	
Less: amount subsequently lent back		100,000	
		60,000	
June 2004	Gift to trust	294,000	16,800*
		354,000	
July 2008	Estate at death	50,000	20,000
		404,000	36,800

(* 354,000 – 312,000 = 42,000 @ 40%)

Tax payable by trust	16,800	
Less: tapering relief 40% (4 to 5 yrs)	6,720	
	10,080	
Less: tax already paid at time of gift	6,200	3,880
Tax payable by estate		20,000
Total tax payable as a result of Andrew's death		£23,880

(2)   *Charging full gift in May 2004 and allowing debt as a deduction in Andrew's death estate*

		Gross £	Tax on 2008/09 scale £
May 2004	Gift to Barry	160,000	–
June 2004	Gift to trust	294,000	56,800*
July 2008	Estate at death (50,000 – 100,000, see note 7)	–	–
		454,000	56,800

(* 454,000 – 312,000 = 142,000 @ 40%)

Tax payable by trust	56,800	
Less: tapering relief 40% (4 to 5 yrs)	22,720	
	34,080	
Less: tax already paid at time of gift	6,200	27,880
Total tax payable as a result of Andrew's death		27,880

The second calculation shows the higher amount of tax payable, therefore that is the calculation used to compute the tax liability.

Explanatory Notes

Relief for double charges

1.   There are several occasions within the inheritance tax legislation where it is possible to get a double charge to tax. Double charges occur where there are gifts with reservation, under the pre-owned asset rules, where there are 'mutual transfers' (ie where a gift is made and the donee makes a gift back), and where a gift is made and the donee then lends money to the donor. The debt is disallowed in the donor's estate at death.

A debt is only deductible from an estate if

(i)   it was incurred for full consideration and wholly for the benefit of the deceased, and

(ii)   it is not connected with any gifts received directly or indirectly by the lender from the deceased. (However this restriction does not apply if it can be shown that the loan was not made out of the property derived from the deceased and was not facilitated by the deceased's gifts.)

If a borrower repays a loan which would otherwise not be a deductible loan he is treated as making a potentially exempt transfer of the amount repaid at the time of repayment (FA 1986 s 103).

2.   Regulations have been made under the authority of FA 1986 s 104, by SI 1987/1130, to eliminate double charges. In each case two calculations are made, and the calculation that produces the higher amount of tax is the one used. If both produce the same amount of tax, the first calculation stipulated in the regulations is treated as producing the higher amount and is thus the calculation used to determine the liabilities. Whether or not the total amount of tax works out the same, the burden of the tax may fall on different people (see note 4 below).

Double charges relief for gifts with reservation

3.   A lifetime gift with reservation may be either potentially exempt, for example the gift of a house while reserving the right to live in it, or immediately chargeable, for example where a gift is made to a discretionary trust in which the donor is a beneficiary. The method laid down in the double charges regulations for gifts with reservation is firstly to charge the gift with reservation in the deceased's estate and ignore the lifetime transfer. The second calculation is to charge the lifetime transfer and leave the gift with reservation out of the deceased's estate. If the gift was a chargeable transfer on which inheritance tax had been paid when it was made, and the first calculation produces the higher figure, the tax paid in lifetime is deducted from the tax payable on death (but not exceeding the part of the death tax payable that relates to that transfer).

The rules are illustrated in Examples 19, 24 and 32.

Double charges relief for pre-owned assets

4.   Where a taxpayer has a liability to income tax under the pre-owned assets rules (see Example 23 and Tolley's Taxwise I 2008/09) and elects to eliminate that charge by deeming the gifts with reservation provisions for inheritance tax to apply, then, a double charge to inheritance tax could arise. This would occur if the taxpayer died within seven years of the original gift. Tax would arise on the original potentially exempt transfer, and also on the property subject to the reservation. As in note 3 two calculations are made. The first is to charge the gift with reservation in the deceased estate and ignore the lifetime transfer. The second calculation charges the lifetime gift and excludes the value of the reservation. The higher tax liability applies.

These provisions only apply where both the lifetime gift and the reservation relate to the same individual. Therefore, where in certain schemes, such as 'Eversden', one spouse or civil partner makes the lifetime gift, but the election under the pre-owned asset rules places the property in the estate of the other spouse or civil partner, no double charge relief is available.

Double charges relief for gift and gift back

5.   With regard to a gift and gift back where the first gift was initially potentially exempt but then becomes chargeable, the regulations provide for the first calculation to include the gift back in the estate of the original donor and ignore the potentially exempt gift, and the second calculation to charge the potentially exempt gift and ignore the value of the gift back in the hands of the original donor.

This is illustrated in part (a) of the example in relation to the gift by Albert to Beryl and her bequest to him of the debt owing from her son. The first calculation showed the higher amount of tax payable, so that calculation was used to calculate the tax liabilities.

Note how the incidence of tax may vary:

	Calculation 1 £	Calculation 2 £	Saving/(Loss) £
Payable by trust	–	5,380	5,380
Payable by estate	105,400	74,000	(31,400)

Double charges relief for gift and loan back

6.   Where a gift is made, followed by a loan to the donor by the donee, with the donor dying within seven years when the debt is still outstanding, the first calculation under the regulations is to ignore the debt and the part of the gift equal to the loan. The second is to charge the gift and also allow the debt. This is illustrated in part (b) of the example, where the second calculation (charging the full gift to Barry and allowing the debt to Barry as a deduction in Andrew's estate) showed the higher amount of tax payable and was thus used to calculate the tax liabilities. Where the first calculation shows the higher amount, credit may be due for all or part of any tax paid on the gift in lifetime.

7.   Normally Andrew's estate would be considered to be insolvent as the debt to Barry exceeds the available assets. This does not prevent a liability to inheritance tax arising on earlier gifts as that charge is made on the donees. The rules relating to gifts followed by subsequent loanbacks are designed to prevent avoidance of tax by the making of potentially exempt transfers at a time when death is very unlikely within seven years (and therefore term assurance is very cheap) followed by a loan of a similar amount thus removing assets from the tax computation whilst retaining effective control of both the capital and the income arising therefrom.

More than one double charge

8.   The double charges regulations do not cover the possibility of a single donor being affected by more than one double charge, and no guidance has been given as to the procedure to be followed.

Transfers to trusts

9.   Where transfers are made to most trusts (before 22 March 2006, only discretionary trusts), tax liabilities may arise within the trust if there are any exits from the trust within ten years. For details see Examples 59 to 63. There will be no such liabilities in this example, since the transfers in both parts (a) and (b) were of cash and were below the nil threshold at the death of the donor.

Question

On 6 April 2003 Basil made gifts to his brothers Simon and Charles of £144,000 each.

Basil died on 26 November 2005 leaving an estate of £200,000.

By his will he provided for a legacy to Charles of £90,000 with the residue to Simon.

On 12 March 2006 Simon died. His estate was valued at £312,000 including the residuary legacy from Basil. He left the whole of his estate to his surviving brother Charles.

Charles died on 10 May 2008 when his estate was worth £469,000.

Compute the tax payable by the personal representatives of each of the brothers on the assumption that none of the brothers had made any lifetime transfers other than those stated.

Note that in 2008/09, inheritance tax will be payable on transfers of value in excess of £312,000.

Answer

Death of Basil — 26 November 2005

Tax on gifts made within seven years before death:

			Gross £	Tax on 2005/06 scale £
6 April 2003	Gift to Simon		144,000	
	Gift to Charles		144,000	
			288,000	
	Less: Annual exemptions			
	2003/04	3,000		
	2002/03	3,000	6,000	
PETs now chargeable			282,000	2,800*

(* 282,000 − 275,000 = 7,000 @ 40%)

The £2,800 is not reduced by tapering relief since the gifts are within three years before death.

		£
Tax payable —	Simon	1,400
	Charles	1,400
		2,800

Inheritance tax on Basil's Estate

	Gross £	Tax £
Cumulative transfers within seven years before death	282,000	2,800
Estate on death	200,000	80,000
	482,000	82,800

Division of Estate

	£
Pecuniary legacy to Charles	90,000
Inheritance tax	80,000
Balance to Simon	30,000
	200,000

Death of Simon — 12 March 2006

	Gross	Tax on 2005/06 scale
Inheritance tax on death	£	£
Cumulative transfers within seven years before death	–	–
Estate on death	312,000	14,800*

(* 312,000 – 275,000 = 37,000 @ 40%)

Inheritance tax payable:

	£	£
Due on estate		14,800

Less: Quick succession relief
Gift from Basil 6 April 2003

$$60\% \times \frac{139,600}{141,000} \times 1,400 \qquad\qquad 832$$

Legacy from Basil's estate 26 November 2005

$$100\% \times \frac{30,000}{50,000} \times 20,000$$

	£	£
	12,000	12,832
Inheritance tax payable by personal representatives of Simon		1,968

The estate passing to Charles is:

	£
Estate	312,000
Less: Inheritance tax	1,968
	310,032

Death of Charles — 10 May 2008

	Gross £	Tax on 2008/09 scale £
Inheritance tax on death		
Cumulative transfers within seven years before death	–	–
Estate on death	469,000	62,800*

(* 469,000 – 312,000 = 157,000 @ 40%)

Inheritance tax payable:

	£	£
Due on estate		62,800

Less: Quick succession relief
Gift from Basil 6 April 2003

	£	£
Over five years before Charles's death	–	
Legacy from Basil's estate 26 November 2005		

$$60\% \times \frac{90,000}{150,000} \times 60,000 \qquad\qquad 21,600$$

Legacy from Simon's estate 12 March 2006

$$60\% \times \frac{310,032}{312,000} \times 1,968 \qquad\qquad 1173 \qquad 22,773$$

Inheritance tax payable by personal representatives of Charles		40,027

Explanatory Notes

Quick succession relief

1. Where a person dies shortly after receiving a chargeable transfer, the transfer has increased the estate at death and therefore attracts tax in the deceased's estate, as well as having been taxed at the time of the transfer. Relief is provided where the *death occurs* within five years after the chargeable transfer, known as quick succession relief (s 141). There is no requirement to retain the asset obtained by that transfer.

2. The first step is to calculate the tax payable on the original transfer. A potentially exempt transfer becomes a chargeable transfer on the death of the donor within seven years. Although the tax is calculated using the rates applicable at the time of death, the date of transfer is relevant in calculating quick succession relief. The part of the transfer covered by the annual exemption does not bear tax and is therefore excluded from the QSR calculation. As the donee pays the tax on a PET, grossing up is not required.

3. The inheritance tax payable on the death of Basil is a charge on the residue (see Example 5 explanatory note 8). Thus the amount receivable by Simon is the net £30,000. The estate rate is 40% so that the figures to use in the calculation of quick succession relief are a gross legacy of £50,000 (£30,000 × 10/6) with tax paid of £20,000.

4. The total tax on the deceased's estate is reduced by the quick succession relief.

5. Where death occurs within one year of the transfer the relief is 100% of the *tax paid on the previous transfer*, reduced in the proportion of net value transferred to the deceased over the gross chargeable transfer.

    Where the period between transfer and death is over one year, the percentage becomes:

1+ to 2 years	80%
2+ to 3 years	60%
3+ to 4 years	40%
4+ to 5 years	20%

Donee dying before donor

6. If the donee dies before the donor then the original gift will continue to be a potentially exempt transfer at that time. Tax will be charged on the estate of the donee (including the gift) without relief. If the donor subsequently dies within seven years of the original gift then the original gift becomes a

chargeable transfer, with the tax payable being a liability of the executors of the donee, and the inheritance tax due on the death of the donee recomputed. Furthermore quick succession relief may then be available. See Example 55 for an illustration of this point.

Quick succession relief on trust property

7.   Quick succession relief is also available where there are successive charges within five years on trust property in which there is an interest in possession. The rates of relief are the same as those in note 5 above, with the percentage relief depending on the period between the successive charges (s 141). For a more complex example of quick succession relief, showing the treatment of settled property and giving further detailed notes, see Example 53.

Other double charges reliefs

8.   Quick succession relief applies where as in this example successive transfers are charged in the estates of different donors. There are other occasions under the inheritance tax rules where property can be charged twice in the same estate. Regulations have been made by the Board of HMRC under the authority of FA 1986 s 104 to avoid double charges to tax (SI 1987/1130). This will normally be where there are gifts with reservation, pre-owned assets or liabilities are created which are non-deductible debts in calculating inheritance tax (see Example 19).

Question

In order to reduce the potential liability to inheritance tax on his accumulated wealth, Henry, aged 80, proposes the following:

(a)   To sell one of a pair of antique objects to his daughter at its market value of £40,000, and then in a year's time to give her the other of equal value.

   The value of the pair is £130,000.

(b)   To sell 2% of his holding of 51% of the shares of Henry Ltd, a property investment company, to John, an unconnected friend, for its market value, then to give the remaining 49% of the shares to his son, Simon, who already holds 35% of the shares.

   The market value of the shares in Henry Ltd is:

51%	holding	£800,000
49%	holding	£500,000
15–20%	holding	£100,000
2%	holding	£5,000

(c)   If the scheme in (b) above is unsuitable, Henry proposes giving 2% of his shares to 'Help the Aged', a recognised charity, then to give the remaining 49% of the shares to Simon.

(d)   A further suggestion is that next winter while Henry is on a cruise around the world Henry Ltd should make a rights issue of four shares for every one share held. Henry will not be back until after the issue has been made and will not be able to take up his entitlement.

Henry has made cash gifts every year to use up his annual exemption.

Advise him of the inheritance tax effect of each of the above proposals.

Answer

(a) **Pair of antiques — sale followed by gift to daughter**

There are two problems in relation to Henry's proposed sale and gift of the two antique objects.

The first is whether the sale at full value to his daughter will itself escape being treated as a transfer of value at that time, since although she would be paying full price for the object, his estate would actually fall by £50,000 (£130,000 – cash received £40,000 and value of remaining object £40,000). A sale at full value is not a transfer of value if it was not intended to confer a gratuitous benefit on anyone and was either made at arm's length (which this transaction is not) or was such as might be expected to have been made at arm's length (s 10). Since the daughter would be paying the full market price, which is the same amount as a stranger would have paid, the transaction will probably not be treated as a transfer of value at that time.

But when Henry gives his daughter the other object the Revenue may use the associated operations rules of s 268 to treat the two events as one. There would then be a potentially exempt transfer on the second occasion of £90,000 (£130,000 – £40,000 cash received) which would become a chargeable transfer if Henry dies within seven years of the gift of the second object.

It would have been better for Henry to sell the pair of objects to his daughter for £40,000 in the first place, because the potentially exempt transfer of £90,000 would then be made one year earlier and the seven year survivorship period would start at that time.

(b) **Shares – sale followed by gift to son**

Again HMRC may use s 268 in determining the inheritance tax position on the gift of shares to Simon. The reason they might do so is that no inheritance tax implications would arise on the sale of shares to John, because in isolation this is a commercial transaction at arm's length and not a transfer of value and on the gift of shares to Simon inheritance tax would ordinarily be payable on death within seven years on a transfer of £500,000 (the value of a 49% holding), whereas but for the earlier sale the transfer would have been valued at the difference between a 51% holding (£800,000) and a 2% holding (£5,000), ie at £795,000.

If HMRC applied s 268 the value transferred to Simon would be as follows:

	£
Value of 51% before first of associated operations	800,000
Value of 0% after second of associated operations	–
	800,000
Less: Cash received (on the sale of the 2% holding)	5,000
Value transferred (potentially exempt transfer)	795,000

(c) **Shares — gift to charity followed by gift to son**

If Henry adopts the alternative of giving 2% of the shares to 'Help the Aged' the related property rules will be applied. These are contained in s 161. The rules provide (inter alia) that where property is transferred to a charity, political party etc by the taxpayer or his spouse/civil partner, such property is related to any other property of the taxpayer and his spouse/civil partner.

The property will continue to be related until five years after it is disposed of by the charity etc.

The value of appropriate parts of the related property is proportionate to the value of all related property, if this produces a higher value than the value of the appropriate part on its own.

Consequently the value transferred by Henry will be:

2% to charity — exempt transfer
49% to son — value before transfer

Own holding	49%	
Related holding	2%	

Value of $\overline{51\%}$ = £800,000

Henry's 49% holding is therefore worth $\dfrac{49}{51} \times £800,000$ = 768,627

Value of Henry's holding after transfer   nil

Value of transfer (which is a potentially exempt transfer)   £768,627

The above computation would apply unless Henry deferred the gift of shares to Simon until five years after 'Help the Aged' had disposed of their shares. If the transfer took place after that time the potentially exempt transfer would be:

Value transferred (49% holding — assuming no change in values)   £500,000

(d) **Failure to take up rights shares**

Henry's proposal concerning the rights issue is covered by s 3(3), which provides that the deliberate omission to exercise a right is a transfer of value.

The issue of rights shares in the circumstances outlined would be caught by this subsection.

The value transferred would be:

     £

Value before transfer (51%)   800,000

Value after transfer:

	Original Shares	Rights Shares	Total
Henry	51	–	51
Son	35	140	175
Others	14	56	70
	100	196	296

Value of

$\dfrac{51}{296} = 17.23\%$ holding   100,000

Value transferred (potentially exempt transfer)   700,000

Because s 3(3) treats the deliberate omission as a disposition such an act would constitute an actual transfer of value and s 3A would apply treating the transfer as potentially exempt.

There would also be a CGT liability.

Explanatory Notes

Associated operations

1.   The associated operations rules are contained in IHTA 1984 s 268. Certain associated operations are specifically covered by other legislation, viz:

Related property — s 161 (see note 5)

Omission to exercise a right — s 3(3) (see part (d) of the example)

Alteration of capital — s 98 (see note 7)

2.   One cannot be certain whether the Revenue will seek to use the associated operations rules in any particular case, but IHTA 1984 s 268 covers:

    (i)   Two or more operations of any kind affecting the same property or property which represents whether directly or indirectly that property, or income arising from that property, or property representing accumulations of such income (s 268(1)(a)).

    (ii)   Any two operations of which one is effected with reference to the other, or with a view to enabling the other to be effected, or facilitating its being effected and any further operation having a like relation to any of those two and so on (s 268(1)(b)).

The operations might be effected by the same person or different persons and might or might not be simultaneous (s 268(1)).

'Operation' includes an omission (s 268(1)).

3.   Where a transfer of value is made by associated operations carried out at different times, it is treated as made at the time of the last of them (s 268(3)). But where one or more of the earlier operations also constitutes a transfer of value made by the same transferor, the value transferred by the earlier operations is treated as reducing the value transferred by all the operations taken together, except to the extent that the earlier operations were exempt because of the spouse transfer rules (s 18) but all operations taken together were not so exempt (s 268).

Series of settlements

4.   The taxpayer was successful in the Court of Appeal, in the case of *Rysaffe Trustee Co (CI) Ltd v IRC 2003* in contending that the associated operations provisions did not apply where five separate identical settlements were created on five separate dates within the same month (see Example 62 explanatory note 12). A subsequent decision of a Special Commissioner (*Smith v IRC (2007)*) distinguished the *Rysaffe* decision where three annuities and three life assurance policies were issued on the same date: in that case the associated operations provisions did apply.

Interaction of associated operations and related property provisions

5.   HMRC Capital Taxes have indicated (in correspondence with Butterworths Tolley – see Taxation 15 February 1996) how the related property and associated operations provisions would interact where assets were transferred in stages, with some being routed via a spouse (or, now, a civil partner). The example illustrated is of a set of four antique chairs, of which two are given by husband to wife, and each then gives one to their son in successive years. The related property rules would value each of the first transfers to the son at half of the value of the set of four less half the value of a set of two, and the second transfers at half the value of a set of two, thus bringing into account the whole of the value of the set of four, half being a transfer by the husband and the other half a transfer by the wife.

If the associated operations rules were invoked at the time the son became the owner of the set, the transfers by the wife would be treated as made by the husband (and so would not be taken into account in her own inheritance tax calculations). The overall effect would be the same in terms of the value transferred, but the whole of the transfer would affect the husband's estate.

See Example 23 for other illustrations of associated operations.

Grant of a lease

6. The granting of a lease for full consideration in money or money's worth is not associated with any operation effected more than three years after the grant (s 268(2)).

    By granting a lease, even for full value, a property owner restricts his rights over that property. If he were then to make a gift of those rights (ie the right to receive the rent under the lease and the freehold reversion) the full value of both rights might be less than that of the unencumbered freehold. He might therefore first grant a lease followed by a gift, instead of giving the freehold out of which the donee could grant the lease.

    The associated operations rules will not apply if the gift is more than three years after the grant of the lease.

Alteration of rights re shares

7. If, instead of a rights issue being made that is available equally to all shareholders, the unquoted share or loan capital of a close company is altered (or there is any alteration in the rights attaching to such shares or debentures) then s 98 applies. This provides that such a change is to be treated as a disposition made by the participators. Such a transfer cannot be a potentially exempt transfer (s 98(3)).

    Where there are deferred shares, an alteration of rights within s 98(1)(b) takes place when the deferred shares come to rank equally, or become merged, with shares of another class.

Business property relief

8. Business property relief is not available on the shares in Henry Ltd because it is a company that invests in land and buildings (s 105(3)).

Gifts with reservation etc

9. In addition to the associated operations legislation donors must also be fully aware of the rules relating to gifts with reservation and the treatment of certain debts. These are illustrated in Examples 19, 20 and 23.

Question

A.

Lucton, a widower aged 80, lives with his unmarried and only daughter Frances at 1 Hayseech, a bungalow currently valued at £250,000.

His only other asset of significance is £300,000 invested in a building society account.

He has already made a transfer of £80,000 in the last but one tax year, £6,000 of which was covered by annual exemptions and the balance of £74,000 was a potentially exempt transfer.

He is conscious that the value of the bungalow is likely to increase, thus worsening the potential inheritance tax position upon his death, when the bungalow is to devolve upon Frances.

Three schemes have been suggested to him for the mitigation of inheritance tax:

(a)   That the bungalow is given to Frances now, but that he continues to live in it with her, since at least this would ensure that whilst the gift less the annual exemption would be a chargeable transfer if he died within seven years, future growth would be in the hands of Frances and not his own.

(b)   That the bungalow is sold to Frances for its current market value but that the purchase price would be left on loan to her. Lucton would then waive £3,000 of the loan each year, the waiver being covered by his annual exemption for inheritance tax.

(c)   That the bungalow is retained by Lucton and instead £300,000 in cash is given to Frances. As Lucton would then have no liquid assets, Frances would each year lend £20,000 to Lucton to enable him to maintain his present lifestyle.

Discuss whether any of these schemes will be successful in mitigating inheritance tax.

B.

A wealthy client, Mr Douglas, who is *not* a farmer, has been involved in the following transactions during the current tax year. All land has been owned by Mr Douglas for more than ten years.

(a)   He divided his land at Ambridge into Upper and Lower Ambridge. He gave Lower Ambridge to his son Kirk and he and Kirk commenced to use the two properties in partnership. None of the land is partnership property.

(b)   He granted a lease of Green Gables at a nominal rent to his wife and himself as tenants in common; he then gave the freehold reversion to his daughter Anne. Thereafter he occupied Green Gables with his wife.

(c)   He granted a landlord's repairing lease of Blackacre at a commercial rent to his wife and himself. He then gave the freehold reversion to Anne.

Explain, with references to statute and case law as appropriate, whether any of these transactions are likely to constitute a gift with reservation for inheritance tax purposes.

C.

Mrs Jones, a wealthy widow, wishes to reduce her estates' liability to inheritance tax. In order to do so she gives Catherine, her only daughter, £500,000 in cash in May 2006. Her daughter then buys a property in Cornwall in February 2007 for £700,000. Mrs Jones visits this property and in 2008 decides that she would like to live there each summer, taking up residence on 6th April 2009. For the remainder of the year Mrs Jones continues to live in her London residence. Although Mrs Jones is aged 72 she is in good health and would be expected to live for another 15+ years. She is a 40% income taxpayer. For 2009/10 the annual rental value of the Cornwall property would be £36,000 pa and its open market value on 6 April 2009 is £900,000. Mrs Jones has no legal obligation to contribute towards the costs of that property.

(a)   Compute the income tax liability arising based upon the above facts.

(b)   Set out any available election to mitigate that charge (assuming that inheritance tax rates and rules remain unchanged).

(c)   Explain why the income tax charge arises and set out how long Mrs Jones could spend at the Cornwall property before a pre-owned assets charge arises.

Answer

A. **Lucton — proposals to mitigate inheritance tax**

(a) **Gift of property while continuing to live in it**

By continuing to live in the bungalow with Frances, Lucton will be retaining a benefit from the gift.

In order to make an effective transfer it is necessary to show that the subject matter of the gift is enjoyed to the entire or virtually the entire exclusion of the donor and of any benefit to him by contract or otherwise. The transfer of ownership to Frances, with Lucton continuing to live there, would not, therefore, be a viable way of mitigating the inheritance tax position, since in the case of land or a chattel the actual occupation or possession is only disregarded if it is made for full consideration.

In this case no consideration is proposed. If a full rent was paid by Lucton for his occupation of the bungalow this could give rise to a charge to income tax on Frances (subject to any 'rent a room' relief) and could also affect her capital gains exemption in respect of owner occupation of the bungalow.

Occupation of land is also disregarded where the occupation by the donor results from a change of circumstances arising since the time of the gift, being a change which was unforeseen at that time and was not brought about by the donor to save inheritance tax. Furthermore the occupation must occur at a time when the donor has become unable to maintain himself through old age or infirmity and must represent a reasonable provision by a donee who is a relative for the care and maintenance of the donor. Clearly Lucton would not qualify under this heading as he already occupies the bungalow and will continue to live there.

The original transfer to Frances, less the current and previous years' annual exemptions, will be a potentially exempt transfer, becoming chargeable if Lucton dies within seven years. As a gift with reservation the property will, however, continue to form part of Lucton's estate. The value of the property will only be taken out of Lucton's estate if it ceases to be property subject to a reservation. In that event Lucton would be deemed to make a potentially exempt transfer to Frances equal to the value of the property at that time, in addition to the potentially exempt transfer made when he gave her the property (and without the benefit of any annual exemptions). There are regulations to eliminate any double tax charge.

If Lucton made a gift of an *undivided share of the bungalow* to Frances and both she and Lucton continue to live at 1 Hayseech then the reservation of benefit rules will not apply provided the gift is unconditional and there is no collateral benefit to Lucton (see Example 19 explanatory note 7). The payment by Frances of Lucton's share of the running costs would be such a benefit.

(b) **Sale of property with purchase price left on loan**

If the bungalow were sold to Frances at its current market value, the purchase price being left on loan to her and then waived at £3,000 per annum, HMRC would probably argue that the associated operations rules should apply.

This means that the value at the time of the last waiver would have to be ascertained and any excess of that value over the value at the time of the actual transfer would be treated as a potentially exempt transfer at the time of the last of the waivers.

Thus, the mitigation of the potential inheritance tax liability by disposing of an appreciating asset for its present value in consideration for a non-appreciating loan debtor would be negated. The annual exemptions will, however, have been used against any waivers, avoiding them being wasted if there was no other facility for using them, and effectively limiting the potential chargeable transfer to the increase in value between the time of the last waiver and that of the actual transfer (the amount of the debt not waived at the time of death would itself form part of the estate). However in view of Lucton's age, it is probable that most of the value will fall to be charged to inheritance tax on death.

The fact that interest on the loan was or was not charged does not apparently affect HMRC's attitude.

(c) Cash gift followed by loans back

The gift of £300,000 cash by Lucton to Frances less the current and previous years' annual exemptions totalling £6,000 would be a potentially exempt transfer provided possession and enjoyment is fully assumed by Frances. This means that there would be no immediate liability to tax. If Lucton died within seven years of his earlier potentially exempt transfer of £74,000, tax would be payable on the gift to Frances, unless the nil threshold had in the meantime increased above £368,000 (ie £294,000 + £74,000). Tapering relief would reduce any tax payable if Lucton survived the gift to Frances by three years, and after seven years the gift would cease to be potentially liable to tax.

However, if Lucton retains a benefit by way of contract or otherwise the gift is negated. If the amount repaid to Lucton is by way of loan then this will also affect the position, as any debt incurred after 17 March 1986 that arises from a disposition made by the borrower will not be a deductible debt on death. (But if, as is implied, Lucton uses the £20,000 cash each year to support his lifestyle, he will not have accumulated that money as savings upon which inheritance tax could be levied.) Furthermore any repayment of that debt by Lucton will be a further transfer, albeit potentially exempt.

If the amounts paid to him by Frances after his gift to her could be treated as a disposition made in favour of a dependent relative for his reasonable care and maintenance they would not be a transfer of value by Frances (s 11(3)), and may not be regarded by HMRC as a reservation of benefit to Lucton.

B.   Douglas — land transactions

(a)   Gift of land subsequently used by partnership of donor and donee

Unless the use of Lower Ambridge by Mr Douglas (through the partnership) is for full consideration then the transfer would appear to be a gift with reservation, as the property is not enjoyed to the entire (or virtually entire) exclusion of the donor (FA 1986 s 102). If, however, the two properties are of similar value and profit sharing and capital sharing ratios are equal, then full consideration would appear to be given and the gifts with reservation rules and pre-owned asset provisions would not apply (FA 1986 Sch 20.6).

All of the relevant circumstances would have to be taken into account to determine full consideration. These would include profit shares, values, actual input to the partnership and any actual rent paid.

(b)   Division of asset followed by gift of part

Where a donor splits an asset into parts and then makes a gift of the whole of a part without retaining an interest in that part then the gifts with reservation rules have previously been avoided. In this example Mr Douglas has divided Green Gables into a leasehold interest and a freehold reversion and then given the freehold reversion to his daughter Anne. Mr Douglas and his wife continue to occupy Green Gables under the leasehold interest.

Until FA 1999 this would have been outside the rules for gifts with reservation, although unless the grant of the lease and the subsequent gift of the freehold reversion were independent transactions, the Revenue might have sought to use the associated operations rules of s 268 to say that the grant of the lease and the gift of the freehold reversion were a single transaction occurring at the time of the gift of the freehold, so that the lease at a nominal rent would be a benefit retained by Mr Douglas. Under FA 1986 s 102A, from 9 March 1999 it is no longer possible to avoid the gifts with reservation rules by taking a leasehold interest and giving away the freehold (see explanatory note 6). Mr Douglas's gift of the freehold of Green Gables to Anne will therefore be treated as a gift with reservation.

(c)   Grant of lease followed by gift of freehold

In giving away a freehold reversion Douglas must not reserve a benefit in that gift. In the case of *Nichols v CIR 1975* it was held that where a gift was made of freehold land, subject to an obligation on the donee to grant an immediate lease back and to keep the property in full repair, this amounted to a gift with reservation. But in Mr Douglas's case he is paying a full commercial rent, so it is considered that the daughter's obligation to repair the property would be reflected in the rent and that no benefit would be regarded as having been reserved. The FA 1999 changes referred to in (b) above do not apply where the donor occupies the land to the exclusion of the donee for full consideration.

C.   Mrs Jones – pre-owned assets

(a)   Income tax liability on pre-owned asset

Mrs Jones has provided funds of £500,000 which have been used to buy the Cornwall property she now occupies. The appropriate rental value is:

$$£36,000 \times \frac{500,000}{900,000} = £20,000$$

which gives an income tax liability of:

£20,000 @ 40% = £8,000 per annum from 6 April 2009.

(See explanatory note 11)

(b)   Election to mitigate charge

Mrs Jones could elect by 31 January 2011, by completing form IHT500, that the Cornwall property is not subject to an income tax charge, but instead, for so long as she continues to occupy the property, the relevant proportion of the property value will be treated as part of her estate. The proportion is as above, that is:

$$\frac{\text{Consideration provided by chargeable person (£500,000)}}{\text{Value of property at valuation date (£900,000)}}$$

Valuation date for this purpose is the first date of occupation.

If Mrs Jones ceases to occupy the Cornwall property then, as for a gift with reservation, the appropriate proportion of the value of the property at the date she ceases to occupy will be included in her estate for the following seven years.

(See explanatory note 13)

(c)   Attribution of gift towards property now occupied

A charge to income tax arises because Mrs Jones has contributed towards a property she now occupies.

An absolute gift of cash is not normally subject to the inheritance tax gifts with reservation provisions. However under the pre-owned asset income tax rules a charge will apply where it is reasonable to attribute the gift as a contribution directly or indirectly, towards the acquisition of the property now occupied. This does not apply if the outright gift of money was made at least seven years before the taxpayer first occupied the premises. For Mrs Jones the period is only 2 years 2 months.

Occupation is a very wide term and could even include usage for storage or sole possession of the means of access linked with occasional use of the property. Incidental usage is not considered to be occupation. This could include:

- Stays not exceeding two weeks each year (one month if the owner is present and it is the owner's residence).

- Social visits that do not include overnight stays.

- Domestic visits eg babysitting the owner's children.

- Temporary stays eg for convalescence after medical treatment or to look after the owner whilst they are convalescing.

However if the property is a holiday home which is only used on an occasional basis by the owner then even occasional visits by the donor could be deemed to be occupational.

It would appear that Mrs Jones wishes to use the Cornwall property for a number of weeks each year. Unless she pays full market rent for that occupation (which would be liable to income tax in the hands of her daughter) she will be liable to a pre-owned asset income tax charge.

If her occupation was for less than one month per year no charge would arise provided her daughter lived in the property as her residence and was present, otherwise occupation could cause the charge to occur.

In practice it would be advisable to pay full market rent for limited occupation of holiday accommodation.

If Mrs Jones is unlikely to occupy the property for more than two or three years it would be beneficial to elect for inheritance tax to apply as there is a high probability that she would live more than seven years after vacating the property and therefore no tax charge would arise.

If Mrs Jones intends to remain in residence indefinitely it is possible that even 15+ years of charge to income tax would be less than the initial inheritance tax saving of £200,000 (£500,000 @ 40%). The actual inheritance tax payable would, of course, be higher if the value of the property increased over that period. For example if on the death of Mrs Jones the Cornwall property was worth £1,800,000 then the inheritance tax liability on her death in respect of her use of the pre-owned asset would be:

$$1,800,000 \times \frac{500,000}{900,000} = £1,000,000 @ 40\% = £400,000$$

Explanatory Notes

Associated operations

1. Where a transfer of value is made by associated operations carried out at different times, it is treated as made at the time of the last of them (s 268). For the meaning of 'associated operations' see Example 22.

2. Where any one or more of the earlier operations also constitutes a *transfer of value* made by the same transferor, the value transferred by the earlier operations is treated as reducing the value transferred by all the operations taken together (s 268).

3. Thus, the annual waivers in part A (b) of the example, being themselves *transfers of value*, albeit potentially exempt, reduce the value transferred by taking all the operations together. The fact that the waivers are not chargeable does not alter the fact that they were transfers of value (as distinct from chargeable transfers), a chargeable transfer being a transfer of value other than an exempt transfer (s 2(1)).

Ensuring that gifts are properly made

4. Care should always be taken to ensure that a gift is properly made. Whilst title to certain assets passes by delivery (eg a watch) there are legally proper ways of transferring title to other assets, such as company shares by a properly constituted and stamped form of transfer and freehold and leasehold properties by deed (and registration where appropriate). An intended but incomplete gift will not therefore be sufficient for tax purposes, although in fact the donee might enjoy the benefit of the gift. If the donor has done all in his power to perfect a gift, an omission by the donee will not make it imperfect for tax purposes (eg if the donor has delivered a properly constituted and stamped share transfer but the donee has failed to have it registered or the company concerned has refused to register it). A cheque only constitutes a valid gift after it has been cleared by the donor's bank, so that if the donor dies before the cheque has been presented the gift is not complete.

    In the 2004 case before the Special Commissioners of Sellars & Anor (SpC 401) it was held that where a building society account was changed to the name of a mother and two daughters, but mother was the only person who made transfers into the account and made withdrawals, that the whole of the balance remained in mother's estate even though one third of the interest had been declared for income tax on the returns of each of the daughters. This was held to be a gift with reservation, not an account held as tenants in common.

    As far as loan waivers are concerned, HMRC Capital Taxes consider that they are not effective for inheritance tax unless the waiver was effected by deed.

Gifts with reservation

5. FA 1986 ss 102 and 103 introduced anti-avoidance legislation relating to gifts with reservation and debts, applicable to events occurring on and after 18 March 1986. These rules apply where a donor reserves a benefit from a gift or subsequently enjoys the benefit of the gifted property (eg gift of a house that the donor continues to occupy, or a settlement into a discretionary trust where the settlor is also a beneficiary).

    Under these rules a gift with reservation is treated in the same way as any other gift at the time it is made, but special rules apply on the death of the donor. If the reservation was released more than seven years before death then no charge arises on death. If the reservation was released within seven years before death then the gift is taxed as if it had been made at the time of release, on the basis of its value at that time (but without the benefit of any annual exemptions), even though the original gift will also be taxed if it was made within seven years before death. There are regulations to eliminate the double charge to tax. For details see Example 19.

    Debts are not deductible from the estate of a deceased person unless they were incurred for full consideration for the deceased's own use or benefit and were not created out of property derived from the deceased as a transfer of value or part of an associated operation. Again there are regulations to prevent double charges to tax, which are dealt with in Example 20.

6. In relation to gifts of land, the gifts with reservation rules are extended by FA 1986 ss 102A, 102B and 102C. The background to the legislation is the 1999 House of Lords' decision in *Ingram v CIR* and the effect of old estate duty law on the inheritance tax provisions.

    Some of the estate duty cases drew very fine distinctions. In *Chick v Commissioners of Stamp Duties of New South Wales* 1958, a farmer had made a gift of grazing land to his son in 1934 and in 1935 the land was brought into a partnership in which the farmer was a partner. The farmer was deemed to have reserved a benefit in the land because of his partnership interest. The Chick case was followed by legislation under which no reservation was assumed if the later benefits were only available because of full consideration provided by the donor. In *Munro v Commissioners of Stamp Duties of New South Wales 1934*, a farmer gave away land but continued as a partner in the family partnership that farmed the land. He was considered not to have given the land itself, but his interest in the land subject to the rights of the partnership, so that no benefit had been retained. The difference between the two cases is that the Chick gift was initially unfettered but the farmer later enjoyed a benefit from the gifted property, whereas the Munro gift was subject to the partnership interest at the time it was made. It was stated by Lord Simonds in *St Aubyn v AG 1952* that a donor does not bring himself within the provisions 'by retaining something which he has never given'.

This principle was considered in the case of *Ingram v CIR*, decided by the House of Lords in 1999. Lady Ingram conveyed the freehold of her property to a bare trustee, who then granted a lease to her and conveyed the freehold reversion to a trust for the family. The High Court held that there was no reservation of benefit, although it was also held that someone could not grant a lease to a nominee, since this would amount to contracting with himself. The Court of Appeal held that the lease was a nullity as the interposing of a mere nominee did not alter the fact that Lady Ingram was effectively both landlord and tenant of the property (*Rye v Rye* 1962). It was also noted that a nominee cannot effectively contract with his principal (following the Scottish case of *Kildrummy (Jersey) Ltd v CIR* 1990). This was overruled by the House of Lords, where it was held that 'if the benefits which the donor continues to enjoy are by virtue of property which was never comprised in the gift, he has not reserved any benefit out of the property of which he disposed'. The House of Lords unanimously declined to follow Kildrummy, stating that 'a trustee in English law is not an agent for his beneficiary'.

This decision has led to the changes in the law referred to above where a gift is made of an interest in land (for details see Example 19 explanatory notes 5 to 7).

Pre-owned assets

7. With effect from 6 April 2005 a free-standing income tax charge applies to the benefit of using an asset that was formerly owned by the taxpayer. A similar charge will apply to the use of assets at low cost or to the use of assets purchased with funds provided by the taxpayer. The charge applies to tangible and intangible assets.

8. The income tax charge does not apply:

   (i) To property given away before 18 March 1986 (FA 2004 Sch 15.3(2); 15.6(2) and 15.8(2)).

   (ii) If the property was transferred to a spouse/civil partner (or to a former spouse/civil partner under a Court Order) (Sch 15.10(1)(c)). This also applied where the property is held in trust and the spouse/civil partner or former spouse/civil partner has an interest in possession (Sch 15.10(1)(d)).

   (iii) If the property remains within the estate of the former owner under the 'Gift with Reservation' rules (Sch 15.11). Note that FA 2006 s 80 amended FA 2004 Sch 15.11 with retrospective effect to provide an exception from the exemption provisions in respect of some interests in possession including those which arose before the exception was introduced.

   (iv) If the property was sold by the taxpayer at an arm's length price (Sch 15.10(1)(a)).

   (v) Where the assets of an estate have been redirected by a deed of variation (ss 142–147) then the deed of variation applies to the asset from date of death for the pre-owned asset rules (Schs 15–16).

   (vi) To property transferred into an interest in possession trust for the benefit of the former owner. This is excluded from the income tax charge because the property remains in the estate of the donor for inheritance tax purposes (Sch 15.10). However the exemption ceases when the interest in possession comes to an end (Sch 15.10(2)) although this would now amount to a gift with reservation under FA 1986 s 102ZA.

   (vii) Where the gift is of property and the former owner has given part of their interest to someone with whom they share occupation or the former owner needs to move back into the gifted property following changes in circumstances (Sch 15.11(1)). These rules are the same as gift with reservation rules for inheritance tax.

(viii) The disposal was an outright gift covered by annual exemption, small gifts or was for the maintenance of the family (Sch 15.10(1)(d), (e)).

(ix) An outright gift of money made more than seven years before the first date of enjoyment of property/chattels acquired with the funds will not be deemed to be consideration (Sch 15.10(2)(c)).

(x) Use of a commercial equity release scheme.

9. The pre-owned asset charge does not apply in any fiscal year:

(a) Where the former owner is not resident in the UK, or

(b) Where the former owner is resident in the UK but domiciled elsewhere for inheritance tax purposes and the property is not UK property, or

(c) Where the former owner was previously domiciled outside the UK for inheritance tax purposes the charge does not apply to property disposed of before becoming domiciled in the UK (Sch 15.12).

10. The income tax charge applies to the use of land or enjoyment of land, chattels and intangible assets.

For the charge to apply to land the taxpayer must:

● occupy the land (wholly or with others) and either

● the disposal condition, or

● the contribution condition must apply (Sch 15.3(1)).

The disposal condition is that after 17 March 1986 the taxpayer owned the relevant property or property the disposal of which has directly or indirectly funded the relevant property and has disposed of all or part of that interest otherwise than by an excluded transaction (see note 8 above).

The contribution condition is that the taxpayer has since 17 March 1986 contributed directly or indirectly to the purchase of the relevant property otherwise than by an excluded transaction (see note 8 above).

11. The charge for land is calculated by taking the appropriate rental value less any amount that the chargeable person is legally obliged to pay the owner of the relevant land in the period in respect of its occupation. The appropriate rental value is:

$$R \times \frac{DV}{V}$$

where:

R is the rent that might reasonably be expected to be obtained on a year to year letting where tenant pays all rates, charges and council taxes and the landlord bears the cost of repairs, maintenance and insurance.

DV is the contribution by the former owner that can reasonably be attributed to the cost of the relevant property.

If the property, or a property that this property replaced, was previously owned by the taxpayer, it is its value on valuation date. If the taxpayer only owned, or disposed of, a part of the land, it is the relevant proportion of its value.

V is the value of the relevant land at the valuation date.

For example, John gave a property worth £100,000 to his son Peter in 1994. Peter sold the property for £350,000 in 1999 buying a further property for £400,000. John moves into the relevant property in 2007 when it had an annual rental value of £36,000. The contribution that could reasonably be attributed to the gifted property would be:

$$\frac{350,000}{400,000}$$

(being the proportion of the cost of the relevant property funded by John's gift)

That proportion is then applied to the annual rental value of the property as at the valuation date of £36,000.

$$\frac{350,000}{400,000} \times 36,000 = £31,500 @ 40\% = £12,600 \text{ pa tax payable at the 40\% rate}$$

Contrast this with the example at C where cash was given. In the example the gift of cash is compared with the current value of the property, whereas it would appear that if property is given then the DV value is increased by the increase in value of the property between gift and commencement of enjoyment. Although the legislation is unclear in the case of a cash gift it is difficult to see how any increase in the value attributed to the investment decision of the recipient can be said to be reasonably attributed to the donor of the cash.

Valuation date is set out in SI 2005/724 para 2 being 6 April in the relevant year, or if later the first day in the year on which enjoyment of the asset occurs.

The first valuation date occurs when use commences, and thereafter the valuation date is the first valuation date for a further four years and then the valuation on the previous fifth anniversary.

The income tax payable is calculated by adding the appropriate rental value to the taxable income of the donor.

In the case of chattels the charge is based upon 5% pa of the value of the chattel at valuation day with similar rules to land applying to replacement chattels and cash.

For intangibles a charge only arises where they are held within a settlement and the settler retains an interest. Again the liability is based upon 5% pa of the value at valuation date.

Where the asset is only enjoyed for part of a year the charge is reduced accordingly. There is no charge if open market rent is paid for use of the asset, and the charge is reduced by payments made under a legal obligation for the use of the asset.

12. If the aggregate notional values before contribution do not exceed £5,000 then this is *de minimus* and there is no charge (Sch 15.13).

    There are provisions preventing a double charge to income tax under both the benefit in kind rules and the pre-owned asset rules (Sch. 15.18).

13. Where a taxpayer is potentially chargeable to income tax by reference to their enjoyment of any land, or chattels, or intangible property for the first time, then they may make an election. The effect of which is that the asset is deemed to be in their estate for inheritance tax and therefore no income tax charge arises. This is a deeming provision, the asset does not actually form part of their estate and therefore there is no uplift in value for capital gains tax when death occurs.

    If the taxpayer permanently ceases to have occupation or use and enjoyment of the asset then the gifts with reservation rules apply so that a potentially exempt transfer is deemed to have occurred at the cessation of use. If more than seven years have elapsed since last enjoyment of the asset then no charge arises.

    The election is required by 31 January following the end of the fiscal year of first use. If use first commenced in 2005/06 or earlier the election was required by 31 January 2007 (Sch 15.21–23). Schedule 15.23(3)(a) expressly permits HMRC to accept late elections. For HMRC's approach see: Income tax and pre-owned assets guidance section 3 which can be found at http://www.hmrc.gov.uk/poa/poa_liable.htm.

Where the whole of the asset would not be attributed to the donor then a similar restriction will apply to the chargeable amount; ie: Chargeable proportion of Asset Value is:

$$\text{Value} \times \frac{DV}{V}$$

where DV and V have the meaning set out in note 11 above.

Value is at death (if use continues) or at cessation of use if within seven years of death.

14. The charge is intended to penalise users of inheritance tax avoidance schemes, such as the double trust home loan scheme (the intention of which is to remove the value of the principal private residence from the donors' estate but to enable continued use of the property), or, where the full consideration for the use of the asset is negligible as compared with the open market value of the asset.

15. However, the charge will also apply to situations where a taxpayer would not expect a charge to arise. For example where a donor gives away assets (eg cash) and then in the future uses property acquired with those assets without paying a full commercial consideration, and does not fall within any of the exceptions for inheritance tax set out at note 4 (i) or pre-owned asset exceptions at note 8. Previously if the gift was at least seven years before the death of the donor there were no tax consequences. Now an income tax charge will arise.

Example

John gave £300,000 in cash to his daughter, Wendy, on the occasion of her marriage in 2002. She used £200,000 to buy a picture. In May 2008 Wendy moves to Australia on a temporary contract for three years. She leaves the picture with John who hangs it in his hall. The open market value as at May 2008 is £500,000. Wendy returns in May 2011 reclaiming possession of the picture. John is still alive in 2018. Assume an Official Rate of 5% throughout, and that John pays tax at 40%.

The valuation date is May 2008. The charge for 2008/09 is:

$$11/12 \times 5\% \times 500,000 \times \frac{200,000\,(DV)}{500,000\,(V)} = 9.166 \text{ @ } 40\% = £3,666$$

For 2009/10 and 2010/11 a full year's charge of £10,000 @ 40% = £4,000 applies

For 2011/12 the charge is:

$$1/12 \times 5\% \times 500,000 \times \frac{200,000\,(DV)}{500,000\,(V)} = 834$$

Tax charged is NIL.

(Amounts below £5,000 are not charged)

The cash/picture cannot be included in John's estate because Wendy took full bona fide possession and enjoyment of the cash in 2002. Because the picture is not included in the estate of John for inheritance tax it is not excluded from the pre-owned asset charge. An income tax charge arises because John has the use of property purchased with funds provided by him within the last seven years.

The income tax charge would be avoided if John elected by 31 January 2010 for gifts with reservation rules for inheritance tax to apply. As he is alive in 2018 no charge would ever arise.

Alternatively John could pay full rental value for the use of the picture. If he is responsible for insurance this could be very low.

16. See also the companion book, Tolley's Taxwise I 2008/09, for calculation of the rate of income tax payable by a donor.

Question

Agnes Brown was a wealthy widow who doted on her nephew Simon. Having not made any gifts previously, she decided in 2001 to begin passing on some of her wealth to Simon and on 17 October 2001 she made a gift to him of a number of investments as follows:

1.   3,000 shares out of her holding of 16,500 shares in Brown Retailing Ltd, a trading company with an issued share capital of 30,000 shares. The other 13,500 shares are already held by Simon.

2.   15,000 shares in Landy plc, which were quoted at 180–188p with marked bargains at 180 and 182p.

On 11 November 2003, following the birth of Simon's first child, Agnes settled her remaining shares in Brown Retailing Ltd on discretionary trust, including herself, Simon and his child amongst the class of beneficiaries.

Feeling that perhaps she had favoured Simon to an unfair extent, she gave £100,000 to her niece Pauline on 21 December 2003.

On 10 March 2004 upon the advice of her professional adviser, she excluded herself from all benefit under the discretionary trust dated 11 November 2003.

An offer of £1 million for the whole of the issued share capital of Brown Retailing Ltd was received on 14 November 2006. This was accepted by all shareholders. The discretionary trust reinvested its proceeds into quoted shares which were all held on 26 September 2009.

Agnes died on 30 September 2008, leaving an estate valued at £700,000 including the following assets:

(i)   a 30% holding valued at £50,000 in Blue Ltd, an unquoted investment company;

(ii)   a 5% holding valued at £60,000 in Pink plc, a trading company on the Alternative Investment Market;

(iii) a 60% holding valued at £100,000 in Green Ltd, an unquoted investment company; and

(iv)   a 40% holding valued at £200,000 in Black Ltd, an unquoted trading company.

Under the terms of her will Agnes added a further £100,000 cash to the discretionary trust. The rest of her estate was divided equally between Simon and Pauline.

On 26 September 2009 the trustees of the discretionary trust appointed £50,000 from the cash received from the executors to Simon on the basis that he was to pay any tax due.

The value of an ordinary share in Brown Retailing Ltd at the relevant times was as follows:

	17.10.01 £	11.11.03 £	10.3.04 £
75–100%	25	42	40
50–74%	20	31	30
25–49%	15	24	23
0–24%	10	16	15

There are no other relevant transfers of shares in Brown Retailing Ltd.

Calculate the inheritance tax payable in respect of the above events.

Answer

Agnes Brown — inheritance tax position in lifetime

	£
17 October 2001	
Gifts to Simon:	
3,000 shares in Brown Retailing Ltd	
16,500 shares at £20 (55% holding)	330,000
13,500 shares at £15 (45% holding)	202,500
Loss to estate	127,500
Less: Business property relief 100%	
(see explanatory note 1)	127,500
Transfer of value	–
15,000 shares in Landy plc @ ½ (180 + 182) = 181p, giving transfer of value of	27,150
Less: Annual exemptions 2001/02 and 2000/01	6,000
Potentially exempt transfer	21,150
11 November 2003	
Settlement on discretionary trust	
13,500 shares in Brown Retailing Ltd	
at £24 per share (45% holding)	324,000
Less: Business property relief 100%	
(see explanatory note 2)	324,000
Transfer of value	–
21 December 2003	
Gift to Pauline	100,000
Less: Annual exemptions 2003/04 and 2002/03	6,000
Potentially exempt transfer	94,000
10 March 2004	
Release of reservation —	
13,500 shares in Brown Retailing Ltd at	
£23 per share (45% holding) – potentially	
exempt transfer (see explanatory note 4)	310,500

On death of Agnes Brown — 30 September 2008

	Gross £	Tax on 2008/09 scale £
Transfers within seven years before death:		
Accumulation in seven years before gift on 17 October 2001*	–	–
17 October 2001		
Gifts to Simon (see explanatory note 1):		
Shares in Brown Retailing Ltd 122,553		
Shares in Landy plc 26,097		
	148,650	–

Accumulation in seven years before transfer to trust on 11 November 2003 (to calculate additional tax only, cumulative transfers not affected — see explanatory note 2):

		Gross £	Tax on 2008/09 scale £
17 October 2001			
Gift previously potentially exempt		148,650	–
11 November 2003			
Settlement on discretionary trust as above	–		
Add business property relief no longer available			
(see explanatory note 2)			
	324,000		
Less: Annual exemptions 2003/04 and 2002/03	6,000	318,000	61,860*
		466,650	61,860

(* 466,650 – 312,000 = 154,650 @ 40%)

As death takes place between 4 and 5 years after the transfer, the tax payable is reduced by 40% to £61,860 × 60% = £ <u>37,116</u>.

Accumulation in seven years before gift to Pauline on 21 December 2003:

	Gross £	Tax on 2008/09 scale £
17 October 2001	148,650	–
11 November 2003 (see above)	–	–
21 December 2003		
Gift to Pauline (annual exemptions reallocated to trust as above —		
see explanatory note 2)	100,000	–*
	248,650	–*

(* 248,650 – 312,000 = Nil)

10 March 2004
   Release of reservation — total inheritance tax payable will be the
   higher of:
   (i)   Disregarding the original gift and charging the potentially
       exempt transfer on release, or
   (ii) Charging original gift and disregarding subsequent potentially
       exempt transfer.

	Gross £	Tax on 2008/09 scale £
Accumulation in seven years before gift on 17 October 2001	–	–
17 October 2001		
Gift to Simon — as above	148,650	–
11 November 2003		
Settlement on discretionary trust — ignored	–	–
21 December 2003		
Gift to Pauline — as above	100,000	–
10 March 2004		
Release of reservation		
Potentially exempt transfer now chargeable		
(13,500 shares @ £23 per share)	310,500	98,860*
	559,150	98,860

(* 559,150 – 312,000 = 247,150 @ 40%)

As death takes place between 4 and 5 years after release of reservation, tax payable is 60% × £98,860 = £59,316

The second calculation is as already calculated above, ie cumulative transfers of £466,650 and tax payable of £37,116

The tax due on death must then be taken into account in both calculations. In the first case, however, the lifetime transfers exceeded the nil threshold at death, so the tax payable on the death estate would be:

		£	£
30 September 2008 — death of Agnes Brown			
Estate on death		700,000	
Less: Business property relief			
100% × £60,000 (shares in Pink plc)	60,000		
100% × £200,000 (shares in Black Ltd)	200,000	260,000	
		440,000	
Tax @ 40%			176,000

In the second case the tax would be:

	Gross £	Tax on 2008/09 scale £
30 September 2008 — death of Agnes Brown — accumulation in seven years before death		
17 October 2001	148,650	–
11 November 2003 (see above)	–	–
21 December 2003	100,000	–
	248,650	–
Estate on death (less business property relief)	440,000	150,660*
	688,650	150,660

(* 688,650 – 312,000 = 376,650 @ 40%)

Total tax payable on lifetime gifts and death is:

First calculation	(59,316 + 176,000)	£235,316
Second calculation	(37,116 + 150,660)	£187,776

The first calculation therefore shows the higher total tax liability, and inheritance tax is therefore payable as follows:

	£
By Agnes Brown on creation of discretionary trust	–
By Simon	–
By Pauline	–
By trustees of discretionary trust	62,196
By personal representatives	176,000
On appointment by discretionary trust to Simon on 26 September 2008 (being within two years of death — s 144 — see explanatory note 5)	–

Explanatory Notes

Same day transfers

1. Where two or more transfers of value are made on the same day, the annual exemption is apportioned between them (s 19(3)(b)). Business property relief is deducted in arriving at the amount of a transfer of value. The treatment of the annual exemption in relation to potentially exempt transfers outlined in Example 1 makes the calculation of the potentially exempt transfers by Agnes Brown in this example particularly difficult. The gift of the shares in Brown Retailing Ltd on 17 October 2001 qualifies for 100% business property relief (see Example 25 part A(c) for rates of business property relief) so that the transfer of value is reduced to nil as shown. On the same day as the gift of the Brown Retailing Ltd shares, Agnes made the gift of the shares in Landy plc, the transfer of value being £27,150, which is not eligible for business property relief. Annual exemptions for 2001/02 and 2000/01 are therefore allocated to the gift of shares in Landy plc.

    When Agnes Brown died on 30 September 2008, the shares in Brown Retailing Ltd no longer qualified for business property relief. It is understood to be the view of HMRC that the annual exemption should then be reallocated between the gifts as follows:

$$\text{Brown Retailing Ltd shares} \frac{127,500}{154,650} \times 6,000 \qquad \text{£4,947}$$

$$\text{Landy plc shares} \frac{27,150}{154,650} \times 6,000 \qquad \text{£1,053}$$

The revised potentially exempt transfers would then be:

Brown Retailing Ltd shares	127,500	– 4,947	122,553
Landy plc shares	27,150	– 1,053	26,097
			£148,650

Alternatively it could be argued that the original allocation of the annual exemption stands despite the withdrawal of business property relief. The gifts to Simon would then be £127,500 in respect of the shares in Brown Retailing Ltd and £21,150 in respect of the shares in Landy plc. In this instance the tax position is the same in any event, as both gifts were made to Simon and there is no inheritance tax liability. However, if a tax liability arose payable by different persons, this point may be taken. The total gifts to Simon would still amount to £148,650 and this amount is included in subsequent calculations.

Business property relief

2.   For detailed notes on business property relief see Example 25. The relief is not available when calculating the tax on a potentially exempt transfer that becomes chargeable as a result of the donor's death within seven years if the relevant conditions are no longer satisfied (s 113A(1)). Similarly, where business property relief has been given against a transfer that was a chargeable transfer in lifetime, the relief is not available when calculating any additional tax payable as a result of the death of the transferor within seven years unless the conditions for the relief are satisfied at that time (s 113A(2)) (see Example 25 part A(c)). Note that the withdrawal of business property relief on a transfer that was a chargeable transfer in lifetime only affects the calculation of any additional tax payable on that transfer. The original chargeable transfer is taken into account in the accumulation for the purpose of working out the position on later transfers and on the death estate. In this example the original chargeable transfer to the discretionary trust on 11 November 2003 qualified for 100% relief so it did not increase the cumulative total at that time. The cumulative total taken into account in calculating the tax on the later gift to Pauline at 24.3 therefore shows the 11 November transfer at nil. For a further illustration see Example 25.

The wording of the legislation supports the view that business property relief is effective immediately to the extent that the original transfer is covered by the annual exemption and that only the balance can be affected by the withdrawal of business property relief if the donor dies within seven years. For transfers on or after 28 November 1995, subsection (7A) was introduced into s 113A, which provides that when applying the rules for withdrawing business property relief on transfers within seven years before death, the relief is disregarded in establishing whether there is a potentially exempt or chargeable transfer. The reason for the change is that it had been contended that a transfer that initially qualified for 100% business property relief became a transfer of nil, and was therefore wholly within the £3,000 annual exempt limit, so no chargeable or potentially exempt transfer remained to be reconsidered if the donor died within seven years and no withdrawal of relief could therefore take place. The Revenue did not agree with this view, and the FA 1996 change was made 'for the removal of any doubt'. A similar change was made to s 124A (in subsection 7A) in relation to agricultural property relief.

The change is intended only to establish that a transfer exists, and does not seek to quantify the amount of the transfer. It is considered, therefore, that it does not affect the view stated above that if a slice of the original transfer is covered by the annual exemption, the business property relief on that slice cannot later be withdrawn. This is not relevant where the original transfer qualified for 100% relief, because the annual exemption would not be used against a nil transfer.

Care needs to be taken in relation to the treatment of the annual exemption when business property relief is withdrawn. Note 1 deals with the situation where the 100% relief is withdrawn from a transfer that was originally potentially exempt, ie the gift to Simon of shares in Brown Retailing Ltd, with the additional complication that another transfer was made on the same day. The example also illustrates the 100% relief being withdrawn from a transfer that would otherwise have been a chargeable transfer, ie the transfer to the discretionary trust on 11 November 2003. The annual exemptions of 2003/04 and 2002/03 were originally given against the 2003/04 gift to Pauline. When the business property relief is withdrawn at Agnes's death, the annual exemptions will be reallocated to the transfer to the discretionary trust, since the trust transfer occurred earlier in the tax year than the transfer to Pauline.

3.   No business property relief is available on Agnes Brown's holdings in:

Blue Ltd — an *investment* company

Green Ltd — an *investment* company.

Business property relief of 100% is available on the holding in Pink plc as it is a trading company on the Alternative Investment Market (AIM), and on the investment in Black Ltd, an unquoted trading company.

Double charges relief

4. The situations when a double charge to tax occurs and the reliefs under the Inheritance Tax (Double Charges Relief) Regulations 1987 (SI 1987/1130) are dealt with in Examples 19 and 20. The regulations apply to the release of reservation on 10 March 2003 in this example, when Agnes Brown excludes herself from benefit under the discretionary trust. The release is specifically treated as a potentially exempt transfer by FA 1986 s 102(4), despite the fact that someone else's estate has not been increased, nor has an interest in possession in the trust been created.

In this example no tax was payable by the trustees of the discretionary settlement in the settlor's lifetime. If any lifetime tax had been payable on such a transfer, then where, as in this example, the first calculation produced the higher figure, the lifetime tax (up to but not exceeding the part of the death tax payable relating to the transfer) would be deducted from the tax payable by the trustees following Agnes Brown's death (see Example 20 explanatory note 3).

Post-death variations of a will

5. The assets of the discretionary trust following Agnes Brown's death consist of shares acquired on the takeover of Brown Retailing Ltd in November 2006 and £100,000 added in cash under the terms of Agnes Brown's will. The appointment of £50,000 to Simon on 26 September 2009 is in cash, the shares being retained in full. Accordingly it is a variation of the property settled by will within two years of the date of death and is treated as a disposition at death for inheritance tax and not as a distribution out of the discretionary trust (s 144). (Section 144 applies where a distribution is made out of property settled by will within two years after the death and before any interest in possession has subsisted in the property. The distribution is treated as if it had been made under the terms of the will.) See Example 60 explanatory note 9 for a problem where such a distribution is made within the first three months after death.

6. For detailed notes on post-death variations of a will see Example 34.

Question

A.

Relief from inheritance tax is available on 'relevant business property'.

(a)   What is relevant business property?

(b)   What types of business do not qualify for this relief?

(c)   What is the nature of the relief and at what rates is it given?

B.

Relief from inheritance tax is also available for 'agricultural property'.

(a)   Under what circumstances is a transferor entitled to inheritance tax relief when transferring agricultural property and what is the nature of the relief?

(b)   Is the relief available to a transferor of shares or debentures in a farming company?

(c)   Whiteacre is a farm of 200 acres which for the last ten years has been owned and farmed by Arthur personally with assistance from his son.

It has been proposed that Arthur should form a partnership with his son because of his advancing age, failing health and the necessity of providing for his wife when he dies.

Arthur would then grant a lease of the land at full rent to that partnership so that on his death the land will be valued at tenanted value.

The current agricultural value of the land is £2,000 per acre vacant possession; £1,400 per acre tenanted.

Advise Arthur as to the viability of the above proposal, quantifying the value chargeable to inheritance tax on Whiteacre on his subsequent death.

(d)   X owned 800 acres of freehold farmland known as Greenacre let to and farmed by the partnership of X himself, Mrs X and their son Y. The tenancy was granted in 1973.

In July 2008 X died leaving his interest in Greenacre to his son Y (subject to Y paying the inheritance tax thereon). It was valued (tenanted) at £479,000. X left the residue of his estate (including his interest in the partnership) to his wife. He had not made any previous lifetime gifts.

After an accident on the farm Y, who was unmarried, died in September 2008.

Y's estate consisted of:

	£
Greenacre Farm (let to the farming partnership of himself and his mother)	479,000
Interest in the farming partnership	60,000
Other assets	76,000

Compute the inheritance tax payable

(i)   on the death of X

(ii)   on the death of Y assuming he had not made any lifetime transfers and that he left the whole of his estate to his mother.

Answer

A. Business property relief

(a) Relevant business property

Relevant business property means (s 105):

(i) A sole trader's business, or a partnership share, including professions and vocations.

(ii) Unquoted *securities* of a company which, together with any unquoted *shares* of the company (including related property in both instances), give the transferor control immediately before the transfer.

(iii) *Any* unquoted *shares* in a company.

(iv) Quoted shares and/or securities of a company which, together with any related property, give the transferor control immediately before the transfer.

(v) Land, buildings, plant or machinery which immediately before the transfer were used wholly or mainly for the purposes of a business carried on by a company of which the transferor then had control, or by a partnership of which he was then a partner.

(vi) Any land or buildings, machinery or plant which, immediately before the transfer, was used wholly or mainly for the purposes of a business carried on by the transferor and were settled property in which he was then beneficially entitled to an interest in possession.

Quoted shares and securities are defined as shares and securities listed on a recognised stock exchange (ss 105(1ZA), 113A(3B)). Shares or securities on the Alternative Investment Market (AIM) are treated as unlisted and therefore qualify as unquoted under (ii) and (iii) above.

In the case of *CIR v Mallender and others (exors of Drury-Lowe decd)* (2001), it was held that an asset (which in this case was land) used as security for a guarantee was not itself used in the business and was not therefore part of the relevant business property.

The relevant business property concerned must have been owned by the transferor throughout the two years preceding the transfer (s 106) or be property replacing relevant business property where the combined period of ownership of the original and replacement property is at least two years out of the last five years (but relief is then granted only on the lower of the value of the original or replacement property) (s 107). Property acquired as a result of death is deemed to have been owned from the date of death, or for property acquired by a spouse, from the date the deceased spouse acquired it (s 108). The two year rule does not apply where the property was eligible for business property relief on an earlier transfer and either the earlier transfer or the subsequent transfer was made on the death of the transferor (s 109). Where a person starts up a new business, however, (rather than inherits it) and then dies within two years, business property relief is not available.

(b) Non-qualifying businesses

A business, or an interest in a business, or shares in or securities of a company, are not relevant business property if the business, or as the case may be, the business of the company, consists wholly or mainly of:

(i) Dealing in securities, stocks or shares (except for market makers and discount houses)

(ii) Dealing in land or buildings

(iii) Making or holding investments (see explanatory note 21 re land which is let).

George & Anor (Exors of Stedman dec'd) v IRC concerned a claim for business property relief by the executors where the deceased owned 85% of the shares in a company carrying on the business of running a caravan park. The Inland Revenue contended the business of the company was making or holding investments. The Court of Appeal allowed the executors' claim on the ground that making or holding investments was only one (and not the main) component of a composite business.

(c)   Nature and amount of relief

The relief applies to transfers of value in lifetime or on death or to the 10 yearly charge on discretionary trusts, the value attributable to relevant business property being reduced by 100% in respect of (a) (i) to (iii) above and 50% in respect of (a) (iv) to (vi) (s 104).

Before 6 April 1996, unquoted shares qualified for relief at only 50% unless, together with related property, they gave the transferor control of *more* than 25% of the votes of the company (and the 25% control had to have been held *throughout* the two years before the transfer, or shorter period under the successions rules in (a) above — s 109A). For chargeable events occurring on or after 6 April 1996 (lifetime transfers, tax uplift on death, etc), 100% relief is available on qualifying unquoted shares regardless of the size of the holding.

The relief is applied automatically without the need for a claim and is given before applying any other relief (eg annual exemptions, as indicated below).

Meaning of control

Control means control of voting on all questions affecting the company as a whole. In considering which shares give control care must be taken with shares that only have votes in special circumstances (eg preference shares entitled to votes when the preference dividends are in arrears). When voting rights relate only to the question of winding-up, or to questions primarily affecting shares of a particular class, then such rights are ignored (s 269(4)). Otherwise the rights are included in determining control. For example, say an unquoted company had a total issued share capital of £100, consisting of 25 ordinary shares of £1 held by A, and 75 preference shares of £1 held by B, the preference shares having votes when the preference dividends were in arrear and on reduction of capital. Neither A nor B *controls* the votes on *all* questions affecting the company as a whole, so neither would qualify for business property relief on any land etc owned personally and used by the company. If the voting rights on the preference shares related only to winding-up, A would then control the company and would be entitled to the 50% relief on land etc owned personally. B's position would be unchanged.

Death of donor within seven years

For lifetime gifts made after 17 March 1986, whether chargeable at the time or potentially exempt, where the death of the donor occurs within seven years, business property relief is available when calculating the tax/additional tax arising as a result of the death providing that:

1.   the original property (or qualifying replacement property — see below) was owned by the transferee throughout the period beginning with the date of the chargeable transfer and ending with the death of the transferor, and

2.   immediately before the death of the donor the original property (or qualifying replacement property) is relevant business property in the hands of the transferee (ignoring the two year period of ownership rule), except that where property qualified as a transfer out of a controlling holding, it is only necessary for the transferee to retain what he was given (which may not give control). In order for unquoted shares to be relevant business property they must still be unquoted when the donor dies (s 113A(3A)).

If the transferee dies before the donor then the property must qualify at the date of his death rather than the date of the donor's death.

Proportionate relief is available where only part of the property is owned at the date of death (s 113A).

To the extent that the original transfer was covered by annual exemptions, whether the balance was chargeable at the time or potentially exempt, it is considered that the business property relief relating to that part of the transfer is not affected by the death of the donor within seven years. See Example 24 explanatory note 2, and the illustration in that example.

It should be noted that if business property relief is not available in calculating additional tax on a *chargeable* lifetime transfer resulting from the donor's death within seven years, it is only that tax calculation that is affected. The donor's total of cumulative transfers is not altered.

> ## Example
>
> A donor who had made no other transfers settled a building worth £324,000 and used for business purposes into a discretionary trust in July 2008. If it qualified for 50% business property relief, £12,000 of the transfer, reduced to £6,000 after 50% business property relief, would be covered by annual exemptions and the balance of £312,000 would, after 50% business property relief, be a chargeable transfer of £156,000. No tax would be payable because the transfer was below the then nil threshold of £312,000. If the donor died within seven years and the trustees had in the meantime disposed of the property, they would pay tax on £312,000 less the nil threshold at the date of the donor's death, but the donor's lifetime transfers to be aggregated with any subsequent transfers and with his estate would remain at £156,000.
>
> By comparison, if the donor had instead gifted the same building to his son in July 2008 it would be a potentially exempt transfer. On the donor's subsequent death within seven years (son having sold the property), the son would similarly be liable to tax on £312,000 less the nil threshold at the date of the donor's death, but the lifetime transfer to be aggregated with subsequent transfers and with the donor's estate would be £312,000, the business property relief available at the time of the gift not being available to compute the *chargeable transfer* resulting from the donor's death.

Qualifying replacement property

Provision is made for property that replaces all or part of the original property to satisfy the continuing ownership test up to the donor's (or donee's) death providing the replacement property also qualifies as business property, and providing the whole of the proceeds of the original property are used in the purchase of the replacement property within three years after the disposal of the original property, or such longer period as HMRC may allow (s 113B).

If unquoted shares in trading companies (for example on AIM) are sold and replaced with other such shares, then it is understood that the new shares will be treated as replacement property under s 107(1). Replacement shares or property must not be acquired in advance of the disposal of the original property.

Excepted assets

For the purpose of calculating the relief the value of the relevant business property excludes *excepted assets*, ie assets which were neither used wholly or mainly for the purposes of the business throughout the two years preceding the transfer, nor required at the time of the transfer for future use for those purposes.

See the Special Commissioners' case of *Barclays Bank Trust Co Ltd* (SpC 158) for the denial of relief to the extent that there were substantial cash balances held within a company. Note also the Special Commissioners' case of *Farmer & Giles (Farmer's Executors) v CIR* 1999 (SpC 216), which held that in determining whether assets were relevant business property the whole business should be considered 'in the round'. This includes turnover, profits and assets used in the business and investment sides of the business. It could also include time spent by the owners, employees and others on the respective parts of the business. It would appear that if a single set of accounts is prepared for the whole business, there is unified management and the majority of the above tests point to business, then there is a single business for inheritance tax, and let property within the balance sheet is not therefore treated as an excepted asset but as an integral part of the qualifying business.

B.   **Agricultural property relief**

(a)   **Availability of agricultural property relief**

Agricultural property relief is available on the transfer of agricultural property (that is, agricultural land or pasture; also woodland and any building used in the intensive rearing of livestock or fish if the occupation of the woodland or building is ancillary to that of the agricultural land or pasture; and also such cottages, farm buildings and farmhouses occupied with the agricultural land as are of a character appropriate to the property) (s 115).

The cultivation of short rotation coppice (ie the harvesting of trees planted at high density at intervals of less than ten years) is regarded as agriculture, therefore the land used for this purpose is agricultural land and ancillary buildings are farm buildings (FA 1995 s 154).

Agricultural property relief is also available on land taken out of farming and dedicated to wildlife habitats under the Government Habitat Schemes, together with buildings used for the management of the land (s 124C).

The provisions for agricultural property relief are very similar to the rules for business property relief, in that the agricultural value is reduced by (s 116):

(i)	Where the transferor had the right to vacant possession immediately before the transfer or the right to obtain such possession within the next twelve months, extended to 24 months by HMRC Concession F17; or (also by Concession F17) the property is valued at an amount broadly equivalent to the vacant possession value	100%
(ii)	Where the agricultural property transferred is let on a tenancy granted on or after 1 September 1995 (including successions to tenancies following the death of the previous tenant on or after that date – see explanatory note 14)	100%
(iii)	Where the transferor has been beneficially entitled to his interest in the property since before 10 March 1981 and satisfies certain conditions (see explanatory note 10)	100%
(iv)	Otherwise.	50%

For transfers before 10 March 1992 the rates of relief were 50% for the first and third categories and 30% otherwise.

The percentage deduction only applies to the agricultural value of the property transferred, ie its value on the assumption that the property was subject to a perpetual covenant prohibiting its use otherwise than as agricultural property. In arriving at the agricultural value any loan secured on the agricultural property must be deducted.

Meaning of agricultural land or pasture

The term 'agricultural land or pasture' is given the narrow meaning of bare land. Therefore to obtain relief for any farmhouse etc, it is necessary to show that its occupation is ancillary to that of agricultural land (*Starke (Brown's Exors) v CIR* 1994). Furthermore in *Exor of Higginson v IRC* 2002 it was held that the farmhouse must be of a character and size appropriate to the property and the requirements of the farming activities conducted on the agricultural land.

The agricultural value of qualifying for agricultural relief of a farmhouse which is a historic building in an attractive location with a value as a residence independently of its merits as a farmhouse may be much lower than the open market value of the property as in *Lloyds TSB Private Banking Plc v Peter Twiddy (Inland Revenue Capital Taxes)* (10 October 2005, unreported), where the agricultural value was 30% less than its market value. Another decision can be found in *Arnander v HMRC* [2006]

STC (SCD) 800 in which the Special Commissioner held that a seven bedroom Grade 2* listed manor house owned together with 110 acres of agricultural land failed to attract relief.

A further recent case on the interaction of farmhouses and agricultural property relief is *Lloyds TSB (personal representatives of Antrobus dec'd) v IRC 2002* (SpC 336). This case set out five principles which had been established for deciding whether a farmhouse is of a character appropriate to the property. The requirement that the buildings are occupied for agricultural purposes is satisfied if they are tenanted by a person employed solely for agricultural purposes, or by retired farm workers or their widow(er)s, and such occupation is a statutorily protected tenancy or the lease was granted to the employee for life as part of his/her terms of employment.

In the case of *Rosser v IRC* (2003) SpC 368 the Inland Revenue refused a claim to agricultural property relief on a house and barn owned by the deceased on the basis that they were not agricultural land. The case was subsequently referred to the Special Commissioners who allowed the appeal in part — the barn was of a character appropriate to the property and was owned and occupied for the relevant period. Relief was granted on the barn but not the house.

Qualifying conditions

The agricultural property must at the time of the transfer have been either:

(i)   occupied by the transferor for the purposes of agriculture throughout the period of two years ending with the date of the transfer or have replaced other agricultural property which, together with the replacement property, was occupied for agricultural purposes for at least two years out of the last five years ending with the date of transfer, or

(ii)   owned by the transferor throughout the period of *seven years* ending with the date of transfer and occupied for the purposes of agriculture by him or another throughout that period. In the case of replacement property this condition is satisfied if the other property and the replacement property were owned by him and occupied for the purposes of agriculture by himself or another for at least seven years out of the period of ten years ending with the date of transfer.

The two year rule in (i) or seven year rule in (ii) does not apply where: the property was eligible for agricultural property relief on an earlier transfer; either the earlier transfer or the subsequent transfer was made on the death of the transferor; and the property is occupied by the second transferor for agricultural purposes at the date of the subsequent transfer.

Where the transferor had acquired the agricultural property on the death of his spouse/civil partner, their respective periods of occupation and/or ownership are aggregated to determine whether the transferor meets the occupation/ownership requirements (ss 117 to 121).

For lifetime gifts, whether chargeable at the time or potentially exempt, where the death of the donor occurs within seven years, agricultural property relief is only available when calculating the tax/additional tax arising as a result of the death providing that:

(a)   the original property (or qualifying replacement property) was owned by the transferee throughout the period beginning with the date of the chargeable transfer and ending with the death of the transferor, and

(b)   immediately before the death of the donor the original property (or qualifying replacement property) is relevant agricultural property in the hands of the transferee (ignoring the two year or seven year period of ownership rule).

If the transferee dies before the donor then the property must qualify at the date of his death rather than the date of the donor's death.

Proportionate relief is available where only part of the property is owned at the date of death (s 124A).

Annual exemptions and effect of donor's death

The same provisions apply as for business property relief in relation to annual exemptions, and also for calculating the additional tax payable on a chargeable lifetime transfer as a result of the donor's death within seven years, where the agricultural property is no longer owned by the donee (see part A(c)).

Provision is made for property that replaces all or part of the original property to satisfy the continuing ownership test providing the replacement property also qualifies as agricultural property, and providing the whole of the proceeds of the original property are used in the purchase of the replacement property within three years after the disposal of the original property, or such longer period as HMRC may allow (s 124B).

Business property relief on non-agricultural value

Where agricultural property satisfies the conditions for business property relief, business property relief is available in respect of any part of the value transferred that does not qualify for agricultural property relief (s 114). Since agricultural property relief is given only on the agricultural value of the land then business property relief where applicable will be given on any excess over that value.

Where agricultural property is replaced by business property, then providing the agricultural property is qualifying property for business property relief, the period of ownership of the agricultural property will be taken into account in deciding whether the conditions for business property relief are satisfied.

(b)   Transfer of shares or debentures in farming company

Agricultural property relief is available on the transfer of shares or debentures in a farming company, providing the holding gave the transferor control of the company immediately before the transfer and the agricultural property forms part of the company's assets (s 119). Relief is given only on that part of the value of the holding that reflects the agricultural value of the underlying property. The rate of relief is 100% where the company occupies the property or where the property is let on a tenancy granted on or after 1 September 1995, and 50% for property let before that date, and the two year/seven year rules in (i) and (ii) in part (a) above apply as if the company were the transferor. (For this purpose the company is treated as having occupied the property at any time when it was occupied by a person who subsequently controls the company.) Furthermore the shares or securities must have been owned by the transferor throughout the two year or seven year period.

Business property relief is available on the non-agricultural value of a holding where the relevant conditions are satisfied at 100% on holdings in unquoted farming companies and at 50% on quoted controlling holdings.

Both agricultural property relief and business property relief are given automatically without the need for a claim.

(c)   Mitigation of inheritance tax through lease of land

The immediately perceived advantage of the proposal is that the value of the agricultural land would be reduced from £400,000 (200 × £2,000) to £280,000 (200 × £1,400) on the granting of the tenancy. This act by itself would not have any inheritance tax consequences providing the grant is for full consideration in money or money's worth (s 16).

Furthermore, the rate of agricultural property relief on tenanted property for tenancies granted on or after 1 September 1995 was increased from 50% to 100%, so that unless there are adverse changes in the agricultural property relief provisions, there will be no disadvantage in terms of the rate of relief available. Unless the conditions for agricultural relief were no longer satisfied at the time of Arthur's death, there would therefore be no charge to inheritance tax at that time. If the conditions were not satisfied, then providing the property remained tenanted, the proposal would achieve the objective of reducing the value of the property in the death estate.

(d)

Inheritance tax payable on the death of X in July 2008

	Gross £	Tax £
Inheritance tax accumulation prior to death	–	–
Estate on death		
Freehold property – Greenacre		
Agricultural value (tenanted)	479,000	
Less: 100% agricultural property relief (note 13)	479,000	–	–
Residue of estate to spouse — exempt	–	–
	–	–
	–	–

Inheritance tax payable on the death of Y in September 2008

	£	£
Greenacre (tenanted since 1973)	479,000	
Less: 50% agricultural property relief (note 13)	239,500	239,500
Interest in farming partnership	60,000	
Less: 100% business property relief	60,000	–
Other assets		76,000
		315,500
Tax thereon (no lifetime transfers)		
(315,500 – 312,000 = 3,500 @ 40%)		£1,400

Explanatory Notes

Business property and agricultural property relief legislation

1. The provisions relating to business property relief are contained in ss 103–114B and those for agricultural property relief in ss 115–124C.

2. The main provisions are dealt with in the example, other points of importance being covered in the following notes.

Meaning of control

3. Control of a company means the control of voting on all questions affecting the company as a whole, subject to what is said in part A(c) of the example (s 269).

    Shares or securities which are related property under s 161 are taken into account in determining whether a person controls a company (s 269(2)), except where related property is left out of account under s 176 because of a sale after death (ss 105(2), 122(2)) (see Example 10 for the related property rules, explanatory note 4 of that example dealing with s 176).

    The voting powers attaching to shares or securities comprised in a settlement are deemed to be exercisable by the person beneficially entitled in possession to the shares or securities (broadly the person entitled to the income for the time being) (s 269(3)).

Business property relief and agricultural property relief are also available on the occasion of a ten yearly charge on a settlement without an interest in possession. For this purpose the trustees are deemed to be a transferor (ss 66, 103(1)(b), 115(1)(b)).

Agricultural value

4. Agricultural value is that which would be the value of the property if it were subject to a perpetual covenant prohibiting its use otherwise than as agricultural property (s 115(3)). The relief does not therefore extend to any value in excess of the agricultural value as defined. For example, if the value was £100,000 because it was hoped that permission would shortly be forthcoming for a caravan site, but the value on the basis that it must be used perpetually for agriculture was £10,000, the agricultural relief would only be available on the lower £10,000.

Occupation by company

5. Occupation of agricultural property by a company controlled by the transferor is treated as occupation by the transferor for the purpose of the minimum two year period of occupation or seven year period of ownership (s 119(1)).

    Hence agricultural property owned by a controlling shareholder and occupied by his farming company qualifies for relief.

Parcels of shares acquired over a period of time — matching provisions

6. As indicated in the example, an asset is not relevant business property unless it has been owned by the transferor throughout the two years before the transfer (or it is qualifying replacement property). As far as shares are concerned, they may have been acquired in separate parcels over a period of time and some of the acquisitions may have been within the last two years.

    Unlike the capital gains position, there are no matching rules in the inheritance tax legislation, so that there is uncertainty over which shares are contained in a transfer. In practice this may be overcome either by the separate parcels of shares having been originally registered in the names of different nominees or by the share certificates that are cancelled as a result of the gift being those acquired more than two years previously.

Binding contract for sale

7. Property that is subject to a binding contract for sale at the time of the transfer is not relevant business or agricultural property unless:

    (a) the sale is to a company that is to carry on the business, the consideration being wholly or mainly shares or securities in the company (which, in the case of agricultural property relief, will give the transferor control of the company), or

    (b) the property is shares or securities of a company and the sale is made for the purpose of reconstruction or amalgamation (ss 113 and 124).

    Where partners or company directors have entered into 'buy and sell' agreements whereby on their death the personal representatives are *obliged* to sell and the survivors *obliged* to buy the deceased's interest (funds often being provided by life assurance policies), such an agreement in HMRC's view constitutes a binding contract for sale and business property relief or agricultural relief is not available (Statement of Practice 12/80). If, however, a double option agreement is entered into under which the surviving partners or shareholders have an option to buy and the deceased's personal representatives an option to sell, such options to be exercised within a stated period after the partner's death, this does not cause business or agricultural relief to be lost.

Other reliefs and exemptions

8.   Business and agricultural property relief are given before any exemptions since they apply to transfers of value (ss 104(1) and 115(1)), such transfers being calculated before reliefs and exemptions (s 3(1)). In relation to potentially exempt transfers that become chargeable transfers, neither relief is available unless the relevant conditions are satisfied at the time of death, as indicated in the example (ss 113A(1) and 124A(1)).

Gifts subject to a reservation

9.   Where a gift of business or agricultural property is subject to a reservation, and a transfer of value is treated as made by the donor on his death (or on the donee's death, if earlier), then in considering the availability of business or agricultural relief the donor's transfer is treated as made by the donee (otherwise the donor would not usually be able to satisfy the ownership/occupation requirements) (FA 1986 Sch 20.8). Where the requirements for 100% relief are satisfied, the fact that a gift of qualifying property was subject to a reservation will not result in any extra tax charge on death.

As far as the donee's entitlement to relief is concerned, there are provisions to enable him to satisfy the occupation/ownership requirements by reference to the occupation/ownership of the donor (FA 1986 Sch 20.8).

For the gifts with reservation provisions see Example 19.

Pre 10 March 1981 transfers of agricultural property and transitional relief

10. For transfers prior to 10 March 1981, agricultural property relief was 50% of the agricultural value of the agricultural property after reduction for exempt transfers. The relief had to be claimed within two years of the transfer and was limited to relief on £250,000 or on 1,000 acres, whichever was the greater (counting rough grazing land as one-sixth of its actual area).

In order to be eligible to claim relief the transferor had broadly to be a working farmer, although relief could still be claimed after the farmer retired, providing the property had been occupied for agricultural purposes by his family throughout the period between his retirement and the date of the transfer, either under a lease or under some informal arrangements.

Relief was not available on let agricultural land except where it was let to a member of the family (as above) or where it was let to a farming partnership of which the transferor was a member or to a farming company controlled by the transferor.

As a transitional measure, where the transferor has been beneficially entitled to his interest in the property since before 10 March 1981, he is entitled to 100% agricultural property relief providing the following conditions are satisfied:

(a)   He would have been entitled to claim the (then) 50% agricultural property relief had he disposed of his interest before that date, and

(b)   His interest did not at any time between 10 March 1981 and the date of transfer carry a right to vacant possession and did not fail to carry such a right through any act or deliberate omission of his.

Where the former relief would have been limited by reference to value or acreage, the 100% relief is available up to the limit and any excess agricultural value attracts relief at 50%.

Where a transferor has acquired agricultural property on the death of his spouse/civil partner on or after 10 March 1981, the transitional 100% relief is available where the spouse/civil partner satisfied condition (a) above and both spouses/civil partners satisfy condition (b) above.

These transitional provisions thus enable relief to be claimed on the first subsequent transfer at the 100% rather than the 50% rate by retired farmers whose families have continued to work the farm and by partners or controlling directors who let land to the partnership or company.

The transitional relief will not be relevant where a tenancy commences on or after 1 September 1995, because relief is now available on such tenanted property at the 100% rate in any event. Had Arthur in part B(c) of the example not been entitled to the 100% relief under the normal provisions, he would not have been able to claim the transitional relief because he had the right to vacant possession after 9 March 1981 and before the transfer (on his death) on which relief is to be claimed.

Formation of partnership

11. The formation of a partnership between Arthur and his son would not give rise to any current or potential liability to inheritance tax provided that any reduction in the value of the estate of either resulted from an agreement that was not intended to confer any gratuitous benefit and was such as would have occurred in an agreement made at arm's length between unconnected persons (s 10).

Grant of agricultural tenancy

12. The grant of the tenancy of Whiteacre by Arthur in part B(c) of the example will not give rise to any liability to inheritance tax because of the exemption provided by s 16 for agricultural tenancies if the grant is made for full consideration. It should be noted, however, that the rent receivable by Arthur will be investment income whereas previously the income was earned income, being embraced in the profits of a farming business carried on by Arthur personally. This will reduce the Class 4 national insurance contributions payable, but will affect the future earnings on which Arthur can claim income tax relief for personal pension premiums (but note that a personal pension premium of up to £3,600 a year may be paid with basic rate tax relief at source by someone who has no earnings). If the tenancy was not granted for full rent, a charge to inheritance tax could arise on the reduction in the value of Arthur's estate and the 'gift' could be 'with reservation' as Arthur would still have a benefit in the land and accordingly could be valued at vacant possession value at the date of Arthur's death.

See Example 10 part A regarding the valuation of tenanted agricultural property.

13. On the death of X in part B(d) of the example Greenacre qualifies for 100% relief because the tenancy was granted before 10 March 1981 and all of the conditions mentioned in explanatory note 10 are satisfied.

On the death of Y Greenacre qualifies for relief even though Y only owned it for three months because the minimum occupation/ownership rules do not apply on a succession where all of the following conditions are satisfied:

 (i)   The value transferred by the earlier transfer qualified for relief

 (ii) The property became that of the later transferor as a result of such an earlier transfer and at the time of the subsequent transfer was *occupied* by the later transferor or the personal representative of the earlier transferor for the purposes of agriculture

 (iii) The property would have qualified for relief if the normal minimum ownership and occupation conditions had been met

 (iv) Either the earlier or later transfer was a transfer on death.

Alternatively Y would still have qualified under the two year occupation test as Y occupied the land as a tenant farmer in the farming partnership for two years even though his ownership did not commence until the death of his father.

The rate of relief on Y's death is only 50%, because the tenancy was granted before 1 September 1995 and Y does not satisfy the conditions for the transitional relief, having not become the owner of Greenacre until his father's death.

Although Y's death is within twelve months of X's death, quick succession relief is not relevant because no tax was payable on X's estate.

14. The availability of 100% agricultural relief in relation to tenanted property was extended by FA 1996. Where a tenant dies on or after 1 September 1995 and someone else succeeds to the tenancy, the new tenancy is deemed to commence on the date of the first tenant's death. Accordingly, if the landlord dies after the death of the first tenant, but before the succession by the second tenant, 100% agricultural property relief is available on the landlord's death. 100% relief is similarly available where a succession to a tenancy is triggered by a notice of retirement given by the retiring tenant to the landlord, and the succession takes effect after the landlord's death (on or after 1 September 1995) and within 30 months of the notice (s 116(5A), (5B) and (5D)).

Deed of variation

15. The tax on the death of Y in part B(d) of the example (£1,400) could be avoided by a deed of variation under which the executors of X and of Y agreed to vary the terms of X's will so that the freehold property devolved to X's widow instead of to Y. This would save the whole of the tax on the death of Y since his estate would then only amount to £76,000 (£239,500 for the farm property no longer being in his estate) which is below the taxable threshold.

The respective executors should have no reservations about this variation, since the estate of Y has in any event been left to his mother, who would simply take the farm property on the death of her husband rather than of her son. See Example 34 for details of deeds of variation.

Furthermore the income tax 'pre-owned' asset rules will not impose an income tax charge on Y as FA 2004 Sch 15.16 provides that a party to a deed of variation is not taxed as a former owner simply because of having an interest which they have now signed away (Y's Executor signing on behalf of Y).

Exempt and partially exempt estates

16. Where business or agricultural property forms part of an estate at death, the benefit of the business or agricultural property relief will be lost if the property is left to an exempt beneficiary. Even if it is not left to an exempt beneficiary, part of the relief will be wasted where there are exempt legacies and the business or agricultural property forms part of the residue of the estate, rather than being left as a specific gift, because the relief is then regarded as applying to the whole estate, including the exempt part of it, so that again relief is wasted to the extent that it is allocated to the exempt legacies. For further notes on this point see Example 15 explanatory notes 6 to 9.

Gifts out of and into trusts

17. Business and agricultural property relief is available on transfers of trust property providing the conditions are satisfied. For life interest trusts, the person with the interest in possession is treated as the beneficial owner of the property (s 49) and when the interest comes to an end, he is treated as having made a transfer at that time (s 52). For discretionary trusts, the relief is available when relevant property is transferred out of the trust and on the occasion of the ten yearly charge, the trustees being treated as the transferor (ss 103, 113) (see Example 62 explanatory note 5).

Detailed notes on the inheritance tax treatment of trusts are contained in Examples 52 to 65. See Examples 60 and 62 in particular for the treatment of business and agricultural property.

Various points need to be borne in mind when placing business or agricultural property into a trust, and the possible effects for the different types of trust need to be carefully considered.

18. Before 22 March 2006, if property was placed into a life interest trust, the transfer was potentially exempt and will only become chargeable if the donor dies within seven years after the transfer. If the property is business or agricultural property, the relief would be taken into account in arriving at the amount of the potentially exempt transfer. The trustees need to hold the property for two years before any transfer by them would qualify for relief.

If the donor dies within seven years after transferring the property to the trust, so that the potentially exempt transfer becomes a chargeable transfer, the trustees still need to hold the property at that time in order for the relief to be available. (If the donor died within two years this would not prevent the relief being available providing the property was still held in the trust.) If the trust does not satisfy the conditions at the donor's death, the relief is not available against the now chargeable transfer, and the donor's 'clock' of cumulative transfers will include that chargeable transfer.

19. Since 22 March 2006, the transfer of property into most types of trust is now an immediately chargeable transfer (at half of the rates of tax payable on death) after being reduced by business or agricultural property relief where available. The trustees need to retain the property for two years before being entitled to relief on any appointments of the property out of the trust. Furthermore, if there are any appointments of the property after that time but within ten years after the trust's creation, then although the relief is available on the transfer the *rate of tax* is based on the full value of the property when settled (see Example 62 explanatory note 5). This would not be a problem, however, if the property qualified for 100% relief because the amount chargeable would be nil. If the donor dies within seven years after the transfer, the tax on the lifetime transfer is recalculated on the death scale, additional tax being payable accordingly. As with life interest trusts, the trustees still need to hold the property when the donor dies in order for the relief to remain available on the donor's transfer (and they would be entitled to the relief even if the donor died within two years providing the property was still held in the trust). If the trust does not satisfy the conditions for relief when the donor dies, the relief is not taken into account in calculating the additional tax on the lifetime transfer, but the amount of the donor's cumulative transfers would not be affected (see the example on page 25.4). Relief will not be available against the lifetime transfer to the trust because the trustees have disposed of the property between the time of the gift and the time of death.

Let property, including holiday lettings

20. Holiday lettings are not agricultural property. HMRC take the view that a property letting business will not usually qualify for business property relief, because it will be regarded as a business of making or holding investments (s 105(3)). This is supported by the Special Commissioners' decisions in Exors of Moore decd and Exor of Burkinyoung decd (1995). In both cases business property relief was denied, even though the taxpayers (or in the Burkinyoung case, the managing agents) carried out considerable work as part of the lettings, eg repairs, decoration and maintenance.

Hotels, bed and breakfast and residential homes will usually qualify for relief because of the level of services provided. In the case of *short-term* holiday lettings (eg weekly or fortnightly), where the property owner or his agent is substantially involved with the holidaymakers during the holiday, business property relief will normally be available even if the lettings were for part of the year only (HMRC's Inheritance Tax Manual IHTM25278). Most furnished holiday lettings should satisfy these tests.

In a decision of the *Special Commissioners (Furness v CIR 1999)*, it was held that a caravan park business qualified for business property relief. Although there were both static and touring caravans, the larger part of the profits came other than from renting out caravan pitches, and the activities of the owner and his staff were greatly in excess of what one would expect in a business concerned wholly or mainly with investments.

The opposite decision was reached in *Weston (exor of Weston decd) v CIR 2000*, where the Court confirmed the Special Commissioner's decision that the greater part of a caravan park's profits came from pitch fees and bank interest rather than caravan sales, so that the business was mainly one of making or holding investments. The same conclusion was reached in *IRC v George & Anor (Exors of Stedman dec'd)* 2002 where the main activities were the letting of sites for 167 residential mobile homes; storage of touring caravans; letting of a shop and warehouse and fields let on grazing licences. This outweighed the ancillary activities of a country club and an insurance agency, so the business was mainly one of making or holding investments. However, that decision was subsequently overturned by the Court of Appeal which reinstated the Special Commissioner's finding that the company was mainly trading.

The comments in the Farmer & Giles case mentioned in part A(c) of the example provide a good basis on which to judge whether a business consists mainly of making or holding investments. Once the hurdle of qualifying for business property relief is crossed then, as the example indicates, the assets used for the investment side of the business will probably not be regarded as 'excepted assets' and will not therefore be excluded from relief.

Question

On 19 July 2003 Stanley (who has never made a lifetime gift before) gave Elizabeth (his granddaughter) the whole of his shares in Printers Ltd, a trading company, together with the freehold of the land and buildings occupied by the company, but which he owned personally.

On the same day Peter (who has made chargeable transfers within the previous seven years amounting to £180,000 and has fully utilised his exemptions for 2003/04 and 2002/03) gave Elizabeth (his daughter) his shareholding in Printers Ltd.

Prior to the above transfers the shareholdings in Printers Ltd (which had remained unchanged for many years) were:

		Shares
Stanley		4,000
Phyllis	(Stanley's wife)	4,000
Peter	(Stanley's son)	1,000
Barbara	(Peter's sister)	900
Elizabeth	(Peter's daughter)	100
		10,000

and the agreed values for inheritance tax purposes were:

100% holding	£1,600,000	51% holding	£900,000
80% holding	£1,400,000	40% holding	£300,000
60% holding	£1,000,000	10% holding	£40,000

The value of the land and buildings transferred by Stanley was agreed at £774,000.

On 13 November 2008 Stanley died. Elizabeth still owned the property and shares at that date.

(a)   Compute the inheritance tax payable by Elizabeth;

(b)   Assuming that the instalment option will be used, state the date on which the first instalment is due, and the amount payable on that day;

(c)   Explain under what circumstances interest will be payable on the instalments (without calculating the amount of any interest).

Answer

(a)   **Inheritance tax payable by Elizabeth as donee of lifetime transfers:**

On death of Stanley 13 November 2008

Potentially exempt transfers 19 July 2003, now chargeable transfers (see explanatory notes 2 and 3):

	Gross £	Tax £
Shares in Printers Ltd	–	–
Land and buildings (see note 2)	381,000	27,600*

(* 381,000 – 312,000 = 69,000 @ 40%)

Tax payable (after 60% tapering relief) is 40% of £27,600 = £11,040, which is payable over 10 annual instalments.

Peter — inheritance tax accumulation

	Gross £	Tax £
Previous transfers	180,000	–

19 July 2003 — potentially exempt transfer £40,000 less 100% business property relief £40,000 = nil. (No tax payable even if Peter dies within seven years and business property relief is not then available, since cumulative transfers total of £180,000 plus £40,000 is within nil rate band. See explanatory note 4.)

(b)   The first instalment of the tax of £11,040 in respect of the land and buildings, amounting to £1,104, is payable on 31 May 2009.

(c)   Interest is payable on the tax in respect of land and buildings from 31 May 2009 to the date of the instalment, calculated on the full amount of tax for the time being unpaid. In addition interest is paid on the instalment from its due date to the actual date of payment of the instalment.

Explanatory Notes

Business property relief

1.   A transfer of a business or an interest in a business qualifies for business property relief of 100% where the business is carried on for gain (ss 103(3), 104 and 105(1)(a)). Transfers out of a holding of unquoted shares also qualify for business property relief of 100% (ss 104(1)(a) and 105(1)(bb)).

Controlling holdings of quoted shares qualify for business property relief of 50% (ss 104(1)(b) and 105(1)(cc)).

Business property relief of 50% is available on the transfer of land and buildings used for the business of a company of which the transferor has control.

Related property

2.   Using the related property rules (s 161) (see Example 10), Stanley's gift of shares on 19 July 2003 must be valued as a proportion of an 80% holding (ie his own plus his wife's holding), of which one-half relates to him. The related holding determines the size of the holding for the purposes of the rate of business property relief (s 269(2)). The rate of business property relief at 19 July 2003 was 100% on the shares and 50% on the land and buildings, so the original calculation would be:

£

$$\text{Value of shares (80\%) } 1,400,000 \times \frac{4,000 \text{ shares}}{8,000 \text{ shares}} = \qquad 700,000$$

Less: Business property relief (100%)	700,000
Transfer of value	–

The transfer of value on the same day in respect of the land and buildings was:

£

Value of property		774,000
Less: Business property relief (50%)		387,000
		387,000
Less: Annual exemptions 2003/04	3,000	
2002/03	3,000	6,000
Chargeable transfer		381,000

For the position where business or agricultural property relief is withdrawn at death because the conditions are no longer satisfied see Example 24 explanatory note 2.

Availability of business property relief

3.   To get the 100% business property relief on the *shares*, Elizabeth merely needs to retain the shares that were transferred to her out of Stanley's holding (s 113A).

To get the 50% relief on the *land and buildings*, Elizabeth needs to *control* Printers Ltd when Stanley dies (s 113A(3)).

The shares owned by Elizabeth following the gifts on 19 July 2003 and still held by her at 13 November 2008 were:

Original shareholding	100
Gift from Stanley	4,000
Gift from Peter	1,000
Total shares held	5,100

so she has control of Printers Ltd and is therefore entitled to business property relief on the land and buildings.

Because Stanley died more than five but less than six years after the date of gift, tapering relief of 60% applies to the tax payable.

4.   Peter's gift of his Printers Ltd shareholding to Elizabeth on 19 July 2003 qualified for 100% business property relief. The whole of the gift is a potentially exempt transfer. If he should die before 19 July 2010, the potentially exempt transfer will become chargeable, and the business property relief will only then be available if Elizabeth satisfies the qualifying conditions at that time. In fact no tax will

be payable on Peter's gift in any event, since the cumulative transfers are within the nil rate band, but if 100% business property relief was not available the gift would be taken into account in the cumulative total for a death within seven years.

5.   Detailed notes on business property relief are given in Example 25.

Instalment option

6.   Inheritance tax payable on certain assets on death (or on lifetime chargeable transfers where the transferee pays the inheritance tax) may be paid by ten annual instalments (ss 227 and 228). See Examples 5 and 9.

The instalment option is available on potentially exempt transfers that become chargeable because of the donor's death within seven years providing the donee still owns the gifted property (or, for transfers of property qualifying for business or agricultural relief, replacement property) at the time of the donor's death.

Unquoted shares and securities (including shares which do not qualify for business property relief, eg shares in property investment companies) that do not represent a controlling holding only qualify as instalment assets if:

(a)   the inheritance tax cannot be paid in one sum without undue hardship, or

(b)   (for shares only) they are valued at more than £20,000 and their nominal value is at least 10% of the nominal value of all the company's shares (or if they are ordinary shares, 10% of the nominal value of the company's ordinary shares), or

(c)   in the case of a transfer on death, the tax payable on the shares or securities, together with the tax on other instalment assets, amounts to 20% or more of the tax payable by the same person on the same transfer.

Furthermore the instalment option on unquoted shares is not available for tax payable in consequence of the donor's death unless the shares are still unquoted when the donor dies (or if earlier, when the donee dies).

The gift of 10% of the shares in Printers Ltd by Peter to Elizabeth would not satisfy any of the conditions listed above so that had tax become chargeable the instalment option would not have been available.

The instalment option is available as indicated in respect of Stanley's gift to Elizabeth of the land and buildings.

Question

A.

To what extent is domicile relevant for inheritance tax purposes?

Explain the extended meaning given to domicile for the purposes of inheritance tax.

B.

Leonardo, who was born in, and whose home country is, Italy, has lived in the UK since 1992, but plans to return to Italy following his retirement.

On 31 January 2009 he made a chargeable transfer of £320,000 before deducting exemptions, paying the inheritance tax due himself on the due date, having made no earlier transfers.

His remaining assets, at current values, comprise:

(a)   10,000 £1 shares in Exodus plc quoted on the Stock Exchange at 134p–140p with recorded bargains at 134, 135 and 136.

(b)   10,000 no par value bearer shares in Canadian Timber Limited. The company register is in Ontario, Canada, and the shares are quoted on the Ontario Stock Exchange at the sterling equivalent of 90–92.

(c)   A half share in a painting in the UK which Leonardo and his brother, Vincento, had bought in 1976, each providing one half of the purchase money. Its value is £48,000 but a half share is worth £22,000.

(d)   A house in Pisa, Italy, valued at €200,000.

(e)   Three insurance policies with a UK insurance company on his life:

    (i)   taken out in 1978; the proceeds of £50,000 will be left to his wife, who will receive nothing else,

    (ii)   taken out in 1984 on which he had paid the premiums and under which £15,000 will become payable to his executor,

    (iii)   taken out in 1988 for the benefit of his grand-daughter under which £30,000 becomes payable on his death. Leonardo had paid each annual premium of £600 himself.

(f)   Debts owing to him of:

    (i)   £1,500 by Michael living in the UK, and,

    (ii)   €1,000 by Manolo living in Italy.

(g)   Cash held in bank accounts:

    (i)   in the UK £4,250,

    (ii)   in Italy €3,000.

(h)   His gold watch valued at £800 and gold ring valued at £1,450, both held in the UK.

(i)   His private dwelling-house in London valued at £370,000 plus furniture valued at £20,000.

(j)   His UK trading business which he has run as a sole trader since his arrival in the UK, valued at £160,000.

Assume the current rate of exchange to be €1.50 = £1.

All share certificates and house deeds are held by Leonardo's solicitor at his office in Italy.

Leonardo is considering making further gifts during his lifetime as follows:

(i)   his Canadian Timber Ltd shares to his niece living in Canada,

(ii)   his half share in the painting to his brother, Angelo, living in London,

(iii)   his house in Pisa, Italy, to his daughter living in London,

(iv)   his gold ring to his grandson, living in London, in consideration of his forthcoming marriage,

(v)   his business in the UK to his son, living in London.

1.   Compute the inheritance tax payable by Leonardo following the January 2009 transfer, stating the date it falls due, and the inheritance tax which would be payable if Leonardo were to die unexpectedly within the week following the transfer, not having made any further gifts, his estate (after the 1978 insurance policy proceeds to his wife) being left to his grandchildren. In the case of tax payable on death, identify the amounts which can be paid in instalments, the period over which instalments are payable, and the extent to which relief from interest is given on tax so payable.

2.   State whether any amounts would become chargeable to inheritance tax if Leonardo, not having died in February 2009, had made the further gifts in (i) to (v) above in March 2009 and whether any additional tax would arise if Leonardo were then to die at any time in the eight years following the making of those gifts (assuming the inheritance tax legislation remains unaltered).

Answer

A. **Relevance of domicile for inheritance tax**

Domicile is relevant for inheritance tax purposes because, whilst the tax is charged on gratuitous transfers of UK assets regardless of the domicile of the transferor, it is also charged on gratuitous transfers of assets by persons of UK domicile regardless of where the property is situated.

Therefore it is necessary to know the domicile of the transferor when the transfer involves assets situated outside the UK.

Until the Domicile and Matrimonial Proceedings Act 1973 s 1 a married woman acquired the domicile of her husband. However, that ceased to apply with respect to marriages after 31 December 1973. Accordingly in the case of transfers between spouses/civil partners it is necessary to know the domicile of both parties because if the transferor is domiciled in the UK but the transferee is domiciled abroad then the spouse/civil partner exemption is limited to £55,000 (s 18(2)).

A person's country of domicile is usually the country that he regards as his natural home, and a change of domicile requires a high standard of proof. A domicile of origin is acquired at birth. This may be abandoned and a domicile of choice acquired. To do so requires positive action, eg changing residence, making a new will in the country of choice, obtaining citizenship etc, and abandoning the previous country. However, retaining electoral voting rights will not be taken into account (FA 1996 s 200). If the domicile of choice is lost without a new domicile being established then the domicile of origin is revived. (It is considered that Leonardo would have retained his domicile of origin in this example, as he was born in Italy and intends to return there on retirement. He also retains a house and a bank account in Italy and keeps his documents with his Italian solicitor.)

For inheritance tax purposes domicile has an extended meaning and the following persons are treated as domiciled in the UK (s 267):

(i)   Persons who on or after 10 December 1974 were domiciled in the UK and were so domiciled within the three years preceding the transfer.

(ii) Persons who were resident in the UK on or after 10 December 1974 and in not less than seventeen out of the twenty income tax years ending with the tax year of transfer.

B. **Leonardo — inheritance tax payable**

1. **Inheritance tax payable re January 2009 transfer**

Leonardo is domiciled in Italy, therefore property located outside the UK is excluded property. (If he was still in the UK in the year ending 5 April 2010 he would have been UK resident for 17 years and would be deemed to be UK domiciled, as indicated in A above.) The inheritance tax position on the transfer on 31 January 2009 is as follows:

			Gross	Tax (2008/09 scale)	Net
			£	£	£
31 January 2009					
Gifts within previous seven years			–	–	–
Chargeable lifetime transfer		320,000			
Less: Annual 2008/09	3,000				
exemptions					
2007/08	3,000	6,000			
Net transfer grossed up*			314,500	500	314,000
			314,500	500	314,000

*Net				Gross
312,000	×	100		312,000
2,000		80		2,500
314,000				314,500

Inheritance tax payable by Leonardo on 31 July 2009 = £500.

If Leonardo died in February 2009

	Gross	Tax (2008/09 scale)
	£	£
Gifts within seven years before death:		
31 January 2009		
Chargeable transfer	314,500	1,000*
Cumulative transfers in seven years prior to death	314,500	1,000

(* 314,500 – 312,000 = 2,500 @ 40%)

Inheritance tax payable by donee on 31 January 2009 transfer:

On death	1,000
Less: due on lifetime transfer	500
Due from donee 31 August 2009	£500

Estate on death would be

	£
Shares in Exodus plc (UK listed company)	
10,000 £1 shares @ 135 (midpoint between 134 and 136,	
being less than 134 + (¼ × (140 – 134) = 135½))	13,500
Canadian Timber Limited shares — excluded property	–
Painting held in UK — one half share	22,000
House in Italy — excluded property	–
Insurance policies — 1978	50,000
— 1984	15,000

			£
Loans	— Michael		1,500
	— Manolo	— excluded property	–
Cash at bank	— UK		4,250
	— Italy — excluded property		–
Possessions	— gold watch		800
	— gold ring		1,450
UK house			370,000
Furniture			20,000
Business		160,000	
Less: 100% business property relief		160,000	–
			498,500
Less: Debts — inheritance tax due on chargeable gift made 31.1.09			500
			498,000
Less: Exempt legacy — widow (1978 insurance policy)			50,000
			448,000

Note

The 1988 life policy for the benefit of Leonardo's grand-daughter does not form part of the estate, the annual premiums having been exempt as gifts out of income.

As business property is left as part of residue to non-exempt beneficiaries and there is a specific gift to an exempt beneficiary (widow), business property relief will be reduced rateably (s 39A):

		£
Estate before reliefs and exemptions (448,000 + 160,000 + 50,000)		658,000
Less: Business property relief		(160,000)
		498,000
Less: Exempt legacy to widow	50,000	
Restricted by reference to business property relief		
$160,000 \times \dfrac{\text{Exempt estate } 50,000}{\text{Total estate} 658,000}$	12,158	(37,842)
Estate chargeable to inheritance tax		460,158
Tax thereon @ 40% (lifetime transfers being above nil threshold)		£184,063

Amount payable by instalments

$$\text{UK house} \ \frac{370,000}{498,000} \times 184,063 = £136,754$$

Payable by ten equal yearly instalments of £13,675 from 1 September 2009 plus interest on the full outstanding balance.

2. **Inheritance tax position if gifts in (i) to (v) were made in March 2009 and Leonardo died within following eight years**

   (i)   As the Canadian Timber Ltd shares are situated outside the UK, they are excluded property and not chargeable to UK inheritance tax on transfer.

(ii)   The transfer of the half-share of the painting to Angelo would be a potentially exempt transfer of £22,000 (no annual exemptions being available since they are already fully used). No inheritance tax would be due providing Leonardo lived for seven years, otherwise the gift would be added to the transfers of £314,500 made within seven years before the date of the gift and inheritance tax would be due based upon the scale and rate of tax applicable at the date of death.

(iii)   The transfer of the house in Pisa to Leonardo's daughter would be excluded as Leonardo is not domiciled in the UK.

(iv)   The gift of the ring valued at £1,450 to Leonardo's grandson, whilst not excluded property, would be exempt as a gift of not more than £2,500 made by a grandparent in consideration of the grandson's marriage.

(v)   The transfer of the business to Leonardo's son would attract 100% business property relief, so that the potentially exempt transfer would be nil. The transfer would not be liable to inheritance tax unless Leonardo died within seven years after making the transfer. If death occurred within the seven year period, the entitlement to business property relief would have to be reconsidered at that time. The relief would only continue to be available providing the son continued to satisfy the qualifying conditions up to the date of Leonardo's death.

If Leonardo died more than three but less than seven years after giving away the painting or business, any tax payable upon the potentially exempt transfers becoming chargeable would be reduced as follows:

Death more than	3 years but less than	4 years after gift	— 20%
	4 years	5 years	— 40%
	5 years	6 years	— 60%
	6 years	7 years	— 80%

After seven years no liability would arise on death in respect of these gifts.

Explanatory Notes

Situation of property

1.   The normal rules of English law apply to determine where property is situated.

(a)   Land is in the country where it is physically situated (but mortgages of land are treated as debts).

(b)   Debts are in the country where the debtor resides.

(c)   Shares are located where the share register is kept.

(d)   Life insurance policies are situated where the proceeds are payable (unless under seal, in which case they are situated where the policy is).

(e)   Business property is situated where the business is carried on.

(f)   Tangible property (including currency) is wherever it is physically situated.

(g)   Bank accounts are situated at the branch at which the deposits are payable (subject to what is said in note 4 re foreign currency accounts).

Excluded property

2.   Foreign property in foreign ownership is excluded property for inheritance tax purposes. The property must be situated outside the UK and the person beneficially entitled to it must be non-UK domiciled (s 6(1)).

3. The following is also excluded property:

   (a) National Savings etc owned by persons domiciled in the Channel Islands or Isle of Man (s 6(3)).

   (b) Certain government securities issued as being exempt from tax where they are owned by persons of a description specified in the conditions of issue of the security concerned (s 6(2)) (see Example 3 part (a)(ii)). The specified conditions prior to FA 1996 required the holder to be neither domiciled nor ordinarily resident in the UK, but the reference to domicile is excluded in current issues.

   In these two cases domicile has its ordinary meaning and not the extended inheritance tax meaning.

   For further notes on the meaning and treatment of excluded property see Example 3.

Foreign currency bank accounts

4. Where a person who is *neither resident, ordinarily resident nor domiciled* in the UK dies, any foreign currency bank accounts with the Bank of England, the Post Office, or an institution authorised under the Banking Act 1987 are left out of account in valuing the estate immediately prior to death. This also applies to such accounts held by trustees of settled property in which the deceased held a beneficial interest in possession unless the settlor was domiciled in the UK at the date of the settlement or the trustees are UK domiciled, resident and ordinarily resident at the time of the beneficiary's death (s 157) (the provision in FA 1989 s 110 deeming trustees of whom one or more is UK resident all to be UK resident regardless of how many foreign resident trustees there are does not apply to this provision). The individual's residence status will be determined using the normal income tax rules.

Works of art

5. Where a work of art is normally kept overseas, but becomes liable to inheritance tax on the owner's death solely because it is physically situated in the UK, that liability will be waived by Concession F7. This relief is only available if the work of art was brought into the UK solely for public exhibition, cleaning or restoration. The liability will similarly be waived if a work of art which would otherwise have left the UK to be kept overseas is retained in the UK solely for those purposes.

Business property relief

6. For further examples and notes on the interaction of exempt legacies and business property relief see Examples 15 and 17. For details of business property relief, see Example 25.

Types of domicile

7. For detailed notes on the possible types of domicile an individual might see Example 3.

Question

David, domiciled in England, who had worked a small agricultural holding for many years, died on 1 May 2008 leaving the following estate in England:

Freehold agricultural land extending to 30 acres and buildings together valued at £123,500 of which the agricultural value was £92,000.

Farming machinery and stores valued at £24,884.

Timber (growing on separate freehold land) valued at £123,000, being operated on a commercial basis. The land itself was valued at £150,000 but was subject to a mortgage of the same amount, for which the lender held no security other than the land.

Leasehold house valued at £157,500.

Household chattels and car valued at £22,850.

A quoted shareholding valued at £80,822 (being a 20% holding that David had owned for many years).

Bank balance £2,303.

English debts and funeral expenses (all allowable) totalled £7,233.

In addition David owned the following property in Afaria:

Freehold house valued at 74,500 fars.

Furniture valued at 28,750 fars.

Bank balance 9,580 fars.

His gardener was owed wages of 830 fars.

He also owned the following property in Nyria:

Leasehold house valued at 22,450 nyrs.

Furniture valued at 12,250 nyrs.

Bank balance of 3,750 nyrs.

There were no outstanding liabilities in Nyria.

Death duties abroad, with no interest if paid within six months of death, are calculated on total assets less liabilities at the following flat rates:

Afaria 10%; Nyria 8%.

The UK and Afaria (but not Nyria) have a double taxation agreement.

On 1 May 2008 exchange rates were:

Afaria 1 far = 100/120p; Nyria £1 = 0.48/0.50 nyrs.

On 1 July 2008 the executor obtained probate by presenting a provisional account in which, after appropriate reliefs, realty was included at £75,000, instalment option personalty at £200,000 and non-instalment option personalty at £171,000.

Inheritance tax was not paid on realty or the instalment option personalty.

The timber was sold standing for £127,500, which was received on 1 August 2008, no election having been made for the value at death to be left out of account under ss 125 to 130.

On 20 June 2006 David had made a potentially exempt transfer (after exemptions) of £119,000 to his sister, which was his only lifetime transfer.

By his will he left £30,000 to his brother, with the residue to his sister.

On 30 November 2008 the executor presented a corrective account.

Prepare statements showing:

(a)   Death duty payable in Afaria and Nyria.*

(b)   Any balance of inheritance tax and interest payable in England on 30 November 2008 on the assumption that the minimum amount of inheritance tax was paid at that time, the balance being deferred.

(c)   The amount of tax that can be deferred.

* Assuming the rates of exchange when the duty was paid were unchanged from 1 May 2008.

Answer

(a)   **Death duty payable overseas**

		Fars		£
Afaria	— House	74,500		74,500
	Furniture	28,750		28,750
	Bank balance	9,580		9,580
		112,830		112,830
	Less: Debts	830		830
		112,000	@ 1 far = 100p	112,000
	Death duty in Afaria @ 10%	11,200	@ 1 far = 120p	£13,440

		Nyrs		£
Nyria	— Leasehold house	22,450		44,900
	Furniture	12,250		24,500
	Bank balance	3,750		7,500
		38,450	@ £1 = 0.5 nyrs	76,900
	Death duty in Nyria @ 8%	3,076	@ £1 = 0.48 nyrs	£6,408

(b)   **Computation of inheritance tax due on 30 November 2008 (Death 1 May 2008)**

Inheritance tax paid on account 1 July 2008 on non-instalment option personalty of £171,000:

		Gross	Tax
		£	£
Potentially exempt transfers within seven years before death, now chargeable:			
20 June 2006		119,000	–
Estate on death per provisional account:			
Realty after reliefs	75,000		
Instalment option personalty after reliefs	200,000		
Non-instalment option personalty after reliefs	171,000	446,000	101,200*
		565,000	101,200*

(* 565,000 – 312,000 = 253,000 @ 40%)

Tax paid 1 July 2007 on £171,000 non-instalment option personalty:

$$\frac{171,000}{446,000} \times £101,200 = £38,801$$

			Date of death 1 May 2008		
			£	£	£
Freehold agricultural land and buildings				123,500	
Less:	Agricultural property relief	100% × £92,000	92,000		
	Business property relief	100% × £31,500	31,500	123,500	
				–	
Freehold land less mortgage thereon (£150,000 – £150,000)				–	
Freehold house in Afaria				74,500	74,500

	£	£	£
brought forward			74,500
Personalty — with instalment option			
Farm machinery and stores	24,884		
Less: Business property relief — 100%	24,884	–	
Leasehold house in England		157,500	
Leasehold house in Nyria		44,900	202,400
Personalty — without instalment option			
Timber (sold)	123,000		
Less: Business property relief — 100%	123,000	–	
Quoted shares (20% holding)		80,822	
Chattels		22,850	
Bank balance		2,303	
In Afaria — chattels	28,750		
bank balance	9,580	38,330	
In Nyria — chattels	24,500		
bank balance	7,500	32,000	
		176,305	
Less: Debts and funeral expenses — UK	7,233		
Debts in Afaria	830	8,063	168,242
Chargeable estate			445,142

	Gross £	Tax £
Inheritance tax accumulation in seven years before death	119,000	–
Estate chargeable on death and tax thereon	445,142	100,857*
	564,142	100,857*

(* 564,142 – 312,000 = 252,142 @ 40%)

Estate rate is $\dfrac{100,857}{445,142} \times 100 = 22.657\%$

Since this average rate clearly exceeds the rates paid overseas, the double taxation relief will be the duty paid overseas.

	£	£	£
Liability on estate		100,857	
Less: Double tax relief —			
Afaria	13,440		
Nyria	6,408	19,848	
		81,009	
Less: Paid on account (see page 28.3)		38,801	42,208
Less: Tax deferred (at estate rate of 22.657%)			
Realty			
House in Afaria £74,500	16,880		
Less: Double tax relief:			

	£	£	£
$\dfrac{74,500}{112,000} \times £13,440$	8,940	7,940	
Instalment option personalty £202,400	45,858		
Less: Double tax relief on house in Nyria:			
$\dfrac{44,900}{76,900} \times £6,408$	3,741	42,117	50,057

Tax repayable to personal representative on non-instalment property   (7,849)

Being: Tax on non-deferred personalty of
£168,242 at estate rate of 22.657%   38,119

     Less: Double tax relief:

Afaria	$\dfrac{37,500}{112,000} \times £13,440$	4,500
Nyria	$\dfrac{32,000}{76,900} \times £6,408$	2,667

     7,167

     30,951

Less: Paid on account (see page 28.3)   38,801

     £(7,849)

Tax payable by personal representative on deferred property

$$\frac{1}{10} \times 50,057$$

     5,006

Total amount repayable 30 November 2008 (no interest due)   (2,843)

(c)

Tax deferred   50,057
Less: First instalment   (5,006)
Amount deferred as at 30 November 2008   £45,051

Explanatory Notes

Converting values of foreign assets and foreign tax

1.   Foreign assets are valued by using the lower value of the exchange rate quoted, ie the more advantageous to the taxpayer. Where foreign tax is paid it is converted to sterling by using the higher value of the exchange rate on the date of payment (restricted to the amount paid if in sterling).

Agricultural and business property relief

2.   (a)   Agricultural property relief at 100% is available under s 116 on the agricultural value of the farm land and buildings. Business property relief at 100% is available under s 104 on the excess over the agricultural value and on the farming machinery and stores.

(b)   Business property relief is also available at 100% on the growing timber. An election could have been made under s 125 for the timber (but not the land on which it stands) to be left out of account on David's death, but with business property relief at 100% there is no point in doing so. Had it been left out it would have had to be brought in later at its sale value, and only 50% business property relief would have been available on the subsequent sale (s 127(2)) (see Example 31 explanatory note 10).

Business property relief is also available on the land on which the timber stands but it is only given on the value of business assets less liabilities so that the land does not attract the relief in this case because its value is wholly eliminated by the mortgage.

Where the only security for the mortgage is the business land, it is not possible to reduce the business property by business property relief and then deduct the mortgage from other assets.

(c)   For detailed notes on agricultural and business property relief and growing timber see Examples 25 and 31.

Instalment option

3.   The option for tax to be paid by ten yearly instalments is available on the following assets in this example:

Land in the UK and abroad (including leaseholds)

Business and agricultural property

The first instalment is due six months after the end of the month in which the death occurred, ie on 30 November 2008 (s 227(3)).

Payment of tax and interest on underpaid/overpaid tax

4.   Inheritance tax on death is payable on presentation of the HMRC Account (s 226(2)), ie on 1 July 2008 in this example, the tax then accounted for being on the provisional amount of £171,000 non-instalment option personalty. The inheritance tax, however, is not due until six months after the end of the month in which the death occurred, ie by 30 November 2008, so the corrective account showing the revised amount payable was submitted in time to stop any interest arising on unpaid tax. In fact the provisional amount paid exceeded the actual liability, so that a refund of £2,843 is due and the question of interest on unpaid tax does not arise.

The amount overpaid on the presentation of the account on 1 July 2008 does not attract an interest supplement. This is not overpaid tax but tax paid in advance of the due date. The amount of £2,843 found to be overpaid at 30 November 2008, on the other hand, will attract interest from that date until it is repaid.

Interest on unpaid tax on instalment assets is charged only from the date the instalment is payable, except for land which, unless the land is agricultural property or part of an interest in a business, attracts interest on the whole of the tax unpaid.

The first instalment due on 30 November 2008 was paid on time and accordingly no interest was payable thereon.

Interest will therefore arise from 1 December 2008 to the date of payment on the remainder of the tax on the freehold house in Afaria, the English leasehold and the leasehold house in Nyria, whether or not the instalments are paid on time.

In this example the inheritance tax payable on the estate is less than the amount payable on the provisional account that the personal representatives had submitted. Personal representatives need to be aware that HMRC are taking a harsher attitude to penalties where a provisional account understates the values of the assets — see Example 33 explanatory note 9.

Overseas liabilities

5.   Overseas liabilities are allowable as a deduction from the deceased's estate providing such debts would be allowable if UK debts. Normally the liabilities are deducted primarily from the value of overseas assets with any surplus deductible from UK assets (s 162(5)). If the liability is secured on UK property or is payable in the UK then the debt is deductible from UK property.

Double tax relief

6.   (a)   Double tax relief is available where the same property is charged to tax both in the UK and overseas. Relief is given under s 158 where the UK has a double tax agreement with the country concerned and otherwise unilaterally under s 159. Where there is a double tax agreement it will usually give greater relief than that available under s 159, but if it does not, the taxpayer is given the benefit of the unilateral relief of s 159.

        (b)   Section 159 enables the overseas duty paid to be deducted provided that this does not exceed the UK tax on the same property. In determining whether the UK tax is greater than the overseas tax, the average rate of UK tax is taken. This differs from double taxation relief for income tax where the UK tax applicable to overseas income can be taken as the highest rate of UK tax which applies to that taxpayer in that year of assessment.

                The UK tax on the overseas property in this example is clearly greater than the overseas tax on the same property, the UK average rate being 22.657% compared with 10% in Afaria and 8% in Nyria.

        (c)   Section 159 also gives relief where both the UK and another country impose tax on property situated in a third country, or where property is situated in the UK under UK law and in another country under that country's law. Relief is calculated by the formula:

$$\frac{A}{A + B} \times C$$

                where A is the inheritance tax, B is the overseas tax and C is whichever of A and B is smaller.

        (d)   For a further account of the interaction beween Double Taxation and IHT see Example 3(c) and Example 15 note 4.

Question

A has made cumulative chargeable transfers amounting to £199,000, all in the year ending 5 April 2002.

In May 2002 he gave a fine painting that he had owned for the last ten years to his son S. The picture was worth £95,000 in the open market at the time of the gift.

In November 2002 he gave a similar picture, then worth £100,000 in the open market, to his daughter D.

In both cases any liability for capital gains tax was held over.

On 20 March 2004 S gave his picture, then valued at £117,500, to his wife W, who is an American citizen but domiciled and resident in the UK. She immediately took it to New York to hang in the family gallery.

A died in December 2006 leaving an estate valued at £400,000 equally to his son S and daughter D.

An undertaking was given by the daughter that she would keep the picture in the UK; that she would take reasonable steps for its preservation; and that she would allow reasonable access to the public to view it.

On 3 April 2009 D sold her painting at an international auction room for £150,000, out of which the auctioneers took £15,000 in fees, and capital gains tax on the sale amounted to £8,800.

Both pictures were designated by the Treasury as being of national, scientific, historic or artistic interest. Appropriate claims for relief are made in connection with all transfers.

Calculate the inheritance tax payable as a result of these events.

Answer

A.

Inheritance tax

May 2002	Picture to S	95,000
	Less: Annual exemption 2002/03	3,000
	Potentially exempt transfer	92,000
November 2002	Picture to D — potentially exempt transfer	100,000

On death of A – December 2006

		Gross £	Tax on 2006/07 scale £
Gifts in lifetime:			
Cumulative transfers (year ended 5.4.2002)		199,000	–
May 2002			
Gift of picture to S (potentially exempt transfer now chargeable)		92,000	2,400*
		291,000	2,400*

(* 291,000 – 285,000 = 6,000 @ 40%)

		Gross £	Tax on 2006/07 scale £
November 2002			
Potentially exempt transfer of picture to D, now a chargeable transfer	100,000		
Less: Conditional exemption	100,000	–	
Inheritance tax accumulation at death		291,000	2,400
Estate on death		400,000	160,000
		691,000	162,400

Tax payable by S (with interest on unpaid tax from 1 July 2007) after 40% tapering relief
60% × £2,400   £1,440

Tax payable by personal representatives (with interest on unpaid tax from 1 July 2007)   £160,000

Breach of conditional exemption — sale of picture by D 3 April 2009

			Gross £	Tax at half rate (2008/09 scale) £
A's inheritance tax accumulation (* 691,000 – 312,000 = 379,000 @ 20%)			691,000	75,800*
Value of picture (sale proceeds)		150,000		
Less: Fees	15,000			
Capital gains tax	8,800	23,800	126,200	25,240
			817,200	101,040
Tax payable by D (with interest on unpaid tax from 1 November 2009)				£25,240

Explanatory Notes

Conditional exemption for works of art etc

1.   Conditional exemption from inheritance tax for works of art etc is provided in ss 30 to 35A. Eligible assets are:

Works of art and other objects or collections or groups of objects that are pre-eminent for their national, scientific, historic or artistic interest

Land of outstanding scenic, historic or scientific interest

Buildings of outstanding historic or architectural interest together with their amenity land and objects historically associated with them.

2.   Transfers are conditionally exempt if designated by the Treasury *following a claim* made within two years of the event (for example following death), providing an appropriate undertaking is given by such person as the Treasury consider appropriate (usually the transferee).

3.   The undertaking depends upon the category, but generally requires reasonable public access, preservation and in the case of objects, retention in the UK, until death or further disposition (s 31). Public access cannot be by prior appointment only, and the owner may be required to publicise information about the conditionally exempt asset.

4.   The conditional exemption is not available if the transfer would be exempt anyway by reason of transfers to charities or one's spouse/civil partner (s 30). But on a transfer to a spouse/civil partner of property that is the subject of an earlier conditional exemption, the spouse/civil partner would have to renew the undertaking to retain the conditional exemption (s 32).

Availability of conditional exemption

5.   Conditional exemption is available upon:

(i)   Death.

(ii)   Lifetime transfers where transferor and spouse/civil partner have between them been beneficially entitled to the subject matter throughout the preceding six years.

(iii)   Lifetime gifts not qualifying under (ii) where the transferor acquired the subject matter on an inheritance tax/capital transfer tax conditionally exempt death transfer (s 30(3)).

Potentially exempt transfers

6.   When a potentially exempt transfer of heritage property is made, no claim for conditional exemption may be made until the transferor dies, and a claim will not then be relevant if the transferor has survived the gift by seven years. If he dies within seven years, s 26A provides that the potentially exempt transfer will nonetheless be exempt if the property has in the meantime been sold by private treaty to an approved body (Sch 3) or surrendered to HMRC in satisfaction of tax (s 230). If the property has been sold other than to an approved body, no claim for conditional exemption may be made. The circumstances at the transferor's death will determine whether conditional exemption is available, and if an undertaking is already in force for capital gains tax or for maintenance fund purposes it will be treated as an undertaking under s 30.

In this example both gifts in 2002 are potentially exempt (after deducting the annual exemption from the earlier gift), so claims for conditional exemption for inheritance tax would not be made at the time of the gifts. In order to avoid capital gains tax arising on the gifts, however, it would have been necessary to make conditional claims to treat the gifts as being on a no loss no gain basis under the provisions of TCGA 1992 s 258, the appropriate undertaking as indicated in note 3 being required (see explanatory note 13).

The removal of the picture to America by W in 2004 does not affect a potentially exempt transfer.

On the death of A the potentially exempt transfers become chargeable. S cannot claim conditional exemption (because the conditions are not satisfied at the time of A's death) and tax is payable. (The transfer from S to W was an exempt transfer and therefore did not affect the inheritance tax accumulation of S.) D can claim conditional exemption, thus saving inheritance tax of 40% × £100,000 = £40,000 less tapering relief of 40% = £24,000 at that time.

Chargeable events

7.   Inheritance tax is payable following a conditionally exempt transfer when a chargeable event occurs.

A 'chargeable event' is:

(i)   Material breach of undertaking.

(ii)   Death (when a new conditionally exempt transfer might occur).

(iii)   Disposal by sale, gift (when a new conditionally exempt transfer might again occur) or otherwise.

In cases (ii) and (iii), that is death or disposal, a surrender to the Board of HMRC to pay inheritance tax, or a sale by private treaty to an approved body (eg museum) is not a chargeable event (s 32). A private treaty sale to an approved body would be below market value, but above the after tax sum that would arise on an open market sale, thus dividing the benefit of the tax saving between the vendor and the approved body.

8.   Inheritance tax is chargeable on the value of the subject matter at the time of the chargeable event. The value is the sale proceeds or market value as appropriate. An unconnected sale will usually fix the value at the sale proceeds (s 33(1)(a) and (3)).

9.   The tax is calculated according to the inheritance tax accumulation of the 'relevant person' at the date of the chargeable event. The relevant person is the person who made the conditionally exempt transfer of the property. If there have been two or more such transfers, but only one within the last thirty years ending with the event then the relevant person is that last person. Otherwise HMRC may select the accumulation of any transferor out of those making appropriate claims in the last thirty years (s 33(5)).

If the relevant person is alive at the time of the chargeable event (which cannot apply in the case of a potentially exempt transfer, because such a transfer only becomes chargeable, and therefore eligible for conditional exemption, on the donor's death), half the scale rate is used, and the rate is not increased to the full rate even if the donor then dies within seven years of the date of the conditionally exempt transfer. If the relevant person is dead at the time of the chargeable event, the full scale rate is charged if the transfer was made on death, and the half scale rate if it was made in lifetime (s 33(1)(b) and (2)).

10. When D sold her picture, this was a chargeable event giving rise to a charge under s 32, with inheritance tax payable by her on the net proceeds of sale (s 33(3)). The half rate applies as the conditional exemption was given on a lifetime potentially exempt transfer that became chargeable because of the death of A within seven years after the gift. The tax has therefore been calculated by adding the proceeds to A's lifetime and death transfers, but using half the scale rates in force at the date of A's death. If, however, the rates of tax have reduced between death and the date of the chargeable event, the rates at the time the asset ceases to qualify for exemption apply (Sch 2.5). There appears to be an anomaly here in that the half scale rate can never apply in normal circumstances to a potentially exempt transfer. It appears therefore that tax could be avoided by claiming conditional exemption on death, if the undertakings were breached soon afterwards. It may be that such conduct would be attacked by HMRC as a composite transaction under the Ramsay doctrine, thus treating the chargeable event as occurring on the death and attracting tax at the full rate.

Variation of undertakings

11. Once given, an undertaking may be varied by agreement between HMRC and the person bound by the undertaking (s 35A). If that person does not agree with a variation proposed by HMRC within six months, and the Special Commissioners consider it to be just and reasonable, they may direct that it should be made, with effect from a date not less than 60 days after the date of the direction.

Due date of payment of tax

12. Where tax becomes payable as a result of the occurrence of a chargeable event, such as the breach of an undertaking as in this example, the due date is six months after the end of the month in which the event by reason of which it is chargeable occurs (s 226(4)). Interest on overdue tax runs from that due date (s 233(1)(c)).

Capital gains tax

13. As far as capital gains tax is concerned, a gift of heritage property in lifetime that is potentially exempt from inheritance tax does not qualify for the gifts holdover relief of TCGA 1992 s 260. The gain may, however, escape tax conditionally under TCGA 1992 s 258 if the appropriate undertaking described in IHTA 1984 s 31 is given as indicated in note 6. The effect for capital gains tax purposes is that the person making the disposal by way of gift and the person acquiring it are treated as if the asset was acquired from the one making the disposal for a consideration of such an amount as would secure that on the disposal neither a gain nor a loss would accrue to the one making the disposal (TCGA 1992 s 258(4)).

On sale (other than to an approved body) or material breach the asset is treated as sold for its market value and capital gains tax arises (TCGA 1992 s 258(5)), taper relief for capital gains tax being given according to the period of ownership of the donee. If inheritance tax is chargeable on the same occasion, any capital gains tax payable reduces the value to be included as a chargeable transfer for inheritance tax (TCGA 1992 s 258(8)).

In the example, claims for conditional no gain no loss treatment for capital gains would have needed to be made by S and D to avoid an immediate capital gains tax charge on the 2002 gifts. When S gave his picture to his wife W, the gift would be a breach of the undertaking unless the undertaking was renewed by W. If it was not, S would be deemed to have sold and reacquired the asset at market value. If W made the undertaking, it would be breached when she took the asset out of the UK and the deemed disposal and reacquisition would be made by her. Although S also becomes liable to inheritance tax on the 2002 gift of the painting because of his father's death within seven years, he cannot deduct the capital gains tax paid by him (if any) from the inheritance tax value, because the occasion of the inheritance tax charge is the 2002 gift from the father, not the 2004 breach of the undertaking by S.

As far as D is concerned, she still held the painting at her father's death and the conditional exemption for inheritance tax will therefore apply, the capital gains tax undertaking being treated as an undertaking under s 30 (see note 6). When she breached the undertaking by selling the painting, both inheritance tax and capital gains tax are charged on that occasion, so the capital gains tax may be deducted from the value of the inheritance tax, as shown in the example.

Question

Mackenzie Ltd is a property holding and investment company.

The following is a summary of its balance sheet at 31 December 2008:

	£			£
Issued Capital: shares of £1 each	10,000	Freehold Properties (Market value £3,000,000)		1,720,000
Reserves	1,420,000			
		Quoted Investments (Market value £1,250,000)		1,200,000
Loan Accounts:				
Robert Mackenzie 1,200,000				
James Mackenzie 200,000		Bank Deposit Account	200,000	
Duncan Mackenzie 300,000	1,700,000			
		Bank Current Account	10,000	210,000
	3,130,000			3,130,000

The issued capital had since December 1982 been held by:

Robert Mackenzie			4,000
James Mackenzie	) Robert's sons		3,500
Duncan Mackenzie	)		2,500
			10,000

On 11 January 2009 Mrs Newman, Robert Mackenzie's daughter, and her three children returned to this country from overseas. To provide for them, Robert withdrew £400,000 from his loan account with the company, which enabled him on 15 January 2009 to give £437,500 to Mrs Newman. Some of the company's investments were sold to produce sufficient cash to pay the £400,000 to Robert.

A meeting of the members was held on 18 January 2009 at which it was resolved that one of the freehold properties owned by the company and valued at £900,000 should be conveyed to Miss Diana Crawley, a very close friend of Robert's. The house was conveyed to her on 20 January 2009 without payment.

Assuming that Robert had made previous chargeable transfers totalling £317,000 in 2004/05, that James had made a gift of £81,000 to his son on 31 December 2008 and that Duncan had made no gifts other than £200,000 to his wife in December 2005, calculate the inheritance tax payable in connection with the above.

Answer

Mackenzie Ltd — apportionment of transfer of value on 20 January 2009

Transfer of value by close company on 20 January 2009 apportioned amongst participators:

Robert Mackenzie	0.40 ×	900,000	=	360,000
James Mackenzie	0.35 ×	900,000	=	315,000
Duncan Mackenzie	0.25 ×	900,000	=	225,000
				£900,000

Inheritance tax payable:
Robert Mackenzie

Inheritance tax accumulation

			Gross £	Tax on 2008/09 scale £	Net £
Previous transfers within seven years			317,000	1,000*	316,000
(* 317,000 – 312,000 = 5,000 @ 20%)					
15 January 2008					
Gift to daughter			437,500		
Less: Annual exemptions	2008/09	3,000			
	2007/08	3,000	6,000		
Potentially exempt transfer			431,500		
20 January 2008					
Apportioned from Mackenzie Ltd (net amount)					360,000
Grossed up			450,000(*)	90,000	
			767,000	91,000	676,000

(*)   £360,000 is wholly within the tax band of 20% for lifetime gifts.

$$\text{The gross transfer is therefore: } 360,000 \times \frac{100}{80} = \text{£}450,000.$$

James Mackenzie

Inheritance tax accumulation

			Gross £	Tax on 2008/09 scale £	Net £
Gift to son on 31 December 2008 is a potentially exempt transfer of:					
Gift			81,000		
Less: Annual exemptions	2008/09	3,000			
	2007/08	3,000	6,000		

		Gross £	Tax on 2008/09 scale £	Net £
	75,000			
20 January 2009 Apportioned from Mackenzie Ltd (net amount)				315,000
Grossed up		315,750(*)	750	
		315,750	750	315,000

(*)   £315,000 – £312,000 = £3,000 is within tax band of 20% for lifetime gifts.

$$\text{The gross transfer is therefore: } 3,000 \times \frac{100}{80} = 3,750$$

312,000	@ nil rate		312,000
315,000			£315,750

Duncan Mackenzie

Inheritance tax accumulation

			Gross £	Tax on 2008/09 scale £	Net £
Previous transfer to wife — exempt			–	–	–
20 January 2009 Apportioned from Mackenzie Ltd (net amount)		225,000			
Less: Annual exemptions 2008/09	3,000				
2007/08	3,000	6,000	219,000*	0	219,000
Net gift grossed up			219,000	0	219,000

* £219,000 – £312,000 = nil within 20% tax band for lifetime gifts. The transfer is wholly within the nil-rate band.

Inheritance tax payable

	£
On conveyance by company	
Robert Mackenzie	90,000
James Mackenzie	750
Duncan Mackenzie	0
Payable by Mackenzie Ltd	90,750
By Robert Mackenzie on gift to his daughter (£6,000 of transfer covered by annual exemptions, balance of £431,500 potentially exempt transfer)	£nil

Explanatory Notes

Apportionment of close company transfers of value

1.   Where a close company makes a transfer of value, the transfer is apportioned amongst the participators and each participator is deemed to have made a net transfer of the amount apportioned to him (s 94(1)). HMRC take the view that only actual transfers (as distinct from those apportioned to participators from a close company) can be potentially exempt transfers, so that the apportioned amounts in this example are immediately reckoned for inheritance tax.

   If, however, the estate of a participator increases in consequence of the transfer, that increase is deducted from the amount chargeable on him, because his personal wealth has only decreased by his share of the close company transfer less the consequential increase in his wealth.

2.   The exempt transfer reliefs for small gifts, normal expenditure out of income and marriage gifts are not available, but the annual exemption is (s 94(5)).

3.   The surrender of losses under the corporation tax group relief provisions (TA 1988 s 402) does not constitute a transfer of value (s 94(3)).

4.   Where an asset is transferred between group companies on a no loss no gain basis under the provisions of TCGA 1992 s 171, the rights of minority participators are not taken into account for the purpose of apportioning transfers of value under s 94 providing the transfer has only a small effect on the value of the minority participators' rights (s 97). The provisions of s 97 have been extended by FA 2001 s 106 to cover *deemed* intra-group no loss no gain transfers on or after 1 April 2000 under the provisions of TCGA 1992 s 171A. For detailed provisions relating to the tax treatment of groups of companies see the companion book Tolley's Taxwise I 2008/09.

Transfers liable to income tax or corporation tax

5.   The apportionment rules do not apply to any part of the transfer that is liable to income tax or corporation tax in the recipient's hands (s 94(2)(a)). This will eliminate transfers of assets to participators who are employees earning £8,500 or more and to directors, which would be charged to income tax as employment income under the benefits code (ITEPA 2003 s 206) and also transfers to other participators, because they would be charged as distributions (TA 1988 s 418). A transfer by a close company to an Employee Benefit Trust may give rise to a transfer of value.

   In the circumstances of this example, HMRC would arguably seek to treat the value of the property as a benefit chargeable to income tax as employment income on the directors, in that an asset has been transferred out of the company at their direction without payment. If this were the case then the inheritance tax apportionment provisions would not apply.

Alterations of capital etc

6.   Changes in the rights or number of unquoted shares of a close company are treated as if made by a disposal at that time by the participator and are chargeable accordingly (s 98). Such transfers cannot be potentially exempt (s 98(3)).

Effect of apportionment on participators

7.   The apportioned amounts are included in the inheritance tax accumulations of the participators, unless an individual has not more than 5% of the transfer apportioned to him, in which case although the tax is computed by reference to his inheritance tax accumulation at that time, the transfer is not added to his cumulative total (s 94(4)).

Liability for payment of tax

8.   The liability to pay the inheritance tax is primarily that of the company, but if the company does not pay by the due date, liability extends to the participators and to the person who received the property transferred, except that a participator to whom not more than 5% of the transfer has been apportioned has no liability (s 202).

Capital gains tax

9.   Transfers at an undervalue by a close company also have a capital gains tax effect, in that the difference between the price paid (if any) and the market value is apportioned amongst the shareholders and regarded as reducing the capital gains tax base cost of their shares (TCGA 1992 s 125).

10. The realisation of investments by the company has nothing to do with the inheritance tax position of any of the shareholders. It is just exchanging one asset for another (but it might trigger a charge to corporation tax on a capital gain).

11. The gift of the property to Miss Crawley by the company is a disposal for capital gains purposes. Since the disposal is not at arm's length the company has a chargeable gain of the difference between the market value of the property and its cost plus indexation allowance to date (TCGA 1992 s 17).

     The 'loss to the donor', ie the company, in respect of the gift comprises the net of tax proceeds that the property would have realised if sold plus the tax the company has to pay on the gain, which together amount to the sum of £900,000 that is treated as a transfer of value.

Withdrawals from loan account

12. The withdrawal by Robert of £400,000 from his loan account with the company does not comprise a transfer of value by him. He has simply put himself in cash funds by exchanging one asset for another.

     The conveyance of the property to Miss Crawley would have been better arranged as a withdrawal of Robert's loan account. The personal capital gains effect at note 9 would have been avoided, and the gift of the property *by him* to Miss Crawley would have been a potentially exempt transfer. An immediate tax cost of £90,750 would have been avoided and the inheritance tax accumulations of all three shareholders not affected.

Question

In 1986 Mr and Mrs John Webb acquired shares in Pirling Ltd, a small private investment company, of which they have since been directors.

The shares in the company are held as follows:

	Shares held	% of issued share capital
Mr Webb	1,201	26.69
Mrs Webb	1,199	26.64
	2,400	53.33
Others (not related persons)	2,100	46.67
	4,500	100.00

Mr and Mrs Webb are each considering transferring out of their respective holdings 350 shares to their adult son David by way of gift. In the event that they proceed, the transfers will be effected on the same day in January 2009, but Mrs Webb will execute her transfer first.

It is expected that HMRC Shares Valuation Division will agree valuations as follows:

53.33% holding	£500 per share
45.55% holding	£315 per share
37.77% holding	£250 per share

Mr Webb's father died in 2003 when his estate comprised an investment in standing timber valued at £120,000, which he left to John, and other assets of £418,000. An election was made to leave the timber out of account and inheritance tax was paid on the £418,000 at the death scale applicable at that time.

Mr Webb now proposes to sell the timber for £220,000 during 2008/09.

He estimates that felling expenses will amount to £24,000 and that the subsequent cost of restoring roads and fences will be £16,000.

The potentially exempt transfers (after exemptions) made up to 5 April 2008 by Mr and Mrs Webb were £356,000 and £171,000 respectively, all made between 6 April 2006 and 5 April 2007.

Assuming the legislation remains unchanged for future years, calculate:

(i)   The potential liability to inheritance tax of Mr and Mrs Webb resulting from their proposals if they die during 2010/11.

(ii) The inheritance tax liability in respect of the disposal of the timber.

Answer

(i) **Mr and Mrs Webb — Potential liability to inheritance tax on death in 2010/11 following gifts of shares**

Mr Webb

		Gross £	Tax on 2010/11 scale £
Potentially exempt transfers at 5.4.08 now chargeable		356,000	2,400*
(* 356,000 – 350,000 = 6,000 @ 40%)			
January 2009			
Gift of shares in Pirling Ltd to son			
(working note (b))	165,565		
Less annual exemptions 2008/09 and 2007/08	6,000		
Potentially exempt transfer now chargeable		159,565	63,826
		515,565	66,226

Inheritance tax payable:

By donees of potentially exempt gifts made in 2006/07 (ie more than three years before Mr Webb's death)		
Tapering relief of either 20% or 40% would be available depending on the dates of the gifts and the date of Mr Webb's death. If he died less than four years after making the gifts the amount payable would be 80% × £2,400		£1,920
By David on gift of shares (within three years before death therefore no tapering relief)		£63,826

Mrs Webb

		Gross £	Tax on 2010/11 scale £
Potentially exempt transfers at 5.4.08 now chargeable		171,000	–
January 2009			
Gift of shares in Pirling Ltd to son			
(working note (a))	332,065		
Less: annual exemptions 2008/09 and 2007/08	6,000		
Potentially exempt transfer now chargeable		326,065	58,826*
		497,065	58,826*

(* 497,065 – 350,000 = 147,065 @ 40%)

		Gross £	Tax on 2010/11 scale £

Inheritance tax payable:
No tax is due from the donees of the gifts made in
2006/07 because the amount chargeable is below the
nil threshold.
By David on gift of shares (within three years before
death therefore no tapering relief) — £58,826

(ii) **Liability to inheritance tax on sale of timber in 2008/09**

			Gross £	Tax on 2008/09 scale £
Father's estate at death (excluding timber)			418,000	42,400
(418,000 – 312,000 = 106,000 @ 40%)				
Sale of timber		220,000		
Less: Expenses				
Felling	24,000			
Restoration*	16,000	40,000	180,000	72,000**
			598,000	114,400

The person who is entitled to the sale proceeds, ie Mr Webb, is liable to pay the tax, although the tax is calculated by reference to the father's estate.

Inheritance tax payable by Mr Webb is therefore £72,000.

* Allowable expenses are expenses of disposal and of replanting. It is considered that the restoration of the roads and fences would form part of the disposal expenses.

** If the timber constituted 'relevant business property', 50% relief would be available, which would halve the tax payable (see explanatory note 10).

Working Notes

Computation of gifts

(a) *Mrs Webb* (using related property rules)

Value of shares before transfer (53.33% holding) — £

$$\frac{1,199}{2,400} \times (2,400 @ £500) \qquad = \qquad 599,500$$

Value of shares after transfer (45.55% holding)

$$\frac{849}{2,050} \times (2,050 @ £315) \qquad = \qquad 267,435$$

Reduction in estate   332,065

(b)   *Mr Webb* (using related property rules)

Value of shares before transfer (45.55% holding)

$$\frac{1,201}{2,050} \times (2,050 @ £315) \qquad = \qquad 378,315$$

Value of shares after transfer (37.77% holding)

$$\frac{851}{1,700} \times (1,700 @ £250) \qquad = \qquad 212,750$$

Reduction in estate   165,565

Explanatory Notes

Business property relief on shares

1.   Business property relief is not available in respect of the transfer of shares by Mr and Mrs Webb because they are shares in an investment company. See Example 25 for detailed notes on business property relief.

Consecutive transfers

2.   Care must be taken to calculate the transfers in the correct order. The example states that Mrs Webb makes her transfer first, thus her accumulation must be used to record the loss in value attributable to the loss of control. Note that although the shares held by Mr Webb also lose value that loss is not due to a transfer of value made by Mr Webb and is therefore not chargeable. HMRC could use the associated operations provisions to counter the loss to the Exchequer but do not normally do so unless the transactions are actually linked or form part of an avoidance package.

For notes on associated operations, see Examples 22 and 23.

Even though the associated operations provisions may not apply, the related property provisions will apply. See notes to Example 10 for further details.

3.   If Mr Webb were to make his transfer of shares first then the potential liabilities (using related property rules) would become:

Mr Webb

£

Value of shares before transfer (53.33% holding)

$$\frac{1,201}{2,400} \times (2,400 \ @ \ £500) =$$

600,500

Value of shares after transfer (45.55% holding)

$$\frac{851}{2,050} \times (2,050 \ @ \ £315) =$$

268,065

Reduction in estate

332,435

Inheritance tax payable on death in 2010/11

		Gross £	Tax on 2010/11 scale £
Cumulative chargeable transfers (as before)		356,000	2,400
January 2009			
Gift of shares in Pirling Ltd to son	332,435		
Less annual exemptions 2008/09 and 2007/08	6,000		
Potentially exempt transfer now chargeable		326,435	130,574
		682,435	132,974

Mrs Webb

£

Value of shares before transfer (45.55% holding)

$$\frac{1,199}{2,050} \times (2,050 \ @ \ £315)$$

377,685

Value of shares after transfer (37.77% holding)

$$\frac{849}{1,700} \times (1,700 \ @ \ £250)$$

212,250

Reduction in estate

165,435

Inheritance tax payable on death in 2010/11

		Gross £	Tax on 2010/11 scale £
Cumulative chargeable transfers (as before)		171,000	–
January 2009			
Gift of shares in Pirling Ltd to son	165,435		
Less annual exemptions 2008/09 and 2007/08	6,000		
Potentially exempt transfer now chargeable		159,435	–
		330,435	–

(* 330,435 – 3050,000 = nil)

A comparison of the potential inheritance tax liabilities is:

	Mrs Webb makes first transfer £	Mr Webb makes first transfer £
On death in 2010/11 of		
Mr Webb	63,826	130,574
Mrs Webb	58,826	–
	122,652	130,574

This illustrates that the order in which transfers are made may alter not only the potential total liabilities, but also where the burden of the tax falls and the future accumulation for inheritance tax. This will be particularly important not only where there are different beneficiaries but also in the context of future gifts.

Growing timber

4.   Where an estate *on death* includes growing timber, an election may be made under s 125 to leave the timber (but not the land on which it stands) out of account in valuing the estate at death. The election must be made within two years of the date of death and is only available if the deceased either had been beneficially entitled to the land throughout the previous five years, or had become entitled to it without consideration (for example, by gift or inheritance).

5.   The election may not be made if the woodland is occupied with agricultural land and the occupation is ancillary to that of the agricultural land. In those circumstances, however, agricultural relief would be given if the necessary conditions were fulfilled.

For details of agricultural relief, see Example 25.

6.   Following an election, the subsequent disposal by sale or gift of the timber gives rise to a charge to inheritance tax under s 126 on the sale price less allowable expenses, or if the disposal is for less than full consideration, the market value (s 127(1)). Allowable expenses are the costs of sale and expenses of replanting within three years of disposal, or such longer time as the Board allows (s 130(2)).

7.   The disposal proceeds are treated as value transferred at the date of *death*, forming the top slice of the property passing on death and thus attracting the highest rates of tax (s 128). But where there have been reductions in the rates of tax, the death scale current at the time of *disposal* is used (Sch 2.4). The tax is due six months after the end of the month in which the disposal takes place, with interest payable from that date. Section 208 provides that the person entitled to the proceeds of sale (or the person who would be entitled if the disposal were a sale) is liable for the tax.

Instalment option

8. If the disposal of the timber was itself a chargeable transfer, or a potentially exempt transfer that becomes chargeable because of the donor's death within seven years, the value transferred thereby is reduced by the tax charged under explanatory note 7 in arriving at the chargeable transfer (s 129). Section 229 provides that a claim may be made for the tax chargeable on such a transfer to be paid by ten equal annual instalments, commencing six months after the end of the month in which the transfer is made. Although this would be possible for a chargeable lifetime transfer, such as to a discretionary trust, it could not apply to a potentially exempt transfer, nor to any additional tax on a chargeable lifetime transfer, because the liability would not exist until after the donor's death. It appears, therefore, that this provision should have been amended to take account of the current treatment of potentially exempt transfers and additional liabilities on chargeable lifetime transfers. It is considered that the instalment option would in practice be available, with the first instalment being due six months after the end of the month in which the donor died. If any instalment is paid late, interest is payable only on the late instalment and not on the full amount outstanding (s 234).

Death before disposal

9. If the person who inherits woodlands on which an election has been made dies before the timber is disposed of, no inheritance tax charge can arise in respect of the earlier death (s 126(1)).

    Furthermore, a new election may then be made on the second death.

Business property relief for growing timber

10. Where woodlands constitute 'relevant business property', ie where they are operated on a commercial basis, they qualify for 100% business property relief. But if an election is made to leave such timber out of account on a death, the net sale proceeds on subsequent sale are reduced by only 50% (s 127(2)). Elections should not therefore be made where the 100% relief is available (although part of the 100% relief may not be effective because of the way the estate devolves — see Examples 15 and 17). Where an election has already been made, as in this example, and the timber is subsequently sold, the relief can only be given at the 50% rate.

    For notes on business property relief see Example 25.

Transitional estate duty provisions

11. Under the transitional provisions that were introduced when estate duty was replaced by capital transfer tax (now inheritance tax), a liability to estate duty will arise on the sale of timber that was left out of account on a pre 13 March 1975 death. But if an inheritance tax transfer of value (other than to a spouse) intervenes (for example, the death of the person beneficially entitled) estate duty will not be chargeable at all and the transfer will be dealt with under the inheritance tax provisions (Sch 7.2). Such a transfer cannot be a potentially exempt transfer and will therefore be a chargeable transfer unless covered by exemptions (FA 1986 Sch 19.46). This provision strictly applies to the whole of any property of which any part, however small, is subject to the deferred estate duty charge. By HMRC Concession F15, any part of the property that is not subject to the deferred charge will not be prevented from being a potentially exempt transfer.

Question

Mr Rosewell, a UK domiciled individual, owned a set of four Rennie Mackintosh chairs which he wanted to give to his son. Rather than gift them as a set, he gifted them individually to his son in August 2004, 2005, 2006 and 2007 so as to lower the gifted value.

The relevant values were:

Number of chairs	2004 £	2005 £	2006 £	2007 £
Four	40,000	44,000	48,000	52,500
Three	30,000	33,000	36,500	40,000
Two	17,500	19,250	21,000	23,500
One	6,250	6,875	7,500	8,250

In September 2007 Mr Rosewell gifted £310,500 cash into a discretionary trust of which he is a beneficiary. The trustees agreed to pay any tax due.

Mr Rosewell's father (a widower) had died in May 2000. In his will he left woodlands including standing timber with a then value of £125,000 to Mr Rosewell. The father's estate was worth £575,000 excluding the timber and the executors elected to exclude the timber from the chargeable estate. In February 2007 Mr Rosewell gifted the woodland to his son, who agreed to pay any tax due. The land was then worth £350,000 and the timber £150,000. The woodland was not run as a business.

After the transactions detailed above Mr Rosewell's estate was worth £200,000. Under his will he left half of the estate to his wife and the balance equally between his son and daughter.

Mr Rosewell is concerned about the inheritance tax exposures were he to die, for example, in December 2009. His health has significantly deteriorated in the last few months. He has made no other gifts or transfers apart from those stated above.

Explain the inheritance tax implications of the above transactions if Mr Rosewell were to die on 30 December 2009 (assuming all assets retain their current values and that the legislation remains unchanged).

Answer

Inheritance tax implications of transactions by Mr Rosewell in the event of his death on 30 December 2009

Position on gifts in lifetime

Gifts of Rennie Mackintosh chairs to son (using associated operations rules for second and subsequent gifts)

			£	£
August 2004	Value of set of four chairs		40,000	
	Value of three chairs		30,000	
	Transfer of value		10,000	
	2004/05 annual exemption	3,000		
	2003/04 annual exemption	3,000	6,000	
	Potentially exempt transfer			4,000
August 2005	Value of four chairs		44,000	
	Value of two chairs		19,250	
	Loss to donor		24,750	
	Less: earlier transfer		10,000	
	Transfer of value		14,750	
	2005/06 annual exemption		3,000	
	Potentially exempt transfer			11,750
August 2006	Value of four chairs		48,000	
	Value of one chair		7,500	
	Loss to donor		40,500	
	Less: earlier transfers (10,000 + 14,750)		24,750	
	Transfer of value		15,750	
	2006/07 annual exemption		3,000	
	Potentially exempt transfer			12,750
August 2007	Value of four chairs		52,500	
	Less: earlier transfers			
	(10,000 + 14,750 + 15,750)		40,500	
	Transfer of value		12,000	
	2007/08 annual exemption		3,000	
	Potentially exempt transfer			9,000

Gift with reservation to discretionary trust

		Gross £	Tax (2007/08 scale) £
Sept 2007	Settlement on trust	310,500	2,100
(* 310,500 – 300,000 = 10,500 @ 20%)			

Tax payable by trustees £2,100

Gift of woodlands to son

The gift of the woodlands to Mr Rosewell's son would trigger a charge to inheritance tax in respect of the timber in Mr Rosewell's father's estate, based on the value at the date of disposal. Since the estate was well in excess of the inheritance tax threshold the tax charge would be £150,000 @ 40% = £60,000, payable by Mr Rosewell six months after the end of the month of disposal, ie by 31 August 2008. The tax would reduce the value of the transfer to the son, as follows:

		£	£
February 2008	Market value of woodlands (350,000 + timber 150,000)	500,000	
	Less: Tax payable re father's estate	60,000	
	Potentially exempt transfer		440,000

On Mr Rosewell's death – 30 December 2009

Since Mr Rosewell made a gift with reservation to the discretionary trust, the double charges regulations must be used when computing the tax following his death. The first calculation is to charge the gift in the death estate and ignore the transfer to the trust, and the second to charge the gift to the trust and exclude it from the death estate.

First calculation (ignoring gift to trust)

			Gross £	*Tax (on 2009/10 scale)* £
Gifts within seven years before death:				
August 2004	PET re gift of chairs		4,000	–
August 2005	PET re gift of chairs		11,750	–
August 2006	PET re gift of chairs		12,750	–
August 2007	PET re gift of chairs		9,000	–
Sept 2007	Gift to trust — ignored		–	–
Feb 2008	Gift of woodlands		440,000	61,000*
(* 477,500 – 325,000 = 152,500 @ 40%)			477,500	61,000*
Value of estate on death:				
Free estate		200,000		
Less: Spouse exemption		100,000	100,000	
Settled property			308,400** 408,400	163,360
			885,900	
Total tax payable				224,360

** Initial value of trust £310,500 less tax of £2,100 paid by trustees out of the amount settled.

Second calculation (excluding value of trust from death estate)

			Gross £	Tax (on 2009/10 scale) £
Gifts within seven years before death:				
August 2004	PET re gift of chairs		4,000	–
August 2005	PET re gift of chairs		11,750	–
August 2006	PET re gift of chairs		12,750	–
August 2007	PET re gift of chairs		9,000	–
Sept 2007	Chargeable transfer to discretionary trust		310,500	8,400*
(* 348,000 – 325,000 = 21,000 @ 40%)			348,000	8,400*
Feb 2008	Gift of woodlands		440,000	176,000
Value of estate on death		200,000		
Less: Spouse exemption		100,000	100,000	40,000
			888,000	
				224,400
Less tax paid in lifetime				2,100
Total tax payable				222,300

Since the first calculation shows the higher tax figure, that calculation applies. The tax of £2,100 paid by the trustees in lifetime is, however, allowed as a credit against the tax payable in respect of the trust property at death, reducing the total payable to £222,260 (see explanatory note 5). Inheritance tax is therefore payable as follows:

By son re woodlands		61,000
By trustees of discretionary trust 308,400 @ 40%	123,360	
Less paid in lifetime	2,100	121,260
By personal representatives		40,000
		222,260

Explanatory Notes

Associated operations

1. The attempt by Mr Rosewell to reduce the value of the gift of the chairs by giving them in different tax years is blocked by the associated operations provisions of s 268 (for details see Examples 22 and 23). Spreading the gifts does, however, enable the annual exemptions to be used.

Growing timber

2. The provisions enabling growing timber to be left out of a deceased's estate are dealt with in Example 31. Where the disposal of the timber is a chargeable transfer or, as in this example, a potentially exempt transfer that becomes a chargeable transfer, the tax charged in respect of the original estate as a result of the disposal of the timber reduces the value transferred, as illustrated for Mr Rosewell (s 129). See Example 31 explanatory note 8 re paying tax by instalments.

Gifts with reservation and double charges regulations

3. By including himself as a beneficiary of the discretionary trust, Mr Rosewell has made a gift with reservation. The effect is that the gift to the trust is chargeable when made, but the value of the trust is still included in his estate for inheritance tax purposes so long as he is included as a beneficiary. See Example 24 for an illustration of the release of such a reservation in lifetime.

4. The effect of the gifts with reservation rules is to charge tax twice, and the double charges regulations (SI 1987/1130) give relief for the double charge by providing for tax to be charged at the higher of two calculations, the first being to charge the gift in the death estate and ignore it in lifetime and the second to charge the gift in lifetime and exclude it from the death estate. For the detailed provisions and further illustrations see Examples 19, 20 and 24.

5. When making the first calculation, in which the gift to the trust in lifetime is ignored and is included in the death estate at its then value, the tax paid on the gift in lifetime is not taken into account. If, however, the first calculation proves to give the higher figure of tax payable, the tax paid in lifetime is credited against the tax attributable to the gift. Note, however, that this credit is taken into account *after* deciding which of the two calculations shows the higher figure (SI 1987/1130 reg 5(4)). In this example, had the lifetime tax been deducted before making the comparison, the second calculation would have shown the higher tax figure (£222,300 compared with £222,260).

    When giving credit for the tax paid in lifetime in the second calculation, that figure will be restricted to the tax payable on death shown in the earlier part of the calculation. That restriction does not apply in this example.

Capital gains tax implications of gift of chairs

6. Mr Rosewell's gifts of the chairs to his son also have implications for capital gains tax. There are two separate provisions affecting the capital gains calculations. The first is the connected persons provisions of TCGA 1992 ss 19 and 20. Where assets are disposed of within a period of six years to one or more connected persons (such as Mr Rosewell's son in this example) and their value taken together is higher than their separate values, the disposal value is taken to be a proportionate part of the aggregate value, and the legislation provides that earlier tax charges should be adjusted appropriately. The second is the chattels exemption of TCGA 1992 s 262, which provides that chattels such as antiques are exempt if sold for £6,000 or less, with marginal relief for proceeds above £6,000. If articles that constitute a set are sold on different occasions to the same person (or connected persons) the transactions are treated as a single transaction for the purpose of the exemption, earlier tax charges similarly being required to be adjusted appropriately. See the companion to this book, Tolley's Taxwise I 2008/09, for full details of the capital gains tax provisions.

Question

(a) In relation to inheritance tax there is a statutory duty laid on solicitors, accountants and others (except barristers) to make a return to the Board of HMRC when they have been acting in a professional capacity on behalf of a settlor in certain given circumstances.

When does that statutory duty arise and what are its limitations?

(b) A client who has undertaken to discharge any inheritance tax payable informs you that he has received a Notice of Determination from HMRC in which it is specified that the value of a holding of 2,500 shares in T Ltd (25% of the equity) which he had transferred to a discretionary settlement, has been determined at £20 per share.

If your client considers that the value of the shares is not more than £5 each, what advice would you offer?

(c) As in (b) above, a client who has undertaken to discharge any inheritance tax payable informs you that he has received a Notice of Determination from HMRC in which it is specified that the value of a plot of land (Blackacre), transferred to the trustees of a discretionary settlement, should be £250,000.

If your client considers that the value of Blackacre is overstated in the Notice of Determination, what further advice would you offer?

(d) When and in what circumstances is it possible to obtain a grant of representation to a deceased person without first delivering an HMRC Account?

How is the legal personal representative protected against any subsequent claim from the Revenue for inheritance tax in connection with the death when a grant has been issued in this way, and in what circumstances is such protection lost?

Can he still be called on to complete an HMRC Account?

(e) When and in what circumstances is it necessary to render an account of transfers of value made during the lifetime of the transferor?

Answer

(a) **Duty to make return to Revenue re settlements**

Section 218 provides that where any person, other than a barrister, has in the course of his trade or profession been concerned with the making of a settlement where the settlor is domiciled in the UK and the trustees are not or will not be resident in the UK, he must within three months of the making of the settlement make a return to the Board of HMRC. The return must state the names and addresses of the settlor and of the trustees.

For this purpose the trustees are regarded as non-resident unless the general administration of the settlement is carried on in the UK and the trustees or a majority of them are also resident in the UK (s 218(3)).

A return is not required where the settlement was created by a will or where such a return has already been made by another person, for example the trustees (s 218(2)).

(b) **Notice of Determination relating to value of shares**

The client should be advised to appeal in writing against the determination of the value of the shares specified in the notice. The appeal must be made within thirty days of service of the notice and must state the client's grounds of appeal, ie that the true value of the shares is not more than £5 each (s 222(1)).

The appeal will normally be made to the Special Commissioners, but it may be made to the High Court if either:

(i) it is agreed between the client and HMRC that the appeal will be to the High Court, or

(ii) following an application by the client, the High Court is satisfied that the matters to be decided are substantially questions of law (s 222(2) and (3)).

If the client makes the appeal outside the thirty day limit it will be allowed to proceed providing there is a reasonable excuse for the delay (s 223).

(c) **Notice of Determination relating to value of land**

The client should be advised to appeal in writing against the determination of the value of Blackacre as at (b) above. However, because the question in dispute is a question as to the value of land in the United Kingdom, it may be made to the Lands Tribunal in the first instance and on any appeal under s 222 to the Special Commissioners or the High Court, the question will be determined on a reference to the Lands Tribunal (s 222(40–(4B)).

(d) **Grant of representation to deceased's estate, exempt and excepted estates**

Personal representatives are not required to produce an account to the probate registry to obtain a grant of representation; instead they complete a Probate Summary in the form of supplementary page D18 to the form IHT200 (previously form P26A). The HMRC account must be sent to HMRC Capital Taxes and the inheritance tax on the non-instalment property must be paid before the grant is issued.

Excepted estates

To apply for a grant of representation for an excepted estate the personal representative completes form IHT 205 (C5 in Scotland) or IHT 207 for those domiciled abroad. The form is given to the Probate Registry.

There is an excepted estate where the conditions set out below are satisfied.

There are three types of excepted estate set out in SI 2004/2543 applicable from 1 November 2004 with respect to deaths on or after 6 April 2004 and this is further amended with respect to deaths on or after 1 September 2006 by SI 2006/2141. The three types of excepted estate are: low value excepted estates; exempt excepted estates and excepted estates of foreign domiciliaries.

A. Low value excepted estates: Under paragraph 4(2) the conditions are:

  (i) the deceased was domiciled in the UK at the date of death;

  (ii) the estate consists only of property passing under the deceased's will or intestacy or under a trust, nominated property, or joint property passing by survivorship;

  (iii) where any trust assets were held in a single trust in which the deceased had an interest in possession with a value not exceeding £150,000;

  (iv) not more than £100,000 represents the value of property situated outside the UK;

  (v) the deceased is not a person by reason of whose death one of the alternatively secured pension fund provisions applies;

  (vi) the deceased died without having made any chargeable transfer in the seven years before his death except cash, quoted shares or quoted securities, or land and buildings (and contents), with a total gross value not exceeding £150,000. For this purpose paragraph 4(7) indicates that business property relief and agricultural property relief shall not apply;

  (vii) the gross value of the estate plus transfer within seven years of death plus exempt transfers to spouse/civil partner, charities etc within seven years of death do not exceed the nil rate band at death.

B. Exempt excepted estates: Under paragraph 4(3) the conditions are:

  (i) the deceased was domiciled in the UK at the date of death;

  (ii) the conditions set out in A above at (ii) to (vi) apply;

  (iii) the gross value of chargeable assets of the estate (before deducting liabilities, reliefs or exemptions), when added to the cumulative chargeable gifts made in the seven years before death, does not exceed £1,000,000 and the net chargeable estate after deduction of spouse/civil partner and charity exemptions only does not exceed the nil rate band.

C. Under paragraph 4(5) the estate is exempt if the deceased was never domiciled (or deemed domicile) in the UK, the estate consists only of cash or quoted shares the alternative pension fund provisions do not apply and the gross value does not exceed £150,000.

The requirement for an HMRC account to be submitted is relaxed by regulations issued under the provisions of s 256. The regulations enable a grant of representation to be issued without the completion of an HMRC account in the case of excepted estates. The procedures are explained in HMRC's Customer Guide to Inheritance Tax.

An estate is not an excepted estate if the deceased had made a gift with reservation of benefit which either continued until death or ceased within seven years before death.

Protection from liability to inheritance tax:

After thirty-five days (the 'prescribed period') from the issue of the grant all persons potentially liable for inheritance tax in respect of the excepted estate are automatically discharged from liability and any charge for such tax on any property comprised in the estate is removed.

The protection is lost:

1. in the case of fraud or failure to disclose material facts or

2.   if it subsequently comes to light that there is further property which causes the excepted estate conditions not to be satisfied (eg the gross value exceeds £1,000,000, or other property exceeds the stipulated limits) or

3.   if within the 'prescribed period' a notice in writing is issued by HMRC to the personal representatives requiring delivery of an HMRC account.

If it is discovered at any time that the estate is not an excepted estate then the personal representative must deliver a Corrective Account (C4) to the Revenue within six months of the discovery.

If an estate ceases to be an excepted estate because of a deed of variation then again a C4 is required within six months of the date of variation. HMRC say it will help them process accounts more quickly if copies of the signed IHT 205/C5 or if appropriate the instrument of variation are attached to the C4.

The Revenue have agreed to adopt this procedure instead of insisting on a full form IHT 200 being delivered (see HMRC IHT Newsletter Aug 2004).

(e)   **Rendering an account of chargeable transfers**

Under section 216 persons liable to inheritance tax are required to submit an account in respect of *chargeable transfers* made in lifetime before the end of twelve months from the end of the month in which the transfer is made unless the transfer is an excepted transfer or excepted termination (in relation to life interest trusts) or, in the case of discretionary trusts, the settlement is an excepted settlement. There were previously no provisions excepting trustees of discretionary trusts from making returns of chargeable transfers (ie ten yearly charges or exit charges), even though the trust funds were too small to give rise to any tax liability. Provisions for 'excepted settlements' were introduced for chargeable events on or after 6 April 2002 (SI 2002/1732) and these have now been replaced by SI 2008/606 with effect in respect of chargeable events occurring on or after 6 April 2007.

An account is also required in the case of alternatively secured pension funds following the death of a member of the scheme or a relevant dependant of the member. The account is required from the scheme administrator of a registered pension scheme within 12 months of the end of the month in which the individual died.

Whilst a potentially exempt transfer is a transfer of value it is not a chargeable transfer unless the transferor dies within seven years. Accordingly there is no requirement to notify HMRC Capital Taxes on the making of such a transfer. On the death of the transferor the transferee is primarily liable for any inheritance tax on the potentially exempt transfer and is obliged to submit an account within twelve months from the end of the month in which the transferor died (s 216(6)). The personal representatives of the transferor have a secondary liability for any inheritance tax arising, and they are required under s 216 to give details of all chargeable transfers made by the deceased with the seven years before his death. If they cannot establish the exact value of any property, the account may contain a provisional figure, but they must undertake to deliver a further account as soon as the exact amount is ascertained.

Where a person holds property subject to a reservation (or within seven years after the release of a reservation) then on the death of the donor that person must deliver to the Board an account of such property within twelve months from the end of the month in which the donor died (s 216(6)(ab)).

An 'excepted termination' is the termination of a life interest in a trust where the life tenant has given notice to the trustees of the availability of annual or marriage exemptions and the value transferred is covered by the exemptions.

An 'excepted settlement' is a settlement in which no qualifying interest in possession subsists in relation to which there are no related settlements (ie settlements created by the settlor on the same day) and in respect of which:

(i) the assets have always comprised only cash (and the settlor has not added any capital to the trust after its creation)

(ii) the trustees have been UK resident throughout the trust's existence

(iii) the total value of the assets at the time of the chargeable event is less than £1,000.

If someone who has submitted an account discovers that it is materially incorrect, he must submit an amended account within six months after the discovery of the defect (s 217).

Under s 219A HMRC may require anyone liable to deliver an account under s 216 or 217 to produce relevant documents and accounts. The person receiving the notice may appeal against it within thirty days from the date on which the notice was given (s 219B).

Explanatory Notes

Accounts, returns and provision of other information

1. An *Account* is a document completed by a transferor (or other taxable person) providing details of a transaction to which a liability to inheritance tax may apply.

    A *Return* is a document submitted by a person about transactions affecting others.

2. In addition to the returns dealt with in part (a) of the example, the Board has power to require a person to provide information as specified in a notice under s 219. This does not extend to information in respect of which a lawyer could maintain a claim of professional privilege, except that solicitors may be obliged to disclose the names and addresses of clients. There is no right of appeal against a s 219 notice.

    A notice under this paragraph may be combined with one relating to income tax.

    The s 219 requirement to provide information is extended by FA 1990 s 125 to require someone to provide information in respect of tax liabilities outside the UK that are of a similar nature to inheritance tax if this is provided for in a double tax agreement, and the s 219 requirements also apply from 28 July 2000 where a tax information exchange agreement has been made by the UK with the country concerned (s 220A).

    Both double taxation and information exchange agreements may provide that information may not only be exchanged with, but also obtained for, the relevant overseas country.

3. The Board also has power (under s 219A) to require a person to produce documents or provide accounts for the purposes of enquiring into an account; determining whether an account is correct; and making determinations. An appeal against such requirements lies to the Special Commissioners under s 219B, but no further appeal is permitted.

Notice of Determination

4. The notice of determination by the Board under s 221 dealt with in part (b) of the example may be issued to the transferor, or to any person liable for any of the tax chargeable on the value transferred, or to anyone making a claim in respect of the value transferred.

    The notice may specify all or any of the following:

    (a) Date of transfer

    (b) Value transferred and value of any property to which the value transferred is wholly or partly attributable

    (c) Transferor

    (d)   Tax chargeable and persons liable

    (e)   Tax overpaid and date from which interest will be added on overpayment (and rate of interest)

    (f)   Any other relevant matter (s 221(1) and (2)).

5.   The determination of any fact relating to a transfer is to be in accordance with the account or return submitted if the Board is satisfied that it is correct but otherwise is to be made by the Board to the best of their judgment (s 221(3)).

Appeals against Notices of Determination

6.   Appeals are to the Special Commissioners or High Court unless the notice is in connection with the value of land, when the appeal is to the Lands Tribunal (s 222(4)). The Special Commissioners may refer any question as to the value of land directly to the Lands Tribunal, rather than the taxpayer being required to make a fresh appeal.

7.   An appeal on the determination of the Special Commissioners may be made on a point of law by requesting a 'case stated' for the opinion of the High Court (s 225).

     The procedure is the same as that relating to income tax appeals on a point of law.

Excepted estates

8.   Where an estate is an excepted estate the personal representatives will swear a revised form of oath stating that the gross value of the estate does not exceed the appropriate amount.

Persons required to deliver an account

9.   The provisions requiring those liable to inheritance tax in lifetime to render an account are dealt with in part (d) of the example.

     The personal representatives of a deceased person must deliver an account of all property which formed part of the estate at death unless the estate is an excepted estate. Where there are no personal representatives then:

    (a)   every person in whom property of the estate vests, or who is beneficially entitled to an interest in possession on or after the deceased's death, and

    (b)   where property passes to a settlement without an interest in possession, every person for whose benefit any of that property, or income from it, is applied

     must deliver an account to the Board specifying the property in which he has an interest.

     The account is submitted on HMRC account form IHT200. This is accompanied by a worksheet (IHT(WS)). HMRC produce a booklet IHT210 (How to fill in form IHT200), individual guidance notes for each of the supplementary pages and booklet IHT213 (How to fill in form IHT(WS)). A practitioner's guide booklet IHT215 collects all the guidance together in a single volume.

Penalties

10.   The legislation imposes various penalties in relation to inheritance tax as follows (ss 245, 245A, 247):

    (a)   Under s 247, someone liable for tax on a chargeable transfer who fraudulently or negligently provides any incorrect account, information or document, is liable to a penalty not exceeding £3,000 (unless no additional inheritance tax is payable as a result of the misinformation).

         Where the person who provided the incorrect information is not liable for the tax, a penalty is payable of up to £3,000 for fraud or negligence.

    (b)   The penalties for negligence apply equally to someone who discovers that information has been supplied that is incorrect in a material respect (regarded by HMRC as involving a tax error of £1,000 or more) and fails to notify HMRC without unreasonable delay (considered by

HMRC to be within 30 days), whether that person is the person who supplied the information or the person who is liable for the tax (s 248). HMRC have, however, stated that if incorrect accounts result from an innocent error they will not seek a penalty if they are notified within six months after the error is discovered.

(c)   Anyone who assists in or induces the delivery of information known to be incorrect is liable to a penalty of up to £3,000 (s 247(4)).

(d)   Under s 245, a penalty of £100 (restricted to tax due) applies if someone fails to deliver an account under s 216 or s 217 unless there is a reasonable excuse.

A further penalty of up to £60 a day may be charged if the failure continues after it has been declared by a court or by the Special Commissioners. If daily penalties have not been sought, and the account is more than six months late, a further penalty of £100 may be charged.

(e)   Under s 245A, a person who fails to make a return under s 218 relating to a trust with non-resident trustees (as to which see part (a) of the example), or to comply with a notice requiring information under s 219 (see explanatory note 2), is liable to a penalty of up to £300 plus a further penalty of up to £60 a day if the failure is declared by a court or by the Special Commissioners. A penalty of up to £3,000 will apply where the failure continues one year after the due date. The section also provides for a penalty of up to £50 plus a daily penalty of up to £30 for failing to comply with a notice under s 219A (see part (d) of the example).

For deeds of variation made on or after 1 August 2002, s 245A has been amended by FA 2002 s 120 to include a penalty where personal representatives fail to send the Revenue a copy of the variation and notify the amount of additional tax payable (see Example 34 explanatory note 5). The penalty is an amount of £100 plus a further penalty of up to £60 a day if the failure is declared by a court or by the Special Commissioners.

The penalties under (d) above cannot exceed the tax chargeable, and penalties will not be charged under (d) or (e) if there is a reasonable excuse for the delay. The daily penalties are not imposed if the fault is remedied before proceedings have started.

HMRC's stated practice is to mitigate penalties according to the degree of disclosure, the cooperation given and the gravity of the offence. Further details are in the penalties leaflet IHT13 issued by HMRC Capital Taxes.

Personal representatives should be aware that HMRC are taking a harsher attitude to the question of penalties where they consider that an HMRC Account containing estimated valuations has been submitted without the personal representatives having made 'the fullest enquiries that are reasonably practicable in the circumstances' as required by s 216(3A). In a case before the Special Commissioners (*Robertson v CIR, SpC 309*, 2002), they sought to impose a penalty of £10,000 on an executor who had submitted an account within six weeks after the testator's death containing estimated figures which were later found to be substantially understated, even though corrective accounts had been submitted less than six months after the death. The Special Commissioners found in favour of the executor, commenting that the Revenue had wholly failed to show that the executor was guilty of negligence. He had acted in accordance with accepted practice in submitting estimated figures and making prompt arrangements for professional valuations. The Revenue were held to have acted wholly unreasonably and the executors were entitled to costs in connection with the hearing. Despite the executor's success in this case, it would be advisable for personal representatives to ensure that they have made all enquiries that are *reasonably practicable* before including estimated figures in HMRC Accounts.

Question

Dr and Mrs Slowe made their wills without professional advice, each leaving the whole of his/her estate to the surviving spouse with the proviso that should the spouse predecease him/her the estate should be divided between their children.

On 31 December 2008 they were involved in a road accident in which Dr Slowe (aged 50) died instantly. Mrs Slowe (aged 51) was seriously injured and died seven days later. They had two children, John (aged 25) and Jill (aged 18).

At death Dr Slowe's interest in the group practice in which he was a partner was valued at £250,000. He also owned assets valued at £50,000, and the family home, valued at £500,000, was in his sole ownership. He had no interest in any settlements nor had he made any lifetime gifts.

Mrs Slowe had assets of her own valued at £75,000 and was the life tenant of the estate of her late father, who died on 20 February 1986, the reversionary interest passing to her children equally. The settlement was valued at £312,000 on 7 January 2009. During her lifetime Mrs Slowe had made chargeable transfers amounting to £85,000 (all less than three years before death).

(a) Compute the inheritance tax payable by reason of the deaths of Dr and Mrs Slowe taking into account any possible transfer of their nil-rate bands.

(b) Consider whether it would be possible to mitigate that liability.

(c) Comment on what the tax position would have been if they had died simultaneously.

(d) Assuming professional advice had been obtained before death so that the wills had included an appropriately worded survivorship clause, recompute the inheritance tax payable consequent upon their deaths.

(e) Prepare a table comparing the tax payable at (a) and (d), and comment on the difference in tax payable at (d) with what would have been payable under (b) and (c).

Answer

(a) **Inheritance tax payable on death of Dr Slowe — 31 December 2008**

Nil, since all property passes to Mrs Slowe which is an exempt transfer.

Inheritance tax payable on death of Mrs Slowe — 7 January 2009

		£	£
Free estate			
Family home			500,000
Other assets —	Own	75,000	
	Husband's estate:		
	Assets from partnership	250,000	
	Other assets	50,000	375,000
			875,000
Settled property			
Life interest in estate of late father			312,000
Amount subject to inheritance tax			1,187,000

Inheritance tax accumulation

	Gross £	Tax £
Cumulative transfers prior to death	85,000	–
Amount liable on death	1,187,000	259,200*
	1,272,000	259,200*

(* 1,272,000 – 624,000 (see note 10) = 648,000 @ 40%)

Estate rate $\dfrac{259,000}{1,187,000} \times 100 = 21.8366\%$

Inheritance tax payable:		
By personal representatives	875,000 @ 21.8366%	191,070
By trustees of settled property	312,000 @ 21.8366%	68,130
		£259,200

(b) **Mitigating Mrs Slowe's inheritance tax liability**

The personal representatives of Mrs Slowe could, within two years after Dr Slowe's death, make a written disclaimer of the gift to her under his will (s 142). This would result in an intestacy, and under the intestacy rules a 28 day survivorship period applies to the spouse entitlement, so the effect of such a disclaimer would be that Dr Slowe's estate would pass to the children. The same effect would be obtained if, again within two years of Dr Slowe's death, Mrs Slowe's personal representatives entered into a written variation under s 142 to redirect the assets to the children.

If a deed of variation or disclaimer is executed, it will not be a transfer of value and inheritance tax will be calculated as though the deed displaced the provisions of the will (ie computed as in part (d) of the example) *providing* in the case of a variation (not a disclaimer) that the instrument of variation contains a statement that the variation is intended to have that effect.

Since additional tax would be payable on Dr Slowe's estate, then within six months after the date of such a variation Dr Slowe's personal representatives, together with Mrs Slowe's personal representatives, would have to notify HMRC Capital Taxes of the amount of extra tax and send a copy of the variation. See explanatory note 5 for further details.

(c)   **Simultaneous deaths (commorientes)**

Where two or more persons die at the same time or in circumstances where it cannot be known which survived the other(s), it is assumed under the rule of commorientes that the elder died first and accordingly that the younger is deemed to have survived the elder (Law of Property Act 1925 s 184). However, for inheritance tax purposes s 4(2) provides that they shall be assumed to have died at the same instant.

Any bequest from one to the other will accordingly be ignored for inheritance tax purposes since neither survived the other. Therefore if Dr and Mrs Slowe had both died at the same time (or if it could not be determined who died first) then for the purposes of general law (ie the actual devolution of the assets) Mrs Slowe (being the elder) would be deemed to have died first, and her estate would pass under her will to her husband. On the death of Dr Slowe his estate (now including his wife's estate) would pass under his will to the children.

For inheritance tax purposes, however, Dr Slowe would be deemed to have died at the same time as Mrs Slowe and his estate for inheritance tax would not include his wife's assets.

Even so, when computing the inheritance tax liability on the estate of Mrs Slowe the assets other than the settled property would in fact pass to Dr Slowe's estate and therefore would be exempt (s 18), whereas the settled property would revert under the terms of the settlement to the children and a liability would arise as follows:

Inheritance tax payable on simultaneous deaths

	£	£
Mrs Slowe (elder)		
Free estate	75,000	
Less: Exempt transfer to Dr Slowe	75,000	nil
Settled property		
Life interest in estate of late father		312,000
Amount subject to inheritance tax		312,000

Inheritance tax accumulation

	Gross £	Tax £
Cumulative transfers prior to death	85,000	–
Amount liable on death	312,000	34,000*
	397,000	34,000*

(* 397,000 – 312,000 = 85,000 @ 40%)

	£
Inheritance tax payable:	
By personal representatives	nil
By trustees of settled property	34,000

Dr Slowe (younger)	£	£
Family home		500,000
Interest in practice	250,000	
Less: 100% business property relief	250,000	–
Other assets (excluding Mrs Slowe's assets of £75,000)		50,000
Amount subject to inheritance tax		550,000

Inheritance tax accumulation

	Gross £	Tax £
Cumulative transfers prior to death	–	–
Amount liable on death	550,000	95,200*
Inheritance tax payable by personal representatives		95,200*

(* 550,000 – 312,000 (see note 10) = 238,000 @ 40%)

(d)   **Survivorship clauses**

To prevent devolution and taxation problems relating to deaths at or near the same time, it is common to include a survivorship clause in a will. For example, the bequest to the spouse is made conditional upon that person surviving for a specified period such as thirty days after the first death. Such clauses are effective for inheritance tax purposes providing the specified period does not exceed six months (s 92) and tax is computed as if the dispositions which take effect at the end of the period (or on the earlier death of the contingent legatee) had taken place at the first death. If survivorship clauses had been included in the wills of Dr and Mrs Slowe (or if Mrs Slowe's personal representatives had disclaimed the inheritance or entered into a variation as indicated in part (b) above) the tax position on their deaths would have been as follows:

Inheritance tax payable on death of Dr Slowe — 31 December 2008

		£
Family home		500,000
Interest in practice	250,000	
Less: 100% business property relief	250,000	–
Other assets		50,000
Estate on death for inheritance tax		550,000

Inheritance tax accumulation

	Gross £	Tax £
Cumulative transfers prior to death	–	–
Estate on death	550,000	95,200
Inheritance tax payable by personal representatives (as in (c))		95,200

Inheritance tax payable on death of Mrs Slowe — 7 January 2009

	£
Free estate	
Assets	75,000
Settled property	
Life interest in estate of late father	312,000
Estate on death	387,000

Inheritance tax accumulation

	Gross £	Tax £
Cumulative transfers prior to death	85,000	–
Estate on death	387,000	64,000*
	472,000	64,000*

(* 472,000 – 312,000 (see note 10) = 160,000 @ 40%)
Estate rate

$$\frac{64,000}{387,000} \times 100 \ = 16.5375\%$$

Inheritance tax payable:

		£
By personal representatives	£75,000 @ 116.5375%	12,403
By trustees of settled property	£312,000 @ 16.5375%	51,597
		64,000

(e)   **Comparison of tax payable**

	Under (a) above (*without variation*) £	With *survivorship clause* £
By personal representatives of Dr Slowe	–	95,200
By personal representatives of Mrs Slowe	191,070	12,403
	191,070	107,063
By trustees of settled property	68,130	51,597
	259,200	159,200

Tax of £159,200 would also be payable if a disclaimer or variation as at (b) were executed.

The tax payable in the event of simultaneous deaths (c) is £129,200 (£34,000 + £95,200). The difference of £30,000 compared with the tax payable had the survivorship clause or a family deed operated is because Mrs Slowe's own assets of £75,000 are in the event of simultaneous deaths exempt from inheritance tax since they none the less pass under her will to her husband (but are not reckoned in his estate for inheritance tax purposes); whereas they are chargeable in her estate if they pass directly to her children as they would under the survivorship clause or family deed, and attract tax at 40% = £30,000.

Explanatory Notes

Inheritance tax on estates of Dr and Mrs Slowe

1. Because Dr Slowe predeceased his wife the whole of his estate passed to her under the will. This is an exempt transfer and no inheritance tax is payable (s 18). Accordingly when Mrs Slowe died there was no quick succession relief because her estate had not been increased by a chargeable transfer (s 141).

   Conversely, Mrs Slowe will benefit from 100% of Dr Slowe's unused nil-rate band. This means that if the increase is claimed, her nil-rate band will be increased by £312,000 for 2008/09 – the year of her death (see note 10).

2. Mrs Slowe's estate includes the value of her husband's share in the professional partnership. As she is not a partner this does not qualify for business property relief. For notes on business property relief see Example 25.

3. The wording of the wills resulted in the second estate being increased in value and attracting a large amount of tax, whilst the first estate failed to utilise its nil rate band. The benefit from the deed of variation would be very substantial because the total inheritance tax payable would be reduced from £259,200 to £159,200, giving an overall saving of £100,000. Such a deed would not have been necessary if the wills had contained a survivorship clause.

Deeds of variation

4. In this example the use of the provisions in s 142 (alteration of dispositions taking effect on death) would be fairly straightforward and could be used to rewrite the provisions of Dr Slowe's will to advantage. In practice complications can occur if the family cannot agree on a revised disposition of the estate, or if one or more of the original beneficiaries is an infant and therefore does not have the legal capacity to agree to a variation. Court consent would be needed to reduce an infant beneficiary's entitlement.

5. As indicated in part (b) of the example, a variation of the way in which a deceased's estate is distributed, either under a will or under an intestacy, is effective for inheritance tax providing the instrument of variation includes a statement that it is intended to have that effect, made by those making the variation, and by the personal representatives of the deceased whose estate is subject to the variation if additional tax is payable (s 142(2), (2A)). The personal representatives can only refuse to make the statement if they hold insufficient assets to discharge the additional tax liability (s 142(2A)). If a beneficiary has died before the date of the variation, his personal representatives can act in his stead.

   Where the effect of a variation is that additional tax is payable, the beneficiaries and the personal representatives of the deceased whose estate is subject to the variation must notify IR Capital Taxes of the amount of extra tax and send a copy of the variation within six months after the date it is made (s 218A). Penalties apply for failure to comply (s 245A(1A)).

   Instruments of variation are also effective for capital gains purposes providing the instrument contains a statement by those making it that it is intended to have that effect (TCGA 1992 s 62(7)).

6. The property which may be subject to variation or disclaimer under s 142 includes 'excluded property' (as to which see Example 3) but not property in which the deceased had retained a benefit (see Example 19) or settled property in which the deceased at the time of his death had a life interest (s 142(5)) (someone who *becomes entitled* to an interest in settled property may disclaim, but not vary, his entitlement under s 93). Where an asset is held jointly as joint tenants, and one of the joint tenants dies, then even though the survivor acquires the deceased's share automatically, he may use a deed of variation to redirect his entitlement to someone else (see Revenue's Tax Bulletin October 1995). Section 142 can also be used in cases of intestacy. The provisions do not, however, apply to any disclaimer or variation which is made for consideration in money or money's worth (s 142(3))

(the same applies to a disclaimer under s 93). Where a variation results in property being held in trust for not more than two years from the date of death, the disposition at the end of the trust is treated as made by the deceased at the date of death (s 142(4)). This provision prevents a variation being used to obtain the benefit of the surviving spouse exemption by redirecting property left as part of the chargeable estate to the spouse, who then, within the two year period, disposes of it by potentially exempt transfer. A disposal outside the two year period would not be caught.

7. The survivorship clause and a deed of variation affect the devolution of the property itself. The treatment for inheritance tax purposes where there are deaths at the same instant does not, however, affect the provisions of the will, commorientes applying where relevant and thus making a survivorship clause valuable from the devolution point of view, quite apart from for tax purposes.

Commorientes

8. The deeming provisions of s 4(2) apply when it is not known which of two or more persons have died first (see part (c) of the example). They do not, however, apply where there is evidence that one died before the other(s) when, in the absence of a survivorship clause or a family deed, the best one can hope for in terms of tax relief is quick succession relief. The insertion of a survivorship clause in a will is therefore most important since as indicated earlier a deed of variation is not always practicable.

For notes on quick succession relief see Example 21.

Deeds of variation — effect on other taxes etc

9. It should be noted that a deed of variation is effective both for inheritance tax and capital gains tax (providing the variation includes a statement to that effect) and does not give rise to a charge to stamp duty. The inheritance tax effect is valid for all purposes of inheritance tax (s 142). In the case of *Marshall v Kerr* (HL 1994), it was held that the capital gains tax effect was restricted to eliminating a capital gains charge by not treating the redirection of the assets as a disposal by the original beneficiaries, and that it did not affect other capital gains tax provisions (so that if, for example, the variation consisted of creating a trust in which the original beneficiary had an interest, the beneficiary would be regarded as a settlor for TCGA 1992 s 77 and would be charged on the trust's gains — see Example 50 part C).

It is possible to make a deed of variation effective for capital gains tax and not inheritance tax, or vice versa. If the variation was not effective for inheritance tax, the redirected assets would be treated as being transferred under the normal inheritance tax rules, so that the transfers would be potentially exempt unless they were to a discretionary trust. Where a discretionary trust is created through a deed of variation, the settlement is regarded as commencing at the date of death, so that the ten-year anniversaries date from that time.

The deed of variation does not affect the income tax position. Any income arising before variation is charged to tax on the original beneficiary. Furthermore, if a parent varies in favour of his/her infant child, this constitutes a settlement within the terms of ITTOIA 2005 ss 620, 648 and any subsequent income arising before the child becomes 18 or marries under that age is chargeable as income of the parent under ITTOIA 2005 ss 629, 631, 632.

TCGA 1992 s 68C (and ITA 2007 ss 472, 473) affects variations of wills or intestacies etc occurring on or after 6 April 2006, irrespective of the date of death of the deceased person in question.

Section 68C applies where a transfer of property following a death is varied in circumstances where TCGA 1992 s 62(6) applies. The main conditions for section 62(6) to apply in respect of a variation are that the variation is made within two years after the deceased person's death, and the instrument of variation contains a statement that the provision is to apply.

The section also applies in any case where property becomes settled property in consequence of the variation but would not otherwise have become settled property. In such circumstances, a person listed below will be treated for TCGA purposes (except where the context otherwise requires) as having made the settlement and as having provided the property for the purposes of the settlement.

Four categories of person are identified in this context:

1.   The first category comprises anyone who, immediately before the variation, was entitled to the property (or to property from which it derives) absolutely as legatee.

2.   The second category relates to a person who would have become entitled to the property (or to property from which it derives) absolutely as legatee but for the variation.

3.   The other two categories relate to individuals who would have fallen into either of the first two categories were they not to have been infants or other persons under a disability.

The legislation applies in any case where property which is not settled property immediately before the variation would have become comprised in a settlement (whether it is a settlement which arose on the deceased person's death or a pre-existing settlement), but the effect of the variation is that the property, or property derived from it, becomes comprised in a different settlement. In such circumstances, the deceased person will be treated for TCGA purposes (except where the context otherwise requires) as having made that other settlement.

Where, immediately before the variation, property is comprised in a settlement and is property of which the deceased person is a settlor, and the effect of the variation is that the property, or property derived from it, becomes comprised in another settlement the deceased person is to be treated for TCGA purposes as having made that other settlement.

Where the deceased person is treated as having made a settlement, he or she is treated for TCGA purposes as having made the settlement in question immediately before their death. This will not apply in any case where the settlement in question arose on the death of the deceased person.

Transfer of the nil-rate band

10.   FA 2008 s 10 and Sch 4 introduces legislation to allow a claim to be made to transfer any unused IHT nil-rate band on a person's death to the estate of their surviving spouse or civil partner who dies on or after 9 October 2007. This will apply where the IHT nil-rate band of the first deceased spouse or civil partner was not fully used in calculating the IHT liability of their estate. When the surviving spouse or civil partner dies, the unused amount may be added to their own nil-rate band.

Where a valid claim to transfer unused nil-rate band is made, the nil-rate band that is available when the surviving spouse or civil partner dies will be increased by the proportion of the nil-rate band unused on the first death. For example, if on the first death the chargeable estate is £162,500 and the nil-rate band is £325,000, 50% of the nil-rate band would be unused. If the nil-rate band when the survivor dies is £350,000, then that would be increased by 50% to £525,500.

The amount of the nil-rate band that can be transferred does not depend on the value of the first spouse or civil partner's estate. Whatever proportion of the nil-rate band is unused on the first death is available for transfer to the survivor.

It is important to remember that even if all the assets passing under the will are left to the surviving spouse or civil partner, there may be other components of the aggregate chargeable 'estate' on death for IHT purposes (such as assets in trust, or gifts to other people made within seven years of death). If present, these may use up some or all of the nil-rate band in the normal way, and so reduce the amount of unused nil-rate band that may be available for transfer.

In this case in (a) none of his nil-rate band was utilised on the death of Dr Slowe so 100% of the rate in force at the date of Mrs Slowe's death is available ie £312,000. The amount to be taken off her estate before the application of IHT is therefore £624,000 (£312,000 × 2).

In (c) Mrs Slowe dies first but she has used all of her nil-rate band – her estate is £397,000 and therefore none is available on the subsequent death of Dr Slowe.

In (d) again Dr Slowe dies first but as his estate on death amounts to £550,000 the nil-rate band will have been fully utilised on his death with no surplus available to Mrs Slowe.

Question

Edward (aged 65 and just retired) is considering settling his assets worth £715,000 on his wife Mary for life with the remainder to their only son, Brian (to be held on trust with powers to apply capital and accumulated income), completely excluding himself from any interest in the settlement.

The settlement may either be made now or included in Edward's will to take effect after his death.

Edward had made lifetime gifts of £306,000 to his brother Jon on 5 September 2007 utilising his unused annual exemptions and part of the nil-rate band. He had made no gifts in the year to 5 April 2007, but had used his annual exemptions for years prior to that. Edward died on 12 December 2009.

The value of the trust at the date of Mary's death on 3 February 2011 is £900,000. The nil-rate band for 2010/11 is £350,000.

Indicate the taxation implications of Edward's proposals, and explain the general principles governing the taxation of such settlements.

The taxation implications of Edward's proposals are as follows:

Answer

Inheritance tax

Settlement on spouse during lifetime

The settlement of his assets by Edward on Mary will be a chargeable transfer and subject immediately to IHT because it falls outside the provisions of s 5(1A).

	Gross	*Tax on 2008/09 scale*
2007/08		
Gift to Jon – potentially exempt transfer £306,000		
2008/09		
Transfer of assets to settlement	715,000	
Less: Annual exemption 2008/09	(3,000)	
	712,000	80,000

*£712,000 – 312,000 @ 20%

Settlements made on or after 22 March 2006 are now generally subject to the rules which previously applied only to discretionary trusts. Therefore, the assets held by the trustees of an interest in possession settlement will not usually form part of the estate of the life tenant provided that the settlement was made after 21 March 2006. So on Mary's death her life interest will not form part of her estate.

This, however, has its drawbacks. In particular, as seen above the creation of the settlement will represent a chargeable event (previously, lifetime transfers into interest in possession settlements constituted PETs). Furthermore, the settlement will be subject to the ten-year charge and exit charge rules for relevant property trusts.

The following trusts will remain outside the rules previously limited to discretionary trusts:

(a) Bare trusts (where the beneficiary continues to be treated as entitled to the assets held under the bare trust).

(b) Interest in possession trusts where the interest in possession is:

(i) an immediate post-death interest (IPDI) (see below);

(ii) a disabled person's interest (broadly an interest in possession for a person incapable of looking after their affairs because of mental disorder, or a person in receipt of an attendance allowance or a disability living allowance); or

(iii) a transitional serial interest (TSI) (see below) (s 49(1A)).

To be a transitional serial interest in a settlement (s 49B–E):

(i) the settlement must have been set up before 22 March 2006; and

(ii) immediately before 22 March 2006, there must have been an individual with a beneficial interest in possession in the settlement;

(iii) that person's interest must have come to an end after 21 March 2006 but before 5 October 2008; and

(iv) the person with the current interest in the settlement became beneficially entitled to that interest at that time; and

(v)   the interest is not a disabled person's interest or an interest of a bereaved minor (IHTA 1984 s 49B).

The rules for bereaved minors are found in s 71A. They apply only for settlements which:

(a)   are set up by:

    (i)   a parent of the beneficiary in their will, or

    (ii)   the Criminal Injuries Compensation Scheme,

(b)   give the minor the capital and income of the trust absolutely when the minor reaches the age of 18.

Settlement on spouse on death of settlor

An immediate post-death interest (IPDI) under s 49A occurs where an individual becomes beneficially entitled on or after 22 March 2006 to an interest in possession in settled property provided certain conditions are met:

(a)   the interest in settled property arises immediately on the death of the settlor by reason of will or intestacy; and

(b)   the person becomes beneficially entitled to an interest in possession on the death of the settlor whether or not he or she dies intestate;

(c)   the trust is not a bereaved minor's or disabled person's trust.

If the conditions are met the new trust will not be subject to the rules applying to relevant property trusts.

Edward has already made gifts of £306,000. His estate is valued at £715,000.

On Edward's death

5 Sept 2007	Gift to Jon		306,000
Less:			
Annual exemptions	2006/07	3,000	
	2007/08	3,000	6,000
			300,000

The chargeable gift of £300,000 after exemptions is charged within the nil-rate band of £312,000. The balance of the estate held on trust for Edward's wife is exempt under s 18.

On Mary's death

There is an IHT charge based on the value of settled property when a beneficiary disposes of their interest or it comes to an end, eg on death. As Mary did not survive seven years but dies within two years of her husband's death, the interest in possession that forms part of her estate is chargeable at 40% after deduction of her nil-rate band.

Value of Mary's estate at 3 February 2011 (s 49(1)(1A))   900,000

Tax due (£900,000 – 350,000) @ 40% = £220,000

Prior to FA 2006 Sch 20 para 4 the settlement of the trust assets in Brian would have been treated as an interest in possession. As Brian's interest in possession is created out of an existing settlement after 6 October 2008 it is neither a transitional serial interest (TSI) or an immediate post-death interest (IPDI). Whilst the assets remain on trust the relevant property rules for taxing discretionary trusts will apply.

Release of life interest

If, prior to her death, Mary relinquished her life interest in the settlement in favour of Brian, this would be a transfer of value, against which her annual exemptions for the year of release and previous year would be available unless otherwise used (s 57) and the balance would be a potentially exempt transfer and therefore not chargeable to tax if she survived the transfer by seven years. If she died within seven years, any tax payable would still come out of the trust fund, the trustees retaining sufficient funds to deal with that contingency, and Brian receiving a correspondingly lesser amount in that event. Tapering relief would be given if the death occurred more than three years after the life interest was relinquished.

Release to settlor

However this is not the case where the release takes the form of a transfer to spouse (who was the original settlor).

The law relating to settlements on spouses was amended following the decision of the Court of Appeal to find in favour of the taxpayer in the case of *IRC v Eversden* [2003] EWCA Civ 668 and [2003] STC 822.

The normal 'gift with reservation' charge applies to gifts made on or after 20 June 2003 where:

- the gift is made into trust and the donor's spouse enjoys an interest in possession;

- the interest in possession comes to an end (whether on the donee's death or otherwise); and

- the subsequent use of the gift is such that it would count as a 'gift with reservation' if the gift had been made at the time the interest in possession comes to an end (FA 2006 s 102).

FA 1986 s 102ZA brings into line the treatment of cases involving trust property formerly subject to an interest-in-possession (and treated at that time as owned for IHT purposes by the person owning the interest) with the treatment where the property was formerly owned outright. In either case, there can be an IHT charge where the former owner or holder of the interest continues to enjoy the property after they have given it away or their interest has terminated.

These rules would therefore apply if Mary relinquished her life interest in the settlement to Brian.

Capital Gains Tax

Settlement by will

If Edward waits until his death to make the transfer into the settlement for Mary, there will be no capital gains tax payable because death is not a chargeable occasion for capital gains tax, although the deceased's assets are regarded as acquired at probate value by those on whom they devolve (ie legatees, trustees, or personal representatives as the case may be) (TCGA 1992 s 62). The trustees would therefore be deemed to acquire the trust property at probate value.

Lifetime settlement

If Edward makes the transfer into the settlement for Mary during his lifetime, then the capital gains tax exemption for absolute transfers between spouses does not apply. Gift relief under TCGA 1992 s 165 or s 260 is not available in respect of disposals of assets to the trustees of a trust in which the settlor has an interest where the disposal is made on or after 10 December 2003. Section 169F provides that any interest of the spouse is to be treated as the interest of the settlor.

These provisions also claw back or prevent any gifts relief in relation to disposals to trusts which become settlor-interested settlements within a certain time period. This period begins immediately after the disposal and ends immediately before the sixth anniversary of the start of the tax year next following that in which the disposal is made.

As Mary will have a life interest in the new settlement, Edward will be deemed to have an interest in the settlement and holdover relief will not be available.

Death of life tenant

When a life tenant dies, the trust property is treated as having been disposed of and immediately reacquired at probate value, but as with the death of someone owning assets absolutely, there is no capital gains tax charge on the trust assets. (If the settlement had been made in lifetime, however, and any gains had been deferred under the holdover provisions of s 165 or s 260 prior to 10 December 2003, the deferred gains would become chargeable on the life tenant's death, any available taper relief being given by reference to the period of ownership by the trust. If any of the property is qualifying property for holdover relief under s 165, the deferred gains on that property could be the subject of a further claim for holdover relief.)

When Mary dies, therefore, neither the trustees nor Brian will be liable to capital gains tax in respect of the assets in the settlement. Those assets which devolve upon Brian (some may have to be sold in order to pay inheritance tax unless Brian wishes to retain all the assets and fund the tax by other means — perhaps by instalments if the property is instalment option property) will do so for capital gains purposes at their market value at the date of his mother's death, and those retained by the trustees in order to sell them to raise cash for the payment of inheritance tax will also have a base value equivalent to their market value at that time (TCGA 1992 s 73).

Release of life interest

If, after Edward's death, Mary relinquishes her entitlement during her lifetime, Brian then becoming absolutely entitled to the trust property, the trustees will be deemed to make a disposal at that time at the then market value, any gains held over if the settlement was created in lifetime becoming chargeable, and capital gains tax will be payable accordingly (less any taper relief and annual exemption available to the trustees and subject to any available holdover relief) (TCGA 1992 s 71).

Trustees' own gains

If, during the continuation of the trust, the trustees themselves realise capital gains on the disposal of trust assets, for example on the switching of investments, then if this occurs during Edward's lifetime, the gains are treated as Edward's gains, on which he is liable to pay the tax (TCGA 1992 s 77). He is entitled, however, to recover the tax from the trustees (TCGA 1992 s 78). If gains are realised after Edward's death, the trustees are liable to tax on the gains at 18%, subject to availability of the annual exemption (TCGA 1992 Sch 1.2(1)). The annual exemption for an interest in possession trust is half that available to individuals (£4,800 for 2008/09), providing it is the only settlement created by the settlor since 6 June 1978 (see Example 50 part C).

Enterprise investment scheme relief

Providing the beneficiaries of the trust are confined to individuals and charities, then the gains may be deferred to the extent that they are reinvested in cash by subscribing for ordinary shares in a qualifying unquoted trading company under the enterprise investment scheme, the money raised being used within twelve months for a qualifying business activity (TCGA 1992 Sch 5B).

For further notes on the capital gains tax position of trusts see Example 50.

Income Tax

Lifetime settlement

If the settlement is made by Edward in his lifetime, then since Mary is entitled to the income it will be treated as a settlement in which he retains an interest, and all income arising, whether distributed by the trustees or retained by them, will be liable to income tax as part of Edward's statutory total income during his lifetime (ITTOIA 2005 s 624). The settlement is not sufficient to transfer income from Edward to Mary for income tax purposes because he is giving her only a right to income and not outright ownership of the assets. Following Edward's death, the income whether distributed or not will be treated as Mary's income. This will also apply if the settlement is made on Edward's death.

Tax liability of trustees

The trustees in each case will have a basic rate liability (or lower rate or dividend ordinary rate liability if the income is savings income) unless the income is mandated direct to Mary in order to save administrative cost and inconvenience, any liability at the higher rate (or dividend upper rate) being assessed on Edward or Mary his widow as the case may be. Edward would be entitled to recover any tax paid by him from the trustees or from Mary (ITTOIA 2005 s 646).

Charge on Edward and Mary after his death

Where income is treated as Edward's income, the amount on which he is charged to tax cannot be reduced by any trust expenses, since he is only permitted to deduct amounts that would have been deductible if he had received the income directly (ITTOIA 2005 ss 619, 621, 623). Furthermore, for income other than dividends, the income is taxed as miscellaneous income, so it cannot be taxed at the savings rate of 20% whether or not Edward is liable at higher rates. Dividend income is, however, charged at the dividend ordinary rate of 10% or upper rate of 32½% (ITTOIA 2005 ss 619, 621, 623.

After Edward's death, Mary is taxed as the beneficiary of an interest in possession trust. Unless the income has been mandated direct to her, the trust expenses will be paid out of the taxed income of the trust, and the balance remaining will be paid to her, the trustees giving her a certificate indicating the amounts of tax deducted at the basic, lower or dividend ordinary rate of tax as the case may be. The tax deducted will count towards the tax payable by her or will be repayable if it exceeds her liability. This does not apply to dividend tax credits, which are not repayable.

Question

Your client, Charles, a wealthy widower, is a director and majority shareholder in an unquoted trading company that was established many years ago.

His wife died suddenly six months ago, leaving her estate comprising shares in quoted companies, life insurance policies, cash, jewellery and personal possessions, valued in total at £335,000, to Charles.

Charles is aged sixty-two and is considering retiring within the next year or so. He is also considering disposing of some of his assets, either by sale or possibly by gift, but is undecided whether to dispose of them during his lifetime or by will on his death.

Taxation will be a major factor influencing his decision regarding the disposition of his assets, and he has stated that he wishes to minimise any tax liability arising.

He has estimated his total estate to have a value of approximately £1,140,000, including the £335,000 left to him by his deceased wife, broadly comprised as follows:

His 70% shareholding in the unquoted family trading company, valued at £140,000

His 18% shareholding in an unquoted company which supplies the family company, valued at £60,000, (the other shares being held by his brothers and sister)

Quoted shares valued at £108,000

His private residence valued at £495,000

A plot of land on which he and his wife had planned to build a bungalow for their retirement valued at £40,000

A life insurance policy on his life with a market value of £40,000 and a surrender value of £36,000

Furniture, jewellery and other chattels with a total value of £25,000, the highest value item being valued at £2,500

Cash at bank, building society and at home — total value £232,000

Private motor car valued at £9,000

He has one daughter and two grandsons, one of whom joined him last year in the family company. He has also developed a considerable interest in Heartbeat (UK) — a registered charity.

(a)   In relation to both capital gains tax and inheritance tax, summarise:

    (i)   the events giving rise to a charge

    (ii)   the amount chargeable

    (iii)   the rates of tax

    (iv)   some common exemptions and reliefs

    (v)   whether phasing of disposals is advantageous

    (vi)   the advantages/disadvantages of lifetime disposals as compared to a transfer on death

    (vii)   the benefits, if any, of Charles emigrating.

(b)   Suggest action that Charles might take and disposals he might make which would result in a nil or small tax liability, and which would reduce the tax payable on his eventual death.

Answer

(a)   **Capital gains tax summary**

   (i)   **Chargeable disposals**

   The capital gains tax provisions apply to the disposal of chargeable assets during lifetime. No charge is made on death. 'Disposal' includes sales, gifts and loss or destruction of assets; chargeable assets are all assets other than those that are specifically exempt. Options, debts, currency other than sterling, and rights are included, but not bettings winnings or damages for personal or professional injuries.

   (ii)   **Calculation of gain or loss**

   The chargeable gain (or allowable loss) is calculated by comparing the value on disposal with the sum of the cost price, costs of acquisition and costs of sale. All assets owned on 31 March 1982 will be deemed to have had a cost equivalent to their market value at that date.

   Treatment of losses

   Chargeable gains are reduced by losses of the same year. In addition, they are reduced by losses brought forward (or carried back from the year of death), but not so as to waste the annual exemption of the year of disposal.

   (iii)   **FA 2008 changes to CGT**

   Under FA 2008 s 8 and Sch 2, the taxation of capital gains has been radically reformed for 2008/09 and later years. The annual exemption and the rules for losses will remain.

   The annual exemption for 2008/09 is set at £9,600 for individuals and £4,800 for trustees.

   The rate of tax on capital gains is set at 18% for individuals, personal representatives and trustees. On some disposals entrepreneurs' relief applies and a lower effective rate of 10% will be applicable (see below and Chapter 40 note 10).

   A number of other changes to simplify the capital gains tax regime will be made, including:

   ● the withdrawal of taper relief;

   ● the withdrawal of indexation allowance;

   ● the abolition of the 'kink test' for assets held at 31 March 1982;

   ● abolition of halving relief; and

   ● simplification of the share identification rules.

   Other CGT reliefs will continue to have effect. For example:

   ● private residence relief will continue to be available for principal private residences;

   ● business asset roll-over relief continues to be available;

   ● business asset gift hold-over relief also continues to apply;

   ● any unused allowable losses from past years will continue to be allowed to be brought forward in order to reduce any gains.

   Where gains are to be deferred until the occurrence of a later event, the effect of the changes is that, where a gain that arises in a tax year earlier than 2008/09 is deferred; the computation of the deferred amount will take account, if appropriate, of the kink test, halving relief and indexation allowance. This figure of deferred gain will not be affected by these changes.

However, taper relief will not be due if these gains come into charge in 2008/09 or a later tax year. This is because taper relief is due only when a gain is brought into charge, and the deferred amount does not include taper relief.

In the case of an unconditional contract to sell made before 5 April 2008 to take effect after this date – the existing pre-5 April 2008 rules will apply and taper relief and/or indexation may be available. This is because the contract is deemed to be made at the date it was entered into.

In the case of a conditional contract to sell made before 5 April 2008 – the disposal date will be treated as the date that the conditions were satisfied. If this is post-5 April 2008 then the new rules will apply.

UK resident settlor-interested settlements

Sch 2 para 5 repeals TCGA 1992 ss 77 to 79. These provisions had the effect that gains in respect of which the trustees of a UK resident settlor-interested settlement would otherwise have been chargeable to CGT are in certain circumstances charged on the settlor. The introduction of a single rate of CGT for trustees and individuals means that the application of ss 77 to 79 would have no effect on the rate at which the gains were charged to CGT.

Settlements for vulnerable persons

For details of the FA 2008 changes to capital gains see Chapter 47 note 4.

Entrepreneurs' relief

Under FA 2008 s 9 and Sch 3 entrepreneurs' relief will apply to individuals and trustees who dispose of the whole or part of a trading business, or of shares in a trading company in which they have a qualifying interest.

Entrepreneurs' relief may be available in respect of gains made by individuals on the disposal of:

- all or part of a trading business the individual carries on alone or in partnership;
- assets of the individual's or partnership's trading business following the cessation of the business;
- shares in (and securities of) the individual's 'personal' trading company (or holding company of a trading group);
- assets owned by the individual and used by his/her 'personal' trading company (or group) or trading partnership.

The first £1 million of gains will qualify for the relief which effectively taxes qualifying gains at 10%. Gains in excess of £1 million will be charged to CGT at the rate of 18%.

The relief works as follows:

1. Schedule 3 introduces a new section 169N into TCGA 1992. Where a claim is made in respect of a qualifying business disposal the relevant gains (see s 5) are to be aggregated, with any relevant losses (see s 6) being deducted.

2. The resulting amount is to be reduced by 4/9ths.

3. But if the total of current gains less losses and the amounts resulting in relation to earlier relevant qualifying business disposals (if any), exceeds £1 million, the reduction is to be made in respect of only so much (if any) of the amount resulting as (when added to that total) does not exceed £1 million.

HMRC have produced a number of useful examples that can be accessed at: http://www.hmrc.gov.uk/budget2008/cgt-entrepreneurs-relief-eg.pdf.

The amount arrived at is to be treated as a chargeable gain accruing at the time of the disposal to the individual or trustees by whom the claim is made.

An individual will be able to make claims for relief on qualifying disposals made on or after 6 April 2008. Claims may be made on more than one occasion up to a 'lifetime' limit of £1 million. Disposals on or before 5 April 2008 do not affect the lifetime limit. The £1 million limit will only begin to diminish when the relief is claimed.

Trustees will be able to claim relief on certain disposals of business assets and company shares and securities where a 'qualifying beneficiary' has a qualifying interest in the business in question. Trustees must make claims jointly with the 'qualifying beneficiary'. Any relief given on the trustees' gains will reduce a beneficiary's £1 million lifetime limit on relief.

If, on the same day, there is both a disposal of trust business assets in respect of which an individual is the qualifying beneficiary and a qualifying business disposal by the individual, s 7 applies as if the disposal of trust business assets were later.

There is more detail on the relief in Chapter 40 note 10.

See page (vii) for the rates applying to personal representatives and trustees.

(iv) Exemptions and reliefs

Exempt assets include:

Principal private residence (subject to certain conditions)

Private motor cars

Tangible movable assets (chattels) that are wasting assets, including racehorses, but excluding chattels used in a business on which capital allowances have been or could have been claimed

Other chattels (including business chattels) if sold for less than £6,000

Gifts of assets to charities.

Reliefs include:

Rollover relief or holdover relief enabling gains to be deferred when qualifying business assets are sold and replaced. Where gains are rolled over to reduce the cost of the replacement asset, taper relief (see (ii) above) is available when the replacement asset is disposed of, based upon the period of ownership of the *new* asset. Where gains are held over against the acquisition of depreciating assets, the taper relief when the replacement asset is disposed of is based on the period of ownership of the *original* asset.

Deferral relief when a gain is reinvested by a cash subscription either for unquoted shares in a qualifying trading company under the enterprise investment scheme or for shares in a venture capital trust. The gain is deferred until the qualifying shares are sold or replaced, taper relief being based on the period of ownership of the *original* asset.

Gifts holdover relief enabling gains to be regarded as reducing the donee's acquisition cost for capital gains tax, in respect of gifts of business assets, agricultural land, shares giving 5% voting control in an unquoted trading company, or gifts subject to an immediate charge to inheritance tax.

(v) Advantages of phasing disposals

By disposing of assets over a period of years a number of annual exemptions may be used. Note that unused annual exemption cannot be carried forward, and unused losses cannot be carried back (except losses of the year of death, which may be carried back against gains in excess of the annual exemption in the three previous years, latest first). But this does not apply to disposals of items to the same person if they form part of a set.

(vi) Disposals in lifetime or on death

On death there is no charge to capital gains tax and there is an automatic uplift to market value at that time for those entitled to the assets, whereas a disposal in lifetime may give rise to a charge. If a gain has been rolled over or held over against the cost of qualifying replacement business assets, the death of the taxpayer means that the gain never gets charged to tax. By contrast, where holdover relief has been claimed on a gift of an asset, the donee's capital gains tax cost is reduced as indicated in (iv), thus resulting in a higher gain when the donee disposes of the asset. The donee's acquisition cost is not affected by the subsequent death of the donor.

(vii) Effect of emigration

Capital gains tax is chargeable on worldwide assets of taxpayers who are resident or ordinarily resident in the UK.

If a taxpayer ceases to be both resident and ordinarily resident then he will not be liable to UK capital gains tax unless the assets are situated in the UK and are used in a trade carried on in the UK. A charge can also occur on accrued gains on the export of a UK company or trust.

Charles can therefore avoid UK capital gains tax by emigration if gains are realised after he has become neither resident nor ordinarily resident, except in relation to any assets used in the UK for the purposes of a trade. If, however, he returned to the UK and became resident or ordinarily resident within five complete tax years of the date of departure, gains on assets held on emigration that were realised while he was non-resident would be chargeable in the tax year of return. Any such gains realised in the tax year of departure would be taxed as gains of that tax year. Finance (No 2) Act 2005 provisions prevent the exploitation of double tax agreements during the period of absence. If a gain has been charged to tax in another country, and is also charged in the UK on the taxpayer's return within five years then the tax paid overseas is deductible from the UK liability. If a taxpayer is resident or ordinarily resident in the UK, but under a double tax treaty would be treated as non-resident (such that a gain would be taxed at a low or nil rate) then UK capital gains tax will be payable overriding the DTA provisions (F(No 2)A 2005 s 32 amending TCGA 1992 s 10A). Similar provisions were introduced for trustees (F(No2)A 2005 s 33 introducing TCGA 1992 s 83A).

Inheritance tax summary

(i) Chargeable transfers

Inheritance tax is chargeable on certain lifetime gifts, on wealth at death and on certain transfers into and out of trust. If a taxpayer makes a lifetime gift to an individual, or to certain trusts such as a trust for the disabled, then provided the donor survives the gift by seven years or more, it is not liable to inheritance tax. This is known as a potentially exempt transfer, and it covers virtually all lifetime gifts that an individual might make, except to a discretionary trust, which are chargeable at the time they are made. Certain gifts are totally exempt from tax (see (iv) below).

(ii) Chargeable amount

Where a lifetime gift is immediately chargeable, the chargeable amount is the difference between the value of the donor's estate before the transfer and its value after the transfer. If the donor bears the inheritance tax then that tax will reduce the value of the estate after the transfer, increasing the chargeable transfer. This is known as grossing up the gift.

(iii) Rates of tax

Any *chargeable* transfers of the last seven years are added together. To that total is added the value of the current chargeable transfer, which is charged to tax as the highest part of the total. For 2008/09 there is no inheritance tax on the first £312,000 of cumulative transfers. Lifetime chargeable transfers in excess of £312,000 are taxed at 20%, which is half of the full rate.

The nil-rate band for 2009/10 has been set at £325,000 and for 2010/11 at £350,000.

Potentially exempt gifts made within seven years before death become chargeable transfers on death, any chargeable transfers within the seven years before the gift being taken into account in calculating the tax payable. The value taken into account is that at the time of the gift, but the rate of tax used is the full rate (not the half rate) applicable at the date of death (currently 40%). If the gift was made more than three years before death then any tax payable on the gift is reduced by a tapering relief.

Where a transfer was chargeable in lifetime, and the donor dies within seven years, tax is recalculated at the full rate on the scale in force at the date of death, tapering relief being available as for potentially exempt transfers, and the tax payable, if any, being reduced by the tax paid in lifetime, but no repayment being available if the lifetime tax exceeds the tax due at death.

Tax on the death estate is calculated by adding the estate to chargeable transfers within the seven years before the death.

(iv) Exemptions and reliefs

Exemptions include:

Transfers between spouses and civil partners (unless transferee is not UK domiciled, when exempt limit is £55,000)

Annual exemption for lifetime gifts	— £3,000 p a
Small lifetime gifts to same person	— not exceeding £250 p a
Normal expenditure out of income	
Gifts in consideration of marriage or registration of a civil partnership	— £5,000 by a parent
	— £2,500 by a grandparent or a party to the marriage/civil partnership
	— £1,000 by any other person

Gifts to charities, political parties, housing associations, or for national purposes

Conditional exemption for heritage property

Gifts made more than seven years before death (see (i) above).

Reliefs include:

Business property relief (relief being at 100% on an interest in a business or unquoted shareholdings; controlling holdings in quoted companies qualify for 50% relief)

Agricultural property relief (at 100% for owner-occupied property and property let on leases granted on or after 1 September 1995 and 50% for other let property)

Quick succession relief, reducing the tax payable where a donee dies within five years after receiving a chargeable transfer.

It is also possible to use a deed of variation within two years after death to alter the way a deceased person's estate is distributed (see Example 34).

(v) Advantages of phasing disposals

Regular gifts could be covered by the exemption for normal expenditure out of income providing they are habitual (eg by payments of regular premiums under an insurance policy), and leave the taxpayer with sufficient income to live in his normal style.

Other lifetime gifts would be potentially exempt in so far as they are not covered by the annual exemption of £3,000. If the previous year's annual exemption was not used, that would also be available to reduce the transfer. The earlier year's annual exemption is only available after the later year has been used in full. Any of the previous year's exemption not then utilised will be lost. Potentially exempt transfers only become chargeable transfers if the donor dies within seven years. Transfers that are not potentially exempt are taxed at one-half of the full rate once the nil threshold is exceeded.

Even though a gift is not covered by a specific exemption, no tax is payable in lifetime or on death to the extent that the gift is covered by the nil threshold (taking into account gifts made within the previous seven years).

(vi)   Disposals in lifetime or on death

Although gifts made more than three but less than seven years before death attract tapering relief, that is irrelevant unless the cumulative total at the time of the lifetime gift exceeds the nil threshold applicable at the date of death, since no tax will be payable to which any tapering relief can apply.

Because lifetime gifts are accumulated with earlier chargeable transfers (made within seven years before the date of the gift) it is possible for gifts made within seven years before death to increase the overall burden of inheritance tax.

Subject to the above, potentially exempt lifetime gifts are normally advantageous as they are completely exempt after seven years, are not chargeable in any event if covered by the nil threshold, and if chargeable, possibly attract tapering relief. Any part of the nil threshold used to cover such transfers would, however, reduce the amount available on the death estate.

In the case of assets attracting 100% business property relief it may not be advantageous to make a lifetime transfer. This is because a liability to capital gains tax can arise on the gift. The gain may be held over for capital gains purposes (see point (iv) under capital gains tax summary above), but it will reduce the base value to the donee (point (vi) of the capital gains tax summary above), whereas on death there is an automatic uplift to market value for capital gains tax purposes without any capital gains tax being payable. There would, however, be no liability to inheritance tax at the time of a lifetime gift because of the 100% relief, nor if the donor died within seven years, providing the gifted business assets were still held and still qualified.

(vii)   Effect of emigration

Inheritance tax is chargeable on worldwide assets of a person domiciled in the UK. To emigrate without changing domicile has no effect.

Even if Charles changes his domicile he will still be deemed UK domiciled for three years, and thereafter will be liable to inheritance tax on UK based property no matter where his domicile is.

See Chapter 3(c) on page x for more information on deemed domicile.

(b)   **Suggested course of action for Charles**

Although the transfer to Charles on his wife's death was exempt because of the spouse exemption, her nil-rate band has been wasted (unless she had made chargeable or potentially exempt gifts in the seven years before her death). The following points should be considered in order to improve the present and potential future tax position.

(i)   Charles should consider a deed of variation to redirect some of the assets left to him by his wife. This could go directly to his daughter, or to the grandchildren, thus utilising the nil rate threshold of his wife at her death and avoiding the value of the appropriate assets becoming part of his estate. Alternatively he could direct his wife's estate to a discretionary trust, for which he is a trustee, so that he can still exercise some control over the assets.

The deed would also be effective for capital gains tax (providing the deed contains a statement that it is intended to have that effect), avoiding any tax if the assets have increased in value since the wife's death (although if the variation included a trust in which Charles had an interest, he would be regarded as the settlor and would be charged on the trust's gains).

(ii) Charles could make transfers of his shareholding in the family trading company in 2008/09, covering any capital gains tax liability with gifts holdover relief. The gifts would initially be potentially exempt transfers covered by 100% business property relief for inheritance tax. If Charles died within seven years, then providing the donees had retained the shares given to them, business property relief of 100% would still be available so long as the company's activities still qualified. If Charles does not wish to give all of the shares directly to his family, trusts could be used.

(iii) Further gifts could be made in so far as no liability to capital gains tax is crystallised (eg cash gifts; chattels worth less than £6,000; possibly the land owned if it has a high base value); or on which gifts holdover relief would be available (eg shares in supplier company or gifts to a discretionary trust; although the latter would be chargeable transfers for inheritance tax, the gifts could be restricted so that they were covered by available reliefs and the nil threshold).

(iv) Thereafter annual gifts could be made utilising the capital gains tax annual exemption, currently £9,600. For inheritance tax, such gifts would be reduced by the £3,000 annual exemption. Gifts could include quoted shares and/or the unquoted shares in the supplier company. The latter would attract 100% business property relief for inheritance tax.

(v) Care must be taken not to allow the taxation advantages of a gift to outweigh the personal requirements of the taxpayer.

(vi) Either in lifetime or on death Charles could make gifts to charity. These would reduce the estate without giving rise to a liability either to capital gains tax or inheritance tax, and he can make gift aid payments of any amount to charity and save higher rate tax on the gross equivalent, providing he makes an appropriate gift aid declaration. He can also obtain higher rate relief for gifts to charities of quoted stocks and shares, and also shares on the Alternative Investment Market (AIM), and this also applies to gifts of UK land and buildings. All such gifts are valued at their open market value plus any incidental costs of making them.

Supplementary Note

For further notes on liability to inheritance tax see Examples 1 to 4; business property relief see Example 25; deeds of variation see Example 34; and domicile see Example 27. Capital gains tax is dealt with in detail in the companion book Tolley's Taxwise I 2008/09.

Question

Mr Gregory is a 68-year old widower for whom you act as tax adviser. He came to see you on 31 May 2008 and told you that he had just been informed by his doctor that he had only a few months left to live. He intends that all his wealth should pass to his only son Neil (who will be his sole executor). He has heard that in some circumstances it might be advantageous either to transfer some of his assets immediately to Neil as a gift or alternatively to sell some of his assets and then to transfer the sale proceeds to Neil as a gift.

Mr Gregory is not currently in a position to make cash gifts as he has just drawn out the last of his savings from his bank account. He provides you with the following information concerning his assets:

(i)   He owns 2,000 shares in Bingo plc, a quoted company, currently valued at £480. He had acquired the shares for £14,350 in December 1990.

(ii) He had acquired 20,000 £1 shares at par out of an issued share capital of 200,000 shares in Peck Limited, a retail company, in February 2006. His shares have been valued recently at £1.20 each. The investment qualified for income tax relief at 20% under the enterprise investment scheme.

(iii) He had acquired 10,000 £1 shares out of an issued share capital of 10,000,000 shares in Zingo plc, a quoted land dealing company, for £7 each in November 1992. The shares are currently worth £30 per share.

(iv) All tax liabilities have been agreed and paid on the due date up to 5 April 2008. Mr Gregory does not expect to have any income tax liabilities outstanding on his death, as his income should be just enough to cover his outgoings up to that time. It is estimated that the income tax computation up to the date of his death will show a repayment due of £1,250.

Other relevant information is as follows:

(v)   He had taxable capital gains in the previous four years of assessment as follows:

	2004/05 £	2005/06 £	2006/07 £	2007/08 £
Net gains	12,400	11,500	–	11,925
Less: Annual exemption	(8,200)	(8,500)	–	(9,200)
Taxable gains	4,200	3,000	nil	2,725

(Mr Gregory's rate of capital gains tax was 40% throughout and he was not entitled to any taper relief on the gains made in the four years.)

(vi) In January 2007 he had made an outright gift of his principal private residence to his son Neil who now resides there. Mr Gregory went to live with his brother. The value of the residence at that time was £250,000 but it has since risen to £400,000. Neil has now suggested that Mr Gregory should come to live with him rent-free. Mr Gregory has refused to go to live with Neil partly on personal grounds, but also because he believes that if he does, problems might arise in connection with inheritance tax. The gift of his residence is the only gift which Mr Gregory has made so far.

(vii) His son Neil, who is due to get married shortly, has recently started up in business and has indicated that he will need to convert any assets which he receives from his father into cash by 31 December 2008 at the latest, in order to invest in the business.

(a)   Indicate the optimum tax strategy for Mr Gregory regarding lifetime gifts.

(b)   Assuming that Mr Gregory had in fact gone to live with Neil in his former private residence, state the inheritance tax consequences which would have arisen.

(c)   Assuming that Mr Gregory adopts the strategy suggested under (a) above, calculate the inheritance tax liability arising on the basis that he died on 30 September 2008.

Answer

(a) **Tax strategy re lifetime gifts**

Disposals of assets in lifetime may attract capital gains tax on their growth in value. Furthermore, if the disposal is a gift, it may be reckonable for inheritance tax.

Mr Gregory is almost certain to die within seven years, and therefore even if a gift was initially a potentially exempt transfer for inheritance tax, it would become chargeable on his death. The tapering relief for inheritance tax applicable after three years will almost certainly not be available.

By comparison, assets retained until death obtain a capital gains tax free uplift to probate value, thus avoiding a liability to capital gains tax. A gift in lifetime may therefore attract a liability to both capital gains tax and inheritance tax, whereas the same asset given on death would only be liable to inheritance tax.

Against that double charge, a gift in lifetime attracts any unused inheritance tax annual exemptions or marriage exemption and the value subsequently chargeable on death because the seven year period has not been survived is the value at the date of the gift. Mr Gregory gave his house to his son in January 2007. The value at that date of £250,000 will be reduced by the annual exemptions for 2006/07 and 2005/06 and will be included in calculating the inheritance tax on Mr Gregory's death at £250,000 – £6,000 = £244,000, not at its current value of £400,000.

As Mr Gregory does not have long to live, the increase in value up to the date of death of any asset given away now is likely to be minimal, but the inheritance tax annual exemptions of 2007/08 and 2008/09 are available. In ordinary circumstances an exemption is available for gifts that are normal expenditure out of income. Although there is no fixed minimum period during which regular gifts have to have been made to constitute 'normal expenditure', it is necessary that a pattern of actual or intended payments has been established (*Bennett & Others v CIR* (1994)). Thus a 'death bed' resolution to make periodic payments for life does not create an exemption for such payments under the normal expenditure out of income provisions.

To create a liability to capital gains tax would not be advisable. If, however, the disposals realised net capital losses, any losses in the tax year of death may be carried back against the capital gains liabilities of the three preceding years, latest first, tax being repayable accordingly. The loss carryback relief is not wasted against gains already covered by the annual exemption. As Mr Gregory is likely to die before 5 April 2009, immediate crystallisation of losses would be useful. Care must be taken not to give loss-producing assets to connected persons such as Neil, as a loss on a disposal to such a person can only be utilised against future gains on disposals to the same person, which are very unlikely if death is imminent.

The recommended stategy would be to:

(i) Sell the shares in Bingo plc, realising a capital loss as follows:

	£
Cost of shares December 1990	14,350
Sale proceeds in say July 2008	480
Loss on Bingo plc shares	13,870

(ii) Relieve the loss on the Bingo plc shares against gains of the three years preceding death (assuming death in 2008/09):

	2007/08 £	2006/07 £	2005/06 £	£
Gains	11,925*	–	11,500*	
Loss re Bingo plc shares	(2,725)		(3,000)	(5,725)
	9,200		8,500	
Less: Annual exemption	(9,200)		(8,500)	
	–		–	
Available loss (as above)				13,870
Unused losses				8,145

* Before taper relief

The tax saving from carrying back the loss to 2007/08 is £2,725 @ 40% = £1,090. The due date of payment for the 2007/08 tax is 31 January 2009, so if Mr Gregory died before that date the capital gains tax originally due would not be paid. Otherwise it would be repaid. The repayment due as a result of carrying back the loss to 2005/06 is £3,000 @ 40% = £1,200.

As far as repayment supplement is concerned, although the *tax saving* is calculated by reference to the tax position of the earlier year, the claim relates to the later year, and repayment supplement is payable only if the repayment is made after 31 January following that later year. Where losses are carried back from the year of death, the deduction is made automatically without the need for a claim (TCGA 1992 s 62(2)). TMA 1970 Sch 1B.2(7) provides, however, that for supplement purposes the carryback is treated in the same way as if a claim was required. In this example, supplement would only be payable if the tax was repaid after 31 January 2010. The tax will almost certainly have been repaid by that date, but if it has not been, repayment supplement will be payable from that date at 4% per annum (based on the current rate from 6 January 2008).

(iii)   Make a gift during 2008/09 to Neil of the appropriate number of shares in Zingo plc.

	£	£
The gain on each Zingo plc share would be:		
Market value		30.00
Less: Cost	7.00	7.00
Gain per share		23.00

The available capital loss in 2008/09 after carry back against 2007/08 and 2005/06 is £8,145 as indicated in (ii) above, which covers a gift of 354 shares (@ £23.00 gain per share). The available exemptions for inheritance tax are:

	£
Annual 2008/09	3,000
2007/08	3,000
Marriage (on gift to Neil)	5,000
	11,000

This covers a gift of 366 shares (@ £30 each). Mr Gregory should therefore give Neil 366 shares in Zingo plc.

(Note that the sale or gift of shares in Peck Limited would give rise to a clawback of enterprise investment scheme relief at 20%, since they will not have been held for three years until February 2009.)

By gifting 366 shares instead of 354 (see above re maximum gift for CGT purposes) the loss to be set back is restricted by £276 (12 × £23.00). This however is better than paying inheritance tax on £360 (12 shares @ £30).

If larger gains than £8,145 were made, the losses available to carry back would be reduced to below £5,725 and the capital gains tax repayment for earlier years would be reduced accordingly. As a result Mr Gregory's annual capital gains tax exemption cannot be used in 2008/09, because to use the annual exemption, gains would need to exceed the losses of £13,870, and no losses would be left to carry back. The executors are unlikely to make losses when they convert assets to cash for Neil because they take the assets at probate value, and even if they did, those losses are not available to carry back against Mr Gregory's gains.

(b) **Inheritance tax consequences of Mr Gregory going to live with Neil**

It is reasonable to assume that Mr Gregory's illness is such that he is unable to maintain himself. Provided such an eventuality was not foreseeable in January 2007 (at the time of the original gift of the property), then Mr Gregory could return to his former residence without breaching the gifts with reservation rules or the use of pre-owned asset provisions.

FA 1986 Sch 20.6(1)(b) provides such an exemption in relation to gifts of an interest in land when the donor's circumstances change in a way that was unforeseen at the time of the original gift and the benefit provided by the donee to the donor represents reasonable provision for the care and maintenance of an elderly or infirm relative. This provision also applies to prevent a pre-owned asset charge (FA 2004 Sch 15.11(5)(d)).

Without such exemption Mr Gregory's return to his former residence would nullify the original gift and would return the value of the house to his estate. In addition the original gift, which was a potentially exempt transfer, would still be included in the lifetime chargeable gifts if death occurred within seven years after the original gift. However, relief is given to prevent double charging (FA 1986 s 104 and SI 1987/1130).

(c) **Inheritance tax as a result of Mr Gregory's death on 30 September 2008**

		£	Gross £	Tax (2008/09 scale) £
Gifts in lifetime:				
January 2007				
Gift to Neil — house		250,000		
Less: Annual 2006/07	3,000			
exemptions				
2005/06	3,000	6,000		
Potentially exempt transfer now chargeable			244,000	–
July 2008				
Gift to Neil				
366 shares in Zingo plc @ £30 per share		10,980		
Less: Marriage exemption	5,000			
Annual exemptions 2008/09	2,980			
2007/08	3,000	10,980	–	–
			244,000	–
Mr Gregory's estate at death —				
30 September 2008				
Proceeds of sale of Bingo plc shares		480		
Income tax repayment		1,250		

	£	Gross £	Tax (2008/09 scale) £
Capital gains tax repayment**		1,090	
Shares in Zingo plc			
10,000 – 366 = 9,634 @ £30		289,020	
Shares in Peck Limited			
20,000 @ £1.20	24,000		
Less: Business property relief 100%	24,000	–	291,840	89,536*
			535,840	89,536*

Inheritance tax liability on death of
Mr Gregory — £89,536

(* 535,840 – 312,000 = £233,840 @ 40%)

**   Assuming that the 2007/08 tax of £1,090 was discharged, the repayment will consist of 2005/06 gains of £3,000 less loss used in 2008/09 of £276 = £2,724@ 18% = £490

Supplementary note

The general principles of inheritance tax are dealt with in earlier examples. In particular normal expenditure out of income is dealt with in Example 1, gifts with reservation in Example 19 and pre-owned assets in Example 23. The capital gains tax provisions are outlined in Example 36. Capital gains tax is dealt with in detail in the companion to this book, Tolley's Taxwise I 2008/09.

Question

Thomas and Maria have been married for many years. Their daughter, Julia, was born in February 1968 and their son, Edmund, in October 1969. Thomas, who was born in 1934, started in business on his own account in 1958 as a manufacturer of domestic hardware. Their relevant financial history is as follows:

March 1965	—	The family home is bought by Maria for £6,000.
May 1979	—	Thomas buys 100,000 ordinary shares in Huntingdon Ltd, a trading company that has since become listed on the Stock Exchange. The value at 31 March 1982 was 25p per share.
September 1988	—	Thomas buys 25,000 ordinary shares in Portsmouth plc for £45,000.
31 March 1989	—	Thomas transfers all his business assets (except plant of £30,000 which he retains personally) to a new company, Thomas Ltd, in consideration for ordinary shares valued at £300,000 (Maria holding one share as nominee). Business assets immediately before the transfers were:

	£
Goodwill	110,000
Plant, at cost less depreciation	55,000
Vehicles, at cost less depreciation	30,000
Stock, at cost or lower market value	65,000
Debtors	90,000
Cash	40,000
Creditors	(60,000)
	330,000

Thomas Ltd continues the trade without a break.

November 2001	—	Maria gives the family home (then valued at £80,000) in equal shares to Julia and her husband Henry. Maria and Thomas then move to their second home (which cost £62,000 in 1988, at which time an election had been made for capital gains tax that the original home remained the principal private residence).
June 2004	—	Maria places £32,500 cash into trust for Edmund for life, with remainder to Julia or her children (Julia has a son and a daughter). The trustees invest the money in a building society account which pays interest monthly. Thomas gives 70% of the shares in Thomas Ltd to Edmund. Company assets, at historical cost, are:

	£
Goodwill on acquisition from Thomas	110,000
Freehold factory bought July 1989	225,000
Shares in 100% subsidiary, allotted May 1992	100,000
Other non-chargeable assets	368,000
	803,000

In June 2004 goodwill is valued at £400,000. The factory is used for the trade (which is to continue) and is worth £600,000. The subsidiary's only assets are a portfolio of investment properties worth £230,000. (Ignore deferred tax.)

October 2004	—	Thomas places his holding of shares in Huntingdon plc (then valued at £130,000) into a discretionary trust. The beneficiaries are Julia, Edmund and all their descendants. Thomas's holding was less than 5% and he did not work for the company. The trustees decide to accumulate all the income arising. The gain arising on the transfer was £60,402 after available reliefs.

May 2008   —   Edmund dies intestate. He is unmarried and without children. In addition to his shares in Thomas Ltd (which have not changed in value since June 2004) he leaves a house worth £165,000 and other investments of £70,000. Under the rules of intestacy his estate will pass to Thomas and Maria.

No person elects to rebase all their chargeable assets to 31 March 1982 values.

Shares in Thomas Ltd at June 2004 are to be valued:

 (i)   as to a 100% holding, on an assets basis;

 (ii)   as to a 70% holding, on an assets basis discounted by 20%;

 (iii) as to a 30% holding, £225,000 for the holding.

Any inheritance tax on lifetime transfers is paid by the donor.

(a)   Work out the gain on the gift by Thomas of 70% of his shares in Thomas Ltd taking into account any available CGT reliefs.

(b)   Identify and quantify all chargeable and potentially exempt transfers, advising how much inheritance tax is payable on chargeable transfers, when it is payable, and any other factors that may be relevant.

(c)   Advise the beneficiaries under Edmund's intestacy of the main planning points that arise on his death.

Answer

(a)   **Capital gains tax liabilities 6 April 2001 onwards**

November 2001 — Gift of family home by Maria — covered by principal
private residence exemption — no chargeable gain.

June 2004 — Cash into trust by Maria — no chargeable disposal.
Gift by Thomas to Edmund of 70% of shares in
Thomas Ltd:

Valuation of Thomas Ltd — assets basis

	£
Factory	600,000
Subsidiary	230,000
Non-chargeable assets	368,000
Goodwill	400,000
	1,598,000
Valuation of gift: 70% × (1,598,000 × 80%)	894,880
Cost — March 1989 (70% × 300,000)	210,000
Gain	684,580

Holdover relief will be available, for any gain relating to the chargeable business assets – restricted to
the fraction:

$$\frac{\text{Chargeable business assets}}{\text{Total chargeable assets}}\text{ ie }\frac{600,000 + 400,000}{600,000 + 400,000 + 230,000}$$

Available for relief:

$$\frac{1,000,000}{1,230,000} \times 684,580$$

	£
Heldover gain	556,569
Gain chargeable on Thomas for 2004/05 (684,580 – 556,569)	£128,011

October 2004 — Gift by Thomas of shares in Huntingdon plc to
discretionary trust

The gain of £60,402 can be held over under TCGA 1992 s 260, as disposition
is immediately liable to inheritance tax.
Note The base cost of shares in Huntingdon plc to the trustees is 130,000 –
60,402 = £69,598.

May 2008 — No liability to capital gains tax on death of Edmund.

(b)   **Inheritance tax**

Inheritance tax position of Maria

November 2001

		£	£
— Gift of house			80,000
Less: Annual exemptions	2001/02	3,000	
	2000/01	3,000	6,000
Potentially exempt transfer			74,000

The transfer will only become chargeable if Maria dies before November 2008, but no tax will be payable in any event, since the transfer is below the nil threshold (although the nil threshold available against Maria's estate at death would be correspondingly reduced).

			£	£
June 2004 —	Gift of cash into interest in possession trust			32,500
	Less: Annual exemptions	2004/05	3,000	
		2003/04	3,000	6,000
	Potentially exempt transfer			26,500

Again the transfer will only become chargeable on the death of Maria, this time before June 2011, but again the cumulative transfers are in any event covered by the nil threshold.

Inheritance tax position of Thomas

		£
June 2004 —	Gift of 70% of shares in Thomas Ltd to Edmund.	
	Valuation of gift:	
	Holding before gift — 100% of 1,598,000	1,598,000
	Holding after gift — 30% minority	225,000
	Loss to estate	1,373,000
	Less: business property relief	
	100% × 1,373,000 1,368,000*	
	1,598,000	1,175,384
		197,616

(* The investment holding subsidiary is an excepted asset for business property relief)

		£	£
	Less: Annual exemptions 2004/05	3,000	
	2003/04	3,000	6,000
	Potentially exempt transfer		191,616

Note   The shares that were returned to Thomas following the death of Edmund would also form part of Thomas's estate. However should he die within seven years, i.e. before June 2011, relief will be given to prevent double charging. No liability will arise on the potentially exempt transfer itself, since it is below the nil threshold.

October 2004 — Gift of shares in Huntingdon plc to discretionary trust

Value of gift   £130,000

No inheritance tax is payable at the time of the gift as the cumulative total of gifts immediately liable to inheritance tax is below the 2004/05 threshold of £263,000. If Thomas should die before June 2011, the gift would be aggregated with the June 2004 potentially exempt transfer that then became chargeable and inheritance tax would be payable to the extent that the aggregate amount exceeded the nil threshold at the time of death. If he should die after June 2011 but before October 2011 no tax would be payable on the gift to the discretionary trust, but it would be aggregated with later gifts and the death estate, thus increasing the inheritance tax payable.

Inheritance tax position re death of Edmund in May 2008

	£	£
Value of free estate:		
Shares in Thomas Ltd (70% holding) (1,598,000 × 70%, less 20%)	894,880	
Less: Business property relief (100% available as second transfer was on death even though not owned for two years)		
$100\% \times 894,880 \times \dfrac{1,368,000^*}{1,598,000}$	766,080	128,800

(*The investment holding subsidiary is an excepted asset)

	£
House	165,000
Other investments	70,000
	363,800
Settled property — trust of Maria	32,500
	396,300

Inheritance tax payable (396,300 − 312,000) @ 40% = £<u>33,720</u>

Payable by:
Personal representatives:

$$\dfrac{363,800}{396,300} \times 33,720 = \quad\quad 30,955$$

Trustees:

$$\dfrac{32,500}{396,300} \times 33,720 = \quad\quad 2,765$$

<u>33,720</u>

Of the total liability, the tax relating to the Thomas Ltd shares can be paid by instalments without interest to the due date and that relating to the house by instalments with interest from 1 December 2008; therefore the amount actually due from the personal representatives on application for probate will be:

Shares

$$\frac{128,800}{363,800} \times 30,955 \times \frac{1}{10} \qquad = 1,096 \qquad \text{(with interest on balance only if paid late)}$$

$$\text{House}\frac{165,000}{363,800} \times 30,955 \times \frac{1}{10} \qquad = 1,404 \qquad \text{(with interest on balance from 1 December 2008)}$$

$$\text{Other investments}\ \frac{70,000}{363,800} \times 30,955 \qquad = 5,956$$

$$\underline{£8,456}$$

(c)   **Advice to Thomas and Maria as beneficiaries of the estate of Edmund**

The value in Edmund's estate is reverting to yourselves. As the oldest generation, you are likely to die before other members of the family. It may be preferable for Edmund's estate to go to your daughter Julia or to your grandchildren. If this course of action is decided on then it could be achieved by use of a deed of variation. Such a deed would not save inheritance tax on Edmund's death but might significantly reduce the potential liability on your own deaths. The deed must be executed within two years of Edmund's death.

It should be noted that if an instalment option asset (ie either the Thomas Ltd shares or Edmund's house) is sold, the outstanding instalments of inheritance tax become payable immediately.

The funding of the inheritance tax could be achieved by Thomas Ltd purchasing its own shares from the estate. This would qualify for special treatment and HMRC clearance should be obtained for the purchase not to be treated as a distribution by Thomas Ltd.

If no deed of variation occurs then should either of you die within five years after Edmund's death (ie before May 2013) quick succession relief would be available in your estates in respect of the assets inherited from him. In the same way, should the devolution of Edmund's estate be varied in favour of Julia and she were to die or make a chargeable transfer of her interest in the settled property devolving on her following Edmund's death, before May 2013, quick succession relief would be available by reference to the tax payable on Edmund's death.

Explanatory Notes

Valuation of assets for capital gains tax and inheritance tax

1.   This example shows the way in which both capital gains tax and inheritance tax may be relevant when gifts are made, and the different rules that apply when dealing with each tax. Note particularly that in valuing a shareholding, the open market value of the holding is taken for capital gains tax (TCGA 1992 s 272), hence the gift of 70% of Thomas's 100% holding in Thomas Ltd to Edmund in June 2004 is discounted by the 20% reduction for a 70% holding, whereas for inheritance tax the 'loss to the donor' principle applies, the shares therefore being taken into account for inheritance tax as a 100% holding, reduced to a minority holding. (See Revenue's Tax Bulletin August 1996 concerning when two or more separate assets may be treated as a single unit of property for valuation purposes.) The value of the gift is therefore different for capital gains tax and inheritance tax, ie:

Capital gains tax	£894,880
Inheritance tax	£1,373,000

When considering the capital gains tax acquisition value for those who inherit a deceased's assets, on the other hand, TCGA 1992 s 274 provides that where the value of an asset has been *ascertained* (whether in any proceedings or otherwise) for the purposes of inheritance tax, that value is taken to be the market value of the asset at the date of death for capital gains tax (overriding the normal 'open market value' provisions in TCGA 1992 s 62). This enables the higher 'loss to the donor' amount to be used in those circumstances, including any value attributable to related property.

Where, however, no tax is due because of reliefs or exemptions, the value of assets will not be *ascertained* for inheritance tax, so their capital gains acquisition value would be the open market value. This would apply, for example, where 100% business property relief is available on family company shares, or where a transfer of such shares is covered by the nil threshold. It has been suggested that where this would give lower acquisition values, the problem could be overcome by having a minimal amount of 'excepted assets', not qualifying for business property relief, within the company (see note 2), so that a valuation would then be necessary. The Revenue have, however, stated that if very little or no tax was at stake, it was unlikely that an ascertained value would be negotiated by Shares Valuation Division (Tax Bulletin April 1995).

In the case of *Stonor & Mills (Dickinson's Executors) v CIR* (SpC 288, 2001), no inheritance tax was payable on the estate because of the nil rate band and the charities exemption. The executors sold freehold properties from the estate for significantly more than the probate value, resulting in large capital gains. They tried to get the Revenue to accept the sale values as amended probate values, but the Revenue refused on the grounds that an investigation into values was not necessary since charity relief had been claimed. The executors then made a claim under s 191 (land sold within three years after death – see Example 10 part B) to substitute the sale proceeds for the probate value, thus increasing the capital gains tax base cost and eliminating the gains. It was held that since no one was liable to pay any tax on the estate no one was entitled to make a s 191 claim.

Investment assets

2. Capital gains tax holdover relief on gifts under TCGA 1992 s 165 is also available only on business assets and not on assets held as investments (other than farming land owned by an agricultural landlord, which can qualify for s 165 relief). Gifts relief under TCGA 1992 s 260 is available on any asset, providing the gift is immediately liable to inheritance tax, hence the relief on the October 2004 gift by Thomas to the discretionary trust.

Transfer of business to company

3. Thomas will not have been able to hold over the chargeable gains on the transfer of his personal business to Thomas Ltd in 1989, since not all of the assets were transferred in consideration for shares. Hence the value of the shares received, £300,000, is not reduced by holdover relief.

Cross references

4. See Example 4 explanatory note 7 for the position when both capital gains tax and inheritance tax are payable on the same transfer. For detailed notes on business property relief see Example 25, on quick succession relief see Example 21, on the instalment option see Example 5 and on deeds of variation in relation to a deceased's estate see Example 34. Note in this example that a variation would not result in additional tax payable on Edmund's estate, since there are no exempt beneficiaries. Had additional tax been payable, the amount would have had to be notified to HMRC Capital Taxes and a copy of the variation sent, within six months after the deed was effected. Capital gains tax is dealt with comprehensively in the companion to this book Tolley's Taxwise I 2008/09.

Question

Y died on 5 April 2007 leaving small bequests to each of three friends and the residue to his son X, for life.

The administration of the estate was completed by the personal representatives on 5 April 2009.

Details of the estate income (which is wholly interest) are as follows:

	Expenses borne £	Leaving residuary income		Payments to X £	made on
		Net £	Gross equivalent £		
2007/08	1,130	1,760	2,200	1,600	3 March 2008
2008/09	1,150	2,880	3,600	3,040	20 June 2009

(a) Indicate the tax liability of the personal representatives in relation to the estate income and state what their responsibilities for reporting the income are under self-assessment.

(b) Calculate for 2007/08 and 2008/09 the amounts of estate income to be included in X's taxable income.

(c) State whether the estate income that would have been included in X's taxable income would have been different had he been absolutely entitled to the residue (as compared with his limited (life) interest).

Answer

(a) **Personal representatives — income tax liability and self-assessment**

Tax rates (FA 2008 s 4, s 5 and Sch 1)

For 2008/09 and subsequent years there has been a change to the tax rates applying for personal representatives:

Tax on non-savings income up to £36,000 is taxed at the rate of 20% (basic rate). The 10% starting rate band has been abolished (FA 2008 s 4).

Savings income (broadly bank and building society interest) is regarded as the part of taxable income which is taxed next. Savings income will be taxed in full at 20% (FA 2008 s 5).

If the personal representatives do not pay tax at 40% (see below) then all dividends or distributions from unit trusts (but not interest) are taxable at the 10% rate only. They form the top slice of income and so are taxed at the highest rate of tax. If the executors pay tax at 40% on other taxable income they will pay tax at 32.50% on dividends.

Taxable income over £36,000 will be taxed at the 40% higher rate (apart from dividends) whether or not it is savings income.

Changes to the Trust and Estate return (SA900) rules

Different filing dates for paper and online returns

Paper returns will now have to be filed by 31 October. This is earlier than the existing deadline and consequently for the 2007/08 return it means filing the form by 31 October 2008. An automatic penalty will be charged if a paper return is received after this date.

Online returns must be filed by 31 January. If it is intended to file a return after 31 October it will need to be filed online. So the deadline for filing the 2007/08 return online is 31 January 2009. Once again, an automatic penalty will be charged if it is received after this date.

The filing obligation is satisfied by the first return received by HMRC and this also triggers any late filing penalty. So if, for example, a paper 2007/08 return is filed after 31 October 2008, it is not then possible to avoid a late filing penalty by filing the return online.

Online filing has the obvious advantage of an immediate acknowledgement of receipt. However, as far as the Trust & Estate return is concerned, it does not provide an automatic tax calculation. HMRC still has to process online Trust & Estate returns in the same way as paper returns.

It is necessary to register first to use the online facility at online.hmrc.gov.uk. However, HMRC does not provide an online version of the Trust & Estate Tax Return series (SA900+) and so proprietary software will be necessary. From April 2008 it is possible to amend returns online.

For HMRC to calculate the liability – the return must be filed by 31 October, whether it is a paper or online return. This is later than the existing deadline.

If HMRC receive the return after 31 October they will apparently still calculate the liability, if asked but they cannot guarantee to do so before the 31 January payment date.

The deadlines for paying tax are unchanged.

Withdrawal of substitute returns

From April 2008 HMRC no longer accept or approve computer generated substitute versions of the Trust & Estate Tax Return series (SA900+). This means that either a paper return must be filed or the return filed online.

Change to the enquiry window

The closure of the enquiry window, the statutory period in which HMRC may open an enquiry into a return, will be linked to the date on which that return is delivered.

Where a return is filed on time, the enquiry window will close 12 months after the return is delivered. This applies to the 2007/08 return and later years. So where a return is received before the filing deadline, the enquiry window will close earlier than under the existing legislation.

(b) **Estate income to be included in taxable income of life tenant, X**

Where a person has a life interest in a will settlement, the amounts to be included in his statutory income during the period of administration are the grossed up equivalents of the net income payments actually made to him in the tax year (ITTOIA 2005 ss 649–662). The amount of the grossing addition depends on the rate of tax on the underlying income, ie for 2007/08 – 10% for dividend income, 20% for other savings income and the basic rate of 20% for non-savings income. For 2008/09 see (a) above.

Thus the amount to be included in the statutory income of X in 2007/08 is £1,600 × 100/80 = £2,000.

Upon the completion of the administration, any amounts due to the life tenant which remain unpaid are deemed to be paid as income of the tax year in which the administration is *completed* (ITTOIA 2005 ss 649–662).

Since the administration is completed in 2008/09, X will be deemed to have received the balance due to him in that tax year, ie £3,040 × 100/80 = £3,800.

(c) **Effect on X's estate income if he had had an absolute interest in residue**

Where a person has an absolute interest in the residue of an estate, the amounts to be included in his statutory income during the period of administration are the same as for a life tenant, ie the net income payments actually made to him, grossed up at the appropriate rate. However, the maximum amount that can be included is the 'aggregated income entitlement' to date, that is the total amount taxable in any year cannot exceed the aggregate amount of the residuary income to which the person is entitled, less amounts paid in previous tax years (ITTOIA 2005 s 668).

Upon the completion of the administration, any amounts not paid, up to the aggregated income entitlement, are deemed to be paid to the beneficiary immediately before completion.

The amounts taxable on X would therefore be the same as in (b) above, ie a gross amount of £2,000 in 2007/08 and a gross amount of £3,800 in 2008/09.

Explanatory Notes

Self-assessment position of personal representatives

1. If all the estate income is taxed income and there are no capital gains, then in most cases no amounts have to be entered on the return and only the information section needs to be completed (see Example 41 re Mrs Daley).

   The personal representatives supply beneficiaries with form R185 (estate income) showing income payments split according to whether the underlying income was taxed at the basic, lower or dividend ordinary rate of tax and whether the tax is repayable or non-repayable (see note 7).

Income of beneficiaries

2. All payments made to a beneficiary with a limited interest (usually a life interest) will be income. For a beneficiary with an absolute interest, payments must be treated as being liable to income tax in the hands of the beneficiary, up to the gross equivalent of the amount of income received by the estate. In the legislation references to amounts paid include assets transferred to beneficiaries, or debts set off or released, the amount for such items being their value at the relevant date (ITTOIA 2005 s 681).

    Where assets have been transferred to absolute beneficiaries during the administration period, therefore, the gross equivalent of their value must be taken into account as a distribution of estate income even though the distribution was of capital, so particular care must be taken in calculating the amount to be shown on forms R185 (estate income). See Example 40 for the capital gains implications of transferring assets to a beneficiary during the administration period.

Beneficiaries with an absolute interest

3. For someone with an absolute interest in the estate, if the amounts to be deducted from the income of the estate exceed the income in any year, the excess is carried forward and deducted from future income in computing the aggregated income entitlement (ITTOIA 2005 s 666(2), (6)).

4. If, when the administration is completed, it is found that the total residuary income of the estate is less than the amounts paid to someone with an absolute interest (for example, because large bills are paid in the later stages of the administration), then the amount included in the statutory income of the person concerned is reduced to the actual net income. This is done by reducing the income of the tax year in which the administration is completed, then, if necessary, the previous year, and so on (ITTOIA 2005 s 668).

Identification of income received by beneficiaries

5. The rate of tax for the different categories of income is known as the 'applicable rate' (ITTOIA 2005 ss 663, 670, 679).

    'Just and reasonable' apportionments of income bearing tax at different rates are to be made between beneficiaries with interests in residue. After making any such apportionments, payments to beneficiaries are regarded as being out of brought forward and current income charged at the basic rate in priority to other income, and as being out of brought forward and current savings income charged at the 20% rate (which will include pre 6 April 1999 dividends) in priority to dividends charged at the ordinary rate of 10% (ITTOIA 2005 ss 670, 679).

Changes in the applicable rate

6. As indicated in the example, amounts payable on completion of the administration are deemed to be income of the tax year in which the administration is completed, and they are therefore regarded as having been taxed at the applicable rate in force for that year, even if the rate of tax actually deducted from the income was different. This treatment applies only where the *applicable rate* changes. Where income was previously treated as being subject to a *different* applicable rate, any brought forward amounts are still regarded as having been taxed at the applicable rate that was relevant when they were received. For dividends received before 6 April 1999, the applicable rate was 20%, and that rate has remained unchanged. If any pre 6 April 1999 dividends were undistributed and were therefore brought forward to 1999/2000 or a later year, they would be regarded as distributed (along with any other savings income) in priority to post 5 April 1999 dividends and the applicable rate would be 20%.

Forms R185

7. Personal representatives supply beneficiaries with an income certificate form R185 (estate income) showing the amounts paid as income and tax deducted (or treated as deducted), split between savings

income (with tax at the lower or dividend ordinary rate) and other income (with tax at the basic rate). The beneficiaries include the information from the R185 in the trusts etc pages in their personal returns.

The tax on some of the income may be shown as non-repayable (ITTOIA 2005 s 680). Non-repayable tax at the 20% rate arises on life policy gains. From 6 April 1999 (ITTOIA 2005 s 680) provides that non-repayable tax also includes tax credits on dividends, and the applicable rate for all non-repayable tax except that on life policy gains is the dividend ordinary rate of 10%.

This also applies to beneficiaries with only a limited interest in residue.

Completion of administration

8.   When the administration of the estate is complete, the personal representatives will have assigned the interest in the assets to the trustees of the life interest settlement, who take those assets for capital gains tax purposes at their value at the date of death. This will normally be the probate value, but where a probate value was not *ascertained* for inheritance tax (because no inheritance tax was payable) the capital gains 'open market value' rule applies (see Example 38 explanatory note 1). Once the interest in the assets has been assigned to the trustees, the trustees are responsible for making the relevant income tax self-assessment returns, using forms R185 (trust income) and paying any tax due. The beneficiary is then liable to tax on the amount shown on the R185. See the examples in the book relating to trusts and Example 43 in respect of the income tax position of a life interest will trust.

Enterprise investment scheme and venture capital trusts

9.   Where someone has invested under the enterprise investment scheme or venture capital trust scheme, their death does not trigger the withdrawal of the income tax relief on the shares nor will it cause deferred gains to become chargeable. The personal representatives would be liable to capital gains tax on sale of the shares, the acquisition cost being the market value at the date of death.

Question

John Bird died on 30 September 2008. By his will he left one half of his estate to his wife (aged 65) and one half to his son (aged 42). His executors, Mrs Bird and her son Rupert, obtained probate on 1 February 2009. There was no inheritance tax payable. The estate, which was valued at £500,000 (gross), included the following assets:

Asset	Probate value £
950 shares of £1 each in Bird Enterprises Ltd, a trading company (the other 50 shares being owned by Mrs Bird, who was a director working part-time and had subscribed for the shares at par in February 1990). Rupert was an employee in the company.	235,000
10,000 shares in Computer Games plc, a quoted company	17,500
3,600 shares in Midwest Bank plc held in an ISA following the flotation of the former building society	10,200

Mrs Bird and her son decided to sell Bird Enterprises Ltd because without its founder, Mr Bird, they were too dependent on the skills of individual employees. Although a number of outside offers were made, on 31 March 2009 they accepted a bid of £332,500 from the management for the whole of the company.

The Midwest Bank received a takeover offer of £2.50 per share from a High Street bank on 3 April 2009 which Mrs Bird and her son accepted.

On 10 February 2009 Micro plc made a cash offer of £3.30 per share or 4% Redeemable Loan Stock to the same value in any proportions for each share in Computer Games plc (the loan stock is within the definition of qualifying corporate bonds (QCB)).

The administration of the estate was completed late January 2009.

Neither Mrs Bird nor her son will have any further capital disposals in 2008/09.

(a)   State the capital gains tax payable for 2008/09 if all of the above transactions are undertaken by Mrs Bird and her son as executors (and they accept cash for the Computer Games shares).

(b)   Set out alternative suggestions which would have mitigated the tax payable.

Answer

(a) **Capital gains tax payable for 2008/09**

Estate of John Bird deceased

	£	£	£
Bird Enterprises Ltd — sale proceeds 950 shares March 2009		332,500	
Probate value September 2008	235,000		
Costs of title 0.75%	1,763	236,763	95,737
Midwest Bank plc —			
Sale proceeds April 2009 3,600 shares @ £2.50		9,000	
Probate value	10,200		
Costs of title 0.75%	77	10,277	(1,277)
Computer Games plc —			
Sale proceeds February 2009 10,000 shares @ £3.30		33,000	
Probate value	17,500		
Costs of title 0.75%	132	17,632	15,368
			109,828
Annual exemption			(9,600)
Chargeable gains for the year			100,228
Capital gains tax payable by executors @ 18% (see Chapter 36 a (iii))			£18,041

Mrs Bird

	£	£	£
Bird Enterprises Ltd —			
Sale proceeds 50 shares March 2009		17,500	
Cost		50	
		17,450	
Annual exemption			(9,600)
Qualifying chargeable gains for the year			7,850
Less: 4/9 of the gain			(3,489)
Capital gains tax payable by Mrs Bird @ 18% on £4,361 (see note 10 re: entrepreneurs' relief)			4,361
* Note that this is effectively the same as charging the whole gain to CGT @ 10%			£785*
Total capital gains tax payable by executors and Mrs Bird			£18,826

(b) **Ways of mitigating tax payable**

The overall tax payable could be mitigated as follows:

Transferring shares in Bird Enterprises Ltd to beneficiaries before sale

If Mrs Bird and her son as executors had transferred the shares to themselves as individuals prior to the sale, the transfer would be deemed to occur at the date of death (TCGA 1992 s 62(4)). Their revised personal capital gains tax position for 2008/09 (subject to any losses arising to them as individuals) would be:

Mrs Bird

	£	£	£
Bird Enterprises Ltd —			
Sale proceeds 525 shares March 2009 (166,250 + 17,500)		183,750	
Cost of 50 shares in February 1990	50		
Probate value of 475 shares September 2008	117,500	117,550	
			66,200
Annual exemption			(9,600)
Qualifying chargeable gains for the year			56,600
Less: 4/9 of the gain			£(25,156)
Capital gains tax payable by Mrs Bird @ 18% on £31,444 (see note 10 re entrepreneurs' relief)			31,444
* Note that this is effectively the same as charging the whole gain to CGT @ 10%			£5,660

Rupert Bird

	£	£	£
Bird Enterprises Ltd —			
Sale proceeds 475 shares March 2009		166,250	
Probate value September 2008		117,500	48,750
Annual exemption			(9,600)
Qualifying chargeable gains for the year			39,150
Capital gains tax payable by Rupert:			
Less: 4/9 of the gain			(17,400)
Capital gains tax payable by Rupert @ 18% on £21,750 (see note 10 re entrepreneurs' relief)			21,750
* Note that this is effectively the same as charging the whole gain to CGT @ 10%			£3,915

Such a transfer would, however, be taken to be a distribution of income, giving rise to taxable income in the hands of the beneficiaries to the extent that undistributed income had arisen in the estate, and would therefore trigger a charge to higher rate tax. Since the administration was completed within the same tax year as the transfer, however, this is irrelevant, since the income would already have been distributed.

Shares in Computer Games plc

The executors could transfer the whole of the shares to themselves as beneficiaries, enabling the beneficiaries to take loan stock, or they could take loan stock themselves as executors and pass it on to themselves as beneficiaries, thus deferring the capital gain. On 3 April 2009, however, they had incurred a loss on the disposal of the Midwest Bank plc shares. To use that loss and also their annual exemption, the executors could take the cash offer on 7,077 Computer Games plc shares and loan stock in respect of 3,183 shares, giving the estate a capital gains liability of:

	£	£
Sale proceeds 7,077 shares @ £3.30	23,355	
Proportion of probate value:		
$\dfrac{7,077}{10,000} \times 17,632$	12,478	10,877
Loss on Midwest Bank plc shares as in (a) above		(1,277)
		9,600
Annual exemption		(9,600)
Chargeable gains		–

This enables both the executor's annual exemption and the loss on the Midwest Bank shares to be fully utilised. (Losses incurred by executors can only be offset against a gain accruing to them as executors in the same or a future year and cannot be transferred to beneficiaries. A similar tax saving could have been achieved if the Midwest Bank shares had been transferred to the beneficiaries before the Bank was taken over, so that the loss would arise to Mrs Bird and Rupert. The Computer Games plc shares on which the cash offer was taken could then be reduced so as to realise gains of approximately £9,600 as before.)

Effect of above suggestions

As a result of the above, the capital gains tax payable for 2008/09 would be reduced from £18,826 to (5,660 + 3,915) £9,575, ie by £9,251. Mrs Bird and Rupert would, however, each have redeemable loan stock in Micro plc with accrued gains of:

*   See explanatory note 4.

	£
1,721 shares @ £3.30	5,679
Proportion of probate value $\dfrac{1,721}{10,000} \times 17,500*$	(3,012)
Accrued gain	2,667

*   See explanatory note 4.

Even so, if the loan stock was redeemed in a year in which the beneficiary had no other gains, the accrued gain would be covered by the annual exemption of the year of disposal. (Taper relief will not be available, since it would be taken into account in calculating the accrued gains on the shares at the time of the takeover, at which time the shares had been held for less than twelve months since the date of Mr Bird's death.)

Explanatory Notes

Treatment of personal representatives

1. On death the deceased's assets are acquired by the personal representatives at market value, but there is no deemed disposal by the deceased and no capital gains tax is payable as a result of the death.

2. The personal representatives — the executors in this example — are treated as a separate single and continuing body of persons. All their dealings as personal representatives are completely separate from their dealings as individuals. Capital gains and losses are accordingly computed and assessed on them as personal representatives. Under self-assessment any tax due on capital gains is payable on 31 January following the end of the tax year. The rate of tax on personal representatives' gains is 18% (TCGA 1992 s 4). See Chapter 36 a (iii).

3. The personal representatives are entitled to an annual exemption of the same amount as an individual for the tax year of death and the following two tax years. If the administration of the estate has not been completed in that time there is no annual exemption for later years and any gains arising are chargeable at the 18% rate.

Probate valuation costs

4. When computing the gain or loss on sales of assets by the personal representatives, the cost of acquiring the assets can be increased by the costs incurred in valuing them for probate (*CIR v Richards' Executors* 1971).

    SP2/04 sets out the scale of expenses allowable under TCGA 1992 s 38(1)(b) for the costs of establishing title in computing the gains or losses of personal representatives on the sale of assets comprised in a deceased person's estate.

	Gross value of estate	Allowable expenditure
A	Not exceeding £50,000	1.8% of the probate value of the assets sold by the personal representatives.
B	Over £50,000 but not exceeding £90,000	A fixed amount of £900, to be divided between all of the assets of the estate in proportion to the probate values and allowed in those proportions on assets sold by the personal representatives.
C	Over £90,000 but not exceeding £400,000	1% of the probate value of the assets sold.
D	Over £400,000 but not exceeding £500,000	A fixed amount of £4,000, to be divided as at B above.
E	Over £500,000 but not exceeding £1,000,000	0.8% of the probate value of the assets sold.
F	Over £1,000,000 but not exceeding £5,000,000	A fixed amount of £8,000, to be divided as at B above.
G	Over £5,000,000	0.16% of the probate value of the assets sold, subject to a maximum of £10,000.

    The scale has effect where the death in question occurred on or after 6 April 2004.

    A deduction for probate valuation costs only applies where the sale is by the personal representatives and not where the sale is by the beneficiaries themselves. It should be noted that the actual costs, if any, of the *beneficiary* relating to the acquisition of the asset are deductible (TCGA 1992 s 64(1)(a)), and also any costs of the personal representatives *in transferring* assets to them (s 64(1)(b)). As Mrs Bird and Rupert have undertaken the transactions themselves it is unlikely there are any such costs.

HMRC have agreed the following scale of allowable expenditure under TCGA 1992 ss 38 and 64(1) for expenses incurred after 6 April 2004 by corporate trustees in the administration of estates and trusts. The Commissioners for Revenue and Customs will accept computations based either on this scale or on the actual allowable expenditure incurred.

The scale is as follows:

Transfers of assets to beneficiaries etc

(i)   *Publicly-marketed shares and securities*

    (A)   One beneficiary – £25 per holding transferred.

    (B)   Two or more beneficiaries between whom a holding must be divided – as (A) above to be divided in equal shares between the beneficiaries.

(ii)   Other shares and securities – as (i) above with the addition of any exceptional expenditure.

(iii)   Other assets – as (i) above with the addition of any exceptional expenditure.

For the purpose of this statement of practice, shares and securities are regarded as marketed to the general public if buying and selling prices for them are regularly published in the financial pages of a national or regional newspaper, magazine, or other journal.

Actual disposals and acquisitions

(i)   Publicly-marketed shares and securities – the investment fee as charged by the trustees.

(ii)   Other shares and securities – as (i) above, plus actual valuation costs.

(iii)   Other assets – the investment fee as charged by the trustees, subject to a maximum of £75, plus actual valuation costs.

Where a comprehensive annual management fee is charged, covering both the cost of administering the trust and the expenses of actual disposals and acquisitions, the investment fee for the purposes of (i), (ii) and (iii) above will be taken to be £0.25 per £100 on the sale or purchase moneys.

Deemed disposals by trustees

(i)   Publicly-marketed shares and securities – £8 per holding disposed of.

(ii)   Other shares and securities – actual valuation costs.

(iii)   Other assets – actual valuation costs.

Valuation for capital gains tax where no inheritance tax payable

5.   Where no inheritance tax is payable on death, the values included in the application for probate will not be binding on HMRC for capital gains tax unless specifically agreed with them (see Example 38 explanatory note 1). The personal representatives may therefore wish to file form CG34 after the sale of shares in Bird Enterprises Ltd to agree the acquisition cost and gain prior to the submission of the self-assessment return.

Shares held in a PEP

6.   Although the shares in Midwest Bank plc were held in a single company PEP and were not therefore liable to capital gains tax, that treatment ceases on death. The shares are held by personal representatives as a normal chargeable asset. Therefore the loss between death and disposal is available for relief (a gain would have similarly been a chargeable gain).

Considerations to be taken into account on deciding appropriate course of action

7.   The executors must carefully consider the taxation implications of selling assets themselves or transferring them to the beneficiaries. These include:

Sale by executors

Capital gains tax rate is 18%

Annual exemption is available in year of death and two following years only

Base costs of assets include costs of the estate (SP 2/04)

Losses are only available against gains of the estate

Sale by beneficiaries

Capital gains tax rate is 18% (or 10% if entrepreneurs' relief applies)

Each beneficiary has own annual exemption

Acquisition value is probate value (subject to what is said in Example 38 explanatory note 1)

Acquisition date is date of death

Personal losses may be offset against gains on assets acquired; losses on assets acquired may be offset against personal gains

The distribution of a capital asset triggers an income tax charge in the hands of the beneficiary to the value of any undistributed income arising in the estate (see Example 39 explanatory note 2).

Furthermore, the tax may be borne by different beneficiaries. In this example the cash to be distributed following a sale by the executors in respect of the three shareholdings held in the estate would be:

		£
Sale proceeds:	Bird Enterprises Ltd	332,500
	Computer Games plc	33,000
	Midwest Bank plc	9,000
		374,500
Less: Capital gains tax		18,041
Divided equally		356,459

Thus Mrs Bird has suffered capital gains tax of half of £18,041 = £9,020. Rupert's share of the tax is £9,021.

If the proposals in (b) had taken place the tax would have been:

	Mrs Bird £	Rupert £
Re Bird Enterprises Ltd	5,660	3,915
Re estate	–	–
	5,660	3,915
Tax saved	3,660	5,105

Thus Rupert would have had a larger saving compared with Mrs Bird.

Because Rupert has not used his annual exemption for 2008/09 it would be better for the beneficiaries to make the disposals than the executors.

Private residence exemption

8.   Where following a death, the private residence is to be sold by the personal representatives, a chargeable gain may arise between death and sale. Under TCGA 1992 s 225A, the private residence exemption is available if the property has both before and after the death been used as the main residence of individuals who are entitled to 75% or more of the sale proceeds either absolutely or for life.

Gifts holdover relief

9.   Personal representatives do not qualify for gifts holdover relief under TCGA 1992 s 165 or s 260, but trustees do. Where the residue of the estate is left on trust, the personal representatives should ensure that assets on which gifts holdover relief is to be claimed have been formally appropriated to the trustees before being gifted. The trustees are then treated as acquiring the assets at the date of death.

The Finance Act 2006 changes to IHT for trust also impinge on the CGT holdover provisions in so far that:

- transfers into and out of trusts that now come within the 'relevant property' rules will automatically be eligible for hold-over relief under TCGA 1992 s 260(2)(a);

- hold-over relief under TCGA 1992 s 260(2)(d) is restricted to trusts that meet the IHT rules for trusts for minor children;

- the special rules in TCGA 1992 ss 72, 73 relating to the death of a person entitled to an IIP are restricted to assets that are subject to an IIP which meets the revised IHT rules.

Entrepreneurs' relief (FA 2008 Sch 3 amends TCGA 1992 s 169)

10.   Under FA 2008 s 9 and Sch 3 entrepreneurs' relief will apply to individuals and trustees who dispose of the whole or part of a trading business, or of shares in a trading company in which they have a qualifying interest.

Entrepreneurs' relief is to be given only on the making of a claim. A claim for entrepreneurs' relief in respect of a qualifying business disposal must be made:

(a)   in the case of a disposal of trust business assets, jointly by the trustees and the qualifying beneficiary; and

(b)   otherwise, by the individual.

The claim for relief in respect of a qualifying business disposal must be made on or before the first anniversary of the 31 January following the tax year in which the qualifying business disposal is made.

A claim for entrepreneurs' relief in respect of a qualifying business disposal may only be made if the amount resulting under TCGA 1992 s 169N(1) is a positive amount.

Entrepreneurs' relief may be available in respect of gains made by individuals on the disposal of:

- all or part of a trading business the individual carries on alone or in partnership;

- assets of the individual's or partnership's trading business following the cessation of the business;

- shares in (and securities of) the individual's 'personal' trading company (or holding company of a trading group);

- assets owned by the individual and used by their 'personal' trading company (or group) or trading partnership.

The first £1 million of gains will qualify for the relief which effectively taxes qualifying gains at 10%. Gains in excess of £1 million will be charged to CGT at the rate of 18%.

The relief works as follows:

(a) Where a claim is made in respect of a qualifying business disposal the relevant gains (see s 5) are to be aggregated, with any relevant losses (see s 6) being deducted.

(b) The resulting amount is to be reduced by 4/9ths.

(c) But if the total of current gains less losses and the amounts resulting in relation to earlier relevant qualifying business disposals (if any), exceeds £1 million, the reduction is to be made in respect of only so much (if any) of the amount resulting as (when added to that total) does not exceed £1 million.

HMRC have produced a number of useful examples that can be accessed at: http://www.hmrc.gov.uk/budget2008/cgt-entrepreneurs-relief-eg.pdf.

An individual is able to make claims for relief on qualifying disposals made on or after 6 April 2008. Claims may be made on more than one occasion up to a 'lifetime' limit of £1 million. Disposals on or before 5 April 2008 do not affect the lifetime limit. The £1 million limit will only begin to diminish when the relief is claimed.

Trustees will be able to claim relief on certain disposals of business assets and company shares and securities where a 'qualifying beneficiary' has a qualifying interest in the business in question. Trustees must make claims jointly with the 'qualifying beneficiary'. Any relief given on the trustees' gains will reduce a beneficiary's £1 million lifetime limit on relief.

If, on the same day, there is both a disposal of trust business assets in respect of which an individual is the qualifying beneficiary and a qualifying business disposal by the individual, s 7 applies as if the disposal of trust business assets were later.

As mentioned above, the relief has effect for qualifying disposals made on or after 6 April 2008. Transitional provisions will also allow relief to be claimed in certain circumstances where gains that have been deferred from disposals made on or before 5 April 2008 become chargeable after that date.

Shares and securities

The relief will have effect for gains on disposals of shares in (and securities of) a trading company (or the holding company of a trading group) provided that throughout a one-year qualifying period the individual making the disposal:

• is an officer or employee of the company, or of a company in the same group of companies;

• owns at least 5% of the ordinary share capital of the company and that holding enables the individual to exercise at least 5% of the voting rights in that company.

Where the company (or group) does not cease to trade, the one-year qualifying period is the year ending on the date the shares or securities are disposed of. Where the company (or group) ceases to trade before the disposal of the shares or securities, the one-year qualifying period ends on the date trading ceased, and the disposal must be made within three years of the date of cessation.

In this case Mrs Bird and Rupert are director and employee respectively and have shareholdings in excess of 5% which they have owned for over one year. Entrepreneur's relief therefore applies to the gains on their disposal of Bird Enterprises Ltd shares.

Question

Mr and Mrs Daley were killed in a road accident on 18 August 2008. Under their wills each appointed their son Arthur as executor. They had each left their entire estate to the other, subject to a 30 day survivorship clause. As default beneficiaries, Mr Daley left his used car business to his son together with one half of residue, the other half being divided between various charities. Mrs Daley, who only had building society investments worth £50,000, named her son as the only beneficiary in default of her husband.

Mr Daley's estate is expected to be valued for probate at:

	£	£
Used car business		900,000
Private residence		240,000
Quoted securities		8,900
National Savings Certificates		41,600
ISA at Midnorth Building Society		10,100
Government securities (interest paid gross)		26,800
Life policies		82,500
Pension policies		104,200
Bank accounts		1,400
Premium bonds		20,000
		1,435,500
Less: Mortgage	125,000	
Other debts, funeral expenses	10,500	135,500
		1,300,000

Because of business property relief and exemption for charities, no inheritance tax will be payable. Arthur, as executor, will convert all his father's assets (including the business) to cash, and pay the liabilities and legacies. He will use a current account with his bank, and will invest surplus funds on the money market. A premium bond prize of £100,000 was received after his father's death. Arthur anticipates completing the administration of the estate by the end of 2009.

Arthur will also obtain probate on his mother's estate, and will cash the investments and pay all debts and legacies by March 2009.

Arthur has contacted your firm for advice as to his obligations as executor under self-assessment. Set out the taxation points to be considered from death to the completion of the administration of the estate for both Mr and Mrs Daley.

Answer

Tax liabilities of Mr Daley deceased — executor's obligations

Arthur should notify HMRC as soon as possible after his father's death. They will send form R27 asking if probate is to be applied for. Arthur will return the form marked accordingly and in due course he will forward probate, together with a copy of the will, to HMRC.

Cessation of used car business

The death of Mr Daley will denote a cessation of the business for income tax purposes. Ideally accounts should be drawn up to the date of death and submitted with the final self-assessment return, otherwise the accounts covering the date of death must be apportioned.

2007/08 tax return

If the 2007/08 tax return of Mr Daley had not been filed before his death, Arthur as executor is responsible for filing it by 31 October 2008 if filing a paper return or 31 January 2009 for a return filed online. See note 4. He is also responsible for paying the outstanding tax for 2007/08 by that date. Interest will be charged on tax paid late, although by Concession A17, interest on tax falling due after death will not start to run until thirty days after the grant of probate.

If the tax is not paid by 28 February 2009 (ie 28 days after the due date), a surcharge of 5% is payable. This increases to 10% if the tax is still unpaid by 31 July. Interest is also payable on any surcharge not paid within thirty days. If there was a reasonable excuse for non-payment throughout the period of default, HMRC (or Commissioners) may set aside the surcharge. Inability to pay is not in itself a reasonable excuse.

FA 2007 s 96 amended the enquiry window for income tax self-assessment tax returns for 2007/08 and subsequent tax years.

For 2007/08 returns and those of later years, the enquiry window will close one year after delivery of the return. Therefore, where a return is received before the filing deadline the enquiry window will close earlier than under current legislation. For example, if the 2008/09 return was received by HMRC on 31 August 2009, HMRC will have until 31 August 2010 to enquire into the form.

If deliberate errors both concealed and not concealed are discovered, HMRC can issue an assessment for years ending not earlier than six years before death (ie for 2001/02 onwards) and such assessments must be issued not later than three years after 31 January following the end of the tax year in which the death occurred, ie three years after 31 January 2009 (TMA 1970 s 40). Normally penalties may be charged where there are deliberate errors. Under the Human Rights legislation, however, it is probably not possible to impose tax geared penalties on personal representatives in respect of tax evasion by the deceased. See Chapter 5 (c) for more detail on the FA 2008 legislation on penalties.

However, it appears that consequent to guidance given to HMRC, penalties will still be sought from personal representatives in these situations by way of addition to the settlement offer. Upon request HMRC will issue a letter stating that if in the future there is an adverse decision on the matter in the courts, the penalty will be repaid with interest.

2008/09 tax return

Following Mr Daley's death in August 2008, HMRC will, on request, issue a tax return for 2008/09 before the end of that tax year (and also before the end of the tax year in which the administration of the estate will be completed). When returns have been submitted HMRC will give early confirmation if they do not intend to enquire into the return.

Because of Mr Daley's death it will be appropriate for Arthur to apply to HMRC to reduce the payment on account due on 31 January 2009 in respect of 2008/09. The application should be made on the return, or on form SA 303.

Any tax due for the year of death (or earlier years) will be a liability of the estate.

Tax position on investments

The ISA investment retains its tax exemption until death. Thereafter the normal income and capital gains tax rules apply. An ISA insurance policy will pay out on death and consequently the personal representatives will need to claim the death benefit. Before the claim is accepted by the insurer there are no income tax or capital gains tax implications but any interest paid as a result of late settlement of the claim will be taxable and paid net of tax.

The premium bond continues to be tax-exempt, including the prize received. The amount received will add to the residue of the estate and be distributed accordingly as capital.

Under ITA 2007 s 636 (2) (based on ICTA s 721), if Arthur as personal representative transfers securities to a beneficiary in the interest period in which Mr Daley died, neither Arthur nor the legatee are treated as making or receiving payments. Therefore, in these circumstances no accrued income profit or accrued income loss can arise. However, because the transfer itself is not excluded, ITA 2007 s 681 (exemption for unrealised interest received after a transfer) may still be an issue.

Interest on investments and dividends on shares are taxable when received. They are *not* apportioned for income tax over the period to which they relate. For probate and inheritance tax purposes, however, dividends receivable after death on ex dividend shares (exclusive of the tax credits) and amounts of interest accrued to the date of death on securities (less lower rate tax) are included in the value of the estate. ITA 2007 s 640 introduces rules for small holding of securities and excludes interest on securities that form part of a deceased person's estate, unless the nominal value of securities held by the personal representatives as such exceeds £5,000 on any day:

(a)   in the tax year in which the interest period ends; or

(b)   in the previous tax year.

In relation to a transfer with unrealised interest of securities that form part of a deceased person's estate, the deceased's personal representatives are an excluded transferor or excluded transferee unless the nominal value of securities held by the deceased's personal representatives as such exceeds £5,000 on any day:

(a)   in the tax year in which the settlement day falls; or

(b)   in the previous tax year.

Where there is a transfer of variable rate securities that form part of a deceased person's estate, the deceased's personal representatives are an excluded transferor unless the nominal value of securities held by the deceased's personal representatives as such exceeds £5,000 on any day in the relevant tax year or the previous tax year (see Example 43).

Relief is given where an absolute beneficiary is liable to higher rate tax and the estate paid inheritance tax on net accrued income (see Example 43 explanatory note 4 on page 43.5).

Tax liabilities of Arthur as executor of Mr Daley's estate

Arthur will receive a trust and estate self-assessment return (form SA 900) for the period 19 August 2008 to 5 April 2009, and in due course for the period 6 April 2009 to the date of completion of the administration of the estate. The returns must be filed by 31 October for a paper return or 31 January 2009 for a return filed online (see note 4) following the end of the relevant tax year, or by 30 September following the tax year if HMRC are to compute the tax liabilities.

Personal representatives are not entitled to personal allowances and are charged tax on the estate income at the basic rate if it is non-savings income, the lower rate if it is savings income other than dividends, and the dividend ordinary rate on dividends. Any capital gains arising on the disposal of assets in excess of probate values are liable to tax at 18%, after deducting an annual exemption (£9,600 for 2008/09) in the tax year of death and the next two tax years.

Used car business

Because the period of trading by the estate will be less than two years the actual basis of assessment will apply, ie:

2008/09	19 August 2008 to 5 April 2009
2009/10	6 April 2009 to date of sale

Supplementary pages will be required to be completed. If only one set of accounts is prepared details will be shown on the first return, with the profits for the period after 5 April 2009 deducted. On the second return the box indicating that all details have been shown on the previous return will be ticked. The profits (after capital allowances) will be shown with the exclusion of the amount assessed in the earlier year. There is no liability for Class 4 national insurance contributions.

Investment income

Investment income received gross must be declared and tax paid at the savings rate. This will include interest on government securities, on investments for a fixed term over £50,000, and on overseas investments. Interest is also paid gross on all quoted eurobonds, now defined as interest-bearing securities issued by a company (or building society) and listed on a recognised stock exchange (ITA 2007 s 882). Other interest will have had tax deducted at source. This is also shown on the self-assessment return.

Any charge arising under the accrued income scheme on a sale by the executor will be taxed at 20%. Where there is any accrued income relief, the relief is given by deducting it from the gross income received, thus reducing the amount chargeable at 20%.

Changes to self-assessment payments on account limits

SI 1996/1654 – Income Tax (Payments on Account) Regulations 1996 is amended by the making of a regulation to raise the figure at regulation 3 from £500 to £1,000.

This will come into force for self-assessment payments on account (POA) from 2009/10 and later years.

The regulation has effect on and after 6 April 2009 for income tax due for 2009/10. The first payments on account affected will therefore be those due in January 2010 and July 2010.

Payment of tax

If the net income tax payable for 2008/09 exceeds £500 for years up to and including 2008/09), or 20% of the total income tax liability for the year (including tax deducted at source), then payments on account will be required for 2009/10.

Capital gains tax is not included in calculating payments on account. The 2008/09 income tax and capital gains tax will be due on 31 January 2010. As the administration of the estate is likely to be almost complete at that time it should be possible accurately to determine the actual liability for 2009/10. Unless covered by the de minimis limits, one half of that liability (excluding capital gains tax), or one half of the 2008/09 net tax liability if less, will be due on 31 January 2010. The second instalment will be due on 31 July 2010 and the balance, together with any capital gains tax, on 31 January 2011.

Arthur as executor may prefer to pay the whole amount at an early date in order to complete the administration of the estate.

The same provisions as to interest on overdue tax and surcharges apply as stated above in relation to the tax position of Mr Daley deceased.

Tax liabilities in relation to Mrs Daley

Tax position of Mrs Daley deceased

Arthur has similar obligations as stated above in respect of his mother's estate. Since her only assets are building society accounts, however, it may be that it will only be necessary to submit a tax repayment return to the date of her death. Even that will not be necessary if Mrs Daley had elected to receive interest gross.

Tax position in relation to Mrs Daley's estate

Following a taxpayer's death, any election to receive interest gross ceases to have effect and all subsequent payments are made net of tax at the savings rate. Since Mrs Daley's only asset is building society interest, Arthur will be able to tick the second box in Step 1 on the trust and estate tax return confirming that he is the personal representative of a deceased person and that all the following points apply:

All the income arose in the UK

He does not wish to claim reliefs

No annual payments have been made out of capital

All income has had tax deducted before it was received (or is UK dividends with tax credit)

There are no chargeable disposals

There are no accrued income charges or reliefs, no income from relevant discounted securities, offshore income gains or gains on life insurance policies etc.

Arthur can then go straight to Question 19 in the return to give his, or his agent's, telephone number and sign the declaration at Question 22. When the administration of the estate is complete the date of completion is shown at Question 21.2. It is likely that this will occur in 2008/09, so that only one return will be required in relation to Mrs Daley's estate.

Supplementary Notes

1. Where HMRC enquire into a return, they will issue a closure notice stating their conclusions and showing the revisions to the self-assessment and the additional tax due (TMA 1970 s 28A). The personal representatives then have thirty days in which to appeal in writing against conclusions stated or amendments made by the closure notice, giving the grounds of appeal (TMA 1970 ss 31, 31A).

2. The personal representatives may give HMRC notice of an amendment to the self-assessment return (within the permitted twelve months after the filing date for the return) whilst an enquiry is in progress. The amendment will not restrict the scope of the enquiry but may be taken into account in the enquiry. If it affects the tax payable, it will not take effect unless and until it is incorporated into the s 28A closure notice (see note 2 above) (TMA 1970 s 9B).

3. Questions relating to the subject matter of an enquiry may be referred to the Special Commissioners for their determination while the enquiry is in progress on a joint written application by the personal representatives and HMRC. Either party may withdraw from the referral process providing they give

notice before the first hearing of the matter by the Special Commissioners. The determination will be binding on both parties as if it were a decision on a preliminary issue under appeal (TMA 1970 ss 28ZA–28ZE (and ss 31A–31D for companies)).

Revised filing dates for paper and online self-assessment returns

Paper substitutes for SA returns

4.   From 2007/08 onwards computer generated substitute versions of the SA Return will no longer be approved or accepted for:

- SA Individual Returns – (SA100 series)

- SA Trust Returns – (SA900 series)

For the time being, HMRC will continue to accept approved substitutes for the remaining SA returns (including those for trustees of registered pension schemes) and for all other forms they currently approve substitutes for.

Changes to SA filing dates

For 2007/08 and subsequent years' returns, anyone who required to file a self-assessment tax return will have:

- until 31 October to do so, if they choose to send a paper return; or

- until the following 31 January if they file online.

This allows an additional three months for online filing compared with paper.

The filing obligation is satisfied by the first return received by HMRC and this also triggers any late filing penalty. So if, for example, a paper 2007/08 return is filed after 31 October 2008, it is not then possible to avoid a late filing penalty by filing the return online.

In addition, in certain other cases, HMRC will allow extra time beyond the statutory deadline of 31 October – until 31 January – for paper filing without incurring a penalty. These include:

- trustees of registered pension schemes; and

- SA taxpayers (see below), for whom facilities to file online are not yet available.

In the event that there are problems with HMRC systems close to the filing deadline, taxpayers will not be penalised for late submission of a return due to such problems provided that they, or their agent, file within a reasonable period once the service is restored.

FA 2007 s 88(1F) – if a notice is given after 31 July the return must be submitted during the period of three months beginning with the date of the notice (for paper returns) or on or before 31 January (for online returns).

FA 2007 s 88(1G) – if a notice is given after 31 October the return (whether paper return or electronic) must be submitted within three months from the date of the notice.

SA taxpayers who are unable to file online

Those SA taxpayers who do not have the choice of online filing, will be allowed to file on paper up to 31 January, without incurring any penalty that might otherwise be due for paper filing after 31 October.

If such paper output is used for returns which could be filed online, it will be accepted provided it is identical to the official HMRC return but must be submitted to HMRC by the paper filing date of 31 October.

5.   For detailed notes on the self-assessment provisions see the companion to this book, Tolley's Taxwise I 2008/09.

Question

Outline the provisions determining the rates of tax applicable to trust income and the way in which the tax payable is accounted for.

Answer

Rates of tax on trust income

Certain trust income is taxed as income of the settlor. Certain other trust income is charged at the 'trust rate' of 40%, or in the case of dividend income, the dividend trust rate of 32.5%.

Under ITA 2007 s 491, the first £1,000 of relevant income is not charged at the special trust tax rates, but is instead charged at the income tax rate appropriate to the type of income, known as standard rate band. Therefore, if payments are received net of tax (for example, building society interest) up to the limit of the standard rate band, then the trustees have no further tax to pay.

For more detailed information see page 47.4.

Otherwise trustees are liable to tax at the dividend ordinary rate of 10% on tax credit inclusive dividend income, the basic rate of 20% on other savings income and non-savings income. The trust income is determined using the principles applicable to each type of income.

Trustees in their capacity as such are not entitled to personal allowances, nor are they liable to pay income tax at the higher rate.

Treatment of expenses

Any expenses applicable to the particular income are deducted in arriving at the assessable income, but there is no relief for the general trust expenses. Such expenses are regarded as paid first out of dividend income, then out of other savings income, then out of non-savings income (ITA 2007 s 486 — see Example 43 at page 43.4 note 10 for details of relief for expenses when the rate applicable to trusts or the dividend trust rate applies).

HMRC have confirmed that the standard rate band set out in FA 2005 s 14 will apply to trust income *net* of trust management expenses so potentially it will apply to other charges as well.

Although the management expenses are deducted from the trust income taxed at the lowest rate first, the standard rate band will apply in the order — basic rate income at 20% first, followed by dividends at 10%.

Income certificates to beneficiaries (forms R185)

At the end of each tax year the trustees give income beneficiaries a certificate of their entitlement to trust income (form R185), and of income tax paid thereon by the trustees, and that income will be included in the statutory income of the beneficiary, whose unused personal allowances and starting rate band, if any, will be available to give an income tax repayment, and upon whom any higher rate or dividend upper rate tax will be charged. The trustee's certificate will show the rates at which tax has been paid. For trusts liable to the trust rate, the tax rate shown will be 40%. For other trusts the rates will be 20% on non-savings income and non-dividend savings income. A 10% tax rate is charged on dividends, distributions on which tax is treated as paid (ie dividends on which a non-resident is not entitled to a tax credit (ITTOIA 2005 s 399), bonus issues of redeemable securities (ITTOIA 2005 s 400(4), (5)), scrip dividends (ITTOIA 2005 s 411), close company loans written off or released (ITTOIA 2005 s 416), and dividends from abroad. The 10% tax credits will be shown as non-repayable.

Trust rate and dividend trust rate

ITA 2007 ss 9, 479–483 provide that distribution income received by trusts is chargeable at the 'dividend trust rate' of 32.5% and at the 'rate applicable to trusts' of 40% otherwise. These rates are not fixed annually and will remain in force unless changed in a subsequent Finance Act.

Trustees are liable at the s 9 rates where they have a power to accumulate income or where they have a discretion as to whether or not the income is made available to income beneficiaries.

With effect from 6 April 2006

Trustees of settlor-interested trusts are taxed at the special trust rates instead of at only up to basic rate.

The dividend trust rate applies to distribution type income, ie UK dividends, dividends from abroad taxed as miscellaneous income, qualifying distributions arising to non-UK resident trustees, non-qualifying distributions (ie bonus issues of redeemable securities — ITTOIA 2005 s 400(4), (5)), scrip dividends (ITTOIA 2005 s 411 — but see Example 49 part B(a)), close company loans written off or released (ITTOIA 2005 s 416), and amounts taxable under ITA 2007 ss 481 and 482 (purchase by company of own shares etc — see below). In each case there is an actual or notional tax credit to reduce the tax payable by the trustees (except for dividends from abroad).

The additional tax of 22.5% is payable by trustees on distributions in respect of the balance of the dividend trust rate of 32.5%.

This could also be seen as taxing the net dividend at 25%. For example, a dividend of £90 carries a tax credit of £10 and the trustees have to pay a further 22.5% of (90 + 10), or 25% of 90, = £22.50, leaving a net amount of £67.50.

If the trustees make discretionary payments to beneficiaries, however, they must make the payments net of 40% tax and they cannot treat the dividend credit as tax already paid in calculating how much of the tax at 40% has already been paid by them. This significantly increases the tax burden on such payments. For the detailed provisions see Example 48.

Purchase by company of own shares etc

Where a company redeems, repays or purchases its own shares from trustees of a settlement, ITA 2007 ss 481 and 482 (purchase by unquoted trading company of own shares to be treated as a capital payment rather than a distribution) does not apply and the payment is treated as income of the trustees liable at the dividend trust rate of 32.5% on the grossed up equivalent, as indicated above. This treatment applies to life interest trusts as well as accumulation/discretionary trusts, but not to unit trusts, charitable trusts, pension funds or where the income is treated as belonging to the settlor (ITA 2007 ss 481 and 482).

Income not liable to ITA 2007 ss 479–483 rates

Where someone has a life interest in a trust fund, or part thereof, or is entitled to an annuity from the fund, that person cannot avoid liability at the higher rate of tax simply because the trustees do not pay out all of the trust income to which that person is entitled, since the income is in any event included in his statutory income, by reference to the statement of trust income and form R185 (trust income), and he will be a creditor of the trust for any balance of income due to him. Liability at the ss 479–483 rates does not therefore apply to income to which someone is absolutely entitled as against the trustees.

Nor do the ss 479–483 rates apply to income treated for tax purposes as that of the settlor *before* it is distributed (eg where the settlor has settled funds and he and/or his wife are discretionary income beneficiaries — in that event all income is assessable on the settlor under ITTOIA 2005 ss 625–629). The rates *do* apply to income paid to infant, unmarried children of the settlor, even though such income is treated as the settlor's under ITTOIA 2005 ss 629–632 (see below).

The rate applicable to trusts does not apply to capital receipts such as lease premiums, even though they are partly charged to income tax (see Example 48 for an illustration).

Income of charitable trusts ITA 2007 s 524 and income from property held for certain occupational and personal pension funds is also excluded from ss 479–483 (see Example 48 explanatory note 6).

Income taxed as income of settlor

Income taxed as the settlor's income under ITTOIA 2005 ss 629–632 or ITTOIA 2005 ss 625–629 (see above under *Income not liable to ITA 2007 ss 479–483 rates*) is treated as the highest part of the settlor's income (other than employment income lump sum compensation payments under ITEPA 2003 s 403 and life policy gains under ITTOIA 2005 s 465). The settlor can recover any tax paid by him from the trustees or from the person who received the income (ITTOIA 2005 s 646).

Where the settlor has retained an interest in the trust, and income is therefore taxed as his income before distribution, the charge under ITTOIA 2005 ss 619, 621, 623 on dividend income is at the dividend ordinary rate of 10% or upper rate of 32½% as the case may be. Any other income is charged as miscellaneous income at 20% or 40%.

By comparison, if income is treated as the settlor's income under ITTOIA 2005 ss 629–632, ie because it is paid to his infant, unmarried child, it will have been liable to tax in the hands of the trustees when it arose at either 40% for non-dividend income or 32.5% for dividend income. When any distribution is made, however, it will come out of the general pool of trust income and it will not be dividend income. The distribution will be made net of 40% tax, but the trustees will not be able to include the 10% dividend tax credit in accounting for that tax. This will therefore result in a higher tax charge where a dividend is paid to an infant child via a discretionary trust compared with a direct settlement by the parent on the child. Using the example above of a net dividend of £90 paid to a discretionary trust with a tax credit of £10, the net distribution to the child would be 60% of £90 = £54 (tax £36). If the settlor had made a direct settlement on the child the additional tax payable would be only £22.50, ie:

Gross income (90 dividend + tax credit 10)	100.00
Tax @ 32½% (£22.50 payable after tax credit)	32.50
Net receipt	£67.50

This principle applies even where the first £1,000 of income is taxed at the standard rates as only the tax paid is included within the tax pool to frank distributions to beneficiaries.

Filing dates for self-assessment returns

Paper substitutes for SA returns

From 2007/08 onwards computer generated substitute versions of the SA return will no longer be approved or accepted for:

- SA individual returns – (SA100 series)
- SA trust returns – (SA900 series).

For the time being, HMRC will continue to accept approved substitutes for the remaining SA returns (including those for trustees of registered pension schemes) and for all other forms they currently approve substitutes for.

Changes to SA filing dates

For 2007/08 and subsequent years' returns, anyone who is required to file a self-assessment tax return will have:

- until 31 October to do so, if they choose to send a paper return; or
- until the following 31 January if they file online.

This allows an additional three months for online filing compared with paper.

The filing obligation is satisfied by the first return received by HMRC and this also triggers any late filing penalty. So if, for example, a paper 2007/08 return is filed after 31 October 2008, it is not then possible to avoid a late filing penalty by filing the return online.

In addition, in certain other cases, HMRC will allow extra time beyond the statutory deadline of 31 October – until 31 January – for paper filing without incurring a penalty. These include:

- trustees of registered pension schemes; and

- SA taxpayers (see below), for whom facilities to file online are not yet available.

In the event that there are problems with HMRC systems close to the filing deadline, taxpayers will not be penalised for late submission of a return due to such problems provided that they, or their agent, file within a reasonable period once the service is restored.

FA 2007 s 88(1F) – if a notice is given after 31 July the return must be submitted during the period of three months beginning with the date of the notice (for paper returns) or on or before 31 January (for online returns).

FA 2007 s 88(1G) – if a notice is given after 31 October the return (whether paper return or electronic) must be submitted within three months from the date of the notice.

SA taxpayers who are unable to file online

Those SA taxpayers who do not have the choice of online filing, will be allowed to file on paper up to 31 January, without incurring any penalty that might otherwise be due for paper filing after 31 October.

If such paper output is used for returns which could be filed online, it will be accepted provided it is identical to the official HMRC return but must be submitted to HMRC by the paper filing date of 31 October.

Payment dates

All sources of income, and also any capital gains, are dealt with in the self-assessment, and trustees make payments on account of income tax (not capital gains tax) in the same way as individuals.

The tax payment dates are:

31 January in the tax year	1st payment on account, being one half of the total tax payable for the previous tax year (including the tax at the rate applicable to trusts or dividend trust rate where appropriate but excluding capital gains tax), as reduced by any tax deducted at source
31 July after end of tax year	2nd payment on account (same amount as 1st payment)
31 January after end of tax year	Full liability for year (including capital gains tax) less payments on account and tax deducted at source

For a detailed illustration see Example 47.

Question

T, a widower, who had been in business as a sole trader for many years, died on 6 April 2007.

By his will S, his accountant, was appointed executor and trustee and the whole estate was left in trust to his son, U, absolutely, with a charity being the longstop beneficiary.

The will did not bar the application of the Apportionment Act 1870, and empowered S to continue T's business so that it could be sold as a going concern.

By the will, S is allowed a fixed annual sum of £1,500 for his services as executor and trustee.

T's income-producing assets apart from the business consisted of:

£20,000 listed 10% loan stock in X plc — interest receivable 31 July and 31 January. Interest was received on the due dates and S apportioned it between capital and income under the Apportionment Act 1870.

Building society deposit — net interest receivable 30 June and 31 December. Interest of £160 was received in June and £64 in December 2008. S apportioned the June interest between capital and income under the Apportionment Act 1870.

Property let unfurnished producing rental income during 2008/09 of £1,130 with allowable expenses of £430. At 5 April 2008, there were unutilised losses arising from this property of £100.

The business accounts were made up to 5 April each year. Accounts were produced for the two years to 5 April 2008 and 2009 showing tax adjusted profits of £17,200 and £16,420 respectively.

The deceased had a mortgage of £16,000 on his home, provided by a relative. The interest paid by S for the period from 6 April 2008 until December 2008, when the property was sold, was £900.

T, until his death, had been the life tenant of a settled fund, the sole asset of which was an investment of £40,000 listed 8% debenture stock in Z plc. The due dates for receipt of the interest were 6 April and 6 October. The trustees normally paid the income to T shortly after it was received, and paid to S the income due until T's death, on 31 July 2008.

A loan was taken out by S to enable inheritance tax to be paid on the estate personally. The loan interest charged for 2008/09 was £500.

Certain administration expenses were paid on 31 March 2009. These were allocated as to £500 for capital and £1,195 for income. On that date S was paid the annual sum of £1,500 due to him.

(a)   Prepare a statement showing the trust income for 2008/09 together with supporting notes explaining your treatment of each of the items mentioned above.

(b)   Show the entries on the R185 (trust income) to be given to U for 2008/09.

(c)   Explain the manner in which double taxation has occurred in respect of the income reported for U. Outline any tax relief U may be entitled to under ITTOIA 2005 s 669. The taxable estate was £500,000 and IHT paid was £75,000.

Answer

(a)   **Statement of trust income 2008/09**

Refer to note

		£	£	Tax £
1	Trading profit	16,420		
2	Unfurnished lettings	700	17,120	
	Savings income			
3	£20,000 10% loan stock, X plc	2,000		
4	Life tenancy (debenture interest)	1,600		
5	Building society interest ((160 + 64) × 100/80)	280	3,880	56
			21,000	56
	Less charges on income:			
6	Executor's remuneration (annuity)	1,500		
7	Loan interest re payment of IHT	500	2,000	
	Total income of trust		19,000	56
	Tax thereon:			
	Non-savings income 15,120 @ 20%	3,024		
	Savings income			
	(non-dividend) 3,880 @ 20%	776		
	19,000	3,800	3,800	
6	*Add:* Tax deducted from executor's remuneration (1,500 @ 20%)	300		
	Total tax due	4,100		4,100
	of which tax payable by self-assessment is (see explanatory note 7)			4,156
			15,200	
	Less trust expenses:			
8	Mortgage interest	900		
9	Administration expenses	1,195	2,095	
	Net income of trust		13,105	
	Less apportioned to capital per (b)		1,652	
	Net income available for beneficiary		11,453	
	Comprising:			
	Non-dividend savings income (3,880 – 776)	3,104		
	Less apportioned to capital	1,652		
		1,452		
10	Used to pay trust expenses (part)	1,452	–	
	Non-savings income (15,120 – 3,024)	12,096		
10	Used to pay trust expenses (balance)	643	11,453	
	Gross equivalent is 11,453 × 100/80 =		14,316	

(b) **Computation of income treated as capital**

Refer to note		£
3	£20,000 10% loan stock X plc	
	1 February 2008 to 6 April 2008 66/182 × £1,000	359
4	Life tenancy	
	7 October 2007 to 6 April 2008	1,600
5	Building society interest received	

$$1 \text{ January } 2008 \text{ to } 6 \text{ April } 2008 \ 97/182 \times \left(£160 \times \frac{100}{80}\right)$$ 106

	£
	2,065
Income tax @ 20%	413
Net income apportioned to capital	1,652

Form R185 (trust income) to be given to U for 2008/09

11	Gross	Tax	Net
Savings income	–	–	–
Non-savings income	£14,316	£2,863	£11,453

(c)

Where, owing to the apportionment rules, income is included in the estate and charged to inheritance tax, and is also charged as income after death, an absolute beneficiary may claim to reduce his income for higher rate or upper rate purposes (not for savings, basic or dividend ordinary rate tax) by the inheritance tax charged on the grossed-up amount of the accrued income (ITTOIA 2005 s 669).

As a beneficiary with an absolute interest in a share of his late father's estate, U has been assessed on income that arose in the period prior to death but which was received after death.

This has resulted in an element of double taxation as this income was also taken into account when establishing the value of his father's estate on death and therefore was also subject to inheritance tax.

However, if U is a higher rate taxpayer, an element of tax relief is available. The relief is computed by multiplying the income taxed twice by the average rate of inheritance tax on T's estate.

This amount is deducted from U's share of the estate income in determining the amount of income to be taxed at higher rates.

For a more detailed explanation see note 9

Estate taxable	£500,000
Inheritance tax paid	£75,000
Average rate	15%
Income treated as capital from (b)	£1,652
IHT attributed @15%	£248
Gross up at 20%	£62
	£310
Tax credit	£62

To deduct from R185 figures to give

	Gross	Tax	Net
Non-savings income	14,296	2,863	11,453
Less: s 669 relief	(310)	(62)	(248)
	£14,006	£2,801	£11,205

This will need to be shown on the trust tax return – stating that s 699 relief of £248 (net) has been claimed.

Notes relating to statement of trust income

1. The death of T constitutes a cessation of the sole trade for tax purposes. The trustees are regarded as commencing the business from that date The first year of charge is 2008/09. Tax will be charged on the profit from 7 April 2008 to 5 April 2009. (Trustees are not liable to Class 4 national insurance contributions – Social Security Contributions and Benefits Act 1992 Sch 2.5.)

2. The income from lettings is:

Rent income in 2008/09	1,130
Allowable expenses	430
	£700

   The unutilised losses of T personally are not available for carry forward against the income of the will trust.

3. Despite the income from the 10% loan stock having to be allocated to the capital of the estate in so far as the proportion up to the date of death of T is concerned (Apportionment Act 1870), the entire income *received* after death has to be included for *income tax purposes* as that of the will trust. (See explanatory note 7.)

4. The settlement income is *received* after death, and despite the allocation to estate capital under the Apportionment Act, is for *income tax purposes* regarded as income of the will trust. (See explanatory note 7.)

5. Building society interest will partly have to be allocated to capital of the estate under the Apportionment Act, but since it is *received* after death it is for *income tax purposes* regarded wholly as income of the will trust.

   The interest is paid after deduction of lower rate tax, except where the recipient is unlikely to be a taxpayer and has provided an appropriate certificate to the building society. As a trust is not entitled to personal allowances it cannot give such a certificate.

6. The £1,500 p a payable to S as executor is regarded as an annuity, from which income tax at the basic rate must be deducted when making the payment (ITA 2007 s 449). See explanatory note 6 for the way in which the tax is accounted for.

   Had the will contained a professional executor's charging clause, the amount paid to S would be an administration expense, payable out of the net income.

7. The interest paid on the loan to pay inheritance tax is allowable in calculating the trust income (ITA 2007 s 383).

8. The mortgage interest paid is a trust expense payable out of taxed income.

9. Administration expenses have to be paid out of taxed income.

10. Trust expenses are the expenses of administration and as such are regarded as paid out of income which has already suffered tax. They must be distinguished from expenses relating to a

particular source, like those of the trade and of the lettings in this case which are allowable in computing the income from that particular source.

Trust expenses are treated as being set against income in the following order (ITA 2007 s 486):

(i) Income carrying non-repayable credits (ie dividends, dividends on which a non-resident is not entitled to a tax credit (ITTOIA 2005 s 399), bonus issues of redeemable securities (ITTOIA 2005 s 400(4), (5)), scrip dividends (ITTOIA 2005 s 411), and close company loans written off or released (ITTOIA 2005 s 416).

(ii) Taxed dividends from abroad.

(iii) Non-savings and savings income other than that in (i) and (ii).

The set-off order is in fact the most beneficial, in that it maximises the amount of tax paid by the trust that may be passed on to beneficiaries.

11. Although for income tax purposes, any income received after death is treated as income of the estate and charged on the trustees, as stated in notes 3, 4 and 5, any part of that income that has been apportioned to trust capital is not available to the life tenant and is excluded from his income. The form R185 therefore excludes the net amount of £1,652 apportioned to capital.

Explanatory Notes

Apportionment of income

1. The Apportionment Act 1870 requires income accrued up to the date of death to be taken into the estate. This is compulsory for inheritance tax, but for succession purposes the Act may be excluded, so that, for example, all income received after death goes to the life tenant, rather than some being treated as part of estate capital. For income tax purposes, any income received after the date of death is regarded as income of the estate. Note that the date of death is counted as one of the days prior to the date of death.

   This may lead to double taxation, ie for inheritance tax in the estate and for income tax.

   Most modern and competently drafted wills or trust deeds will specifically exclude the application of all apportionments.

   Where the deceased was life tenant of a trust fund, any income accrued to the date of death (net of tax) is part of his estate for inheritance tax, the settled fund being reduced accordingly. Again this may result in double taxation.

   Where double taxation occurs, some relief is available to an *absolute* beneficiary (not a beneficiary with a life interest) in respect of higher rate tax — see Example 43 (c) and explanatory note 9.

2. Where income is received prior to death it is not apportioned even if all or part of it relates to a period after death. Where income received after death is to be accrued up to the date of death as indicated in note 1 above, the amount to be included in the estate for inheritance tax is as follows:

Shares

Where the shares are cum dividend, no apportionment is necessary. Where they are ex dividend, the forthcoming dividend (exclusive of the tax credit) is taken into the estate.

Other securities

The price must include the accrued interest (less tax at the lower rate) as at the date of death.

Rents

Where the amount received after death relates wholly or partly to a period before death it must be apportioned on the basis that the income accrues evenly from day to day.

Salaries, pensions, annuities

These are again accrued on a day-to-day basis and the amount receivable (net of tax) must be apportioned to the periods before and after death.

Income of life tenant during administration of estate

3.   Where a person has a life interest in the residue of an estate, the amounts to be included in his statutory income during the period of administration are the grossed up equivalents of the actual income payments made to him (see Example 39 for further details). Where part of the income has been apportioned to trust capital under the provisions of the Apportionment Act 1870, the amounts actually paid to the life tenant will be less than the net income of the trust, as shown in part (b) of the example.

Income of beneficiary with absolute interest during administration of estate

4.   Where a person has an absolute interest in the residue of an estate (ie a right to capital as well as to income) again the amounts included in total income during the administration period will be the grossed up equivalent of the actual income payments made to him (see Example 39).

If interest is paid on overdue inheritance tax, it is not an allowable deduction for someone with an absolute interest (IHTA 1984 s 233(3)). (For someone with a life interest, his income is the gross equivalent of the amounts actually paid to him, so that interest on overdue tax is effectively allowed for higher rate purposes.)

Nature of payments from estate to beneficiaries

5.   Payments from the estate to beneficiaries are treated as made first from income taxed at the 20% basic rate, then savings income (excluding dividends) taxed at the 20% basic rate, then dividend income taxed at 10% (ITTOIA 2005 s 679).

The different types of income (net of expenses) and the tax deducted therefrom are shown separately on forms R185, with tax relating to the income in note 10(i) of the example shown as being non-repayable.

Executor's remuneration

6.   The executor's remuneration of £1,500 represents an annuity, which is a charge on income and reduces the trust's income for tax purposes. Tax relief has, however, already been retained out of the payment at 20%. In order to ensure that the tax retained is balanced by an equivalent amount of tax payable (so that the trust suffers no tax on that slice of its income), the trust's income is first reduced by the annuity, and tax is calculated on the resulting trust income at the appropriate rates. The tax payable is then increased by basic rate tax on the amount of the annuity. For an illustration of the treatment where charges exceed the trust income see Example 44 part B.

Changes to self-assessment payments on account limits

7.   SI 1996/1654 – Income Tax (Payments on Account) Regulations 1996 is amended by the making of a regulation to raise the figure at regulation 3 from £500 to £1,000.

This will come into force for self-assessment payments on account (POA) from 2009/10 and later years.

The regulation has effect on and after 6 April 2009 for income tax due for 2009/10. The first payments on account affected will therefore be those due in January 2010 and July 2010.

Self-assessment

8. The self-assessment provisions apply to trustees and personal representatives in the same way as for individuals. Payments on account are due on 31 January in the tax year and 31 July following, each equal to half of the total income tax payable (net of tax deducted at source) for the previous tax year (unless it was below the de minimis thresholds). A balancing payment is then due on the following 31 January (which will include any capital gains tax payable). At the same time the first payment on account for the next year is due.

    Payments on account will not be made for the tax year in which a trust commences, since no tax was payable for the previous year. In this example therefore all the tax payable by self-assessment, amounting to £4,100, will be due for payment on 31 January 2009. Note that this tax figure is made up of the tax of £3,024 on the non-savings income plus the tax of £776 on the savings income of £3,600 not taxed at source plus the tax of £300 deducted at source from the executor's remuneration.

    The first payment on account for 2009/10 is also due on 31 January 2010. Since there is no capital gains tax in the tax figure of £4,100, the first payment on account for 2009/10 will be half of that figure, ie £2,050. The total amount payable by the trustees on 31 January 2010 is therefore £6,150.

    ITA 2007 s 882 now provides that tax is not deducted from payments of interest on quoted eurobonds, which are defined as interest-bearing securities issued by a company and listed on a recognised stock exchange.

    For further notes on self-assessment see Examples 41, 46, 47 and 48.

Will trusts

9. Often it will be necessary for the executors to administer the estate of a deceased person and then to transfer their responsibilities to the trustees of the life interest settlement in respect of the residue of the estate. In this example the trustees and personal representatives are the same. Furthermore the whole of the estate is left in trust to the son. In practice in these circumstances, it is usual to treat all of the income as belonging to the trustees from the date of death and to allow the expenses of administration etc against that income. More correctly the executor should issue a form R185 (estate income) and complete a self-assessment return for the period of administration of the estate and then do the same as trustee, ie issue form R185 (trust income) and complete a further self-assessment return for the remaining part of the same tax year.

Relief for inheritance tax attributable to income accrued at death (ITTOIA 2005 s 669)

10. Income that accrued during the lifetime of the deceased but was paid after death is treated under inheritance tax rules as part of the estate of the deceased person. The same income is treated as part of the net statutory income of the estate and therefore enters into the computation of residuary income.

    Where this happens, a residuary beneficiary D who is liable to tax at the higher rate may claim a deduction from the residuary income of an amount equal to the inheritance tax applicable to the accrued income (ITTOIA 2005 s 669).

    Instructions for working out the deduction are set out in the legislation as follows:

    A reduction is made in the residuary income of D's estate for that tax year in ascertaining the extra liability, if any, of a person with an absolute interest in the whole or part of the residue of D's estate or any other estate to which that residuary income is relevant.

A person's extra liability is the amount by which the person's liability to income tax exceeds the amount it would be if:

(a)   income charged at the higher rate were charged:

    (i)   in the case of income chargeable at the lower rate instead of the basic rate, at the lower rate, and

    (ii)   in any other case, at the basic rate, and

(b)   income charged at the dividend upper rate were charged at the dividend ordinary rate.

The amount of the reduction under subsection (2) is calculated as follows:

Step 1

Calculate the net pre-death income by subtracting from the pre-death income any liabilities which have been taken account both:

(a)   in determining the value of D's estate for the purposes of inheritance tax, and

(b)   in calculating the residuary income of D's estate for the tax year.

Step 2

Calculate the inheritance tax attributable to net pre-death income by multiplying the inheritance tax to be charged by:

where:

NPDI is the net pre-death income, and

VE is the value of D's estate.

Step 3

Gross up the inheritance tax attributable to net pre-death income by reference to the basic rate for the tax year.

The amount of pre-death income taken into account in determining the value of D's estate is taken to be the actual amount of income accruing before D's death, less income tax at the basic rate for the tax year in which D died.

Question

A.

Herbie Fritter is the life tenant of a trust fund set up by his grandfather.

The trust income in 2008/09 consisted of taxed interest on £80,000 3% Treasury Stock which had been held for a number of years.

Trust expenses amounted to £320.

Herbie is a widower aged seventy, whose only other income in 2008/09 is a state retirement pension of £7,250.

(a)   Prepare a statement showing the trust income and show the details to be stated on the income certificate given to Herbie.

(b)   Compute Herbie's income tax repayment for 2008/09.

B.

Assume the same facts as above except that Herbie is an annuitant entitled to an annuity from the trust amounting to £3,200 per annum gross.

The trustees paid the full annuity in 2008/09, being authorised to use capital to make up the deficiency.

(a)   Show the position of the trustees and the figures on the certificate to be given to Herbie.

(b)   Compute Herbie's income tax repayment for 2008/09.

Answer

A.   Herbie Fritter — Trust Income

(a)   Statement of trust income 2008/09

	Net £	Tax £	Gross £
3% Treasury Stock interest	1,920	480	2,400
Trust expenses paid therefrom	320		
Regarded as net amount with tax deduction of		80	
and a gross equivalent of			400
Net amount, tax thereon and gross equivalent remaining	1,600	400	2,000

Certificate by trustees to Herbie (R185 (non-discretionary trusts))

Gross	Tax	Net
£2,000	£400	£1,600

(b)   Herbie's income tax repayment claim 2008/09

	£	Tax £
Retirement pension	7,250	
Trust income	2,000	400
	9,250	
Age allowance	9,030	
Taxable income	220	
Tax payable @ 10% starting rate for savings (see note 6)		22
Repayment due		378

B.   Tax payable by trustees under ITA 2007 s 963

(a)   Statement of trust income 2008/09

	Net £	Tax £	Gross £
Trust income after expenses as before	1,600	400	2,000
Annuity to Herbie	2,560	640	3,200
Further tax to be paid by trustees		240	

The annuity is income in Herbie's hands, even though part of it was paid out of capital. Having accounted for tax at 20% on the full amount of the payment, the trustees will give Herbie the appropriate certificate on form R185 as follows:

	Gross	Tax	Net
	£3,200	£640	£2,560

B.   (b)   Herbie's income tax repayment claim 2008/09

	£	Tax £
Retirement pension	7,250	
Annuity	3,200	704
	10,450	
Age allowance	9,030	
Taxable income	1,420	
Tax payable @ 10% on £1,420 (see note 6)		142
Repayment due		562

Explanatory Notes

Paying expenses out of capital

1.   Had the trustees been empowered to pay the expenses from capital, their income of £2,400 would have been intact. In part A of the example, Herbie would have received £1,920 net, the gross equivalent of which would have been the full £2,400 received by the trustees.

   If Herbie had been liable to tax at 40%, his higher rate liability would be increased if the trust expenses were paid out of the trust capital.

Payment of annuities

2.   Annuities reduce the payer's income for tax purposes (the payer being the trust in part B of the example). It is, however, provided by ITA 2007 s 901 that tax must be deducted from annuities at the basic rate. The tax relief is therefore normally given by allowing the payer to retain the tax deducted, but an equivalent amount of the payer's income must be taxed at the *basic rate*. The net result is that no tax is suffered on that part of the payer's income. If there is insufficient income to cover the annuity, tax must be accounted for at the basic rate on the excess under ITA 2007 s 963, and no tax relief is available on the payment, since it is made out of trust capital.

Assessments under ITA 2007 s 963

3.   Where tax is payable under ITA 2007 s 963 as indicated in note 2 above, HMRC issue assessments outside the self-assessment system for the amount due. Interest on such assessments runs from 31 January after the tax year to which the assessment relates, regardless of when the assessment is issued.

Interest on government stocks

4.   From 6 April 1998, interest on all government stocks is paid gross where the stocks are acquired on or after that date, unless the holders apply to receive the interest net (ITA 2007 s 892). Those like Herbie's trustees who already hold such stocks are treated as having *opted* for net payment, but they may apply for the gross payment rules to apply. If such an application has been made, the interest

received would normally be taken into account in calculating the half-yearly payments on account, but in this example it would be covered by the de minimis limit of £500 so that half-yearly payments would not be required.

It is worth noting that SI 1996/1654 – Income Tax (Payments on Account) Regulations 1996 is amended by the making of a regulation to raise the figure at regulation 3 from £500 to £1,000. This will come into force for self-assessment payments on account (POA) from 2009/10 and later years. The regulation has effect on and after 6 April 2009 for income tax due for 2009/10.

The first payments on account affected will therefore be those due in January 2010 and July 2010.

Self-assessment

5. See Example 47 for detailed notes on the treatment of trusts under self-assessment.

Tax on savings income – FA 2008 s 5 & Sch 1

6. This is tax on taxable income such as earnings, pensions, taxable state benefits, self-employed profits up to £34,800 at the rate of 20% (now basic rate) except income from savings (FA 2008 s 4).

    Savings income (broadly, bank and building society interest) is regarded as the part of taxable income which is taxed next. The definition of income to be treated as savings income is contained in ITA 2007 s 18. FA 2008 s 5 introduces a new 10% starting rate for savings income only, with a limit of £2,320. If taxable non-savings income (ie earnings and pensions etc as mentioned above) is more than this limit, then the 10% savings rate will not be applicable and savings income will be taxed in full at 20%.

    What this means is that if an individual has total income including savings of between £6,035 and £8,355 – the 10% rate will apply to at least part of their savings income. For people over 65 who are receiving the higher personal allowance these limits will be increased.

    However, if the personal allowance has been utilised against non-savings income (as explained above) but the remaining non-savings income is less than £2,320 – the balance of the £2,320 against can be used to tax savings income at the 10% rate. Only the balance of savings income remaining is then chargeable at 20%.

    For example – Keith aged 60, has taxable employment and pension income of £6,600 and savings interest (before any tax is taken off) of £1,000. Keith's tax free personal allowance for 2008/09 is £6,035 so he only has tax to pay on £565 (6,600 – 6,035) on his non-savings income. This means that he has used up £565 of the £2,320 starting rate band of 10% for savings leaving £1,755 available. His savings of £1,000 will be taxed in full at 10% only.

    However, if Keith's non-savings income amounted to £25,000 (before tax) – he will be taxed in full at 20% on his savings income as taxable non-savings income is more than his allowance £6,035 and the savings rate band of £2,320.

    There are no changes to the taxation of dividends or distributions from unit trusts (but not interest) – they are taxable at the 10% rate and form the last tranche of income and so are taxed at the highest appropriate rate of tax. For an individual paying tax at 40% on their other taxable income they will pay tax at 32.50% on their dividends.

    Taxable income over £34,800 will be taxed at the 40% higher rate (apart from dividends) whether or not it is savings income.

Question

A and his wife died in a car crash on 6 April 2007, being survived by their four children C, D, E and F.

The children's dates of birth are:

C	20 January 1987
D	6 October 1990
E	11 November 1992
F	23 May 1994

By his will, in addition to bequests to more distant relatives and friends, A created the following separate trusts for his children:

For C, an annuity of £1,500 to be paid out of the income from 20,000 £1 shares in X plc. It is stipulated that if the income of any year is insufficient to meet the annuity in full, capital is to be used to make good the deficiency. Because of falling profits, X plc was only able to pay a 4% dividend during 2008/09.

For D, 10,000 shares in Y plc if he attains 25 years of age. By Trustee Act 1925 s 31, the income may, at the discretion of the trustees, be applied for D's maintenance. When D attains 18 years of age the income has to be paid to him. The dividends received from Y plc shares in 2008/09 (exclusive of tax credits) totalled £1,600, of which £800 was in the period to 6 October 2008. Maintenance paid to D until 5 October was £240. £500 was paid to D between 6 October and the end of the tax year.

For E, a vested interest in 10,000 8% preference shares of £1 each in Z plc. The capital cannot be paid to E until the child's 18th birthday, but power is given for payments to be made for E's maintenance out of income. Any income not distributed will be accumulated until E becomes 18. £700 was paid to E during 2008/09.

For F — Rannoch House — if he attains 18 years of age. The house is currently let at an annual rent of £7,500 from 6 April 2008 but was empty in the period from 1 May 2005 until 5 April 2008 for major renovation work so no rents were received in this period. Consequently no election for the special income tax treatment for trust with vulnerable beneficiary was made for 2007/08 but an election has been made for 2008/09 before the deadline of 31 January 2010.

No maintenance was paid to F during 2008/09 as he has a part time job from which he earns £2,500 a year with no tax deducted. He has no other income.

By 5 April 2008 the estate had been administered and the funds to satisfy the bequests to C, D and E had been set aside.

(a)   Calculate the income tax payable by the trustees of each of the above funds for 2008/09.

(b)   State the amounts which will be treated as taxable income of each beneficiary for 2008/09.

Answer

(a)   Income tax payable by trustees for 2008/09

C Trust:

			Gross £	Tax £
Dividends (20,000 × 4% = 800 + 89 (tax credit of 1/9))			889	
Less charges: Annuity (part)			889	
			—	
Tax on trust income			—	
Tax on charges	889	@ 20%	178	178
Tax payable by trustees under self-assessment (due 31 January 2009)				89
Tax payable by trustees under ITA 2007 s 963 assessment re annual payment made out of capital (see explanatory note 1):				
Balance of annuity of (1,500 − 889)	611	@ 20%		122

Form R185 to the annuitant will show:

	Gross £	Tax £	Net £
Annuity	1,500	300	1,200

D Trust:

Trustees are liable to tax in respect of dividend income at the dividend trust rate of 32.5% on the tax credit inclusive amount until the beneficiary has an absolute interest in income (6 October 2008). From that date the trust becomes an interest in possession trust until D reaches age 25. The tax payable on the dividends is then covered by the tax credits, so the trustees are not liable to pay any tax thereon. The position is therefore as follows.

Dividend income (6 April 2008 to 5 October 2008)	800		
Tax credits £800 × 1/9	89		
	£889		
Tax payable at dividend ordinary rate	500	@ 10% =	50
dividend trust rate	389	@ 32.5% =	126
			176
Less: Tax credits			89
Tax payable by trustees under self-assessment (due 31 January 2010)			£87
Tax Pool			
Tax added	87		
Tax on distribution	160		
Further tax due under ITA 2007 ss 497/498	73		

No election can be made to treat the trust as one with a vulnerable beneficiary since D does not become entitled to the settled property until he is 25. To qualify as a trust for a vulnerable person, D would need to become entitled to all the trust assets on reaching the age of 18.

Until Finance Act 2006, there were special rules for accumulation and maintenance (A&M) trusts. Lifetime transfers into these trusts were exempt from IHT if the settlor survives seven years, and the trusts are not subject to the periodic or exit charges.

FA 2006 Schedule 20 restricted the favourable rules to trusts that are created:

- on death by a parent for a minor child who will be fully entitled to the assets in the trust between the age of 18 of 25; or

- on death for the benefit of one life tenant in order of time only (more than one such interest may be created on death as long as the trust capital vests absolutely when the life interest comes to an end); or

- either in the settlor's lifetime or on death for a disabled person. Trusts for *disabled persons* will also continue to enjoy special treatment, as will existing regular premium life insurance policies written into trust.

The IHT treatment for trusts which do not come within these rules will in future fall within the IHT rules for 'relevant property' trusts.

These changes took effect from 22 March 2006, but Schedule 20 provided transitional arrangements for existing trusts.

Broadly, where existing A&M trusts provide that the assets in trust will go to a beneficiary absolutely at 18 — or where the terms on which they are held were modified before 6 April 2008 to provide this — their current IHT treatment continues.

For a new A&M trust if the capital is left on fully flexible trust with no set date for the beneficiary to become absolutely entitled, the trust will become subject to the 6% rule on the death of the parent and will remain so until the beneficiary is paid out.

For new and old A& M type arrangements, the trusts will not become subject to the 6% regime until the child reaches age 18 and this will continue until they become absolutely entitled at age 25. There will be no 20% entry charge. However, for new arrangements (ie trust property settled after 21 March 2006), this applies only if one of the child's parents has died and the trust was established under the will of the parent or under the Criminal Injuries Compensation Scheme.

For existing A&M settlements where beneficiaries are under age 18 at the end of the transitional period on 6 April 2008, they will not be subject to the 6% charge until they reach age 18 provided the trust was modified before 6 April 2008.

Therefore, the trustees of the D settlement arranged that the trust deed was modified so that the assets devolve absolutely in D by 6 April 2008 to avoid the new interest in possession settlement being treated as a relevant property trust and not as previously when he reached his 18th birthday.

E Trust:

Income received

10,000 × £1 × 8% = £800 + tax credit £89 = £889.

Tax at the dividend trust rate does not apply as E has an absolute right to the income.

The tax liability on the dividend income is at 10%, covered by the tax credit. Although the trustees will have to send in a tax return form SA 900, they will not need to make any income entries since the tax on the income was covered by tax credits. The due date for submitting the return is 31 January 2010.

F Trust:

Because F is absolutely entitled to all of the trust assets on reaching 18 an election can be made for special income tax treatment (FA 2005 Chapter 4). The tax liability is then calculated by reducing the normal trust tax payable (referred to in FA 2005 s 27 as TQTI) by the excess of that figure over the extra amount of tax the vulnerable beneficiary would pay (FA 2005 s 28 VQTI) on the assumption that the trust income is the highest part of his or her income and disregarding any relief given by way of a reduction of income tax (eg married couple's allowance).

The calculation of the trustees tax liability, as set out in FA 2005 ss 26–28 is:

2007/08
Steps

TLV2	Compute F's liability to income and capital gains tax on the basis that any income distributed to him by the trustees is disregarded and that any reliefs given by way of an income tax deduction (for example – married couple's allowance) are also ignored for this purpose.
TLV1	This is the tax due computed by assuming that the trust income relating to the vulnerable beneficiary was in fact charged on F as the highest part of his income.
VQTI	VQTI = TLV1 – TLV2
TQTI	This is the tax due on the trustees without reference to the vulnerable person rules.
The relief	The trustees' income tax liability is reduced by TQTI – VQTI. This gives the answer of VQTI as trustees reduced liability.

F's Trust calculation of relief

TLV2   F's income ignoring the trust income is £2,500 which is within his personal allowance – no tax is payable on this.

	£
Earnings	2,500
Personal allowance (restricted)	2,500
	0

	£
TLV1 Earnings	2,500
Trust income	7,500
	10,000

	£
Income including trust (TLV1)	10,000
Personal allowance	6,035
Taxable income	£3,965

Tax payable thereon

	£		£
	3,965	@ 20%	793

VQTI   TLV1 minus TLV2 equals VQTI (793 – 0 = 793)
So VQTI is £793

TQTI   Tax on trustees (assumes no management expenses for purpose of this example)

	£		£
	1,000	@ 20%	200
	6,500	@ 40%	2,600
	7,500		2,800

	The relief	Trustees' income tax liability reduced by TQTI – VQTI		
				£
		TQTI		2,800
		The relief (2,800 – 793)		2,007
		Revised liability		793

(b)   **Amounts treated as taxable income of the beneficiaries for 2008/09**

C	Annuity		£1,500	Tax deducted	£300
D	Maintenance to 5.10.08				
	$£240 \times \dfrac{100}{60} =$		400	Tax deducted	£160
	Income of trust from 6.10.08 — Dividends				
	$£800 \times \dfrac{100}{90} =$		889	Tax credit (non-repayable)	£89
			£1,289		
E	Income vested (that is, an absolute entitlement to it whether or not distributed)		£889	Tax credit (non-repayable)	£89
F	Nil				

In all cases the beneficiary's income is below the level of the single personal allowance. Dividend tax credits are, however, not repayable. Unless their personal allowances are covered by other income, C will be able to reclaim the whole of the tax deducted of £300 and D will be able to reclaim the tax of £160 deducted from his maintenance. Neither D nor E will be able to reclaim the tax credits of £89.

The tax paid by the trustees of F trust will equal the liability on trust income.

Explanatory Notes

Payment of annuities

1.   Where an annuity is payable, tax must be deducted at the basic rate, and tax must be accounted for at that rate on an equivalent amount of income. The effect is to cause tax to be charged on the dividend income of the C trust at 20% rather than the dividend rate of 10%. ITA 2007 s 963 provides that tax also has to be paid at the basic rate on the part of the annuity paid out of the capital of the trust. HMRC issue assessments outside the self-assessment system in respect of such tax. Although the tax on such an assessment is payable thirty days after it is issued (unless an appeal and postponement application is made) (TMA 1970 s 59B(6)), interest on unpaid tax runs from 31 January after the tax year to which the assessment relates (see Example 44 explanatory note 3).

Now that dividend credits are not repayable, the fact that the trust's dividend income is effectively taxed at 20% will not disadvantage C.

For a further illustration of the treatment of an annuity see Example 44 part B.

Contingent interest

2. At present D only acquires shares in Y plc provided he attains the age of 25 but see 45.2(a). Until age 18 the trustees have the power to accumulate income and therefore the dividend income received by the trust before D's 18th birthday on 6 October 2008 is chargeable to tax at the dividend trust rate (currently 32.5%). As and when payments are made to D during that time, they are net of tax at 40%, and the tax may be reclaimed by D if appropriate, as indicated in the example. The trustees must, however, account for the 40% tax deducted from the payments and they cannot treat the dividend credit relating to the amount distributed as tax paid by them when calculating how much tax they must pay. They could not, therefore, have paid a distribution of more than £800 gross (£480 net), to D before 6 October 2008, ie:

	£	Available income £
Trust income		
Dividend 800 × (100/90)	889	800
Tax due (per 45.2 at D)	176	
Less tax credit	89	
Tax payable	87	(87)
If £800 gross distributed		
Tax at 40% on £800	320	
Already paid	87	
Further tax payable	233	(233)
		480

For a more detailed illustration of these provisions see Example 48.

From his 18th birthday D is entitled to the income whether it is actually distributed or not. The amount of £500 paid to him after his 18th birthday in the tax year is irrelevant, since he is entitled to and will eventually receive the rest.

Vested interest

3. Although E is under 18, he has a vested interest in the preference shares in Z plc. Whilst the capital cannot be distributed, the income can. As the settlors (E's parents) are dead, ITTOIA 2005 s 629 (which treats income from a parental settlement on an infant child as belonging to the parent) cannot apply and therefore this income is taxed on E personally.

Contrast the interest of E (vested) with that of D (contingent). Although E cannot personally have the shares in Z plc until he is 18, or even the income for his personal unrestricted use, the shares belong to him. If he dies the asset will form part of his estate. The income from the shares forms part of his statutory income. By comparison D's interest in the shares of Y plc is conditional upon his living to age 25. If he dies then the asset will revert to the will trust. D has no right to the income until he is 18 (other than at the discretion of the trustees). Thereafter he has an absolute right to income which is taxed in his name. Only after the contingency has been eliminated (ie on attaining age 25) will the shares vest in D. There is a considerable body of case law on the question of whether an interest under a will is vested or contingent, and it involves a detailed knowledge of the general law of trusts, which is outside the scope of this book.

Trust with vulnerable beneficiary

4. The rate applicable to trusts (40%) and the dividend trust rate (32.5%) were raised in FA 2004 with effect for the tax year 2004/05 as a tax avoidance deterrent. To prevent these changes having an

adverse effect on trusts with vulnerable beneficiaries, particularly trusts for disabled people and for children with a deceased parent — FA 2005 Chapter 4 (ss 23–45) brought in provisions to protect such individuals.

Income tax

FA 2005 ss 25–29 sets out the special tax treatment rules. The mechanics of working out the reduction in the trustees tax liability are set out in detail for the F trust in (a) but basically the trustees will be able to take account of the vulnerable beneficiary's personal allowances and starting and basic rate income tax bands to reduce the amount of income tax paid.

For income tax purposes, the trustees therefore include in their return the tax that would normally be due by them and then calculate what the tax would be if the income had been given directly to F, taking into account his other income, gains and allowances. The difference is claimed as a deduction — see the calculations for F on 45.3–45.4.

Capital gains

If a trust has any capital gains, and the trustees and the vulnerable beneficiary are UK resident then an election for special tax treatment by the trustees would mean that the gain would be treated as arising to a settlor in a settlor-interested trust (s 31). The trustees are not chargeable to capital gains tax — instead the gain is charged on the vulnerable person who should return it in their tax return. Clearly this may pose a problem for some vulnerable beneficiaries who have not been required to submit a self-assessment return previously and suddenly find themselves confronted with the need to work out their capital gain.

This provision does not apply in the tax year of the death of the vulnerable beneficiary (s 30).

FA 2008 Sch 2 paras 11 to 20 amend the rules in FA 2005 Chapter 4 Part 2 for the taxation of the income and gains of settlements for vulnerable persons. The tax paid in respect of such income and gains should be no higher than would be the case if the income and gains arose directly to the vulnerable person. A vulnerable person is broadly, a person suffering from a significant mental or physical disability, or a minor child who has lost a parent through death.

For most cases, the rules in FA 2005 result in the trustees' liability to income tax or CGT being reduced by sums computed in accordance with particular formulae. But where capital gains arose to trustees and the vulnerable beneficiary was resident in the UK, the rules used TCGA 1992 ss 77–79 to charge gains directly on the vulnerable person. Paragraphs 13 and 14 amend the rules for computing the amount by which the trustees' income tax liability is reduced.

FA 2008 Sch 2 paras 15 to 18 amend the rules for the special treatment of chargeable gains of trustees of a settlement for a vulnerable person.

The result of the changes to FA 2005 s 31 made by para 16 of the Schedule is that where the vulnerable person is resident in the UK, the trustees' liability to CGT in respect of chargeable gains on the disposal of settled property held for the benefit of the vulnerable person (described as 'qualifying trust gains') is reduced to the amount of CGT that would have been payable by the vulnerable person in respect of those gains if they had arisen directly to the vulnerable person. This replaces the previous rule, which used TCGA 1992 s 77 so that the vulnerable person was charged to CGT as though the qualifying trust gains arose directly to him.

Where the vulnerable person is not resident in the UK, the same principle applies, that the trustees' CGT liability in respect of qualifying trust gains is reduced to the amount that would have been payable had they arisen directly to the vulnerable person. This rule already applied in these cases, but the removal of the link between the CGT and income tax rates means that the calculation process can be simplified, as only CGT liability needs to be taken into account.

Non-UK resident beneficiaries and trustees

Where the beneficiary is non-UK resident for the tax year for the purposes of Chapter 4, the trustees' tax liability in respect of the gains will be whatever the vulnerable beneficiary's tax liability in respect of the gains would have been had the gains arisen to him or her directly.

The special capital gains tax regime does not apply in any case where, in the tax year in question, the trustees are not, for TCGA 1992 purposes, resident in the UK during part of the year, or ordinarily resident in the UK during the year (ss 32, 33 and Sch 1).

Election for special tax treatment

The trustees of relevant trusts will be able to make an irrevocable joint election with a vulnerable beneficiary which will have effect, for any tax year for which the election is in force, to allow the trustees to make a claim for the special tax treatment provided by FA 2005 Chapter 4 to apply for that year.

The election must state the date from which it is to be valid and must be made no later than 12 months after 31 January following the tax year in which that date falls.

If the election becomes invalid, the trustees have 90 days from the time of the change in circumstances to notify HMRC (s 37).

Disabled person

A disabled person is defined in FA 2005 s 38 as a person with a mental disability who is incapable of administering his property or managing his affairs, or, a person in receipt of attendance allowance or disability living allowance at the middle or highest rates (or who would be so entitled to such an allowance if they were UK resident).

Relevant minor

A child is a relevant minor if aged under 18 *and* at least one of their parents has died (s 39).

Qualifying trust — disabled persons

To be a qualifying trust for a vulnerable disabled person that person must be entitled to all of the income arising from the trust fund, or, no income of the trust may be applied for the benefit of any other person. Any capital distribution must be for the benefit of the disabled person (s 34).

Qualifying trust — relevant minor

A trust is a qualifying trust for a relevant minor if it is:

– a statutory trust for a minor on an intestacy, or

– a trust established under the will of the deceased parent of the relevant minor, or

– a trust established under the Criminal Injuries Compensation Scheme.

To qualify the trust must provide that the relevant minor will be absolutely entitled to income and capital including accumulations at age 18. Before that age any distribution must be applied for the benefit of the relevant minor and no income may be applied for the benefit of any other person (s 35).

It must therefore be noted that any trusts established by parents, by will or intestacy, for their minor children, where the children do not become entitled to the settled property until age 25 (eg accumulation and maintenance settlements) will not qualify. Hence the D settlement does not qualify but that for F does.

Part qualification

References to qualifying trusts include trusts where only part of the property qualifies provided that part and any income arising from that asset can be identified (s 36). In such cases only the relevant proportion of management expenses will be allowed against the income of each part. The proportion being the amount of qualifying income as a proportion of total income allowed against qualifying income (s 27(2)).

Part years

Where the trust only qualifies for part of a tax year then income and expenses are related to the qualifying and non-qualifying periods based upon when income arises (s 29).

Self-assessment

5.   See Example 47 for further details on the way in which income is shown in the self-assessment tax return of the individual.

Question

Garth, a bachelor aged 45, was injured in a road accident some years ago and the Court awarded the sum of £50,000 compensation to be paid to him.

Garth created a settlement of this sum under which he was himself to receive the income for life, the capital upon his death being divisible amongst certain relatives.

The trust income for the year ended 5 April 2009 comprised:

		£
Building society interest (amounts received)		1,280
Taxed interest from government stocks (gross amounts)		660
National Savings Bank interest (investment account)		76
Rents receivable		4,739
Repairs and maintenance of rented property	329	
Insurance	205	(534)
Dividends from UK companies (amount received)		1,800

Trust expenses amounted to £450. There was a loss brought forward of £205 on the rented property.

In 2008/09 Garth's only personal income, other than non-taxable social security allowances, consisted of National Savings Bank Income Bonds of £4,000 (paid gross).

(a)   Prepare a statement showing the trust income for 2008/09.

(b)   Compute Garth's personal tax position for 2008/09.

Answer

Garth — Trust Income

(a) **Garth's Trustees — Statement of Trust Income 2008/09**

				Gross	*Tax*
			£	£	£
Rent receivable			4,739		
Less: Expenses			(534)		
Loss brought forward			(205)	4,000	
Savings income					
Building society interest					
(1,280 × 100/80)			1,600		320
Government stocks interest			660		132
NSB interest			76	2,336	
Dividends (1,800 + 200)				2,000	200
Total income of trust				8,336	652
Tax thereon:					
Non-savings income	4,000	@ 20%	800		
Non-dividend savings income	2,336	@ 20%	467		
Dividend income	2,000	@ 10%	200	1,467	1,467
	8,336				
of which tax payable by self-assessment is					815
Net income of trust treated as Garth's income				6,869	

(b) **Garth — Income tax liability 2008/09**

		Tax
	£	£
NSB interest	4,000	–
Trust income (both savings and non-savings)	6,869	1,467
	10,869	1,467
Personal allowance	6,035	
	4,834	
Tax payable thereon @ 20%. (The 10% starting rate for savings will not apply as taxable income is more than the notional limit of £2,320.)		967
		500
Non-repayable dividend tax credits (200 – 29)		171
Repayment due		329

Explanatory Notes

Settlement in which settlor retains an interest

1. For income tax purposes, income from a settlement is treated as the settlor's income if he or his wife has retained an interest in the settlement (ITTOIA 2005 s 625).

    Garth is therefore assessable on the trust income whether he receives it or not, since he was the settlor, and no relief is available for the trust expenses of £450. Furthermore, income other than dividend income is treated as miscellaneous income, so the savings rate of 20% does not apply to the non-dividend savings income. This makes no difference in Garth's case, since dividend income is treated as the top slice of taxable income and the income remaining chargeable after deducting his personal allowance is part of his dividend income of £2,000, so it is taxed at 10% in any event. For further notes on settlements in which the settlor retains an interest, see Example 35.

    ITTOIA 2005 ss 622–627 is part of the anti-avoidance legislation in ITTOIA 2005 Part 5 Chapter 5, which also provides, in ITTOIA 2005 ss 629, 631, that payments to unmarried minor children of the settlor are treated as the settlor's income (see Example 42).

2. Where a settlor retains an interest in a discretionary settlement, the income is not liable to the trust rate or the dividend trust rate — see Example 42 under the headings *Income not liable to ITA 2007 ss 479–483 rates* and *Income taxed as income of the settlor*.

3. Special provisions apply for capital gains tax where a settlor retains an interest in a non-resident settlement — see Example 51 for details.

4. ITTOIA 2005 s 685A gives statutory effect to an existing practice of not taxing beneficiaries of settlor-interested settlements on discretionary income payments they receive from the trustees where the underlying income has already been taxed in the hands of the settlor.

    ITTOIA 2005 s 685A applies where a person receives a discretionary income payment from the trustees of a settlement, and where the settlor is also chargeable to tax under ITTOIA 2005 s 619(1) on the income arising to the trustees of the settlement, whether income of the current year of assessment or of a previous year of assessment.

    The section applies only to a proportion of the discretionary annual payment corresponding to the proportion of the trustees' income (of current and previous years of assessment) that has been charged to income tax under ITTOIA 2005 s 619 in the hands of the settlor. In such circumstances the recipient of the annual payment is treated as having paid income tax at the higher rate in respect of the annual payment.

    The beneficiary who receives the discretionary annual payment is to be treated as receiving the sum with a higher rate tax credit, to the extent that the section applies to the income he receives (see note 10).

    The tax which the beneficiary is treated as having paid is not repayable, and prevents the tax that s 685A(3) treats as having been paid from being used to reduce a tax bill on other income. It also provides for the annual payment to be treated as wholly payable out of profits or gains not brought into charge to income tax.

    Where the recipient of the annual payment is the settlor then the annual payment is not a taxable receipt in the settlor's hands, and the rule that the beneficiary who receives the discretionary annual payment is to be treated as receiving the sum with a higher rate tax credit, to the extent that the section applies to the income he receives does not apply.

    ITA 2007 ss 497–498 will not apply in relation to the payment, or to so much of the payment as falls within the terms of s 685A.

Gifts to charity

5.   Where a UK resident trust that is caught by the anti-avoidance legislation of ITTOIA 2005 Part 5 Chapter 5 (see note 1) gives money to a charity, the amount taxable on the settlor is reduced by the amount (plus tax) given to the charity (ITTOIA 2005 ss 628, 630).

This means that the income given to the charity will be net of tax at the relevant rate applicable to the trustees, ie 40% for discretionary trusts and the basic, lower or dividend ordinary rate for interest in possession trusts. Where the trust's income exceeds the amount given to the charity, the amount given to the charity is treated as made rateably out of the trust's different sources of income (unless the trust stipulates that the charity should receive certain sources of income). Trust management expenses are similarly allocated between income that goes to the charity and the remainder of the trust income.

The rate of tax recoverable by the charity depends on the tax payable by the trust. Say a trust gives a charity bank interest of £500. If the trust is a discretionary trust with income (after management expenses) of £10,000, the interest would be net of 40% tax, so that the tax thereon would be (500 × 40/60 =) £333. The charity would receive £500 plus a tax refund of £333, making £833 in all. If the trust is an interest in possession trust, the tax on the gift of £500 would be (500 × 20/80 =) £125. The charity would receive £500 plus a tax refund of £125, making a total of £625.

6.   For the purpose of the anti-avoidance provisions mentioned in note 1, an interest free or low interest rate loan is an 'arrangement' that is within the definition of settlement, so that income from the investment of such a loan is treated as the settlor's income. It is provided by ITTOIA 2005 ss 628, 630 that this does not apply where the loan is made to a charity.

Self-assessment

7.   See Example 47 explanatory note 7 for the entries on self-assessment returns in relation to trusts in which the settlor retains an interest. HMRC Helpsheet IR 270 contains detailed information on how to decide whether an interest has been retained and also relating to parental settlements on minor children (as to which see Example 64). Where gifts or loans are made to charity as outlined in notes 5 and 6 above, the income does not have to be included in the settlor's self-assessment return.

Settlor-interested trusts

8.   A settlement may be made by a settlor on himself for a number of reasons. In this example Garth may well have made the settlement so that trustees can administer his assets on his behalf whilst he is suffering from a mental or physical disability. Other reasons for such settlements would include:

   (a)   A couple with no children, but each having relatives, wishing to ensure that each set of relatives obtained the appropriate share of their respective estates (rather than the whole devolving upon the relatives of the spouse/civil partner who died last as could occur in intestacy).

   (b)   To provide certainty for the next generation(s) by creating a settlement under which each of husband and wife would receive the income during their lifetime, their children having the knowledge that the destination of the capital could not be altered by such events as the remarriage of a widow/widower.

   (c)   A couple with children from different relationships who wish to ensure that their own offspring obtain the appropriate share of their respective estates (removing the possibility that the destination of the capital could be altered after their own deaths, whilst providing income for their co-habitee in the meantime).

Settlor-interested trust – FA 2008 amendments

FA 2008 s 67, which will have effect on or after 6 April 2006, has been introduced to rectify an anomaly of the trusts modernisation legislation in FA 2006. It affects individuals who receive discretionary income payments from a settlor-interested trust and who also receive savings or dividend income.

The income of a 'settlor-interested' trust is deemed, for the purposes of income tax, to be the settlor's income. Tax paid by the trustees of such trusts is treated as paid on behalf of the settlor. This is in contrast to other trusts where the tax paid by trustees is available to the beneficiaries.

To avoid the double taxation which would otherwise result, ITTOIA 2005 s 685A provides that income paid by trustees of a settlor-interested trust to (non-settlor) beneficiaries comes with a non-repayable 'notional' tax credit equal to the higher rate of tax (currently 40%) which covers all the tax liability on that income.

However, under current statutory ordering rules income from a trust is charged before savings and/or dividend income. The result is that a beneficiary of such a trust who also has savings and/or dividend income may find that the non-trust income is pushed into higher rates so that more tax is due overall.

The measure amends this ordering rule, such that income from a settlor-interested trust is treated within ITA 2007 s 1012 as one of the highest slices of income.

Trustees

FA 2006 s 89 made a change to the way trustees of settlor-interested accumulation and discretionary trusts are taxed. Until FA 2006, trustees of settlor-interested trusts were exempt from the special trust rates. FA 2006 withdrew the exemption, so that from 6 April 2006 trustees of settlor-interested accumulation/discretionary trusts are liable at the special rates for trustees: the trust rate (40%) and the dividend trust rate (32.5%).

Trustees should make returns as before, but now tick both box 8.12 and box 8.16 on the trust and estate return.

The settlor is still taxable on the income, and gets a credit for the tax paid by the trustees. It is just that the tax will have been paid at higher rates.

FA 2006 s 89 made a change to the way income is taxed on the settlor. From 6 April 2006 the income taxed on the settlor retains its original character. So it is treated as dividend type income or other income, depending on the source. Consequently the dividend, savings or basic rate will now apply to the settlor (subject to starting and higher rates).

ITTOIA 2005 s 685A means that discretionary payments to non-settlor beneficiaries are properly outside the tax pool arrangements. Such payments are shown separately in both the trustees' and the non-settlor beneficiary's returns.

They do not carry a repayable 40% tax credit and so trustees do not need to gross up the payments or account for additional tax to cover the credit. Because of this, such payments should not be shown in Q14 – they should instead be shown in the 'Additional information' box.

Where the settlement is partly settlor-interested and partly not, there must be a distinction in the way discretionary payments are dealt with. Rather than try to attribute them to the underlying income, ITTOIA 2005 s 685A provides for a statutory apportionment. The amount of the discretionary payments from the settlor-interested part is the same proportion of the total discretionary payments as the proportion of total income that is chargeable on the settlor.

So, for example, if the trustees' total income is £5,000, of which £1,500 is chargeable on the settlor and they make discretionary payments of £2,000, then the entry in 21.11 is:

$2,000 \times (1,500/5000) = 600$

The difference $(2,000 - 600 = 1,400)$ goes in Q14 as normal.

Beneficiaries

From 6 April 2006, in the hands of the beneficiary, discretionary payments from a settlor-interested settlement do not carry a repayable 40% tax credit. Instead, the payment is treated as though tax has been paid at 40%. This is notional tax, which is ring-fenced – it cannot be set sideways against any other income of the beneficiary and cannot be repaid. There is a new box (7.3A) for such payments on the SA107 – the R185 (Trust Income) has been amended to reflect this.

The beneficiary returns the actual amount they receive – there is no grossing up. So whatever the beneficiary's marginal rate, the notional tax covers their liability on that income – if they are anything other than a higher rate taxpayer, part of the notional tax will be lost. While the beneficiary has nothing further to pay on the trust payment itself, it is nevertheless included in the their total income and may push other income/gains into a higher tax rate bracket.

The layout of the personal return has changed for 2007/08 and later years. The SA107 has a separate section for settlor income. The three box format (net, tax credit and gross) is replaced with a single box for the net amount. The underlying calculation will apply the correct tax credit but this does mean there will be separate boxes for income chargeable at the three standard and two special trust rates, as well as for income where no tax has been suffered/deducted.

Interest on government stocks

9. Garth's trustees could make an election to receive interest on the government stocks gross (see Example 44 explanatory note 4 for details). If this was done in relation to interest receivable from 2008/09, tax would not be payable on the 2008/09 interest until 31 January 2010, but the tax would be included in payments on account for later years, unless covered by the de minimis limits.

Question

The Colenso Trust was created in 1985 by a settlor who had already created five other trusts since 6 June 1978. Under the terms of the trust deed the trustees have discretionary power to pay income to any of the named beneficiaries and to accumulate any income that is not so applied.

The income and expenses of the trustees for the year ended 5 April 2009 were as follows:

Income

	£
Dividends from UK companies (amount received)	2,520
Rent of property let unfurnished	2,850
Interest on National Savings investment account	465

Expenses

		£
Property expenses	— ground rent	34
	— repairs	646
Accountancy fees		588

The income tax liability of the trust for 2007/08 amounted to £1,696, of which tax credits covered £546. In addition the trustees had made payments on account of £486 on each of 31 January 2008 and 31 July 2008.

The trustees had a tax pool brought forward at 6 April 2008 of £326. During the year the trustees had net capital gains of £3,290, before deduction of the annual exemption.

One of the beneficiaries of the trust is Clery, a widower who was born in 1924.

The trustees paid £4,200 to Clery out of the trust income in 2008/09.

His other income for that year was a state pension of £4,372 and income from purchased life annuities totalling £20,000, of which the capital content was £16,000.

(a)   Prepare a statement of income and gains for the Colenso Trust for 2008/09.

(b)   Compute the tax pool to carry forward to 2009/10 or s 497 tax payable.

(c)   Show the tax payable by the trustees under self-assessment.

(d)   Calculate Clery's repayment of income tax for 2008/09.

Answer

The Colenso Trust

(a) **Statement of trust income and gains 2008/09**

	£	Gross £	Tax £
Rent receivable	2,850		
Less: expenses	680	2,170	
Savings income			
NSB interest		465	
Dividends (2,520 + 280)		2,800	280
Total income of trust		5,435	280

Tax thereon:

	£		Gross £	Tax £
On amount equal to grossed up trust expenses (paid out of dividend income and not chargeable at dividend trust rate) (588 × 100/90) =	653	@ 10%	65	
On balance of dividends at dividend trust rate (2,800 − 653)	2,147	@ 32.5%	698	
On £1,000 @ standard rate (see explanatory note 1)	1,000	@ 20%	200	
On remaining income at rate applicable to trusts	1,635	@ 40%	654	
	5,435		1,617	1,617
Of which tax payable by self-assessment is				1,337
Used to pay trust expenses		588	2,205	
Net income of trust			3,230	

Capital gains:

	£
Net gains for 2008/09	3,290
Less: Annual exemption (see explanatory note 13)	960
Chargeable gains	2,330
Capital gains tax thereon @ 18%	419

(b) **Tax pool and position under ITA 2007 ss 497–498**

		£
Unutilised tax brought forward at 6 April 2008		326
Tax already accounted for by trustees at:		
Standard rate	200	
Rate applicable to trusts	654	
Dividend trust rate, net of tax credits (2,147 @ 22.5%)	483	
		71,337
		1,663

Tax on payments made out of income to Clery:

$$4,200 \times \frac{40}{60} \qquad 2,800$$

Tax payable under ss 497–498	1,137

(c) **Tax payable by trustees under self-assessment (POA — payment on account)**

		£	£	Tax payable £	Re 2008/09 £
31.1.08	1st POA 2007/08			486	
31.7.08	2nd POA 2007/08			486	
31.1.09	Balancing payment 2007/08:				
	Tax due (1,696 – tax credits 546)	1,150			
	Less POAs	972	178		
	1st POA 2008/09 (½ × 1,150)		575	753	575
31.7.09	2nd POA 2008/09			575	575
31.1.10	Balancing payment 2008/09:				
	Income tax as in (a)	1,617			
	ss 497–498 liability as in (b)	1,137			
	Capital gains tax as in (a)	419			
	Total liability	3,173			
	Less tax credits	280			
	Tax due	2,893			
	Less POAs	1,150	1,743		1,743
	1st POA 2009/10 ½ × (2,893 – CGT 419)		1,237	2,980	
	Total tax paid directly for 2008/09				2,893
31.7.09	2nd POA 2009/10			1,237	

(d)   Clery's income tax repayment claim 2007/08

		£	Tax £
Trust income £4,200 $\times \dfrac{100}{60}$		7,000	2,800
State pension		4,372	
Savings income:			
Purchased life annuities (income element)		4,000	800
		15,372	3,600
Age allowance (over 75)		9,180	
		6,192	
Tax payable thereon:			
On non-savings income	2,192 @ 20%	438	
On savings income	4,000 @ 20%	800	1,238
Repayment due			2,362

Explanatory Notes

Rates applicable to trusts

1. For 2008/09 the income of accumulation and discretionary trusts is liable to tax at the dividend trust rate of 32.5% if it is distribution income (see Example 42 for details) and otherwise at the rate applicable to trusts of 40% (ITA 2007 s 9).

    Under ITA 2007 s 491, the first £1,000 of relevant income will not be charged at the rate applicable to trusts, but will instead be charged at the income tax rate appropriate to the type of income. Therefore, if payments are received net of tax (for example, building society interest) up to the limit of the standard rate band, then the trustees will have no further tax to pay.

    ITA 2007 s 492 applies s 491 where a settlor has made more than one settlement. The reference to £1,000 is replaced by £200, or by an amount obtained by dividing £1,000 by the number of settlements made by the same settlor, provided that amount is not less than £200.

    The section sets out the position where there is more than one settlor of a settlement, and in such circumstances the amount is the amount obtained in relation to the largest class of settlements.

    HMRC have confirmed that the new standard rate band will apply to trust income *net* of trust management expenses so potentially it will apply to other charges as well.

    Although the management expenses are deducted from the trust income taxed at the lowest rate first, the standard rate band will apply in the order – basic rate income at 20% first, followed by dividends at 10%.

    Trustees are liable to tax at the rate applicable to trusts or dividend trust rate on income as the case may be if:

    (a)   the income is to be accumulated or payable at the discretion of the trustees, and

    (b)   it exceeds the trust expenses paid out of income, grossed up at the appropriate rate of tax. The expenses are treated as coming first out of dividends and other income carrying a non-repayable tax credit, then out of dividends from abroad, then out of non-dividend savings income, then out of non-savings income (see Example 43 note 10 at page 43.4). The grossing up rate for the expenses is 10% for dividend income, 20% basic rate for non-dividend savings income and for non-savings income. The expenses are not allowable deductions for basic or for dividend ordinary rate tax, so tax is charged on an equivalent amount of income at the appropriate rate (10% in this example).

2.   See Example 48 for an illustration of a trust liable at the rate applicable to trusts where there is a non-UK resident beneficiary.

3.   In this example, it may be possible to agree that some of the accountancy fees relate to the property income, rather than treating them as general trust expenses, thereby reducing the assessable income and the overall tax liability of the trust.

Self-assessment returns

4.   The HMRC Trusts, Settlements and Estates Manual — Section TSEM 1405 states that a new trust that does not have any income or gains does not have to notify them of the existence of the trust. Existing trusts who do not have any income or gains may ask HMRC to close the trust's record. The trustees are, of course, obliged to notify HMRC by 5 October following the relevant tax year in the same way as individuals if they do have income and/or gains chargeable to tax (TMA 1970 s 7).

5.   Where a self-assessment return is required, all types of trusts and estates complete the same return (SA 900).

Revised filing dates for paper and online self-assessment returns

Paper substitutes for SA returns

6.   From 2007/08 onwards computer generated substitute versions of the SA return will no longer be approved or accepted for:

   • SA Individual Returns – (SA100 series);

   • SA Trust Returns – (SA900 series).

For the time being, HMRC will continue to accept approved substitutes for the remaining SA Returns (including those for trustees of registered pension schemes) and for all other forms they currently approve substitutes for.

Changes to SA filing dates

For 2007/08 and subsequent years' returns, anyone who is required to file a self-assessment tax return will have:

   • until 31 October to do so, if they choose to send a paper return; or

   • until the following 31 January if they file online.

This allows an additional three months for online filing compared with paper.

The filing obligation is satisfied by the first return received by HMRC and this also triggers any late filing penalty. So if, for example, a paper 2007/08 return is filed after 31 October 2008, it is not then possible to avoid a late filing penalty by filing the return online.

In addition, in certain other cases, HMRC will allow extra time beyond the statutory deadline of 31 October – until 31 January – for paper filing without incurring a penalty. These include:

   • Trustees of Registered Pension Schemes; and

   • SA taxpayers (see below), for whom facilities to file online are not yet available.

In the event that there are problems with HMRC systems close to the filing deadline, taxpayers will not be penalised for late submission of a return due to such problems provided that they, or their agent, file within a reasonable period once the service is restored.

FA 2007 s 88(1F) – if a notice is given after 31 July the return must be submitted during the period of three months beginning with the date of the notice (for paper returns) or on or before 31 January (for online returns).

FA 2007 s 88(1G) – if a notice is given after 31 October the return (whether paper return or electronic) must be submitted within three months from the date of the notice.

SA taxpayers who are unable to file online

Those SA taxpayers who do not have the choice of online filing, will be allowed to file on paper up to 31 January, without incurring any penalty that might otherwise be due for paper filing after 31 October.

If such paper output is used by taxpayers or their agents, for returns which could be filed online, it will be accepted provided it is identical to the official HMRC return but must be submitted to HMRC by the paper filing date of 31 October.

Interest in possession trusts are not required to show any *taxed* income in the return, except where accrued income relief is due on the income. (Accrued income *charges* are untaxed income and must be shown.) The trustees will still, however, need to know the overall tax position in order to be able to ascertain the income payable to the life tenant to be shown on form R185 (trust income) (see note 8). The returns for discretionary trusts show both taxed and untaxed income and the amount of the unused tax pool (if any) brought forward from the previous year. For both types of trust, supplementary pages have to be completed where income arises from a trade, partnership, land and property or from abroad, or where there are capital gains, or where the trust is non-resident or dual resident.

7.   To minimise administration burdens, HMRC have a scheme under which trustees responsible for at least 50 trusts dealt with in a single tax office may receive a single notice calling for trust returns and may make a single declaration when submitting a batch of returns. Trustees wishing to operate the scheme must make a written application. More information can be found in the HMRC Trusts, Settlements and Estates Manual at TSEM 3052.

Changes to self-assessment payments on account limits

8.   SI 1996/1654 – Income Tax (Payments on Account) Regulations 1996 is amended by the making of a regulation to raise the figure at regulation 3 from £500 to £1,000.

This will come into force for self-assessment payments on account (POA) from 2009/10 and later years.

The regulation has effect on and after 6 April 2009 for income tax due for 2009/10. The first payments on account affected will therefore be those due in January 2010 and July 2010.

Trusts in which settlor retains an interest

9.   Where the settlor retains an interest in the trust, all income (other than certain income derived from charitable gifts and loans — see Example 46 explanatory notes 5 and 6), *before* deducting expenses, is taxable on the settlor. The amount included on the trust pages of the settlor's personal tax return depends on whether the settlor also has an absolute entitlement to income.

Where the settlor does have an absolute entitlement, the amounts of income will be entered on the trust pages of the settlor's return net of management expenses. The management expenses must, however, also be treated as his income, so they have to be entered as 'other income' under Question 13 in the main part of the return, grossed up by the appropriate tax rate (dividend rate, lower rate or basic rate according to the income used to meet the expenses). Exceptionally, tax may not have been deducted from the income at all, for example if the trustees are non-resident. Even if the expenses are grossed up at the dividend or lower rate, the rate of tax payable by the settlor will be the non-savings rate.

If the settlor is not absolutely entitled to income, then the amounts entered in the trust pages of the return will be the whole of the trust income *before* management expenses.

See HMRC Help Sheet IR 270 for further details.

Forms R185 and beneficiaries' own tax returns

10.   It is advisable for trustees to compute the overall tax position of the trust as quickly as possible after 5 April each year to comply with their responsibilities under self-assessment.

Where the beneficiary is absolutely entitled to the income it will be essential to do so, in order that the R185 may be completed and forwarded to the beneficiary in plenty of time for him to complete his own self-assessment return or to claim a repayment as the case may be. For such beneficiaries, if all the income is taxed at source and there are no expenses, it is usual to mandate the income directly to the beneficiary and to include the income in the beneficiary's return as if it was his own income. In the case of a bare trust, ie where the beneficiary has an absolute right to both income and capital, all of the trust income is deemed to be that of the beneficiary and entered as such on the beneficiary's tax return. Trustees of bare trusts are not required to send trust returns but may, if they wish, send a trust return of the trust income, but not capital gains. This does not affect the beneficiary's liability to make his own returns.

Income paid out to discretionary beneficiaries

11.   Under ITA 2007 ss 497–498, trustees are required to account for tax at the 40% rate applicable to trusts on income paid out in exercise of their discretion to beneficiaries, and the beneficiaries will be given form R185 showing the income as non-savings income with tax deducted at 40%. The tax suffered is available for repayment, as illustrated in the example.

Tax does not have to be accounted for under ss 497–498 on capital payments, nor on payments of accumulated income that have become part of capital. If, however, the payment is advanced in such a way that it becomes income in the hands of the beneficiary, ss 497–498 applies. For example where trustees are empowered to make payments to bring a beneficiary's income up to a certain level, such payments will be income whether paid out of current or accumulated income or capital.

The trustees can reduce the tax to be accounted for under ss 497–498 by the following (excluding any tax on income that has been used to cover trust expenses (see note 1(b)):

(i)   Tax paid on income liable to the rate applicable to trusts, including tax deducted at source.

(ii)   The excess of the tax paid at the dividend trust rate on distributions and dividend type income over the dividend ordinary rate.

(iii) The whole of the tax paid at the dividend trust rate on dividends from abroad.

(iv)   Any pool of unused tax brought forward at 5 April 1999 (see note 11).

(v)   Tax at the basic or lower rate on the first £1,000 of trust income.

12.   If a beneficiary of a discretionary trust has not received a form R185, he should gross up the income received for tax deducted at 40%. If there is any doubt that part of the payment received is not income, the amount should be shown on his personal return as a provisional figure with a tick in box 23.2 and the reason for the figure being provisional should be shown in the additional information box at 23.5. The beneficiary should not delay submitting his return because of the failure of the trustees to provide a form R185.

Ss 497–498 tax pool

13. In many instances, the pool of tax under ss 497–498 will exceed the amount that is due, so no amount will be payable. Furthermore tax could be paid on income that is used to cover non-deductible expenses (see Example 48). From 6 April 1999, however, none of the tax credits on dividends are included in the tax pool, whereas the payments out of income will still have repayable tax of 40% (34% prior to 5 April 2004) deducted. Except to the extent that there is an unused pool of tax brought forward, this will restrict the maximum payment out of dividend income to 60% of the net dividend, giving a ss 497–498 liability of 40% of the net dividend (see Example 45 explanatory note 2 for an illustration). Although any excess of tax paid over tax on distributions can be carried forward to a later year, no credit is given for ss 497–498 tax paid if the tax paid at the rate applicable to trusts exceeds the tax on distributions in later years. That surplus is carried forward as unutilised tax in the pool.

     Note that the unused pool brought forward at 6 April 1999 will include tax credits on any pre 6 April 1999 dividends that have not been paid out to beneficiaries, and those credits are available to cover ss 497–498 tax on discretionary payments after 5 April 1999.

14. The ss 497–498 tax payable is added to the tax due under self-assessment and is accounted for in the balancing payment. It also counts, however, in the calculation of the payments on account for the following year. Thus it can increase the tax payable on 31 January following the end of the tax year by 150% of the ss 497–498 liability.

     The trustees may not intend to make distributions to beneficiaries in the following tax year and may be tempted to apply to reduce the payments on account by the amount of the ss 497–498 tax. Payments on account are, however, compared with the actual tax due for the subsequent year, and if the reduced payment is below the actual liability for that year, interest is payable on the difference (restricted to the amount of the reduction). It does not matter that the claim to reduce the payments on account was in respect of ss 497–498 tax and the additional liability arises because of an increase in tax because of increased income, tax rate increases, reduced expenses or for any other reason.

Capital gains tax

15. FA 2008 s 8 and Schedule 2 radically amends the regime for capital gains for 2008/09 onwards. The annual exemption and the rules for losses will remain.

     The current annual exemption for 2008/09 is £4,800 for trustees.

     The rate of tax on capital gains is set at 18% for individuals, personal representatives and trustees.

     A number of other changes to simplify the capital gains tax regime will be made, including:

     ●   the withdrawal of taper relief;

     ●   the withdrawal of indexation allowance;

     ●   the abolition of the 'kink test' for assets held at 31 March 1982;

     ●   abolition of halving relief; and

     ●   simplification of the share identification rules.

     Other CGT reliefs will continue to have effect. For example:

     ●   private residence relief will continue to be available for principal private residences;

     ●   business asset roll-over relief continues to be available;

     ●   business asset gift hold-over relief also continues to apply;

     ●   any unused allowable losses from past years will continue to be allowed to be brought forward in order to reduce any gains.

Where gains are to be deferred until the occurrence of a later event, the effect of the changes is that, where a gain that arises in a tax year earlier than 2008/09 is deferred; the computation of the deferred amount will take account, if appropriate, of the kink test, halving relief and indexation allowance. This figure of deferred gain will not be affected by these changes.

However, taper relief will not be due if these gains come into charge in 2008/09 or a later tax year. This is because taper relief is due only when a gain is brought into charge, and the deferred amount does not include taper relief.

In the case of an unconditional contract to sell made before 5 April 2008 to take effect after this date – the existing pre-5 April 2008 rules will apply and taper relief and/or indexation may be available. This is because the contract is deemed to be made at the date it was entered into.

In the case of a conditional contract to sell made before 5 April 2008 – the disposal date will be treated as the date that the conditions were satisfied. If this is post 5 April 2008 then the new rules will apply.

UK resident settlor-interested settlements

16.   FA 2008 Sch 2 para 5 repeals TCGA 1992 ss 77 to 79. These provisions had the effect that gains in respect of which the trustees of a UK resident settlor-interested settlement would otherwise have been chargeable to CGT are in certain circumstances charged on the settlor. The introduction of a single rate of CGT for trustees and individuals means that the application of ss 77 to 79 would have no effect on the rate at which the gains were charged to CGT.

As mentioned above, a trust is liable to capital gains tax at 18% from 6 April 2008 on the gains less the annual exemption. The exemption for a trust is one half of that applicable to individuals (half of £9,600 for 2008/09 = £4,800), but it is further reduced where the settlor has created more than one settlement after 6 June 1978 (see Example 50 part C). The limit is divided between the settlements, with a minimum exemption of one tenth of the amount available to individuals, ie £960 for 2008/09. In this example, the £960 limit applies since it is higher than one sixth of £4,800 = £800.

The tax applies to the gains less losses of the year, as reduced by losses brought forward (but not so as to lose the annual exemption).

The amount due is payable on 31 January following the tax year, but is not included in the calculation of payments on account for the following year, nor is it available for inclusion in the tax pool for ss 497–498 liability.

Question

A trust was established on 6 April 1991. The trust deed stipulates that after paying an annuity of £6,500 per annum to the settlor's sister, the remaining income of each year is to be distributed or accumulated as the trustees deem fit.

The assets placed into the trust consisted of certain properties let unfurnished on landlord's repairing short leases, and cash. The latter was placed on bank deposit and used to fund investments in government securities and quoted shares.

At 6 April 2007 the pool of unutilised tax brought forward under ITA 2007 ss 497–498 was £3,750.

The receipts and payments of the trust for 2007/08 and 2008/09 were as follows:

	2007/08 £	2008/09 £
Receipts		
Rents receivable	11,300	11,300
Premium received on granting of 21 year lease	–	10,000
Interest on £10,000 9% Government Stock (gross amount)	900	900
Bank interest received (see below)	1,400	1,500
Dividends from quoted UK companies (including tax credits)	2,762	2,762
Payments		
Trustees' expenses properly chargeable to income	405	450
Trustees' expenses re investment advice	–	100
Loan interest (see below)	200	550
Repairs to the let properties	100	400
Annuity to settlor's sister (gross amount)	6,500	6,500
Discretionary payments of cash from the trust income:		
to A, who is resident in the UK	3,366	–
to B, who is neither resident nor ordinarily resident in the UK	–	3,700

The amounts stated in respect of bank interest received are the gross amounts. The interest was received net of tax. The loan was obtained to finance an extension to one of the let properties. Interest on the 9% Government Stock, which is received net of 20% tax, is exempt from tax in the hands of a non-resident. The trustees' expenses for investment advice have been charged to income by authority of the trust deed.

For 2006/07, the amount of income tax paid on account equalled the liability for the year of £4,208.

Calculate:

(1)   The income of the trust for 2007/08 and 208/09, showing any liability in respect of income chargeable at the trust rate under ITA 2007 s 9, and the due dates of payment of tax.

(2)   The income available for distribution to discretionary beneficiaries for 2007/08 and 2008/09.

(3)   The trust's position under ITA 2007 ss 497–498 at the end of 2008/09.

(4)   Any income tax that may be reclaimable by the non-UK resident beneficiary in respect of the discretionary payment made to him.

Note:

Ignore capital gains tax.

Answer

(1)   **Statement of trust income**

2006/07

2007/08

			Gross £	Tax deducted or credited £
Property income (see explanatory note 6)			11,000	
Savings income				
Interest on Government Stock			900	180
Bank interest			1,400	280
Dividends			3,200	320
			16,500	780
Less: Charges (annuity)			6,500	
Net total income of trust			10,000	

Tax thereon:

On amount equal to grossed up trust expenses, excluding those for investment advice (450 × 100/90) =	500	@ 10%	50	
On lease premium (see explanatory note 6)	6,000	@ 20%	1200	
On £1,000 of income at standard rate under FA 2005 s 14 (20% on property income)	1,000	@ 20%	200	
On dividend income at dividend trust rate (2,762 − 500)	2,262	@ 32.5%	735	
On balance at trust rate	238	@ 40%	95	
	10,000			
Tax deducted from annuity	6,500	@ 20%	1,300	
Total income tax due			3,580	3,580
Of which tax payable by self-assessment is				2,800

Amounts of income tax payable by trustees direct to HMRC under self-assessment for 2007/08 and payments on account for 2008/09 are as follows:

		£	£
31 January 2008:			
½ × 4,208			2,104
31 July 2008:			
½ × 4,208			2,104
31 January 2009:			
Total income tax payable for 2007/08		2,800	
Less: Payments on account	4,208		
Tax/tax credits at source	780	4,988	
		(2,188)	(2,188)
			2,020
First payment on account for 2008/09 (½ × 2,800)		1,400	
Total amount re-payable		(788)	

31 July 2009:
Second payment on account for 2008/09 (see explanatory note 6)

			Gross £	Tax deducted or credited £
31 July 2009: Second payment on account for 2008/09 (see explanatory note 6)			1,400	
2008/09			Gross	Tax deducted or credited
			£	£
Property income (see explanatory note 6)			16,350	
Savings income				
Interest on Government Stock			900	180
Bank interest			1,400	300
Dividends			2,762	276
			21,512	756
Less: Charges (annuity)			6,500	
Net total income of trust			15,012	
Tax thereon:				
On amount equal to grossed up trust expenses, excluding those for investment advice (450 × 100/90) =	500	@ 10%	50	
On lease premium (see explanatory note 6)	6,000	@ 20%	1,200	
On £1,000 of income at standard rate under FA 2005 s 14 (22% on property income)	1,000	@ 20%	200	
On dividend income at dividend trust rate (2,762 – 500)	2,262	@ 32.5%	735	
On balance at trust rate	5,250	@ 40%	2,100	
	15,012			
Tax deducted from annuity	6,500	@ 20%	1,300	
Total income tax due			5,585	5,585
Of which tax payable by self-assessment is				4,829

Amounts of income tax payable by trustees direct to HMRC under self-assessment for 2008/09 and payments on account for 2009/10 are as follows:

31 January 2009:		£	£
As above ½ × 2,800			1,400
31 July 2009:			
½ × 2,800			1,400
31 January 2010:			
Total income tax payable for 2008/09		5,585	
Less: Payments on account	2,800		
Tax/tax credits at source	756	3,556	
		2,029	2,029
			4,829
First payment on account for 2009/10 (½ × 4,829) (see explanatory note 13)		2,415	
Total amount re-payable		4,444	
31 July 2010:			
Second payment on account for 2009/10 (see explanatory notes 6 and 13)		2,414	

(2)   **Income available for distribution to discretionary beneficiaries**

		2007/08 £		2008/09 £
Trust income (excluding lease premium) after annuity and expenses		9,550*		8,512**
Less: Tax at Standard Rate (20%) under FA 2005 s 14	200		200	
Tax at trust rate per part (1)	95		2,100	
Tax at dividend trust rate per part (1)	735		735	
Trustees' expenses for investment advice (see explanatory note 7)	100	1,130	–	3,035
Available for beneficiaries		8,420†		5,477†
Amount actually distributed was		£3,366		£3,700
Leaving undistributed income of		£5,054†		£1,777†

* £10,000 net total income as at part (1) less expenses £450.

** £15,012 net total income as at part (1) less lease premium £6,000 and expenses £500.

† Note that in so far as the amount shown as available to the beneficiaries includes dividend income, it cannot all be distributed without the trustees incurring a further tax liability, except to the extent that there is unutilised tax brought forward (see explanatory note 9).

(3)   **Trust's position under ITA 2007 ss 497–498 at end of 2008/09**

		2007/08 £		2008/09 £
Tax at 40% on amounts paid at trustees' discretion to beneficiaries:				
$£3,366 \times \dfrac{40}{60}$		2,244		
Tax at 40% on amounts paid at trustees' discretion to beneficiaries:				
$£3,700 \times \dfrac{40}{60}$				2,467
Less: Tax already accounted for by trustees: on trust income charged at standard rate under FA 2005 s 14	200		200	
on trust income chargeable under ITA 2007 s 9 –				
at trust rate, ie 40%	95		2,100	
at dividend trust rate excluding non-repayable tax credits (2,262 @ 22.5%)	509			
(2,262 @ 22.5%)			509	
Unutilised tax bf	3,750		2,330	
	4,554		5,139	
Utilised	2,244	2,244	2,467	2,467

	2007/08 £		2008/09 £	
Unutilised tax c/f	2,310	–	2,672*	–
Amount due from trustees under ITA 2007 ss 497–498		–		–
		–		–

* The amount of £2,672 carried forward represents tax paid at the trust rate plus the excess of the dividend trust rate over the dividend ordinary rate, and it can be used to cover tax at 40% on the gross equivalent of future income distributions.

(4) **Tax reclaimable by non-resident beneficiary (see explanatory note 10)**

2007/08	No distribution to B – no repayment.
2008/09	Distribution of £3,700 to B (who is neither resident nor ordinarily resident in UK) comes from trust income that includes £900 from Government Stock that is exempt from tax in B's hands.

The part of the total tax paid on the discretionary payment of trust income in 2007/08, ie £2,467, that represents the interest on the Government Stock is therefore repayable, thus:

$$£2,467 \times \frac{900}{15,512*} = £143$$

* Being taxable income of £21,512 before charges, less lease premium of £6,000 which is a capital receipt.

Explanatory Notes

Trusts liable to the trust rate and dividend trust rate (special trust rates)

1. A trust that can accumulate income, or pay income to the beneficiaries at the discretion of the trustees, is liable to tax on non-dividend income at the rate applicable to trusts, currently 40%, and at the dividend trust rate of 32.5% on 'distribution income', ie UK dividend income and certain other income carrying non-repayable tax credits, and foreign dividends (ITA 2007 s 9). In the case of UK dividends and other income carrying a non-repayable tax credit of 10%, the trustees have to pay the balance of 22.5% for 2007/08 and 2008/09 of the tax credit inclusive amount. In the case of dividends from abroad, the trustees have to pay the full 32.5% for 2007/08 and 2008/09 (subject to a claim for double tax relief where foreign tax has been paid). See Example 42 for details of income carrying non-repayable tax credits and for details of amounts that are not chargeable at the trust rate.

    In this example, the amounts excluded from the charge under s 9 are the lease premium (see note 6) and the annuity to the settlor's sister. The trustees have to account for tax on such amounts at the basic rate. Under self-assessment, tax is not charged separately for each source of income, and the tax under s 9 is accounted for as part of the overall figure.

Amount on which special trust rates are charged

2. The liability under s 9 applies to the *income* of the trust after deducting any excluded amounts per note 1 and allowing for the trustees' expenses of managing the trust. Trust expenses are regarded as being met first from income taxed at the dividend trust rate, then other savings income, then non-savings income, grossed up appropriately. See Example 43 note 10 at page 43.4 for further details.

Non-resident discretionary trusts and non-resident life tenants

3.   Where a discretionary trust has income not chargeable to UK income tax, because it is not resident in the UK, or deemed to be not resident under a double tax treaty, the management expenses must be apportioned between the taxable and non-taxable income of that year, and only the proportion applicable to taxable income is allowable in computing the tax under ITA 2007 s 487(1)–(4). (Income which is strictly taxable income may not be charged to tax on non-residents because of FA 1995 s 128, which broadly limits the charge to the tax, if any, deducted at source. Any such income from which tax is *not* deducted is treated by s 487(5)(6) as non-taxable income for the purposes of s 487(1)–(4).)

Similar provisions disallow a proportion of trust expenses in computing the income of a non-resident beneficiary with a life interest (ITA 2007 s 501).

Interest on government stocks

4.   If the trustees had so elected, the interest on the Government Stock in the example would have been paid gross. There is a cash flow advantage of receiving gross interest, because payments on account are made half-yearly on 31 January in the tax year and 31 July following, with a later balancing payment (or repayment), on the next following 31 January. See Example 44 explanatory note 4 for the rules for paying gross interest on *all* government stocks.

Bank and building society interest

5.   Tax is deducted from both building society interest and bank interest paid to trustees of discretionary trusts, providing in the case of bank interest on deposits made before 6 April 1995 that the trustees or HMRC have notified the bank since that date that the income is income of a discretionary trust (ITA 2007 Sch 2 para 154(1)(2)(3)).

Lease premiums

6.   In relation to the let property, although the lease premium is a capital amount, it is chargeable in part to income tax under ITTOIA 2005 s 277 thus reducing the amount of the credit to capital.

Therefore the taxable property income is:

			2007/08 £		2008/09 £
Rents receivable			11,300		11,300
Premium				10,000	
Less:	Treated as part disposal for capital gains tax 2% for (21 − 1) yrs = 40%			4,000	6,000
			11,300		17,300
Less:	Expenses	– Repairs	100	400	
		– Loan interest	200	550	
			300		950
			11,000		16,350

As a capital receipt, however, the lease premium is not subject to the rate applicable to trusts, and is therefore deducted in calculating the tax payable under ITA 2007 s 9 (see note 1).

Since the lease premium is a non-recurring item, the trustees might think it appropriate to apply to reduce the payments on account for 2009/10. If, however, the final liability proves to be higher than the payments on account actually made (up to the total of the payments due without a claim, ie £4,829), interest would be charged on the shortfall from the half-yearly payment dates, the rate of interest at the time of writing being 7.5% per annum (from 6 January 2008).

If the payments on account had exceeded the liability for 2008/09, interest at the appropriate rate (3% per annum from 6 January 2008) would be paid on the overpayment from the respective dates that the half-yearly instalments were paid to the date the repayment order was issued. There should therefore be a non-taxable credit to income in the trust accounts, equal to the interest that would have been received, the credit to capital for the lease premium being reduced accordingly (in addition to being reduced by the income tax on the premium plus capital gains tax, if any).

Investment advice

7.   The cost of investment advice is of a capital nature and is not allowable for additional rate tax notwithstanding the authority of the trust deed to charge it to income (*Carver v Duncan* and *Bosanquet v Allen* 1985). Nonetheless, the trust deed authorises the expenses to be charged to income, so that the amount available for distribution to income beneficiaries is reduced accordingly.

Income payments to discretionary beneficiaries

8.   Any income payments made to beneficiaries of discretionary trusts are treated for income tax as being amounts paid net of 40% tax.

Under ITA 2007 ss 497–498 trustees are required to account for tax at the rate applicable to trusts on income paid out in exercise of their discretion to beneficiaries. In arriving at the amount payable, they may deduct the tax that has been accounted for already on the trust non-dividend income that is liable to the rate applicable to trusts and on the trust dividend income at the excess of the tax at the dividend trust rate of 32.5% over non-repayable tax credits (see Example 47 explanatory note 11 for further details). Note that the amount of tax deductible will not always cover the full amount of tax paid by the trustees, because the trustees' expenses have to come out of the taxed income of the trust. This is not relevant, however, where, as in the example, the expenses have come out of dividend income, so that the dividend credits are used to cover the tax, because the dividend credits, being non-repayable, are not taken into account under ss 497–498 in any event.

In many instances the 'pool' of tax under ss 497–498 will exceed the amount that is due, so that no amount will be payable, as shown in part (3) of the example. In this example there is the further point that the cost of investment advice was not allowable in calculating the tax due at the rate applicable to trusts, but nevertheless reduced the income available for distribution.

9.   From 6 April 1999 the fact that dividend credits are not repayable means that unless there is an unused pool of tax brought forward, the maximum distribution that can be made out of dividend income is 60%.

The effect on the amount available for beneficiaries in part (2) of the example is as follows:

	2007/08 £	2008/09 £
Tax credit inclusive dividend income (net of trust expenses)		
(2,762 – 500)	2,262	
(2,762 – 500)		2,262
Less: Tax credits 10%	226	226
Tax credit exclusive amounts	2,036	2,036
60% thereof	1,222	1,222
Amount shown as available for beneficiaries per part (2)	8,400	5,457
Dividend income included therein as above	2,262	2,262
Less: Tax at dividend trust rate of 32.5%	735	735
	1,527	1,527
Actual amount available as above	1,222	1,222

	2007/08 £	2008/09 £
Further reduction required	305	305
Reducing amount available for distribution to	8,095	5,152

As stated above, higher distributions could be made to the extent that the tax was covered by the pool of unutilised tax brought forward.

Tax credits on pre 6 April 1999 dividends *were* repayable and were thus included in the ss 497–498 pool. If those dividends had not been distributed before 6 April 1999, therefore, the credits will be available to cover tax on a post 5 April 1999 distribution.

FOTRA securities

10.   Government securities held by someone who is neither resident nor ordinarily resident in the UK are free of UK tax, such securities being referred to as FOTRA securities (ITTOIA 2005 ss 713–716 and ITTOIA 2005 ss 153, 713). If a discretionary trust holds such securities and makes distributions to beneficiaries who are both not resident and not ordinarily resident in the UK, then under Concession B18, a repayment claim may be made based upon the proportion of exempt income over total income (before charges) of tax credits attributed to distributions. Under the concession, the distribution is treated as made rateably out of income on a last in first out basis. Relief is available for payments out of income arising not earlier than 6 years before the end of the tax year of payment, providing the trustees have filed tax returns and paid all tax, interest, surcharges and penalties due. Claims must be made within five years from 31 January following the relevant tax year.

The claim by B re the distribution of £3,700 to him in 2008/09 will be regarded as relating wholly to the 2008/09 trust income, since that income exceeds the amount of the distribution.

The tax accounted for by the trustees for 2008/09 on the distribution of £3,700 is £2,467 per part (3) of the example. The repayment available to B is the proportion of that amount that the £900 interest on the Government Stock bears to the 2008/09 total income before charges of (21,512 − 6,000 =) £15,512 (the lease premium not being taken into account since it is a capital receipt). This amounts to £143 as shown in part (4) of the example.

Income paid to settlor's children

11.   Where income is paid to an unmarried minor child of the settlor, it is treated as income of the settlor in the year of distribution (ITTOIA 2005 ss 629, 631) and taxed as the highest part of that income (ITTOIA 2005 ss 619, 621, 623 – see Example 42 for details). Provided the trust is UK resident, full credit is given to the settlor for the tax paid by the trustees at the trust rate (ITA 2007 ss 497–498).

By Revenue concession A93 this treatment is extended to tax paid by non-resident trusts to the extent that the distribution to the child is made out of income that arose not earlier than 6 years before the end of the year of distribution (on a last in first out basis). Credit will be given to the extent that the distribution is made from income chargeable to UK tax and the trustees have complied with their UK obligations, ie filed tax returns and paid all tax, interest, surcharges and penalties due. No credit will be given for non-repayable tax, eg on dividends. Such tax will not, however, be taken into account in calculating the gross income taxable on the settlor under the concession. Claims under the concession must be made within five years from 31 January following the tax year in which the beneficiary received the payment from the trust.

Anti-avoidance provisions re payments made by discretionary trusts to companies

12.   To prevent companies circumventing the rules by routing dividends through discretionary trusts, thus receiving the income not in the form of dividends but as annual payments from which income tax had been deducted, ITA 2007 ss 497–498 provides that payments made to a *company* by a

discretionary trust are not liable to corporation tax in the receiving company's hands, but the income tax deducted from the payments by the trustees is not repayable. This does not apply if the recipient company is a charity, heritage body etc, and it only applies to a non-resident company if the payments would otherwise be chargeable to corporation tax as income of a UK branch or agency. It is not common for companies to receive payments from discretionary trusts, but these provisions are aimed at preventing possible abuse.

Changes to self assessment payments on account limits

13. SI 1996/1654 – Income Tax (Payments on Account) Regulations 1996 is amended by the making of a regulation to raise the figure at regulation 3 from £500 to £1,000.

    This will come into force for self-assessment payments on account (POA) from 2009/10 and later years.

    The regulation has effect on and after 6 April 2009 for income tax due for 2009/10. The first payments on account affected will therefore be those due in January 2010 and July 2010.

Question

A.

Mrs Spencer, who was born on 3 April 1937, has a life interest in income under a will trust established by her late husband who died on 30 May 2007.

The trust fund consists of loan stocks and similar securities having a nominal value of £50,000, the interest on which is received gross. In addition a small building society deposit account is held on which interest is received net of income tax.

During the year to 5 April 2009 the trustees had the following transactions:

(i)   On 16 December 2008 contracted to purchase £69,780 nominal of 7% Treasury Stock for settlement on 17 December 2008. The interest payment dates of this stock are 22 May and 22 November.

(ii) On 5 May 2008 contracted to sell £2,059 nominal National Midland 9% Unsecured Loan Stock for settlement on 6 May 2008. The interest payment dates of this stock are 30 June and 31 December.

During the year to 5 April 2009 the trustees received the following income (no expenses being incurred):

	£
Building society interest received (net)	400
Gross income from securities	5,000

Mrs Spencer's only other income comes from state and occupational pensions totalling £17,000 gross less tax deducted of £2,000 for 2008/09.

(a)   Compute the accrued income relief or charge on the will trust and state how this will be dealt with.

(b)   Compute the income tax payable by or repayable to Mrs Spencer for 2008/09.

B.

Outline the tax problems for trusts in relation to:

(a)   Scrip dividends.

(b)   Demergers.

Answer

A.   **Mrs Spencer – accrued income scheme**

(a)   **Accrued income relief or charge on will trust**

Purchase of Treasury Stock:

Interest accrued to date of settlement	23.11.08 to 17.12.08	=	25 days

$$\text{Accrued } 7\% \times £69,780 = £4,885 \times \frac{25}{365} \qquad = \qquad £334$$

Trustees are entitled to accrued income relief on this amount.

Sale of National Midland Stock:

Interest accrued to date of settlement	1.1.08 to 6.5.08	=	127 days

$$\text{Accrued } 9\% \times £2,059 = £185 \times \frac{127}{366} \qquad = \qquad £64$$

Trustees are liable to an accrued income charge on this amount.

Taxation treatment:

Accrued income charges and reliefs are taken into account in the tax year in which the next interest payment date falls after the settlement date. Accrued income charges are taxed at the rate applicable to trusts (see note 1). Accrued income relief is given by reducing the assessable interest. Charges and reliefs are not netted off unless they relate to the same kind of stock with the same interest payment dates.

The first receipt of interest on the 7% Treasury Stock will be in May 2009. From that income accrued income relief of £334 will be deducted, the balance being taxable as trust income of 2009/10. If the stock is sold before May 2009 then the accrued income relief will be deducted from the accrued income charge on sale.

The next interest payment date on the National Midland Stock was June 2008, so the £64 is taxed in 2008/09 and is liable to tax at the rate applicable to trusts of 40%. By ITA 2007 s 491(3)(5) accrued income is to be treated as income chargeable at the lower rate for the standard rate band charge. Accordingly the liability will be £64 @ 20%. The accrued income will not be assessed on Mrs Spencer, because although it is taxed as income it actually represents an accretion to capital (which is why it is taxed at the rate applicable to trusts).

As both stocks are exempt from capital gains tax no related adjustments for that tax are required.

(b)   Income tax payable by or repayable to Mrs Spencer for 2008/09

			£	Tax paid £
Pension income			17,000	2,000
Will trust (savings income):				
Securities		5,000		
Building society interest		500	5,500	100
Total income			22,500	2,100
Age allowance 9,030 less half of (22,500 – 21,800)			8,680	
			13,820	
Tax thereon:	8,320	@ 20% basic rate	1,664	
Savings income	5,500	@ 20%	1,100	2,764
Tax payable				664

B.   (a)   Scrip dividends

Where a UK resident company offers scrip shares as an alternative to a cash dividend, certain shareholders taking the scrip option are treated as having income equal to the 'appropriate amount in cash' (ITTOIA 2005 s 411). This means the amount of the cash option, unless it differs by more than 15% from the market value of the shares (ITTOIA 2005 ss 410–413), in which case the deemed income is the market value of the shares on the first day of dealing. The notional income is deemed to be net of the dividend ordinary rate of tax of 10% and is grossed up accordingly. The grossing addition represents a notional tax credit, which is not repayable to non-taxpayers.

This treatment applies where an *individual* is beneficially entitled to the *shares*, or where the shares are received by personal representatives or by trustees for whom a cash dividend would be liable at the 'dividend trust rate' under ITA 2007 s 9.

Where the shares are treated as income, the 'appropriate amount in cash', before grossing up, is treated as the capital gains cost of the scrip shares. Such scrip dividend shares are treated as a separate free-standing acquisition and are not added pro-rata to existing holdings (TCGA 1992 s 142).

As far as life interest trusts are concerned, the trustees must decide whether, in the light of trust and general law and the terms of the particular trust, the shares are received as capital or income.

HMRC's Statement of Practice (SP 4/94) gives their view of the position. They will not seek to challenge the view taken by the trustees (providing the facts support that view) if they have treated the scrip shares either as belonging to the life tenant, or as belonging to trust capital, or as being part of trust capital, but with the life tenant being compensated for the loss of the cash dividend he would have had.

If life tenant is treated as beneficially entitled to the shares

If the life tenant is treated as beneficially entitled to the shares, the trustees would be regarded as holding the shares as bare trustees (except in Scotland, where different rules apply). Any transfer to the beneficiary would therefore be disregarded. For income tax purposes the life tenant would have notional income equal to the appropriate amount in cash. For capital gains tax, the shares would not form part of the trust holding and the life tenant would be regarded as having purchased the shares separately for the 'appropriate amount in cash'. Any sale of the shares by the trustees would be regarded as a sale by the life tenant, so if the shares were sold at the time of issue under the terms of a cash offer from a broker, the last in first out identification rule would apply (see below), there would be no taper relief and there would in fact be an allowable loss because the amount paid by the broker would be less than the issue price of the shares.

If shares are treated as belonging to trust capital

If the trustees treat the shares as belonging to trust capital, there are no income tax implications and the shares are treated as normal scrip shares for capital gains tax and added to the trust's existing holding at a *nil cost*, so that the whole of their value will represent a capital gain on disposal. The trust's position when the shares are disposed of will depend on whether they have exemptions etc available to cover the potential gain. The tax liability (at present tax rates) could be nil or 40%.

If shares are treated as belonging to trust capital with cash payment to life tenant

If the trustees treat the shares as capital, but make a cash payment to the life tenant to compensate him for not getting the dividend, the treatment of the shares is the same as in the previous paragraph. The cash payment to the life tenant is not, however, an income dividend but a payment out of trust capital, so that income tax must be deducted at 20%. There may still be a problem with how much cash to pay, because if the life tenant is a basic rate taxpayer, the effective tax rate on actual dividends is only 10%. The trustees must account for the tax on the payment under ITA 2007 s 963 (see Example 44 part B), and will show the payment separately on the form R185 issued to the life tenant.

If shares are treated as belonging to capital and immediately sold

FA 2008 s 8 and Sch 2 simplifies the rules for pooling of shares.

The changes mean that in identifying securities disposed of after 5 April 2008, all identical securities owned are treated as part of a single pool (a *section 104 holding*), and the allowable expenditure in respect of that holding will be the sum of:

- the market value at 31 March 1982 of all securities in the section 104 holding that were held at that date; and

- the actual cost or CGT acquisition value of all securities in the section 104 holding acquired from April 1982 onwards.

Where there is an existing section 104 holding at 5 April 2008, the record of the holding should distinguish between the original cost and indexed cost. It is the original cost (not the indexed cost) of an existing section 104 holding that is taken into account in computing the allowable expenditure in a revised section 104 holding from 6 April 2008 onwards.

Where there were any additions to a section 104 holding between 30 November 1993 and 5 April 2008 under transactions (such as transfers between husband and wife or post-December 2005 – civil partners) that are treated for capital gains tax purposes as giving rise to neither a gain nor a loss to the person making the disposal, the amount of the original cost will not include any element of indexation allowance. (In such cases the indexation element was added to the indexed cost of the holding separately from the original cost.)

The abolition of the kink test, indexation allowance, and taper relief simplifies the existing pooling rules. The single *section 104 holding* includes all shares acquired before the date of disposal, and the order of matching is now:

- assets acquired on the date of disposal;

- assets acquired in the 30 days following the date of disposal; and

- assets in the enlarged section 104 holding.

The primary effect of s 104 (as amended by para 85) is to provide that a holding of 'securities' (s 104 uses 'securities' to refer to assets such as shares) is treated as a single asset, growing or diminishing as securities are acquired and disposed of. Before the changes, for CGT purposes a section 104 holding could not contain securities acquired before 6 April 1982, nor after 5 April 1998.

Para 85 adds a new subsection (3A) to s 104. The effect of this subsection is that TCGA 1992 s 35(2) of applies to securities in a section 104 holding that were held at 31 March 1982. This means that the acquisition cost of those securities taken into account in computing the allowable expenditure in relation to the section 104 holding is their market value at 31 March 1982.

Para 87 amends s 106A, which gives the identification and ordering rules for CGT purposes and provides and similarly para 86 amends s 105 in that securities acquired that are identified under s 106A(5) with securities disposed of in the 30 days preceding that acquisition, cannot form part of a section 104 holding.

The simplification of the rules for identification of securities means that the LIFO rule is no longer required for securities in a section 104 holding, as there is a single asset, the section 104 holding, and no ordering rules are required.

Discretionary and accumulation trusts

The treatment of scrip dividends received by discretionary and accumulation trusts is not clear. As indicated in the second paragraph of this section, such trusts are treated as having notional income under ITTOIA 2005 ss 409–414) if a cash dividend would have been income to which ITA 2007 s 9 applies, the notional income being regarded as accompanied by a notional tax credit at 10% of the tax credit inclusive amount. If, however, the scrip dividend is required under the terms of the trust to be treated as trust capital, there is an argument that it cannot be charged to the dividend trust rate under ITA 2007 s 9 (but that even so, since the scrip shares are within ITTOA 2005 ss 409–414, they would be treated as a free-standing acquisition for capital gains tax with a base cost equal to the 'appropriate amount in cash'). The Revenue do not share this view, and consider that the trustees are liable to tax at the excess of the dividend trust rate of 32.5% over the grossed up amount of the scrip dividend, so that a further 22.5% tax is payable. Only the tax actually paid is taken into account when calculating how much tax is payable by the trustees under ITA 2007 ss 497–498 on distributions to beneficiaries (see Example 42 for further details). The shares have a base cost for capital gains tax equal to the appropriate amount in cash and are treated as a free-standing acquisition, disposals being matched with acquisitions according to the rules of TCGA 1992 s 106A outlined above.

In the case of *Red Discretionary Trustees v HMIT* (2003) Sp C 397, IHT, the discretionary trust received a stock dividend. The settlement trustees elected to receive dividends consisting of further shares in the relevant company. The market value of the stock dividends represented taxable income — the Trust return was submitted on the basis that the stock dividend was taxable at the ordinary trust rate but the Inland Revenue amended the return to increase income tax payable to the dividend trust rate. The Special Commissioners dismissed the trustee's appeal and confirmed that the dividends were taxable at the higher dividend trust rate. This decision was confirmed by the Court of Appeal in *Howell v Trippier* (2004).

(b) Demergers

Demergers treated as exempt distributions

There is specific legislation in relation to demergers in TA 1988 ss 213–218. The legislation prevents some of the tax problems that a demerger would otherwise cause. Providing the relevant conditions are satisfied, a demerger may be classed as an 'exempt distribution', and in that event the distribution is not treated as income in the hands of the shareholders. For capital gains tax it is treated either as a reorganisation under TCGA 1992 ss 126–131 (by s 192) or a reconstruction under TCGA 1992 ss 136 and 139, depending on the type of demerger, and there is therefore neither chargeable gain nor allowable loss.

Direct demergers and indirect demergers

Demergers may either be direct demergers, where a company distributes shares in one or more 75% subsidiaries direct to its shareholders, or indirect demergers, where a company transfers either a trade or shares in its 75% subsidiaries to another company and that other company makes an issue of shares to the transferor company's shareholders.

Where there is a direct distribution in the form of shares, the shares are regarded as income in the hands of trustees (although exempt from tax as indicated above). It was, however, held in the case of *Sinclair v Lee* (1993) that this did not apply to an indirect demerger. The case related to ICI/Zeneca, where ICI transferred shares in its wholly owned subsidiary Zeneca Ltd to Zeneca Group plc (which was not ICI's subsidiary), and Zeneca Group plc issued shares to ICI shareholders. On the facts, this was held to be a capital distribution, the ICI holding being split for capital gains purposes into separate ICI/Zeneca holdings according to the market value of the shares on the first day after the demerger (for unquoted shares the relevant date would be the date of disposal).

This does not, however, determine the treatment of trust holdings for all demergers and it is necessary to look at the particular circumstances, and also the provisions of the particular trust. The Revenue made a detailed statement of their views in the October 1994 issue of the Tax Bulletin, a summary of which follows.

Where there is a direct demerger, the shares are regarded as *income* of the trust, because under company law they are a dividend paid out of accumulated profits. If, exceptionally, they were treated as capital, the capital gains tax treatment for the trustees would be as for individuals.

In an indirect demerger, the Revenue view is that the shares would normally be an addition to capital (following *Sinclair v Lee*), the capital gains treatment of the trustees being the same as for individuals, but this is not necessarily true of all indirect demergers.

Discretionary trusts

The trustees are treated in the same way as individuals, ie they are not liable to income tax or capital gains tax. If shares are then distributed to beneficiaries, they are treated for capital gains tax as a disposal of a proportionate part of the holding at market value, the cost plus the available indexation allowance for that part of the holding being allowed against the deemed proceeds.

If the trustees exercise a power to accumulate the 'income' as part of the trust fund, and later distribute the shares as capital, no income tax arises. If the shares are distributed as income rather than accumulated, the distribution is treated as being net of 40% tax (the value of the distribution being the lower of the value at the date of the demerger and the value when distributed). Since income tax will not have been paid on the demerged shares under ITA 2007 s 9, the trustees may have to pay tax under ITA 2007 s 497/498 (unless there is a sufficient fund of tax already accounted for). (See Example 48 for details of ITA 2007 s 9 and ss 497–498.)

Life interest trusts

The following relates to the treatment of English life interest trusts. (Different rules apply in Scotland.)

In a direct demerger, the shares would belong to the life tenant directly, so they would not form part of the trust's holding, the capital gains tax cost of which is unaffected. The life tenant would be treated for capital gains as acquiring the shares at market value at the date of the demerger (the distribution being other than at arm's length – TCGA 1992 s 17(1)), even though there would have been no reduction of the trustees' allowable cost. (If the trustees retained the shares, there would be a disposal of them by the life tenant to the trustees, and unless he was paid their cash value, he would be the settlor of shares into the trust.)

In an indirect demerger, the shares would usually be treated as capital as indicated above, so that they would not affect the life tenant. If *exceptionally* they were treated as income, the capital gains tax position would be the same as for a direct demerger, except that s 17(1) would not apply (because there would be no disposal by the transferor company *directly* to the shareholder), and the beneficiary's capital gains tax cost would be nil.

For direct demergers, there would be no income tax on the life tenants nor on the trustees under ITA 2007 ss 9, 497, 498, since the shares are treated as belonging to the life tenant. The same would apply where, exceptionally, shares are treated as income in an indirect demerger. If the shares are treated as capital, the trustees would have no income tax liability. If, however, they then distributed the shares under provisions in the trust deed, such that the shares were income in the hands of the life tenant, the trustees would have to deduct tax and pay it over to the Revenue under s 963.

Explanatory Notes

Accrued income scheme

1.   The accrued income scheme provisions are in ITA 2007 ss 616–681.

The accrued income scheme causes particular difficulties in relation to trusts. The scheme treats amounts that are capital sums under the general (and trust) law as being income for tax purposes and tax is charged (or refunded) accordingly.

The fact that the sums are to be accumulated as part of capital, rather than being income of a beneficiary, is, however, recognised by ITA 2007 s 482, which provides that the trustees are taxed in respect of accrued income charges at the rate applicable to trusts, ie 40%. However ITA 2007 s 491(3)(5) provides that for the standard rate such deemed income is chargeable at the basic rate. Mrs Spencer's trust is only liable to tax at special trust rates on accrued income of £64, as this is less than £500. The whole is chargeable at the basic rate (ie 20%).

These rules can lead to an anomaly. The trustees could receive a reduction for accrued income relief at lower rate but be liable at special rate on an amount in excess of £500 and have to pay tax at 40% on the excess. Individuals are charged at the savings rate on accrued interest, but this does not apply to trustees.

Because the accrued income charges represent capital sums, they do not form part of a beneficiary's income and are not shown on form R185.

The trustees then have the problem of how to deal with accrued income charges and accrued income reliefs in the trust accounts. The Accounting Recommendations of the Institute of Chartered Accountants state that where a life tenant may be interested in such accruals, consideration should be given to accounting for the interest and the associated tax on an accruals basis when the securities are purchased and sold. The alternative view, which the authors prefer, is that the accruals treatment should not apply to accrued income charges, and that the tax on accrued income charges should be debited to the capital account of the trust as it would have been if it had been capital gains tax.

There is also doubt as to the treatment of accrued income relief. The relief reduces the trustees' income for tax purposes as shown in part A (a) above, and the beneficiary's income for tax purposes is similarly reduced, so that in 2009/10 Mrs Spencer's interest from the 7% Treasury Stock shown on form R185 will be the gross interest of (7% × £69,780 =) £4,885, reduced by £334, giving taxable income of £4,551. Tax thereon amounts to £910 compared with tax on £4,885 of £977. The reduction of £334 at 20% = £67 in the tax payable will have been reflected in the amount payable by the trustees under self-assessment. If tax had been deducted at source from the interest, the trustees would have a tax refund of £67. The question then is how much should the trustees actually pay to Mrs Spencer. HMRC have stated that this is a matter for the trustees in accordance with the general law, and whatever is paid will not affect the tax treatment. There are several possibilities:

(a)   Taxable income £4,551 less tax £910 = £3,641.

(b)   Actual gross income £4,885 less tax thereon £977 = £3,908.

(c)   As (b) plus tax reduction of £67 = £3,975.

The trustees have actually received net income of £3,908 and have had a tax reduction of £67, and some people therefore favour paying the beneficiary £3,975 as in (c). Before the introduction of the accrued income scheme, however, the part of the purchase price representing accrued interest, ie £334, would have been part of the capital cost of the security. The authors take the view that the logical approach is to regard the £67 as a reduction in the cost and to pay to the beneficiary what would previously have been paid, ie £3,908. Thus both accrued income charges and accrued income reliefs would be dealt with through the trust capital account.

Scope of accrued income provisions

2.   The accrued income provisions apply to 'transfers'. This means 'transfer by way of sale, exchange, gift or otherwise' (ITA 2007 s 620(1)(2)), and would include a settlement of securities by an individual, and a transfer of securities to beneficiaries on termination of a trust, as well as the trustees buying and selling the trust securities. The provisions do not apply where securities are vested in an individual's personal representatives on his death (ITA 2007 s 620(1)(2)). Nor do they apply if the personal representatives transfer the securities to legatees or to those entitled on an intestacy in the interest period in which the individual died (ITA 2007 s 636). There is no exemption for a transfer in a later interest period.

Scrip dividends and demergers

3.   The problems of trustees who receive scrip dividends or shares on a demerger are outlined in part B of the example. The Revenue have given detailed comments on their views, but there are many grey areas which it would be difficult to resolve, even with amended legislation, because of the mismatch between trust law and tax law.

     As far as scrip dividends are concerned, where the shares are worth the same as the cash dividend, the simple way to avoid problems is to take the cash. The enhanced scrip dividends which were offered by listed companies a few years ago were worth half as much again as the cash dividend, and there was the option of obtaining the extra cash by selling immediately, thus giving rise to the particular problems mentioned in the example. Such offers have not been made recently, although enhanced scrip offers may arise in other circumstances.

Purchase by company of own shares etc

4.   Where a company redeems, repays or purchases its own shares from the trustees of a settlement, the excess of the amount paid over the original issue price is treated as if it were an income distribution with a notional tax credit attached, and the trustees are liable to tax at the excess of the dividend trust rate of 32.5% over the tax credit rate of 10%, so that a further 22.5% is payable (ITA 2007 ss 481–482). This does not apply where the trust income is treated as belonging to the settlor, or where the trust is a unit trust, charitable trust, or pension trust (or presumably where the trust is a bare trust — see Example 64 explanatory note 8), but it applies to all other trusts, including interest in possession trusts.

     If the purchase is by an unquoted trading company in order to benefit its trade, and specified conditions are satisfied, the purchase is treated as a chargeable disposal for capital gains tax rather than as an income distribution (TA 1988 ss 219 to 229).

Cross references

5.   See Example 44 explanatory note 4 for the provisions that apply for receiving interest gross on government stocks, Example 43 explanatory note 7 for the provisions that apply for receiving interest gross on listed company securities and Example 47 for the self-assessment provisions in relation to trusts.

Question

A.

The termination of a life interest in settled property can occur in various circumstances, including:

(a)   where, on the death of the life tenant, the settlement (or a part) comes to an end,

(b)   where, on the life tenant's death, there is a successive life tenancy,

(c)   where the life tenant dies and the property passes to the original settlor, and

(d)   where the interest ceases otherwise than on the death of the life tenant.

State the capital gains tax situation in each of the events (a) to (d) above, giving appropriate statutory references.

B.

Where capital gains tax is payable by trustees, state the position regarding the capital gains tax rate and the annual exemption, and indicate the position if the settlor has retained an interest in the settlement.

Answer

A.   Termination of life interests in settled property — capital gains tax treatment

(a)   Where the settlement or part thereof comes to an end on the death of the life tenant

The settled property to which someone becomes entitled is deemed to be disposed of at market value and immediately reacquired by the trustees, but no chargeable gain (or allowable loss) arises on the disposal except as indicated below (TCGA 1992 ss 71–73). In other words there is an adjustment to the base cost of the settled property and the trustees then hold that property as bare trustees for the person entitled thereto.

Where the asset disposed of, or part thereof, was the subject of a claim for gifts holdover relief under TCGA 1992 s 165 or s 260 when the trustees acquired it, then a chargeable gain will arise, restricted to the amount of the heldover gain.

Where the life interest did not extend to the whole of the settled property to which someone became entitled on the life tenant's death, then there is no exemption from the capital gains charge on the deemed disposal, but any gain arising is reduced by a proportion representing the life tenant's interest (TCGA 1992 s 73).

A further instance where a chargeable gain arises is where deferral relief has been claimed in respect of a subscription for enterprise investment scheme shares (see explanatory note 7).

(b)   Where, on the life tenant's death, there is a successive life tenancy

The consequences are similar to those in (a) above. The settled property is deemed to be disposed of at market value and immediately reacquired by the trustees, but no chargeable gain arises on the disposal (TCGA 1992 s 72), other than any gain held over under the gifts holdover provisions (TCGA 1992 s 74) or enterprise investment scheme deferral relief provisions (see explanatory note 7).

(c)   Where the life tenant dies and the property passes to the original settlor

There is a deemed disposal and reacquisition of the settled property as in (a) above, but the consideration is deemed to be such that no gain or loss accrues to the trustees.

Where the property reverts to the settlor after 31 March 1982 then the original settlor is also deemed to have held the assets on 31 March 1982 (providing the settlement actually owned the assets on that date). Therefore on a subsequent disposal by the original settlor it is possible to treat the assets as acquired at market value as at 31 March 1982 even though the assets were actually owned by the settlement on that date.

(d)   Where the life interest ceases otherwise than on the death of the life tenant

Such a termination has no capital gains tax effect if the property remains in trust, and the capital gains tax base value of the property remains the same. If, however, a beneficiary becomes absolutely entitled to any property against the trustees at that time, there is a deemed disposal and reacquisition at market value as bare trustees, and the trustees are chargeable to capital gains tax accordingly (TCGA 1992 s 71). A claim may, however, be made by the trustees and beneficiary jointly for any gain to be held over under the provisions of TCGA 1992 s 165 and Sch 7 if the property consists of any of the following:

Assets used in a business by the trustees or the life tenant

Unquoted shares in a trading company

Shares in a trading company in which the trustees hold 25% or more of the voting rights Property that would qualify for agricultural property relief (Sch 7.1–7.3).

Where a beneficiary becomes absolutely entitled, s 71(2) is amended by FA 1999 s 75 to provide that:

(i)   Losses on actual disposals by the trustees before the beneficiary becomes absolutely entitled cannot be transferred to the beneficiary. Such losses will remain losses of the trustees, for which relief may be obtained within the trust according to the normal rules.

(ii) Losses arising on the deemed market value transfer to the beneficiary that the trustees cannot use against gains arising at the time of the transfer of the property or earlier in the same tax year will be treated as made by the beneficiary who has become absolutely entitled to the asset, but the beneficiary will be able to use the loss only to reduce a gain on the disposal of the asset, or in the case of land, an asset derived from the land.

These changes were made to prevent abuse of the rules by artificial schemes enabling people unconnected with a trust to purchase the trust losses, including schemes set up specifically to manufacture losses within trusts to be used in this way.

See explanatory note 3 re the connected persons rules.

If someone with an interest in a settlement (either a life interest or a reversionary interest) sells his interest, the disposal is not subject to capital gains tax (unless the interest was acquired for money or money's worth) (TCGA 1992 s 76(1)). The exemption does not, however, apply to disposals on or after 6 March 1998 of an interest in a trust whose trustees have at any time been not resident or not ordinarily resident in the UK (s 76(1A), (1B)). If a reversionary interest was purchased, then when the purchaser becomes absolutely entitled to the assets of the settlement, he is deemed to have disposed of his interest for the then market value of the assets (TCGA 1992 s 76(2)). This charge is in addition to any charge on the trustees under TCGA 1992 s 71 (as above). The assets to which the purchaser becomes entitled then have a base value equal to that market value.

If the disposal takes place at a time when the trustees are neither resident nor ordinarily resident in the UK, then the exemption in s 76(1) does not apply, even if the interest in the settlement was not acquired for money or money's worth (TCGA 1992 s 85). Some relief is, however, available in certain circumstances where the trust became non-resident after 18 March 1991 (s 85(2)–(9)).

The treatment of the disposal for a consideration of an interest in settled property was changed for certain disposals on or after 21 March 2000 by TCGA 1992 s 76A and Schedule 4A. The revised provisions apply where the trust is UK resident or ordinarily resident in the tax year of disposal, the settlor is or has been resident or ordinarily resident in the UK in the current year or in any of the previous five tax years (excluding years before 1999/2000), and the settlor has an interest in the trust (or has had an interest at any time in the period commencing two years before the start of the tax year of disposal and ending with the date of disposal, excluding any period before 6 April 1999). Where a beneficiary sells an interest in such a trust, the trustees are deemed to dispose of and reacquire all the trust assets at market value, and the settlor is charged on the resulting gains (unless the disposal is of an interest in a specific fund, in which case the deemed disposal relates to the assets in that fund, or the disposal is an interest in a specific fraction of the income or capital, in which case the deemed disposal is of that fraction of the underlying assets). The settlor will not be able to claim gifts holdover relief in respect of the gains. He may, however, recover from the trustees the tax suffered (TCGA 1992 s 78), and they in turn may recover the tax from the beneficiary who sold the interest (Sch 4A.11).

B.   Capital gains tax rate etc

Charging gains to tax

Subject to what follows, and what is said below regarding trusts in which the settlor retains an interest, trustees are chargeable to tax on their chargeable gains less allowable losses as for individuals. There are anti-avoidance provisions in TCGA 1992 s 79A that prevent losses arising on trustees' disposals being set against gains they make on assets that had been transferred to the trust if the transferor or someone connected with him had bought an interest in the trust and had claimed gifts holdover relief on the transferred assets.

The capital gains tax rate for trusts is 18%, except where gains are taxed on a settlor as indicated below (TCGA 1992 s 4). The 18% rate also applies to personal representatives of a deceased's estate.

Trusts in which settlor retains an interest

Where both the settlor and the trustees are resident or ordinarily resident in the UK and the settlor or spouse has or may have a present or future interest in the income or property of the settlement, or enjoys a benefit from the settlement (eg free use of property or an interest-free loan) then the chargeable gains of the settlement are treated as belonging to the settlor). (This is subject to an exception in respect of income from assets given or interest free or low interest rate loans made to charity – see Example 46 notes 5 and 6. See also Example 51 explanatory note 16 re anti-avoidance provisions to prevent the settlor avoiding the charge to tax.)

Gains in the tax year in which the settlor dies are not attributed to the settlor under the above provisions. In addition if the interest or benefit relates to the spouse (and not the settlor) the provisions do not apply to gains made in the tax year in which the spouse dies or the settlor and spouse divorce.

FA 2004 s 116 and Sch 21 introduce a restriction of gift relief into the provisions of TCGA 1992 s 165 or s 260 in respect of the disposal of assets preventing gift relief being available in respect of disposals of assets to the trustees of a trust in which the settlor has an interest where the disposal is made on or after 10 December 2003.

These provisions claw back or prevent any gifts relief in relation to disposals to trusts which become settlor-interested settlements within a certain time period.

This period begins immediately after the disposal and ends immediately before the sixth anniversary of the start of the tax year next following that in which the disposal is made.

There are exclusions from the provisions in disposals to settlements benefiting disabled persons or which provide maintenance income for historic buildings.

FA 2004 s 117 and Sch 22 are intended to complement and extend s 116 and Sch 21.

The effect is to prevent private residence relief (PPR) being available in certain circumstances where the trustees of a settlement make a disposal.

The circumstances arise where the computation of the amount of any gains arising on the disposal has to take account of gift relief obtained in respect of an earlier disposal.

This is subject to a transitional provision restricting the amount of relief available in respect of the disposal if there has been no earlier disposal on or after 10 December 2003.

These provisions do not apply where the gain arising on the disposal in not in any way affected by a gifts relief claim under TCGA 1992 s 260.

Capital gains tax annual exemption

Where tax is chargeable in the name of the trustees on a heldover gain, or under the provisions in part A (d) above, or on disposals of trust assets by the trustees, the trustees can claim an annual exemption equal to half the amount exempt for an individual, ie £4,800 for 2008/09.

If, however, the same person is the settlor in relation to more than one trust created after 6 June 1978 (excluding charitable trusts), the exemption of £4,800 is divided between those trusts, with a minimum exempt slice for each trust of £960 (TCGA 1992 Sch 1.2(3)). This rule applies to settlements arising under a will or intestacy as well as those created in lifetime.

If the trust is a trust for the disabled, the full annual exemption of £9,600 is available, reduced pro rata if there is more than one disabled trust established by the same settlor after 9 March 1981, with a minimum slice for each trust of £960 (TCGA 1992 Sch 1.1).

No trust annual exemption is available if the settlor has retained an interest in the trust, as indicated above.

Explanatory Notes

Types of trust and amendments to IHT and CGT treatment in Finance Act 2006

1.   The main types of trust are bare trusts, trusts with an interest in possession, discretionary trusts and accumulation and maintenance trusts.

Where someone is a bare trustee this means that the beneficiary is absolutely entitled to the trust property as against the trustee. The capital gains treatment is therefore to look through the trust and to deem the trustee's acts as being those of the beneficiary (TCGA 1992 s 60). For further details see Example 64.

Most interest in possession trusts are life interest trusts, but sometimes an interest may cease earlier, for example if a widow remarries. The treatment of life interest trusts in part A of the example applies to *all* interest in possession trusts and also on the death of an annuitant (TCGA 1992 ss 72, 73).

Inheritance Tax Act 1984 (TA) sets out the rules for discretionary trusts (strictly, 'relevant property' trusts). These include:

- an immediate 'entry' tax charge of 20% on lifetime transfers that exceed the inheritance tax (IHT) threshold into'relevant property' trusts;

- a 'periodic' tax charge of 6% on the value of trust assets over the IHT threshold once every ten years; and

- an 'exit' charge proportionate to the periodic charge when funds are taken out of a trust between ten year anniversaries.

However, there are special rules for 'interest in possession' (IIP) accumulation & maintenance (A&M) trusts, which are now of limited application. Lifetime transfers into some privileged trusts are exempt from IHT if the settlor survives seven years, and the trusts are not subject to the periodic or exit charges.

FA 2006, Sch 20 provides that these special rules will in future be limited to trusts that are created:

(a)   on death by a parent for a minor child who will be fully entitled to the assets in the trust at age 18, or

(b)   on death for the benefit of one life tenant in order of time only (more than one such interest may be created on death as long as the trust capital vests absolutely when the life interest comes to an end), or

(c)   either in the settlor's lifetime or on death for a disabled person.

The IHT treatment for trusts which do not come within these rules have been brought into line with the mainstream IHT rules for 'relevant property' trusts. These changes took effect from 22 March 2006, subject to transitional arrangements for some pre-existing trusts.

IHTA 1984 s 49 (which treats property subject to an interest-in-possession as owned for IHT purposes by the person having the interest) is restricted to a specified class of trusts where the interest arises on or after 22 March 2006, namely:

(i)   an 'immediate post-death interest (49A)',

(ii)   a 'disabled person's interest (89A)', or

(iii)   a 'transitional serial interest (49B–49E)'.

IHTA 1984 s 49A, which sets out the conditions to be satisfied by an 'immediate post-death interest' (IPDI) is expanded: broadly, so that the interest arises immediately on the death of the settlor. This applies to interests created by a will or on intestacy.

Section 49C includes tests for transitional protection as a 'transitional serial interest' (TSI). An interest in possession arising before 6 October 2008 will qualify if it arises on or after 22 March 2006 but follows a previous interest in possession in effect before that date. Alternatively, s 49D covers transitional serial interests where the new interest arises on or after 6 October 2008. This is, however, limited to cases where the second interest is held by the widow or surviving civil partner and acquired on the death of the previous life tenant.

Broadly, where existing A&M trusts provide that the assets in trust will go to a beneficiary absolutely at 18 — or where the terms on which they are held were modified before 6 April 2008 to provide this — their current IHT treatment will continue.

For a new A&M trust if the capital is left on fully flexible trust with no set date for the beneficiary to become absolutely entitled, the trust will become subject to the 6% rule on the death of the parent and will remain so until the beneficiary is paid out.

For new and old A&M type arrangements, the trusts will not become subject to the 6% regime until the child reaches age 18 and this will continue until they become absolutely entitled at age 25. There will be no 20% entry charge. However, for new arrangements (ie trust property settled after 21 March 2006), this applies only if one of the child's parents has died and the trust was established under the will of the parent or under the Criminal Injuries Compensation Scheme.

For existing A&M settlements where beneficiaries are under age 18 at the end of the transitional period on 6 April 2008, they will not be subject to the 6% charge until they reach age 18 provided the trust is modified before 6 April 2008.

The new IHT rules for trusts have consequences for capital gains tax (CGT). Some of the necessary changes will happen automatically — for example, transfers into and out of trusts that will now come within the 'relevant property' rules will automatically be eligible for CGT hold-over relief.

There is an amendment to the current CGT treatment of trust property on the death of a person having an interest-in-possession so that for interests created on or after 22 March 2006 it applies only to the above categories of IIP. The rule at TCGA 1992 s 72 is amended. This applies when a life interest comes to an end but the property continues to be held on trust; and there is a further amendment to the rule at s 73 which applies where the property ceases to be held on trust once the life interest comes to an end.

2.   Trustees are treated as a continuing body of persons distinct from those who may from time to time occupy the position of trustee, and gains arising on the disposal of trust assets are assessable on the trustees (other than bare trustees, as indicated in note 1 above, or trusts in which the settlor retains an interest) (TCGA 1992 s 69).

Creation of settlement

3.   When a settlement is created the settlor is deemed to have disposed of the entire property in the settlement at its market value, even if he retains an interest as beneficiary or is a trustee under the settlement, and he is therefore chargeable to capital gains tax accordingly (subject to any available reliefs and exemptions).

If the assets transferred are business assets (as defined by TCGA 1992 s 165) or the transfer is *immediately* chargeable to inheritance tax (whether or not there is any actual inheritance tax payable (TCGA 1992 s 260)) then the settlor can avoid paying tax on the gain by making an election to hold it over so that it reduces the trustees' base acquisition cost, and unlike other gifts relief elections the donees do not have to join in the election. For gifts into settlement on or after 10 December 2003 this facility is not available if the settlor retains an interest or the trust becomes settlor related within six years. Where the trust is a life interest trust or an accumulation and maintenance trust, gifts holdover relief is not available under s 260 (because the transfers are *potentially exempt* from inheritance tax), so gains on chargeable assets may only be held over if the assets are qualifying business assets under s 165.

In a life interest trust, the heldover gains crystallise when the life tenant dies, as indicated in part A of the example (subject to any further holdover relief claim). In a discretionary trust, the heldover gains are similarly triggered when assets are transferred to beneficiaries (see note 5).

If the settlor's disposal gives rise to losses rather than gains, then under the 'connected persons' rules, the losses can only be set against gains on other disposals to the trustees. The trustees are, however, no longer connected with the settlor's spouse and relatives after the settlor's death. If the trustees and beneficiaries *are* connected, this does not prevent the trustees' losses arising from the disposal to the beneficiaries being transferred to the beneficiaries under TCGA 1992 s 71(2), as indicated in part A (d) of the example.

Emigration of trustees

4. Emigrating trustees are charged not only on gains held over at the time the funds were settled but on the whole of any increase in value of the trust assets up to the time of emigration (TCGA 1992 s 80). For detailed notes on non-resident trusts see Example 51.

Persons becoming absolutely entitled to trust property

5. TCGA 1992 s 71 applies not only when a beneficiary under an interest in possession trust becomes absolutely entitled as against the trustees, as outlined in part A (d) of the example, but also where a beneficiary of a discretionary trust becomes so entitled. The trustees are deemed to have disposed of the assets to the beneficiary at market value at that time and are chargeable to capital gains tax accordingly.

The gifts holdover relief provisions of ss 165 and 260 outlined in note 3 are, however, available if the conditions are satisfied. The distribution from the discretionary trust will be a chargeable event for inheritance tax, triggering an exit charge under IHTA 1984 s 65 and thus satisfying the s 260 requirement, unless it takes place within three months after the creation of the settlement or within three months after a ten-year anniversary.

Where a discretionary trust is created by will, distributions to beneficiaries within the two years after the death (but not within the first three months) are treated as if made under the will for inheritance tax purposes (IHTA 1984 s 144 – see Example 60 explanatory note 9). For capital gains tax purposes, however, if such a distribution was of chargeable assets that had grown in value since the date of death, the trustees would be liable to tax on the gain arising under TCGA 1992 s 71 (subject to any available annual exemption), unless the business gifts holdover relief of s 165 was available. Relief under s 260 would not be available because the distribution would not be a chargeable event for inheritance tax. One way of avoiding a capital gains tax charge in these circumstances would be for the trustees to appoint assets to a beneficiary *before* the assets were appropriated to the trustees by the personal representatives. The trustees would then be bare trustees (as to which see explanatory note 1), and as and when the assets were appropriated to them by the personal representatives, the beneficiary's deemed acquisition cost would be the market value at the date of death.

Creation of life interest out of discretionary trust

6. If property is held under a discretionary trust, and a life interest is created in the property, it has to be established whether a separate settlement has been created or whether the original settlement continues (*Roome v Edwards* 1981 and *Bond v Pickford* 1983). If the original settlement is treated as continuing, there would be no capital gains consequences on the creation of the life interest.

If the creation of the life interest was held to constitute a separate settlement, this would be an occasion of charge under TCGA 1992 s 71, since another 'person', ie the trustees of the new settlement, would become entitled to the trust property as against the trustees of the original settlement. The creation of the life interest would, however, usually result in an exit charge for inheritance tax on the discretionary trust under IHTA 1984 s 65 as indicated in note 5 above, and therefore the capital gain could be held over under TCGA 1992 s 260 and treated as reducing the acquisition cost of the property for the new trustees.

Enterprise investment scheme deferral relief

7. If trustees reinvest gains by making a cash subscription for enterprise investment scheme (EIS) shares, they may claim deferral relief under the provisions of TCGA 1992 Sch 5B (but not EIS income tax relief or capital gains exemption) (Sch 5B.17). This applies to interest in possession trusts in which any of the beneficiaries is an individual or a charity and to discretionary trusts in which all beneficiaries are individuals or charities. Where, however, a life tenant dies and EIS shares pass to a succeeding life tenant or remainderman, the deemed disposal under TCGA 1992 s 71(1) or s 72(1) (see part A(a) of the example) triggers the deferred gain, even though no gain arises on the shares themselves.

Anti-avoidance provisions — apportionment of gains of non-resident companies

8. There are provisions in TCGA 1992 s 13 to attribute gains in a non-resident company to UK resident participators if the company would have been a close company if UK resident. For gains realised after 20 March 2000, where the UK participators are trustees, the gains cannot be prevented from being so attributed by reason of the provisions of a double tax agreement (TCGA 1992 s 79B). For further details of the provisions of TCGA 1992 s 13 see Example 51 explanatory note 18.

Question

A.

In May 1988 Stephen Jones set up a discretionary trust for the benefit of his cousins. The trust paid inheritance tax of £44,000 on a chargeable transfer of £330,000. Stephen acted as trustee, together with his solicitor and a close friend. Capital gains of £110,000 were held over. Stephen had not set up any other trusts.

In February 1989 Stephen emigrated (permanently) and the administration of the trust was transferred to new trustees all of whom were and are resident outside the UK. Had the trust's assets been disposed of at that time capital gains of £155,000 would have arisen (including the gain held over).

The beneficiaries, Matthew, Mark, Mary and Matilda were all minors, resident and ordinarily resident in the UK. However, although all the children were born in the UK, Matthew's father was born in the USA and had retained his American domicile.

The trustees subsequently undertook the following transactions:

June 1997	Disposal of a freehold office property for £360,980 (net of costs). The property was part of the original trust fund. It had cost Stephen Jones £50,000 in March 1982 and was worth £100,000 in May 1988.
September 1997	Disposal of quoted shares in Jonah plc for £25,000. These shares had been acquired by the trustees in March 1990 for £9,650.
May 1998	Purchase of warehouse property in England for £150,000.
June 1998	Sale of UK residential property for £200,000. This property had been bought by the trustees in December 1988 for £62,034 including costs.
June 2008	Sale of chargeable non-business assets for £244,652 which had originally been settled by Stephen. The gain was £111,401. There was no heldover gain in respect of these assets.

In addition to distributing all income, the trustees made capital distributions out of the settlement as follows:

	Matthew £	Mark £	Mary £	Matilda £
May 1996	–	–	60,000	20,000
December 1997	90,000	60,000	–	70,000
May 1999	6,000	6,000	6,000	–
July 2008	10,000	10,000	10,000	15,000

The re-referenced retail prices index for the dates given was:

March 1982	79.44
May 1988	106.2
December 1988	110.3
February 1989	111.82
March 1990	121.4
June 1997	157.5
September 1997	159.3
April 1998	162.6

Calculate the capital gains chargeable on the trustees and the beneficiaries in respect of the above transactions, stating if any supplementary charge will apply.

The capital gains tax annual exemption was as follows:

1997/98	£6,500
1998/99	£6,800
1999/2000	£7,100
2000/01	£7,200
2001/02	£7,500
2002/03	£7,700
2003/04	£7,900
2004/05	£8,200
2005/06	£8,500
2006/07	£8,800
2007/08	£9,200
2008/09	£9,600

The annual exemption for discretionary trusts is half the above amounts (except where several trusts have been made by the same settlor). The rate of capital gains tax payable by such trusts was 34% for 1997/98 to 2003/04; 40% from 2004/05 to 2007/08 and has been 18% since 6 April 2008.

B.

Set out the capital gains that would have been chargeable on the trustees and beneficiaries in respect of the settlement in A if, although Stephen Jones had emigrated in 1989, the trustees had remained UK resident.

C.

Set out the capital gains that would have been chargeable on the trustees and settlor on the assumption that the settlement was on Stephen Jones for life and then to his four cousins absolutely. Assume also that he did not emigrate in 1989, but the administration of the trust was transferred to non-resident trustees in February 1989 (no inheritance tax being payable as the transfer would be a potentially exempt transfer), that the capital payments up to May 1998 were all made to Stephen Jones, that on 1 December 1998 Stephen Jones excluded himself from any further benefit from the trust by releasing his life interest in favour of his cousins and that the capital payments in May 1999 and July 2008 were made to the cousins.

D.

Explain briefly how the rules relating to the residence status of trustees has changed under Finance Act 2006.

E.

How have the rules on non-resident trusts changed as a result of FA 2008 Schedule 7?

Answer

A. **Overseas trusts — capital gains tax treatment — pre 1991 trust**

Capital gains on creation of settlement

When a settlement is created, the settlor is deemed to have disposed of the entire property in the settlement at its market value, even if he retains an interest as beneficiary or is a trustee of the settlement, and he is therefore chargeable to capital gains tax accordingly (subject to available reliefs and exemptions).

When the assets transferred are business assets (TCGA 1992 s 165) or the transfer is immediately chargeable to inheritance tax (TCGA 1992 s 260), then providing the settlement is a UK resident settlement (see TCGA 1992 s 166) and it is not a settlor-interested settlement (within the broad definition of that term employed by TCGA s 169B), the settlor can avoid paying tax on the gains by making an election to hold them over so that they reduce the trustees' base acquisition costs. For disposals prior to 19 March 1989 the holdover relief was under FA 1980 s 79 and covered all assets, although no relief was then available on a subsequent disposal for inheritance tax paid.

Since Stephen Jones had created a UK resident discretionary trust, the transfer of assets to the trust would be chargeable to inheritance tax. (If he had retained an interest in the trust, the trust income would be chargeable on him, as would any capital gains remitted as long as he was resident in the UK — see part C.)

The gain arising on the creation of the settlement was held over under FA 1980 s 79.

Capital gain on emigration of Stephen Jones

The emigration of Stephen Jones in February 1989 did not create a liability for capital gains tax on any gains held over, or on any increase in value to the date of emigration.

Export of trust prior to 19 March 1991

When the trust was taken over by non-resident trustees in February 1989, the gains of £110,000 held over on the creation of the trust became chargeable but the accrued gains of £45,000 on the trust's assets were not chargeable as they were not realised (TCGA 1992 s 168) (see explanatory note 8 for emigration of a trust on or after 19 March 1991). The liability for the capital gains tax on the heldover gains was that of the trustees, although if the amount was not paid within twelve months from the due date then the Revenue could recover the tax from Stephen Jones.

Subsequent disposals

Although the trustees, as non-residents, are not chargeable to UK capital gains tax, the capital gains on disposals by the trustees must still be calculated as though they were still resident in the UK. The gains are then apportioned to beneficiaries in proportion to any capital sums they have received from the trust in that or any earlier year, except to the extent that those capital sums have already been allocated to earlier capital gains. The apportioned amounts cannot exceed the actual capital sums received, and are chargeable on the beneficiaries in the year of apportionment. Only beneficiaries who are resident or ordinarily resident in the UK *and* domiciled in the UK are assessed to capital gains tax on gains apportioned to them (TCGA 1992 s 87). The normal annual exemption for capital gains tax is available to the UK domiciled beneficiaries on the apportioned amounts, and is applied against the gains attributed to them in priority to their own gains. The apportioned gains do not, however, attract taper relief, since the gains will have been reduced by any available taper relief when they arose in the trust. From 6 April 1998 to 5 April 2008 it was not possible to offset a beneficiary's own capital losses against apportioned gains other than to gains attributed to the settlor. The abolition of taper relief and introduction of a flat rate of capital gains tax with effect from 6 April

2008 means that such a restriction is no longer necessary. See explanatory notes 5, 9 and 10 in respect of the attribution of gains to resident settlors and also explanatory notes 16 and 17 re anti-avoidance provisions applicable from 21 March 2000.

The position in respect of the non-resident trust is as follows:

Gains

	£	£
1997/98		
Sale proceeds freehold office property June 1997		360,980
Market value May 1988	100,000	
Indexation allowance $\left(\dfrac{157.5 - 106.2}{106.5}\right) = .484$	48,400	
	———	
		148,400
Gain		212,580
Sale proceeds Jonah plc shares September 1997		25,000
Cost March 1990	9,650	
Indexation allowance $\left(\dfrac{159.3 - 121.4}{121.4}\right) = .313$	3,020	
	———	
		12,670
Gain		12,330
Total gains for 1997/98 (212,580 + 12,330) =		£224,910
1998/99	£	£
Sale proceeds UK property June 1998		200,000
Cost December 1988	62,034	
Indexation allowance to April 1998		
$\left(\dfrac{162.6 - 110.3}{110.3}\right) = .475$	29,466	
	———	
		91,500
Total gains for 1998/99		108,500
2008/09		
		£
Gain on disposal of non-business assets June 2008		111,401
Total gains for 2008/09		111,401

Apportionment of gains

	Matthew £	Mark £	Mary £	Matilda £	Total £
1997/98					
Capital payments to date	–	–	60,000	20,000	80,000
Capital payments in year	90,000	60,000	–	70,000	220,000
	90,000	60,000	60,000	90,000	300,000
Apportioned gain (90:60:60:90)	67,473	44,982	44,982	67,473	224,910
Excess capital payments to date cf	22,527	15,018	15,018	22,527	75,090
1998/99					
Apportioned gain (restricted to actual payments to date)	22,527	15,018	15,018	22,527	75,090
Actual gain					108,500
Apportioned above					75,090
Unallocated gain of 1998/99 cf					33,410
1999/2000					
Capital payments in year	6,000	6,000	6,000	–	18,000
Apportioned gain (restricted to actual payments)	6,000	6,000	6,000	–	18,000
Unallocated gain bf					33,410
Apportioned in 1999/2000					18,000
Unallocated gain of 1998/99 cf					15,410
2008/09					
Capital payments in year	10,000	10,000	10,000	15,000	45,000
Apportionment of unallocated gain bf (10:10:10:15)	3,424	3,424	3,425	5,137	15,410
Apportionment of gain of year (restricted to actual payments)	6,576	6,576	6,575	9,863	29,590
Actual gain					111,401
Apportioned above					29,590
Unallocated gain of 2008/09					81,811

The apportioned gains will be chargeable on the beneficiaries (except Matthew, who is not UK domiciled) in the year of apportionment, eg Mark will be chargeable on £44,982 in 1997/98, £15,018 in 1998/99, £6,000 in 1999/2000, and £10,000 in 2008/09, less his annual exemption in each case unless otherwise used.

In 2008/09 the capital gains tax payable by the beneficiaries other than Matthew on their shares of the apportioned gain of £15,410 is increased by a supplementary charge, as the gain arose in 1998/99, and was not distributed in that year, or the following year (1999/2000). The charge runs from 1 December in the tax year following that in which the gain was made to 30 November in the tax year following that in which the capital payment was made (although the period cannot start earlier than six years before that 30 November date). The charge therefore runs from 1 December 2000 to 30 November 2008 = 7 years but limited to six years (maximum period) @ 10% per annum, so the capital gains tax payable by each beneficiary other than Matthew is increased by 60% (see note 13). The apportioned gain may, however, be treated as the lowest part of the chargeable gains of the year. For example:

Assume Matilda has no gains in her own right in the year 2008/09. Her liability will be:

Total apportioned gains	15,000			
Less Annual exemption	9,600			
Capital gains tax @ 18% on	5,400	=	£	972
Of which proportion relating to 1998/99 is 5,137/15,000		=	£	333
Supplementary charge re 1998/99	£333 @ 60%	=	£	200

(to be shown in box 8.9 on the capital gains supplementary sheets of the self-assessment tax return).

By comparison, if in 2008/09 Mary had capital gains of £7,100 in her own right, her liability would be:

Total apportioned gains	10,000			
Less annual exemption	9,600			
	400			
Own gains	7,100			
	7,500			
Capital gains tax	7,500	@ 18%		1,350
Tax relating to apportioned gains	£400	@ 18%	£	72
Of which proportion relating to 1998/99 is 3,425/10,000		=	£	25
Supplementary charge re 1998/99	£25	@ 60%	= £	15

B.   Position if trust had remained UK resident after Stephen Jones emigrated

If the trustees had remained UK resident, the gain held over when the trust was created would not be chargeable until the underlying assets were disposed of. The revised capital gains on the trustees' disposals would be chargeable on them in the tax year in which the disposal took place. The trust would have an annual exemption of one half of the exemption for individuals and tax would be payable on the remaining gains at the rate applicable to trusts of 40% prior to 6 April 2008 and at the rate of 18% since then. There would be no relief by reference to the non-resident beneficiary, Matthew. The position would therefore be:

		£	£
1997/98			
Sale proceeds freehold office property June 1997			360,980
Market value May 1988		100,000	
Less heldover gain:			
Cost March 1982	50,000		
Indexation allowance			
$\left(\dfrac{106.2 - 79.44}{79.44}\right) = .337$	16,850		
	66,850		
Market value on transfer to trust	100,000		
Gain held over	33,150		
		66,850	
Indexation allowance .484 as in A		32,355	99,205
Gain (cf)			261,775

	£	£
1997/98		
Gain (bf)		261,775
Gain on Jonah plc shares acquired by trustees in March 1990		
(as in A)		12,330
Total gains		274,105
Less annual exemption (½ × 6,500)		3,250
Gains chargeable at 34%		270,855

Note No capital gains relief for inheritance tax paid is given for gains held over before 19 March 1989.

1998/99		
Gain on sale of UK property bought by trustees in December 1998 (as in A)		108,500
Less annual exemption (½ × 6,800)		3,400
Gains chargeable at 34%		105,100
2008/09		
Gain on sale of non-business chargeable assets June 2008 as in A		111,401
Less annual exemption (½ × 9,600)		4,800
Gains chargeable at 18%		106,601

C.   **Position if Stephen Jones had been life tenant and had remained UK resident but the trust had emigrated**

The creation of a life interest settlement on Stephen Jones in May 1988 would give rise to chargeable gains which could be held over under FA 1980 s 79 as before. The heldover gain would then be chargeable on Stephen Jones on the export of the trust in February 1989 as in A above.

The subsequent disposals by the trust would be treated as in A, ie there would be a capital gains tax computation as though the trustees were still resident in the UK. Since the trust emigrated before 19 March 1991, the provisions of TCGA 1992 s 86 charging a settlor who retains an interest in a trust on gains as they arise would not apply before 1999/2000, in respect of gains arising on or after 17 March 1998 (see below). Gains arising before 17 March 1998 would be chargeable on Stephen Jones when remitted, with a supplementary charge if not remitted in the tax year in which the gain arose or the following tax year (as in A above).

By FA 1998 s 132 any gain arising on or after 17 March 1998 on a pre 19 March 1991 settlement will be chargeable on the settlor if he or his immediate family (or companies they control) can benefit from the settlement. Gains arising between 17 March 1998 and 5 April 1999 were deferred until 6 April 1999 to allow settlors to reorganise their affairs. Stephen Jones did this in December 1998 by releasing his life interest in favour of his cousins. The release would be a potentially exempt transfer for inheritance tax (see Example 55).

The gains attributable to Stephen Jones would be as follows (before his personal annual exemption or any personal losses prior to 6 April 1998):

	£
1997/98	
Capital payments to date	80,000
Capital payments in year	220,000
	300,000
Gains chargeable on Stephen Jones (actual)	224,910
Excess capital payments to date	75,090

	£
1998/99	
Actual gains	108,500
Gains chargeable on Stephen Jones — excess capital payments to date	75,090
Unremitted gain of 1998/99 cf	33,410

As Stephen Jones excluded himself from benefit on 1 December 1998, the unremitted 1998/99 gain of £33,410 carried forward would not be chargeable on him, but would be apportioned among the four cousins along with subsequent gains and taxed as and when capital payments were made to them. The first capital payment was made in 1999/2000 and would be treated as in part A of the example.

D.

Until the introduction of FA 2006, there were different rules determining the residence status of trustees for income and capital gains tax. These have been harmonised so that trustees are treated as resident and ordinarily resident in the UK if either:

(a) all the trustees are resident in the UK; or

(b) (i) at least one trustee is resident in the UK, and

(ii) a settlor in relation to the settlement was resident, ordinarily resident or domiciled in the UK when the settlement is made (ICTA 1988 s 685E).

The new rules came into effect on 6 April 2007.

E.

Prior to FA 2008 non-UK domiciled, but UK resident, individuals are exempt from both the settlor charge under TCGA 1992 s 86 and the beneficiary charge in TCGA 1992 s 87.

Under FA 2008 the exemption from the settlor charge for non-UK domiciled settlors of non-UK resident trusts will remain but, as from 6 April 2008, the beneficiary charge in TCGA 1992 s 87 will apply to non-UK domiciled beneficiaries. The charge to tax under TCGA 1992 s 87 will be subject to the remittance basis where the non-UK domiciled beneficiary has claimed the remittance basis under ITA 2007 s 809B or is entitled to it under new ITA 2007 s 809C.

In addition, non-resident trustees are given an option to rebase trusts assets to the market value as at 6 April 2008 so that trust gains accruing, but not realised, prior to 6 April 2008 will not be chargeable if matched to capital payments made on or after 6 April 2008 to non-UK domiciled beneficiaries. This option is open only to the trustees and neither settlor nor beneficiaries have the right to make the election.

As a result of the changes:

Capital payments made from 6 April 2008 to non-UK domiciled beneficiaries will generally be chargeable to tax.

The remittance basis will apply if the non-UK domiciled beneficiary is a remittance basis user in the year when trust gains are treated as accruing to him. This will be so whether the trust gains accrue on UK or non-UK assets. A capital distribution will be treated as remitted if the distributed property is received in or brought to the UK. Benefits in kind will be treated as remitted if enjoyed or used in the UK.

Surplus capital payments brought forward from 2007/08 will not be taxed unless (as now) the non-UK domiciled beneficiary is both resident and domiciled in the UK when trust gains are treated as accruing to him. Surplus capital payments to non-UK domiciled beneficiaries made prior to 12 March 2008 can be franked against future post 5 April trust gains although only to the extent that there are no capital payments made after 5 April 2008 to which the post 5 April 2008 gains can be attributed first and there are no pre April 2008 gains accruing by virtue of the rebasing election.

Capital payments to non-UK domiciled beneficiaries between 12 March and 5 April 2008 which are not matched to pre 6 April 2008 gains will be left out of account in 2008/09 and subsequent years for the purposes of TCGA 1992 s 87.

If the trustees have made a rebasing election, the pre 6 April 2008 element of any gain treated as accruing to the beneficiary will be matched with any surplus capital payments made between 12 March and 5 April 2008.

Trust gains brought forward from 2007/08 and treated under section TCGA 1992 s 87(4) as accruing to non-UK domiciled beneficiaries by virtue of capital payments made on or after 6 April 2008 will not be taxed unless the non-UK domiciled beneficiary has become both resident and domiciled in the UK. Although the capital payment is received after 5 April 2008, if it is matched to trust gains realised prior to 6 April 2008 or to the pre 6 April 2008 element of any gain on a rebasing election, it is not necessary in this case for the non-UK domiciled beneficiary to be a remittance basis user.

Trusts which are non-UK resident on 6 April 2008 will have the option to elect for rebasing to the market value as at 6 April 2008 in relation to all assets held by the trust both directly and by its underlying companies. The effect is that the pre 6 April 2008 element of any trust gains treated as accruing to non-UK domiciled beneficiaries after that date will not be taxed. This right of election is described further below.

Any supplemental charge under TCGA 1992 s 91 for remittance basis users will be calculated based on the year in which the capital payment is made by the trustees, not the year in which it is remitted to the UK by the non-UK domiciled beneficiary.

A general matching rule is introduced to the effect that a last in, first out rule will be used to match any trust gains with capital payments made on or after 6 April 2008. This applies to all beneficiaries, not just non-UK domiciled beneficiaries, and applies in place of the present first in, first out rule in computing supplemental tax.

Explanatory Notes

Legislation relating to offshore trusts

1.   The capital gains tax charges relating to offshore trusts contain many points of difficulty. On 21 May 1992 the Revenue issued a lengthy Statement of Practice (5/92) and also concession D40 dealing with the approach they will take in applying certain areas of the rules. The Revenue gave additional guidance in their Tax Bulletin of April 1995. The changes made by FA 1998 have, however, introduced many more areas of complexity and anomaly. Significant further changes were introduced by FA 2000, which are dealt with briefly below.

Effect of emigration of trust on trustees

2.   If an election to hold over a settlor's gains had been made under TCGA 1992 s 165 or s 260 (or previously under FA 1980 s 79), the heldover gain crystallised if donee trustees emigrated before 19 March 1991. The amount chargeable was the gain originally held over (TCGA 1992 s 168).

For trusts emigrating on or after 19 March 1991, the emigrating trustees are charged not only on gains held over at the time the funds were settled but on the whole of any increase in value of the trust assets up to the time of emigration (see note 8). Since 19 March 1991 TCGA 1992 s 168 has accordingly no longer applied where a trust becomes non-resident and now relates only to the emigration of donees who are individuals.

3.   Where a heldover gain has been charged under TCGA 1992 s 168 as a result of the emigration of the donee, the base cost at which the donee is deemed to have acquired the asset is its full value at the time of the gift, so that the trustees are treated as having acquired the assets at their value on the creation of the settlement. Where that was before 31 March 1982, HMRC apparently take the view that a general 31 March 1982 rebasing election can only be made by the trustees, even though any charge to capital gains tax will be made on the beneficiaries.

4.   Where a heldover gain is triggered on or after 6 April 1988 and is wholly or partly attributable to a disposal before 6 April 1988 of an asset acquired before 31 March 1982, only half of the heldover gain is charged to tax (TCGA 1992 Sch 4.4).

Attribution of gains of offshore trusts to beneficiaries or settlor

5.   TCGA 1992 s 87 charges beneficiaries to tax on gains made by a non-resident trust to the extent that they receive capital payments from the trust. Before FA 1998 this applied where the trustees were neither resident nor ordinarily resident at any time in the tax year, if at any time in that year or at the time when he made the settlement the settlor was domiciled and either resident or ordinarily resident in the UK. In respect of gains realised and capital payments made on or after 17 March 1998, the conditions relating to the settlor's residence and domicile no longer apply (FA 1998 s 130). Both before and after 17 March 1998, however, a beneficiary is not charged unless he is resident or ordinarily resident in the UK and was domiciled in the UK at some time in the year in which the gains were apportioned to him (TCGA 1992 ss 2(1), 87(7)). Note that where the income tax provisions of TA 1988 ss 739, 740 apply (transfer of assets abroad – liability of non-transferors on benefits received), any remittances are treated as being made first from accumulated income before being treated as capital payments under TCGA 1992 s 87. In this example all income has been remitted in addition to the capital payments made.

       If the settlor retains an interest in the trust, gains are charged on him as and when they arise under the provisions of TCGA 1992 s 86 if the settlement becomes non-resident on or after 19 March 1991, or if funds are added or the beneficiaries are varied on or after that date, and in any event from 6 April 1999 in respect of gains arising on or after 17 March 1998 (see explanatory notes 9 and 10). Gains taxed on the settlor are not charged on the beneficiaries (s 87(3)).

       As and when chargeable gains are made that are not taxed on the settlor, they are apportioned to the beneficiaries and charged to tax, but only to the extent that capital payments of an equivalent amount have been paid to the beneficiaries, either in the year in which the gains are made or in an earlier year. (See notes 16 and 17 for anti-avoidance provisions to counter schemes to avoid the charge on the beneficiaries.) Any gains that have not been distributed in this way are carried forward and apportioned as and when capital payments are made, as in 1999/2000 and 2007/08 in part A of the example. The capital payments carried forward at the end of 1997/98 represented amounts that the beneficiaries had already received in respect of which no chargeable gains had arisen. When chargeable gains next arose in 1998/99 they were apportioned to the beneficiaries because of the excess capital payments at 5 April 1998.

6.   It should be noted that the chargeable gains can exceed the capital payments received in a year because of amounts received in prior years (but not before 10 March 1981) (TCGA 1992 s 87(4), (5), (10)). Therefore Mary, who does not receive any capital payments in 1997/98, has a liability in that year on gains of £44,982, since she had received capital payments in excess of that amount in earlier years. On the other hand, a charge to tax may occur in a year in which no gains are made, because capital payments are made when there are unallocated gains brought forward. In 1999/2000 there are no gains but Mark and Mary are charged on brought forward gains because of the capital amounts received. Furthermore, if those unallocated gains brought forward were realised in an earlier year than the immediately previous year, a supplementary charge is payable, as shown (see note 13).

7.   Matthew is not chargeable on the gains apportioned to him as, although he is resident and ordinarily resident in the UK, he is not UK domiciled.

Emigration of trust on or after 19 March 1991

8.   In part A of the example the trust became non-resident in February 1989 and the gains held over on creation of the settlement became chargeable at that time, but not accrued gains on the trust's assets, as they had not been realised. If trustees of a settlement become non-resident on or after 19 March 1991, then they are deemed to have disposed of and immediately reacquired the settled property at market value on the day they become non-resident, so that not only any heldover gains but also accrued gains become chargeable at that time (TCGA 1992 s 80). TCGA 1992 s 168 imposing a separate charge on heldover gains, as illustrated in part A, therefore no longer applies where trustees become non-resident on or after 19 March 1991.

       The deemed disposal under TCGA 1992 s 80(2) does not apply to trading assets of a branch or agency which remain chargeable to UK capital gains tax under TCGA 1992 s 10. Rollover relief on replacement of business assets under TCGA 1992 ss 152–156 cannot be claimed if the new assets are acquired after the trust becomes non-resident and are outside the UK tax charge. These provisions also apply to dual resident trusts that are exempt from UK tax on gains because of a double tax treaty.

       On the emigration of a trust, beneficiaries would normally be treated as having acquired their interest in the trust at the market value at the date of the trust's emigration. Where a trust becomes non-resident on or after 21 March 2000, this uplift to market value does not apply where the trust has a stockpile of gains at the date of emigration that have not been attributed to beneficiaries (TCGA 1992 s 85).

Trusts in which the settlor retains an interest

9.   Where a settlement with non-resident trustees is made on or after 19 March 1991, or becomes non-resident on or after that date, and the settlor is resident or ordinarily resident and domiciled in the UK, and the settlor or his spouse/civil partner, children, children's spouses/civil partners, a company controlled by one or more of those persons, or an associated company, can benefit from the settlement, then the gains of the settlement are attributed to the settlor (TCGA 1992 s 86). For settlements with non-resident trustees made on or after 17 March 1998, grandchildren and their spouses (and, since 5 December 2005, their civil partners) are added to the list of defined persons for s 86 (FA 1998 s 131). This also applies to pre 17 March 1998 trusts if they become non-resident or if funds are added or grandchildren become beneficiaries on or after that date (or a grandchild who was already a beneficiary enjoys a benefit for the first time on or after that date that he would not have been able to enjoy under the terms of the settlement as it stood at that date) (FA 1998 Sch 22).

       Before FA 2002 a trust's gains were reduced by taper relief before being attributed to a settlor and the settlor could not use his personal losses to reduce the gains. The abolition of taper relief with effect from 6 April 2008 simplifies this calculation.

       The settlor can recover the tax he has paid from the trustees without that amount being treated as a capital payment by the settlement. For this purpose he may require the Revenue to issue him with a certificate of the tax paid (TCGA 1992 Sch 5.6). There is no provision for the settlor to obtain payment from the trustees before he has paid the tax, even though the disposal proceeds relating to the gains will be in the trust. If the settlor fails to recover the tax, then that amount will be considered to be an addition to the settlement unless the trust is unable to remit the amount because of local restrictions.

       The provisions of s 86 do not apply in a tax year in which the settlor dies, nor in which all those individuals who cause him to have an interest die, or, where the interest is that of a spouse/civil partner, they cease to be married/the civil partnership is dissolved.

10.   Before FA 1998 a non-resident trust made before 19 March 1991 was only subject to the provisions of TCGA 1992 s 86 outlined in note 9 if funds were added or the beneficiaries were varied to include any of the defined persons.

With effect from 6 April 1999, gains of pre 19 March 1991 non-resident trusts are no longer excluded from the provisions of TCGA 1992 s 86 (TCGA 1992 Sch 5). Unremitted gains of the period 17 March 1998 to 5 April 1999 were deemed to arise on 6 April 1999, thus bringing them within the provisions. The charge was delayed to enable trusts to reorganise their affairs, for example by excluding the range of defined persons as beneficiaries, or by becoming resident or by winding up the trust. There are, however, anti-avoidance provisions in Sch 23 to prevent exploitation of the transitional period.

The revised provisions do not apply to 'protected settlements', ie where the beneficiaries are confined to:

(i)   Children of the settlor or his spouse/civil partner who are under 18

(ii)   Unborn children of the settlor or his spouse/civil partner

(iii)   Future spouses/civil partners of the settlor or his children

(iv)   Persons outside the defined categories (eg cousins, as in part A of the example).

This protection ceases, however, when the child reaches age 18. Furthermore, distributions to grandchildren are caught as a result of FA 1998 s 131 (see note 9). The Revenue have, however, stated that the existence of grandchildren (of whatever age) as beneficiaries of a pre 19 March 1991 settlement at 6 April 1999 will not cause the settlement to fall outside the 'protected' category (Tax Bulletin December 1998).

11.   Where capital payments are made on or after 6 April 1999 to beneficiaries of pre 19 March 1991 trusts in which the settlor has an interest, they will be matched with any unallocated gains that arose before 17 March 1998, earliest first (attracting the supplementary charge if appropriate – see note 13), and only when all such unallocated gains have been matched with capital payments will capital payments to beneficiaries be regarded as having been already charged on the settlor.

Settlor who is temporarily non-resident

12.   To be liable to UK capital gains tax the settlor must be UK resident or ordinarily resident in the tax year that gains arise. Under TCGA 1992 ss 10A and 86A, however, a UK domiciled settlor can also be liable if after becoming non-resident he returns to the UK having been away for fewer than five complete tax years. The charge is made in the tax year of return to the UK, but it is reduced by any gains that have been charged on UK resident beneficiaries during his period of non-residence.

From 2003/04 (or earlier by election), gains will not normally be reduced by a trust's taper relief *before* being attributed to a settlor (FA 2002 s 51 and Sch 11) (see explanatory note 9). This does not, however, apply where the gains on which a returning settlor is charged have been reduced by gains already attributed to UK resident beneficiaries during the settlor's absence. The gains in such circumstances will continue to be reduced by the trust's taper relief before they are attributed to the settlor and will not be able to be reduced by the settlor's losses (TCGA 1992 s 86A as amended by FA 2002 Sch 11.5).

Supplementary charge

13.   Before FA 1991 it was possible to defer payment of capital gains tax on gains realised by offshore trusts by not remitting the gains. Where such gains are assessable on beneficiaries for 1992/93 onwards, the tax payable is increased by a supplementary charge (TCGA 1992 ss 91–97). The charge runs from 1 December in the tax year following that in which the trustees' gains arose to 30 November in the tax year after that in which the gain is apportioned to the beneficiary as a result of a capital payment (any capital payments being regarded as applying to the earliest unallocated gains first). If the period would otherwise exceed six years, however, it starts on 1 December six years before the 30 November charging date (TCGA 1992 s 92(4)(5)). The supplementary charge does not apply where gains are matched by capital payments in the same or following tax year. Gains made before 6 April 1990 were treated as made in 1990/91. Trustees could distribute such gains before

6 April 1992 without any supplementary charge on the beneficiary. Later gains may be distributed in the same or the following tax year without the supplementary charge becoming payable, subject to the 6 April 1990 fund of undistributed gains being matched with payments first. The charge is at an annual rate of 10% of the tax on the capital payment, giving an overall maximum possible rate of 60% of 18% = 10.8%, in addition to the capital gains tax of 18% already payable.

In part A of the example, the 1997/98 capital gain is more than matched by capital payments made in or before that year, so that the whole gain is apportioned to beneficiaries in that year. The 1998/99 gain of £108,500 is distributed as to £75,090 in that year and £18,000 in 1999/2000, but £15,410 remains unallocated until 2008/09, so that the supplementary charge arises on the 2008/09 assessable gains.

14. Prior to 6 April 2008 careful planning of capital payments could, in some cases, reduce the overall amount of supplementary charge payable. Say, for example, an overseas trust has two beneficiaries, one liable to capital gains tax at 20% and the other at 40%, and the trustees were to make a capital payment which would partly relate to gains of a year to which the supplementary charge would apply and partly to a later year for which the supplementary charge was not relevant. If a capital payment was made to the lower taxed beneficiary first, this would relate to earlier gains before later gains, so that any part of the payment that attracted the supplementary charge would suffer the additional charge on a 20% tax bill. A subsequent payment could then be made to the higher taxed beneficiary out of gains not liable to the supplementary charge. This is no longer the case now that capital gains tax is charged at a flat rate of 18%. Similar planning points will apply where there is a non-UK domiciled beneficiary, like Matthew in this example, or where, although UK domiciled, a beneficiary is not resident or ordinarily resident in the UK.

Treatment of interest-free loans

15. Many non-resident trustees have regarded payments to beneficiaries to be by way of loan (often interest-free), rather than capital payments to which gains would be apportioned. Such a loan was considered in a criminal case in relation to a confiscation of property order (*R v Harvey* 1998). The loan was secured by way of a charge on the offender's property. The loan was disregarded, because it was stated to be in reality a gift and that the charge was unlikely to be enforced. The Revenue have taken a similar view for tax purposes in relation to offshore trusts, and succeeded in the cases of *Billingham v Cooper* and *Edwards v Fisher*, heard by the Court of Appeal in 2001. In both cases overseas trustees had made interest-free loans, repayable on demand, to UK resident (settlor) beneficiaries of pre March 1991 trusts. Although the Revenue conceded that such loans had little initial benefit, they contended that the continuation of the loans meant that the benefit was provided on a continuing basis. The Court of Appeal agreed, stating that in giving effect to the purpose of TCGA 1992 ss 87 and 97, it needed to be considered what benefit a beneficiary actually received, so that the 'loan' payments to beneficiaries were within the capital payments and supplementary charges rules.

Apportionment of gains of non-resident companies

16. A chargeable gain that arises in a non-resident company which would be a close company if resident in the UK is apportioned between its participators. In so far as a participator has at least 10% (5% prior to 7 March 2001) of the gain apportioned to him, and is UK resident or ordinarily resident (and, if an individual, domiciled) in the UK, he is chargeable to capital gains tax on the apportioned amount. These provisions apply to UK resident trustees as well as to individuals (see Example 50 explanatory note 8 for special anti-avoidance provisions for trustees). Although chargeable to capital gains tax, the gain is computed using corporation tax rules, with indexation allowance but not taper relief applying (see Tolley's Taxwise I 2008/09 Example 70 for details) (TCGA 1992 s 13).

Such gains may also be apportioned to non-resident trustees (s 13(10)), and may in turn be chargeable on the settlor or beneficiaries under the provisions in note 5 above.

These provisions do not apply to gains on the disposal of an asset used for the purposes of a trade carried on by the non-resident company wholly outside the UK, or to trading currency.

If the gain is distributed within four years of the date the gain is realised or, if earlier, three years after the end of the accounting period in which the gain is realised (within two years after the gain was realised for gains realised before 7 March 2001), then the capital gains tax on the apportioned amount can be offset against the income tax on the distribution (or capital gains tax if a capital distribution). If not so relieved the tax is treated as an expense for capital gains tax in computing any subsequent gain on the disposal of the participator's interest in the company (TCGA 1992 s 13).

Question

Explain, with appropriate reference to both statute and case law, what is meant by an 'interest in possession' in settled property, commenting specifically on the impact that powers granted to the trustees may have on the position.

Summarise the ways in which settlements with an 'interest in possession' are treated for inheritance tax purposes and explain the position both before and after the changes made by Finance Act 2006.

Answer

Meaning of 'interest in possession'

The Inheritance Tax Act 1984 uses the term 'interest in possession' but it is not defined clearly in the legislation.

The definition put forward by the Revenue is that 'an interest in possession in settled property exists where the person having the interest has an immediate entitlement .... to any income produced by that property as the income arises; but that a discretion or power, in whatever form, which can be exercised after income arises so as to withhold it from that person negatives the existence of an interest in possession. For this purpose a power to accumulate income is regarded as a power to withhold it, unless any accumulations must be held solely for the person having the interest or his personal representatives.'

The Revenue's view was upheld by the *House of Lords in Pearson and Others v CIR* 1980 in which it was stated that it is the present right of present enjoyment that constitutes an interest in possession.

What is meant is that a beneficiary has an interest in possession in settled property if he has a present right of present enjoyment of the net income of the settled property without any further decision of the trustees being required.

Having the present right of present enjoyment means that the beneficiary must have a right to enjoy the income of the settlement as it arises. A beneficiary may have an interest in possession in property which produces no income. It is not necessary for the beneficiary to be entitled to the gross income from the settled property and the fact that the trustees may deduct their administrative expenses from the gross income does not defeat a beneficiary's interest in possession. Because of this a beneficiary will still have an interest in possession even if he has to wait until expenses have been deducted before receiving the income.

An interest in possession may not subsist in settled property if the trustees have powers affecting the net income after payment of administration expenses. Purely administrative powers such as power to pay taxes, to charge fees or pay insurance do not defeat an interest in possession. The existence of dispositive powers such power to accumulate income or a power to appoint or pay or apply income to or for the benefit of another beneficiary will prevent an interest in possession from subsisting on the settled property.

Inheritance tax treatment of settlements

Where property is held in trust, the inheritance tax treatment of that property depends on the type of trust. The Inheritance Tax Act 1984 divides trusts into three categories: those where there is an interest in possession (meaning a beneficiary taxed interest in possession); those where there is no interest in possession; and those which are given privileged status.

Since 22 March 2006 many trusts in which there is an interest in possession will be taxed as trusts in which there is no interest in possession under the mainstream IHT rules for 'relevant property' trusts such as discretionary trusts. Relevant property is settled property in which there is no interest in possession or there is an interest in possession but no beneficiary is treated as beneficially entitled to the property in which the interest subsists.

Under the mainstream IHT rules for relevant property trusts:

(a)   The trust has its own inheritance tax accumulation, the method of calculating the rate of tax on a transfer of trust funds depending upon the date the settlement was created.

The tax scale used is one half of the normal scale applicable at the date of charge.

(b) On the tenth anniversary of the creation of the settlement it is subject to a ten-year charge (s 64).

The charge is 30% of the tax that would be payable on the relevant property in the trust if the whole of the trust property were distributed on that day.

A further charge will occur every ten years thereafter.

(c) There is also an exit charge when property in such a settlement ceases to be relevant property (either because the property leaves the settlement or for any other reason, for example the property becoming subject to an interest in possession) (s 65).

Where the trust is one which is still, since 22 March 2006, taxed as an interest in possession trust, the beneficiary with that interest is treated as if the trust fund was part of his estate.

Inheritance tax treatment of settlements with an interest in possession

The term 'interest in possession' is crucial to the taxation treatment of these settlements for inheritance tax.

Where an interest in possession exists in respect of a settlement made before 22 March 2006, then the person beneficially entitled to that interest is treated for inheritance tax purposes as being beneficially entitled to the underlying property in which the interest subsists (s 49).

Thus the value of the settled property in which a person has an interest in possession is deemed to be part of the estate of that person and any transfer of that interest will appear on his inheritance tax accumulation if chargeable.

Although the actual tax may well be paid by the trustees, the effect of this treatment is to increase the rate of tax on any subsequent chargeable transfer by the person in possession or, in the case of a liability on death, to increase the estate rate and therefore the tax payable on the free estate at death by reason of the aggregation of the free estate and the interest in possession.

Inheritance tax treatment of trusts post 22 March 2006

Settlements made on or after 22 March 2006 are now generally subject to the mainstream rules which apply to relevant property even if there is an interest in possession in the trust property. Therefore, if the settlement was made after 21 March 2006, the assets held by the trustees of an interest in possession settlement will not usually form part of the estate of the person beneficially entitled to an interest in possession.

This, however, has its drawbacks. In particular, the creation of the settlement will represent a chargeable event (previously, lifetime transfers into interest in possession settlements constituted PETs). Furthermore, the settlement will be subject to the ten-year charge and exit charge rules described above.

Since 22 March 2006 only the following interest in possession trusts will remain outside the mainstream rules for charging relevant property trusts previously limited to discretionary trusts:

(a) Pre-22 March 2006 interest in possession trusts to which the beneficiary became beneficially entitled to an interest in possession before 22 March 2006.

(b) Bare trusts (where the beneficiary continues to be treated as entitled to the assets held under the bare trust). A bare trust is not a settlement for IHT purposes.

(c) Interest in possession trusts where the interest in possession is:

    (i) an immediate post-death interest (see below);

    (ii) a disabled person's interest (broadly an interest in possession for a person incapable of looking after their affairs because of mental disorder, or a person in receipt of an attendance allowance or a disability living allowance); or

(iii)   a transitional serial interest (see below) (IHTA 1984 s 49(1A)).

An immediate post-death interest is one:

– created on an individual's death under the deceased's will or under the law of intestacy,

– which gave the life tenant the beneficial entitlement to the trust fund on the individual's death, and

– which is not and has not been a disabled person's interest or an interest of a bereaved minor (IHTA 1984 s 49A).

A trust may be an immediate post-death interest whether created before or after 22 March 2006.

To be a transitional serial interest in a settlement:

(i)   the settlement must have been set up before 22 March 2006; and

(ii)   immediately before 22 March 2006, there must have been an individual with a beneficial interest in possession in the settlement; and

(iii)   that person's interest must have come to an end after 21 March 2006 but before 6 October 2008; and

(iv)   the person with the current interest in the settlement became beneficially entitled to that interest at that time; and

(v)   the interest is not a disabled person's interest or an interest of a bereaved minor (IHTA 1984 s 49B).

The rules for bereaved minors are found in IHTA 1984 s 71A. They apply only for settlements which:

(a)   are set up by:

(i)   a parent of the beneficiary in their will, or

(ii)   the Criminal Injuries Compensation Scheme

(b)   give the minor the capital and income of the trust absolutely when the minor reaches the age of 18.

Explanatory Notes

Effect of having an interest in possession in a settlement in a pre-22 March 2006 settlement

1.   Inheritance tax cannot be avoided on a capital sum simply because the person presently entitled to the income has no recourse to the capital.

The supporting capital is deemed to be part of his wealth for inheritance tax (s 49(1)).

2.   There are two consequences:

First, a cessation of the interest in possession attracts an inheritance tax charge by reference to the accumulated transfers of the taxpayer who ceases to have possession.

Second, an advance of capital to a person presently entitled to the income does not attract an inheritance tax charge. The supporting capital was previously part of the taxpayer's estate in the form of trust property and is now part of his estate in the form of free estate.

Since 22 March 2006, such a transfer is a PET only if made to

– another individual,

– a disabled trust, or

–   a bereaved minor's trust on the coming to an end of an immediate post-death interest (IHTA 1984 s 3A(1A))

so that if the potentially exempt transfer becomes chargeable because of the taxpayer's death within seven years, it increases his cumulative transfers for the purpose of calculating tax on later transfers.

3.   Thus, contrast the position where trustees use their powers to pay a capital sum to:

(a)   The person presently enjoying the income — no inheritance tax charge.

(b)   The person eventually entitled to the capital (ie when the interest in possession comes to an end) — there is a potential inheritance tax charge.

Creation of interest in possession settlement

4.   It was thus possible for a transferor to make an immediate transfer into a trust fund and thereby fix the value of the transfer at that time. Such a transfer would have been a potentially exempt transfer for inheritance tax (after deducting annual exemptions if available), providing another individual was beneficially entitled to the interest in possession. Accordingly inheritance tax would have been payable only if the settlor died in the next seven years. If the period between settlement and death is more than three years the tax charge, if any, on the transfer would have been reduced by tapering relief. There would have been no inheritance tax charge upon the funds leaving the trust so long as their destination was the person presently entitled to the interest in possession. This was particularly useful if one wished to transfer appreciating assets (ie to trustees) without the intended beneficiary being able to have absolute personal control of them. Further transfers into the trust, and the termination of the life interest during the lifetime of the person entitled to the interest, followed either by another life interest or by someone becoming absolutely entitled to the trust property, would all have been potentially exempt transfers (again subject to any available annual exemptions).

There would, however, have been a chargeable event for capital gains tax on the termination of the interest in possession (TCGA 1992 s 71) unless occasioned by the death of the life tenant (TCGA 1992 s 73), or where the property remained in trust (TCGA 1992 s 72), subject to the trustees and the transferee being able to make a claim under TCGA 1992 s 165 or s 260 for the gain to be held over in appropriate circumstances (for detailed notes see Example 50).

Interest in possession and residential property

5.   The capital gains tax exemption for only or main residence is extended by TCGA 1992 s 225 to a beneficiary who is entitled to occupy a property owned by a trust. The view of the Revenue is that non-exclusive occupation of a property would not constitute an interest in possession (Statement of Practice 10/79), but a lease for life for less than full consideration will create an interest in possession. Thus obtaining the capital gains tax exemption means that a charge to inheritance tax can arise as set out above.

Where substantially the whole of the assets of a married couple consist of the matrimonial home, it is often difficult to utilise both nil rate bands. A possible solution is for the home to be held by the couple as tenants in common, and for the half share to be left on the first death to a discretionary trust, the surviving spouse then buying the trust's half share at full price with the consideration left outstanding. On the second death full capital gains tax exemption applies, but there is a deduction in the inheritance tax computation for the outstanding loan. If the property had remained in the trust it would appear that only one half of the value of the property should be included in the inheritance tax computation, as the surviving spouse had occupied the property with the permission of the trustees and this may not equate to an interest in possession of the whole (*Woodhall v CIR, SpC*, 2000).

Discretionary or relevant property trusts

6.   Detailed notes on the tax treatment of discretionary trusts are given in Examples 59 to 63.

Interests in possession post 22 March 2006

7.   Settlements made on or after 22 March 2006 are now generally subject to the rules which previously applied only to discretionary trusts. Therefore, the assets held by the trustees of an interest in possession settlement will not usually form part of the estate of the life tenant.

The following interests in trusts form part of the estate of the life tenant:

(a)   bare trusts (where the beneficiary continues to be treated as entitled to the assets held under the bare trust);

(b)   interests in possession which commenced before 22 March 2006;

(c)   later interests in possession trusts where the interest in possession is:

    (i)   an immediate post-death interest (see below)

    (ii)   a disabled person's interest (broadly an interest in possession for a person incapable of looking after their affairs because of mental disorder, or a person in receipt of an attendance allowance or a disability living allowance) or

    (iii)   a transitional serial interest (see below) (IHTA 1984 s 49(1A)).

As has been seen, an immediate post-death interest (IPDI) is one:

(a)   created on an individual's death under the deceased's will or under the law of intestacy,

(b)   which gave the life tenant the beneficial entitlement to the trust fund on the individual's death, and

(c)   which is not and has not been a disabled person's interest or an interest of a bereaved minor (IHTA 1984 s 49A).

Most notably, lifetime transfers into interest in possession settlements will constitute chargeable transfers but the life tenant will not be treated as beneficially entitled to the trust fund. This can lead to multiple taxation. See Example.

Example

Hardy settles £500,000 for himself for life, the remainder for his wife. The transfer is a chargeable lifetime settlement and so inheritance tax will be payable at the lifetime rates. The settlement will be subject to ten-year and exit charges as appropriate. However, because Hardy still has the use of these funds, the transfer will be treated as a gift with the reservation of benefit. Consequently, the £500,000 will form part of Hardy's estate when he dies. The problem would have been worse had Hardy settled assets which gave rise to a chargeable gain. The transfer would have given rise to a capital gains tax liability with no scope for any holdover relief (because the donee trust was settlor-interested).

Question

Robin died on 30 June 2004 and the inheritance tax on his estate was payable out of residue, at an estate rate of 25%.

His will provided for the following:

(1) A bequest to his married daughter Merle of 25,000 shares of £1 each in Fieldfare plc, quoted on the Stock Exchange at 398–406p.

(2) The creation of a settlement, the assets of which amounted to £30,000, under which the income was payable to Merle for life, then to Merle's daughter Jenny for life, with remainder to Merle's son Martin.

On 1 September 2007 Merle gave Jenny 12,500 of the shares in Fieldfare plc that she had inherited from her father. The shares were quoted on that day at 272–276p. She had made previous potentially exempt transfers amounting to £286,000 (after exemptions), all on 30 September 2002.

Merle and Jenny were involved in an accident and as a result Merle died on 30 September 2008, leaving her free estate to her son Martin. Jenny died on 31 October 2008, having made no lifetime transfers, and leaving her estate to her brother Martin.

Their respective estates were valued for probate as follows:

	Merle 30.9.08 £	Jenny 31.10.08 £
12,500 shares each in Fieldfare plc	36,750	38,000
Other assets (net of liabilities)	24,025	263,250
Settled fund (net of liabilities)	32,000	22,750

Compute the inheritance tax payable:

(a) on the death of Merle

(b) on the death of Jenny.

Jenny's date of birth is 15 January 1981.

Answer

(a) **Inheritance tax payable on death of Merle (30 September 2008)**

			Gross £	Tax on 2008/09 scale £
Gifts within seven years before death:				
During 2002/03			286,000	–
1 September 2007				
Gift to Jenny 12,500 shares @ 273		34,125		
Less: Annual exemptions 2007/08	3,000			
2006/07	3,000	6,000		
Potentially exempt transfer now chargeable			28,125	850*
Cumulative transfers in seven years prior to death			314,125	850*

(* 314,125 – 312,000 = 2,125 @ 40%)

Estate of Merle deceased

	Date of death 30 September 2008 £
Free estate:	
12,500 shares in Fieldfare plc	36,750
Other assets (net of liabilities)	24,025
	60,775
Settled property (Robin's will trust) (net of liabilities)	32,000
Chargeable to inheritance tax on death	92,775

	Gross £	Tax on 2008/09 scale £
Cumulative transfers in seven years prior to death	314,125	850
Chargeable estate on death	92,775	37,110*
	406,900	37,960

(* £92,775 @ 40% = £37,110)

Inheritance tax payable:

On gifts within seven years before death

Payable by transferees of gifts in 2002/03 (previously potentially exempt transfers) .... nil

Payable by Jenny (or her executors) re gift of shares on 1 September 2007, previously potentially exempt £850

On estate at death as computed 37,110

Less: Quick succession relief re gift of shares from Robin (see explanatory note 6)

$$20\% \text{ of } \left(\frac{100,000}{133,333} \times 33,333 \right) \qquad\qquad 5,000$$

Quick succession relief re settled property (see explanatory note 7)

$$20\% \text{ of } \left(\frac{30,000}{40,000} \times 10,000 \right) \qquad\qquad 1,500 \qquad 6,500$$

Inheritance tax payable on Merle's estate £30,610

Payable by executors:

$$\frac{60,775}{92,775} \times £30,610 \qquad\qquad\qquad £20,052$$

Payable by trustees of settled property:

$$\frac{32,000}{92,775} \times £30,610 \qquad\qquad\qquad £10,558$$

(b)   **Inheritance tax payable on death of Jenny (31 October 2008)**

Estate of Jenny deceased

	Date of death 31 October 2008
Free estate:	
12,500 shares in Fieldfare plc	38,000
Other assets (net of liabilities)	263,250
	301,250
Settled property (Robin's will trust) (net of liabilities)	22,750
	£324,000

Inheritance tax payable:

	£
On £324,000 (324,000 − 312,000 = 12,000 @ 40%)	4,800

Less: Quick succession relief re gift of shares from Merle (see explanatory note 9)

		£
80% of	$\left(\dfrac{27,275}{28,125} \times £850\right)$	659

Quick succession relief re settled property (see explanatory note 10)

		£
100% of	$\left(\dfrac{21,442}{32,000} \times £10,558\right)$	7,075

	£	£
Total quick succession relief available	£7,734	
But relief restricted to total tax chargeable		4,800
		−

Accordingly no inheritance tax is payable on Jenny's death.

Explanatory Notes

Quick succession relief

1.   Under the provisions of s 141, quick succession relief applies where the value of a person's chargeable estate for inheritance tax purposes was increased by a chargeable transfer made not more than five years before

(a)   his death

or

(b)   a lifetime charge on settled property in which the deemed transferor had an interest in possession (where the earlier transfer was or included the making of the settlement or was made after the making of the settlement).

The rates of quick succession relief are as follows:

Period between transfer and death	*Percentage relief*
1 year or less	100%
1+ to 2 years	80%
2+ to 3 years	60%
3+ to 4 years	40%
4+ to 5 years	20%

The percentage relief is calculated on the part of the tax paid on the previous transfer that the net value then transferred bears to the gross chargeable transfer at that time.

Where the later transfer is made on death, whether it relates to free estate or settled property, the quick succession relief reduces the total tax chargeable because of the death, as shown in the example, so that the apportionment of the tax payable between free estate and settled property is of the tax as reduced by quick succession relief.

Successive transfers

2.   Where an individual who has a life interest in possession in settled property transfers parts of his interest therein at different times and more than one later transfer occurs within five years of his acquisition of the life interest, then quick succession relief is available on the second and subsequent transfers within the five years, but only to the extent of any tax not used up on the earlier transfers. In this connection a transfer uses up the full amount of tax paid on the earlier transfer of which the tax relievable on the later transfer is a percentage (s 141(4)(5)).

        For example:

        A grants a life interest to B by will trust. Within two years B releases part of his interest to a discretionary trust (C), then in the fifth year after A's death B releases the remainder of his interest to a second discretionary trust (D).

        Proportion of tax on A's transfer relevant to the increase in B's estate is say £25,000. Transfer of part interest within two years to C trust attracts tax of say £8,000 and transfer of remainder to D trust within five years tax of say £7,000.

        The quick succession relief available on the transfer to C trust is 80% × £25,000 so the amount of £8,000 is fully covered by quick succession relief, representing £10,000 of the original £25,000 (£8,000 = 80% × £10,000) leaving £15,000 still available. The transfer to D trust attracts quick succession relief of 20% of £15,000 = £3,000 to set against the tax payable of £7,000.

Valuation of quoted securities

3.   Quoted securities are valued one quarter up from the lower of the two quoted prices. Thus on Robin's death a quotation of 398–406p per share becomes 400p.

Gift by Merle to Jenny of inherited shares

4.   Quick succession relief was not available on the Fieldfare plc shares given by Merle to Jenny despite Merle having acquired the shares by a chargeable transfer less than five years earlier, because it only applies where the *later transfer* is on death or termination of an interest in possession in settled property.

Position on death of Merle

5.   As Merle's death occurred more than four years but within five years after Robin's death, quick succession relief is available at 20%. The quick succession relief applies both on the shares transferred to her and on the life interest in the settled fund that passes to Jenny on Merle's death.

6.   The value of the shares transferred to Merle on Robin's death was:

25,000 shares in Fieldfare plc @ 400p (see explanatory note 3)	100,000
Tax thereon (25% of gross = 25/75 of net)	33,333
Gross transfer	£133,333

7.   The value of the assets transferred to the settled fund on Robin's death was:

Assets	30,000
Tax thereon (25% of gross = 25/75 of net)	10,000
Gross transfer	£40,000

Position on death of Jenny

8.   The liabilities in Jenny's estate will have included the inheritance tax on the gift from Merle and the value of the settled property will have been reduced by the inheritance tax payable by the trustees because of the death of Merle.

9. Jenny's death occurred within two years after the gift of shares from Merle, so 80% quick succession relief is available thereon.

   The value of the shares transferred was:

Chargeable transfer – gross	28,125
Less: Inheritance tax on death of Merle	850
Net chargeable transfer	£27,275

10. Jenny's death occurred within one year of Merle's death, so the rate of quick succession relief on the assets in the settlement is 100%.

    The net value transferred on Merle's death was:

Settled fund	32,000
Inheritance tax payable thereon	10,558
	£21,442

    The value of £22,750 at Jenny's death reflects the movement in the value of the fund for reasons other than the liability for tax.

11. Jenny is not a minor and therefore the interest she acquired in her mother's estate is not subject to the rules in section 71A.

    However, the interest in Robin's will trust is a transitional serial interest because:

    (i)   the settlement was set up before 22 March 2006 (on Robin's death); and

    (ii) immediately before 22 March 2006, there was an individual (Merle) with a beneficial interest in possession in the settlement; and

    (iii) that person's interest must have come to an end after 21 March 2006 but before 6 October 2008 (on 30 September 2008 on Merle's death); and

    (iv) Jenny became beneficially entitled to that interest at that time; and

    (v)   the interest is not a disabled person's interest or an interest of a bereaved minor.

    Consequently, Jenny is treated as beneficially entitled to the assets in the fund at her death.

Question

Mr Maxford died on 7 January 2009. He was UK domiciled. The following information is held:

(1) He had previously owned a 14% shareholding (70,000 shares) in Maxford plc, an unquoted trading company, for many years.

(2) In February 1999 he gifted 30,000 of the Maxford plc shares to trustees of a discretionary trust for his children.

(3) In May 2003 he gifted 20,000 of the Maxford plc shares to a trust in which his daughter has a life interest. (He was excluded from benefit under both trusts and the trustees retained the shares.)

(4) The agreed share values at the time of both gifts were:

Shareholding	Per share value £
11% to 15%	10.00
5% to 10%	5.00
Below 5%	3.00

In February 2005 Maxford plc was listed on the Alternative Investment Market. All donees had retained their shares.

(5) In 1992 he had inherited a 51% shareholding in Minota plc, a company whose shares are listed on the London Stock Exchange. In July 2005 he gifted a 10% shareholding then worth £654,000 to his daughter and she held them at his death when they were worth £200,000.

(6) No other transfers had been made. Donees agreed to pay any tax due in respect of transfers to them.

His estate at death comprised:

(i) His house worth £800,000.

(ii) A life interest in his uncle's estate. The uncle had died in June 2004 with an estate worth £235,000 on which inheritance tax of £27,500 was suffered. On Mr Maxford's death his daughter became entitled to the capital, which was then worth £300,000.

(iii) 20,000 shares in Maxford plc valued at £10 per share.

(iv) Holdings of quoted shares as follows:

Number/%	Company	Value at death £
7,000	Green plc	107,000
3,500	Blue plc	42,000
6,000	Red plc	8,000
41%	Minota plc	850,000

In the six months following death the following share sales occurred:

Shares sold	Company	Gross proceeds £
6,000	Green plc	84,000
2,000	Blue plc	35,000
600	Red plc	950

54.2 TAX ON DEATH — BUSINESS PROPERTY RELIEF, SETTLED PROPERTY, QUICK SUCCESSION RELIEF

In his will, Mr Maxford left his Maxford plc shares to his daughter. His house was left equally to his widow and daughter, subject to his widow having full use and enjoyment of the house for her lifetime or for so long as she wished. The balance of his estate went to his son.

(a)   Calculate the inheritance tax payable as a result of the death of Mr Maxford.

(b)   Calculate the allocation of any tax due between the free estate and settled property.

Answer

(a) **Inheritance tax payable as a result of death of Mr Maxford**

Position on gifts in lifetime

		Gross £
February 1999	Gift of 30,000 Maxford plc shares to discretionary trust –	
	Value of 70,000 shares @ £10	700,000
	Value of 40,000 shares @ £5	200,000
	Loss to estate	500,000
	Less: business property relief	500,000
	Transfer of value	–
May 2003	Gift of 20,000 Maxford plc shares to life interest trust –	
	Value of 40,000 shares @ £5	200,000
	Value of 20,000 shares @ £3	60,000
	Loss to estate	140,000
	Less: 100% business property relief	140,000
		–
July 2005	Gift of 10% holding of Minota plc shares to daughter	654,000
	Less: 50% business property relief	327,000
		327,000
	Less: Annual exemptions 2005/06 and 2004/05	6,000
	Potentially exempt transfer	321,000

On Mr Maxford's death 7 January 2009

Lifetime transfers in seven years before death

No additional tax is payable on the February 1999 gift, since this was more than seven years before Mr Maxford's death. (It is, however, included in the inheritance tax accumulation until February 2006, affecting the July 2005 gift accordingly.)

Business property relief remains available on the other gifts providing the transferees have retained what they were given and the property still qualifies as relevant business property. A listing on the Alternative Investment Market does not affect the status of unquoted shares, so that the May 2003 gift to the life interest trust will still retain entitlement to the 100% relief. The position on the July 2005 gift of Minota plc shares to the daughter is as follows:

	Gross £	Tax on 2008/09 scale £
Cumulative transfers in previous seven years	–	–
July 2005 PET now chargeable	321,000	3,600*
	321,000	3,600*

(* 321,000 – 312,000 = 9,000 @ 40%)

As the Minota plc shares have fallen in value at the date of death, the daughter may claim to have the tax on her gift recomputed as follows:

Value of gift as above		321,000
Value on death	200,000	
Less: 50% business property relief	(100,000)	
Annual exemptions	(6,000)	94,000
Reduce transfer by		227,000

This reduces the tax figure to nil. The amount included in the inheritance tax accumulation, however, remains at £321,000.

Estate at death

	£	£
House	800,000	
Less: Spouse exemption (see explanatory note 4)	800,000	–
20,000 shares in Maxford plc @ £10	200,000	
Less: 100% business property relief	200,000	–
Quoted shares**:		
Green plc 7,000 shares	107,000	
Blue plc 3,500 shares	42,000	
Red plc 6,000 shares	8,000	
Minota plc 41%	850,000	1,007,000
Free estate		1,007,000
Settled property – life interest in uncle's estate		300,000
		1,307,000

** See explanatory note 5.

	£	£
Inheritance tax thereon:		
Cumulative transfers in previous seven years	321,000	–
Estate at death	1,307,000	526,400*
	1,628,000	526,400

(* 1,628,000 – 312,000 = 1,316,000 @ 40%)

Tax on estate	526,400
Less: Quick succession relief re uncle's estate (4 to 5 years)	
$20\% \times \dfrac{207,500}{235,000} \times 27,500$	4,856
	521,544

(b) **Allocation of tax between free estate and settled property**

	£
Tax on estate as above	521,544

$$\text{Estate rate} = \frac{521,544}{1,307,000} \times 100 = 39.904\%$$

	£
Tax on free estate 1,007,000 @ 39.904%	401,832
(payable by personal representatives)	
Tax on settled property 300,000 @ 39.904%	119,712
(payable by trustees, reducing daughter's entitlement accordingly)	
	521,544

Explanatory Notes

Business property relief

1. Business property relief increased to 100% on 6 April 1996.

    Thus the Maxford plc shares retained by Mr Maxford until his death qualify for 100% business property relief in the death estate. Since they were left as a specific gift to his daughter, there is no restriction of the exempt legacy of the house to the spouse by reference to the business property relief (see Example 15 for further details).

2. From 10 March 1992 quoted shares qualify for business property relief of 50% if they give the transferor control immediately before the transfer, hence the relief in respect of the gift of the Minota plc shares to the daughter. There is no relief in the death estate on the Minota plc shares retained by Mr Maxford, since he no longer had a controlling holding.

Fall in value of gift

3. The claim for tax to be computed on the value of a gift at death where that is lower than the value at the time of the gift does not affect the cumulative transfers figure for the purpose of later transfers, so the amount included in lifetime transfers remains at £321,000. For detailed notes on such claims see Example 12.

Legacy of house to spouse and daughter

4. The stipulation in Mr Maxford's will that his spouse was entitled to full use of the property created a life interest in the daughter's share of the property (*CIR v Lloyds Private Banking* 1998). Mrs Maxford therefore owns half the property outright and has a life interest in the other half. In both cases the spouse exemption applies. For detailed notes on interests in possession and property see Example 52.

Sale of quoted shares at a loss within twelve months after death

5. Although 6,000 of the Green plc shares were sold at a loss within twelve months after death, no relief may be claimed, since the overall result of the sales was a profit as follows:

			Death Value £	Realised Value
Green plc	6,000 shares	6,000/7,000 × 107,000	91,714	84,000
Blue plc	2,000 shares	2,000/3,500 × 42,000	24,000	35,000
Red plc	600 shares	600/6,000 × 8,000	800	950
			116,514	119,950

For detailed notes on claims for a loss on quoted shares see Example 8.

Question

A.

(a)   Brian is the life tenant of a settlement valued at £159,000 and on 31 December 2005 he released his life tenancy for the benefit of the succeeding life tenant, Carol.

Brian made a previous transfer in the form of a gift to his brother on 26 March 2004 of £173,000.

After relinquishing his interest in the settlement he made a gift of £60,000 to a friend on 8 June 2006.

On 2 April 2009 Brian died leaving free estate of £120,000.

Calculate the inheritance tax payable.

(b)   Carol, who succeeded to the life tenancy from Brian in (a) above, died on 1 February 2007, having made no previous transfers.

The settlement was then valued at £182,000. On the death of Carol the property passed to David, the remainderman, absolutely.

Carol left free estate of £114,000.

Calculate

(i)   the inheritance tax position on her death, and

(ii)   the effect of the subsequent death of Brian.

B.

Antony and Benjamin each have a life interest in trust funds, with remainder to Denis, the assets of each fund consisting entirely of a loan of £60,000 to a close company, repayable at seven days' notice.

On 30 June 2005 Antony sold his interest to Clive for its full market value of £20,000.

Before Antony sold his interest to Clive he had made chargeable transfers of £281,000 in August 1999, but had not made any later transfers of value.

Antony died on 30 September 2008 leaving an estate of £435,000.

Clive, before his acquisition of Antony's interest, had made a potentially exempt transfer (after exemptions) of £200,000 in February 2003 and made no further gifts.

Benjamin died on 30 December 2008. Before his death he had made potentially exempt transfers (after exemptions) in the previous seven years amounting to £213,000 and his estate was valued at £100,000, excluding his interest in the trust.

Sufficient of the loans was repaid for the trustees of each fund to meet their inheritance tax liabilities on each occasion.

Compute the inheritance tax payable by the trustees of each fund by reference to the above events.

Where relevant, proper notice was given to the trustees of availability of exemptions within the appropriate time limit for both part A and part B of the example.

Answer

A. (a) **Brian**

Inheritance tax accumulation

26 March 2004			
Gift to brother			173,000
Less: Annual exemptions	2003/04	3,000	
	2002/03	3,000	6,000
Potentially exempt transfer			£ 167,000
31 December 2005			
Release of life tenancy			159,000
Less: Annual exemptions	2005/06	3,000	
	2004/05	3,000	6,000
Potentially exempt transfer			£153,000
8 June 2006			
Gift to friend			60,000
Less: Annual exemption 2006/07			3,000
Potentially exempt transfer			£57,000

Death of Brian — 2 April 2009

Inheritance tax payable on gifts within seven years before death

	Gross £	Tax (on 2008/09 scale) £
26 March 2004		
Gift to brother	167,000	–
31 December 2005		
Release of life tenancy	153,000	3,200*
	320,000	3,200*
(* 320,000 – 312,000 = 8,000 @ 40%)		
8 June 2006		
Gift to friend	57,000	22,800
Cumulative chargeable transfers at death	377,000	26,000
Free estate on death	120,000	48,000
	497,000	74,000

Inheritance tax payable

		£	By
Re 26 March 2004 gift		nil	
Re 31 December 2005 release of life interest			
(3–4 years before death)	3,200		
Less: Tapering relief 20%	640	2,560	trustees of settlement
Re 8 June 2006 gift		22,800	friend

	£	By
(less than 3 years before death)		
On free estate	48,000	personal representatives

A. **(b)**

(i) Estate of Carol — Inheritance tax position as at date of death 1 February 2007

	£
Free estate	114,000
Settled property	182,000
	296,000

	£	
Inheritance tax on 2006/07 death scale (no previous transfers)	£	4,400*

(* 296,000 – 285,000 = 11,000 @ 40%)
Payable by:

$$\text{Personal representatives} \frac{114,000}{296,000} \times £4,400 = \qquad 1,695$$

$$\text{Trustees of settlement} \frac{182,000}{296,000} \times £4,400 = \qquad 2,705**$$

	£	4,400

(ii) Estate of Carol — Revision of inheritance tax position following death of Brian

	£	£
Free estate		114,000
Settled property	182,000	
Less: Inheritance tax payable by reference to now chargeable transfer dated 31.12.05	2,560	179,440
		293,440*
Inheritance tax payable (* 293,440 – 285,000 = 8,440 @ 40%)		3,376*

Quick succession relief by reference to
earlier chargeable transfer on 31.12.05:
80% ×

$$\frac{150,440}{153,000} \times £2,560 \qquad 2,014$$

Tax payable	£	1,362

Payable by:

$$\text{Personal representatives} \frac{114,000}{293,440} \times 1,362 = 529$$

	£	£

$$\text{Trustees of settlement} \frac{179,440}{293,440} \times 1,362 = 833$$

		£
Repayable to: Personal representatives (1,695 – 529)		1,166
Trustees of settlement (2,705 – 833)		1,872**
	£	3,038

** See also explanatory note 11.

B. Antony

Inheritance Tax Accumulation

Cumulative transfers to date			281,000
30 June 2005			
Sale of life interest in trust			
Value transferred		60,000	
Less: Proceeds of sale		20,000	
		40,000	
Less: Annual exemptions 2005/06	3,000		
2004/05	3,000	6,000	
Potentially exempt transfer		£34,000	

30 September 2008 — Death of Antony

	Gross £	Tax (on 2008/09 scale) £
Tax payable by trustees on potentially exempt transfer 30 June 2005:		
Cumulative transfers within seven years before 30 June 2005 –		
Chargeable transfers in August 1999	281,000	–
Potentially exempt transfer 30 June 2005	34,000	1,200*
	315,000	1,200*

(* 315,000 – 312,000 = 3,000 @ 40%)

	Gross £	Tax (on 2008/09 scale) £
Tax payable by personal representatives on estate at death:		
Cumulative transfers within seven years before 30 September 2008	34,000	–
Estate on death	435,000	62,800*
	469,000	62,800*

(* 469,000 – 312,000 = 157,000 @ 40%)

Inheritance tax payable:	
By trustees (3–4 years before death)	
1,200 subject to tapering relief at 20%	£960
By personal representatives	£62,800

Clive

Inheritance Tax Accumulation

Potentially exempt transfer February 2003			£200,000

30 September 2008

Transfer of life interest because of death of Antony			60,000
Less: Annual exemptions	2008/09	3,000	
	2007/08	3,000	6,000
Potentially exempt transfer			£54,000

Benjamin — Date of death 30 December 2008

Inheritance Tax Accumulation

		Gross £	Tax (on 2008/09 scale) £
Potentially exempt transfers within seven years before death, now chargeable		213,000	–
Value chargeable on death:			
Free estate	100,000		
Settled property	60,000	160,000	24,400*
		373,000	24,400*

(* 373,000 – 312,000 = 61,000 @ 40%)

Tax payable:
By personal representatives

$$\frac{100,000}{160,000} \times £24,400 =$$
                                              15,250

By trustees

$$\frac{60,000}{160,000} \times £24,400 =$$
                                              9,150

£24,400

Summary of Inheritance Tax payable by Trustees

	£
By trustees of Antony's trust fund	
On sale of Antony's life interest to Clive 30 June 2005	nil
On Antony's death 30 September 2008:	
Re potentially exempt transfer 30 June 2005	960
Re termination of life interest	
(by reference to inheritance tax accumulation of Clive who is in possession, providing Clive lives until after 30 September 2015)	nil

£

By trustees of Benjamin's trust fund
On Benjamin's death 30 December 2008   9,150

Explanatory Notes

Disclaiming interest in a settlement

1.   A person who becomes entitled to an interest under a settlement (any type of interest, not just a life interest) may disclaim his entitlement and providing this is not done for money or money's worth, he is treated as never having become entitled to the interest (s 93). This only applies where an interest is disclaimed *before* any benefit is accepted, and the disclaimer must be of the whole interest and not just part of it. Once benefits have been accepted the normal tax consequences follow.

Termination of interest in possession

2.   Where a person, before 22 March 2006, had an interest in possession in the whole or any part of a settlement, the appropriate part of the trust fund continues to be treated for inheritance tax purposes as belonging to that person absolutely (s 49(1)). (An interest in possession broadly means an entitlement as of right to *income* from a settlement. For further notes on this point see Example 52.)

     Clive acquired his interest before 22 March 2006 and, therefore, is treated as beneficially entitled to the assets in the fund until Antony's death.

     Had Clive acquired his interest in the fund after 21 March 2006, it would not have been treated as part of his taxable estate as the limited exceptions discussed in Example 52 do not apply.

     Therefore, for pre-22 March 2006 interests, if the person with the interest dies (s 4(1)) or terminates that interest by releasing or selling it (s 52) there will be a potential charge to inheritance tax. It would be unfair for the person in possession of the interest to have to pay any inheritance tax arising as that person has no control over the assets of the settlement. The tax is therefore payable by the trustees (s 201(1)). If the transfer is or becomes a chargeable transfer, however, it is added to the inheritance tax accumulation of the person with the interest in possession (s 52) and the tax is calculated as though the transfer had been made by that person.

3.   The termination of an interest in possession during the lifetime of the person beneficially entitled to that interest is treated under s 52(1) as a transfer of value equal to the value of the property in which the interest in possession subsisted. The estate of the transferor immediately before the transfer is deemed to include the whole of the property in which he had an interest in possession and therefore the reduction in value of the estate as a result of the assignment is the full value of the property in which he had an interest in possession less any amount received as consideration for the assignment (s 52(2)). Where consideration is received, exemption cannot be claimed as a commercial transaction because s 52(1) and (2) expressly provide for tax to be payable. The easiest way to look at it is that whilst the life tenant's reservoir of assets has been depleted by the underlying value of the trust fund which it is deemed to contain, the free estate included in the reservoir has increased by the proceeds received, so that the transfer of value is the difference between the two.

Availability of exemptions

4.   For events after 21 March 2006, if the termination occurs during the person's lifetime and the property devolves upon

     (i)   a gift to another individual,

     (ii) a gift into a disabled trust, or

    (iii)   a gift into a bereaved minor's trust on the coming to an end of an immediate post-death interest

then the transfer is a potentially exempt transfer and will only become a chargeable transfer should the former life tenant die within seven years. The transfer is, however, a *deemed* transfer of value and accordingly the small gifts exemption and exemption for normal expenditure out of income do not apply (ss 20(3), 21(5)). The annual and marriage gifts exemptions are, however, available providing the transferor gives the trustees of the settlement a notice informing them of the availability of the exemptions, within six months after the date of *termination*, in a form prescribed by HMRC (s 57). Notice is required within that period even though the transfer is a potentially exempt transfer. Both the annual and marriage exemptions would be taken into account in arriving at the potentially exempt transfer (ss 51(2), 57). Other exemptions are also available (see explanatory note 6).

After the transfer the interest in possession does not concern the transferor, but instead forms part of the inheritance tax reservoir of assets of the transferee. If, however, the transferor dies within seven years after the date of transfer the potentially exempt transfer rules apply in the normal way and tax on the potentially exempt transfer is chargeable on the normal scale, any tax arising being payable by the trustees (or the transferee if the trust came to an end as a result of the transfer).

5.   Even though any tax that may arise on the termination of the life interest is payable by the trustees and not by the transferor, his accumulation is increased by the amount of the transfer if it becomes a chargeable transfer, thus increasing his tax liability on any later transfers. Brian in part A and Antony and Clive in part B of the example would therefore surrender their annual exemptions to the trustees for use against the transfers if they had made no other transfers against which the exemptions could be utilised.

6.   If the termination of the life interest occurs on the life tenant's death, the value of the assets in the settlement is added to the free estate and tax calculated on the aggregate. The trustees are then liable to pay a proportionate part of the total inheritance tax payable.

For both lifetime and death terminations the exemptions for transfers to spouse/civil partner, charities or political parties are available.

For most life interests formerly qualifying as interests in possession created on or after 22 March 2006, the death of the life tenant will not give rise to any inheritance tax consequence as the trust fund would not be deemed to form part of the life tenant's estate.

Release of Brian's life interest

7.   On the release of Brian's life interest in part A of the example there is a transfer of value based on the underlying assets in the settlement. Since Brian is entitled to the whole of the income of the trust, the whole capital value of the fund is deemed to be transferred. Because the release is to another interest in possession settlement in which an individual, Carol, is beneficially entitled, the transfer is at that point potentially exempt (after deducting annual exemptions, following notice by Brian to the trustees of their availability).

On the death of Brian his accumulation is recomputed for the seven years prior to death, with the potentially exempt transfers now being treated as chargeable transfers. The rates used for the recomputation are those applicable on 2 April 2009. In the case of transfers occurring more than three years before death, tapering relief reduces the tax on those particular transfers without affecting the overall computation.

Death of Carol

8.   In part A (b) Carol has not made any previous transfers and her free estate of £114,000 is below the threshold for inheritance tax on her death. But the estate for inheritance tax purposes includes both free and settled property. The possession of the life interest therefore causes tax to be payable on the free estate, as well as giving rise to a liability in the settlement. A tax liability of £1,695 therefore arises on the free estate at the time of Carol's death. This liability is, however, reduced to £529

through a combination of less tax being payable because of the tax debt which has to be deducted from the settled property and quick succession relief when the position is recomputed on the subsequent death of Brian (see note 10).

Quick succession relief etc

9. If, on death, a person's estate has been increased by a chargeable transfer within the previous five years then quick succession relief is available. The total tax chargeable on death is reduced by a percentage of that part of the tax charged on the previous transfer that the net value then transferred bore to the gross chargeable transfer at that time. The percentage is as follows:

Time between transfer and death	*Percentage relief*
1 year or less	100%
1+ to 2 years	80%
2+ to 3 years	60%
3+ to 4 years	40%
4+ to 5 years	20%

The release of the life interest by Brian in part A of the example on 31 December 2005 was potentially exempt so that no quick succession relief was due on Carol's death on 1 February 2007. However, when Brian dies on 2 April 2009 his release of his life interest which was previously potentially exempt becomes chargeable (s 3A(4)) with tax payable of £2,560.

Quick succession relief is then available by reference to the death of Carol on 1 February 2007, giving a repayment of inheritance tax to the trustees and her personal representatives.

The time between the two chargeable transfers is just over one year, and the percentage is therefore 80% (s 141).

The tax of £2,560 charged on the earlier transfer reduces the gross chargeable transfer of £153,000 so that the increase in the estate of Carol resulting from that chargeable transfer is only £150,440.

For further notes on quick succession relief see Example 53.

10. On the subsequent death of Brian the inheritance tax liability of the trust fund on the original transfer is £2,560. Whilst this liability does not arise until the death of Brian on 2 April 2009, it nonetheless affects the value of the trust property on Carol's earlier death on 1 February 2007 since it derives from the now chargeable transfer by Brian on 31 December 2005.

The inheritance tax liability on the death of Carol is therefore not only recomputed by quick succession relief, but also by the inclusion of a different figure for the value of the trust property itself.

Retaining funds to meet potential liabilities

11. This example illustrates that trustees of settlements will have a potential tax liability for seven years after a release of a life interest although this will become less relevant now that most post-22 March 2006 settlements are no longer treated as part of the life tenant's estate. Accordingly funds must be retained for that period to meet those liabilities. Thus on the death of Carol the trustees should not distribute to the remainderman, David, all of the assets remaining after the tax of £2,705 on her death since by doing so they would find themselves with a personal liability for tax on the subsequent death of Brian should they be unable to recover from David the tax due of £1,727 (£2,560 – £833) by reference to Brian's death.

12. In part B of the example, when Antony dies, Clive's reservoir of assets is reduced as the property passes to the remainderman, Denis. This is a potentially exempt transfer after deduction of annual exemptions for 2007/08 and 2006/07 and provided Clive lives for at least a further seven years, it will not give rise to a charge. If, however, Clive died within that time the transfer would become

chargeable by reference to his accumulation. The tax would be payable out of the trust funds, and in transferring the trust assets to the remainderman Denis, the trustees should provide for this contingent liability.

On the death of Benjamin his interest in possession is chargeable in the normal way, that is by aggregation with the free estate and the tax on the total is apportioned rateably to the various parts of his estate.

Reversion to settlor or spouse/civil partner

13. If an interest in possession comes to an end during the settlor's lifetime, and the settled property reverts to the settlor, tax is not chargeable (s 53(3)). Furthermore tax is not chargeable if the settlor's spouse/civil partner (or widow/widower or surviving civil partner if settlor had died less than two years earlier) becomes beneficially entitled to the property and is domiciled in the UK (s 53(4)).

Tax is chargeable if the settlor or spouse/civil partner acquired the reversionary interest for a consideration in money or money's worth (s 53(5)).

Anti-avoidance provisions

14. When property is transferred to a discretionary trust, the transfer cannot be potentially exempt. And since 22 March 2006 it is no longer possible for a settlor, whilst alive, to make a potentially exempt transfer into an interest in possession trust, on which no tax would be payable if he survived seven years.

Question

(a) Fred, an annuitant under a settled fund, died on 31 August 2008. The amount of the annuity was £5,000. The value of the fund as a whole on that date was £500,000 and it produces an average annual income yield of 10%. Assume the current yield shown in the FT Actuaries Share Index was 4.17% for British Government Stocks (Irredeemables).

Calculate the value of the annuity fund for inheritance tax purposes on the death of Fred.

(b) Jim, the life tenant of a settled fund, died on 31 August 2008. His life tenancy was subject to an annuity of £5,000. The value of the fund as a whole was £500,000 on that date and the annual income yield was 6%. Assume the current actual dividend yield of the FT Actuaries All Share Index was 3%.

Calculate the value of the life tenancy for inheritance tax purposes on the death of Jim. Assume Jim acquired his interest in the fund before 22 March 2006.

Answer

(a) **Fred deceased — 31 August 2008**

Value of Annuity Fund

	£

Without s 50(3)
Annuity £5,000
Income of fund (£500,000 × 10%) £50,000
Share of capital attributable to Fred

$$\frac{5,000}{50,000} \times 500,000 \qquad\qquad 50,000$$

With s 50(3)
Annuity £5,000
Notional income of fund (£500,000 × 4.17%) £20,850
Minimum share of capital attributable to Fred

$$\frac{5,000}{20,850} \times 500,000 \qquad\qquad 119,904$$

Value for inheritance tax of Fred's annuity fund — £119,904

(b) **Jim deceased — 31 August 2008**

Value of part remaining after an annuity

	£

Without s 50(3)
Annuity £5,000
Income of fund (£500,000 × 6%) £30,000
Share of capital attributable to Jim
(ie after annuity of £5,000)

$$\left(\frac{30,000 - 5,000}{30,000}\right) \times 500,000 \qquad\qquad 416,667$$

With s 50(3)
Annuity £5,000
Notional income of fund (£500,000 × 3%) £15,000
Value of fund   500,000
Less: Maximum value of annuity fund

$$\frac{5,000}{15,000} \times 500,000 \qquad\qquad 166,667$$

Minimum value of part remaining   333,333

	£
Value for inheritance tax of Jim's life tenancy	£416,667

Explanatory Notes

1. A person who has a life interest in settled property is treated for the purposes of inheritance tax as owning it absolutely provided the interest was acquired before 22 March 2006 (s 49(1)).

    Where one beneficiary of a settlement is entitled to a fixed amount of income and another to the remainder of the income, then to arrive at their respective shares of the trust fund the fund is divided in proportion to their shares of income (s 50(1)). The income arising over the previous twelve months is usually used for this purpose.

2. However, if only one of the interests in the settlement is to be valued for the purpose of calculating a chargeable transfer, s 50(3) contains anti-avoidance provisions to prevent loss of tax to HMRC where the yield of the fund may have been arranged to reduce the taxable amount.

    The anti-avoidance provisions *do not apply* where chargeable transfers of *both* of the interests are made *at the same time*, since the whole of the supporting capital will in those circumstances be caught in any event.

3. The value of the annuity fund becomes:

    (a)   In the case of a transfer of the annuity — not *less* than its capital value using the current yield on the FT Actuaries Index for British Government Stocks (Irredeemables).

    (b)   In the case of a transfer of the remainder — not *more* than its capital value using the current actual yield on the FT Actuaries All Share Index.

    The use of these particular indices is prescribed by SI 2000/174, effective from 18 February 2000. The figures are obtainable from the Financial Times.

4. The value of Fred's annuity fund included in his estate is therefore the higher of £50,000 (arrived at using the actual income yield of the fund) and £119,904 (arrived at using the notional income yield of 4.17% being the yield on British Government Irredeemable Stocks).

    In arriving at the value of Jim's life tenancy, the value of the annuity fund using the actual income yield is 1/6th of £500,000 = £83,333. Since this is less than the maximum permitted value of £166,667 using the All-Share Index, the anti-avoidance provision in s 50(3) does not apply in valuing Jim's interest for inheritance tax purposes on his death.

5. For interests created on or after 22 March 2006 the rules apply only to

    –   interest in possession trusts where the interest in possession is:

        –   an immediate post-death interest (see below)

        –   a disabled person's interest (broadly an interest in possession for a person incapable of looking after their affairs because of mental disorder, or a person in receipt of an attendance allowance or a disability living allowance) or

        –   a transitional serial interest (see below) (IHTA 1984 s 49(1A)).

    An immediate post-death interest is one:

    (a)   created on an individual's death under the deceased's will or under the law of intestacy,

    (b)   which gave the life tenant the beneficial entitlement to the trust fund on the individual's death, and

(c)   which is not and has not been a disabled person's interest or an interest of a bereaved minor (IHTA 1984 s 49A).

To be a transitional serial interest in a settlement:

(a)   the settlement must have been set up before 22 March 2006; and

(b)   immediately before 22 March 2006, there must have been an individual with a beneficial interest in possession in the settlement; and

(c)   that person's interest must have come to an end after 21 March 2006 but before 6 October 2008; and

(d)   the person with the current interest in the settlement became beneficially entitled to that interest at that time; and

(e)   the interest is not a disabled person's interest or an interest of a bereaved minor (IHTA 1984 s 49B).

The rules for bereaved minors are found in IHTA 1984 s 71A. They apply only for settlements which:

(a)   are set up by:

    (i)   a parent of the beneficiary in their will or

    (ii)   the Criminal Injuries Compensation Scheme

(b)   give the minor the capital and income of the trust absolutely when the minor reaches the age of 18.

Question

Amelia Dobbin, a widow, died on 15 July 2008.

Her first husband, George Sedley, who died in 1971, had by his will left the residue of his estate to her absolutely. In 1973 she made a settlement of this absolute interest under which she took a life interest with remainder to her son.

At her death the settled fund consisted of investments valued at £249,000.

Her second husband, William Dobbin, who died in July 1974, settled the residue of his estate on her for life with the remainder to Rebecca, his daughter by a previous marriage.

This settled fund on Amelia Dobbin's death was valued at £300,000.

Amelia had made two transfers of value prior to her death.

On 1 January 1998 she transferred assets to Rebecca's husband, the value of the transfer being £70,900. On 10 June 2006 she gave £159,000 to her son.

For many years up to the date of her death Amelia had owned and farmed 200 acres of agricultural land, the open market value of which is £400,000 and the agricultural value £300,000. The farm's business assets are valued at £96,000.

Amelia's free estate at death, apart from the farm land and business assets, consisted of £40,000 Crawley Corporation 6% Stock 2004, quoted at 92–94 ex div (interest paid 15 February and 15 August), furniture and effects valued at £13,500, income due to her from the settlements £4,320 and a bank balance of £8,590.

Her liabilities and funeral expenses amounted to £4,370.

By her will she left £50,000 to a registered charity, £2,000 to a major British political party, and the residue to a close friend.

(a)   Prepare a statement of the amount on which inheritance tax is chargeable on Amelia's death.

(b)   Compute the inheritance tax payable, stating by whom it will be borne.

Answer

Amelia Dobbin deceased

(a) Calculation of amount on which inheritance tax is chargeable on death — 15 July 2008

Free estate

			£
Agricultural property:			
Agricultural value	300,000		
Less: Agricultural property relief 100%	300,000	–	
Business property:			
Non-agricultural value (£400,000 – £300,000)	100,000		
Farm business assets	96,000		
	196,000		
Less: Business property relief 100%	196,000	–	
£40,000 Crawley Corporation 6% stock @ 92½% ex div	37,000		

Interest due (half year)	1,200		
Less: Income tax @ 20%	240	960	37,960
Furniture and effects		13,500	
Income due from settlements		4,320	
Bank balance		8,590	
		64,370	
Less: Funeral expenses and liabilities		4,370	60,000

Settled property

1973 Settlement by Amelia on herself for life Investments			249,000
1974 Surviving spouse settlement Transitional exemption (see explanatory note 4)			–
			309,000
Less: Exempt legacies			
Charity		50,000	
Political party		2,000	
		£52,000	

Giving a deduction after agricultural and business property relief attributable thereto of

$$£52,000 \times \frac{60,000 \ (\text{free estate } after \ \text{APR/BPR})}{556,000 \ (\text{free estate } before \ \text{APR/BPR})}$$ 5,612

Chargeable to inheritance tax on Amelia's death 303,388

(b) **Inheritance tax payable at death — 15 July 2008**

On potentially exempt transfers within seven years before death (ie 16 July 2001 to 15 July 2008):

				Gross £	Tax £
10 June 2006					
Gift to son			159,000		
Less: Annual exemptions	2006/07	3,000			
	2005/06	3,000	6,000		
Potentially exempt transfer now chargeable				153,000	–
				153,000	–

On estate at death:

	Gross £	Tax £
Inheritance tax accumulation within seven years before death as above	153,000	–
Chargeable assets at death and tax thereon	303,388	57,755*
	456,388	57,755*

(* 445,388 – 312,000 = 144,388 @ 40%)
The inheritance tax of £57,755 is borne as follows:
By personal representatives

Value of free estate (as reduced by APR and BPR)	60,000
Less: Exempt transfers (as reduced by APR and BPR)	5,612
	£54,388

$$£57,755 \times \frac{54,388}{303,388} = \qquad 10,354$$

By trustees of 1973 settlement

Value of settled property £249,000

$$£57,755 \times \frac{249,000}{303,388} = \qquad 47,401$$

£57,755

Explanatory Notes

Valuation of quoted securities

1. Quoted securities are valued at a quarter up from the lower of the quoted prices (or halfway between the highest and lowest bargains marked if less), any accrued income therefore being included in the quotation. If quoted ex interest, the whole of the forthcoming income (net of lower rate income tax) must be added to the resultant valuation, since the whole of that income would have been forthcoming had a sale been made at the point of death, not just the part accrued on a day to day basis up to the death.

Agricultural and business property relief

2.   For detailed notes on agricultural property and business property relief see Example 25.

3.   The free estate is reduced by the exempt legacies to the charity and political party. Such legacies are completely exempt (ss 23, 24). However unless agricultural and business property is left as a specific legacy rather than as part of the residue of the estate, the benefit of agricultural property and business property relief is allocated over the exempt and chargeable free estate, thus effectively reducing the value of those reliefs where there are exempt legacies (see Examples 15 and 17).

     For detailed notes on the charity and political party exemptions see Example 1.

Estate duty — surviving spouse exemption

4.   Where one party to a marriage died before 13 November 1974 and the other dies after 12 March 1975 (the date on which estate duty was abolished and capital transfer tax/inheritance tax commenced to be chargeable on death) any property which would have been exempt from estate duty under the 'surviving spouse' exemption of FA 1894 s 5(2) is left out of account for inheritance tax (Sch 6.2).

     The estate duty exemption applied only to property in which the spouse had a limited interest (eg for life or widowhood) and of which she/he was at no time competent to dispose, and not to property that passed absolutely. The property comprised in the settlement established by Amelia's second husband on his death in July 1974 is therefore left out of account for inheritance tax under this transitional provision.

5.   Although Amelia at her death only had a life interest in the 1973 settlement comprising the assets from her first husband's estate, she did at one time (between 1971 and 1973) have an absolute interest in those assets, having herself created the settlement in her own favour. The transitional relief at note 4 does not therefore apply. A settlement upon oneself with remainder to specified persons is a useful way of determining in one's lifetime the destination of specified property upon death. For further notes on this point see Example 46 explanatory note 8.

     The assets comprised in the settlement itself remain in the reservoir of assets of the settlor through the interest in possession rules, so there is not even a potentially exempt transfer when the settlement is made, no transfer of value having taken place.

     The settled fund remains chargeable to inheritance tax on the death of the settlor, so no tax is avoided, but the lifetime settlement has determined the devolution on death, thus safeguarding against any possible family problems arising, say, from remarriage or other doubts within a family.

     For an account of the new provisions relating to the transfer of the nil-rate band from one spouse to another see Example 1 (iii).

Potentially exempt transfers

6.   Amelia made potentially exempt transfers on 1 January 1998 and 10 June 2006. The earlier transfer became completely exempt on 1 January 2005. The second transfer became a chargeable transfer by reason of her death on 15 July 2008, but since it is below the nil threshold no tax is payable (and tapering relief is not therefore relevant). It does, however, reduce the nil band available against the death estate.

Question

Richard died in 1994 and left his estate consisting of marketable securities in trust for his brother Alan for life and thereafter absolutely to Alan's son, Lawrie.

Lawrie died on 1 June 2008. His estate, including his interest in expectancy on the death of Alan, was left to his only daughter Gladys for life and thereafter to his nephew John absolutely.

Lawrie's estate comprised:

Personal assets £322,000

Interest expectant on the death of Alan valued at £32,000.

His funeral expenses amounted to £1,700 and his debts, including £100 owed to his turf accountant, amounted to £3,400. He had made no lifetime transfers.

Alan died on 31 December 2008, the value of the settled property on that date amounting to £55,000. Alan's personal estate was valued at £233,000. He had made one previous transfer on 6 October 2005, being a gift of quoted shares then valued at £130,000.

Calculate the inheritance tax payable on the above events.

Answer

Inheritance tax computation on death of Lawrie (1 June 2008)

Value of estate for inheritance tax

			£
Free estate			322,000
Reversionary interest:			
Interest in expectancy on death of Alan – excluded property, therefore			Nil
			322,000
Less: Funeral expenses		1,700	
Debts	3,400		
Less: Turf accountant	100	3,300	5,000
Chargeable to inheritance tax			317,000
Inheritance tax on 2008/09 scale (317,000 – 312,000 = 5,000 @ 40%)			2,000

Inheritance tax computation on death of Alan (31 December 2008)

Inheritance tax accumulation

			Gross £	Tax £
6 October 2005				
Shares transferred		130,000		
Less: Annual exemptions 2003/06	3,000			
2004/05	3,000	6,000	124,000*	–
Estate at death:				
Free estate		233,000		
Settled property – Richard's settlement		55,000	288,000	40,000**
			412,000	40,000**

(** 412,000 – 312,000 = 100,000 @ 40%)

> * This will have been a potentially exempt transfer when it was made, but becomes a chargeable transfer since death occurred within seven years. No tax is payable, however, because it is below the nil threshold.

Tax of £40,000 on estate is payable as follows:

By trustees of settled property

$$\frac{55,000}{288,000} \times £40,000$$

7,639

By personal representatives

$$\frac{233,000}{288,000} \times £40,000$$

32,361

£40,000

Explanatory Notes

Reversionary interests

1. A reversionary interest in a settlement is excluded property whether it is transferred in lifetime or on death unless it was acquired for a consideration, or unless it is one to which the settlor or his spouse/civil partner is beneficially entitled (or for interests acquired on or after 10 March 1981, has been at any time beneficially entitled (s 48)). Accordingly the value of the reversion in this example is excluded from Lawrie's estate for inheritance tax purposes.

    For detailed notes on excluded property see Example 3.

2. The reason for excluding reversionary interests from a person's estate for inheritance tax purposes was that the capital value of the settlement (as distinct from the value of the right to receive the income for the time being) is included in the estate of the person presently entitled to receive the income for interests in possession created before 22 March 2006 and for some interests in possession created after that date.

    For other interests in possession created on or after 22 March 2006, the settlement is subject to a separate charging regime based upon the value of the trust property and, therefore, it is still unnecessary to tax reversionary interests.

Quick succession relief

3. The settled property does not give rise to quick succession relief on the death of Alan since it was *not* chargeable on the death of Lawrie (see Examples 53 and 55).

    The settlement made by Richard granted a life interest to Alan and a reversion to Lawrie.

    That made by Lawrie granted a life interest to Gladys with reversion to John.

    The fund left by Richard therefore devolves as follows:

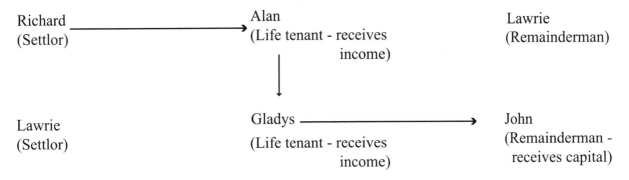

    Lawrie therefore never had an interest in the income of the settlement made by Richard and was therefore not chargeable to inheritance tax on the transfer of the reversion on his death. This passed as part of his estate from which Gladys is to enjoy the income for her life and will not be chargeable to inheritance tax until Gladys's interest in the fund ceases (ordinarily upon her death). On Alan's death on 31 December 2008, however, the trust fund created by Richard is reduced by inheritance tax of £7,639, reducing the value in the estate of Lawrie from which Gladys is to enjoy the income. It does not reduce the inheritance tax payable on Lawrie's death, because the trust fund is excluded property.

Treatment of debts in deceased's estate

4. Debts may be deducted from the chargeable estate if they are:

    (i)   Reasonable funeral expenses, including the cost of a tombstone (s 172).

(ii)   Liabilities imposed by law or incurred for a consideration in money or money's worth (including income and other taxes) (s 5(3), (5)).

(iii)   Liabilities for inheritance tax providing they are paid from the estate (ss 5(4) and 174(2)).

A debt may not be deducted, however, to the extent that the creditor has received gifts from the deceased (FA 1986 s 103). For details see Example 20.

The amount due to the turf accountant is not incurred for consideration in money or money's worth and cannot therefore be deducted in arriving at the chargeable estate of Lawrie.

Powers over trust property

5.   The inheritance tax treatment of powers over trust property had become uncertain following the decision of the Court of Appeal in *Melville v CIR* (2001). The case concerned a scheme to obtain capital gains tax gifts holdover relief under TCGA 1992 s 260. In order for the relief to be available, the gift had to be a chargeable transfer for inheritance tax (see Example 50 explanatory note 3). The donor therefore made the gift to a discretionary trust. The aim was, however, to obtain the capital gains relief without attracting a large amount of inheritance tax. This was achieved by giving the settlor the power, after 90 days, to direct the trustees to exercise various powers, including the power to direct them to transfer all or part of the fund back to him. Since the settlor could effectively revoke the trust after 90 days, the value of the power (and hence the chargeable transfer) was claimed to be the income arising in the 90-day period. The Revenue argued that the power was not 'property' for inheritance tax, being similar to that of a reversionary interest, and should therefore be ignored, so that the value transferred was the full value of the property transferred into the trust. The Court of Appeal found in the taxpayer's favour. Although this decision enabled the taxpayer to avoid capital gains tax, it had adverse inheritance tax implications, in particular for offshore trusts.

The position was amended by FA 2002 s 119, which provides that the definition of 'property' in IHTA 1984 s 272 does not include a 'settlement power'. A settlement power is defined in new s 47A as 'any power over, or exercisable (whether directly or indirectly) in relation to, settled property or a settlement'. To prevent the revised provisions being used for tax avoidance, s 55A provides that someone who *purchases* a settlement power will be treated as making a transfer of value equal to the decrease in value of his estate as a result of the transfer, and no exemptions will be available against the transfer. The revised provisions apply for transfers of value on or after 17 April 2002, but the definitions of settlement power and property are deemed to apply in relation to deaths before that date (to avoid adverse effects of the *Melville* decision).

Question

The trustees of a discretionary settlement made on 1 November 1967 make the following appointments under powers given to them in the settlement, the cumulative transfers in the ten years prior to 1 November 1997 being £181,000.

(i)	1 July 2000	£40,000	cash to A absolutely
(ii)	1 April 2007	£60,000	cash to the settlor's wife

All the beneficiaries are domiciled and resident in the United Kingdom.

Any tax payable is to be paid by the beneficiaries.

(a) Calculate the inheritance tax payable (if any) as a result of each of the above appointments and also the amount payable on the ten-year anniversaries up to and including 1 November 2007.

The value of relevant property on 31 October 1997 was £162,000 and on 31 October 2007 £290,000.

(b) If the original settlor added £25,000 to the original settlement on 1 November 2003 (at which time his gross chargeable transfers for the seven years to that date amounted to £240,000 including the £25,000 then transferred) calculate the revised tax liabilities assuming that the value of relevant property at 31 October 2007 was £306,000, including the addition to the settlement which was valued at £16,000 on that date.

The payment of £60,000 to the settlor's wife on 1 April 2007 is to be deemed to be wholly attributable to the funds in the original settlement.

Answer

(a)   **Inheritance tax position of settlement made 1 November 1967**

	Gross £	Tax £
1 November 1997		
Ten-yearly charge (see explanatory notes 3 and 4):		
Distributions in previous ten years (ie amounts subject to		
exit charges)	181,000	–
Value of relevant property on 31 October 1997	162,000	25,600*
	343,000	25,600*

Actual rate is 30% of effective rate

$$\frac{25,600}{162,000} \times 30\% = 4.741\%$$

Tax payable by trustees is £162,000 × 4.741% =   £7,680

* Tax is calculated on 1997/98 scale
   (343,000 – 215,000 = 128,000 @ 20%)

1 July 2000
   Exit charge – on distribution to A
   Amount chargeable = £40,000
   Actual rate at previous ten-year anniversary recomputed for
   change of rates
   2000/2001 scale 343,000 – 234,000 = 109,000 @ 20% = £21,800
   Actual rate is 30% of effective rate

$$\frac{21,800}{162,000} \times 30\% = 4.03\%$$

Number of complete quarters between 1 November 1997
and 30 June 2000 = 10
Tax payable by A

$$£40,000 \times 4.03\% \times \frac{10}{40} = £403$$

1 April 2007
   Exit charge – on distribution to settlor's wife
   Amount chargeable = £60,000
   Actual rate at previous ten-year anniversary recomputed
   for change of rates
   2006/07 scale 343,000 – 285,000 = 58,000 @ 20% = £11,600
   Actual rate is 30% of effective rate

$$\frac{11,600}{162,000} \times 30\% = 2.15\%$$

	Gross £	Tax £

Number of complete quarters between 1 November 1997 and
31 March 2007 = 37
Tax payable by settlor's wife

$$£60,000 \times 2.15\% \times \frac{37}{40} = £1,193$$

1 November 2007
    Ten-yearly charge
    Distributions in previous ten years (ie between

	Gross £	Tax £
1 November 1997 and 31 October 2007)	100,000	–
Value of relevant property on 31 October 2007	290,000	18,000**
	390,000	18,000**

(** 390,000 – 300,000 = 90,000 @ 20%)
Actual rate is 30% of effective rate

$$\frac{18,000}{290,000} \times 30\% = 1.86\%$$

Tax payable by trustees is £290,000 × 1.86% =   £5,394

(b)   **Additions to existing settlement**

1 November 2003
    Recalculation of distributions at previous ten-year
    anniversary because of addition to property in the
    settlement:

	Gross £	Tax £
Distributions in ten years to 31 October 1997		181,000
Value of relevant property at 31 October 1997	162,000	
Value of property added 1 November 2003	25,000	187,000
		368,000

1 April 2007
    Exit charge – on distribution to settlor's wife
    Amount chargeable = £60,000
    Revised rate at previous ten-year anniversary following addition to
        settlement, using 2006/07 scale:
        368,000 – 285,000 = 83,000 @ 20% = £16,600
    Actual rate is 30% of effective rate

$$\frac{16,600}{187,000} \times 30\% = 2.663\%$$

Number of complete quarters between 1 November 1997
and 31 March 2007 = 37

Tax payable by settlor's wife

$$£60,000 \times 2.663\% \times \frac{37}{40} = £1,478$$

	Gross £	Tax £
1 November 2007		
Ten-yearly charge (see explanatory note 7)		
Distributions in previous ten years subject to an exit charge	100,000	–
Chargeable transfers made by settlor in seven years preceding addition to settlement (2405,000 – 25,000)	215,000	3,000*
	315,000	3,000
Value of relevant property on 31 October 2006	306,000	61,200
	621,000	64,200 †

(* 315,000 – 300,000 = 15,000 @ 20% = £3,000)
(† 621,000 – 300,000 = 321,000 @ 20% = £64,200)
Actual rate is 30% of effective rate

$$\frac{61,200}{306,000} \times 30\% = 6\%$$

proportionately reduced where relevant property added in previous ten years.
Tax payable by trustees:
On relevant property held for preceding ten years
(£306,000 – £16,000) = £290,000 @ 6%   17,400
On relevant property added 1 November 2003

$$£16,000 @ 6\% \times \frac{16}{40} \text{ (see explanatory note 7)}$$

384
—————
£17,784
—————

Explanatory Notes

Discretionary settlement — deemed chargeable transfers

1.   Where a settlement has an interest in possession which was created before 22 March 2006, the person with that interest is deemed to be beneficially entitled to the underlying assets, and chargeable transfers affecting his interest are deemed to be made by him (s 49).

This is also the case for subsequent interests in possession if they are:

(a)   an immediate post-death interest;

(b)   a disabled person's interest (broadly an interest in possession for a person incapable of looking after their affairs because of mental disorder, or a person in receipt of an attendance allowance or a disability living allowance); or

(c)   a transitional serial interest (IHTA 1984 s 49(1A)).

See Example 52.

In other cases this deemed ownership cannot apply, nor can the trustees make transfers of value or chargeable transfers. They are, however, deemed to make chargeable transfers when they make capital distributions.

Pre 27 March 1974 discretionary settlements

2.   Where a settlement without an interest in possession was created before 27 March 1974 it has an inheritance tax accumulation of its own commencing at nil on 27 March 1974 (s 66(6b)). The rules for such settlements were changed from 9 March 1982. Under the old rules, tax was charged by taking into account 'distribution payments', which broadly meant capital distributions, although the term was more widely defined. From 9 March 1982 tax is charged at ten-yearly intervals and also when property leaves the settlement, as detailed below.

Ten-yearly charge

3.   On the tenth anniversary of the creation of the settlement and every subsequent tenth anniversary (but not before 1 April 1983) a charge to inheritance tax arises. This is known as the principal or 'ten-yearly' charge (s 64).

The charge is made on any *relevant property* held in the trust at the anniversary. This means property in which there is no interest in possession (subject to certain exclusions – see note 8). See note 9 re reducing the tax on relevant property that has not been relevant property throughout the ten-year period.

The trust is deemed to make a notional transfer immediately before the anniversary, having previously made chargeable transfers of a specified amount, and *one half* the normal scale rate in force at the date of the charge is used to arrive at the tax on the transfer. There is no grossing up (s 64). The rate of tax charged on the relevant property in the trust is 30% of the effective rate of tax on the notional transfer. With the current half scale rate of 20% this gives a maximum charging rate of 6% (see note 11 re business or agricultural property relief and the instalment option).

The rules for arriving at both the notional transfer and the previous transfers are different for pre 27 March 1974 trusts and trusts made on or after that date. For the detailed rules relating to post 26 March 1974 trusts see Example 60.

Cumulative transfers at ten-year anniversary

4.   For pre 27 March 1974 trusts, the inheritance tax accumulation at the anniversary date will normally only show transfers occurring during the preceding ten years. Those transfers will comprise:

(a)   At the first ten-year anniversary, distribution payments (as defined under the old rules) up to 8 March 1982. These are not included at later ten-year anniversaries.

(b)   The amounts on which exit charges have been made under s 65 (see notes 5 and 6).

Thus the charge in 2007 uses the exit charges of the preceding ten years:

	£
1 July 2000	40,000
1 April 2007	60,000
	100,000

These previous transfers are cumulated with the relevant property in the trust at the anniversary to compute the tax at one half normal rates on the notional transfer and arrive at the effective rate. The tax charge on the relevant property is then at 30% of the effective rate (s 66). In each case the tax is calculated at the rates in force at the date of the charge.

Special rules apply when property has been added to the settlement during the ten-year period. These are detailed in note 7.

Exit charges

5.   In addition to the ten-yearly charge (explanatory notes 3 and 4) a charge to inheritance tax arises when property in a settlement ceases to be relevant property (s 65). This charge is known as the exit charge. If the tax is payable out of the relevant property remaining in the trust, the distribution is grossed up using the rate of tax payable on the distribution (ie after reducing it under note 6 below, if appropriate, according to the complete quarters since the last ten-year anniversary) (s 65(2)). (For an illustration of grossing up see Example 60.) The method of computing exit charges occurring after the first post 1 April 1983 ten-year anniversary of the settlement is the same for both pre 27 March 1974 settlements and settlements made on or after that date.

6.   The charge on distributions after the first ten-year anniversary is found by using the rate of tax computed at the previous ten-year anniversary (but where the scale of rates has been reduced the rate deemed to have applied at that anniversary is recalculated using the revised scales (Sch 2.3), as shown in part (a) of the example). The exit charge rate is arrived at by applying to that previous rate the fraction x/40 where x is the number of complete quarters in the period since the previous ten-year anniversary (s 69). If, therefore, the distribution occurs at the anniversary, or within three months thereafter, no exit charge is payable. The charge is levied on the difference between the value of relevant property before the distribution and its value thereafter. Thus the 'loss to the donor' principle applies to discretionary settlements. The maximum rate for an exit charge is 5.85%, ie 6% (maximum rate at previous ten-year anniversary) × 39/40.

Special rules apply where property has been added to a settlement since the date of the last ten-year charge (see note 7).

Added property

7.   Where property has been added to a pre 27 March 1974 settlement after 8 March 1982 as a result of a chargeable transfer by the settlor, then on the occasion of the following ten-year anniversary the inheritance tax accumulation is deemed to commence with the distributions subject to an exit charge in the previous ten years, plus the aggregate of the values transferred by the settlor in the seven years preceding the date of the addition to the settlement disregarding transfers made on that day. Where two or more additions have been made then the higher of the two (or more) possible figures will be used (s 67(4)). Thus a modest addition to an existing settlement can give rise to a substantial increase in the tax payable. In the example the ten-yearly charge on 1 November 2007 would increase from £5,394 to £17,784 if £25,000 was added to the settlement on 1 November 2003.

Although the total value of relevant property added in the previous ten years is chargeable to tax and is added to the accumulation to arrive at the rate of tax, the rate of tax chargeable on that added property is reduced by one-fortieth for each complete quarter before the date that the property became relevant property. In the example the property was added after six years (24 quarters) and therefore tax was payable on the added property of £16,000 @ 6% × 16/40 = £384; being a charge for the last four of the ten years (16 quarters) (s 66(2)).

In addition to affecting the subsequent ten-year charge the addition will also increase the exit charge on any distribution occurring after its settlement. This is because it is necessary both for pre and post 27 March 1974 settlements to recompute the tax rate on the previous ten-year anniversary by including in the calculation the value of property added subsequently as though it were relevant property at that time (s 69(2), (3)). This is illustrated by the difference in rates in part (b) of the example in relation to the distribution on 1 April 2007 to the settlor's wife where the tax increased from £1,193 to £1,478.

If the £60,000 paid to the settlor's wife on 1 April 2007 had come partly from the original settlement and partly from the added property then two separate computations would be required. The fraction applicable to the added property will not take into account the complete quarters (since the date of the previous anniversary) occurring before the day that the property was added (ss 68(3), 69(4)).

Thus, assuming that £54,000 came from the original settlement and £6,000 from the added property, the computation would be:

1 April 2007   £
    Exit charge – on distribution to settlor's wife
    Original property = £54,000
    Revised rate at previous ten-year anniversary 2.663%
    Number of complete quarters = 37
    Tax payable:

$$£54,000 \times 2.663\% \times \frac{37}{40} =$$ 1,330

    Added property – £6,000
    Complete quarters 1 November 1997 to 1 November 2003 = 24

$$\text{Appropriate fraction is} \frac{37-24}{40} = \frac{13}{40}$$

Tax payable:

$$£6,000 \times 2.663\% \times \frac{13}{40} =$$ 52

                                                                                                        ———
                                                                                                        1,382
                                                                                                        ———

Where there is no indication as to whether a distribution is paid out of the original property or added property, it is treated as coming out of each proportionately.

Property will be deemed to have been added if the settlor makes any chargeable transfer which results in the value of the property in the settlement increasing, unless it can be shown that the transfer was not primarily intended to increase the value of the settlement and the actual increase was not more than 5% of its original value (s 67(2)).

Meaning of 'relevant property'

8.   Relevant property is defined in s 58 as settled property in which there is an interest in possession created on or after 22 March 2006 other than:

    1.   An immediate post-death interest

    2.   A disabled person's interest (broadly an interest in possession for a person incapable of looking after their affairs because of mental disorder, or a person in receipt of an attendance allowance or a disability living allowance) or

    3.   A transitional serial interest

    or there is no qualifying interest in possession, other than:

    (i)   Charitable trusts

    (ii) Property held on accumulation and maintenance trusts (see Example 64) set up before 22 March 2006 or trusts for a bereaved minor

> (iii) Maintenance funds for historic buildings etc
>
> (iv) Pension funds
>
> (v) Employee and newspaper trusts unless there is a post 22 March 2006 interest possession and the interest in possession is:
>
>> – not an immediate post-death interest,
>>
>> – not a disabled person's interest, and
>>
>> – not a transitional serial interest.
>
> (vi) Trade or professional compensation funds
>
> (vii) Protective trusts where the discretionary trust was triggered before 12 April 1978
>
> (viii) Privileged trusts for disabled persons where funds were settled before 10 March 1981
>
> (ix) Excluded property.

9. If property in a settlement has not been relevant property throughout the whole of the period then the charge on that property will not take into account the complete quarters (since the date of the previous anniversary) occurring before the day that the property became relevant property (s 68(3)). See Example 61 for an illustration of this point.

Conversion of relevant property into non-relevant property

10. An exit charge can (and in certain cases does) arise if trustees convert relevant property into property that is not relevant property. Such a charge is prevented in most instances, however, by specific provisions. Thus there is no exit charge when property ceases to be relevant property because it is transferred to an employee trust (subject to detailed conditions – see s 75), or is held for an unlimited period for charitable purposes, or becomes the property of a national body such as a museum or the National Trust, or a political party or a non-profit making body (s 76). This is subject to the proviso that the property does not cease to be used for the purposes of the body concerned.

Although an exit charge does not arise when a distribution is made from a charitable trust if it is for that purpose, a special charge is made under s 70 on the cessation of the trust or on a non-privileged distribution. This is calculated by reference to the time that the property has been held (but not before 13 March 1975) and is the sum of

0.25% for each of the first forty quarters

0.20% for each of the next forty quarters

0.15% for each of the next forty quarters

0.10% for each of the next forty quarters

0.05% for each of the next forty quarters

Thus the maximum rate of 30% cannot apply until 2025.

If the trust pays the tax then the amount must be grossed up.

Instalment option

11. It should be noted that where inheritance tax is payable on property eligible for the instalment option, that option is available to trustees of a settlement, provided that the property remains in the settlement (s 227(1)(c)). For details of property eligible see Example 5 at explanatory note 5. If the property is business or agricultural property qualifying for 50% relief, the 6% maximum rate of charge for discretionary trusts is effectively 3% on that property, and when paid by instalments over ten years this becomes 0.3% a year.

Question

Nicholas Carraway, whose gross chargeable transfers in the preceding seven years totalled £122,000 and who had no available annual exemptions, settled a sum of £100,000 on 6 April 1989 in a discretionary trust, personally paying the inheritance tax chargeable on the scale at that time.

On 21 September 1991 the trustees made a distribution of £4,000 to A, subject to payment of tax out of that amount.

On 1 April 1993 the trustees made a distribution of £6,000 to B, subject to payment of tax out of that amount.

The market value of the trust fund on 5 April 1999 was £150,000.

On 27 May 2003 the trustees made a distribution of £20,000 to C, paying the tax out of the remainder of the settled fund.

The market value of the trust fund on 5 April 2009 was £300,000.

On 10 October 2012 the trustees made a final distribution of £330,000 to D, subject to payment of tax out of that amount.

Compute the inheritance tax payable on each chargeable occasion.

Assume for this purpose that the inheritance tax legislation remains unchanged for later years.

Also assume that the 2010/11 rates will continue into 2011/12 and 2012/13.

Answer

Tax position of settlement (settlor having paid the tax on the settlement)

Initial value of settlement = £100,000

Inheritance tax – effective rate (originally calculated using FA 1988 scale but revised using 1991/92 scale to calculate tax on distribution 21 September 1991):

	Gross £	Tax £
Settlor's previous transfers within seven years before commencement of settlement	122,000	–
Initial value of settlement	100,000	16,400*
	222,000	16,400*

(* 222,000 – 140,000 = 82,000 @ 20%)
Actual rate is 30% of effective rate

$$\frac{16,400}{100,000} \times 30\% = 4.92\%$$

21 September 1991
    Exit charge on distribution to A
    Amount chargeable = £4,000
    Actual rate applicable at formation of settlement
        (revised using 1991/92 lifetime scale) – 4.92%
    Number of complete quarters between 6 April 1989
        and 21 September 1991 = 9
    Tax payable by A out of the distribution

$$£4,000 \times 4.92\% \times \frac{9}{40} = £44$$

1 April 1993
    Exit charge on distribution to B
    Amount chargeable – £6,000
    Actual rate applicable at formation of settlement
        (revised using 1992/93 lifetime scale):
    222,000 – 150,000 = 72,000 @ 20% = £14,400
    Actual rate is 30% of effective rate

$$\frac{14,400}{100,000} \times 30\% = 4.32\%$$

Number of complete quarters between 6 April 1989
    and 31 March 1993 = 15
Tax payable by B out of the distribution

$$£6,000 \times 4.32\% \times \frac{15}{40} = £7$$

	Gross £	Tax using FA 1999 scale £
6 April 1999		
Ten-yearly charge (using one half of rate at 6.4.99)		
Settlor's previous transfers within seven years before commencement of settlement	122,000	
Distributions subject to exit charges in previous ten years (£4,000 + £6,000)	10,000	
	132,000	–
Value of relevant property – 5 April 1999	150,000	10,200**
	282,000	10,200**

(** 282,000 – 231,000 = 51,000 @ 20%)

Actual rate is 30% of effective rate

$$\frac{10,200}{150,000} \times 30\% = 2.04\%$$

Tax payable by trustees is £150,000 × 2.04% =   £3,060

27 May 2003

Exit charge on distribution to C
Actual rate at previous ten-year anniversary
  (revised using 2003/04 lifetime scale):
282,000 – 255,000 = 27,000 @ 20% = £5,400
Actual rate is 30% of effective rate

$$\frac{5,400}{150,000} \times 30\% = 1.08\%$$

Number of complete quarters between 6 April 1999 and
  26 May 2003 = 16
Rate of exit charge applicable

$$1.08\% \times \frac{16}{40} = 0.432\%$$

Distribution (net) – £20,000

Gross equivalent thereof £20,000 × $\frac{100}{99.568}$ = £20,087

Exit charge payable by trustees £20,087 × 0.432% =   £87

	Gross £	Tax using FA 1999 scale £
6 April 2009		
Ten-yearly charge (using one half of rate at 6.4.09)		
Settlor's previous transfers within seven years before commencement of settlement	122,000	
Distributions in preceding ten years subject to an exit charge	20,087	

	Gross £	Tax using FA 1999 scale £
	142,087	–
Value of relevant property – 5 April 2009	300,000	26,017 †
	442,087	26,017 †

(† 442,087 – 312,000 = 130,087 @ 20%)

Actual rate is 30% of effective rate

$$\frac{26,017}{300,000} \times 30\% = 2.602\%$$

Tax payable by trustees is £300,000 × 2.602% =   £7,806

10 October 2012
   Exit charge on distribution to D
   Amount chargeable – £330,000
   Actual rate at previous ten-year anniversary
   revised using 2012/13 lifetime scale:
   442,087 – 350,000 = 92,087 @ 20% = £18,417
   Actual rate is 30% of effective rate

$$\frac{18,417}{300,000} \times 30\% = 1.8417\%$$

Number of complete quarters between 6 April 2009 and
      9 October 2012 = 14
Tax payable by trustees on final distribution

$$£330,000 \times 1.8417\% \times \frac{14}{40} = £2,127$$

Explanatory Notes

Ten-yearly charge on post 26 March 1974 discretionary settlements

1.   The rules relating to discretionary settlements were amended from 9 March 1982. Those relating to pre 27 March 1974 settlements are dealt with in Example 59.

2.   A charge arises under the 1982 legislation on each tenth anniversary of the settlement. This charge is applied to the *relevant property* held in the trust at the anniversary date, without grossing up (s 64).

   Relevant property used to mean (ie before 22 March 2006) property without an interest in possession. It is defined in detail in Example 59 explanatory note 9.

   For post 26 March 1974 settlements the charge is arrived at as follows (s 66):

   (a)   The settlement is deemed to make a notional transfer immediately before the anniversary comprising:

(i) the value of the relevant property immediately before the anniversary, ie its value on the day before the anniversary

(ii) the value immediately after it became comprised in the settlement of any property which was not then relevant property and has not subsequently become relevant property whilst remaining comprised in the settlement (eg where part of the settled property has always been subject to an interest in possession)

(iii) the value of the property in any related settlement at the time the related settlement commenced (s 66). A related settlement is a settlement made by the same settlor and commencing on the same day (excluding settlements in which all the property is held without time limit for charitable purposes) (s 62). (Such a settlement might originally be a potentially exempt transfer but might then become chargeable because of the donor's death within seven years.)

(b) The notional transfer in (a) is added to the notional previous transfers to arrive at the effective rate of tax on the notional transfer in (a) (i).

The notional previous transfers are:

(i) Any chargeable transfers made by the settlor in the seven years prior to the creation of the settlement (excluding transfers made on the day the settlement commenced), except where (e) below applies. (It should be noted that if any potentially exempt transfers made before the transfer into settlement become chargeable because of the donor's death within seven years, this will affect the cumulative total of chargeable transfers. This could happen before or after the date of the ten-year charge, and if it was after, the ten-year charge would have to be recomputed accordingly.)

(ii) In the case of the first ten-year anniversary if it occurred before 9 March 1992, any distribution payments made under the old rules before 9 March 1982 and within the ten years before the anniversary.

(iii) Any amounts on which exit charges have been levied under s 65 within the previous ten years (see note 4).

To compute the tax charge one half of the normal rate of tax is used.

(c) Having arrived at the effective rate of tax on the notional transfer, take 30% of that effective rate to arrive at the actual rate (unless the chargeable relevant property had not been relevant property throughout the ten-year period, in which case the rate on such property is further reduced by 1/40th for each complete quarter that had elapsed in the ten-year period before the property became relevant property). At current rates this gives a maximum charging rate of 6% (or 3% on property that qualifies for 50% business or agricultural property relief, further reduced to 0.3% a year if the instalment option is available – see Example 5 explanatory note 5).

(d) Apply the *rate* arrived at in (c) above to the *relevant property* in the trust at the anniversary, ie to the property at (a) (i) above. Note that the effect of including (a) (ii) and (iii) in the notional transfer is to give a higher cumulative total and thus possibly a higher tax rate, but the charge is levied on the relevant property (a) (i) only.

(e) Where property has been added to the settlement within the previous ten years then although the charge on that property is proportionately reduced as indicated in (c) above, the settlor's previous cumulative transfers at (b) (i) become the chargeable transfers made by him in the seven years preceding the addition to the settlement, if that gives a higher total. Where more than one addition has taken place then either the commencement date or any one of the addition dates is used, whichever gives the highest cumulative total for the previous seven years (s 67).

Where the total used is at one of the addition dates then it is possible that this total will include transfers to the settlement. This would result in a transfer being included twice, eg if the addition was made less than seven years after the commencement of the settlement, the settlor's seven year cumulative total at the date of the addition will include the original chargeable transfer on the creation of the settlement, and (unless it has been the subject of an exit charge) that property will also form part of the relevant property in the settlement (ie included at (a) (i) above). In such circumstances the seven year cumulative total is reduced by the net amount put into the settlement.

Similarly that seven year cumulative total may include the value of property which has ceased to be relevant property at the date of the ten-year charge and has been the subject of an exit charge under s 65 (ie included at (b) (iii) above). Then the seven year cumulative total is reduced by the value attributable to the property subject to that exit charge (s 67(3)(b), (5)).

A double counting relief also applies where property has been the subject of an exit charge (eg on the creation of an interest in possession within the last ten years) but has since become relevant property again. Thus its value would appear both as relevant property (under (a)(i) above) and also as property on which an exit charge had been levied in the last ten years (under (b)(iii) above). In such circumstances the latter amount is reduced by the smaller of:

the value at the time of the exit charge; or

the value on the day before the ten-year anniversary (s 67(b)).

3. Under the pre 9 March 1982 rules, a proportional periodic charge was payable annually where trustees were not resident in the UK but this charge was abolished when the rules were changed. Any unused tax credit arising from the payment of such annual charges is available against *any* payments under the revised rules, ie both ten-yearly charges and exit charges (s 85).

Exit charges

4. A further charge to inheritance tax arises when property in a settlement ceases to be relevant property. This is known as the 'exit charge'. For both pre and post 27 March 1974 settlements where a ten-yearly charge has already been made, the exit charge is calculated by using the rate of tax computed at the previous ten-year anniversary, recalculated using one half of the scale in force at the date of the distribution (if lower). This charge is further reduced by applying the fraction of x/40 where x is the number of *complete* quarters in the period since the preceding ten-year anniversary (s 69) (no charge therefore arising if the distribution is made within the first three months after the anniversary, since x would be nil). The value transferred is the difference between the value of relevant property before the distribution and its value after the distribution. Thus the 'loss to the donor' principle applies and grossing up is necessary if the trustees pay the tax (see note 6). Special rules apply when property has been added to a settlement since the date of the last ten-year charge (s 69). For details see Example 59 at explanatory note 8.

Exit charge before first ten-year anniversary

5. Where an exit charge arises before the first anniversary to which a ten-year charge applies then for post 26 March 1974 settlements the rate of tax is 30% of the effective rate, reduced by applying the fraction of x/40 where x is the number of *complete* quarters in the period since the creation of the settlement (and again no charge arises on a distribution in the first three months after the creation of the settlement since x is nil) (s 68(2)).

The effective rate of tax is found by applying one half of the rates of inheritance tax then applicable to a notional chargeable transfer which is the sum of:

(a) the value of all the property in the settlement, whether it is relevant property or not, immediately after the settlement commenced,

(b) the value of the property in any related settlement immediately after it commenced,

(c)   the value of any added property at the time of its addition to the settlement (this includes accumulated income that has been treated as an accretion to capital, the date of addition being the date that the accumulation was so treated)

and assumes previous chargeable transfers equal to any chargeable transfers made by the settlor in the seven years prior to the day on which the settlement was created. Note that the charge may be affected if potentially exempt transfers become part of the settlor's cumulative chargeable transfers because he died within seven years of making them. Various problems arise in respect of a settlor's premature death within seven years of making a settlement. These include additional tax being due when the original transfer to settlement was at lifetime rates, or a failed PET made by the settlor prior to the set up of the settlement increasing the tax on the transfer which created the settlement.

If a gift into settlement was free from IHT because of the availability of BPR or APR, and the property involved was subsequently disposed of, the trustees should have replaced it with other agricultural or business property so as to shelter any charge within IHTA 1984 ss 113B and 118.

The problems can be illustrated in this brief example:

A always used up his annual exemption by a gift of £3,000 to his nephew on 20 May each year. A died on 1 May 2008.

On 1 May 2002 A gave his daughter £65,000

On 12 June 2003 he gave his son £100,000

On 1 September 2005, he set up a discretionary settlement with funds of £311,000, paying the tax due.

Original IHT position:

Gifts to son and daughter – PETs – Set up of discretionary trust

This is a chargeable transfer of £311,000. A has a nil cumulative total and the nil-rate band for 2005/06 was £275,000. The excess of £36,000 is grossed up as tax is paid by the settlor (36,000 × 100/80 = 45,000).

Chargeable transfer (gross)	£320,000
Tax paid by settlor (320,000 – 275,000 = 45,000 @ 20%)	£9,000

On subsequent death of Mr A

PETs to son and daughter

Transfers of £100,000 to his son and £65,000 to his daughter are within Mr A's nil-rate band for 2008/09 so no further tax payable. The cumulative total of transfers is however now increased to £165,000.

Transfer to discretionary trust

	£
Chargeable transfer to trust	320,000
Cumulative transfers	165,000
	485,000
Tax at death rate (485,000 – 312,000 @ 40%)	69,200
Less: paid in 2005/06	9,000
Additional tax payable by trustees	60,200

If the settlor's death occurs before a distribution out of the trust, the charge on the distribution is calculated accordingly. If the settlor dies after the distribution is made the exit charge may be increased and additional tax will then be payable. This is because any failed PETs on death will increase the amount of the settlor's previous transfers in the seven years before the commencement of the settlement.

The effect of the settlor's death on occasions of charge is considered in more detail in Example 62. The rate so calculated is applied to the relevant property leaving the settlement using the 'loss to the donor' principle.

If the property was not relevant property throughout the period since the settlement commenced the rate of tax on that property is reduced according to the complete quarters that had expired before it became relevant property.

Grossing up

6.   If the exit charge is paid by the donee then no grossing up is necessary (s 65(2)(a)) but if the tax is paid by the settlement then the chargeable amount must be grossed up (s 65(2)(b)). In the example the distributions to A, B and D did not require any grossing up as they paid the tax out of the distribution. C, however, received £20,000 after payment of tax. The fund has therefore been reduced by £20,000 plus the tax thereon £87, a total transfer of £20,087.

This is calculated by using the formula of:

$$\text{Net transfer} \times \frac{100}{(100 - \text{rate of tax})} = \text{gross transfer}$$

In this example the rate of tax is 0.432% and therefore the calculation is:

$$£20,000 \times \frac{100}{(100 - 0.432)} = £20,087$$

Tax planning

7.   Although the treatment of discretionary trusts is complex, they have a useful role to play in tax planning.

If a settlor has not made any chargeable transfers, nor used his annual exemptions, he can presently transfer assets to the value of £318,000 into a discretionary trust without paying either inheritance tax or capital gains tax (since the holdover relief in TCGA 1992 s 260 is available on *chargeable* transfers, whether any inheritance tax is payable on those transfers or not). Any transfers out of the trust in the first ten years will then not attract tax (subject to what is said below about business and agricultural property). Care needs to be taken, however, if the settlor has already made potentially exempt transfers, because a liability on the transfer to the trust could then arise if he died within seven years, and also on distributions out of the trust.

Furthermore, now that all lifetime transfers into trust are subject to the relevant property regime it will be appropriate in many cases for trusts to maintain the flexibility of discretionary trusts rather than be constrained by the use of interest in possession settlements or accumulation and maintenance trusts.

If the property transferred into trust qualifies for 100% or 50% business or agricultural relief, this increases the amount that can be transferred without tax being payable, subject to what is said above about potentially exempt transfers. Distributions of the business or agricultural property out of the trust also qualify for the relief (providing the trustees have owned the property for two years). There is, however, a particular problem where distributions are made out of the trust within the first ten years, because the whole of the value of the business or agricultural property is taken into account in calculating the initial value of the settlement (see note 5(a) above), so any exit charges on distributions within the first *ten* years are based on the full value of the property when settled. For further details see Example 62 at explanatory note 5.

Spouse as discretionary beneficiary

8.   It is possible to include a spouse/civil partner as one of the discretionary beneficiaries, thus ensuring that property is not left directly to the surviving spouse/civil partner to swell that spouse's/civil partner's own estate. Prior to the introduction of a transferrable nil-rate band between spouses and civil partners (announced in the 2007 Pre-Budget Report and incorporated into FA 2008 Sch 4), this was a common ploy for the reduction of inheritance tax on the second death. In most cases it is no longer considered appropriate to make use of a discretionary trust in the will of the first spouse to die because this will not result in any tax saving on the death of the survivor. The following example illustrate the point.

Example A – Use of discretionary trusts prior to transferrable nil-rate band

Mr and Mrs Forster have estates in their sole names of £301,000 and £282,000 respectively. In addition they own a freehold house as joint tenants valued at £400,000. Their wills each leave all of their estate to the other (or to their only child in the case of the second spouse to die). They have not made any lifetime gifts. If both had died before 9 October 2007 their potential liability to inheritance tax would have been:

	£
On first death:	
Inter-spouse transfer – exempt	nil
On second death:	
Estate of Mr Forster	301,000
Estate of Mrs Forster	282,000
House	400,000
	983,000

Tax thereon (983,000 – 300,000 = 683,000 @ 40%) =   £273,200

If, however, their wills had provided for an amount equal to the nil band for inheritance tax to devolve upon a discretionary settlement, from which spouse, child and, say, grandchildren could benefit, with the residue of the estate devolving on the spouse, then the nil-rate band of the spouse dying first would be utilised, viz:

On first death (say Mr Forster)	£
Free assets	301,000
Pecuniary legacy to discretionary trust	300,000
Residue to spouse	1,000
½ share of house (passes to spouse by survivorship)	200,000
Exempt transfer	201,000
Value of Estate	
Own assets	301,000
½ share of house	200,000
	501,000
Less: exempt transfer	201,000
Chargeable estate	300,000

Covered by nil threshold.

On Mrs Forster's death	
Own assets	282,000
Residue from husband's estate	1,000
House	400,000

On first death (say Mr Forster)	£
	683,000

Tax thereon (683,000 – 300,000 = 383,000 @ 40%) =   £153,200

Thus taking both deaths together the discretionary trust would at the time of the second death (before 9 October 2007) save inheritance tax equal to the value of the nil-rate band on the first death (£300,000 @ 40% = £120,000). Provided the value in the discretionary trust does not increase faster than the rate of increase of the nil-rate band, no further tax will be payable on capital distributions from the trust. The surviving spouse would be able to have use of the income (and capital) of the trust with the agreement of the trustees (but distributions must not be made with in first three months – see note 9 below). The income of the trust would be subject to income tax at 40% but this will be recoverable to the extent that it exceeds the beneficiary's personal tax liability if the income is distributed (see Example 47 for further details).

Example B – Use of discretionary trusts after transferrable nil-rate band

Assume the same facts as in Example A but the survivor (Mrs Forster) dies between 9 October 2007 and 5 April 2008). The potential inheritance tax liability without the use of a discretionary trust is:

	£
On first death:	
Inter-spouse transfer – exempt	nil
On second death:	
Estate of Mr Forster	301,000
Estate of Mrs Forster	282,000
House	400,000
	983,000

Tax thereon (983,000 – 600,000* = 383,000 @ 40%) =   £153,200

* Mr Forster has not used his nil-rate band at all so Mrs Forster's nil-rate band is augmented by 100% and she has £600,000 rather than £300,000 available.

If Mr and Mrs Forster's wills had provided for an amount equal to the nil-rate band to devolve upon a discretionary settlement, from which spouse, child and, say, grandchildren could benefit, with the residue of the estate devolving on the spouse, then the nil-rate band of the spouse dying first would be utilised, so the survivor's nil-rate band is not increased at all. Thus, the second calculation produces the same result (inheritance tax of £153,200 is payable on Mrs Forster's death) and there is no advantage in making use of the discretionary trust. Where such trusts are used it is possible to unravel them within two years of the first death (see note 9 below).

Distributions within two years after death

9.   If a discretionary trust is created by will, distributions out of it within two years after the death are treated as having been made under the will (IHTA 1984 s 144) rather than being treated as amounts on which an exit charge is payable. This is a very useful provision enabling maximum flexibility to be built into a will so that the estate may be distributed taking into account the situation at the time of the death, rather than having to review the will regularly to ensure that its provisions are still appropriate.

To be within the provisions of s 144, the distribution must be one on which tax would otherwise be chargeable. It must not therefore occur within the first three months after death, because exit charges do not apply to such distributions (see note 5). In the case of *Frankland v CIR* (CA 1997), within three months after the creation of a discretionary trust by will, the trust property was transferred to a trust in which the surviving spouse had a life interest. The intention was to avoid the inheritance tax on the death estate through the substitution of an exempt spouse transfer for the taxable transfer to the discretionary trust. It was held that s 144 did not apply because there would have been no exit charge on the transfer to the life interest trust.

10. Where distributions of assets from a discretionary trust within two years after death are treated as made at death as indicated in note 9 above, the capital gains tax position must be considered if the assets are liable to that tax and have increased in value since death. The capital gains tax gifts holdover relief of TCGA 1992 s 260 only applies if the transfer is chargeable to inheritance tax (see Example 50 explanatory note 3), which it is not where IHTA 1984 s 144 applies. Capital gains tax cannot therefore be held over unless the assets qualify for business gifts holdover relief under TCGA 1992 s 165 (as to which see Example 50 part A(d)). See Example 50 explanatory note 5 for a way in which capital gains tax may be avoided.

Question

On 6 June 1996 H, who had made no previous transfers of value, settled £80,000 on himself for life, with remainder to his wife, W, for life, with remainder on her death on discretionary trusts for the benefit of their children and grandchildren.

H died on 5 May 1997 when his own assets were valued at £90,000.

His cumulative chargeable transfers at that date were £95,000.

By his will he left all his property to his children equally.

His wife, W, died on 4 April 2000 leaving assets valued at £184,000.

By her will she settled £50,000 cash on discretionary charitable trusts without limit of time, and the residue to her brother for life with remainder to his children.

She had made chargeable transfers of value totalling £111,750, all less than seven years before her death.

The settled fund from her husband's death was valued at £110,000 upon her death.

On 8 August 2002 the trustees appointed £30,000 gross to the eldest child, William, for life with remainder to his children who attained 18 or being daughters sooner married, whom failing to revert to the trust fund.

On 10 April 2005 William and his wife (who had no children) were killed in a car accident.

After payment of inheritance tax and other expenses in connection with his death, the fund appointed to William, which then fell back into the settlement created on 6 June 1996, was valued at only £24,000.

The rest of the property in that settlement was valued at that date at £96,000.

The recombined settlement may be taken to have the following values:

As at 5 June 2006	£113,640
As at 4 May 2007	£125,410
As at 3 April 2010	£157,624

Calculate the inheritance tax payable in connection with the appointment on 8 August 2002 and on the first ten-year anniversary.

(So far as future events are concerned assume that the law set out in IHTA 1984 does not change.)

Answer

6 June 1996	–	H settles £80,000 on himself for life	
	–	No inheritance tax payable as no loss to his estate.	
5 May 1997	–	H dies, settlement passes to spouse for life – exempt transfer.	
4 April 2000	–	W dies, and is deemed settlor of discretionary trust dated 6 June 1996.	

Tax position of deemed settlor W at date of her death, 4 April 2000

		Gross £	Tax on 1999/2000 scale £
Cumulative transfers in seven years to date of death		111,750	–
Free estate on death	184,000		
Less: Charitable settlement (exempt)	50,000		
	134,000		
Interest in possession in husband's 1995 settlement	110,000	244,000	49,900*
		355,750	49,900*

(* 355,750 – 231,000 = 124,750 @ 40%)

Inheritance tax payable: £

By personal representatives	$\dfrac{134,000}{244,000} \times £49,900 =$	27,404
By trustees of settlement	$\dfrac{110,000}{244,000} \times £49,900 =$	22,496
		49,900

Initial value of related settlement (W's 2000 will settlement)

Free estate	184,000
Less: to charitable trusts	50,000
	134,000
Less: IHT payable by personal representatives	27,404
	£106,596

Initial value of discretionary settlement (ie value at time it was deemed to commence)

Value of fund in which W had an interest in possession at her death	110,000
Less: IHT payable by trustees	22,496
	£87,504

8 August 2002 – Exit charge on creation of life interest for William

		Gross £	Tax on 2002/03 scale £
Settlor's seven-year cumulative total at time settlement deemed to commence		111,750	–
Notional transfer			
Initial value of settlement	87,504		
Initial value of related settlement	106,596		
Initial value of added property	nil	194,100	11,170*
		305,850	11,170*

(* 305,850 – 250,000 = 55,850 @ 20%)
Actual rate is 30% of effective rate

$$\frac{11,170}{194,100} \times 30\% = 1.73\%$$

Quarters since settlement deemed to commence
4 April 2000 to 8 August 2002 = 9 quarters
Tax payable:

$$1.73\% \times \frac{9}{40} \times £30,000 = £117$$

6 June 2006 ten-year charge

	£
Assumed cumulative total:	
Settlor's seven-year cumulative total at time settlement deemed to commence	111,750
Exit charges in last 10 years	30,000
	141,750

Less: Amount included in £141,750 and also reflected in value of relevant property of £113,640 below

$$\frac{*24,000}{*24,000 + **96,000} \times 113,640$$

(Value of fund at 10-year anniversary)	22,728
	119,022

    * Property reverting on death of William
    ** Value of rest of property at that time

Assumed transfer at 10-year anniversary:	
Relevant property	113,640
Initial value of related settlement	106,596
	220,236

	Gross £	Tax on 2006/07 scale £
Assumed cumulative total	119,022	nil
Assumed transfer at 10-year anniversary	220,236	10,852*
	339,258	10,852*

(* 339,258 – 285,000 = 54,258 @ 20%)

Actual rate is 30% of effective rate

$$\frac{10,852}{220,236} \times 30\% = 1.478\%$$

Appropriate fraction:

$$\text{Original settlement} \left(4/5 \times 113,640\right) \left(\text{ie} \frac{96,000}{24,000 + 96,000} \text{calculation above}\right) = £90,912$$

Complete quarters until property becomes relevant property
6 June 1996 to 4 April 2000 = 15 quarters reduction
Appropriate fraction – 25/40ths

$$\text{Property returning to settlement} \left(1/5 \times 113,640\right) \left(\text{ie} \frac{24,000}{24,000 + 96,000} \text{calculation above} = £22,728\right)$$

Complete quarters prior to property last becoming relevant property
6 June 1995 to 10 April 2004 = 35 quarters reduction
Appropriate fraction – 5/40ths

Tax payable:			£
Original settlement	1.478% × 25/40 ×	90,912	840
Returned property	1.478% × 5/40 ×	22,728	42
Value of settlement at 10-year anniversary	£	113,640	882

Explanatory Notes

Settlement on self

1. A transfer of value normally occurs when a person transfers property to a settlement.

    However, if the settlor retains an interest in possession in the property in the settlement then there is no loss to his estate and therefore no transfer of value.

    If the property subsequently forms part of a discretionary settlement, or the interest in possession passes to anyone other than the settlor or his spouse, then the settlor or spouse (whoever last had the interest in possession) is deemed to have created a separate settlement at that time (unless the original settlement was made before 27 March 1974) (s 80).

    Accordingly the discretionary settlement is not deemed to be made until W dies, since until then she had an interest in possession, being entitled as of right to the income.

Related settlements

2. Any other settlements created at the time of W's death would normally be related settlements (s 62(1)).

    However the charitable trust is not regarded as related as the assets are held for charitable purposes without limit of time (s 62(2)) – see Example 60 explanatory note 2(a)(iii).

    Furthermore the transfer to the charitable trust is an exempt transfer (s 23) thus reducing the estate chargeable on W's death.

    The inheritance tax payable on the settlement is met by the trustees, thus reducing the initial value of the discretionary settlement from £110,000 to £87,504.

Exit charges

3. The effective rate of tax on an exit depends upon whether the distribution occurs before the first ten-year anniversary (s 68) or after that date (s 69).

    Although the settlement was deemed to be created by the death of W, the anniversary date is fixed by s 61 as being the 10th anniversary of the date when the original settlement commenced (s 61(2)).

4. For the purpose of computing the assumed cumulative total and notional transfer, the date of the deemed creation of the settlement applies and accordingly the settlement commences with W's 7 year cumulative total immediately prior to her death, the settlement created by her will becoming a related settlement.

5. Because the property was not relevant property throughout the whole of the period since the settlement was created, s 68(3) applies and only the period from the deemed creation (4 April 2000) to date of distribution (8 August 2002) is used to compute the appropriate fraction.

Ten-yearly charge

6. On the 10th anniversary of the settlement (6 June 2006) s 66 applies.

    As the property subject to the exit charge (distribution to William) is also included in the value of relevant property (because of the death of William and his wife and the consequent reversion of the property to the discretionary settlement), the assumed cumulative total is reduced by the lower of:

    (a)   the exit charge £30,000; or

    (b)   the proportionate value at the 10-year anniversary of the property which has reverted (s 66(5)).

    At the time the property reverted to the settlement it was valued at £24,000 and the other property in the settlement at £96,000.

    $$\text{Accordingly} \frac{24,000}{120,000} \text{ of the value at 6 June 2006 relates to the exit to William, ie:}$$

    ⅕ × £113,640 = £22,728.

7. The charge at the ten-year anniversary is reduced by the number of complete quarters prior to the appropriate date. Again the appropriate fractions reflect the fact that part of the property only became relevant property on 4 April 2000, and part last reverted to the settlement on 10 April 2005 (s 66(2)).

8. See Examples 59, 60 and 62 for further details of discretionary trusts.

Question

On 6 June 1998 Smith retired from the family farming partnership which had commenced 20 years earlier when he had taken his brother and their sons into partnership.

His cumulative chargeable transfers at that date were £181,352 arising out of transfers of value made in late 1990, and he had not yet made any potentially exempt transfers.

At the time of his retirement he transferred the freehold interest in one of his farms, valued at £100,000, which had been leased for the last 12 years to a non-family tenant farmer, to the trustees of a discretionary settlement he created in favour of the children of his brother, who had recently been killed in a farming accident for which Smith felt some moral responsibility. He agreed to pay any inheritance tax due.

At the same time he settled £100,000 of the cash due to him from the partnership on a second discretionary settlement in favour of his own children.

The trustees of this settlement paid any inheritance tax due.

On 5 May 1999 Smith added £24,000 in cash to the brother's children's settlement (on which the trustees are to pay the inheritance tax due).

On 6 May 1999 Smith gave his own children £195,000 in cash.

On 1 January 2000 the trustees of the brother's children's settlement appointed £18,000 to the late brother's eldest son.

On 9 September 2001 when the brother's children's settlement consisted of the farm and 12,000 £1 shares in ABC plc, Smith added a further 120,000 £1 shares in ABC plc to that trust and paid the inheritance tax himself.

On 2 February 2004 the trustees of the brother's children's settlement appointed 66,000 shares in ABC plc to the eldest daughter absolutely.

The assets in the brother's children's settlement were:

	Market value of farm	Shares in ABC plc at value for inheritance tax
9 September 2001	£200,000	133⅓p each
2 February 2004	£210,000	150p each
5 June 2008	£300,000	200p each
6 June 2008	£300,000	201¾p each

Calculate the inheritance tax payable by the trustees in connection with the two appointments from the brother's children's settlement and on the first 10-year anniversary of that trust.

Ignore capital gains tax.

Answer

Tax position of settlor — Smith

			Gross	Tax (on 1998/99 scale)	Net
Inheritance tax accumulation					
6 *June 1998*			£	£	£
Cumulative transfers to date (1990)			181,352	–	181,352
Brother's children's settlement – Farm		100,000			
Less: Agricultural property relief 50% (see explanatory note 5)		50,000			
		50,000			
Less: Annual exemptions 1998/99	3,000				
1997/98	3,000				
	6,000				
$\left(**\dfrac{50,000}{150,000} \times £6,000 \right)$		2,000			
Net transfer, grossed up (see explanatory note 4)		48,000	49,588	1,588	48,000
			230,940	1,588	229,352
Own children's settlement – Cash		100,000			
Less: Annual exemption					
$\left(**\dfrac{100,000}{150,000} \times £6,000 \right)$		4,000	96,000	19,200	76,800
			326,940	20,788*	306,152

(** see explanatory note 1)
(* 326,940 – 223,000 = 103,940 @ 20%)

Tax position of settlements:

Initial value of brother's children's settlement	£100,000
Initial value of own children's settlement (a related settlement – £100,000 less tax £19,200)	£80,800

5 May 1999 — Property added to brother's children's settlement

Tax position of settlor — Smith

					Gross	Tax (1999/00 scale)
Inheritance tax accumulation					£	£
Cumulative transfers in last 7 years (326,940 – 181,352)					145,588	–
Added property				24,000		
Less:	Annual exemptions	1999/00	3,000			
		1998/99	3,000	6,000	18,000	–
					163,588	–*

(* 163,588 – 231,000 = Nil)

Initial value of added property =   £24,000

Tax position of brother's children's settlement

1 January 2000
Exit charge on distribution to late brother's eldest son (Note – as farm is not sold the distribution must come from property added on 5 May 1999 and the tax calculation is affected accordingly)

		Gross	Tax (1999/00 scale)
		£	£
Settlor's 7-year cumulative total at time settlement commenced (s 68(4)(b))		181,352	–
Notional transfer (s 68(4)(a) and (5))			
Initial value of settlement	100,000		
Initial value of related settlement	80,800		
Initial value of added property	24,000	204,800	31,030
(* 386,152 – 231,000 = 155,152 @ 20%)		386,152	31,030*

Effective rate: $\dfrac{31,030}{204,800} \times 100\% = 15.151\%$

Appropriate fraction (s 68(3)):
Quarters since settlement commenced
    6 June 1998 to 1 January 2000   6 quarters
Less: Complete quarters until property added
    6 June 1998 to 5 May 1999   3 quarters
                                  3

9 September 2001 — further added property

Tax position of settlor — Smith

		Gross	Tax (2001/02 scale)	Net
		£	£	£
Cumulative transfers to date (5 May 1999)		163,588		
Gift to children (6 May 1999) – Potentially exempt		– 163,588	–	163,588
Added property 120,000 shares @ 133⅓p		160,000		
Less: Annual exemptions 2001/02	3,000			
2000/2001	3,000	6,000		
Net transfer				154,000
Grossed up*		172,897	18,897	
		336,485	18,897	317,588

* Cumulative net transfers of £317,588 exceed nil band of £242,000 by £75,588, the gross equivalent of which is 83,588 × 100/80 = £94,485. The tax payable is therefore £18,897 and the grossed up transfer is (154,000 + 18,897 =) £172,897.

Initial value of added property – £160,000 (tax paid by settlor)

Tax position of brother's children's settlement

2 February 2004
Exit charge on distribution to eldest daughter (Shares deemed to have been appropriated pro-rata out of property added on 5 May 1999 and 9 September 2001, since the farm is still owned)

		Gross	Tax (2003/04 scale)
		£	£
Assumed Transfer:			
Settlor's 7-year cumulative total at time settlement commenced (see explanatory note 9)		181,352	–
Notional transfer			
At 1 January 2000 (above)	204,800		
Initial value of further added property	160,000	364,800	56,630
		538,152	56,630*

(* 538,152 – 255,000 = 283,152 @ 20%)

Effective rate: $\dfrac{56,630}{364,800} \times 100\% = 15.524\%$

Actual rate is 30% of effective rate, ie 30% × 15.524% = 4.657%

Appropriate fraction:
Quarters since settlement commenced

6 June 1998 to 2 February 2004	22
Less: Complete quarters until first addition (as above)	3
	19
6 June 1998 to 2 February 2004	22
Less: Complete quarters until second addition 6 June 1998 to 9 September 2001	13
	9

Tax payable on distribution of 66,000 ABC plc shares at £1.50 to daughter – value distributed £99,000: re 1999 addition (12,000 shares)

re 1999 addition (12,000 shares)

$$4.657\% \times \frac{19}{40} \times £99,000 \times \frac{12,000}{132,000} = \qquad 199$$

re 2000 addition (120,000 shares)

$$4.657\% \times \frac{9}{40} \times £99,000 \times \frac{120,000}{132,000} = \qquad 943$$

$$\underline{£1,142}$$

6 June 2008 – 10-year charge (see explanatory notes 8, 9 and 10)

	Gross £	Tax (2008/09 scale) £
Assumed cumulative total:		
Settlor's 7-year cumulative total at time settlement commenced (see explanatory notes 9 and 10)	181,352	
Exit charges in previous 10 years		
1 January 2000	18,000	
2 February 2004	99,000	117,000
		298,352	–
Assumed transfer:		
Relevant property – value as at 5 June 2007		
Farm	300,000	
Less: Agricultural property relief 50%	150,000	
	150,000	
66,000 shares in ABC plc @ 200p	132,000	
	282,000	
Initial value of related settlement	80,800	362,800	70,630*
		661,152	69,830*

(* 661,152 – 312,000 = 349,152 @ 20%)

	Gross £	Tax (2008/09 scale) £

Assumed cumulative total:

Effective rate: $\dfrac{69,830}{362,000} \times 100\% = 19.29\%$

(Note that with the present single rate structure the effective rate will always be 20% if the assumed cumulative total exceeds the nil threshold, and the subsequent calculations are not necessary. It is still, however, necessary to value the respective parts of the settled fund if it has not all been settled for the full 10 years.)

Appropriate fraction

Farm – no reduction (settled for full 10 years)

Shares – 6/66 added 5 May 1999 = 3 quarters reduction giving 37/40

Shares – 60/66 added 9 September 2001 = 13 quarters reduction giving 27/40

Inheritance tax payable:

	Gross £	Tax £
19.29% × 30% × £150,000 (re farm)		8,681
$19.29\% \times 30\% \times \dfrac{37}{40} \times £132,000 \times \dfrac{6,000}{66,000}$		642
$19.29\% \times 30\% \times \dfrac{27}{40} \times £132,000 \times \dfrac{60,000}{66,000}$		4,688
		£14,011

Explanatory Notes

Same day transfers

1. Where two transfers are made on the same day, the annual exemptions are divided between the transfers proportionally to the value transferred, even if one of the transfers was a potentially exempt transfer. In this example both transfers are immediately chargeable.

    The transfer to the brother's children's settlement is added to the inheritance tax accumulation before the gift to the trustees of Smith's own children's settlement because the tax on the former gift is to be met by Smith, whereas the trustees of his children's settlement are to meet the tax due on that later transfer and the total tax on both gifts would be higher if they were included the other way round (s 266(1)).

Related settlement

2. Because his children's settlement is made on the same day as his settlement on his brother's children it is a related settlement (s 62).

Although the amount settled by Smith was £100,000, inheritance tax of £19,200 was payable by the trustees, giving an initial value of £80,800 applicable to that related settlement.

3. The tax on the brother's children's settlement is paid by Smith (the settlor) and therefore its initial value remains at £100,000.

4. The chargeable transfer of £48,000 so far as his own inheritance tax accumulation is concerned has to be grossed up since he bears the tax. Thus, on the scale applicable in 1998/99:

	Net		*Gross*
Cumulative transfers to date	181,352		181,352
Balance of nil band	41,648		41,648
	223,000		223,000
	6,352		
		× 100	
		80	
			7,940
	£229,352		£230,940

giving tax of (7,940 – 6,352 =) £1,588.

Exit charge

5. The rate of tax payable on an exit depends on whether the property leaving the settlement came from the original settlement (or property held at the previous 10-year anniversary) or property added.

In this example the original settlement in favour of his brother's children was a farm which is still owned throughout the period under consideration so therefore the distributions must always be from the added property.

Note however that where property has qualified for annual exemptions and/or business or agricultural relief when it was put into the settlement, this is not taken into account in calculating the initial value of the settlement, so any exit charges on distributions within the first ten years are based on the full value of the property when settled, as shown in the example in relation to the exit charge on 1 January 1999 (s 68). If the distribution itself consists of qualifying business or agricultural property, the relief is available in arriving at the value of the distribution (providing the trustees satisfy the conditions for relief). When calculating the ten-yearly charge, business or agricultural property relief is taken into account in arriving at the value of the trust property, as shown in the example in the calculation on 6 June 2008 (s 66).

The rate of agricultural property relief on the transfer of the farm to the settlement in 1997 was 50% for tenanted agricultural property rather than 100% for owner occupied property etc (see Example 25). Where rates of relief increase after a settlement, the increased rate may be taken into account in computing any *additional* liability to inheritance tax resulting from a death within seven years where the date of death is *after* the date of increase. However the increased rate is *not* applied to calculations of the accumulated transfers brought forward where the original chargeable transfer was before the date of increase even if that amount is used to calculate liabilities after that date.

Agricultural property relief of 50% will be available on 5 June 2008, as the lease was granted prior to 1 September 1995 and vacant possession is not available within twelve months.

Exit charge – rate of tax when property has been added

6. The effective rate of tax on an exit depends upon whether the distribution occurs before the first 10-year anniversary (in which case s 68 applies) or after the first 10 years (then s 69 applies) (see Example 60 explanatory notes 4 and 5).

In this example the exits are both before the first 10-year anniversary, so the effective rate is calculated by adding a notional transfer to the settlor's 7-year cumulative total at the time the settlement commenced.

The notional transfer is the sum of the initial values of the original settlement, related settlements and added property (including accumulated income treated as an accretion to capital).

The effective rate is reduced to an appropriate fraction comprising the number of complete quarters from the date the settlement commenced to the date of the charge, divided by 40.

However when the property leaving the settlement is not part of the original settlement then the numerator is reduced by the number of complete quarters from the date of settlement to the date the property is added.

The tax payable on the distribution is then 30% of the appropriate fraction of the effective rate.

7. On the occasion of the second distribution it should be noted that the rate must be recomputed using the inheritance tax rates then applicable (if lower) and, because further property has been added, the notional transfer has been increased.

Provisions to avoid double counting

8. Where property has been added to the settlement after 8 March 1982 when the law relating to discretionary trusts altered (strictly because 'the settlor has made a chargeable transfer as a result of which the value of the property comprised in the settlement was increased') the rules in s 67 apply when calculating the tax charge on the 10-year anniversary.

The 'assumed cumulative total' to be used includes the highest of the settlor's 7-year cumulative total as at the date the settlement commenced and his 7-year cumulative totals at the time of additions, reduced when appropriate as explained below.

If no reductions were made this procedure might result in double counting, eg if the addition is made less than 7 years after the commencement of the settlement, the settlor's 7-year cumulative total at the date of the addition will include the sum originally settled as well as earlier additions which (unless the property has been the subject of an exit charge) form part or all of the relevant property in the settlement now subject to the 10-year charge. It will also reflect the initial value of any related settlement.

In such circumstances the 7-year cumulation is reduced by so much as is attributable to property whose value is taken into account in the 'assumed transfer' (s 67(5)(a)).

Similarly the 7-year cumulative total at the time of an addition may reflect the value of property which has ceased to be relevant property at the date of the 10-year charge and has been the subject of an exit charge in the previous 10 years. Once again the 7-year cumulation is reduced by the amount attributable to the property in respect of which the exit charge was made (s 67(5)(b)).

Double counting relief also applies where property has been the subject of an exit charge on the creation of an interest in possession within the last 10 years, but has since become relevant property again. Its value would appear both as relevant property and as property on which an exit charge had been levied in the last 10 years. In such circumstances, the latter amount is reduced by the smaller of the value at the time of the exit charge and the value at the time of the 10-year charge (s 67(6)).

9. (i) In the example the settlor's 7-year cumulative total at the time of the first addition and the available reduction in calculating the effective rate on the 10-year charge is:

		Cumulative Total £	Available Reduction £
(a)	his 7-year cumulation prior to the creation of the settlement	181,352	–
(b)	relating to the creation of the settlement of which £1,588 is attributable to the tax paid and £48,000 is attributable to relevant property in the settlement at the time of the 10-year charge (the farm)	49,588	48,000
(c)	by reference to the creation of the related (own children's) settlement. Of this sum £19,200 was used by the trustees to pay the tax so that only £76,800 is attributable to the initial value of the related settlement in the 'assumed transfer'	96,000	76,800
		326,940	124,800
Less:	Transfers more than 7 years prior to the date of the addition, ie prior to 6 May 1992 1991 transfer	181,352	–
		145,588	124,800

(ii) The settlor's 7-year cumulative total at the time of the second addition and the available reduction in calculating the effective rate on the 10-year charge is:

		Cumulative Total £	Available Reduction £
(a)	his 7-year cumulation prior to the creation of the settlement	181,352	–
(b)	relating to the creation of the settlement, as in (i) (b) above	49,588	48,000
(c)	by reference to the creation of the related (own children's) settlement, as in (i) (c) above	96,000	76,800
(d)	by reference to the first addition of £24,000. The chargeable £18,000 is therefore attributable to relevant property in the settlement at the time of the 10-year charge or to property that is the subject of the exit charge on 1 January 2000	18,000	18,000
(e)	Gift to children – potentially exempt	–	–
		344,940	142,800
Less:	Transfers more than 7 years prior to date of second addition	181,352	–
		163,588	142,800

See Example 60 explanatory note 2(e) for the reason why the second addition is not included in the assumed cumulative total.

(iii) The assumed cumulative total is therefore the highest of:

			£	£
(a)	Settlor's 7-year cumulative total prior to the creation of the settlement			181,352
(b)	Settlor's 7-year cumulative total on first addition (see 9(i))		145,588	
	Less: Available reduction		124,800	20,788
(c)	Settlor's 7-year cumulative total on second addition (see 9(ii))		163,588	
	Less: Available reduction		142,800	20,788

Accordingly the cumulative total on creation of the settlement is used.

Effect of settlor's death

10. Note that if Smith had died before 6 May 2006 then the potentially exempt gift of £195,000 to his children would have become chargeable. This would alter the calculation of liability at the time of the second addition (even though death occurred after the tax had been agreed). The 7-year cumulative total would then be:

	Cumulative Total £	Available Reduction £
As 9(ii) (a) to (d) above	344,940	142,800
(e) Gift to children – now chargeable	195,000	–
	539,940	142,800
Less: Transfers more than 7 years prior to date of second addition	181,352	–
	358,588	142,800

The assumed cumulative total would therefore be the highest of:

		£	£
(a)	Settlor's 7-year cumulative total prior to the creation of the settlement		181,352
(b)	Settlor's 7-year cumulative total on first addition	145,588	
	Less Available reduction	124,800	20,788
(c)	Settlor's 7-year cumulative total on second addition	358,588	
	Less Available reduction	142,800	215,788

This would revise the inheritance tax liability on 2 February 2004 and also on subsequent occasions of charge, such as the 10-year anniversary on 6 June 2008, as follows:

Exit charge 2 February 2004

	Gross £	Tax (2003/04 scale) £
Assumed transfer:		
Settlor's cumulative total as above	215,788	–
Notional transfer (see page 62.4)	364,800	65,118
	580,588	65,118*

	Gross £	Tax (2003/04 scale) £

(* 580,588 – 255,000 = 325,588 @ 20%)
Actual rate is 30% of the effective rate

$$\frac{65,118}{364,800} \times 100 \times 30\% = 5.355\%$$

Tax payable:
  re 1999 addition (12,000 shares)

$$5.355\% \times \frac{19}{40} \times £99,000 \times \frac{12,000}{132,000} =$$ 229

  re 2001 addition (120,000 shares)

$$5.355\% \times \frac{9}{40} \times £99,000 \times \frac{120,000}{132,000} =$$ 1,084

     £1,133   (previously £1,142)

6 June 2008 – 10-year charge

	Gross £	Tax (on 2008/09 scale) £
Settlor's cumulative total as above	215,788	–
Exit charges in previous 10 years (see page 62.5)	117,000	
	332,788	4,158*
Assumed transfer (see page 62.5)	362,800	72,560
	695,588	76,718

(* 332,788 – 312,000 = 20,788 @ 20%)

$$\text{Effective rate:} \frac{72,560}{362,800} \times 100 = 20\%$$

Inheritance tax payable:
20% × 30% × £150,000   9,000

$$20\% \times 30\% \times \frac{37}{40} \times £132,000 \times \frac{6,000}{66,000}$$ 666

	Gross £	Tax (on 2008/09 scale) £
$$20\% \times 30\% \times \frac{27}{40} \times £132,000 \times \frac{60,000}{66,000}$$	4,860	
	£14,526	(previously £14,011)

11. The relevant value of the property comprised in the settlement is its value on the day preceding the 10th anniversary – in this case 5 June 2008 (s 64).

Associated operations

12. If two or more settlements of an identical or substantially similar nature were set up over a short term, HMRC Capital Taxes took the view that the associated operations provisions of s 268 (as to which see Example 22) would apply. This would have resulted in the settlements being treated as a single settlement set up at the time of the last settlement, with only one nil rate band. In the case of *Rysaffe Trustee Co (CI) Ltd v IRC* 2002, however, the High Court held that as a matter of general law the creation of five identical settlements must be treated as five separate settlements, not one. It was up to the settlor to determine if he wished to create more than one settlement and the associated operations provisions of s 268 could not apply.

13. For further notes on discretionary trusts see Examples 59, 60 and 61.

Question

A has a protected life interest within Trustee Act 1925 s 33(1) in a trust fund valued at £250,000 created by his uncle and on 1 July 2003 purported to assign that life interest to his brother. The trustees pointed out that the attempted alienation was ineffective and brought the protected life interest to an end, substituting for it a discretionary trust under which the beneficiaries were A, his wife and their children.

The only previous transfer A had made at that date was £108,000 in respect of a gift in July 1996.

A also has a life interest under his father's will trust.

On 1 May 2007 A sold this life interest to a Reversionary Interest Society for £200,000 – the full market value. The assets of the trust fund were worth £552,000 at that time.

He did not advise the trustees of the fund of the availability of annual inheritance tax exemptions.

On 21 April 2008 A sold his house, then valued at £200,000 on a vacant possession basis, to his daughter D for £160,000 but reserving to himself a lease of the property for 99 years determinable on his death. The value of the lease at that time was £80,000.

On 1 May 2008, before his daughter had paid the £160,000 (although all documentation had been completed), A was killed in a car accident. His other assets totalled £30,000 net.

His uncle's discretionary, formerly protective, trust fund was then valued at £305,000.

By his will, A created a discretionary trust of the whole of his free estate in favour of his children. On 12 March 2010 the trustees appointed a sum of £10,000, free of tax, to a son, S, absolutely.

Calculate:

(a)   the inheritance tax payable as a result of these transactions and consequent upon A's death

(b)   the rate at which inheritance tax will be payable on future appointments out of the discretionary trust created by A's will.

Answer

(a) **Inheritance tax accumulation — A**

1 July 2003
   Cessation of protected life interest – No transfer of value –
   A deemed to retain an interest in possession (s 88(2))

	Gross £	Tax on 2007/08 scale £
1 May 2007		
Cumulative chargeable transfers within previous 7 years (ie since 2 May 2000)	–	–
Sale of life interest under father's will trust		
Value of trust fund 552,000		
Less: Amount received 200,000	352,000	10,400*
	352,000	10,400*

(* 352,000 – 300,000 = 52,000 @ 20%)

21 April 2008
   Sale of house to daughter

Market value	200,000	
Less: Amount receivable	160,000	
	40,000	
Less: Value retained through lease for life	80,000	
	No loss to A	–

Accumulation at death on 1 May 2008 — 352,000

Inheritance tax accumulation — daughter

21 April 2008

Amount payable for house		160,000
Less: Value of house to daughter		
Open market value without lease	200,000	
Value of lease	80,000	120,000
'Gift' to father		40,000
Less: Annual exemptions 2008/09	3,000	
2007/08	3,000	6,000
Potentially exempt transfer		34,000

Death of A — 1 May 2008

	£	£
Estate on death		
Net assets	30,000	
Amount due from daughter re house sale	160,000	190,000
Settled property		
Lease for life		
Value of house	200,000	
Less: Amount attributable to consideration received (see explanatory note 3) — one half	100,000	100,000
Deemed life interest in protective trust		305,000
		595,000

Inheritance tax due on death

	Date of death 1 May 2008	
	Gross	Tax on 2008/09 scale
	£	£
On gifts within seven years before death		
Transfers within 7 years before 1 May 2008 (ie on and after 2 May 2001)	–	–
1 May 2007 – sale of life interest	352,000	16,000*
	352,000	16,000*

(* 352,000 – 312,000 = 40,000 @ 40%)

On estate at death
(Nil threshold already exceeded by lifetime transfers)
£595,000 @ 40%   238,000

Tax payable		£
By trustees of father's will trust	16,000	
Less: paid on original transfer	10,400	5,600

By personal representatives:

$$\frac{190,000}{595,000} \times 238,000 \qquad\qquad 76,000$$

By trustees of protective trust

$$\frac{305,000}{595,000} \times 238,000 \qquad\qquad 122,000$$

By daughter re house

$$\frac{100,000}{595,000} \times 238,000 \qquad\qquad 40,000$$

Appointment of £10,000 by the trustees of the will of A to S

12 March 2010 – Appointment is within 2 years after the death and is deemed to have been made by A under his will (s 144). No further tax is payable.

(b)   **Discretionary trust created by A's will**

	£
A's estate	190,000
Less: appointment to son	10,000
	180,000
Less: tax payable by executors	76,000
Net amount transferred to discretionary settlement created by the will	104,000

Rate of tax on distributions before the first ten-year anniversary on 1 May 2018

A's seven-year cumulative total at *commencement of settlement* (ignoring transfers of value made on that day, that is the transfer of value deemed to have been made on A's death), was £352,000. The position of the settlement is therefore as follows:

	£
Cumulative total of settlor	352,000
Net amount transferred as above	104,000
	456,000

As this is above the threshold the 'effective' rate of tax on distributions is 20%.

If the tax rates have been reduced when the distribution occurs, the 'effective rate' is recalculated using the new reduced rates.

Rate of tax at ten-year anniversaries

This is 30% of the 'effective rate' found by assuming a transfer of value equal to the value of the trust fund immediately before the ten-year anniversary (ie on 30 April 2018, 30 April 2028 and so on), made by a transferor whose cumulative total is deemed to be £312,000 *plus* the amounts taxed on exit from the discretionary trust in the preceding ten years, using one half the scale current at the date of the ten-year anniversary.

If any property subject to the ten-year charge was not 'relevant property' throughout the whole of the preceding ten years or was not comprised in the settlement throughout the whole of that period, then in relation to that property alone the 'effective rate' above is reduced by 1/40th for each complete successive quarter which expired before the property became relevant property.

The value charged to tax is the value of the 'relevant property' in the settlement immediately before the anniversary on the appropriate 30 April.

Rate of tax between ten-year anniversaries

This is the 'appropriate fraction' (ie N/40 – where 'N' is the number of completed quarters since the last ten-year anniversary or since the property became relevant property) of the rate charged on the last ten-year anniversary.

If the tax rates have been reduced since the last ten-year anniversary, the current lower rates are substituted.

Explanatory Notes

1. *1 July 2003 – purported assignment to brother*

    When A's life interest comes to an end there is no transfer of value because A is deemed to retain his interest in possession (s 88(2)).

2. *1 May 2007 – sale of life interest*

    Although the sale by A of his life interest to the Reversionary Interest Society is a commercial transaction for full value, s 10 does not prevent its being a transfer of value because s 52(2) expressly provides that a transfer of value arises with an allowance for the sale price received, ie a lifetime transfer of £552,000 (the value of the assets comprising the trust fund) less the £200,000 received = £352,000.

    The transfer is not a potentially exempt transfer because the interest does not become comprised in the estate of another individual, nor is another individual's estate increased as a result of the transfer, and it therefore falls outside s 3A.

    Section 57 allows the annual and marriage exemptions to be applied to events on the happening of which tax is chargeable under s 52 (ie the coming to an end during lifetime of interests in possession in settled property) provided the transferor (the person with the interest in possession which came to an end) gives the trustees a formal notice telling them of the availability of the exemption and the extent to which he is making it available.

    As no such notice has been given the exemptions are not available to the trustees.

3. *21 April 2008 – lease for life*

    For the purposes of inheritance tax a lease for life is deemed to be a settlement of the property leased – s 43(3). Prior to the intervention of FA 2006 s 80, because the value of the property remained in the estate of A no income tax charge would arise under the pre-owned asset provisions of FA 2004. FA 2006 s 80 has now amended FA 2004 Sch 15 para 11 with retrospective effect for the part of the year 2005/06 beginning with 5 December 2005 and for 2006/07 and subsequent years of assessment to provide that where the relevant property has ceased to be comprised in a person's estate for the purposes of IHTA 1984, or he has directly or indirectly provided any consideration for the acquisition of the relevant property, and at any subsequent time the relevant property or any derived property is comprised in his estate because he has an interest in possession in it then the relevant property and any derived property are not treated as comprised in his estate for the purposes of obtaining an exemption from the pre-owned assets charge.

    Although the lease determinable on A's death was not created by his daughter but reserved by A himself, so that strictly no allowance for the consideration given can be made, in such circumstances HMRC will nevertheless treat an appropriate part of the total consideration given as referable to the grant of the lease for life.

    As the value of A's life interest is £80,000, and the difference between the market value and the amount receivable is £40,000, the relevant portion is one half (s 170).

    In so far as the daughter is concerned, far from having purchased the house at an undervalue, she has depleted her own estate in favour of her father when the aggregate of what she has paid him and the value of the lease is taken into account.

    Hence the potentially exempt transfer of value in her case.

4. *1 May 2008 – position on A's death*

    On A's death the tax on transfers of value made within the last seven years is recalculated using the full scale rates in force at the date of death and by accumulation with transfers within the seven years preceding each gift.

The difference between the tax calculated on this basis and the tax originally calculated using the lifetime rates in force at the time of the transfer is due from the trustee of A's father's will trust (s 201).

A's own assets on death include the sum of £160,000 due to him from his daughter.

His estate for inheritance tax purposes (defined in s 5(1) as the aggregate of all the property to which he is beneficially entitled – except excluded property) includes the value of the house in which he has a lease for life less the amount attributable to the consideration received in order to prevent double counting. In this example the gifts with reservation rules do not apply as no transfer of value occurred when A sold the house to his daughter.

His chargeable estate also includes the value of the property in the protective trust in which his life interest is deemed to continue (see explanatory note 1).

5. *12 March 2010 – variation within two years after death*

Example 34 illustrates how s 142 allows beneficiaries within two years after a death to vary the dispositions without that variation being itself a transfer of value, and for the tax payable in connection with the death to be calculated as though the variation had been made by the deceased himself.

Section 144 provides that distributions made within two years after death out of discretionary settlements created by the deceased's will (other than in the first three months after death) are similarly treated as having been made at the time of the death and are not therefore subject to an exit charge. (See Example 60 explanatory note 9 for the position on transfers within the first three months and explanatory note 10 for the interaction of s 144 with capital gains tax.)

The £10,000 appointed by the trustees of A's will to A's son is therefore deemed for the purposes of inheritance tax to have been given to him by his father A under his will and does not give rise to any exit charge under the discretionary trust rules.

Section 144 also provides that distributions out of discretionary settlements within two years after the settlor's death made under s 75 (employee trusts), s 76 (charities, political parties etc) or Sch 4.16(1) (maintenance funds for historic buildings etc) are treated as having been made at the time of death.

6. See Example 60 for the rules for calculating the rate at which inheritance tax will be payable on appointments after the first ten-year anniversary out of the discretionary trust created by A's will.

Question

A.

You receive a letter from a wealthy client:

10 August 2008

Dear William

As you will recall, I had previously intended to transfer £375,000 into a settlement for my minor children. We had discussed creating an accumulation and maintenance settlement in early 2006 but I had a short stay in hospital and when I came out you advised me that the rules had changed and that accumulation and maintenance settlements were no longer be available.

Due to the uncertainties of the Government's proposals you suggested that I write to you again later in the year when things had settled down. I had another bout of illness and with one thing and another it has taken me rather longer to write to you.

I am still interested in making a settlement for my children all of whom are, as you know, still minors. I recall reading that it is now possible to put assets into trust for children which can be kept until they are 25 (rather than the age of 18 as originally proposed). Is this something that you would recommend? As you know I think it highly irresponsible for any parent to let an 18-year old receive substantial capital; whilst not entirely happy about it, I would be less concerned about my children receiving their entitlement at 25.

If not, what other strategies would you suggest I consider.

Please let me know what reporting requirements and other ongoing tax-related responsibilities this will entail.

Yours sincerely

Bernard

PS As you may recall when my wife Celia died in December 2005 she left £250,000 on trust for the children in her will. The terms of the trust mean that the children do not get the money until they are 25. I remember that you advised me at the time that this was not an accumulation and maintenance trust but I wonder if this trust is affected by the changes?

B.

Another of your clients of more modest means than Bernard wants to know whether there would be any tax advantages if he and his wife transferred funds to their children. The children are aged 15, 12 and 10. Prepare notes on the points to be made to the client.

Answer

A. Accumulation and maintenance settlement

31 August 2008

Dear Bernard,

Thank you for your letter of 10 August.

You are quite right in recalling that it is no longer possible to create an accumulation and maintenance settlement of the kind which we had discussed before your hospitalisation in early 2006. Some amendments were made to the Government's proposals as outlined in the 2006 Budget but the benign tax treatment given to accumulation and maintenance settlements has ended.

If it is any consolation, even accumulation and maintenance settlements made before the 2006 Budget were affected by the changes although the previous tax treatment was left in place until 5 April 2008. If you had been able to settle the funds on an accumulation and maintenance settlement before 22 March 2006, the trust would have still been affected by the new rules unless steps had been taken to rearrange with effect from 6 April 2008 so it would have been necessary to rearrange these trusts before 6 April 2008 if at all possible.

You correctly refer to the changes which allow some trusts to retain funds until a child reaches the age of 25 (rather than 18). However, this applies only to certain trusts which were set up under the will of the child's parent (or under the Criminal Injuries Compensation Scheme). The trust set up by Celia for your children will qualify even though it was made before 22 March 2006. Trusts that take advantage of this slight relaxation will suffer from charges when capital is taken from the trust if a beneficiary is over the age of 18. However, this should not be relevant in the case of Celia's trust because the capital in the trust is covered by the nil rate band (currently £312,000) and this has traditionally increased from year to year: it will be £325,000 next year and £350,000 the year after. In saying this I am assuming that Celia made no significant chargeable transfers in the seven years before she died. If that assumption is incorrect, please let me know.

One important consequence of Celia leaving £250,000 to the children in her Will is that she used some of her nil rate band. If she had left everything to you there would have been no inheritance tax to pay because gifts between spouses are exempt for inheritance tax purposes. The practice at the time Celia died was to leave as much of the nil rate band as possible to persons other than the spouse because the nil rate band would otherwise be 'wasted'. You might recall that last year the Chancellor announced that nil rate bands of spouses were to be transferrable so that if Celia had left everything to you, your nil rate band would effectively double on your death. Since Celia has used some of her nil rate band to make a gift to the children your nil rate band will not be enhanced by 100% on your death. Instead, if Celia left the balance of her estate to you, your nil rate band will be enhanced by only 9%. It therefore makes sense for you to consider making lifetime gifts into trusts for your children in the expectation that you survive by a further seven years so that these will no longer be taken into account in assessing the lifetime chargeable transfer on your death.

If you wish to make a lifetime gift to your children, you have broadly two options. First, you can make an outright gift (to a bare trust on behalf of your children). This means that they can get the capital as soon as they are 18. Such a gift would constitute a potentially exempt transfer and will escape inheritance tax altogether provided you live for seven years after the gift. In view of your understandable objections to giving 18-year olds substantial sums of money, I would not recommend that you followed this option. However, you should note that it is the most tax-friendly solution.

Alternatively, you can settle the funds into a trust. Since 22 March 2006, the tax treatment has been the same for both interest in possession trusts (essentially those where the beneficiaries have a right to receive the income from a fixed interest in the trust) and discretionary trusts (those where the trustees have a lot more freedom about paying income and capital to the beneficiaries). In the circumstances I would suggest that you consider using a discretionary trust as that gives you the greatest flexibility in the future.

If you proceed, inheritance tax will be payable at 20% on the funds entering the trust. However, on the basis that you have made no chargeable transfers to date, the first £312,000 will be covered by the nil rate band. The next £6,000 will be covered by your annual exemption for this year and for last year.

Therefore, assuming you were to gift £375,000, the trustees would be required to pay inheritance tax of £11,400 (£369,000 – £312,000 @ 20%).

This tax will be payable (assuming you make the gift before the end of next month) by 30 April 2009. Otherwise, it will be payable six months after the end of the month in which you make the gift.

Further tax will be payable from your estate should you die within seven years of making the gift. This will be payable six months after the end of the month in which you die.

If the tax is not paid on the due date, interest is charged at the rate in force at that time (currently 3%).

This means that even though the trustees will have twelve months in which to report the transfer, the notification will need to be submitted much earlier than that if interest charges are to be avoided.

Initial and ongoing reporting requirements:

In relation to yourself

(i)   In addition to the possible requirement for your personal representatives to report the transfer into settlement as detailed above, you will need to include in your tax return for the year ended 5 April 2009 full details of any chargeable assets disposed of in order to raise the funds for the settlement, so that any chargeable gains arising may be calculated.

(ii) Income arising under the settlement will not affect you in so far as it is accumulated for the benefit of your children but if while the children are under eighteen years of age and unmarried the trustees make any payment for their maintenance, education or benefit the amount so paid will be regarded as your income for tax purposes, and will consequently need to be included in your personal income tax return. You would be entitled to recover any tax paid from the trustees or from the children who receive the income. To the extent that the trust's income consisted of dividend income, there is an increased tax cost of making such payments compared with dividend income received directly (see point (iii) below under the heading In relation to the trustees).

(iii) The same reporting responsibilities will apply if you make any additions to the settlement in future years.

In relation to the trustees

(i)   The trustees should inform HMRC that the settlement has been created and ask for a reference for the settlement.

(ii) Tax return forms must be prepared and submitted by the trustees for each year ended 5 April. The forms give details of the income of the trust, the trustees' expenses and outgoings, disposals and deemed disposals for capital gains tax purposes, details of any distributions made to the children and may include the calculation of the self-assessed tax liability. The income of an accumulation and maintenance settlement is chargeable if the trust rate —currently 32½% for dividends and 40% for other income. The first £1,000 of income, plus the amount used for expenses, is charged at 10% for dividends, 20% for other savings income and 22% for any non-savings income.

The capital gains of the accumulation and maintenance settlement will be chargeable at 18% after the deduction of the annual exemption (£4,800 for 2008/09, reduced if you have created more than one settlement).

(iii) If the trustees distribute any income for the maintenance or education of one or more of the children when they are still under eighteen and unmarried, then as stated above, such income will be treated as your income for tax purposes. Even so, the amount of any such income will be declared in the trust tax return and will be included in calculating the income liable at the 32½% and 40% rates. The trustees will deduct tax at 40% from the payments and if the underlying income includes dividends, the dividend credits cannot be taken into account as tax paid by the trustees, thus increasing their tax liability.

(iv) Inheritance tax will be payable on the 10th anniversary (and every subsequent 10 years) on the value of the trust assets. The top charging rate is currently 6% but the trustees have the benefit of the nil rate band (currently £312,000) before any tax is payable.

(v) Charges will also be payable by the trustees whenever capital distributions are made by the trust. This basic rate of this charge is 6% although in practice the actual rate will be a lot lower. This is because the calculation takes into account the nil rate band at the time of the distribution. Furthermore, the basic rate of the charge is then multiplied by a top rate of n/40 where n is the number of complete quarters since the last ten-year anniversary (or the creation of the trust).

Therefore no exit charge will be payable during the first three months of any ten-year period, and 39/40 of the basic charge will be payable in the final quarter.

In relation to your children

(i) The children have no reporting responsibility until they reach age eighteen.

(ii) When income is distributed to your children, this will be shown on their tax returns (which you will complete whilst they are minors).

I shall be happy to discuss any of the above points with you in more detail if you wish, and to assist in the completion of relevant forms.

Yours sincerely,

William

B.   Transferring funds to infant children

1. Where funds are transferred to children under 18, there is little opportunity to obtain any income tax advantages. The funds transfer would be treated for income tax as a settlement. Unless it is covered by one of the exceptions listed below, settlement income that is paid to or would otherwise be treated as the income of a child of the settlor who is under 18 and unmarried is treated as the parent's income and not the child's (ITTOIA 2005 s 629). A settlement includes 'any disposition, trust, covenant, agreement, arrangement or transfer of assets' (s 620).

2. Each parent may, however, give each such child a capital sum from which not more than £100 gross income arises each year. If income exceeds the limit the whole amount is taxable (s 629(3)).

3. Before 9 March 1999, there were income tax advantages if the parents arranged for funds for each child to be held under a 'bare trust', under which the child had an absolute right to the property and income, but the trustees (who could be the parents) were the legal owners, effectively holding as the child's nominee. The disadvantage of such trusts was that the child could not be prevented from obtaining legal ownership of the funds at age 18.

The income tax advantages of bare trusts by parents in favour of their minor children are no longer available for trusts created on or after 9 March 1999. Subject to the de minimis amount of £100 referred to in note 2 above, the income arising will be taxed as that of the parent under s 629.

4.   The changed rules for bare trusts do not alter the capital gains treatment, which treats gains arising as the child's gains against which the annual exemption (currently £9,600) is available, the rates of tax on any gains above that level being 18%. Funds could therefore be invested for the child purely for capital growth, with no income arising. This does not, however, give the former benefits of being able to use the child's personal allowance and lower tax rates against income.

5.   Other possibilities, which also do not make use of the children's allowances and lower tax rates are as follows (see explanatory note 12):

   (a)   National Savings and Investments Children's Bonus Bonds for children under 16.

   (b)   Friendly society policies (with premiums up to £270 per annum).

   (c)   Contributions of up to £2,880 net per child into a personal pension plan. The basic rate tax relief of 20% is added to the amount invested in the plan, so that for a contribution of £2,880 the plan investment would be £3,600.

6.   Where a child aged 16 or 17 opens a cash individual savings account (ISA) with funds provided by the parents then this will be treated as a settlement and the income arising will be taxable on the parent (subject to the de minimis amount of £100) even though income within an ISA is normally tax free.

Explanatory Notes

Payments re settlor's infant, unmarried children

1.   The income of discretionary and accumulation settlements is charged at the dividend trust rate (currently 32½%) if it is dividend or similar income (see Example 42 for details) and at the rate applicable to trusts (currently 40%) if it is non-dividend income. These rates do not apply to any amount which is treated as the settlor's income *before* it is distributed (ITA 2007 s 480).

Under ITA 2007 s 491 (replacing FA 2005 s 14 with effect from 6 April 2007) the first £1,000 of relevant income will not be charged at the special trust tax rates, but will instead be charged at the income tax rate appropriate to the type of income, known as standard rate band. Therefore, if payments are received net of tax (for example, building society interest) up to the limit of the standard rate band, then the trustees will have no further tax to pay.

The standard rate band will apply to trust income *net* of trust management expenses so potentially it will apply to other charges as well.

Although the management expenses are deducted from the trust income taxed at the lowest rate first, (the basic rate at 20% first, followed by l dividends at 10%).

See Examples 42, 47 and 48 for further details on the standard rate band and its interaction with trust expenses and additional liabilities where amounts are distributed.

Although any payment made by the trustees for the maintenance or education of a child of the settlor who is under 18 and unmarried is deemed to be the settlor's income, it is not so treated *before* the payment is made. The trustees are therefore liable to tax at the 40% rate, and any payments for the children are grossed up at that rate (ITA 2007 ss 493–498). See Example 42 under heading *Income taxed as income of settlor* for the effect of the treatment of dividend income on the overall tax charge where dividend income is paid to minor children via a discretionary trust.

Notification of liability to tax

2.   Since the trustees are chargeable to income tax on the trust income that arises, they must notify HMRC that they are so liable within six months after the end of the first relevant tax year. This is the same requirement as that of an individual taxpayer and carries a penalty of up to 100% of the tax due in the event of failure to notify (TMA 1970 s 7).

Person becoming absolutely entitled as against the trustees; gifts holdover relief

3.   When a person becomes absolutely entitled to trust assets as against the trustees, other than on the death of a life tenant, the assets are deemed to have been disposed of by the trustees at market value for capital gains tax purposes. Any capital gain arising may be held over if the assets are qualifying assets under TCGA 1992 s 165 (see Example 50 part A(d)).

       If the assets are not qualifying assets for TCGA 1992 s 165, there is the possibility of holding over a gain under the provisions of TCGA 1992 s 260, because s 260(2)(d) specifically allows a gain to be held over on a disposal on which inheritance tax is not chargeable by reason of the inheritance tax exemption for trusts for bereaved minors (IHTA 1984 s 71B(2)) or age 18 to 25 trusts (IHTA 1984 s 71E(2)). Hold over relief is also available in respect of the inheritance tax exemption for accumulation and maintenance settlements where a beneficiary becomes entitled to trust property or a life interest therein, or dies before reaching the specified age (IHTA 1984 s 71(4)) although after 5 April 2008 these trusts come under the relevant property regime.

Requirements for and advantages of accumulation and maintenance type settlements

4.   Accumulation and maintenance settlements cannot be established after 21 March 2006. Those already in existence continued until 5 April 2008. From 6 April 2008, with certain exceptions, the capital must be payable to the beneficiaries when they reach the age of 18. The exceptions (which continue to permit capital, but not just income to be taken up to the age of 25) relate to trusts for bereaved minors set up by a bequest from their parent (or under the Criminal Injuries Compensation Scheme).

       If an accumulation and maintenance settlement ceases to qualify as such, either because all beneficiaries are no longer children of a common grandparent or because of the 25-year rule, the trustees are liable to an inheritance tax charge. Thereafter the normal ten-yearly and exit charges apply.

5.   Settlements which ceased to be A&M settlements on 6 April 2008 simply because of the requirement to pay capital by the age of 18 did not incur an inheritance tax charge on that event.

Reporting potentially exempt transfers that become chargeable

6.   Potentially exempt transfers that become chargeable because of the death of the donor within seven years must be included in the account delivered by the personal representatives, along with details of the deceased's estate (IHTA 1984 s 216). Section 216 also requires potentially exempt transfers to be reported by the donee, the donee being primarily liable for payment of the tax.

Bare trusts

7.   Bare trusts used to provide a simple way of enabling children's personal allowances and lower tax rates to be used against funds from the parent, so long as the income merely accumulated for the children's benefit without actually being paid to them. The parents could act as trustees and there thus need be no administration costs.

       The income tax advantages of bare trusts by parents in favour of their children under 18 were blocked by FA 1999 s 64, amending TA 1988 s 660B for trusts created on or after 9 March 1999 or where funds were added on or after that date. The rule is continued by ITTOIA 2005 s 629.

The advantages continue for bare trusts created by parents before that date providing no funds are added. The tax deducted at source from the accumulated income may be reclaimed to the extent that it exceeds the child's liability, except for dividend credits, which are no longer repayable.

The revised rules do not prevent bare trusts being created by a parent's will, or by other relatives. It is not, however, possible for a parent to circumvent the rules by creating a bare trust for a relative's or friend's children and for the relative/friend to do the same for his children by way of a reciprocal arrangement (ITTOIA 2005 s 620).

8.   Property held on a bare trust is in the legal ownership of the trustees and must remain in their ownership if and so long as the beneficiary is a minor (since a minor cannot give a valid receipt). As and when the beneficiary is over 18 he may call for the legal ownership to be transferred to him at any time.

Under self-assessment, trustees are not required to complete tax returns in respect of bare trusts (although they may send a return of *income*, but not capital gains, if they wish – see Example 47 explanatory note 10), and the child must show the income and gains in his own return.

9.   Because the property is held for the beneficiary absolutely, it is not settled property for capital gains tax (TCGA 1992 s 60), and any gains are taxable on the beneficiary, so that the full annual exemption (£9,600 for 2008/09) is available unless used against other gains.

10. There is now an equivalent to TCGA 1992 s 60 in the income tax legislation in the shape of ITA 2007 s 466. The trustee is effectively only a nominee, so the provisions of ITA 2007 s 479 charging tax at the excess of the dividend trust rate of 32½% over the tax credit rate of 10% where a company purchases the trustees' shares (see Example 49 explanatory note 4) do not apply. As far as inheritance tax is concerned, the transfer to the bare trust is a potentially exempt transfer, so that tax will not be payable providing the donor survives the transfer by seven years. In the hands of the beneficiary, the property is not treated as settled property since it is held for him absolutely.

Other tax-efficient ways of benefiting children

11. In addition to creating accumulation and maintenance settlements, which have the inheritance tax advantages outlined in note 4 above, or creating bare trusts that do not produce income but offer capital growth, parents may use funds for the benefit of their children without being caught by the income tax parental settlement rules as follows, as indicated in the example at part B note 5:

(a)   National Savings and Investments Children's Bonus Bonds may be purchased for children under 16 (maximum holding per child £3,000 in latest issue plus holdings in earlier issues). Interest on the bonds is tax-free. They mature at the child's 21st birthday.

(b)   Premiums of up to £270 per annum for each child may be paid on a qualifying friendly society policy. The proceeds of the policy are tax-free and the society does not pay tax on its income and gains in respect of such policies.

(c)   Personal pension contributions of up to £2,880 net, £3,600 gross, per child may be paid each year. The child may not, however, draw any benefits from a pension plan until pension age is reached (age 55 from 2010).

These tax-efficient payments do not, however, give any opportunity for using the child's personal allowance and lower rates of tax.

Question

You were contacted in September 2007 by the trustees of the Green grandchildren's trust, a trust resident in the UK with UK based trustees. They are concerned about the tax treatment of dividends, tax credits on distributions to beneficiaries and capital gains.

The following details are known:

(1)   The trust's main asset is a 27% shareholding in Green plc, an unquoted UK trading company. The shareholding was acquired by gift in 1987 from the settlor. The shares were worth £850,000 at that time and a gain of £650,000 was held over. The settlor had acquired the shares in 1967. This shareholding is now worth about £2 million. It is anticipated that the company may be floated on the London Stock Exchange in the next year or so, in which case the shares could increase in value to over £5 million.

(2)   The trust's main source of income is dividends from its shareholding in Green plc. Normally about half the dividend is distributed to the beneficiaries.

(3)   The trust was created as an accumulation and maintenance trust which provides for a grandchild of the settlor to receive a life interest at age 25 with capital distributions subject to trustees' discretion. No alteration was made to the trust before 6 April 2008.

(4)   There are currently eight grandchildren with age ranges 19 to 26. All of them were 18 or over on 6 April 2008. It is unlikely that any further beneficiaries will come into existence and the trustees have established eight accounts within the trust for administration purposes. Only two of the beneficiaries work for Green plc. The trustees are under pressure to completely wind up the trust and distribute to the beneficiaries. The trustees have already resolved to fully distribute all retained income within the trust.

(5)   The trust had a brought forward tax credit pool for TA 1988 s 687 purposes of £650,000 at 6 April 1999, being mainly tax at the trust rate on dividends.

The trustees wish to call a meeting with their advisers to consider the best way forward. They would like to understand the effect of the changes on trust income, distributions, gains and capital gains tax taper relief, in relation to the question whether to retain in the fund or distribute. They also wish to discuss how the FA 2006 changes have affected their trust.

Draft technical notes for the meeting with the trustees.

Answer

Technical notes for meeting with trustees of Green grandchildren's trust

Tax treatment of dividends from 6 April 1999 to 5 April 2004

1. Before 6 April 1999 dividends carried a repayable tax credit of 25% of the cash dividend (20% of the tax credit inclusive amount), so that a cash dividend of £80 represented a dividend of £100 with a credit of £20, which was repayable to a non-taxpayer. Trust expenses were deducted from net trust income to give the amount available for distribution to beneficiaries.

    A grandchild with a life interest in the trust (ie a grandchild over 25) was (and still is) entitled to the income whether it was distributed or not. If the grandchild's personal allowance covered his income, he could therefore claim repayment of the dividend credit. If the grandchild was a basic rate taxpayer no further tax was payable. A higher rate taxpayer had to pay a further 20% of the tax credit inclusive amount (25% of the cash dividend).

    Where the dividend income was subject to accumulation, it was taxable at the 34% rate applicable to trusts. If any of the dividend income was paid out as maintenance to grandchildren under 25, then since the trust was created by a grandparent rather than a parent, the amount distributed was (and still is) treated as the grandchildren's income, from which tax at 34% had been deducted. Grandchildren not liable to tax would recover the whole of the 34% tax, basic rate taxpayers would recover the difference and higher rate taxpayers would pay an extra 6%.

2. From 6 April 1999 dividend credits are reduced to 1/9th of the cash amount (10% of the tax credit inclusive figure). Trust expenses are deducted from dividend income in priority to other sources of trust income. The dividend tax credits are not repayable. Thus a dividend of £80 carries a non-repayable credit of £9.

    Grandchildren with a life interest will accordingly no longer be able to recover the tax credits. Those liable at the basic rate will still have no further tax to pay and those with income above the basic rate threshold will be liable at the excess of the Schedule F (now dividend) upper rate of 32½% over the tax credit rate of 10%.

3. As far as dividends subject to accumulation were concerned, they were chargeable from 6 April 1999 at a special Schedule F (now dividend) trust rate of 25%. The trustees were left with broadly the same net of tax income as previously, ie:

	Pre-6 April 1999 £	6 April 1999 to 5 April 2004 £
Dividend received	80.00	80.00
Tax credit	20.00	8.89
Trust income	100.00	88.89
Tax at 34%/25%	34.00	22.22
Net of tax income	66.00	66.67

Tax treatment of dividends from 6 April 2004

4. From 6 April 2004 the dividend trust rate for accumulations was increased from 25% to 32½%. This has reduced the amount of income now available for distribution.

	Pre-6 April 2004 £	Post-6 April 2004 £
Dividend received	80.00	80.00
Tax credit	8.89	8.89
Trust income	88.89	88.89
Tax at 25%/32½%	22.22	28.89
Net of tax income	66.67	60.00

Grandchildren with a life interest will continue to receive dividends with a non-repayable tax credit of 10% and to be liable to dividend trust tax of 32½% (less tax credit of 10%) if higher rate taxpayers.

Effect on income available for distribution

5. Distributions out of the trust to grandchildren under 25 are made net of 40% tax and treated as income of the grandchildren as previously. From 6 April 1999, however, the trustees cannot treat dividend credits as tax already paid in calculating how much of the 40%/34% tax on a distribution has already been accounted for, since they may only include in the tax pool the excess of tax at the dividend trust rate of 32½%/25% over the 10% tax credit rate. The effect is that the maximum distribution out of post 5 April 1999 dividend income is 60% (prior to 6 April 2004 – 66%) of the tax credit *exclusive* amount, eg:

	2003/04 £	2004/05 onwards £
Tax credit exclusive dividend income (net of trust expenses), say	1,800	1,800
Tax credit (1/9)	200	200
Trust gross income	2,000	2,000
Tax on income (25%/32½%)	500	650
Net income	1,500	1,350
Maximum gross payment to beneficiaries:		
Tax credit *exclusive* dividend	1,800	1,800
Tax thereon @ 34%/40%	612	720
Distributable amount	1,188	1,080
Tax to be paid by trustees:		
Tax on gross income	500	650
Covered by tax credits	200	200
Payable by trustees on income	300	450
Tax on distributions	612	720
Further tax due from trustees	312	270

Although the trustees received £1,800 as income it is not possible to distribute that amount because of the tax due on income. In fact it is not normally possible to distribute all of the net income because of the additional tax due from the trustees on distribution, however that amount may be covered by amounts brought forward within the tax pool.

The whole of the tax deducted from the distributions may be repaid to non-taxpaying beneficiaries. Thus in 2003/04 non-taxpaying beneficiaries could recover tax of £612 and from 2004/05 tax of £720.

Tax pool brought forward

6. The provisions in note 5 from 6 April 1999 onwards may not apply where there is a tax pool brought forward (£650,000 at 6 April 1999 in the case of the Green grandchildren's trust, although this will have been increased by Schedule F (now dividend) tax paid on dividends received after that date as indicated in note 5). The whole of the brought forward figure, which largely represents dividend credits, is fully available to cover the tax on distributions to the beneficiaries. Thus if the trustees distribute all retained income, the restriction of payments to 60% of the dividends will apply only to the post 5 April 1999 amounts, and even then there may be surplus tax in the tax pool because of earlier changes of rates etc. Any surplus remaining in the tax pool when the last child attains age 25 cannot then be used.

    Although making an income distribution would use some of the tax pool brought forward, the benefit would depend on the tax position of the beneficiaries, since if the distribution was chargeable to higher rate tax in the hands of the grandchild, no tax would be repayable to them.

    To the extent that trust income has been accumulated and thus forms part of the trust capital, it would be paid over to the beneficiaries as capital and no part of the tax suffered could be recovered nor, on the other hand, would any higher rate tax be payable.

Capital gains if trust wound up

7. The Green plc shareholding is currently worth around £2 million, and may increase to over £5 million if the company is floated on the Stock Exchange. Its base cost for capital gains tax in 1987 was (850,000 less heldover gain 650,000 =) £200,000, so that there will be a substantial capital gain on disposal. Indexation allowance and taper relief have been abolished and the gain will be taxed at a flat rate of 18% unless it is possible to attract entrepreneurs' relief in respect of the first £1 million of the gain.

8. For the disposal to qualify for entrepreneurs' relief to a qualifying beneficiary must have been an officer or employee of the company throughout a period of 1 year ending not more than 3 years before the disposal or a qualifying beneficiary must have carried on the business throughout a period of 1 year ending not more than 3 years before the disposal and ceases to do so on the date of the disposal or within 3 years before then. Some relief will be available in respect of any life interest beneficiaries who work for the company if the disposal is of shares or securities or an interest in shares or securities in the company.

9. Assuming entrepreneurs' relief is available the first £1 million of the gain would be taxed at an effective rate of 10% and the remainder at 18%.

10. Business gifts holdover relief under TCGA 1992 s 165 could be claimed in respect of the trustees' gains (providing the shares remained unquoted, or the trustees retained 25% or more of the voting rights), so that the beneficiaries' acquisition costs would be reduced accordingly.

Rules for Accumulation and Maintenance Settlements post FA 2006

11. One of the main changes of the 2006 rules is that new A&M settlements cannot be established on or after 22 March 2006 (IHTA 1984 s 71(1A)).

    Furthermore, existing A&M settlements ceased to be treated as such for IHT purposes on 6 April 2008 when they fell within the relevant property charging regime applied to discretionary trusts unless by 6 April 2008 at least one beneficiary was beneficially entitled to the capital at the age of 18 or IHTA 1984 s 71D applies (but s 71A does not).

    If these new conditions are not met after 5 April 2008, the settlement will be subject to the exit and 10-yearly charges regime.

    The 10-year anniversaries will be based on the date the trust was established in 1987 rather than the date the trust property became 'relevant property' in 2008.

The Green grandchildren's trust was an accumulation and maintenance settlement but nothing was done with it before 6 April 2008. No beneficiary was absolutely entitled to the capital at the age of 18 and IHTA 1984 s 71D will not apply. The settlement will now be within the relevant property regime.

Explanatory Notes

Treatment of dividend income in discretionary trusts

1. The basic income tax treatment of discretionary trusts is that in respect of income which the trustees have the power to accumulate, or which may be distributed at their discretion, the trustees are liable to tax under ITA 2007 ss 479–481 at the dividend trust rate of 32½% on dividend income and at the 'trust rate' of 40% on other income. The tax suffered by the trustees forms a tax pool (ITA 2007 ss 493–498 (replacing TA 1998 with effect from 6 April 2007)), which is available to cover the tax on any distributions to the beneficiaries. From 6 April 2004 only 22½% of the 32½% tax credit on dividends goes into the tax pool, hence the reduced level of possible distribution as indicated in the example.

    Under ITA 2007 s 491 the first £1,000 of relevant income will not be charged at the special trust tax rates, but will instead be charged at the income tax rate appropriate to the type of income, known as standard rate band. Therefore, if payments are received net of tax (for example, building society interest) up to the limit of the standard rate band, then the trustees will have no further tax to pay.

    The standard rate band set out in ITA 2007 s 491 will apply to trust income *net* of trust management expenses so potentially it will apply to other charges as well.

    Although the management expenses are deducted from the trust income taxed at the lowest rate first, the standard rate band will apply in the order – basic rate income at 20% first, followed by dividends at 10%.

    See Examples 42, 47 and 48 for the details of this provision which applies from 6 April 2005.

2. In this example, once a grandchild reaches age 25 and becomes entitled to a life interest in the trust, his share of the trust income is taxable on him, whether it is received or retained within the trust. If there is unutilised tax within the pool of tax under TA 1988 s 687 when the last grandchild reaches age 25 the unused amount will be wasted, although this would not be a disadvantage to the extent that capital distributions were then made to grandchildren who would be liable to higher rate tax on income distributions.

Capital gains tax holdover relief and entrepreneurs' relief

3. There are two holdover reliefs available for capital gains tax, the business assets holdover relief of TCGA 1992 s 165 (see Example 50 part A(d) for the definition of business assets for this purpose) and the holdover relief of TCGA 1992 s 260 for gifts on which inheritance tax is chargeable. Even if inheritance tax is not chargeable, s 260(2)(d) provides that the capital gains holdover relief is still available where a beneficiary becomes entitled to trust property or a life interest therein under IHTA 1984 s 71(4) (accumulation and maintenance trusts) before 6 April 2008. FA 2006 introduced s 260(da) and (db) which extend the relief to the termination of a Bereaved Minor's Trust (IHTA 1984 s 71A) and the termination of an age 18 to 25 trust (IHTA 1984 s 71D). In this example this would only apply in relation to beneficiaries under 25 who had not already attained a life interest (see Example 64 explanatory note 3). So long as the shares remain unquoted, or the trustees retain 25% of the voting rights, however, the Green plc shares will be business assets for TCGA 1992 s 165.

    However see 35.3 and 50.6–50.7 regarding new sections in FA 2004 and FA 2006 restricting gift holdover relief in respect of disposals of assets by trustees of settlor-interested settlements.

4. Taper relief (introduced in FA 1998) has been abolished by FA 2008 s 8 for disposals on or after 6 April 2008. Indexation allowance and halving relief have also been abolished. There is now a uniform rate of capital gains tax at 18%.

5. FA 2008 s 9 and Sch 3 introduce new TCGA 1992 ss 169H to 169S which provide for a new relief ('entrepreneurs' relief') so that the first £1 million of gains arising on or in connection with disposals of the whole or part of a business (including, in certain circumstances, disposals of shares or securities) or of trust business assets ('qualifying business disposals') are charged to capital gains tax at an effective rate of 10% (4/9ths of the 18% rate). The relief has effect for disposals on or after 6 April 2008.

    There is a disposal of trust business assets when:

    (a) there is a disposal by trustees of assets which are part of the settled property of the settlement and are shares in or securities of a company, or interests in such shares or securities; or assets that have been used for the purposes of a business, or interests in such assets ('settlement business assets');

    (b) there is an individual in relation to a the settlement who has have an interest in possession (other than an interest in possession which has a fixed term) in the whole of the settled property of the settlement or in a part of the settled property that contains the settlement business assets (a 'qualifying beneficiary');

    (c) in relation to the disposal of settlement business assets a 'relevant condition' is being satisfied. The nature of the relevant condition depends upon whether the settlement business assets are shares in or securities of a company (or interests in such shares or securities), in which case the company should have been the qualifying beneficiary's personal company and the qualifying beneficiary must have been an officer or employee of the company throughout a period of 1 year ending not more than 3 years before the disposal. If the settlement business assets are assets (or interests in assets) that have been used for the purposes of a business the relevant condition is that the qualifying beneficiary has carried on the business throughout a period of 1 year ending not more than 3 years before the disposal and ceases to do so on the date of the disposal or within 3 years before then.

INDEX

References are to page numbers.

INDEX